A History of the Inquisition of Spain
Volume IV
By Henry Charles Lea, LL.D.
Edited by Anthony Uyl

Woodstock, Ontario, 2017

A History of the Inquisition of Spain: Volume IV
A History of the Inquisition of Spain: Volume IV
By Henry Charles Lea, LL.D.
Edited by Anthony Uyl

Originally Published by:
New York: The MacMillan Company; London: MacMillan & Co., Ltd.; 1922; Copyright, 1907

The text of A History of the Inquisition of Spain - Volume IV is all in the Public Domain. The layout is not in the Public Domain and is Copyright 2017© Devoted Publishing a division of 2165467 Ontario Inc.

Let us hear your philosophies and thoughts!

Contact us at: devotedpub@hotmail.com
Visit us on Facebook at: @DevotedPublishing
Visit our website for a full selection of print products: www.devotedpublishing.com

Published in Woodstock, Ontario, Canada 2017.

ISBN: 978-1-988297-82-8

Table of Contents

- BOOK VIII (Continued) 4
  - CHAPTER V - MYSTICISM 4
  - CHAPTER VI - SOLICITATION 43
  - CHAPTER VII - PROPOSITIONS 60
  - CHAPTER VIII - SORCERY AND OCCULT ARTS 77
  - CHAPTER IX - WITCHCRAFT 88
  - CHAPTER X - POLITICAL ACTIVITY 105
  - CHAPTER XI - JANSENISM 121
  - CHAPTER XII - FREE-MASONRY 127
  - CHAPTER XIII - PHILOSOPHISM 131
  - CHAPTER XIV - BIGAMY 135
  - CHAPTER XV - BLASPHEMY 140
  - CHAPTER XVI - MISCELLANEOUS BUSINESS 144
- BOOK IX - CONCLUSION 164
  - CHAPTER I - DECADENCE AND EXTINCTION 164
  - CHAPTER II - RETROSPECT 201
- APPENDIX 226
  - I. ABJURATION OF JOSEPH FERNANDEZ DE TORO, BISHOP OF OVIEDO 226
  - II. ABSTRACT OF THE CASE OF CATALINA MATHEO IN 1591 227
  - III. LETTER OF THE SUPREMA ON THE TUMULT OF MAY 2, 1808 228
  - IV. DECREE OF FERNANDO VII, SEPTEMBER 9, 1814, RESTORING THE PROPERTY OR THE INQUISITION 228
  - V. DECREE OF SUPPRESSION, MARCH 9, 1820 229
  - VI. THE LAST VOTE OF THE SUPREME COUNCIL, FEBRUARY 10, 1820 229
  - VII. DICTAMEN OF THE CONSEJO DE GOBIERNO ON THE DECREE EXTINGUISHING THE INQUISITION 230
  - VIII. DECREE OF JULY 15, 1834, ABOLISHING THE INQUISITION 231
  - IX. PRAYER RECITED DAILY AT OPENING OF MORNING SESSION 231
- FOOTNOTES: 232

BOOK VIII (Continued)
CHAPTER V - MYSTICISM[1]

The belief that, by prolonged meditation and abstraction from the phenomenal world, the soul can elevate itself to the Creator, and can even attain union with the Godhead, has existed from the earliest times and among many races. Passing through ecstasy into trance, it was admitted to the secrets of God, it enjoyed revelations of the invisible universe, it acquired foreknowledge and wielded supernatural powers. St. Paul gave to these beliefs the sanction of his own experience;[2] Tertullian describes the influence of the Holy Spirit on the devotee in manifestations which bear a curious similitude to those which we shall meet in Spain,[3] and the anchorites of the Nitrian desert were adepts of the same kind to whom all the secrets of God were laid bare.[4] These supernal joys continued to be the reward of those who earned them by disciplining the flesh, and the virtues of mental prayer, in which the soul lost consciousness of all earthly things, were taught by a long series of doctors--Richard of Saint Victor, Joachim of Flora, St. Bonaventura, John Tauler, John of Rysbroek, Henry Suso, Henry Herp, John Gerson and many others. If Cardinal Jacques de Vitry is to be believed, the nuns of Liége, in the thirteenth century, were largely given to these mystic raptures; of one of them he relates that she often had twenty-five ecstasies a day, while others passed years in bed, dissolved in divine love;[5] and Richard Rolle, the Hermit of Hampole, who missed his deserved canonization, was fully acquainted with the superhuman delights of union with God.[6] These spiritual marvels are reduced to the common-places of psychology by modern researches into hypnotism and auto-suggestion. The connection is well illustrated by the Umbilicarii, the pious monks of Mount Athos who, by prolonged contemplation of their navels, found their souls illuminated with light from above.[7]

IMPECCABILITY

Yet there were dangers in the pursuit of the via purgativa and the via illuminativa. The followers of Amaury of Bène, who came to be popularly known in Germany as Begghards and Beguines, invented the term Illuminism to describe the condition of the soul suffused with divine light and held that any one, thus filled with the Holy Ghost, was impeccable, irrespective of the sins which he might commit; he was simply following the impulses of the Spirit which can do no sin. Master Eckhart, the founder of German mysticism, was prosecuted for sharing in these venturesome speculations and, if the twenty-eight articles condemned by John XXII were correctly drawn from his writings, he admitted the common divinity of man and God and that, in the sight of God, sin and virtue are the same.[8] Zealots too there were who taught the pre-eminent holiness of nudity and, in imitation of the follies of early Christian ascetics, assumed to triumph over the lusts of the flesh by exposing themselves to the crucial temptation of sleeping with the other sex and indulging in lascivious acts.[9] The condemnation, by the Council of Vienne in 1312, of the tenets of the so-called Begghards respecting impeccability[10] was carried into the body of canon law and thus was rendered familiar to jurists, when mysticism came to be regarded as dangerous and was subjected to the Inquisition.

That it should eventually be so regarded was inevitable. The mystic, who considered himself to be communing directly with God and who held meditation and mental prayer to be the highest of religious acts, was apt to feel himself released from ecclesiastical precepts and to regard with indifference, if not with contempt, the observances enjoined by the Church as essential to salvation. If the inner light was a direct inspiration from God, it superseded the commands of the Holy See and, under such impulse, private judgement was to be followed, irrespective of what the Church might ordain. In all this there was the germ of a rebellion as defiant as that of Luther. Justification by faith might not be taught, but justification by works was cast aside as unworthy of the truly spiritual man. The new Judaism, decried by Erasmus, which relied on external observances, was a hindrance rather than a help to salvation. Francisco de Osuna, the teacher of Santa Teresa, asserts that oral prayer is a positive injury to those advanced in mental prayer.[11] San Juan de la Cruz says that church observances, images and places of worship are merely for the uninstructed, like toys that amuse children; those who are advanced must liberate themselves from these things which only distract from internal contemplation.[12] San Pedro de

Alcántara, in his enumeration of the nine aids to devotion, significantly omits all reference to the observances prescribed by the Church.[13] In an ecclesiastical establishment, which had built up its enormous wealth by the thrifty exploitation of the text "Give alms and behold all things are clean unto you" (Luke, XI, 41), Luis de Granada dared to teach that the most dangerous temptation in the spiritual life is the desire to do good to others, for a man's first duty is to himself.[14] Yet these men were all held in the highest honor, and two of them earned the supreme reward of canonization.

There was in this a certain savor of Lutheranism, but it was not until the danger of the latter was fully appreciated that the Inquisition awoke to the peril lurking in a system which released the devotee from the obligation of obedience to authority, as in the Alumbrado or Illuminated, who recognized the supremacy of the internal light, and the Dejado or Quietist, who abandoned himself to God and allowed free course to the impulses suggesting themselves in his contemplative abstraction, with the corollary that there could be no sin in what emanated from God. The real significance of that which had been current in the Church for so many centuries was unnoticed until Protestantism presented itself as a threatening peril, when the two were classed together, or rather Protestantism was regarded as the development of mysticism. In the letter of September 9, 1558, to Paul IV, the Inquisition traced the origin of the former in Spain farther back than to Doctor Egidio and Don Carlos de Seso; the heresies of which Maestro Juan de Oria (Olmillos?) was accused and of those called Alumbrados or Dejados of Guadalajara and other places, were the seed of these Lutheran heresies, but the inquisitors who tried those heretics were insufficiently versed in Lutheranism to apply the proper vigor of repression.[15] It is necessary to bear all this in mind to understand the varying attitude of the Inquisition in its gradual progress towards the condemnation of all mysticism.

CONTEMPT FOR THEOLOGY

The distinction at first attempted between the mysticism that was praiseworthy and that which was dangerous was complicated by the recognized fact that, while visions and revelations and ecstasies might be special favors from God, they might also be the work of demons, and there was no test that could be applied to differentiate them. The Church was in the unfortunate position of being committed to the belief in special manifestations of supernatural power, while it was confessedly unable to determine whether they came from heaven or from hell. This had long been recognized as one of the most treacherous pitfalls in the perilous paths of illumination and union with God. As early as the twelfth century, Richard of St. Victor warns his disciples to beware of it, and Aquinas points out that trances may come from God, from the demon or from bodily affections.[16] John Gerson wrote a special tractate in which he endeavored to frame diagnostic rules.[17] The Blessed Juan de Avila emphatically admonishes the devout to beware of such deceptions, but he fails to guide them in discriminating between demonic illusions and the effects of divine grace.[18] Arbiol describes the uncertainty as to the sources of these manifestations as the greatest danger besetting the path of perfection, causing the ruin of innumerable souls.[19] When, in the eighteenth century, mysticism had become discredited, Dr. Amort argues that, even if a revelation is from God, there can be no certainty that it is not falsified by the operation of the fancy or the work of the demon.[20] When to this we add the facility of imposture, by which a livelihood could be gained from the contributions of the credulous, we can appreciate the difficulty of the task assumed by the Inquisition, in a land swarming with hysterics of both sexes, to restrain the extravagance of the devout and to punish the frauds of impostors, without interfering with the ways of God in guiding his saints. It is merely another instance of the failure of humanity in its efforts to interpret the Infinite.

Apart from visions and revelations, there was another feature of mysticism which rendered it especially dangerous to the Church and odious to theologians. Though the mystic might not controvert the received doctrines of the faith, yet scholastic theology, on which they were founded, was to him a matter of careless contempt. Mystic theology, says Osuna, is higher than speculative or scholastic theology; it needs no labor or learning or study, only faith and love and the grace of God.[21] In the trial of María Cazalla, one of the accusations was that she and her brother Bishop Cazalla ridiculed Aquinas and Scotus and the whole mass of scholastic theology.[22] When Gerónimo de la Madre de Dios was on trial, one of his writings produced in evidence was a comparison between mystic and scholastic theology, to the great disadvantage of the latter. Its learning, he says, is perfectly compatible with vice; its masters preach the virtues but do not practise them; they wallow in the sins that they denounce; they are Pharisees, and this is so general a pest that there is scarce one who is not infected with the contagion.[23]

A History of the Inquisition of Spain: Volume IV
COMMENCEMENT OF PERSECUTION

Medieval Spain had been little troubled with mystic extravagance. Eymerich who, in his Directorium Inquisitorum, gives an exhaustive account of heresies existing towards the close of the fourteenth century, makes no allusion to such errors, except in his denunciation of his special object of hatred Raymond Lully, to whom he attributes some vagaries of mystic illuminism, and the Repertorium Inquisitorum of 1494 is equally silent.[24] Spiritual exaltation, however, accompanied the development of the fanaticism stimulated by the establishment of the Inquisition and its persecution of Jews and Moors. Osuna, in 1527, alludes to a holy man who for fifty years had devoted himself to recojimiento, or the abstraction of mental prayer, and already, in 1498, Francisco de Villalobos complains of the Aluminados or Illuminati, derived from Italy, of whom there were many in Spain, and who should be reduced to reason by scourging, cold, hunger and prison.[25] This indicates that mysticism was obtaining a foothold and its spread was facilitated by the beatas, women adopting a religious life without entering an Order, or at most simply as Tertiaries, living usually on alms and often regarded as possessing spiritual gifts and prophetic powers. The first of the class to obtain prominence was known as the Beata de Piedrahita. A career such as hers was common enough subsequently, as we shall see, and the discussion which she aroused shows that as yet she was a novel phenomenon. The daughter of a fanatic peasant, she had been carefully trained in mystic exercises and was wholly given up to contemplative abstraction, in which she enjoyed the most intimate relations with God, in whose arms she was dissolved in love. Sometimes she asserted that Christ was with her, sometimes that she was Christ himself or the bride of Christ; often she held conversations with the Virgin in which she spoke for both. As her reputation spread, her visions and revelations won for her the character of a prophetess. Many denounced them as superstitious and demanded her suppression, but Ximenes who, as inquisitor-general, had jurisdiction in the matter, argued that she was inspired with divine wisdom and Ferdinand, who visited her, expressed his belief in her inspiration. In 1510 the matter was referred to the Holy See, and Julius II appointed his nuncio, Giovanni Ruffo, and the Bishops of Burgos and Vich, as commissioners to examine her and to suppress the scandal if it proved to be only female levity. Peter Martyr, to whom we are indebted for the account, was unable to ascertain their decision but, as they discharged her without reproof, it may be assumed that their report was favorable, for it could scarce have been otherwise with such supporters as Ferdinand and Ximenes.[26] Such success naturally stimulated imitation and was the foreshadowing of wide-spread delusion and imposture.

In this case there appears no trace of carnality, but it is the distinguishing feature of another soon afterwards, reported in 1512 to Ximenes by Fray Antonio de Pastrana, of a contemplative fraile of Ocaña "illuminated with the darkness of Satan." To him God had revealed that he should engender on a holy woman a prophet who should reform the world. He was a spiritual man, not given to women and, in his simplicity, he had written to Madre Juana de la Cruz, apparently inviting her coöperation in the good work. Fray Antonio, who was custodian of the Province of Castile, imprisoned the alumbrado and subjected him to treatment so active that he speedily admitted his error.[27]

Guadalajara and Pastrana were becoming centres of a group of mystics who attracted the attention of the Inquisition about 1521, when it commenced gathering testimony about them. The earliest disseminator of the doctrine appears to have been a sempstress named Isabel de la Cruz, noted for her ability in the exposition of Scripture, who commenced about 1512 and was a leader until superseded by Francisca Hernández, of whom more hereafter. The Seraphic Order of St. Francis naturally furnished many initiates, whose names are included among the fifty or sixty forming the group. The Franciscan Guardian of Escalona, Fray Juan de Olmillos, had ecstasies when receiving the sacrament and when preaching, in which he talked and acted extravagantly. When removed to Madrid, this attracted crowds to watch his contortions and he was generally regarded as a saint; he was promoted to the provincialate of Castile and died in 1529. The Marquis of Villena, at Escalona, was inclined to mysticism, induced perhaps by Fray Francisco de Ocaña, who was stationed there and had prophetic visions of the reform of the Church. Villena, in 1523, employed as lay-preacher Pedro Ruiz de Alcaraz, one of the most prominent of the Guadalajara mystics, who seems to have converted all the members of the household. The name of Alcaraz appears frequently in the trials of the group; he was a married layman, uneducated but possessing remarkable familiarity with Scripture and skilled in its exposition, and he was an earnest missionary of mysticism. When sufficient evidence against him was accumulated, he was arrested February 26, 1524, and imprisoned by the Toledo tribunal. The formal accusation, presented October 31st, indicates that the mysticism, of at least some of the accused, embraced Quietism or Dejamiento to the full extent, with its consequent assumption of impeccability, no matter what might be the acts of the devotee, that mental prayer was the sole observance necessary, that all the prescriptions of the Church—confession, indulgences, works of charity and piety--were useless, and that the conjugal act was Union with God. There was also the denial of transubstantiation and of the existence of hell, which may probably be left out of account as foreign to the recognized tenets of mysticism. The latter, in fact, was presumably an exaggeration of an utterance of Alcaraz, who said that it was the ignorant and children who were afraid of hell, for the advanced served the Lord, not from servile fear but from fear of offending Him whom they loved, and moreover that God was not to be prayed to for anything-- principles subsequently approved in S. François de Sales and condemned in Fénelon. There was no spirit of martyrdom in Alcaraz, and the severe torture to which he was exposed would seem a superfluity. He confessed his errors, professed conversion and begged for mercy. His sentence, July 22, 1529, recited that he had incurred relaxation but through clemency was admitted to reconciliation with confiscation, irremissible prison and scourging in Toledo, Guadalajara, Escalona and Pastrana, where he had disseminated his errors. This severity indicates the inquisitorial estimate of the magnitude of the evil to be suppressed but, after ten years, on February 20, 1539, the Suprema liberated him, with the restriction of not leaving Toledo and the imposition of certain spiritual exercises.[28]

FRANCISCA HERNANDEZ

In the ensuing trials, pursued with customary inquisitorial thoroughness, the question of sexual aberrations constantly obtrudes itself and offers no little complexity. That the majority of the Spanish mystics were thoroughly pure in heart there can be no doubt, but spiritual exaltation, shared by the two sexes, had the ever-present risk that it might insensibly become carnal, when those who fancied themselves to be advancing in the path of perfection might suddenly find that the flesh had deceived the spirit. This was an experience as old as mysticism itself, and the eloquent warning which St. Bonaventura addressed to his brethren shows, by the vividness of its details, that he must have witnessed more than one such fall from grace.[29] The danger was all the greater in the extreme mysticism known as Illuminism, with its doctrines of internal light, of Dejamiento, or abandonment to impulses assumed to come from God, and of the impeccability of the advanced adept, combined with the test of continence. Unquestionably there were cases in which these aberrations were honestly entertained; there were numerous others in which they were assumed for purposes of seduction, nor can we always, from the evidence before us, pronounce a confident judgement.

Of the trials which have seen the light several centre around the curious personality of Francisca Hernández, who succeeded Isabel de la Cruz as the leader of the mystic disciples. She seems to have possessed powers of fascination, collecting around her devotees of the most diverse character. We have seen how she entangled Bernardino de Tovar and how his brother, Juan de Vergara, became involved with the Inquisition, after detaching him from her. Francisco de Osuna, the earliest Spanish writer on mysticism and the teacher of Santa Teresa, was one of her disciples and so was Francisco Ortiz, a Franciscan of the utmost purity of heart. A devotee of a different stamp was Antonio de Medrano, cura of Navarrete, who had made her acquaintance in 1516 when a student at Salamanca. She was attractive and penniless but, through a long career, she always managed to live in comfort at the expense of her admirers. Though she claimed to be a bride of Christ, she practised no austerities; she was fastidious in her diet and slept in a soft bed, which she had no scruple in sharing with her male devotees. This required funds and she and Medrano persuaded an unlucky youth named Calero to sell his patrimony and devote the proceeds to support the circle of Alumbrados whom she gathered around her. The episcopal authorities commenced investigations, ending with a sentence of banishment on Medrano, when the pair betook themselves to Valladolid, whither Tovar followed them, and where the Inquisition commenced proceedings in 1519; it was as yet not aroused to dealing harshly with these eccentric forms of devotion, and it merely forbade him and Tovar from further converse with Francisca; this they eluded, the tribunal insisted and Medrano went to his cure at Navarrete. She was kept under surveillance, but her reputation for holiness was such that Cardinal Adrian, after his election to the papacy, in 1522, ordered his secretary Carmona to ask her prayers for him and for the whole Church.

***

In 1525 the Inquisition again arrested her; she was accused of suspicious relations with men and, when discharged, was obliged to swear that she would permit no indecent familiarities. Meanwhile Medrano, at Navarrete continued his career as an Alumbrado, holding conversations with the Holy Ghost and declaring himself to be impeccable. In 1526 the Logroño tribunal arrested him and, after nearly eighteen months, he was discharged June 4, 1527, with the lenient sentence of abjuration de levi and such spiritual penance as might be assigned to him. This escape emboldened him to greater extravagance and to renewed devotion to Francisca, leading to another prosecution, in 1530, by the Toledo tribunal. There was evidence of highly indecent character as to their relations, but he stoutly denied it, asserting that he was so favored by God that all the evil women in the world and all the devils in hell could not move him to carnal sin--a grace which came to him after he knew Francisca; he could lie in bed with a woman without feeling desire and it gave him grace to do so with Francisca and to fondle and embrace her, which she enjoyed; he believed her to be free from both mortal and venial sin, and he held her to be a greater saint than any in heaven except Our Lady. Under torture, however, he confessed whatever was wanted--that when he told people that she could not sin, because she was illuminated by the Holy Ghost, it was to spread her reputation and gain money for them both; that he was jealous of all her other disciples, among whom he named Valderrama, Diego de Villareal, Muñoz, Cabrera, Gumiel, Ortiz and Sayavedra and his brother, showing that she had a numerous following. He admitted teaching that male and female devotees could embrace each other naked, for it was not clothes but intention that counted. By this time the Inquisition was dealing harshly with these aberrations, and his sentence, April 21, 1532, excused him from relaxation as an incorrigible heretic because he was only a hypocritical swindler whose object was to raise money for a life of pleasure; he was to retract his propositions in an auto de fe, to abjure de vehementi and to be recluded for life in a monastery, with two years' suspension from his sacerdotal functions, and was to hold no further communication with Francisca, under pain of impenitent relapse, but he was not deprived of his cure of Navarrete. In 1537 the Duke of Nájera interceded for his release, with what result the records fail to inform us.[30]

Francisca's strange powers of fascination were manifested by the influence which she acquired over a man of infinitely higher character than Medrano. Fray Francisco Ortiz was the most promising member of the great Franciscan Order, who was rapidly acquiring the reputation of the foremost preacher in Spain. He was not fully a mystic, but his pulpit exhortations, stimulating the love of God, caused him to be regarded as wandering near to the dangerous border. In 1523 he made the acquaintance of Francisca and his feelings towards her are emphatically expressed in a defiant declaration to the Inquisition during his trial.--"No word of love, however strong, is by a hundredth part adequate to describe the holy love, so pure and sweet and strong and great and full of God's blessing and melting of heart and soul, which God in his goodness has given me through His holy betrothed, my true Mother and Lady, through whom I hope, at the awful Day of Judgement, to be numbered among the elect. I can call her my love for, in loving her, I love nothing but God." There can be no doubts as to the purity of his relations with her whom he thus reverenced, but they were displeasing to his superiors who viewed with growing disquiet the distraction of one whom they regarded as a valuable asset of the Order. It was in vain that he was ordered to break off all relations with her; he replied vehemently that God was to be obeyed rather than man and that if he was to be debarred from seeing that beloved one of God he would transfer himself to the Carthusians. To effect the separation the Franciscan prelates induced the Inquisition to arrest Francisca, but the unexpected result of this was that Ortiz, in a sermon before all the assembled magnates of the city April 7, 1529, arraigned the Inquisition for the great sin committed in her arrest. Such revolt was unexampled and he was forthwith prosecuted, not so much to punish him as to procure his retractation and submission, but he was obstinate and defiant for nearly three years. It was in vain that the Empress Isabel twice, in 1530, urged his liberation or the expediting of his case, and equally vain was a brief of Clement VII, July 1, 1531, to Cardinal Manrique, asking his discharge if his only offence was his public denunciation of the arrest of that holy woman, Francisca Hernández.[31] At length, in April 1532, Ortiz experienced a revulsion of feeling, and the same emotional impulsiveness that had led to his outbreak now prompted him to declare that God had given him the grace to recognize his errors and that he found great peace in retracting them. He escaped with public abjuration de vehementi, five years' suspension from priestly functions, two years' confinement in a cell of the convent of Torrelaguna, and absolute sundering of relations with Francisca. He betook himself to his place of reclusion and, although papal briefs released him from all restrictions and his prelates repeatedly urged him to leave his retreat, he seems never to have abandoned the solitude which he said had become sweet to him. Until his death, in 1546, he remained in the convent, the object of overflowing honor on the part of his brethren.[32]

CONNECTION WITH PROTESTANTISM

Francisca herself seems to have been treated with remarkable leniency, in spite of her previous trials and the evidence of Medrano. Her arrest had been merely with the object of separating her from Ortiz, and her trial seems to have been scarce more than formal for, in September 1532, we find her merely detained in the house of Gutierre Pérez de Montalvo, at Medina del Campo, with her maid María Ramírez in waiting on her.[33] Possibly this favor may have been earned by her readiness to accuse her old friends and associates, among whom were two brothers and a sister, Juan Cazalla, Bishop of Troy in partibus, Pedro Cazalla and María Cazalla, wife of Lope de Ruida.[34] The trial of the latter is worth brief reference as it throws some light on the confusion existing at the time between Illuminism and Protestantism.

María Cazalla was a resident of Guadalajara who visited Pastrana, where women assembled to listen to her readings and expositions of Scripture. When proceedings were commenced against the group, in 1524, she was arrested and examined but was discharged. For six years she remained undisturbed, when the testimony of Francisca Hernández caused a second prosecution, in which the heterogeneous character of the fiscal's accusation shows how little was understood as to the heresies under discussion. She was a Lutheran who praised Luther, denied transubstantiation and free-will, ridiculed confession, decried scholastic theology and held indulgences as valueless; she was an Alumbrada who regarded Isabel de la Cruz as superior to St. Paul, who rated matrimony higher than virginity, who wrote letters full of Illuminism and taught the Alumbrados their doctrines from Scripture, decrying external works of adoration and prayer; she was an Erasmist who pronounced Church observances to be Judaism, despised the religious Orders and ridiculed the preachers of sermons.[35] She had been arrested about May 1, 1532, and her trial dragged on as usual. As a solvent of doubts she was tortured smartly and, on December 19, 1534, her sentence pronounced that the fiscal had not proved her to be a heretic but that, for the suspicions arising from the trial, she should abjure de levi and undergo solemn public penance in her parish church, she should avoid all intercourse with Alumbrados or other suspects and pay a fine of a hundred ducats.[36]

An affiliated group comes before us in Toledo, centering around Petronila de Lucena, an unmarried woman of 25, living with her brother, Juan del Castillo. She had a high reputation for sanctity and was credited with thaumaturgic powers; when the Duke del Infantazgo was mortally ill, she was sent for, but too late. We hear of María Cazalla, Bernardino de Tovar and Francisca Hernández; there are allusions to Erasmus, and Diego Hernández had included her in his denunciations of Lutheranism. Letters to her from her brother, Gaspar de Lucena, are mere mystical maunderings, showing the atmosphere in which they lived, but the other brother, Juan del Castillo, then on trial, admitted many Lutheran doctrines--works were not necessary, Church precepts were not binding, man had not free-will, indulgences were useless and a book by OEcolampadius had led him to disbelieve in transubstantiation. Both Juan and Gaspar were on trial, and we hear of another prisoner, Catalina de Figueredo. Petronila was arrested, with sequestration, May 7, 1534, and her trial pursued the ordinary course until March 20, 1535, when, as we have seen (Vol. III, p. 111), it was decided that, as the principal witness against her, Juan del Castillo, had revoked the evidence given under torture, she might be released on bail of a hundred thousand maravedís, which was promptly entered. In June she petitioned to be wholly discharged and that the sequestration be lifted; to this no attention was paid but a second application, October 20, 1536 procured the removal of the sequestration. Gaspar de Lucena was sentenced to reconciliation and this was presumably the fate of Juan del Castillo unless he was impenitent.[37]

PERVADING SUSPICION

These cases show that the prevalence of the mingled heresies of Illuminism and Lutheranism was calling for repression, nor was this confined to Castile. In 1533, Miguel Galba, fiscal of the tribunal of Lérida, in a letter to Cardinal Manrique, declared that only the vigilance of the Inquisition prevented both kingdoms from being filled with the followers of the two heresies.[38] There was of course exaggeration in this, but the fears of the authorities led them to see heresies everywhere. As Juan de Valdés, himself inclined to mysticism, says, when any one endeavored to manifest the perfection of Christianity, his utterances were misinterpreted and he was condemned as a heretic, so that there was scarce any one who dared to live as a Christian.[39] Many suffered from the results of this hyper-sensitiveness. When Ignatius Loyola, after his conversion, came in 1526 to Alcalá to study, he was joined by four young men; they assumed a peculiar gray gown and their fervor brought many to the Hôpital de la Misericordia, where they lodged, to consult with them and join in their spiritual exercises. This excited suspicion and invited investigation. What was the exact authority of Doctor Miguel Carrasco, confessor of Fonseca Archbishop of Toledo, and of Alonso Mexia, who bore a commission as inquisitor, does not appear, but they examined witnesses and the sentence rendered by the Vicar-general, Juan Rodríguez de Figueroa, was merely that the associates should lay aside their distinctive garments. After this the number who went to listen to Loyola continued to increase, and the women had a fashion of falling in convulsions, there was nothing of illuminism in his exhortations, but he was open to suspicion, and it was inadmissible that a young layman should assume the function of a director of souls. This time it was Vicar-general Figueroa who took the matter in hand and threw Loyola into prison, in 1527, finally sentencing him and his companions not to appear in public until they had assumed the ordinary lay garments, nor for three years to hold assemblages public or private and then only with permission of the Ordinary.[40] It was this experience that drove Loyola to complete his studies in Paris, where he was not subject to the intrusion of excitable devotees.

Carranza offered a mark too vulnerable to be spared. He was inclined to mysticism, and there were many passages in his unfortunate Comentarios which, separated from their context, afforded material for reprehension. The keen-sighted Melchor Cano was able to cite isolated texts to prove that he held the alumbrado doctrines of impeccability, of interior illumination, of the supreme merits of contemplation, of despising all exterior works and observances--in short that he defended the errors of the Begghards and Beguines, of Pedro Rúiz Alcaraz and of the Alumbrados who figured in the autos of Toledo.[41] It is significant of the advanced position of Spanish orthodoxy on the subject of mysticism that these accusations had no weight with the Council of Trent, which approved the Comentarios, nor with Pius V, when he permitted the publication of the book in Rome. When, at last in 1576, Gregory XIII yielded and condemned the book and its author, of the sixteen propositions which he was required to abjure only three bore any relation to mysticism, and these were on the border line between it and Protestantism--that all works without charity are sins and offend God, that faith without works suffices for salvation, and that the use of images and veneration of relics are of human precept.[42]

SANCTITY OR HERESY

In this inquisitorial temper it was a matter of chance whether a devotional writer should be canonized or condemned and mayhap both might befall him, as occurred to San Francisco de Borja, whose Obras del Cristiano was put on the Index of 1559, though it disappeared after that of Quiroga in 1583.[43] Santa Teresa herself, the queen of Spanish mystics and, along with Santiago, the patron saint of Spain, was confined in a convent by the Nuncio Sega, who denounced her as a restless vagabond, plunged in dissipation under pretext of religion, and an effort was made to transport her to the Indies, which were a sort of penal settlement. But for the accident that Philip II became interested in her, she would probably have come down to us as one of the beatas revelanderas whom it was the special mission of the Inquisition to suppress. When, in 1575, she founded a convent of her Barefooted Carmelites in Seville, they were denounced as Alumbradas; the inquisitors created a terrible scandal by going to the house with the guards to investigate, but they could substantiate nothing to justify prosecution. So, when in 1574 her spiritual autobiography was denounced to the Inquisition, it was held for ten years in suspense, and the Duchess of Alva, who possessed a MS. copy, was obliged to procure a licence to read it in private until judgement should be rendered--although finally, in 1588, it was printed by Fray Luis de Leon at the special request of the empress. Even after canonization her Conceptos del Amor divino, when printed with the works of her disciple Jerónimo Gracian, were put on the Index and remained there.[44] Her most illustrious disciple, San Juan de la Cruz, escaped prosecution, though repeatedly denounced to the Inquisition, and his writings were not forbidden, but he was most vindictively persecuted as an Alumbrado, first by his unreformed Carmelite brethren and then by the Barefooted Order, and he ended his days in disgrace, recluded in a convent in the Sierra Morena.[45] Yet Francisco de Osuna, the preceptor of Santa Teresa, although his writings are of the highest mysticism, escaped persecution himself, and his Abecedario Spiritual incurred only a single expurgation.[46]

The Venerable Luis de Granada was not canonized, for the proceedings were never completed. He was one of the most moderate of those who taught the supreme virtues of recojimiento and his Guia de Pecadores ranks as one of the Spanish classics, yet his works were prohibited in the Index of 1559.[47] Melchor Cano declared that his books contained doctrines of Alumbrados and matters contrary to the faith, while Fray Alonso de la Fuente, who was a vigorous persecutor of illuminism, endeavored to have him prosecuted and pronounced his De la Oracion the worst of the books which presented these errors so subtly that only the initiated could discover them. It illustrates the difference between Spanish and Roman standards, at this period, that his writings were translated and freely current in many languages and that, in 1582, Gregory XIII wrote to him eulogizing them in the most exuberant terms and urging him to continue his labors for the curing of the infirm, the strengthening of the weak, the comfort of the strong and the glory of both Churches, the militant and the triumphant. When he died, in 1588, it was in the odor of sanctity, and he subsequently appeared to a devotee arrayed in a cloak of glory, glittering with innumerable stars, which were the souls of those saved by his writings.[48]

Ignatius Loyola was inclined to mysticism, and the mental prayer which he taught--the Ejercicio de las tres Potencias or exercise of the memory, intellect and will--differed little from the meditation which, with the mystics, was the prelude to contemplation.[49] Yet he was sceptical as to special graces vouchsafed to mystic ardor; such things were possible, he said, but they were very rare and the demon often thus deludes human vanity.[50] His disciples were less cautious and indulged in the extravagance of the more advanced school, producing many adepts gifted with the highest spiritual graces. Luis de la Puente, who died in 1624, at the age of 69 may be mentioned as an example, for in him the intensity of divine love was so strong that in his ecstasies he shone with a light that filled his cell; he would be elevated from the floor and the whole building would shake as though about to fall; during his sickness, which lasted for thirty years, angels were often seen ministering to him; he had the gift of prophecy and of reading the thoughts of his penitents and, when he died, his garments were torn to shreds and his hair cut off to be preserved as relics. He taught the heretical doctrine that prayer is a satisfaction for sin, while his views as to resignation to the will of God approach closely to the Quietism which we shall hereafter see condemned by the Holy See. Yet he escaped condemnation and his works have continued to the present time to be multiplied in innumerable editions and translations.[51]

It was probably the impossibility of differentiation between heresy and sanctity that explains the vacillation of the Inquisition. During the active proceedings of the Toledo tribunal, the Suprema, in 1530, issued general instructions that there should be appended to all edicts requiring denunciation of prohibited books a clause including mystics given to Illuminism and Quietism.[52] There seem to be no traces of any result from this and the whole matter appears to have ceased to attract attention for many years, until the animosity excited by the Jesuits led to an investigation of the results of their teachings. Melchor Cano, who hated them, denounced them as Alumbrados, such as the Devil has constantly thrust into the Church, and he foretold that they would complete what the Gnostics had commenced.[53]

THE JESUITS

The warning was unheeded and, some ten years later, another Dominican, Fray Alonso de la Fuente, was led to devote himself to a mortal struggle with Illuminism, and with the Society of Jesus as its source. In a long and rambling memorial addressed, in 1575, to Philip II, he relates that, in 1570, he chanced to visit his birth-place, la Fuente del Maestre, near Cuidad Rodrigo, and found there a Jesuit, Gaspar Sánchez, highly esteemed for holiness, but who was blamed for perpetually confessing certain beatas and granting daily communion. Sánchez appealed to him for support and he preached in his favor, which brought to him numerous beatas, whose revelations of their ecstasies and other spiritual experiences surprised him greatly. This led him to investigate, when he found that the practice of contemplation was widely spread, but its inner secrets were jealously guarded, until he persuaded a neice of his, a girl of 17, to reveal them. She said that her director ordered her to place herself in contemplation with the simple prayer, "Lord I am here, Lord you have me here!" when there would come such a flood of evil thoughts, of filthy imaginings, of carnal movements, of infidel conceptions, of blasphemies against God and the saints and the purity of the Mother of God, and against the whole faith, that the torment of them rendered her crazy, but she bore it with fortitude, as her director told her that this was a sign of perfection and of progress on the path.[54]

Thenceforth Fray Alonso devoted himself to the task of investigating and exterminating this dangerous heresy, but the work of investigation was complicated by the concealment of error under external piety. Before discovering a single false doctrine, we meet, he says, a thousand prayers and disciplines and communions and pious sighs and devotions. It is like sifting gold out of sand; to reach one heresy you must winnow away a thousand pious works. So it is everywhere in Spain where there are Jesuits and thus we see what great labor is required to overcome it, since there are not in the kingdom three inquisitors who understand it or have the energy and requisite zeal. Yet he penetrated far enough into it, after sundry prosecutions, to draw up a list of thirty-nine errors, some of which, like those ascribed to witchcraft, suggest the influence of the torture-chamber in extracting confessions satisfactory to the prosecutor. Not only are the adepts guilty of all the heresies of the Begghards, condemned in the Clementines, and of teaching that mental prayer is the sole thing requisite to salvation, but the teachers are great sorcerers and magicians, who have pact with the demon, and thus they make themselves masters of men and women, their persons and property, as though they were slaves. They train many saints, who feel in themselves the Holy Ghost, who see the Divine Essence and learn the secrets of heaven; who have visions and revelations and a knowledge of Scripture, and all this is accomplished by means of the demon, and by magic arts. By magic, they gain possession of women, whom they teach that it is no sin, and sometimes the demon comes disguised as Christ and has commerce with the women.

If Fray Alonso found it difficult to inspire belief in these horrors, it is easily explicable by his account of the origin of the sect in Extremadura, the region to which his labors were devoted. When Cristóbal de Rojas was Bishop of Badajoz (1556-1562) there came there Padre González, a Jesuit of high standing, who introduced the use of Loyola's Exercicios; there were already there two priests, Hernando Alvarez and the Licentiate Zapata, who were familiar with it, and the practice spread rapidly, under the favor of the bishop and his provisor Meléndez, and none who did not use it could be ordained, or obtain licence to preach and hear confessions, for the bishop placed all this in the hands of Alvarez; and when he was translated to Córdova (1562-1571) and subsequently to Seville (1571-1580) he continued to favor the Alumbrados. He was succeeded in Badajoz (1562-1568) by Juan de Ribera, subsequently Archbishop of Valencia, who was at first adverse to the Alumbrados, but they won him over, and he became as favorable to them as Rojas had been, especially to the women, whose trances and stigmata he investigated and approved and rewarded. If any preacher preached against Illuminism, Ribera banished him and, under this protection, the sect multiplied throughout Extremadura. It is true that Bishop Simancas, who succeeded Ribera (1569-1579) was not so favorable, and his provisor, Picado, at one time prosecuted a number of Alumbrados, who took refuge in Seville under Rojas, among whom was Hernando Alvarez, but the Llerena tribunal took no part in this and the great body of the sect was undisturbed.

***

It is easy to conceive, therefore, the obstacles confronting Fray Alonso, when he commenced his crusade in 1570. He relates at much length his labors, against great opposition, especially of the Jesuits, and he found no little difficulty in arousing the Llerena inquisitors to action, for they said that it was a new matter and obscure, which required instructions from the Suprema. It is true that, in February 1572, they lent him some support and made a few arrests, but nothing seems to have come of it. He wished to go to Madrid and lay the matter before the Suprema, but his superiors, who apparently disapproved of his zeal, sent him, in October 1572, to Avila, to purchase lumber, and then to Usagre, to preach the Lenten sermons of 1573. After this his prior despatched him to Arenas about the lumber, and it was a providence of God that this business necessitated action by the Council of Military Orders, so that he had an excuse for visiting Madrid. There he sought Rodrigo de Castro--the captor of Carranza--to whom he complained of the negligence and indifference of the Llerena inquisitors, and gave a memorial reciting the errors of the Alumbrados. This resulted in the Suprema sending for the papers, on seeing which it ordered the arrest of the most guilty, when Hernando Alvarez, Francisco Zamora and Gaspar Sánchez were seized in Seville, where they had taken refuge. This produced only a momentary effect in Extremadura, where the Alumbrados comforted themselves with the assurance that their leaders would be dismissed with honor.

It had been proposed to remove the tribunal from Llerena to Plasencia, where houses had been bought for it, but, early in 1574, Fray Alonso remonstrated with the inquisitor-general, pointing out that the land was full of Alumbrados, many of them powerful, and what preaching had been done against them, under the protection of the Inquisition, would be silenced if it were removed. This brought a summons and in May he appeared before the Suprema, where his revelations astonished the members and they asked his advice. He urged a visitation of the district, to be made by the fiscal Montoya, who had studied the matter and understood it, while the inquisitors did not comprehend the subtle mysteries and distinctions involved. It was so ordered, and Montoya commenced his visitation at Zafra, where, on July 25th he published the Edict of Faith, and a special one against Illuminism and Quietism. At first he was much disconcerted in finding among the Alumbrados nothing but fasts and disciplines, prayers, contemplation, hair-shirts, confessions and communions or, if traces appeared of evil doctrines, so commingled with the words of God and the sacraments that evil was concealed in good. Fray Alonso however encouraged him to investigate the lives and conversation of those who enjoyed trances and visions and the stigmata, when it became evident that all was magic art, the work of Satan and of hell. For four months Montoya gathered information and sent the papers to the Suprema, which ordered the arrest with sequestration of five persons, four of the adepts and a female disciple. Towards the close of December he returned to Llerena, to resume the visitation in March, 1575. During the interval Fray Alonso was summoned to Madrid, where he was ordered to accompany Montoya, and the inquisitors were instructed to pay him a salary; this at first they refused to do and then assigned him four reales a day for each day on which he should preach, but the Suprema intervened with an order on the receiver to pay him a certain sum that would enable him to perform the duty. The visitation lasted from March till the beginning of November, and comprised sixteen places, in which Fray Alonso tells us that there were found great errors and sins. Unfortunately he omits to inform us what were the practical results or what was done with the culprits arrested the previous year, and he concludes his memorial by assuring us that the Jesuits and the Alumbrados are alike in doctrine and are the same, which is so certain that to doubt it would be great sin and offence to God.

THE ALUMBRADOS OF LLERENA

Fray Alonso might safely thus attack the children of Loyola in Spain, but he made a fatal error when his zeal induced him to carry the war into Portugal. In the following year, 1576, he addressed memorials to the Portuguese ecclesiastical authorities, ascribing to the Jesuits all the Illuminism that afflicted Spain; they taught, he said, that their contemplation of the Passion of Christ was rewarded with the highest spiritual gifts, including impeccability, with the corollary that carnal indulgence was no sin in the Illuminated, while in reality their visions and revelations were the work of demons, whom they controlled by their skill in sorcery. The Jesuits, however, by this time were a dominant power in Portugal; Cardinal Henry, the inquisitor-general, transmitted the memorials to the Spanish Inquisition, with a request for the condign punishment of the audacious fraile. It was no more than he had openly preached and repeatedly urged on the Suprema, but the time was fast approaching for the absorption of Portugal under the Castilian crown, and Cardinal Henry was to be propitiated. Fray Alonso was forced to retract, and was recluded in a convent, but this did not satisfy the Cardinal, who asked for his extradition, or that the matter be submitted to the Holy See, when the opportune death of the fraile put a happy end to the matter.[55]

Yet, in Spain, Fray Alonso exerted a decisive influence on the relations of the Inquisition to mysticism and, before this unlucky outburst of zeal, he had the satisfaction of seeing the indifference of the Llerena tribunal excited to active work. In 1576, while preaching in that city, he said that he had heard of persons who, under an exterior of special sanctity, gave free rein to their appetites. On this, an imprudent devotee, named Mari Sanz, interrupted him, exclaiming "Padre, the lives of these people are better and their faith sounder than your own" and, when he reproved her, she declared that the Holy Spirit had moved her. This was a dangerous admission; she was arrested, and her confessions led to the seizure of so many accomplices that the tribunal was obliged to ask for assistance. An experienced inquisitor, Francisco de Soto, Bishop of Salamanca, was sent, who vigorously pushed the trials until he died, January 29, 1578, poisoned, as it was currently reported, by his physician, who was long detained in prison under the accusation. How little the sectaries imagined themselves to have erred is seen in the fact that one of them, a shoemaker named Juan Bernal, obeyed a revelation which directed him to appeal to Philip II, to tell him of the injustice perpetrated at Llerena and to ask him why he did not intervene and evoke the matter to himself--hardihood which earned for him six years of galley-service and two hundred lashes.

The evidence elicited in the trials showed the errors ordinarily attributed to Illuminism, including trances and revelations and sexual abominations unfit for transcription. After three years spent in this work, an auto was held, June 14, 1579, in which, among other offenders, there appeared fifteen Alumbrados--ten men and five women. Of the men, all but the unlucky shoemaker were priests, and among them we recognize Hernando Alvarez, against whom there appeared no less than a hundred and forty-six witnesses. Many were curas of various towns and naturally the illicit relations were principally between confessors and their spiritual daughters. From a doctrinal standpoint, their offence seems not to have been regarded as serious, for none of them were degraded, and the abjurations were for light suspicion, but this leniency was accompanied by deprivation of functions, galley-service, reclusion and similar penalties, while the fines inflicted amounted to fifteen hundred ducats and eight thousand maravedís. The unfortunate Mari Sanz, who had caused the explosion, expiated her imprudence by appearing with a gag and a sentence to perpetual prison, two hundred lashes in Llerena and two hundred more at la Fuente del Maestre, her place of residence.[56] From the number of those inculpated it may be assumed that this auto did not empty the prisons, and that it was followed by others, but if so, we have no record of them. The impression produced by the affair was wide and profound. Páramo, writing towards the end of the century, speaks of it as one in which the vigilance of the Inquisition preserved Spain from serious peril.[57]

HOSTILITY OF THE INQUISITION

In fact, it marks a turning-point in the relations of the Inquisition to Spanish mysticism, of which the persecution became one of its regular and recognized duties. Even before the auto of 1579, the Suprema, in a carta acordada of January 4, 1578, ordered the tribunals to add to the Edict of Faith a section in which the errors developed in the trials were enumerated. These consisted in asserting that mental prayer is of divine precept and that it fulfils everything, while vocal prayer is of trivial importance; that the servants of God are not required to labor; that the orders of superiors are to be disregarded, when conflicting with the hours devoted to mental prayer and contemplation; decrying the sacrament of matrimony; asserting that the perfect have no need of performing virtuous actions; advising persons not to marry or to enter religious Orders; saying that the servants of God are to shine in secular life; obtaining promises of obedience and enforcing it in every detail; holding that, after reaching a certain degree of perfection, they cannot look upon holy images or listen to sermons, and teaching these errors under pledge of secrecy.[58]

It is noteworthy that here there is no allusion to ecstasies or trances or to sexual aberrations, as in subsequent edicts, although Páramo, some twenty years later, in his frequent allusions to the Alumbrados, dwells especially on the latter and on the dangers to which they led in the confessional.[59] That this danger was not imaginary is indicated by the case of Fray Juan de la Cruz, a discalced Franciscan, so convinced of the truth of alumbrado doctrine that, in 1605, he presented himself to the Toledo tribunal with a memorial in which he argued that indecent practices between spiritual persons were purifying and elevating to the soul, and resulting in the greatest spiritual benefit when unaccompanied with desire to sin. He was promptly placed on trial and six witnesses testified to his teaching of this doctrine. Ordinary seduction in the confessional, as will be seen hereafter, when the culprit admitted it to be a sin, was treated with comparative leniency, but doctrinal error was far more serious, and the unlucky fraile, who maintained throughout the trial the truth of his theories, was visited with much greater severity. Humiliations and disabilities were heaped upon him; he received a circular scourging in a convent of his order and a monthly discipline for a year, with six years of reclusion.[60]

Simple mysticism, however, even without the advanced doctrines of Illuminism and Quietism, was becoming to the Inquisition an object of pronounced hostility. The land was being filled with beatas revelanderas; mystic fervor was spreading and threatening to become a part of the national religion, stimulated doubtless by the increasing cult paid to its prominent exemplars, for Santa Teresa was beatified in 1614 and canonized in 1622, while San Pedro de Alcántara was beatified in the latter year.

Apart from all moral questions, the mystic might at any moment assert independence; his theory was destructive to the intervention of the priest between man and God, and Illuminism was only a development of mysticism. The Inquisition was not wholly consistent, but its determination to stem the current which was setting so strongly was emphatically expressed in the trial of Padre Gerónimo de la Madre de Dios by the Toledo tribunal in 1616.

The padre was a secular priest, the son of Don Sánchez de Molina, who for forty-eight years had been corregidor of Malagon. He had entered the Dominican Order, had led an irregular life and apparently had been expelled but, in 1610, had been converted from his evil ways by a vision and, in 1613, obeying a voice from God, he had come to Madrid and taken service in a little hospital attached to the parish church of San Martin. His sermons speedily attracted crowds, including the noblest ladies of the court; his fervent devotion, the austerity of his life, the rigor of his mortifications and the self-denial of his charities won for him the reputation of a saint, which was enhanced by the trances into which he habitually fell when celebrating mass, and popular credulity credited him with elevation from the ground. There is absolutely no evidence that in this there was hypocrisy or imposture, and the most searching investigation failed to discover any imputation on his virtue. All that he received he gave to the poor, even to clothes from his back, and his sequestrated property consisted solely of pious books, rosaries and objects of devotion. He speedily gathered around him disciples, prominent among whom was Fray Bartolomé de Alcalá, vicar of the Geronimite convent; the number of their penitents, all espirituales was large, and these usually partook of the sacrament daily or oftener; many of them had revelations and were consulted by the pious as being in direct relations with God, from whom they received answers to petitions.

GERONIMO DE LA MADRE DE DIOS

In all this there was nothing beyond the manifestations of devotional fervor customary to Spanish piety, but an accusation was brought against Padre Gerónimo, September 20, 1615, for teaching that the soul could reach a state of perfection in which it would be an act of imperfection to ask God for anything. This, which was one of the refinements of mysticism, was subsequently proved by the calificadores to be subversive of existing observances, because the saints in heaven were in a state of perfection and, if they could ask nothing of God, what would become of their suffrage and intercession and what would be the use of the cult and oblations offered to them? Still, at the time, the tribunal took no action beyond examining a few witnesses, and Gerónimo would probably not have been disturbed in his useful career had he not written a book. In his mystic zeal he imagined himself inspired in the composition of a work entitled El Discipulo espiritual que trata de oracion mental y de espiritu, which he submitted to several learned theologians, whose emendations he adopted. This had considerable currency in MS.; a demand arose for its printing, and he laid it before the Royal Council for a licence, when he was informed that the approbation of the episcopal provisor of Toledo was a condition precedent. After sending it to that official and receiving no answer for six months, he submitted a copy to the Suprema, October 20, 1615, explaining what he had done and asking for its examination; if there was in it anything contrary to the faith, he desired its correction, for he wished the work to be unimpeachably orthodox and would die a thousand deaths in defence of the true religion.

He waited some seven months and, on May 17, 1616, he ventured an inquiry of the Suprema, but a month earlier three calificadores had reported on it unfavorably, the Suprema had ordered the Toledo tribunal to act and, on May 28th, the warrant for his arrest with sequestration was issued. A mass of papers, MS. sermons, tracts and miscellaneous accumulations were distributed among fifteen calificadores, who, as scholastic theologians, were not propitiated by his contempt for schoolmen. They performed their task with avidity and accumulated an imposing array of a hundred and eighty-six erroneous propositions--many of them the veriest trifles, significant only of their temper, but, after all his explanations, there was a formidable residuum of twenty-five qualified as heretical, twenty-nine as erroneous, three as sacrilegious, and numerous others as scandalous, rash and savoring of heresy.

Despite the piteous supplications of his aged father, his trial lasted until September, 1618--some twenty-seven months of incarceration, during which his health suffered severely. Throughout it all he never varied from his attitude of abject submission; kneeling and weeping he begged for penance and punishment, as he would rather be plunged in hell than commit a sin or give utterance to aught offensive to pious ears. This availed him little. He was sentenced to appear in the auto of September 2, 1618, as a penitent, to abjure de vehementi and to retract publicly a list of sixty-one errors. He was forbidden for life to preach or to hear confessions, or to write on religious subjects; he was recluded for a year in a designated convent and for five more was banished from Madrid and Toledo, and a public edict commanded the surrender of all his writings. Thus he was not only publicly proclaimed a heretic, but his career was blasted, he was virtually deprived of the means of subsistence, yet his first act on reaching his place of confinement was to write humbly thanking the inquisitors for their kindness. Seven months later he appealed to them, saying that he was sick and enfeebled, he had been bled four times and he begged for the love of God that he might be spared the rest of his reclusion and be allowed to comfort his aged father. To this no attention was paid and we hear nothing more of him.

THE MYSTICS OF SEVILLE

For us the interest of the case lies not so much in the cruelty with which the bruised reed was broken, as in the revelation of the silent revolution in the Spanish Church with regard to mysticism. In the sixty-one condemned propositions there were one or two properly liable to censure, the most dangerous being that ascribed to the Begghards--that the perfected soul enjoys the spirit of liberty, going at will without laws or rules, and that in this state God gives it the power of working miracles. Another which asserted that devotion to images, rosaries, blessed beads etc. was an error so great that souls so employed could have no hope of salvation was scarce more than an exaggeration of the precepts of Francisco de Osuna and Juan de la Cruz. For the most part, the condemned propositions were merely the common-places of the great mystics of the sixteenth century--that the perfected soul enjoys absolute peace, for the appetites and passions are at rest and the flesh in no way contradicts the spirit--that trances are the highest of God's gifts--that the supreme grade of contemplation becomes habitual, and that the soul at will can thus enter God's presence--that, in the trance, God can be seen--that the perfected soul should ask only that God's will be done. Other condemnations were directed against the claims of inspiration and revelation, against the suspension of the faculties in mental prayer, against the Union with God which had been the aim of all the mystics. In short, it was a condemnation of the doctrines and practices which, for centuries, had been recognized by the Church as manifestations of the utmost holiness. Had Francisco de Osuna, Luis de Granada, San Pedro de Alcántara, Santa Teresa, San Juan de la Cruz and their disciples been judged by the same standard, they would have shared the fate of Padre Gerónimo unless, indeed, their convictions had led them to refuse submission, in which case they would have been burnt.[61] This was shown at Valladolid when, in 1620, Juan de Gabana, priest of San Martin de Valverri and Gerónima González, a widow, were prosecuted for mysticism. He died in prison, pertinacious to the last and was duly burnt in effigy, in 1622. She was less firm and was voted to reconciliation, but the Suprema ordered her to be tortured; this she escaped by dying, and her effigy was reconciled.[62]

Yet the mystic cult was too firmly planted in the religious habits of Spain to be readily eradicated, nor was the Inquisition prepared to be wholly consistent. While Padre Gerónimo was thus harshly treated for unpublished writings, the Minim Fray Fernando de Caldera was allowed undisturbed to publish, in 1623, his Mística Teología, perhaps the craziest of the mystic treatises. It is cast in the form of instructions uttered by Christ, in the first person, and teaches Illuminism and Quietism of the most exalted kind. The intellect is to be suspended and the will abandoned to God, who does with it as he pleases, infusing it with divine light and admitting it to a knowledge of the divine mysteries. Lubricious temptations, if they come from the flesh are to be overcome with austerities; if from pride, with humility; if they are passive, they are to be met with patience and resignation, for God who sends them will remove them at his own time and with great benefit to the soul.[63] No teaching more dangerous is to be found in Molinos but, although a translation of the work appeared in Rome in 1658, it escaped condemnation both there and in Spain.

During this time there was a storm gathering in Seville which enabled the Inquisition to impress its definite policy on the mystically inclined. We have seen how mysticism flourished there under the patronage of Archbishop Rojas, and the persecution in Extremadura seems not to have extended to Andalusia, so that it continued unrepressed. While Padre Gerónimo was awaiting his doom in Toledo, a much more extravagant performer was enjoying the cult of the devout in Seville. A priest named Fernando Méndez had a special reputation for sanctity; when celebrating mass he fell into trances and uttered terrible roars; he taught his disciples to invoke his intercession, as though he were already a saint in heaven; fragments of his garments were treasured as relics; he gathered a congregation of beatas and, after mass in his oratory, they would strip off their garments and dance with indecent vigor--drunk with the love of God--and, on some of his female penitents, he would impose the penance of lifting their skirts and exposing themselves before him. His disciples were not drawn merely from the lower classes, for we are told that as many as thirty coaches could be counted of a morning around the gate of the Franciscan convent to which he had retired.[64]

***

This hysteric contagion spread through Seville, affecting a considerable portion of the population. There was no concealment and evidently no thought that it involved suspicion of heresy, or that it departed in any way from orthodoxy. A special group of mystics, known as la Granata, under successive spiritual directors, had long held their meetings in the chapel of Nuestra Señora de la Granada, without exciting animadversion or calling for interference from the Inquisition.[65] When, however, the imperious

Pacheco, in 1622, assumed the office of inquisitor-general, he speedily ordered the Seville tribunal to investigate and report as to the mystic extravagances current in the city, and there could have been no difficulty in collecting ample material for condemnation according to the new standard. This resulted in the publication of a special Edict of Grace, May 9, 1523, granting the customary thirty days in which those feeling themselves inculpated could denounce themselves and their accomplices and be admitted to absolution with salutary penance and without confiscation or disabilities affecting their descendants. That all might understand what these new heresies were, the edict embodied a list of seventy-six errors ascribed to the Alumbrados, which marks the advance made since 1578 in suppressing mysticism in general and in attributing to it additional evil practices. There was a fuller condemnation of the beliefs common to all mystics, which had so often earned canonization--that their trembling or burning or fainting was a sign of grace and of the influence of the Holy Spirit--that a stage of perfection could be reached in which they could see the Divine Essence and the mysteries of the Trinity and that, in this state, grace drowned all the faculties--that they were governed directly by the Holy Spirit in what they did or left undone--that in contemplation they dismissed all thought and concentrated themselves in the presence of God--that, in the state of Union with God, the will is subordinated--that in trances God is clearly seen in his glory--that mental prayer renders other works superfluous--that other duties, both religious and worldly, can be neglected to devote oneself wholly to this supreme devotion.

Besides these, there was an enumeration of the errors commonly attributed to the Alumbrados with more or less justice--impeccability--the elevation of mental prayer to the dignity of a sacrament--communion with more than one wafer--promiscuous intercourse among the elect--indecent actions in the confessional regarded as meritorious--teaching wives to refuse cohabitation--forcing girls to take vows of chastity or to become nuns--requiring vows of absolute obedience to the spiritual director--breathing on the mouths of female penitents to communicate to them the love of God--violation of the seal of the confessional--that the perfected have power of absolution even in reserved cases--that those who follow this doctrine will escape purgatory and that many who refused to do so have returned to beg release, when they give them an Evangelio and see them fly to heaven. One article would indicate that among the devotees, as was usually the case, there was at least one who boasted of bearing the stigmata, of conversing with God and of living solely upon the sacrament, while a clause requiring the surrender of all statutes and instructions for their congregations and assemblies shows that they were organized into more or less formal associations.[66]

The audacious assumption of power in this pronouncement was forcibly pointed out by Juan Dionisio Portocarrero, in an opinion furnished to the Archbishop Pedro de Castro y Quiñones. There was gross disrespect shown to him, who had been kept in ignorance, though it was known that an edict was in preparation, of which the nature was sedulously concealed until it was suddenly published in all the churches. Inquisitors could not decide cases without the participation of the Ordinary, while here the cases were tried and the parties admitted to reconciliation, without calling in the episcopal authority. Similar usurpation was manifested in the definition of heresies, which was the attribute of the Holy See and of general councils, not of the Inquisition. No general council could do more than the inquisitor-general had done in defining the seventy-six errors, and to say that these errors were widely disseminated in Seville, not without fault of those permitting it, and to do so without calling upon the archbishop to explain the condition of his flock, was to condemn him without a hearing. These seventy-six propositions were all styled matters of faith, although many of them were rather matters of discipline, pertaining to the Ordinary, yet all were reserved to the Inquisition. Moreover, the inquisitor-general was not competent to decide the disputed question whether the power assured to bishops to absolve for secret heresy was annulled by the bull in Coena Domini. Then Portocarrero proceeded to examine one by one a considerable portion of the condemned propositions and showed that some of them expressed the accepted teaching of the Church, while many were not cognizable by the Inquisition, because they had nothing to do with faith, and others again he omitted as being unintelligible. He urged the archbishop to vindicate his jurisdiction quietly, without causing scandal, and that the edict be examined and qualified by learned men, not Dominicans, for it had originated with them--the truth being that the inculpated mystics were mostly under the direction of Franciscans and Jesuits and that, in the bitter hatred between the Orders, the Dominicans had stirred up the matter to strike a blow at their rivals.[67]

***

The poor old archbishop, who died in December of the same year, of course did nothing. The edict was published on June 4th and again on the 11th, when the most pious circles in Seville suddenly found themselves arraigned for heresy. Mysticism had become fashionable, especially among the women, from the noblest to the lower classes, and they rushed at once to obtain the pardon promised within the thirty days. A Seville letter of June 15th says that an inquisitor with a secretary established himself in San Pablo (the Dominican church used in autos de fe), eating and sleeping there, and on duty from 5

A.M. until 10 P.M., with an hour's intermission for meals, but that he could not attend to a twentieth part of the applicants, and that another thirty days would have to be granted. In this there is doubtless exaggeration, but another authority states the number of those inculpated at 695.[68] There had of course been no intentional heresy and there were no pertinacious heretics, although among them were impostors who had traded upon popular credulity and love for the marvellous. Still, an auto de fe was necessary to confirm the impression and it was held on November 30, 1624, in which eleven Alumbrados appeared, but eight of them were confessed impostors. Of the remaining three, one was the Padre Fernando Méndez, who in dying had distributed his garments and his virtues among his disciples; no special punishment was decreed against his memory, but his effigy was displayed in the auto, his revelations, trances, visions and prophecies were declared to be fictitious, and his disciples were required to surrender the articles which they had treasured as relics. Another was a mulatto slave named Antonio de la Cruz, who had united to his mysticism some unauthorized speculations respecting the power of Satan; he escaped with abjuration de levi and deprivation of the sacrament except at Easter, Pentecost and Christmas. The third was Francisco del Castillo, a priest whose trances were so frequent and uncontrollable that they would seize him in the act of eating; he was at the head of a congregation, the members of which he boasted were all saved, and through which the Church was to be reformed, he being possessed of the spirit of Jesus Christ and his disciples of that of the Apostles--all of which had not prevented him from maintaining improper relations with his female penitents. He was sentenced only to abjuration de levi, perpetual deprivation of confessing and reclusion for four years in a convent, with exile from Seville--the usual penalty, as we shall see, for solicitation ad turpia in the confessional-- with warning of severer punishment if he did not abandon his visions and revelations.[69]

Evidently the object of the Edict had been to warn rather than to punish; but few examples were deemed necessary, and in these the mildness of the penalties indicates a recognition of the fact that these so-called heresies had not previously been regarded as culpable. It sufficed to set an impressive stamp of reprobation on mysticism without unnecessary severity.

Seville, however, was not yet cleansed of the infection. At an auto held some two years later, on February 28, 1627, there were two conspicuous mystics, Maestre Juan de Villalpando, a priest in charge of one of the city parishes, and Madre Catalina de Jesus, a Carmelite beata. Notwithstanding the Edict of 1623, Villalpando had maintained a congregation of both sexes, who obeyed him implicitly in all things, temporal and spiritual. No less than two hundred and seventy-five erroneous propositions were charged against him, and he was required to retract twenty-two articles. He was deprived of his priestly functions, recluded for four years in a convent and confined subsequently to the city of Seville, with a fine of two hundred ducats. Madre Catalina, for thirty-eight years, had been sick with the love of God, and her continued existence was regarded as a miracle by her numerous disciples, who treasured as relics whatever had touched her person. She was accused of improper relations with a priest--probably Villalpando--who reverenced her as his guide and teacher, and she was a dogmatizer, for her writings, both MS. and printed, were required to be surrendered. On the testimony of a hundred and forty-eight witnesses, she was sentenced to reclusion for six years in a hospital, where she was to earn her support by labor.[70]

This shows increasing severity, and a still more deterrent example was furnished, in 1630, by an auto in which eight Alumbrados, as we are told, were burned alive and six in effigy. There were also sixty reconciliations, of which some were doubtless for the same heresy.[71] We have no further details of this auto, save that Bernino characterizes the victims as obstinate; possibly they may have been relapsed but, as we have seen, the abjurations had been for light suspicion, which did not entail relaxation for relapse. Be this as it may, the affair would indicate that Illuminism was now regarded as formal heresy, not as merely inferring suspicion, and that pertinacity incurred the stake.

TREATMENT

Obstinacy, in fact, converts into formal heresy what may be otherwise regarded as light suspicion, as it infers disobedience to the decisions of the Church. This is seen in an interesting review of the whole subject by an inquisitor about 1640. He describes the evidence customarily brought against alumbrado confessors and preachers, of teaching sensuality under cover of mortification. Some hold that indecent handling and sleeping with a woman are meritorious as trampling on the devil and overcoming temptation; so it is with making the penitent strip and stand against a wall with arms outstretched, and other details that may well be spared. There is also teaching that obedience is better than the sacrament and that it excuses what would otherwise be evil, or that God has revealed to them that such things are not sin, or that interior impulses are to be followed in doing or not doing anything. Such persons, he tells us are confined in the secret prison, without sequestration, although, if there is suspicion of heresy, there is sequestration. If, as usually occurs, they confess to these teachings, extenuating them as the result of thoughtlessness or ignorance without errors of belief, and if they are priests or frailes, the sentence is read in the audience-chamber and the punishment is the same as for solicitation in the confessional--that is to say, reclusion in a monastery for a term of years and deprivation of the faculty of confessing. But, if this evil doctrine has caused much injury, as at Llerena, they appear in a public auto with some years of galley-service and, if they are priests owning property, they are fined at discretion.

If there should be obstinacy and rejection of the arguments of the theologians deputed to reason with them, there is postponement for some months to allow time for conversion, as happened in Logroño with a certain priest, and in Valladolid with a fraile. The priest taught his female penitents that there was no sin in kisses and in indecent handling and in sleeping with a woman so long as the final act was omitted. He revoked repeatedly and varied between submission and persistence, but was convinced at last and appeared in a public auto, abjured de vehementi, was verbally degraded with five years of galleys and ten more of exile, besides perpetual deprivation of confessing. If the culprit is impervious to argument and will not abandon errors of belief, he must be treated as a heretic and be relaxed even if he denies intention. There was one who abjured de vehementi and relapsed. It was alleged by his Order that he was insane, for he was a person of high repute for virtue and learning; he was given secret penance, but so severe that he was never heard of again.[72]

From this statement it would appear that the extreme position assumed by Pacheco had not been maintained and that simple mysticism was tolerated unless it was complicated with the follies of Illuminism, especially as concerned the relations between the sexes. The policy of the Inquisition, in fact, was by no means uniform; for a time many harmless mystics were allowed to enjoy in peace the veneration of their disciples while, if there was scandal or imposture or some ulterior motive, prosecution was easy. One such case was that of Fray Francisco García Calderon whom we have seen (Vol. II, p. 135) concerned with the case of the nuns of San Placido and the Marquis of Villanueva, in 1630. A contemporary was Doña Luisa de Colmenares, popularly known as Madre Luisa de Carrion, a nun of the convent of Santa Clara, at Carrion de los Condes, who, at the age of seventy, had passed fifty-three years in a cloister. She was not strictly an Alumbrado but a mystic of the type of Santa Teresa, and her case is instructive as showing how general was the belief attributing supernatural powers to beings favored by God, how profitably this belief could be exploited by shrewd management, and how effectively the Inquisition could intervene, in the face of the most intense popular opposition. There is no reason to suppose that Madre Luisa was consciously an impostor; she was merely an ignorant old woman, hypnotically habituated to trances and visions like so many others, and the Franciscan Order, to which she belonged, saw in her a speculative value of which they made the most. Philip IV venerated her and popes were her correspondents; there was an immense demand for objects sanctified by her--crosses, beads, images of the Christ-child and similar trifles--the sales of which brought in large profits and, between these and the offerings of pilgrims, the Order was said to have realized two hundred thousand crowns and to look forward to much more if it could secure her canonization after death.

MADRE LUISA DE CARRION

Suddenly, in 1635, the Inquisition undertook to investigate her. There had been nothing exceptional in her career, except its success and, under Franciscan management she had been mostly kept clear of the errors condemned in Pacheco's edict. The motive for action is obscure, and the most probable suggestion is that the opponents of Count-Duke Olivares had sought, after the fashion of the time, to make use, for political ends, of the boundless popular veneration of which she was the object. Yet there was significant caution in the preliminaries. Juan Santos, senior Inquisitor of Valladolid, was ordered to examine her, when he pretended a visit to the Bishop of Palencia and on the road stopped for a fortnight at Carrion. It was not difficult to involve an untutored nun in erroneous theological speculations, and a warrant for her arrest followed; she was placed in a carriage with a female relative of one of the inquisitors, when her journey to Valladolid was a triumphal procession. A pillar of light, changing into a cross, was seen in the sky; everywhere the population gathered in mass, and the precaution of entering Valladolid at night was unavailing, for the crowds were so great that she was with difficulty carried in safety, through the surging mob striving to gather some fragment of her dress as a talisman. She was housed in the Augustinian convent, where she was the object of veneration to the nuns, who declared her destined to be the most powerful saint in the annals of the Church; but it was observed that she no longer had ecstasies, although at Carrion they had been of daily occurrence and were celebrated by sounding the organ, when everyone rushed to see them.

The Franciscans officially undertook her defence; the population of Valladolid, with the bishop at their head, were so demonstrative in her favor that the tribunal hesitated, and the Suprema had to send a special commissioner, who was no other than our old acquaintance Juan Dionisio Portocarrero, soon afterwards rewarded with the bishopric of Guadix. It was easy to make her convict herself of heresy, for she was foolish and ignorant, full of vain-glory, and merely a tool of the rapacious friars who had exploited her. Papers signed by her were in circulation in which she declared that she had seen the Divine Essence, that she was confirmed in grace, that at six years of age Christ had removed her heart of flesh and substituted his own, that he had given her an apple of paradise by which she would remain immortal until the Day of Judgement, when she would accompany Enoch and Elias in the war with Antichrist; that God sustained her without food, and much more that testifies to the incredible credulity of the people, and to the unscrupulous audacity of the friars. Under examination, she declared that she had seen the Divine Essence, but she proved herself wholly ignorant of the orthodox doctrine of the Trinity and uttered a thousand follies, including a revelation from God that all who possessed her crosses, beads, rosaries or other objects of devotion would be saved unconditionally and could rest secure of their predestination.

    The fore-ordained condemnation was preceded by an edict of October 23, 1636, requiring the surrender of all letters, portraits, crosses, beads etc., which were so numerous that in a few days the cura of the parish of San Miguel had a room full of them. The poor old crone was blind, toothless and exhausted with a life of hysteria; the shock of these experiences was too great for her feeble vitality, and she died in November. This was, of course, no impediment to her trial, and the tribunal was justly incensed to learn that the bishop had buried her without its permission. When summoned to answer for this he threatened a popular uprising, but the tribunal held good, exhumed the body and verified its identity, after which the Suprema ordered a second exhumation and burial under its authority.

    It seems that no formal sentence was ever rendered. The Franciscans talked of appealing to the pope, but were only laughed at. Madre Luisa had ceased to be of importance, but that her devotees had not lost all veneration for her is shown by the Inquisition, in 1638, forbidding all discussion of the case. In 1643 it was referred to Arce y Reynoso, together with that of San Placido and, in 1644, he was said to be pushing it with energy, but probably it was wisely allowed to be forgotten, without reaching a conclusion. Yet, notwithstanding the inquisitorial edict, her crosses were not all surrendered and continued to be regarded as enriched with indulgences, for we find them condemned by the Roman Congregation of Indulgences in 1668 and again in 1678.[73]

INFLUENCE OF MYSTICS

    But for the presumably political motive prompting her prosecution it may be assumed that Madre Luisa would have been enrolled in the calendar of saints. Her career was no more extravagant than that of her contemporary, the Blessed María Ana de Jesus, a Madrileña, who was born in 1565 and died in 1624. She belonged to the Order of La Merced, and her biography was written in 1673, by Fray Juan de la Presentacion, official historiographer of Philip IV, who informs us that, when an infant at the breast, she gave evidence of her future sanctity; at the age of four she was constantly at prayer, and at six she had ecstasies, visions and revelations. She says herself that her soul was ordinarily illuminated by God, who manifested his will to her unmistakably. The effort for her canonization began shortly after her death and was renewed at intervals, until she was beatified in 1783.[74] Another contemporary of María Ana de Jesus was she of Peru, known as la Azucena de Quito. Born in 1618 and dying in 1645, her miracles commenced before her birth, and she began to mortify the flesh by refusing to suckle before noon-day. It was in vain that, in her humility, she prayed to be denied the favor of visions and miracles. Efforts were commenced, in 1670, to procure her canonization, but it was not until 1850 that she was beatified by Pius IX.[75]

    These saintly mystics, with their direct communications from God, wielded an influence which we can scarce realize. They had become so numerous and their revelations were so unhesitatingly accepted, that Spain was enveloped in an atmosphere of mysticism, in which the divine guidance was sought, rather than the councils of human wisdom. Olivares might well fear any adverse utterances of Madre Luisa, for his downfall, in 1643, was accelerated by visions enjoyed by Don Francisco de Chiribaga, although the Jesuit Padre Galindo, who was concerned in making them known, was imprisoned by his superiors for acting without their permission.[76] When the affairs of the Spanish monarchy were at their lowest ebb at this time, it is a curious revelation of the impulses under which it was governed to find Philip IV complaining of the perplexities to which he was exposed by the visions brought to him by the frailes; this matter of revelations, he says, is one which requires much consideration, especially when he is told that God orders him to punish those who have rendered him good service, and to elevate those whose methods have not earned them a good reputation. All that is lacking to complete this picture of unreasoning superstition is found in the fact that this utterance is made to another mystic to whom he appeals for guidance and for intercession with God to send him light.[77]

    María de Jesus, commonly known as Sor María de Agreda, to whom Philip thus turned for counsel, was too strongly entrenched in the royal favor to be in danger from the Inquisition yet, notwithstanding that favor, her revelations were rejected by Rome, thus furnishing another example of the difficulty of differentiating between sanctity and heresy. She had practised mental prayer from the time when she was able to use her reason, and she was in constant communication with God, the Virgin and the angels.[78] Her fame filled the land, and her voluminous writings, which claim to be inspired, still form part of the devotional literature of the faithful. She so captured the confidence of Philip that he made her his chief adviser; for twenty-two years, until her death in 1665, four months before his own, he maintained constant correspondence with her by every post. Her influence thus was almost unbounded, but she seems never to have abused it; her advice was usually sound, and she never sought the enrichment of the impoverished convent of Agreda, of which she was the superior.

SOR MARIA DE AGREDA

With all the power of the Franciscan Order and of the Spanish court to sustain her claims to sanctity, the canonization of such a personage would seem almost a matter of course, and it would doubtless have been effected if she had not reduced her revelations to writing. However they might suit the appetite of Spanish piety, nourished so long on mystic extravagance, they did not appeal to the sober judgement of the rest of the Catholic world. In spite of their divine inspiration, her Letanía y nombres misteriosos de la Reina del Cielo and her Mística Ciudad de Dios were condemned in Rome, and the decree as to the latter was posted on the doors of St. Peter's, August 4, 1681. The Mística Ciudad was eminently popular in Spain and, at the instance of the Spanish court, its prohibition was suspended. The Inquisition took advantage of this, in 1686, to issue a decree permitting its circulation, at which the Congregation of the Index was naturally offended and, in 1692, the papal decree of condemnation appeared in the Appendix to the Index of Innocent XI, in spite of which the book was formally permitted by the Spanish Inquisition.[79] When, in 1695, a translation by Père Thomas Croset appeared in France, the Sorbonne, by decree of September 27, 1696, condemned it as containing propositions contrary to the rules of ecclesiastical modesty, and many fables and dreams from the Apocrypha, exposing Catholicism to the contempt of the heretics.[80] The Spanish court labored earnestly to obtain a renewal of the suspension and finally succeeded, so that the book was omitted from the 1716 Index of Clement XI. Then in 1729, the subject was again taken up, when, after a long debate, the book was permitted, though Dr. Eusebius Amort tells us that in Rome, in 1735, he was shown a decree of Benedict XIII renewing the prohibition and asserting that its withdrawal had been obtained fraudulently; still, the book has never since reappeared in the Index.[81] There was a similar struggle over the Letanía, which was still included in the 1716 Index of Clement XI and the first Index of Benedict XIV, in 1744, but has disappeared from all succeeding issues.[82] Less successful thus far has been the persistent effort to procure the canonization of Madre María, leading to a papal decree of April 27, 1773, forbidding all future proceedings in the case. Notwithstanding this, Leo XIII, on March 10, 1884, ordered the Congregation of Rites to consider in secret whether this prohibition could be removed. To suggest such a discussion is almost equivalent to prejudging it affirmatively but, before the decision was reached, chance led to the publication in the Deutscher Merkur of December 29, 1889, of the whole secret history of the case, which has probably put an end, at least for the present, to the prospect of enrolling in the calendar of saints one whose revelations have been so repeatedly condemned as illusory or as emanating from Satan.

***

While, as we shall see, the pest of beatas revelanderas and more or less conscious impostors continued to afflict the land, the cases recognized as Alumbrados are comparatively few during the remainder of the seventeenth century. In a Toledo record, commencing in 1648, the first one occurs in 1679, when the Franciscan Fray Francisco de Toledo was convicted. In this the offence is treated as formal heresy, requiring reconciliation, and the punishment was extremely severe. He was to receive a circular discipline in his convent; he was to be confined in a cell for two years and for two years more was to be recluded, during which time he was to be occupied in works of humility. In addition, he was perpetually suspended from orders, deprived of active and passive voice, and reduced to lay communion. It is possibly to this, or to some movement in which Fray Francisco bore a part, that Miguel Molinos refers, in a letter of February 16, 1680, to the Jesuit General Oliva, saying that when, in 1679, Satan sought to revive the sect of Illuminists in Spain, and they had applied to him, he had given an opinion so contrary to their follies that it frightened them and stopped the attempt.[83]

ITALIAN MYSTICS

While Spain had thus been combatting Mysticism, Rome had remained comparatively indifferent, for in Italy it had not developed into a popular mania to be suppressed irrespective of the immoral extravagances to which it sometimes led. In the Edict of the Inquisition requiring denunciation of all offences subject to its jurisdiction, there is no mention of Mysticism or Illuminism.[84] The elaborate folios of the writers on the Holy Office--Carena, Del Bene, Lupo, Dandino--are silent as to its eccentricities. Yet these were by no means unknown to the Roman Holy Office, which took cognizance of them when brought to its notice. Occasionally some book too extravagant in its teachings was put upon the Index.[85] Cardinal Scaglia ([dagger symbol] 1639), a member of the Congregation of the Inquisition, in his little manual of practice, which was circulated only in MS., when treating of the troubles customary in nunneries, says that through giddiness of brain, or vain-glory, or illusion, nuns often claim to have celestial visions and revelations and intercourse with God and the saints when, if the confessor is imprudently given to spirituality, he reduces their utterances to writing and, if he is learned, he defends them, very often with propositions punishable by the Inquisition. Sometimes, he adds, sensuality is involved, leading to the assertion that carnal acts are not sinful but meritorious, when, if the confessor desires to take advantage of this, he seeks with revelations and false doctrines to prove that they are lawful. Cases of this kind have occurred in the Holy Office, when priests who so justify themselves become liable to the penalties of heresy. Such cases also occur between women assuming to be spiritual and their confessors, who so teach them, even without revelations and visions, leading their spiritual daughters to believe these to be works of merit and mortification.[86]

Bernino tells us that, early in the seventeenth century, Illuminism was widely diffused throughout Italy, where abjurations enforced by the Inquisition were frequent, but this is probably the exaggeration so frequent with heresiologists.[87] A well-marked case, however, startled Florence in 1640, when the Canon Pandolfo Ricasoli, a highly respected member of the noble house of the Barons of Trappola and a man of wide learning and handsome fortune, was arrested with his chief accomplice Faustina Mainardi, her brother Girolamo, and the Maestro Serafino de' Servi, Dottor Carlo Scalandrini, the priest Giacomo Fantoni, Andrea Biliotti, Francesco Borgeschi and two others, Mozzetti and Cocchi. Some nuns of Santa Anna sul Prato were also implicated, but if they were prosecuted no knowledge of it was allowed to reach the public. They seem to have formed a coterie of Illuminists to whom Ricasoli taught that all manner of indecent acts conduced to purity, if performed with the mind fixed on God; they claimed special relations with heaven and were free from sin in whatever they did for the greater glory of God. This continued for eight years; rumors spread abroad and were conveyed to the Inquisition, when Ricasoli came forward and denounced himself with expressions of contrition. A public atto di fede was held, November 28, 1641, in the great refectory of the convent of Santa Croce, attended by the Grand Duke, the Cardinal de' Medici, the nuncio and other notabilities. One of the culprits, Serafino de' Servi, had died in prison and appeared in effigy, the rest abjured de vehementi. Ricasoli, Faustina and Fantoni were condemned to perpetual irremissible prison, others to prison with the privilege of asking for pardon, while two, Cocchi and Borgeschi, had a private atto di fede and were confined in the Stinche prison at the pleasure of the Inquisition. Ricasoli, as he was led away, declared that he had acted foolishly and ignorantly, and he asked pardon of the people for the scandal which he had caused; he lingered in his prison until July 1657, when he died at the age of 78, protesting to the end that he had erred through ignorance and not through lust; there was some question as to his interment, but finally he received Christian burial. The inquisitor, Fra Giovanni Muzzarelli, was sternly rebuked for misplaced mercy by the Roman Congregation and was speedily replaced by one of severer temper.[88]

Impostors likewise were not unknown, as appears in the career of Francesco Giuseppe Borri, a brilliant but dissolute scion of a noble Milanese house. A misadventure in Rome forced him to take asylum in a church where, in recognition of the mercy of God, he changed his life. He soon had visions and revelations, from which he constructed a new theology, showing an intimate acquaintance with the mysteries of the Trinity and of the universe. That St. Anne was conceived by the operation of the Spirit and the Virgin consequently was Deity, was one of the twenty errors set forth in his sentence. Moreover he had been selected to found the Kingdom of the Highest, in which all mankind would be brought under papal rule, and the world would live in peace for a thousand years; the philosopher's stone, of which he had the secret, would furnish the means of raising the papal armies, in the leadership of which he would be guided by St. Michael. Rome soon became dangerous for the new prophet and, in 1655, he transferred his propaganda to Milan, where he founded a secret mystical Order, the members of which were trained in meditation and mental prayer, pledged themselves to shed their blood in the execution of the work and, what was more to the purpose, contributed all their property to the common fund. The Milanese inquisitor got wind of the new sect and arrested some of the members; Borri thought of raising a tumult but decided in favor of the safer alternative of flight. His case was transferred to the Roman Congregation, which cited him, March 20, 1659, to appear within ninety days and then tried him in absentia, with the result that his effigy, with all his impious writings, was burnt on January 3, 1661. His dupes were duly prosecuted, but seem not to have been severely punished.

***

Meanwhile he was starting on a fresh career in Northern Europe, as a man possessed of all the secrets of alchemy and medicine, with a success that even Cagliostro might have envied. Strassburg and Amsterdam had reason to repent of his seductive arts. In Hamburg, Christina of Sweden furnished him with means to prosecute the work of the Grand Arcanum. Frederic III of Denmark lavished large sums on him and even made him chief political adviser, which aroused the hatred of the heir-apparent, Christian V, on whose accession, in 1670, he was obliged to save his life by flight. He sought to find refuge in Turkey, but in Moravia, when within a day's journey of the frontier, he was arrested by mistake, on suspicion of complicity in a conspiracy in Vienna. There the papal nuncio recognized and claimed him, but Leopold I, whose favor he had speedily acquired by his chemical marvels, surrendered him only on condition that his life should be spared. Before the Inquisition he confessed his errors and attributed them to diabolical inspiration, and his sentence, September 25, 1672, was merely to perpetual prison and certain spiritual penances. Even here his good luck befriended him, for Cardinal d'Estrées, the influential ambassador of Louis XIV, in dangerous illness, asked to consult him and, on recovery, procured his transfer to easier confinement in the castle of St. Angelo, where he was allowed special privileges and sometimes to go out and visit the sick. There he remained until his death, August 20, 1695--just a century before Cagliostro came to the same end.[89]

Although the Roman Inquisition issued no general denunciations, there was a surveillance kept over the votaries of mental prayer and contemplation, in view of the extravagances to which they might be led when, abandoning themselves wholly to God, they felt themselves irresponsible for what God might cause them to do, in the rapture of Quietism. There was a little community of this kind formed in Genoa, where they were known as Sequere me, from the phrase used when addressing those whom they elected to join them. Under the lead of a Trinitarian friar, they bought a house in the suburbs, where they lived in the utmost austerity, devoting themselves to contemplation. Thus came visions and revelations that the Church was to be reformed through them by a new pope, of whom they were to be the apostles. One of them communicated this to a vicar of the Inquisition who promptly reported to the tribunal. They were all summoned before it; some went into ecstasies and, as a body, they threatened the inquisitor with the vengeance of God and were thrown into prison. The Congregation of the Inquisition ordered their prosecution, which resulted in their being adjudged to be crazy rather than evil-minded. The friar was deprived of active and passive voice in his Order and the rest were dismissed with threats of the galleys if they reassembled and continued to wear the habit which they had adopted.[90]

More persistent was the sect known as the Pelagini which, about 1650, developed itself in the Valcamonica and spread throughout Lombardy. Giacomo Filippo di Santa Pelagia was a layman of Milan, highly esteemed for conspicuous piety. From Marco Morosini, Bishop of Brescia (1645-1654) he obtained permission to found conventicles or oratories in the Valcamonica, but it shows that mental prayer was regarded as a dangerous exercise when Morosini imposed the condition that it should not be practised in these little assemblies. The prohibition was disregarded and the devotees largely gave themselves up to contemplation, with the result that they had trances and revelations; they threw off subjection to their priests and were accused of claiming that mental prayer was essential to salvation, that none but Pelagini could be saved, that those who practised it became impeccable, that laymen could preach and hear confessions, that indulgences were worthless and that God through them would reform the world. In 1654, Cardinal Pietro Ottoboni (afterwards Alexander VIII) obtained the see of Brescia and by accident discovered some colporteurs distributing the Catechism of Calvin, along with the tracts of the Pelagini. In March, 1656, he sent to the Valcamonica three commissioners with verbal instructions and armed with full powers, who temporarily suppressed the oratories and made a number of arrests, but the Inquisition intervened, taking the affair out of his hands and prosecuting the leaders.[91]

THE PELAGINI

We hear nothing more of Filippo, except that he never was condemned. He probably died early in the history of the sect and his memory was cherished as that of a saint with thaumaturgic power. In 1686, the Archpriest of Morbegno, in the Valtelline, was found to be distributing relics of him and collecting materials for his life and miracles, all of which he was obliged to abandon, after obeying a summons from Calchi, the Inquisitor of Como. There were also inquiries made of the Provost of Talamona as to his motives in keeping a picture of Filippo and whether it was prayed to.[92]

After Filippo's disappearance we hear of Francesco Catanei and of the Archpriest Marc Antonio Ricaldini as leaders of the sect, but Agostino Ricaldini, a brother of the latter and a married layman, was really the centre around which it gathered. In Ottoboni's prosecution, he was imprisoned in 1656 and thrice tortured, and, on September 19, 1660, he was sentenced by the Brescia tribunal to exile from the Valcamonica and was relegated to Treviso. Persisting in his errors, he was again tried in Treviso, obliged to abjure de vehementi and sentenced to perpetual prison, while a book which he had written was publicly burnt. How long his imprisonment lasted does not appear but, in 1680, we find him living in Treviso, under surveillance of the episcopal vicar-general.[93]

If Ottoboni and the Inquisition fancied that they had crushed the sect, they were mistaken. It maintained a secret existence for over twenty years, which enabled it to spread far beyond its original seat and, about 1680, it had associations and oratories for mental prayer established in Brescia, Verona, Vicenza, Treviso, Padua, Pesaro, Lucca and doubtless many other places, while its votaries expected it to spread through the world. Ricaldini, at Treviso, was busy in corresponding with the heads of the associations and receiving their visits. In Brescia, Bartolommeo Bona, priest of S. Rocco, presided over an oratory of sixty members and was even said to have six hundred souls under his direction. They were called Pellegrini di S. Rocco, they practised mental prayer assiduously and had even procured an episcopal licence for the association. In Verona, Giovanni Battista Bonioli guided a membership of thirty disciples, many of them persons of high consideration. For the most part the devotees seem to have been quiet and pious folk, humbly seeking salvation by the interior way, but there were some who were given to extravagance. Margarita Rossi had visions and revelations, strangely repeating portions of the fantastic theology of Borri, and when written out by a believer, Don Giovanni Antonio, it was not difficult to extract from them a hundred and thirty-four errors, concerning which she was tortured as to intention as well as in caput alienum. Two others, Cosimo Dolci and Francesco Nigra had visions and prophetic insight, for which the latter was sentenced, in 1684, to five years' incarceration.[94]

The sect could not continue spreading indefinitely without discovery. In 1682 the Inquisition suddenly awoke to the necessity of action and it repeated an edict which it had issued in 1656, forbidding all oratories and assemblages for mental prayer. Ricaldini felt his position critical, for he had abjured de vehementi and was liable to the stake for relapse. He disappeared from Treviso and all that the Inquisition could learn was that he was somewhere on the Swiss border. At length, in 1684, his retreat was found to be Chiuro, in the Valtelline, and Antonio Ceccotti, Inquisitor of Brescia, made fruitless attempts to induce the authorities of the Valtelline and the Podestà of Brescia to unite in procuring his extradition, but in March, 1685, Ceccotti had the mortification to learn that he had died on the previous October 6th, having received all the sacraments and with the repute of a most pious Christian.[95]

MOLINOS

The prominent Pelagini were duly prosecuted, but there seems to have been little vindictiveness aroused in regard to them and little heresy attributable to them. The punishments inflicted were light, for we hear, in 1685, of Bona, one of the leaders, having returned to his district and living in retirement, and of Belleri, another, being in the Valcamonica, where the bishop had appointed him missionary for the whole district. Evidently the disciples must have escaped with a warning. What the ecclesiastical authorities objected to was not Mysticism and its long-accepted practices, but organization, more or less secret, under leaders outside of the hierarchy and free from its supervision, when heated brains, under divine inspiration, indulged in dreams of regenerating the Church. It was not until the case of Molinos had called attention to other dangers that there came from Rome strict orders for the suppression of all oratories and of the practice of mental prayer--that rapture of meditation which had been the distinguishing habit of mystics through the ages.[96]

***

Miguel de Molinos was a Spaniard, born probably about 1630 at Muniesa (Teruel). After obtaining at Coimbra the degree of doctor of theology, he came to Rome in 1665, in connection with a canonization--probably of San Pedro Arbués, who was beatified in 1668. There he speedily acquired distinction as a confessor and spiritual director. Innocent XI prized him so highly as to give him apartments in the papal palace; the noblest women placed themselves under his care; his reputation spread throughout Italy and his correspondence became enormous. On the day of his arrest it is said that the postage on the letters delivered that day at his house amounted to twenty-three ducats; he made a small charge to cover expenses and, in the sequestration of his property, there were found four thousand gold crowns derived from this source. The letters seized were reported variously as numbering twelve or twenty thousand, of which two hundred were from Christina of Sweden and two thousand from the Princess Borghese. The mysticism which proved so attractive, when set forth by his winning personality, had in it--ostensibly at least--nothing that had not long since received the approbation of the Church in the writings of the great Spanish mystics and of St. François de Sales. It is true that Molinos dropped the machinery of ecstasies and visions, which loom so largely in the writings of Santa Teresa, and confined his way of perfection to the Brahmanical ideal of the annihilation of sense and intellect, the mystic silence or death, in which speech and thought and desire are no more and in which God speaks with the soul and teaches it the highest wisdom.[97] This spiritualized hypnotism was in no way original with Molinos, but was the goal which all the mystic saints sought to attain. To reach it he tells us the soul must abandon itself wholly to God; it must make no resistance to the thoughts or impulses which God might send or allow Satan to send; if assailed by intruding or sensual thoughts, they should not be opposed but be quietly contemned and the resultant suffering be offered as a sacrifice to God.[98] This was the Quietism--the Spanish Dejamiento--which was subsequently condemned so severely; there is no question that it had its dangers if the senses were allowed to control the spirit, and the adversaries of Molinos made the most of it, but he taught that the soul must overcome temptation through patience and resignation. When souls have acquired control of themselves, he says, if a temptation attacks them they soon overcome it; passions cannot hold out against the divine strength which fills them, even if the violence is continued and is supported by suggestions of the enemy; the soul gains the victory and enjoys the infinite resultant benefit.[99]

***

All this Molinos was allowed to teach for years in the Holy City with general applause, though it had been persecuted in the Pelagini. In 1675, at the height of his popularity, he embodied his doctrine in the Guida spirituale, a little volume which came forth with the emphatic approbation of five distinguished theologians--four of them consultors or censors of the Inquisition and all of them men of high standing in their respective Orders of Franciscans, Trinitarians, Jesuits, Carmelites and Capuchins. The book had an immediate and wide circulation and was translated into many languages. Even in Spain there was a Madrid edition in 1676, one at Saragossa in 1677 and another at Seville as late as 1685, without exciting animadversion. Yet such a career as that of Molinos could not continue indefinitely without exciting hostility, none the less dangerous because prudently concealed. His immense success was provocative of envy and, if mystic contemplation was largely adopted as the surest path to salvation, what was to be the result on the infinite variety of exterior works to which the Church owed so much of its power and wealth? It was found that in many nunneries in Rome, whose confessors had adopted his views, the inmates had cast aside their rosaries and chaplets and depended wholly on contemplation. It was observed that at mass the mystic devotees did not raise their eyes at the elevation of the Host or gaze on the holy images, but pursued uninterruptedly their mental prayer. Molinos gave further occasion for criticism by a tract on daily communion, in which he asserted that a soul, secure that it was not in mortal sin, could safely partake of the sacrament without previous confession--a doctrine which, however, theologically defensible, threatened, if extensively practised, largely to diminish the authority of the priesthood, while encouraging the sinner to settle his account directly with God.

To attack as a heretic a man so universally respected and so firmly entrenched as Molinos might well seem desperate, and it is not surprising that the credit for the work was attributed to the Jesuits, as the only body daring and powerful enough. The current story is that, having resolved upon it, they procured Père La Chaise to induce Louis XIV to order his ambassador, Cardinal d'Estrées to labor unceasingly for the removal of the scandal caused by the teaching of Molinos. Whether this was so is doubtful, but it is certain that the first attack came from the Jesuits, and that d'Estrées, who had professed the warmest admiration for Molinos, became his unrelenting persecutor. The campaign was opened in 1678, when Gottardo Bell' Uomo, S. J., issued at Modena a work on the comparative value of ordinary and mystic prayer, which was duly denounced to the Inquisition. Molinos had been made to recognize in various ways the coming storm, and he sought to conjure it in a fashion which revealed his conscious weakness. February 16, 1680, he addressed to the Jesuit General Oliva a long exculpatory letter. He had not attacked the Society but had always held it in the highest honor, and when, in Valencia, the University had forbidden the Jesuit College to teach theology, he was the only one who had disobeyed the order and had come to its aid. He had never decried the Spiritual Exercises of Loyola, but had recognized the vast good accomplished by them, though he held that, for those suited to it, contemplation was better than meditation. He had for some years been persecuted and stigmatized as a heretic, in writing and preaching, by the most distinguished members of the Society, but he rejoiced in this and only prayed God for those who reviled him nor, in his defence of the Guida, had he sought aught but the glory of God and, so far from defending the Begghards and Illuminati, he had always condemned them. Evidently the work of the Jesuits in discrediting him had been active and better organized than the records show, and he thought it wiser to disarm, if possible, rather than to struggle with adversaries so powerful. Oliva's answer of February 28th was by no means reassuring. He complimented Molinos on his Christian spirit in returning good for evil and on the flattering terms bestowed on the Society and its founder. He had never read the books of Molinos and could not speak of them with knowledge but, if they corresponded with his letter, his disciples were doing him great wrong in applying his system of contemplation, of which only the rarest souls were capable, indiscriminately to nuns and worldly young women. Finally, he could not understand why so distinguished a member of the Society as Padre Bell' Uomo should have been brought before the Congregation of the Index, and he gave infinite thanks to God for defending him before it.

Promptly on the next day, February 29th, Molinos replied to this discouraging epistle. At much length he disculpated himself for writings and sayings falsely attributed to him. He held meditation in the highest esteem as an exercise suited to all; the loftiest form of contemplation was a gift of God bestowed on the rare souls fitted for it. He again spoke of the persecution to which he was exposed and, as for Padre Bell' Uomo, whom he did not know, if his doctrine was as sound as represented by Oliva, God would enlighten his ministers to recognize it. Oliva's rejoinder to this, on March 2d, would appear to be written in a style of studied obscurity, saying much and meaning little, but one passage reveals a source of Jesuit enmity, in alluding to the number of convents which had passed out of the direction of the Society to practise the new method.[100]

***

The effort of Molinos to propitiate his enemies had only encouraged them by its confession of weakness. Their next step was a dextrous one. Padre Paolo Segneri was not only the most popular Jesuit preacher in Italy, but his favor with Innocent XI was almost as great as that of Molinos. He was selected as the next athlete and, in 1680, he issued a little volume--"Concordia tra la fatica e la quiete nell' oratione," in which he argued that the highest life is that which combines activity with contemplation. He was promptly answered by Pietro Matteo Petrucci, an ardent admirer of Molinos, who was rewarded by Innocent with the see of Jesi. Segneri rejoined in a "Lettera di riposta al Sig. Ignacio Bartalini" and the controversy was fairly joined. A more aggressive antagonist was the Minorite Padre Alessandro Reggio whose "Clavis Aurea qua aperiuntur errores Michaelis de Molinos" appeared in 1682 and boldly argued that the Guida revived the condemned errors of the Begghards, that Quietism destroyed all conceptions of the Trinity, while the practice of prayer without works was destructive of all the pious observances prescribed by the Church, and the teaching that temptation should be endured without resistance was dangerous and contrary to Scripture and to the doctors. Petrucci responded vigorously, while Molinos remained silent. He had, at least, the advantage of official support, for Bell' Uomo's book was forbidden donec corrigatur; Segneri's "Lettera" and the "Clavis Aurea" were condemned unconditionally, and Segneri's "Concordia," while it escaped the Index, was quietly forbidden and he was instructed to revise it.[101]

The Jesuits, however, were not the only body interested in the downfall of Molinos. There is a curious anonymous tract devoted to explaining what it calls the secret policy of the Quietists, assuming their main object to be the destruction of all the religious Orders and especially of the Dominicans and Franciscans. Apparently taking advantage of the development of the Pelagini about this time, it asserts that the Quietists had organized conventicles and oratories throughout Italy; that they had a common treasury in which 14,000 ducats were found; that they flattered the secular clergy and sought to unite them in opposition to the regulars, whom they systematically decried, raking together all the stories of their corruption and ignorance. In short, Quietism was a deep-laid conspiracy, through which Molinos expected to revolutionize the Church and reduce the religious Orders to impotence.[102] The only importance of the tract is as a manifestation of the attitude of the regulars towards Molinos and the hostility aroused by his success in winning from them, for his disciples, the directorship of souls which was their special province.

The enormous influence of the elements thus combining for his destruction left little doubt of the result. The first open attack was made in June, 1682, when Cardinal Caraccioli, Archbishop of Naples, a pupil of the Jesuits, reported to the pope that he found his diocese deeply infected with this new Quietism, subversive of the received prescriptions of the Church, and he asked instructions for its suppression, nor was he alone in this for similar appeals came from other Italian bishops. Molinos was too firmly established in the papal favor for this to dislodge him, but the hostile forces gradually gathered strength and, in November, 1684, the Congregation of the Inquisition formally assumed consideration of the matter. At its head was Cardinal Ottoboni, a fanatic whose experience with the Pelagini, when Bishop of Brescia, had sharpened his hatred of mysticism. The spirit in which he conducted the inquest is revealed in a memorandum in his handwriting of the points to be elaborated in the next day's meeting of the Congregation--that this heresy is the worst of all and if left alone will become inextinguishable; that it is spreading in Spain through the Archbishop of Seville and in France with many books of the most dangerous nature; that it destroys the Catholic faith and all the religious Orders; that in Jesi the canons and the cura of the cathedral keep a school for its propagation; that a rich and powerful citizen of Jesi threatens the witnesses and that a vigorous commissioner must be sent there; that the monasteries of Faenza and Ravenna are infected and one in Ferrara has a Quietist confessor; that this pestilence calls for fire and steel.[103] In a court presided over by so bitter a prosecutor, the judgement was fore-ordained.

For awhile the contending forces seem to have been equally balanced and eight months were spent in gathering testimony sufficient to justify arrest. At last, on July 3, 1685, at a meeting of the Congregation, Cardinal d'Estrées insisted that no one should leave the chamber until the arrest was ordered and executed. This was agreed to; the sbirri were despatched and Molinos was lodged in the prison of the Inquisition.[104] Yet when, on November 9th the Spanish Holy Office condemned the Guia espirituale as containing propositions savoring of heresy and Illuminism, the Congregation addressed to the pope a vigorous protest against its action on a matter which was still under consideration at headquarters.[105]

***

The influence of Queen Christina, we are told, was exerted to procure for Molinos better treatment than was usual with prisoners. Of the details of the trial we know little or nothing, but, as torture was habitual in the Roman Inquisition, it is not probable that he was spared. As his books had not been condemned, the evidence employed was drawn exclusively from the immense mass of his correspondence and MSS. which had been seized, the depositions of witnesses and his own confessions, so that we are unable to judge how far it justified the conclusions set forth in the sentence, though, from the manner in which that discriminates between what he admitted and what he denied, it is but fair to assume that it represents correctly the evidence before the tribunal. The trial was necessarily prolonged. In his defence interrogatories were forwarded to Saragossa and Valencia, in 1687, where his witnesses were duly examined.[106] Two hundred and sixty-three erroneous propositions were extracted by the censors from the mass of matter before them, to which he of course was required to answer in detail, and these seem to have been condensed into nineteen for the consideration of the Congregation.[107]

Petrucci was threatened and his elevation to the cardinalate, September 2, 1686, was ascribed to the desire of Innocent to save him from prosecution. Shortly afterwards, two of the principal assistants of Molinos, the brothers Leoni of Como, of whom Simone was a priest and Antonio Maria was a tailor, were arrested. Then, on February 9, 1687, followed the arrest of the Count and Countess Vespiniani, of Paolo Rocchi, confessor of the Princess Borghese, and of seventy others, causing general consternation, not diminished by the subsequent imprisonment of some two hundred more. The Congregation was doing its work thoroughly and it was even said that, on February 13th, it appointed a commission which examined the pope himself. A revolution in the traditional standards of orthodoxy could not be effected without compromising multitudes, and the victors were determined that their victory should be complete. On February 15th, Cardinal Cibò, the secretary of the Congregation, addressed to all the bishops of Italy a circular stating that in many places there existed or were forming associations called spiritual conferences, under ignorant directors, who, with maxims of exquisite perfection, misled them into most pernicious errors, resulting in manifest heresy and abominable immorality. The bishops were therefore ordered to investigate and, if such assemblies were found, to abolish them forthwith, taking moreover especial care that this pestilence was not allowed to infect the monasteries.

***

There could be but one end to the trial. Every possible accusation was brought against Molinos, even to a foolish self-laudatory speech made to the sbirri who arrested him, and his admiring certain anagrams made of his name. One charge, which he denied, was his giving to a certain person the soiled shirt in which he had come from Spain, saying that, after his death, it would be a great relic. He seems to have responded with candor to the various articles, denying some and admitting others. Of the articles the most important were his justifying the sacrilege of breaking images and crucifixes; depreciating religious vows and dissuading persons from entering religious Orders; saying that vows destroyed perfection; that, by the prayer of Quiet, the soul is rendered not only sinless but impeccable, for it is deprived of freedom and God operates it, wishing us sometimes to sin and offend him, and the demon moves the members to indecent acts; that the three ways of the spirit, hitherto described by the doctors, are absurd and that there is but one, the interior way; that he had formed conventicles of men and women and permitted them to perform immoral acts and to eat flesh on fast days. He admitted excusing the breaking of images and crucifixes; he denied depreciation of solemn vows, but admitted it as respects private ones, and he had only dissuaded from entering religion those whom he knew would create scandal. He denied teaching that in Quietism the soul becomes impeccable, but only that it did not consent to the act of sin and he said that he knew many persons practising it who lived many years without committing even venial sin. He denied also that Quietism deprived the soul of freewill, but said that, in that perfect union with God, it was God who worked and not the faculties, and when he said that God sometimes wished sin, he meant material sin (as distinguished from formal), and that the demon, as God's instrument to mortify the flesh and purify the soul, causes sometimes the hand and other members to perform lascivious acts. He denied condemning the three ways of the spirit, having meant only that the interior way was so much more perfect that the others were negligible by comparison. He denied forming conventicles in which lascivious acts were permitted and he had excluded some persons who would not refrain from them. He admitted eating flesh on prohibited days, and that he had not perfectly observed a single Lent since he came to Rome, but said that this was by licence of his physician. He confessed that for many years he had practised the most indecent acts with two women, the details of which need not be repeated; he had not deemed this sinful, but a purification of the soul and that in them he enjoyed a closer union with God; these were merely acts of the senses, in which the higher faculties had no part, as they were united with God. When he was told that these were propositions heretical, bestial and scandalous, he replied that he submitted himself in all things to the Holy Office, recognizing that its lights were superior to his own.[108]

A sentence of condemnation was inevitable. It was drawn up, August 20, 1687; on the 28th an inquisitorial decree was signed embodying sixty-eight propositions, drawn from the evidence and confessions, which were condemned as heretical, suspect, erroneous, scandalous, blasphemous, offensive to pious ears, subversive of Christian discipline and seditious; they were not to be taught or practised under pain of deprivation of office and benefice and perpetual disability, and of an anathema reserved to the Holy See. All the writings of Molinos, in whatever language, were forbidden to be printed, possessed or read, and all copies were, under the same penalties, to be surrendered to the inquisitors or bishops, who were to burn them.[109] This was posted in the usual places on September 3d, the day fixed for the atto di fede in which Molinos was to appear.

Under a heavy guard he was brought, on the previous evening, from the inquisitorial prison to the church of Santa Maria sopra Minerva, in which the atto was to be celebrated. In the morning, in a room next to the sacristy, he was exhibited to some curious persons of distinction, eliciting from him an expression of indignation, construed as indicating how little he felt of real repentance. This was confirmed by what followed, explicable possibly by Spanish imperturbability, but more probably by the Quietism which led him to regard himself as the passive instrument of God's will, and superbly indifferent to whatever might befall him, so long as his soul was rapt in the joys of the mystic death, which he had taught as the summum bonum. Called upon to order a meal, he specified one which in quantity and quality might satisfy the most voracious gourmet and, after partaking of it, he lay down to a refreshing siesta, until he was roused to take his place on the platform where, in spite of his manacles, his bearing was that of a judge and not of a convict.

CONDEMNATION OF MOLINISM

The vast church was thronged to its farthest corner with all that was notable in Rome, including twenty-three cardinals, and the spacious piazza in front and all the neighboring streets were crowded. An indulgence of fifteen days and fifteen quarantines had been proclaimed for all in attendance, but in Rome, where plenary indulgences could be had on almost every day in the year by merely visiting churches, this could not account for the eagerness which brushed aside the Swiss guards stationed at the portals, requiring a reinforcement of troops and resulting in considerable bloodshed. As the long sentence was read, with its details of Molinos's enormities, occupying two hours, it was interrupted with the frequent roar of Burn him! Burn him! led by an enthusiastic cardinal and echoed by the mob outside. Through all this, we are told, his effrontery never failed him, which was reckoned as an infallible sign of his persistent perversity. The sentence concluded by declaring him convicted as a dogmatizing heretic but, as he had professed himself repentant and had implored mercy and pardon, it ordered him to abjure his heresies and to be rigidly imprisoned with the sanbenito for life, without hope of release, and to perform certain spiritual exercises. This was duly executed and he lingered, it was said repentant, until his death, December 28, 1696. The day after the atto di fede his disciples performed their abjuration. There was no desire to deal harshly with them, and they were dismissed with trivial penances, except the brothers Leoni. Simone the priest, who had been a popular confessor, was sentenced to ten years' imprisonment; Antonio Maria, the tailor, who had been a travelling missionary and organizer, was incarcerated for life. There was still another victim, the secretary of Molinos, Pedro Peña, arrested May 9, 1687, for defending his master. He was fully convicted of Quietism and, on March 16, 1689, he was condemned to life-long prison.[110]

There still remained the publication to Christendom of the new position assumed by the Holy See towards Mysticism. The sixty-eight propositions, condemned in the inquisitorial decree of August 28th, were printed in the vernacular and placed on sale, but were speedily suppressed. There must still have been opposition in the Sacred College, or on the part of Innocent XI, for the bull Coelestis Pastor was not drawn up and signed until November 20th, and was not finally published to the world until February 19, 1688. This recited the same series of propositions and the condamnation of Molinos and confirmed the decree of August 28th. The propositions condemned consisted, for the most part, of the untenable extravagances of Quietism, including impeccability and the sinlessness of acts committed while the soul was absorbed with God, but it was impossible to do this without condemning much that had been taught and practised by the mystic saints, and there were no saving clauses to differentiate lawful from unlawful converse of the soul with its Creator. The Church broke definitely with Mysticism, and by implication gave the faithful to understand that salvation was to be sought in the beaten track, through the prescribed observances and under the guidance of the hierarchical organization.[111]

This change of front was emphasized in various ways. Innocent's favor saved Cardinal Petrucci from formal prosecution; to the vexation of the Inquisition, his case was referred to four cardinals, Cibò, Ottoboni, Casanate and Azzolini; he professed himself ready to retract whatever the pope objected to and, though the Inquisition held an abjuration to be necessary, he was not required to make it; he was relegated to Jesi and then recalled to Rome, where he was kept under surveillance. He could not, moreover, escape the mortification of seeing the books, which had been so warmly approved, condemned by a decree of February 5, 1688. Many other works, which had long passed current as recognized aids to devotion, were similarly treated--those of Benedetto Biscia, Juan Falconi, François Malaval and of numerous others--even the Opera della divina Gratia of the Dominican Tommaso Menghini, himself Inquisitor-general of Ferrara and author of the Regole del Tribunal del Santo Officio, which long remained a standard guide in the tribunals. What had been accepted as the highest expression of religious devotion had suddenly become heresy.[112] Apparently it was not until May, 1689, that instructions were sent everywhere to demand the surrender of all books of Molinos and to report any one suspected of Molinism.[113]

THE BECCARELLISTI

Persecution received a fresh impulse when Cardinal Ottoboni, as Alexander VIII, succeeded Innocent XI, October 6, 1689. Bernino tells us that he appeared to him an angel in looks and an apostle in utterance when he declared that there was no creature in the world so devoid of sense as a heretic for, as he was deprived of faith so also was he of reason. His first care was to remove from office and throw into irremissible prison every one who was in the slightest degree suspect of Molinism; in this he did not even spare his Apostolic camera, for he arrested an Apostolic Prothonotary and, although in the Congregation of the Inquisition there were four kinsmen of the prisoner, zeal for the faith preponderated over blood.[114] Fortunately his pontificate lasted for only sixteen months, so that he had but limited opportunity for the gratification of his ardent fanaticism and scandalous nepotism.

In spite of all this, there were still found those who indulged their sensual instincts under cover of exalted spirituality. In 1698 there was in Rome the case of a priest, named Pietro Paolo di San Giov. Evangelista, who had already been tried by the tribunals of Naples and Spoleto, so that his career must have been prolonged, while references to a Padre Benigno and a Padre Filippo del Rio show that he was not alone. He had ecstasies and a following of devotees; he taught that communion could be taken without preliminary confession and that, when the spirit was united with God, whatever acts the inferior part might commit were not sins. He freely confessed to practices of indescribable obscenity with his female penitents, whom he assured afterwards that they were as pure as the Blessed Virgin. He was sentenced to perpetual prison, without hope of release, and to a series of arduous spiritual penances, while Fra Benigno escaped with seven years of imprisonment.[115]

Another development of the same tendencies--probably a survival of the Pelagini--was discovered in Brescia in 1708. The sectaries called themselves disciples of St. Augustin, engaged in vindicating his opinions on predestination and grace, but they were popularly known as Beccarellisti, from two brothers, priests of the name of Beccarelli, whom they regarded as their leaders. For twenty-five years-- that is, since the ostensible suppression of the Pelagini--the sect had been secretly spreading itself throughout Lombardy, where it was said to number some forty-two thousand members, including many nobles and wealthy families and ecclesiastics of position. They had a common treasury and a regular organization, headed by the elder Beccarelli as pope, with cardinals, apostles and other dignitaries. The immediate object of the movement, we are told, was to break the power of the religious Orders and to restore to the secular priesthood the functions of confession and the direction of souls which it had well-nigh lost, but there was taught the Quietist doctrine of divine grace to which the devotee surrendered all his faculties. This was allowed to operate without resistance, and Beccarelli held that Molinos was the only true teacher of Christian perfection, but we may safely reject as exaggeration the statement that carnal indulgence was regarded as earning a plenary indulgence, applicable to souls in purgatory. Cardinal Badoaro, then Bishop of Brescia, took energetic measures to stamp out this recrudescence of the condemned doctrines; the leaders scattered to Switzerland, Germany and England, while Beccarelli was tried by the Inquisition of Venice and was condemned to seven years of galley-service.[116]

Probably the latest victims who paid with their lives for their belief in the efficacy of mental prayer and mystic death were a beguine named Geltruda and a friar named Romualdo, who were burnt in a Palermitan atto di fede, April 6, 1724, as impenitent Molinists after languishing in gaol since 1699.[117]

FÉNELON AND BOSSUET

If, in the condemnation of Molinos, Mysticism was not wholly condemned, what was lacking was supplied when the duel between the two glories of the Gallican Church--Bossuet and Fénelon--induced an appeal to the Holy See. Beyond the Alps, mystic ardor was not widely diffused in the seventeenth century, yet there were those who revelled in the agonies and bliss of the interior way. St. François de Sales, who died in 1622, was beatified in 1661 and canonized in 1665, taught Quietism as pronounced as that of Molinos, although he avoided the application to sensuality. The soul abandoned itself wholly to God; when divine love took possession of it, God deprived it of all human desires, even for spiritual consolations, exercises of piety and the perfection of virtue. He said that he had scarce a desire and, if he were to live again, he would have none; if God came to him, he would go to meet him but, if God did not come, he would remain quiescent and would not seek God. Freedom of the spirit consisted in detachment from everything to submit to the will of God, caring neither for places, or persons, or the practice of virtue.[118] It followed that the soul, absorbed in divine love, had nothing to ask of God; it rested in the quiet of contemplation, while vocal prayer and all the received observances of religion were cast aside, as fitted only for those who had not attained these mystic altitudes. Then there was Antoinette Bourignon (1616-1680) who, in her voluminous writings, taught the supremacy of the interior light, the abandonment of the faculties to the will of God, and the utter renunciation of self in the ardor of divine love.[119] There was Jean de Bernières-Louvigny (1602-1659) whose writings had an immense circulation and whose views as to mystic death were virtually the same as those of Molinos.[120] All these and others taught and wrote without interference, save from polemics, such as those of Pére Archange Ripaut, Guardian of the Capuchin convent of S. Jacques in Paris, who devoted a volume of near a thousand pages to their refutation and reprobation. If we are to believe him, these superhuman heights of spirituality were accompanied in France, as elsewhere, with sensuality.[121]

The condemnation of Molinos and the sixty-eight propositions attributed to him naturally attracted attention to the more or less quietistic developments of Mysticism, but it is probable that no action on the subject would have been taken in France had not personal motives suggested the persecution of one who chanced at the moment to be the most prominent representative of the interior way--that very curious personality, Jeanne Marie Bouvières de la Mothe Guyon, whose autobiography, written with a frank absence of reserve, affords a living picture of the self-inflicted martyrdom endured in the struggle to emancipate the soul from the ties of earth. When she reached the final stage she tells us that formerly God was in her, now she was in him, plunged in his immensity without sight or light or knowledge; she was lost in him as a wave in the ocean; her soul was as a leaf or a feather borne by the wind, abandoning itself to the operation of God in all that it did, exteriorly or interiorly. She acquired the faculty of working miraculous cures and her power over demons was such that, if she were in hell, they would all abandon it. At times the plenitude of grace was so superabundant and so oppressive that she could only lie speechless in bed; it so swelled her that her clothes would be torn and she could find relief only by discharging the surplus on others.[122]

It is beyond our province to enter into the miserable story of her persecutions, commenced by some of her relatives and carried on by Bossuet, leading to her reclusion in convents and imprisonment in Vincennes and the Bastile. It suffices for us that her influence stimulated Fénelon's tendency to Mysticism and converted into bitter hostility the friendship between him and Bossuet. A commission, appointed to examine her doctrine and headed by Bossuet, drew up, in 1694, a list of thirty-four errors of Mysticism, which Fénelon willingly signed and which Bossuet and Noailles, then Bishop of Châlons-sur-Marne, issued with instructions for their dioceses, including condemnations of the Guide of Molinos, the Pratique facile of Malaval, the Règle des Associés de l'Enfant Jésus, the Analis of Lacombe and Madame Guyon's Moyen court and Cantique des Cantiques. By this time Madame Guyon had been put out of the way, and the matter might have been allowed to rest under the comprehensive definitions of the bull Coelestis pastor, but Bossuet's combative spirit had been aroused and he was determined to crush out all vestiges of Mysticism, heedless of what the Church had accepted for centuries. He drew up an Instruction on the various kinds of prayer, in which he pointed out, in vigorous terms, the dangers attendant on contemplation. Noailles, now Archbishop of Paris, signed it with him, and they invited Fénelon to join but he refused, in spite of entreaties and remonstrances, for it attributed to Madame Guyon all that was most objectionable in Illuminism.

***

The breach between the friends had commenced and it widened irrevocably when Fénelon, in justification of himself, published, in February 1697, his Explication des Maximes des Saints sur la Vie intérieure, with a letter to Madame de Maintenon animadverting sharply on Bossuet's injustice. The book was based chiefly on the utterances of St. François de Sales, but it carefully guarded the practice of Quietism from all objectionable deductions. There was no self-abandonment to temptations and no claim of impeccability; souls of the highest altitude could commit mortal sin; they were bound daily to ask God for forgiveness, to detest their sins and seek remission, not for the mercenary motive of their own salvation but in obedience to the wishes of God. It is true that they were not tied down to formal observances, but vocal prayer was not to be decried,--though its value depended upon its being animated by internal prayer. The indifference, which was the point most objected to in Quietism, was greatly limited by Fénelon. The senseless determination to wish for nothing was an impious resistance to the known will of God, and to all the impulses of his grace; it is true that the advanced soul wishes nothing for itself but it wishes everything for God; it does not wish perfection or happiness for itself, but it wishes all perfection and happiness, so far as it pleases God to make us wish for these things, by the impulsion of his grace. In this highest state the soul does not wish salvation in its own interest, but wishes it for the glory and good pleasure of God, as a thing which he wishes and wishes us to wish for his sake.

It is difficult to see what objection could be raised to a Quietism thus strictly limited and guarded, and no one who compares the Maximes des Saints with the extravagance of the great mystic saints can fail to recognize that the violent quarrel which arose was a purely personal matter. In this Fénelon defended himself with dignity and moderation, while the violence of Bossuet's attack sometimes bordered on truculence. He was secure in the support of the court. Louis XIV had been won over, and it soon became to him a matter of personal pride to overcome all resistance to his will. Fénelon was banished to his diocese of Cambrai and deprived of his position of preceptor to the royal children, showing that he was in complete disgrace and warning all time-servers to abandon him.

It was soon evident that the matter would have to be settled in Rome. Bossuet sent an advance copy of his Instruction to Innocent XII, pointing out that he was applying in France the principles affirmed in the condemnation of Molinos. Fénelon followed his example and, on April 27th, sent the Maximes, stating that he submitted it to the judgement of the Holy See. The curia gladly accepted the task, rejoiced at the opportunity of intervening authoritatively in a quarrel within the Gallican Church. Fénelon was refused permission to go to Rome and defend himself, but he had a powerful protector in the person of the Cardinal de Bouillon, then French ambassador and a member of the Congregation of the Inquisition, who loyally stood by him even at the expense of a rebuke from his royal master. He also secured the support of the Jesuits, whose Collége de Clermont had approved of the Maximes, and who promised to manifest as much energy in his defence as they had shown in procuring the condemnation of Cornelis Jansen. These weighty influences might secure delay and discussion, but they could not control the result against the overmastering pressure of such a monarch as Louis XIV who, on July 27, 1697, wrote to the pope that he had had the Maximes examined and that it was pronounced "très mauvais et très dangéreux," wherefore he asked to have judgement pronounced on it without delay. Then, on May 16, 1698, the nuncio at Paris reported that the king complained of the delay; it was in contempt of his person and crown, and if Rome did not act promptly he would take such measures as he saw fit. Threats such as this were not to be lightly disregarded, and still more ominous was an autograph letter to the pope, December 23d, expressing his displeasure at the prolongation of the case and urging its speedy conclusion.

***

To Bossuet's representative and grand-vicar, the Abbé Phelippeaux, we owe a minute report of the long contest, which affords an interesting inside view of the conduct of such affairs, showing how little regard was paid to the principles involved and how completely the result depended on intrigue and influence. The case passed through its regular stages. A commission of seven consultors had been found, to whom, after a struggle, three were added. These disputed at much length over thirty-seven propositions extracted from the book and, when at length they made their report to the Congregation of the Inquisition, they stood five to five, showing that each side had succeeded in putting an equal number of friends on the commission. In the Congregation, the struggle was renewed and continued through thirty-eight sessions. Had the fate of Europe been at stake, the matter could not have been more warmly contested. At length the inevitable condemnation was voted, and then came a fresh contest over the phraseology of the decree. Bossuet's agents were not content with the simple condemnation of twenty-three propositions and the prohibition of the book, and they struggled vigorously for clauses condemning and humiliating Fénelon himself, showing how purely personal was the controversy. In this they failed, as well as in the endeavor to have the propositions characterized as heretical; they were only pronounced to be respectively rash, scandalous, ill-sounding, offensive to pious ears, pernicious in practice and erroneous. The principal doctrine aimed at was that the pure love of God should be wholly disinterested, and that its acts and motives should be divested of all mercenary hope of reward. The brief was finally agreed to, on March 12, 1699, and published on the 13th. It was in the form of a motu proprio which, under the rules in force in France respecting papal decrees, precluded its acceptance and registration by the Parlement, but Louis, ordinarily so tenacious about papal intrusion, found indirect means of eluding the difficulty.

Fénelon, however, had not awaited this cumbrous procedure. In a dignified letter of submission to the pope, April 4, 1699, he stated that he had already prepared a mandement for his diocese, condemning the book with its twenty-three propositions, which he would publish as soon as he should receive the royal permission. This was promptly given and, on April 9th he issued it, forbidding the possession and reading of the Maximes, and condemning the propositions "simply, absolutely and without a shadow of restriction." Innocent XII, who had more than once indicated sympathy with Fénelon, responded May 12th, in a brief expressing his cordial satisfaction, bestowing on him his loving benediction and invoking the aid of God for his pastoral labors. Bossuet, with the royal assistance, had triumphed, at the cost of a stain on his reputation; what the Church had gained, in condemning the sublimated speculations of a rarefied and impracticable Mysticism, it would be hard to say.[123]

Yet, as though to indicate that there is no finality in these matters, Pius VI, in 1789, beatified the Blessed Giovanni Giuseppe della Croce ([dagger symbol] March 5, 1734), who was much given to contemplation and to union with God, in which all his faculties were lost, as completely as in the trances of his prototype, San Juan de la Cruz, or as in the mystic death of Molinos. That his Mysticism did not forfeit the favor of heaven was shown by his possessing the gift of bilocation--of being in two places at one time--of which numerous instances were cited in the beatification proceedings.[124]

***

The Spanish Inquisition which had so long carried on single-handed the struggle against Mysticism, watched with satisfaction the Roman proceedings against Molinos. As we have seen, his arrest, on July 3, 1685, was promptly followed, November 9th with a condemnation of the Guida which, for nine years, had been allowed to circulate freely in Spain. The edict pronounced it to contain propositions ill-sounding, offensive to pious ears, rash, savoring of the heresy of the Alumbrados, and some erroneous ones, and the title was denounced as misleading because it spoke only of the interior way.[125] When the sentence of the Roman Inquisition was published, September 3, 1687, although as a rule the Spanish Holy Office paid no attention to its decrees, the sixty-eight propositions were speedily translated into the vernacular and widely distributed. On October 11th, sixty copies were sent to Valencia to be posted, with orders to print more if they should be required. These were accompanied with an edict, commanding obedience and threatening the most rigorous prosecution for remissness, while all persons were ordered to denounce, within ten days, contraventions of any kind coming to their knowledge. This edict was to be published in all churches of the capitals of partidos and an authentic record of such publication was to be affixed to the doors. In due time, when the bull Coelestis pastor was issued, it was circulated with the same prescriptions.[126] There was evidently a determination to make the most of this new ally in the struggle with Mysticism.

MOLINISM

The Seville tribunal, indeed, had not waited for this, as it had already, April 24, 1687, arrested a canon of the church of San Salvador, Joseph Luis Navarro de Luna y Medina, who was a correspondent of Molinos and had sent him his autobiography, in order to obtain instructions for his spiritual guidance. He had previously been deprived of his licence as confessor, on charges of imprudent conduct as spiritual director of a nunnery, but Jaime de Palafox, Archbishop of Seville, who was a warm admirer of Molinos, had restored the licence, introduced him in all the convents and adopted him as confessor of himself and his family. For four years Navarro endured incarceration and the torture which was not spared, but he succumbed at last, confessed and sought reconciliation. His sentence declared him guilty of the errors of the Lutherans, Calvinists, Arians, Nestorians, Trinitarians, Waldenses, Agapetæ, Baianists and Alumbrados, besides being a dogmatizer of those of Molinos, with the addition that evil thoughts arising in prayer should be carried into execution, and also that, when his disciples assembled in his house, the lights would be extinguished and he would teach doctrines too foul for description. The tribunal itself could scarce have believed all this, for he was only required to abjure, to be deprived of benefice and functions, to be recluded for two years and be exiled for six more. When the term had expired he returned to Seville and then, until his death, in 1725, he passed his days in the churches, where the Venerable Sacrament was exposed for adoration, carrying with him a hinged stool on which he sat, gazing at the Host.[127] He was not the only Molinist in Seville for in 1689, after three years' trial, Fray Pedro de San José was condemned as a disciple of Molinos, for committing obscenities with his penitents and foretelling his election as pope and his suffering under Antichrist, who was already in Jerusalem, twenty years old. He was sentenced to abjure de vehementi, to undergo a circular discipline in his convent, to perpetual deprivation of teaching and confessing, and to six years' reclusion in a convent, with the customary disabilities.[128] Soon afterwards there was penanced in an auto, May 18, 1692, a woman named Ana Raguza, popularly known as la pabeza, as an Alumbrada and Molinista. She had come from Palermo as a missionary to convert the wicked, probably in the train of Palafox, who had been Archbishop of Palermo. She called herself a bride of Christ, she had visions and revelations, she denied the efficacy of masses and fasts, and she had the faculty of determining the condition of consciences by the sense of smell. She escaped with two years of reclusion and six more of exile.[129]

MOLINISM

The condemnation of Molinos seems to have stimulated the Inquisition to greater activity in the suppression of mysticism, for cases begin to appear more frequently in the records and henceforth the term Molinism, to a great extent, takes the place of Illuminism. We hear of a Molinist penanced in a Córdova auto of May 12, 1693,[130] and he cannot have been the only one there for Fray Francisco de Possadas of that city tells us that he was led to write his book against the carnal errors of Molinos by his experience in the confessional, showing that some of his penitents had been misled by them.[131] The report of the Valencia tribunal, for 1695, contains three cases then on trial. The Franciscan, Fray Vicente Selles, had been arrested in 1692. He had led a life exteriorly austere, practising meditation and contemplation, and he freely admitted that when Molinos was condemned he held that the pope was wrongly informed. His overwrought brain gave way under the stress of confinement; at times he was full of religious emotion and solicitous as to his salvation, while at others he was violently insane, performing various crazy freaks. On August 24th he attempted suicide by dashing his head against a projecting piece of iron, causing a wound so serious that several pieces of skull were discharged and, on February 6, 1693, the surgeons reported his life to be still in danger. He remained melancolico, variable in mood, confessing and retracting until, on October 23d, he confessed fully to Molinism, naming eleven women with whom he had had relations in the confessional and also admitting unnatural crime and other offences. At the date of the report his trial was still unfinished. Another phase of these eccentric methods of salvation is presented in the case of Vicente Hernan, a hermit of San Cristóbal of Concentayna, accused by three women of teaching them the way of bruising the head of the serpent by sleeping with them and resisting temptation, and of attempting indecencies, which they denied permitting. He was arrested September 23, 1692, and in two audiences he was a negativo. Then on December 17th he asked for an audience in which he said that for eight days some little flies and black pigeons had been biting him and reminding him of things forgotten, whereupon he told of the women whom he had got to sleep with him, sometimes two or three at a time, and he also mentioned numerous miraculous cures which he had wrought. In January 1693, he said that the demons with the voice of flies had been recalling his sins, and he told of three other women. Doubts arose as to his sanity and, at the end of 1693 steps were taken to investigate it, which were still in progress at the time of closing the report. The third case was that of Mosen Antonio Serra, whose doctrines the calificadores reported to be Molinistic. He was arrested December 19, 1695, so that his trial had only begun.[132]

In 1708 the Toledo tribunal arrested Fray Manuel de Paredes, a contemplative fraile, who encouraged mystic practices among his penitents, leading to several trials, which illustrate the increased severity visited upon these condemned forms of devotion.[133] The same tendency is visible soon afterwards at Córdova, where a little conventicle of Molinistas alumbrados was discovered in the Dominican convent of San Pablo, under the leadership of a beata named Isabel del Castillo. Her disciples abandoned to her their free-will and all their faculties; they had no need of fasts and penances but could transfer their sins to her and the path of salvation lay through sensual indulgence. In the auto of April 24, 1718, there were seven of them penanced, Isabel being visited with two hundred lashes and perpetual prison; the friars were reconciled, deprived of their functions and imprisoned, some irremissibly and some perpetually, while the laymen had penances of various degrees of severity.[134]

During this period there occurred a case deserving of consideration in some detail, not only because of the prominence of the culprit but because it affords a clearer view than others of the strange intermixture of sensuality and spirituality, which was distinctly known as Molinism, and of the self-deception which enabled men and women to indulge their passions while believing themselves to be living in the mystic altitude of Union with God. Perhaps this may partly be explicable by the teachings of the laxer morality, current in the sixteenth century and known under the general name of Probabilism, and by the distinction between material and formal sin, whereby that alone was mortal sin which the conscience recognized as such, the conscience being still further eased by refinements as to advertence and consent. In the skilful hands of the casuists, the boundaries between right and wrong became dangerously nebulous, and arguments were plentiful through which men could persuade themselves that whatever they chose to do was lawful.

BISHOP TORO OF OVIEDO

Joseph Fernández de Toro was an inquisitor in Murcia, deeply imbued with quietistic Mysticism. In 1686 he issued anonymously in Seville a little tract with the significant title of "Remedio facilissimo para no pecar en el uso y exercicio de la Oracion," which in time duly found its way into the Index.[135] As inquisitor he had manifested his tendencies, when a prelate of high repute and station in a religious Order was tried before him for solicitation ad turpia in the confessional. Guided by the light within, Toro was satisfied that it was merely a case of obsession by the demon; he persuaded the Suprema to accept this view, and the culprit escaped with suspension from celebrating mass and hearing confessions until the obsession should pass. In 1706, he was promoted to the see of Oviedo, of which he took possession October 1st. Unluckily for him there was at Oviedo the Jesuit college of San Mathias; his reputation for Quietism seems to have preceded him, and the heads of the college resolved themselves into a corps of detectives. Professing the utmost friendship, they speedily acquired his confidence and he talked with them freely. They were prompt in action for, in January 1707, Padre José del Campo drew up for the inquisitor-general an elaborate secret denunciation, setting forth how Toro in conversation had offered to explain to him the contemplation of Molinos; since coming to Asturias, he had spoken to no one about these things, for he knew that they had occasioned much murmuring against him, but he described the mode in which the soul reached the summit of perfection in Union with God, while the inferior sensual part might be abandoned to the foulest temptation. These dangerous speculations were reported in full detail and were accompanied by a long and skilful argument to prove that Toro was in every sense a Molinist.

Other Jesuits drew up similar denunciations, or attested their truth, and the case was fairly before the Holy Office. It was too serious for hasty action and investigation was made in Murcia, where his female accomplices were arrested, and ample confirmatory evidence was obtained from their confessions and from eighteen of his letters. The Carranza case had taught the lesson that bishops could be reached only through papal authority and, on November 7, 1709, Inquisitor-general Ybáñez forwarded to Clement XI the accumulated evidence, to which the pope replied, March 8, 1710, that the matter would be thoroughly examined and the necessary action be taken. Toro had at first been disposed to make a contest, asserting that God would work miracles in defence of the women, and that their imprisonment was a martyrdom; that the light infused in him by God rendered him superior to the Inquisition, and that he was illuminated above all other men. By this time, however, he realized his position; on February 8, 1710, he made, through his confessor, a partial confession, and he followed this with several letters to the pope, begging permission to come to Rome for judgement. Then a papal brief of June 7th ordered Ybáñez, within three years and under the advice of the Suprema, to frame a prosecution, for which full powers were granted; if the evidence sufficed, Toro was to be arrested and the case carried on up to the point of sentence, when all the documents were to be transmitted to Rome, where the pope would render the decision.

Toro was duly imprisoned and his trial proceeded. Ybáñez died, September 3, 1710 and was succeeded by Giudice, who was empowered, by a brief of October 3, 1711, to carry on the process. Toro was found to be diminuto on a hundred and four of the articles of accusation; he was reticent and refused to answer interrogations, begging earnestly to be sent to Rome. His request was granted, by a brief of June 7, 1714, but his departure was delayed, and it was not until June 11, 1716, that he reached Rome and was lodged in the castle of Sant'Angelo. Andrés de Cabrejas, fiscal of the Suprema, accompanied him, to represent the Spanish Inquisition in the trial which proceeded slowly. Toro's confessions and letters were a rich mine for the calificadores, who extracted from them four hundred and fifty-five propositions of various degrees of error--some of them being identical with those of Molinos. Finally he abandoned all defence and acknowledged that he had been a dogmatizing heretic, a soliciting seducer, a blasphemer against the purity of God, Jesus Christ and the Blessed Virgin, a reviver of the filthy sects of the Begghards, Illuminists and Molinists and subject to the same penalties.

MOLINISM

In fact he seems to have recognized his errors and to have confessed with a freedom indicative of sincere repentance. Much of his confessions is unfit for transcription, but a brief extract will indicate the self-deception that reconciled the grossest sensuality with aspirations for perfection. Thus of one of his accomplices he says that, believing himself to be illuminated in the sacrifice of the mass, he had written that none of her directors could estimate her spiritual state as regards her perfection and Union with God, in spite of the concussions of her inferior part, excited by obsession, through which those could be deceived who were unable to understand her interior virtues and perfect state. Although in obscene acts the woman might seem externally to be a sinner, yet, by asserting that she had not yielded consent, she might internally be perfect and be in Union with God. That, as the Incarnate Word did not contract original sin in his union with humanity, so with persons annihilated, purged and perfected, God could direct them to supernatural operations in such wise that the operations of the inferior part worked no prejudice to their state of perfection, and that the woman's obscene acts might proceed from obsession, and she be passive without consent.... That he had believed this doctrine to be infused in him by God, and thus to be true, like the doctrine of the Church, to be held unhesitatingly, especially by those obsessed, and he had written that he was ready to give his life in its defence.... That he had believed the indecencies committed with this same woman might be an exercise and martyrdom sent by God for the humiliation and purification of both, but nevertheless he made confession of them, and took care that she should do so. She was accustomed to say that, in the inferior part, she was without sensuality and in the superior part was absorbed in contemplation and love of God.... That in his oratory after mass and her communion he had embraced her and told her that she received the light and that this was the love of God for his creatures.... That Jesus was in him and worked in him, because neither he nor the woman experienced sensuality in what they did nor did it from corrupt intention.... That he had had this belief for seven years prior to his episcopate, and had maintained it subsequently up to July 1708, but then, in confessing his sins, a worthy confessor enlightened his blindness, and since then he had detested his errors and had followed the way of Catholic truth.

At length the pope designated July 27, 1719 for pronouncing sentence. Cabrejas had the records of Carranza's condemnation looked up, and the same ceremonial was observed. Toro was brought from the castle of Sant'Angelo to one of the halls of the papal palace, and there the sentence was read. It deposed him from his bishopric and all other benefices, it incapacitated him from holding any preferment, and suspended him perpetually from sacerdotal functions; it required him to abjure his heresy and errors, it called upon him to pay for pious uses, as far as he could, all revenues accrued since his lapse into heresy, and it burdened his see with a pension for his support, to be determined by the pope; it condemned him to reclusion, in some convent outside of Spain, when he was to perform perpetual penance, on the bread of sorrow and water of grief, and it prescribed certain spiritual observances. After listening to his sentence, Toro made the required abjuration, accepted the penance and disappeared from view.[136]

Another prominent culprit was the priest, Don Francisco de Leon y Luna, a Knight of Santiago and member of the Council of Castile, who was tried by the tribunal of Madrid for Molinism and formal solicitation. As a negativo he was liable to relaxation but, on November 24, 1721, it was voted to give him nine audiences, in which the inquisitors, with some calificadores, should exhort him to confession and conversion, under threat of administering the full rigor of the law. He seems to have yielded and, on August 11, 1722, his sentence con méritos was read in the presence of twelve members of the Councils of Castile, Indies, Orders and Hacienda. He was required to abjure de vehementi, he was deprived perpetually of confessing men and women, of guiding souls and instructing them in prayer, and of the honors of the Order of Santiago; half of his property was confiscated, and he was recluded for three years with suspension of all sacerdotal functions, to be followed by five years of exile.[137]

***

Llorente gives, in great detail, an account of a Molinist movement which, soon after this, afforded ample occupation to the tribunals of Logroño and Valladolid. Juan de Causadas, a prebendary of Tudela, was an ardent disciple of Molinos and propagator of his doctrines. He was burnt at Logroño, but whether for pertinacity or denial we are not informed. His nephew, Fray Juan de Longas, of the Barefooted Carmelites, was also a dogmatizer and was sentenced, in 1729, to two hundred lashes and ten years of galleys, followed by perpetual prison. This severity seems not to have discouraged the proselytes who, apparently, were not betrayed by Longas. The principal among them was Doña Agueda de Luna, who had entered the Carmelite convent of Lerma in 1712, with the reputation of a saint. Her ecstasies and miracles were spread abroad by Juan de Longas, by the Prior of Lerma, by the Provincial of the Order, Juan de la Vega, and by the leading frailes, who found their account in the crowds of devotees seeking her intercession. Juan de la Vega himself acquired the name of el extático and was represented as the holiest mystic since the days of Juan de la Cruz. A convent was founded at Corella for Madre Agueda, of which she was made prioress, and the nuns were fully indoctrinated in the principles and practice of Molinism. By Madre Agueda, Juan de la Vega had five children who were strangled at birth and, with other untimely fruits of the prevailing licence, were buried in the vicinity. After a long course of iniquity and deception, Madre Agueda was denounced to the Logroño tribunal; her accomplices and disciples were arrested and their trials were pushed with unsparing severity. She perished under torture and, in 1743, the frailes were recluded in various houses and the nuns were distributed among convents of their Order.[138] Madre Agueda's case had been decided some years previously for, in the Supplement to the Index of 1707, published in 1739, the first entry relates to her, "of whom the apocryphal life has been written, and of whom are circulated stones, cloths, medals and papers as relics," all of which were to be surrendered as well as relations of her prodigies and virtues.

The stones here alluded to are evidently those described by Llorente, made of brick-dust and stamped with a cross on one side and a star on the other, which were said to be voided by her with child-birth pains, and were universally treasured as amulets. It may be assumed that this case led to the issue, in 1745, by the Inquisition of an edict directed against five Molinist errors.[139]

Cases still continued to occur, but infrequently and of minor importance. The inquisitors had begun to merge immoral mysticism with solicitation in the confessional, of which more hereafter, while the more harmless kinds were classified as embusteros (impostors) or ilusos (deluded). There is a Mexican case, however, which is so illustrative of the abuses to which inquisitorial methods were liable, that it deserves mention. The Franciscan, Fray Eusebio de Villaroja, was distinguished for learning, eloquence and blameless life. He was inclined to mysticism and had written a work entitled Oracion de Fe interior, which the Inquisition admitted to contain no reprobated doctrine but yet to be dangerous for popular use. The convent at Pachuca obtained his assignment there and in 1783, at the age of 38, he arrived in Mexico, where his kindly earnestness speedily won universal regard. After two or three years he happened to assume the spiritual direction of two girls, Gertrudis and Josefa Palacios, who were adepts in the mystic devices of ecstasies and revelations. Gertrudis died and Villaroja became completely engrossed in Josefa. He reduced to writing her visions and prophecies, until he had filled seventy-six books and, in his ardor, he committed freaks attracting undesirable attention. The convent physician suggested that undue austerity had engendered hypochondriac humors, and the Guardian interposed by ordering him to attend to other duties, to limit Josefa to an hour in the confessional, and never to go to her house. His obedience was implicit and prompt; he ceased to talk of her visions and prophecies, and she naturally ceased to have them. A year later, when questioned by Fray Juan Sánchez, the visitor of the Province, he said that, as soon as the Guardian reproved him, he recognized his error and would not relapse into it--so the affair seemed to have died a natural death.

Unluckily the Guardian, not anticipating such docility, had reported the matter to the Inquisition, which commenced to gather testimony, but when he was, some months later, in the city of Mexico and was summoned as a witness, he stated that Villaroja's eccentricities had ceased, and he evidently regarded the matter as closed. Still the tribunal persisted and, in July 1789, it seized Villaroja's diaries, in which the latest entry was one humbly submitting to the judgement of the Church both himself and the authenticity of the visions.

After a formidable mass of testimony was accumulated, bearing witness to Villaroja's eminent piety and virtue, he was summoned, in July 1790, to present himself. He was not informed that he was on trial for, in his profound humility, he would at once have submitted his opinions to the judgement of the tribunal, but he was drawn into a discussion as to whether God, for the greater perfection of the creature, would permit the demon to incite to foul and obscene actions--a position which he had taken to justify some filthy habits of Josefa. This was, as we have seen, one of the dangerous tenets of Quietism, and over this there was a prolonged and subtle disputation. He subsequently declared that he supposed the inquisitor to be only seeking to learn his opinions when in fact he was being cunningly led to pile up evidence against himself, at the same time arousing the controversial pride of Inquisitor Prado y Obejero, who pronounced futile his efforts to differentiate his doctrine from that of Molinos.

He was thrown into the secret prison, October 13, 1791, and his trial proceeded in regular form. Nothing could exceed his submissive humility. On every fitting occasion he protested that he had been miserably led into error by ignorance; he begged to be undeceived in whatever he had erred and he submitted himself to the correction of the Holy Office, for he desired above all things the discharge of his conscience and the salvation of his soul. It required uncommon perversity in his judges to make a pertinacious heretic out of so humble and contrite a spirit but, when his sentence was pronounced, April 26, 1793, it represented him as a hardened and obstinate Alumbrado and Molinist, condemning him to abjure de vehementi, to be forever deprived of the faculty of confessing, to be recluded for three years in the Franciscan convent of Mexico, and to be sent to Spain whenever the inquisitors should see fit. Had he been an habitual seducer of his spiritual daughters, the sentence would have been less severe.

DELUSION

The treatment of a fraile recluded in a convent of his brethren was usually harsh in the extreme, but Fray Eusebio's kindliness and gentleness so won on his hosts that they declared his daily life to be an edification, while those of Pachuca, who had to bear the expenses of his trial, continued to regard him with undiminished affection. His punishment, however, was far more severe than the mere provisions of his sentence. Incarceration for eighteen months in a humid cell had developed a former rheumatic tendency and he was crippled. His request to be transferred to Pachuca was refused and, in March, 1795, he appealed to Inquisitor-general Lorenzana. His sufferings, he said, were on the increase and, if he were kept in the city of Mexico or sent to Spain, he would surely die. The result of this was a command to transmit him to Spain, which was notified to him, in June 1796, when he protested, to no purpose, that it would kill him. His removal was postponed until October, when he was carried by easy stages to Vera Cruz and placed on board the good ship Aurora, November 9th, consigned to the commissioner at Seville. The Aurora sailed the next day, but his prophetic spirit proved true and, when nine days out, his gentle spirit passed to a judge more merciful than his earthly ones.[140]

***

Fray Eusebio would have fared better in Spain, where there was a growing tendency to regard the accused as subject to delusion, when there was no conscious imposture and no teaching of dangerous Mysticism. Delusion was recognized at an early period, but the first case which I have met in which it formed the basis of prosecution occurs in the Barcelona tribunal which, in 1666, reported that it had found a process brought, in 1659, against Sor María de la Cruz, nun of the convent of la Concepcion of Tortosa, por ilusa, which had never been concluded.[141] In 1694, Don Francisco de las Cuevas y Rojas, of Madrid, was sentenced by the Toledo tribunal, as an iluso pasivo, to reprimand, absolution ad cautelam, retractation of certain propositions, abstention from spiritual matters, and a year's reclusion, during which a calificador would teach him the safest method of prayer, while all his writings were to be suppressed. The same year a beata named María de la Paz, as ilusa, was required merely to abjure de levi, to be severely reprimanded and to be handed over to a calificador for instruction. So, in 1716, Don Eugenio Aguado de Lara, cura of Algete, was sentenced, by the same tribunal, for suspicion of illusion in the direction of a beata, to abjure de levi, with reprimand and prohibition of further communication with her, while he was to abstain from the direction of souls as far as was compatible with his priestly functions. The beata his accomplice, Agustina Salgado, was regarded as more reprehensible for, besides being ilusa, she was held guilty of false revelations; she abjured de levi, with perpetual exile from Algete and reclusion in a hospital for two years, for instruction.[142]

Even this moderation increased with time. In 1785, the Valencia tribunal suspended the case, and sent to an insane hospital, Esperanza Bueno of Puig, popularly known as la Santa, denounced for pretended revelations and asserting that she could absolve from sin.[143] The same tendency appears in the case of María Rivero, of Valladolid, in 1817, whom the Suprema characterized as erroneously and presumptuously believing herself to be adorned with revelations and special graces. She was ordered to place herself unreservedly under the guidance of a spiritual director, with the warning that otherwise she would be treated with judicial rigor, while the director was instructed to disillusion her, and to call in medical advice as to her sanity, which was doubtful.[144]

Although the Inquisition was thus growing rationalistic in its treatment of these cases, it was impossible to eradicate popular credulity with its accompanying temptation to exploitation. In the last case before the Córdova tribunal, it ordered, July 9, 1818, the incarceration in the secret prison, as an ilusa, of the beata Francisca de Paula Caballero y Garrida of Lucena, while her sister María Dominga Caballero was confined in the carceles medias, and the two curas of Lucena, Joaquin de Burgos and Josef Barranco, were recluded in a convent without communication with each other. The beata performed miracles and had revelations, which seem to have found credence among a circle of disciples for when, after full investigation, the Suprema, on July 5, 1819, ordered the prosecution of the four prisoners, it directed proceedings to be commenced against seven other parties, including clerics and laymen of both sexes. Fortunately for this group of ilusos, the revolution of 1820 came to put an end to all proceedings, and when the Córdova tribunal was suppressed, the only inmates found in its prison were the two beatas of Lucena.[145]

IMPOSTORS

While the Inquisition was thus merciful towards those whom it considered to be merely deluded in claiming spiritual graces, it grew to be severe with those who traded on popular credulity. That credulity was so universal and so boundless that the profession of beata revelandera was an easy and a profitable one. The people were eager to be deceived; no fiction was too gross to find ready credence, and the believers invented miracles which they ascribed to the objects of their reverence. The punishment of the impostor and the exposure of the fraud failed to repress either belief or imposition, and the land in time was overrun by a horde of these practitioners, mostly female. It was a spiritual pestilence of the most degrading character, shared by all classes, with the extenuating circumstances that some of the boldest cases of imposture enjoyed the approbation of the Holy See. The Inquisition did good work in its ceaseless efforts to repress this prostitution of Mysticism--a work which no other tribunal could venture to attempt. If it found suppression impossible, at least it checked the development which at one time threatened to render the popular religion of Spain a matter of hysterics.

In its inception, there was some hesitation as to the treatment of these speculators on the credulity of the people. When the Beata of Piedrahita was allowed to continue her career, she naturally had imitators. In 1525, Alonso de Mariana, a Toledan inquisitor, on a visitation of his district, had his attention called to Doña Juana Maldonado of Guadalajara, widow of the alcaide of la Vega de la

Montaña. She was arrested and presented written statements or confessions of her dreams and visions of the Virgin and Christ, St. John the Evangelist and St. Bernard. The proceedings were informal and, in an audience, March 27th, at Alcalá de Henares, after publication of the evidence, she admitted its truth, stating that she had talked about her visions in order to obtain some aid in her poverty and she begged for mercy and penance. There was evidently no desire to treat her harshly or to regard her as an impostor, for she is spoken of as an ilusa or soñadera (dreamer) and she was required only to fast on five Fridays and Saturdays, in honor of Christ and the Virgin, with fifteen Paters and Aves each day, to keep her house as a prison until released by the tribunal, after which, on six Saturdays, she was to visit the church of the Virgin, outside of the town.[146] A century later she would have fared much worse.

The exposure, in 1543, of a more accomplished practitioner, Magdalena de la Cruz, removed any further hesitation in dealing with such cases. She had long been the wonder of Spain and even of Christendom. Tempest-tossed mariners would invoke her intercession, when she would appear to them and the storm would subside. The noblest ladies, when nearing confinement, would send the layette to be blessed by her, as did the Empress Isabel before the birth of Philip II. When, in 1535, Charles V was starting from Barcelona for the expedition to Tunis, he sent his banner to Córdova that she might bestow on it her blessing. Cardinal Manrique, the inquisitor-general, and Giovanni di Reggio, the papal nuncio, made pilgrimages to her, and the pope sent to ask her prayers for the Christian Republic. It is true that Ignatius Loyola was incredulous and, in 1541, severely reproved Martin de la Santa Cruz, who endeavored to win him over, for accepting exterior signs without seeking for the true ones; the Venerable Juan de Avila was also sceptical and, when he was in Córdoba, he was discreetly denied access to her.

***

When, in 1504, at the age of 17, she entered the Franciscan convent of Santa Isabel de los Angeles of Córdova, she was already regarded as a vessel overflowing with divine grace, a belief confirmed by a series of ecstasies, trances, visions, revelations and miracles. Space is lacking to recount the varied series of marvels, many of which do infinite credit to her imaginative invention, while some of them required confederates, who seem not to have been lacking, in view of the benefit to the convent accruing from its containing so saintly a person. Elected prioress in 1533, she retained the position until 1542, and during this time she devoted to it the large stream of offerings which poured in on her. Defeated for re-election in 1542, she no longer made this use of her funds and the successful faction denounced her to the Guardian and the Provincial as an impostor, but the credit of the Order was at stake and they were silenced. She was not destined however to adorn the calendar of mystic saints for, in 1543, she fell dangerously sick and was warned to prepare for death. Under this pressure she made a full confession, ascribing her deceits to demoniacal possession. She recovered and the Inquisition seized her. The trial lasted until May 3, 1546, an immense body of testimony being taken, corroborative of her confession, which was skilfully framed to throw the blame on her demons Balban and Patorrio. In short, she had commenced as a mystic, had been unable to resist the temptation of accepting the miracles thrust upon her by popular superstition, she had stimulated this with her frauds, and finally sought extenuation by alleging demonic influence. An immense crowd attended the auto held May 3, 1546, when the reading of her sentence con méritos occupied from 6 A.M. to 4 P.M., while she sat on the staging with a gag in her mouth, a halter around her neck and a lighted candle in her hand. Her sentence was moderate-- perpetual reclusion in a convent, without active or passive voice, and occupying the last place in choir, refectory and chapter, together with some spiritual penances. She was relegated to the convent of Santa Clara, at Andujar, where she lived an exemplary life and, at her death, in 1560, it was piously hoped that her sins were expiated.[147]

Had human reason any share in these beliefs, such an exposure would have put an end to the industry of the beatas revelanderas, but the popular appetite for the marvellous was insatiable, and there were abundant practitioners ready to dare the attendant risks for the accompanying glory and profit. Everywhere there were women accomplished in these arts and skilled in impressing their neighbors with their revelations and prophecies; every town and almost every hamlet had its local saint, who was regarded with intense veneration and assured of an abundant livelihood.[148] All branches of the supernatural were exploited: some could predict the future; others had prophetic dreams or could expound those of their devotees; others could release souls from purgatory; others could perform curative miracles; popular faith in these gifted spirits was boundless and innumerable sharpers of both sexes fattened upon it.

The people might well be credulous when they but followed the example of those highest in Church and State. Magdalena de la Cruz had a worthy imitator in the Dominican Madre María de la Visitacion, of the convent of the Annunciada of Lisbon, whose intimate relations with Christ began at the age of 16, in 1572. About 1580 Christ crucified appeared to her, when a ray of fire from his breast pierced her left side, leaving a wound which on Fridays distilled drops of blood with intense pain. In

1583 she was elected prioress and, in 1584, in another vision of Christ crucified, rays of fire from his hands and feet pierced hers and thus completed the Stigmata. No time was lost by the Dominican Provincial, Antonio de la Cerda, in spreading the news of this, in a statement dated March 14, 1584, and sent to Rome to be submitted to Gregory XIII. It was corroborated by the signatures of several frailes, among which is the honored name of the great mystic, Luis de Granada.[149] The Provincial followed this, March 30th, with another letter to Rome stating that the impression produced had been so great that many gentlemen had been induced to abandon the world and enter the Order, and even that three Moors had come to look upon Sor María, whose appearance had so impressed them that they sought baptism on the spot--to which he added two miraculous cures effected through articles touched by her.[150]

Sor María's fame penetrated through Christendom and even, we are told, to the Indies. Gregory XIII was duly impressed and wrote to her urging to persevere without faltering in the path which she had entered. She might have continued to do so, with the reputation of a saint, if she had abstained from politics. Unluckily she allowed herself to be drawn into a movement to throw off the Spanish yoke, and the authorities, who had been content to allow her to acquire influence, found it necessary to expose her, when that influence threatened to be potent on the side of rebellion.

***

The Annunciada was not without internal jealousies which facilitated the obtaining of information justifying investigation. A commission was appointed consisting of the Archbishops of Lisbon and Braga, the Bishop of Guarda, the Dominican Provincial, the Inquisitors of Lisbon and Doctor Pablo Alfonso of the Royal Council. Assembling in the convent they took the testimony of many of the nuns that Sor María's sanctity was feigned and her stigmata were painted. She was then brought before them and sworn, when she persisted, in spite of threats and adjurations, in the story of the stigmata and of her communications with Christ. The next day, hot water and soap were called for; she protested and pretended to suffer extreme agony, but a vigorous application of the detergents to the palms of her hands caused the wounds to disappear, when she threw herself at the feet of her judges and begged for mercy. At a subsequent audience she gave a detailed explanation of the devices by which she had deceived the faithful--how she had managed the apparent elevation from the ground and the divine light suffused around her and the cloths stained with blood from her side. The severity of the sentence, rendered December 6, 1588, shows how much greater than mere sacrilegious imposture was the offence of her meddling with politics. She was recluded for life in a convent of a different Order from her own; for a year she was to be whipped every Monday and Friday for the space of a Miserere; in the refectory she was to take her meals on the floor, what she left was to be cast out and, at the end of the meal, she was to lie in the door-way and be trampled on by the sisters in their exit; she was to observe a perpetual fast; she was incapacitated from holding office; she was always to be last and was to hold converse with none without permission of the abbess; she was not to wear a veil; on Wednesdays and Fridays she was to have only bread and water, and whenever the nuns assembled in the refectory she was to recite her crimes in an audible voice. In this living death she is said to have performed her cruel penance with such patience and humility that she became saintly in reality.[151] It is not improbable that she may have been from the beginning a tool in designing hands. A contemporary relates that, before the exposure, he wrote to Fray Alberto de Aguajo in Lisbon, asking whether he should go thither to consult her on a case of conscience, and was told in reply that there was nothing wonderful about her except the goodness of God in granting her such graces, for she was as simple as a child of six. She was, however, a rich source of income, for the Portuguese in the Indies used to send her gold and diamonds and pearls to purchase her intercession with God.[152] Even her condemnation did not wholly disabuse her dupes. Four years later, a certain Martin de Ayala, prosecuted in 1592 for revelations and imposturas, claimed to have spiritual communication with her and foretold direful things about the conquest of Spain by foreigners, when a cave in Toledo would be the only place where the few elect could find safety. He had a colleague, Don Guillen de Casans, who was likewise prosecuted.[153]

One would have supposed that a case like that of Sor María, to which the utmost publicity must have been given, would have discredited the stigmata as a special mark of divine favor, but it seems rather to have stimulated the ambitious to possess them by showing how easily they could be imitated. They became a matter of almost daily occurrence. In 1634 a Jesuit casually alludes in a letter to two new cases just reported--one of a nun of la Concepcion in Salamanca and the other in Burgos--adding that they had become so common that no woman esteems herself a servant of God unless she can exhibit them.[154]

***

When uncomplicated with politics, imposture continued to be leniently treated and it was an exception when, in 1591, the Toledo tribunal visited with two hundred lashes María de Morales for trances and revelations and other deceits to acquire the reputation of a saint.[155] Thus at the Seville auto of 1624, when Pacheco was intent on suppressing the errors of Mysticism, there were eight impostors guilty of every device to exploit superstition, six of whom escaped with a year or two of reclusion. Only two were more severely dealt with. Mariana de Jesus, a barefooted Carmelite, was a Maestra de Espiritu, who taught Illuminism and had a record of endless visions, prophetic inspiration and conflicts with Satan. She maintained herself in luxury by selling her spiritual gifts, and it was in evidence that poor people had pledged their household gear to purchase her intercession for the souls of their kindred, but she was only paraded in vergüenza with four year's reclusion in a convent and perpetual exile from Seville. The heaviest punishment was that visited on Juan de Jesus, known as el Hermito, who professed to be insensible to carnal temptation, for God had deprived him of all free-will and he was governed only by the spirit. Religious observances for him were superfluous, for he was always in the presence of God, and so fervent was his love for God that water hissed when he drank it. He not only claimed that he healed the sick but that once he had prayed eight thousand souls out of purgatory, thirty thousand at another time, then twenty-two thousand and finally all that were left. In general his relations with women are unfit for description, and he shrewdly had a revelation that all who gave him alms would be saved. His devotees were not confined to the ignorant, for he was received in the houses of the principal ladies of Seville and men of high distinction admitted him to their tables. He received less than his deserts when he was sentenced to a hundred lashes and life confinement in a convent or hospital, where he was to work for his board and to pray daily a third of the rosary.[156]

In its persistent and fruitless efforts to stamp out this pestilence, the Inquisition was beginning to adopt severer treatment, as in the case of Sor Lorenza Murga of Simancas, a Franciscan tertiary, who for sixteen years enjoyed great reputation in Valladolid. She had ecstasies and revelations whenever wanted, and her little house was an object of pilgrimage, when she would throw herself into a trance at the request of any one. It was a profitable pursuit, for she rose from abject poverty to comfortable affluence. Her arrest, April 29, 1634, caused no little excitement, and it was whispered that she had been detected in keeping two lovers besides her confessor. In her audiences she persistently maintained the truth of her revelations, constantly adding fresh marvels, till the inquisitors tortured her smartly, when she confessed it to be all an imposture. Her career was cut short with two hundred lashes and exile for six years from all the places where she had lived.[157]

The experienced inquisitor whom I have so often quoted tells us, about this time, that these impostors were very common; that there were rules for teaching them their trade and, as it was so prejudicial and so discreditable, they must be punished with all rigor. He mentions a case at Llerena, where the woman persisted in asserting the truth of her revelations and miracles, until she was tortured, when she confessed the fraud and was condemned to scourging and reclusion, at the discretion of the tribunal, with fasting on bread and water.[158] Yet one cannot help feeling sympathy for María Cotanilla, a poor blind crone, sentenced in 1676, by the Toledo tribunal, to a hundred lashes and to pass four years in a designated place, where she could support herself by beggary, reporting herself monthly to the commissioner.[159]

Severity might check, but could not suppress, a profession which was the inevitable outcome of popular demand. How it was stimulated is well exemplified in the case of María Manuela de Tho--, a young woman of 23, arrested by the Madrid tribunal, in April, 1673. She confessed unreservedly a vast variety of impostures, pretended diabolical possession, visits from the angels Gabriel and Raphael and numerous others. She told how she was venerated as a saint; her signature written on scraps of blank paper was distributed by her confessor and was treasured as though it were that of Santa Teresa; he had crosses made of olive wood which she blessed and they were valued as relics and amulets; she cured the sick and performed many other miracles. The origin of all this, as she related it, is highly illuminating. She chanced to tell certain persons that in a dream she saw a soul in purgatory; they shook their heads wisely and said it was more than a dream and contained great mysteries. Then they began to admire her and she, finding that she was esteemed and admired and regaled with presents, and that money came to her without labor, went on from one step to another with her visions and miracles. She knew that it was wrong but, as there were learned and distinguished persons cognizant of it, who could have undeceived her and did not and, as there was no pact with the demon, she continued for, though she had been a miserable sinner, she had always been firm in the faith of Christ as a true Catholic Christian.[160] When the appetite for marvels was so universal and unreasoning, the supply could not be lacking, no matter what might be the efforts of the Inquisition.

***

These practitioners naturally continued to give occupation to the tribunals, but their cases can teach us little except to note the severity with which they were occasionally treated. In the Madrid auto of 1680 there were four impostors, of whom a carpenter named Alfonso de Arenas was visited with abjuration, two hundred lashes, and five years of galleys followed by five more of exile.[161] In the little conventicle arrested, in 1708, by the Toledo tribunal (p. 71), four women and a man were punished, in 1711, as impostors, the man, Pablo Díez, an apothecary of Yepes, with reconciliation, confiscation and perpetual prison, while one of the women, María Fernández, had two hundred lashes and exile.[162] In 1725, the Murcia tribunal inflicted the same scourging and eight years of exile on Mariana Matozes, who added to her other impostures a claim to the stigmata, and in 1726, in Valencia, Juan Vives of Castillon de la Plana had the same allowance of stripes, with a year's reclusion and eight years' exile from Valencia and Catalonia.[163] It is therefore not easy to understand the clemency shown by the Toledo tribunal, in 1729, to Ana Rodríguez of Madridejos, who is described as a scandalous impostor, deluded and deluding, audacious, sacrilegious, boasting of her exemption from the sixth commandment, heretically blasphemous, vehemently suspect and formally guilty of the heresy of Molinos and the Alumbrados, insulting to the Blessed Virgin and St. Bernard and contumacious in all her errors. Her contumacy gave way, thus saving her from relaxation and she escaped with formal abjuration, reconciliation and confinement for instruction in the Jesuit college of Navalcarnero, during such time as the tribunal might deem necessary for her soul.[164]

Further enumeration of these obscure cases is scarce worth while and we may pass to one which excited lively interest. María de los Dolores López, known as the Beata Dolores, had a successful and scandalous career for fifteen or twenty years, commencing at the age of twelve, when she left her father's house to live as a concubine with her confessor. Her fame spread far and wide and, for ten years, the Inquisition received occasional denunciation of her misdeeds without taking action until, in 1779, one of her confessors, to relieve his conscience, denounced both himself and her to the Seville tribunal. On her trial she resolutely maintained the truth of the special graces which she had enjoyed since the age of four. She had continued and familiar intercourse with the Virgin, she had been married in heaven to the child Jesus, with St. Joseph and St. Augustin as witnesses, she had liberated millions of souls from purgatory, with much more of the kind so familiar to us, to which she added one of the errors of Molinism by maintaining that evil actions cease to be sinful when God so wills it. She was thus not merely an impostor but a formal and impenitent heretic, for whom relaxation was the only penalty known to the Inquisition. Burning, however, had well-nigh gone out of fashion, and the tribunal honestly spared no effort to save her from the stake. Eminent theologians wasted on her their learning and eloquence. Fray Diego de Cádiz, the foremost preacher of his time, labored with her for two months, and finally reported that there was nothing to do but to burn her. It was all in vain. God, she said, had revealed to her that she should die a martyr, after which, in three days, he would prove her innocence. The law had to take its course and, on August 22, 1781, she was formally sentenced to relaxation. As this left her unmoved the execution was postponed for three days to try the effect of fresh exhortations. This failed and, during the sermon and ceremonies of the auto, she had to be gagged to suppress her blasphemy. As so frequently happened however, her nerves gave way on the road to the brasero; she burst into tears and asked for a confessor, thus gaining the privilege of strangulation before the faggots were fired.[165]

***

Imposture continued to flourish. In 1800 the Valladolid tribunal was occupied with an extensive "complicidad," resulting in the prosecution of Madre María Ignacia de la Presentacion, a Mercenarian of the convent of Toro, for pretended miracles, along with nine frailes of the same Order as accomplices.[166] Contemporary with this was a case at Cuenca, which almost transcends belief. The wife of a peasant of Villar del Aguila, Isabel María Herraiz, known as the Beata de Cuenca, who had a reputation for sanctity, announced that Christ had revealed to her that, in order to be more completely united to her in love, he had transfused his body and blood into hers. The theology of the period is illustrated by the learned disputation which arose, some doctors arguing this to be impossible because it would render her more holy than the Blessed Virgin and would deprive the sacrament of the exclusive distinction of being the body and blood of the Lord; others held it to be possible but that the proofs in the present case were insufficient; others, again, accepted it and urged the virtues of the beata and the absence of motive for deception. The people felt no scruple, and were encouraged in their credulity by two Franciscan frailes, Joaquin de Alustante and Domingo de Cañizares, and a Carmelite, Sebastian de los Dolores. Her believers worshipped her, carrying her through the streets in procession, lighting candles before her and prostrating themselves in adoration. The scandal attained proportions calling for repression, and the Inquisition arrested her, June 25, 1801, together with her accomplices. It is possible that she was severely handled, for she died in the secret prison without confession, and was consequently burnt in effigy. The cura of Villar and two of the frailes were banished to the Philippines; two laymen received two hundred lashes each, with service for life in a presidio, and her hand-maid, Manuela Pérez, was consigned for ten years to the Recojidas or house of correction for women.[167]

While this comedy was in progress in Cuenca, a similar one was performing in Madrid, in the highest social ranks. Sor María Clara Rosa de Jesus, known as the Beata Clara, had acquired great reputation by her visions and miracles. She was, or pretended to be, paralyzed and unable to leave her bed and, when she announced that a special command of the Holy Ghost required her to join the Capuchin Order, Pius VI granted her a dispensation to take the vows without residence. Atanasio de Puyal, subsequently Bishop of Calahorra, obtained licence to erect a private altar in her chamber, where mass was celebrated daily, and she received communion, pretending to take no other nourishment. All the great ladies of the court were accustomed to implore her intercession in their troubles and gave her large sums to be expended in charity. It is to the credit of the Inquisition that it broke up this speculative imposture by arresting her, in 1801, together with her mother and confessor as accomplices. It was not difficult to prove their guilt and, in 1803, they were mercifully sentenced to reclusion.[168]

For three hundred years, up to the time of its suppression, the Inquisition, thus vainly labored to put an end to these speculations on the credulity of the faithful. It did its best, but the popular craving for the marvellous, for concrete evidence of divine interposition in human affairs, was too universal and too strong to be controlled, even by its supreme authority. After its downfall, the career of the notorious Sor Patrocinio proves how ineradicable was this and serves to bring medievalism down to our own time.

***

María Rafaela Quiroga, known in religion as Sor María Cipriana del Patrocinio de San José, in 1829 took the veil in the convent of San José, and soon commenced to have visions and revelations, followed by the development of the stigmata. Her reputation spread and cloths stained with the blood of her wounds were in request as curative amulets. When the death of Fernando VII, September 29, 1833 was followed by the Carlist war, the clericals, who favored Don Carlos, saw in her a useful instrument. She was made to prophesy the success of the Pretender and to furnish proof of the illegitimacy of the young Queen Isabel. As in the case of the Portuguese María de la Visitacion, this dangerous factor in the political situation called for governmental intervention and, after some resistance, in November 1835, the Sor was removed from the convent to a private house, where she was kept under the care of her mother and of a priest, while three physicians were summoned to examine the stigmata. They pronounced them artificial and promised a speedy cure if interference was prevented. This was verified and, in spite of a scab being torn off from one of them, they were healed by December 17th. On January 21, 1836, an official inspection by a number of dignitaries confirmed the fact, which was assented to by the Sor and, on February 7th, she made a full confession, stating that a Capuchin, Padre Firmin de Alcaraz, had given her a caustic with directions to use it on hands, feet, side and head, telling her that the resultant pain would be a salutary penance. Prosecution was duly commenced against her and the Vicar, Prioress and Vicaress of the convent, Padre Firmin having prudently disappeared. Sentence was rendered, November 25, 1836, from which an appeal was taken, resulting in a slight increase of rigor. The convent was suppressed; the vicar, Andrés Rivas, was banished from Madrid for eight years, and the three women were sent to convents of their Order, Sor Patrocinio being conveyed, on April 27, 1837, to the nunnery at Talavera.[169]

Years passed away and she seemed to be forgotten when the reaction of 1844 suggested that she might again be utilized. In 1845 the convent of Jesus was built for her; she returned with the stigmata freshened and her saintly reputation enhanced. Imposing ceremonies rendered her entrance impressive, and she was conveyed to her convent under a canopy, like a royal personage. In conjunction with Padre Fulgencio, confessor to Don Francisco de Asis the king-consort, and with her brother Manuel Quiroga, whom she made gentleman of the royal bed-chamber, she became the power behind the throne. Dr. Argumosa, who had cured her stigmata, was persecuted and Fray Firmin Alcaraz, who had emerged from his hiding-place, was made Bishop of Cuenca. In 1849 she was held to have forced Isabel to dismiss the Duke of Valencia (Narvaez) and his cabinet. This was followed by what was known as the Ministerio Relámpago, or Lightning Ministry, which held office for three hours on October 19, 1849, and was forced to retire by the threatening aspect of the people. Narvaez was recalled and forthwith relegated to a distance Sor Patrocinio, her brother, Padre Fulgencio and some of their confederates.

She was soon recalled, however, and wielded an influence which Narvaez could not resist. His successor, Bravo Murillo, sought to get a respite by persuading the Nuncio Brunelli to send her to Rome, but this availed little, for she soon returned, more powerful than ever, with the blessing of Pius IX. Under her guidance, during the remainder of the reign of Isabel II, the camarilla practically ruled the kingdom and precipitated the revolution of 1868, which, for a time, supplanted the monarchy with a republic. With the fall of Isabel she disappeared from public view, in the retirement of the convent of Guadalajara, of which she was the abbess. There she lingered in seclusion, until January 27, 1891, when she died serenely, comforted in her last moments with a telegraphic blessing from Leo XIII.[170]

The Inquisition could suppress Judaism, it could destroy Protestantism, it could render necessary the expulsion of the Moriscos, but it failed when it sought to eradicate the abuses of Mysticism, which not only signalized the ardor of Spanish faith, but were so difficult of differentiation from beliefs long recognized and encouraged by the Church. There seems to be, in the average human mind, an insatiable craving for manifestations of the supernatural. Modern science, with its materialism, may weaken or even eradicate this in the majority, and may explain psychologically much of what seems to be marvellous, but the success in our own land of the curious superstition known as Christian Science shows us how superficial is latter-day enlightenment, and should teach us sympathy rather than disdain for the fantastic exhibitions of credulity which we have passed in review.

Henry Charles Lea, LL.D.

CHAPTER VI - SOLICITATION

The seduction of female penitents by their confessors, euphemistically known as solicitatio ad turpia or "solicitation," has been a perennial source of trouble to the Church since the introduction of confession, more especially after the Lateran Council of 1216 rendered yearly confession to the parish priest obligatory. It was admitted to be a prevailing vice, and canonists sought some opportunity of the evil by arguing that the priest notoriously addicted to it lost his jurisdiction over his female parishioners, who were thus at liberty to seek the sacrament of penitence from others.[171] A Spanish authority, however, holds that this requires the licence of the parish priest himself and, when he refuses it, the woman must confess to him, after prayer to God for strength to resist his importunities.[172]

It was an evil of which repression was impossible, notwithstanding penalties freely threatened. A virtue of uncommon robustness was required to resist the temptations arising from the confidences of the confessional, and so well was this understood that an exception was made to the rule requiring perfect confession, for reticence as to carnal sins was counselled, when the reputation of the priest rendered it advisable.[173] Few women thus approached, whether yielding or not, could be expected to denounce their pastors to the bishop or provisor, and for her who yielded the path to sin was made easy through the universal abuse of absolution by her accomplice, and this, although objected to on ethical grounds, was admitted to be valid.[174] On the other hand, the peccant confessor could rely on obtaining absolution from a sympathizing colleague, at the cost of penance which had become habitually trivial.

The intercourse between priest and penitent was especially dangerous because there had not yet been invented the device of the confessional--a box or stall in which the confessor sits with his ear at a grille, through which the tale of sins conceived or committed is whispered. Seated by his side or kneeling at his feet, there was greater risk of inflaming passion and much more opportunity for provocative advances. It was not until the middle of the sixteenth century that the confessional was devised, doubtless in consequence of the attacks of heretics, who found in these scandals a fertile subject of animadversion. The earliest allusion to it that I have met occurs in a memorial from Siliceo of Toledo to Charles V, in 1547.[175] In 1565 a Council of Valencia prescribed its use and contemporaneously S. Carlo Borromeo introduced it in his Milanese province, while in 1614 the Roman Ritual commanded its employment in all churches.[176] It was easier to command than to secure obedience, for the priesthood offered a passive resistance which even the Inquisition found it almost impossible to overcome. As early as 1625 it forbade parish priests from hearing confessions in their houses; between 1709 and 1720 we find it occupied in endeavoring to enforce the use of confessionals and, to prevent evasions, such as hearing confessions in cells and chapels, and not in the body of the church.[177] How long-continued was the opposition, and how transparent were the artifices to elude the regulations, are visible in an edict of November 3, 1781, which led to considerable trouble. After alluding to the repeated orders on the subject, and the deplorable results of their disregard, it prescribed that women should be heard only through the gratings of closed confessionals, or of open stalls in the body of the churches, or in chapels open and well lighted. It forbade the use of hand-gratings or handkerchiefs, sieves, bundle of twigs, fans, or other derisive substitutes, and it prescribed minute and highly suggestive regulations as to oratories and private chapels, while a similar series concerning male penitents shows the dread of contamination even with them.[178]

TOLERANCE OF SPIRITUAL COURTS

The crime of solicitation was subject to episcopal jurisdiction and, throughout the middle ages, there was no general legislation prescribing its penalties. Some apocryphal canons visited it with well-deserved severity and, in 1217, Richard Poore, the reforming Bishop of Salisbury, threatened it with fifteen years of penance followed by confinement in a monastery.[179] The spiritual courts, however, were notoriously lenient, and the prevalent sexual laxity tended to sympathy which disarmed severity in the rare cases coming before them. When, during the Reformation, this offence afforded a favorite topic for the heretics, there arose a demand for sharper treatment. In 1587, Iñigo López de Salcedo gives this as a reason for rigorous punishment, and he greatly lauds Matteo Ghiberti, the reforming Bishop of Verona ([dagger symbol] 1543) for decreeing a series of heavy penalties for attempts on the virtue of female penitents, culminating in deprivation and perpetual imprisonment when they were successful.[180]

This virtuous rigor, however, was purely exceptional. The usual tolerant view adopted is manifested in a case which, in 1535 at Toledo, came before the vicar-general, Blas Ortiz, a man so respected that he was promoted to the inquisitorship of Valencia soon afterwards. Alonso de Valdelamar, parish priest of Almodovar, was charged with a black catalogue of offences--theft, blasphemy, cheating with Cruzada indulgences, charging penitents for absolution, frequenting public brothels and solicitation. It was in evidence that he refused absolution to a girl unless she would surrender herself to him, that he seduced a married penitent whose husband was obliged to leave Almodovar in order to get her away from him, while Doña Leonor de Godoy admitted that he repeatedly used violence on her in the church itself. His sentence, rendered February 26, 1535, stated that the fiscal had fully proved his charges, but for all these crimes he was punished only with thirty days' penitential reclusion in his church, with a fine of ten ducats, besides four reales to the fiscal, a ducat to the episcopal advocate, ten days' wages to the notary who went to Almodovar to take testimony, and the costs of the trial. From this the fiscal appealed to the archbishop but the next day withdrew the appeal; Valdelamar accepted it and was sent back to his parish to pursue his course of profligacy. Evidently the episcopal tribunal was more concerned with the profits of its jurisdiction than with the suppression of solicitation.[181]

SUBJECTED TO THE INQUISITION

It may be inferred from this that peccant confessors were not likely to be prosecuted, unless there were other circumstances or offences to stimulate action, and this is confirmed by another case, about the same time, which also shows the readiness of the tribunal to claim jurisdiction. Pedro Bermúdez, incumbent of Ciempozuelos, employed a priest named Pareja as vicar, from 1525 to 1529. They quarrelled; Pareja was dismissed, found employment at Valdemoro, and commenced suit against Bermúdez. The latter retorted by instigating a certain Catalina Roldan, who had borne a child to Pareja, and her mother, to complain to Romero, a visiting inquisitor from Toledo, about the seduction, asking that he be forced to provide a dower and find a husband for her. Romero took up the case. Bermúdez busied himself in collecting testimony and was aided by a priest named Solorzano, whose enmity had been excited by Pareja having served as commissioner in taking evidence as to his seduction of a married woman, for which he was prosecuted in Alcalá. The proof collected against Pareja was conclusive. Two of his penitents admitted to having yielded to him, and several others testified as to his advances in the act of confession. When one of them was asked whether she confessed to him their mutual sin, she said that he told her not to do so, and afterwards admitted her to communion. There was also evidence as to his violating the seal of confession, and to irreverence in administering the sacrament. The trial pursued the usual course, the main charges being his misdeeds with his female penitents, which he admitted more or less explicitly. When the papers were sent to the Suprema, it returned them, saying that the charges for the most part were beyond the competence of the tribunal, and appertained to the episcopal court, to which they should be transferred, while the tribunal could proceed with the little that remained. The charges thus, after omitting the solicitation, were reduced to four--that he persuaded his accomplices that their mutual sin need not be confessed, that he told them that they could take the sacrament without confessing, that he said it was better to have masses celebrated than to pay debts, and that almost all the witnesses held him to be a bad Christian, a heretic and an evil man.

Pareja and his advocate argued that the case was outside of inquisitorial jurisdiction, but the tribunal pushed it to the end on these subsidiary points and, on May 23, 1532 sentenced him to perpetual deprivation of hearing the confessions of women, to a fine of twenty thousand maravedís, and to have Toledo as a prison for two years, during which he was to fast and recite psalms on Fridays. As he was not required to abjure, even for light suspicion, the charge of heresy was abandoned, and as solicitation was not included in the sentence, he was liable to further prosecution by the Ordinary. Yet the character of the penalties shows that solicitation was the real gravamen, over which the tribunal was seeking indirectly to acquire jurisdiction.[182]

Evidently, if there was to be any cure or mitigation of this corroding cancer, some less sympathetic tribunal than the episcopal court was requisite, and the Inquisition was eager to supply the want, yet matters were allowed to drift for a quarter of a century longer. Possibly it may have been the Lutheran alarm of 1558 that led Archbishop Guerrero of Granada to seek the remedy and to call to the attention of the Holy See the frequency of the crime and the need of its more energetic repression.[183] His appeal was heard, and Paul IV, in a brief of February 18, 1559, expressed his sorrow at learning that certain priests of Granada misled their penitents and abused the sacraments, wherefore he granted, to the inquisitors of Granada, jurisdiction over the heresy implied in the crime and withdrew all exemptions of the religious Orders.[184] What activity the Granada tribunal manifested in the exercise of its new function is not recorded, but the field thus thrown open was sufficiently inviting for Valdés, in 1561, to obtain from Pius IV a brief granting to him and to his delegates throughout Spain the same faculties.[185] It required some ingenuity to bring the crime within the purview of the Inquisition, but it was alleged that no one whose faith was correct could thus abuse the sacraments of the Church of God. The point is not without importance, for it made the matter one of faith and not of morals, leading, as we shall see, to a notable limitation in the efficacy of the reform attempted.

The regular clergy sought to escape to the milder mercies of their own superiors, and claimed that, in the constitution of Pius IV, in 1562, which subjected them in general to the Inquisition, there was an exception of cases in which the superiors had taken the earlier action.[186] The application, however, of this exception to the crime of solicitation was negatived, in 1592, by a decree of Clement VIII, which declared that the jurisdiction of the Inquisition in this matter was exclusive and not cumulative, and it ordered the members of all privileged Orders to denounce to the Inquisition their guilty brethren.[187] In 1608, Paul V granted the same powers to the Inquisition of Portugal and, in 1612, he settled in favor of the faith a question which had arisen, whether the briefs comprehended the solicitation of men as well as of women.[188] Even before this, solicitation in Italy had been subjected to the Roman Inquisition, for it issued, December 15, 1613 a decree ordering confessors to instruct their penitents that they must denounce to the tribunals all attempts to solicit them to evil and, on July 5, 1614, it included, what it described as a frequent offence, the discussion of indecent matters with women in the confessional, even without confession.[189]

LEGISLATION OF GREGORY XV

Thus the Church was gradually realizing the necessity of more stringent measures to curb the evil propensities of those to whom it confided the salvation of souls, but as yet it had made only local regulations. Gregory XV recognized that a general law was required, to cover all the lands of the Roman obedience, and not merely those possessed of an Inquisition and, at the same time, to define more comprehensively the nature of the offence. The briefs thus far had limited this to seduction in the act of hearing confessions. Papal legislation was always construed in the strictest manner, and confessors felt safe if they confined their seductions to the time preceding and following the actual utterance of the confession. Had the moral and spiritual welfare of priest and penitent been the only matter involved, it would have been easy to include in general terms any indecent or illicit passages between them, no matter when or where committed, but solicitation had been made to involve suspicion of heresy, in order to bring it under the Inquisition, and it became regarded as a purely technical offence, punishable only when it could be connected directly with the sacrament, leading to the unfortunate corollary that otherwise it was a trivial matter, undeserving of special consideration.

Accordingly Gregory, in his brief Universi Dominici Gregis, August 30, 1622, while enlarging the definition, confined it to what was said or done in the place destined to hearing confessions, whether it was before or after confession, or even if there was only a pretext of confession. He extended the provisions of his predecessors to all lands, and delegated all inquisitors and Ordinaries as special judges, with exclusive jurisdiction to inquire into and diligently prosecute such cases, according to the canons in matters of faith. He further decreed the penalties of suspension of functions, deprivation of benefices and dignities with perpetual disability for the same and, for regulars, of active and passive voice; besides these there were the temporal penalties of exile, galleys, perpetual and irremissible imprisonment and, in cases of exceptional wickedness, of degradation and relaxation. In view of the difficulty of proof, single witnesses should suffice for condemnation, when circumstances afforded due presumption. Confessors, who found that their penitents had been previously solicited, were required to admonish them to denounce the offenders, and for neglect of this they were to be duly punished. This latter provision was of difficult enforcement, for Urban VIII, in 1626, felt obliged to address all archbishops, instructing them to call the attention of confessors to it, and to insert a corresponding clause in all licences. The regular clergy seem to have been the subject of special anxiety for, in 1633, the superiors of all religious houses were ordered to assemble the inmates yearly and warn them as to the observance of these decrees, and this was also to be done in all chapters, general, provincial and conventual.[190]

The Holy See was in earnest, but the result did not correspond to its efforts. France and Germany paid virtually no attention to the decrees, and in Spain the Inquisition made no change in its procedure or in the mildness of its penalties. The only effect of Gregory's brief was to raise the question whether it did not confirm, at least cumulatively, to the bishops the jurisdiction of which they had been practically deprived. No distinction was expressed between lands with and those without an Inquisition, and the original briefs of Paul IV and Pius IV had not deprived the bishops of jurisdiction, although the latter had made little effort to assert it against the exclusive claims of the tribunals. We chance to hear of the case of Dr. Miguel Bueso, who was surrendered by the Archbishop of Valencia, in 1608, for trial on this charge and, after punishment, was returned to the archiepiscopal court.[191] Soon after this de Sousa argues that, in spite of the papal decrees, bishops have cumulative jurisdiction, although the inquisitor-general can evoke cases.[192] In 1620, Inquisitor-general Luis de Aliaga had a struggle with his brother Isidor de Aliaga, Archbishop of Valencia, over the case of Gaspar Flori, rector of Urgel, who was on trial by the vicar-general for various offences, including solicitation. The tribunal demanded cognizance of this special charge; the vicar-general asserted cumulative jurisdiction, adding that he had already tried two cases of the kind. The inquisitor-general argued strenuously that, as a matter of faith, it belonged to the Inquisition; if it were not a matter of faith it would go unpunished, for there would be no obligation to denounce, and without this women would never imperil their honor, for experience showed how rarely they did so voluntarily, and they had to be compelled by the refusal of absolution. Notwithstanding all this the archbishop of Valencia held good; his vicar-general tried the case and executed the sentence.[193] There were few episcopal courts, however, so audacious as this, and the claim of the Inquisition to exclusive jurisdiction was generally conceded.

EXCLUSIVE JURISDICTION CLAIMED

The brief of Gregory XV was not published in Spain but, by some means, the Ordinary of Seville obtained a copy and exhibited it to the inquisitors. The Suprema promptly, on January 14, 1623 addressed a consulta to Philip IV, stating that it had not learned that the brief had reached any other bishop and dwelling eloquently on the frequency and heinousness of the crime, the energy and rigor of the Inquisition in its repression, and the disastrous consequences of concurrent episcopal jurisdiction, where the leniency of punishment encouraged evildoers, and the publicity of procedure conveyed knowledge to husbands and kinsmen. The king was therefore asked to apply for the exemption of Spain from the operation of the brief; this was speedily arranged and, on April 10, Ambassador Alburquerque reported the forwarding of a decree of the Congregation of the Inquisition, stating that it was not the papal intention that the brief should apply to the Spanish dominions. Cardinal Millino, at the same time, wrote that the pope had declared that the Inquisition should continue to prosecute such cases in its customary form and manner.[194]

This simply left the matter where it was before, but the Inquisition boldly asserted that it had been given exclusive jurisdiction and, when Urban VIII granted, to the Bishop of Astorga, cognizance of these cases among the regular clergy, it had the effrontery to raise a competencia with him.[195] On May 19, 1629, it sent to the tribunals copies of Gregory's brief, with instructions to follow its prescriptions, as punishment should be uniform in a crime of such frequent occurrence. Although, it added, the brief appeared to confer only cumulative jurisdiction, the pope had declared to the king that in his dominions it was exclusive so that, if any Ordinary should undertake to hear such a case, he was to be inhibited and a prompt report be made to the Suprema. To make matters sure, this was followed by an order of August 9th, that this exclusive cognizance should be asserted in the Edict of Faith.[196]

It was not long before this produced another quarrel with Archbishop Aliaga of Valencia. In 1631, Vicente Palmer, rector of Játiva, was prosecuted in the archiepiscopal court for sundry offences, including a charge of solicitation preferred by Ana Martínez. The notary employed was a familiar who informed the tribunal. It promptly notified the Ordinary to omit that specification, to which Aliaga replied that his court had always possessed jurisdiction over the matter, and the brief of Gregory XV had confirmed the cumulative jurisdiction of both tribunals; if Urban VIII had rendered that of the Inquisition exclusive, he had not seen the brief, but if shown to him he would of course obey it. Then came a pause during which Palmer returned to Játiva and, from the pulpit, denounced all who had testified against him, declaring that all who accused ecclesiastics were excommunicated and he would not hear them in confession, especially Ana Martínez; the town was in an uproar and one man died without confession. After some months the tribunal, in its customary arrogant fashion, with threats of excommunication, summoned the archbishop to surrender the papers and admit that he was inhibited. To this he replied at much length, pointing out that it was unreasonable to ask him to strip himself of an established jurisdiction on the simple assertion of the inquisitors that they held a brief of Urban VIII, which they would not exhibit. He offered to submit the question to the pope or to form a competencia in the regular way, but both suggestions were rejected, although the tribunal adopted a more moderate tone. The records are imperfect and we do not know the outcome, but probably the Suprema quietly let the affair drop out of sight through delay, in preference to provoking an investigation which would have manifested the fraudulence of its claims.[197]

INCLUDED IN EDICT OF FAITH

The audacity of the claim increased with time and, in the formula of the Edict of Faith, in use in 1696, there was an absolute assertion that Gregory XV had declared that, in the Spanish dominions, the offence was subjected to the exclusive cognizance of the Inquisition and not to that of the bishops, their vicars, provisors or ordinaries.[198] Notwithstanding this, when bishops asserted their rights, the Suprema shrank from a direct contest. Thus, in 1755, when the Bishop of Quito undertook to try cases of the kind, the Suprema merely presented a long and argumentative consulta to the king. So, in 1807, the Bishop of Badajoz tried Joseph Méndez Rodríguez, priest of Llerena, for solicitation, apparently without remonstrance on its part and when, in 1816, Rodríguez was prosecuted by the tribunal of Llerena for propositions and mala doctrina, the Suprema ordered it to obtain from the bishop the papers of the former trial and add them to the new proceedings.[199]

***

While the Inquisition was thus aggressive in grasping exclusive jurisdiction, it hesitated for some time as to the vigorous use of its powers. It could evidently do little more than the inert episcopal courts unless it included solicitation in the Edicts of Faith, which specified offences and the obligation of denouncing them, but this involved the ever-present dread of scandal, and the necessity of calling attention to a matter so delicate. This explains the initial fluctuations of policy. When jurisdiction was first conferred, the Suprema ordered the omission of solicitation and then, by edict of July 17, 1562, that it should be included.[200] This speedily brought forth a vigorous remonstrance, which earnestly urged the necessity of secrecy to prevent scandal and the rendering of confession odious. It should never be admitted that such wickedness was possible; it had, in fact, always existed, but such a remedy had never been imagined, which would lead men to keep their wives and daughters from the confessional, nobles to refrain from putting their daughters into convents, religion to be despised and Christianity itself to be abhorred. Good confessors would be driven to abandon the confessional, and the clergy, seeing that their weaknesses were to be punished by the Inquisition, would withdraw their support from it, leading to serious results. At least the punishment should be secret, so that the people, seeing no results, might be led to believe that there were no wicked men administering the sacrament.[201] This final suggestion was superfluous, for clerical offenders, short of those incurring degradation and relaxation, were always punished in secret.

The opposition to this public admission of clerical frailty grew so strong that the Suprema, in a carta acordada of May 22, 1571, stated that, after many discussions, it had been decided that the disadvantages attendant on it required its omission, and inquisitors were told to find some other means, including notice to the Ordinaries to instruct confessors to admonish penitents to denounce offenders to the Holy Office. The exception thus made in favor of soliciting confessors evidently led to a marked diminution in the number of denunciations, causing the Suprema to hesitate for, in a carta of September 20, 1574, repeating the orders to omit, the Suprema spoke of it as possibly a temporary regulation.[202] The conviction seems to have grown that in no other way could the abuse be checked and, in a carta acordada of March 2, 1576, inquisitors were ordered to replace the clause in the Edict of Faith.[203]

REPUGNANCE TO DENOUNCE

Notwithstanding the publicity of the Edict, which imposed excommunication for failure to denounce, the trials show that the most fertile source of denunciation was the refusal of confessors to absolve penitents who had been solicited, unless they would accuse their guilty partners to the Inquisition. In spite of the assurance of secrecy, women were naturally reluctant, whether they had yielded or not, to expose themselves to the necessity of reciting details more or less revolting, and subjecting themselves at least to suspicion. One feature which rendered this exposure peculiarly distressing was the necessity of ratification, when all the foul or incriminating matter was rehearsed in the presence of two more men and, as much of this testimony was taken on the spot, by commissioners and notaries appointed ad hoc, in small places where everything was known, such revelations would only be made under the severest pressure. Again there was the enmity which was sure to be excited for, in these cases, the device of suppressing the names of witnesses was no protection against identification, which was a risk not lightly to be encountered, especially when the culprit was a parish priest, whose capacity for revenging himself was unlimited. The Inquisition sorrowfully admitted that, even when it had one accusing witness, corroborative evidence was almost impossible to obtain.[204]

Even where no direct enmity was excited, the incidental troubles to which a denunciation might give rise are illustrated in the case of Sor María de Santa Rita, a nun, 29 years of age, in the convent of La Magdalena at Alcalá de Henares, in 1737. During the absence of the regular confessor, she confessed thrice a week for five weeks to Maestro Diego de Azumanes, pastor of Alcalá. On her alluding to certain carnal temptations, he pushed his inquiries to the furthest extent and then, day after day, he poured into her ears a flood of foul and indecent talk, with personal applications to her and to himself in a manner most provocative of lust--or disgust. The regular confessor, on his return, instructed her to report Azumanes to the Inquisition. In doing so she unluckily mentioned that the superior of the house, Sor Teresa de San Bartolomé, a virgin with thirty-eight years of conventual experience, observing her repugnance to confess to Azumanes, told her not to mind him; it was true that he was too clear and explicit in discussing such matters, leading to temporary excitement of the passions, but she would soon overcome this. The tribunal ordered a commissioner to examine Sor María and, on receiving his report, instructed him to interrogate Sor Teresa, which he did with a directness that must have been excessively unpleasant, and it is easy to conjecture how miserable must have been Sor María's subsequent life in the convent. The tribunal, it may be added, did nothing, except to ascertain that no other denunciations had been made against Azumanes. He was allowed to go on infecting the minds of his penitents with his obscenity, until his death a few years afterwards, in happy ignorance that any complaint had been made against him.[205] When there were so many reasons to deter women from denunciation, it is easy to understand how small a proportion of the cases of solicitation reached the Inquisition. In 1695, Fray Luis Aritio, a Recollect, was accused to the tribunal of Valencia by two women and, on his trial, he confessed to ten.[206]

IS A TECHNICAL OFFENCE

The most available means of overcoming this repugnance was to render denunciation a binding obligation on the woman. To effect this as far as possible, when, in 1571, the clause in the Edict of Faith was suspended, the Suprema issued an edict requiring confessors, under pain of excommunication, not to absolve penitents confessing to having been solicited, unless they would promise to denounce the offender.[207] It was admitted, however, that there were degrees of danger which would release the woman from the obligation, and casuists endeavored to define this with their usual acuteness and lack of unanimity. One learned writer, about 1620, even laid down the general principle that natural law is superior to positive law, and the preservation of reputation belongs to the former, while the obligation to denounce belongs to the latter.[208] The Roman Inquisition, in 1623, made a concession to this weakness, by providing that, when noble or modest women could not be induced to denounce, there might be granted to their confessors faculties to absolve them, on condition that, when the cause of fear was removed, they would fulfil the duty, but this permission apparently was abused for, in 1626, inquisitors and bishops were warned to grant such faculties only when there were serious grounds.[209] That danger was really sometimes incurred would appear from some fragmentary cases in the Valencia records. In one of these, a baffled confessor threatens his penitent with death if she betrays him; in another a priest, on finding himself denounced, similarly threatens the confessor who had been the medium of denunciation, unless he will write that the women had withdrawn their statements.[210] The Spanish Inquisition, however, made no allowances. It was apparently to put an end to the refinements of casuistry that when, in 1629, it distributed to the tribunals the brief of Gregory XV, it granted to all inquisitors a faculty to punish confessors who taught that penitents were not obliged to denounce such solicitors.[211] To render this more effective, in 1713, it ordered that all women bringing charges of solicitation should be interrogated whether any confessor had neglected to impose on them the obligation of denunciation, and if so his name, residence and all the circumstances were to be ascertained, so that he could be called to account.[212]

While the Spanish Inquisition was thus creditably rigid in exacting denunciations, it was equally strict in construing the limits of the technical offence as defined in the papal decrees. As stated above, morals had nothing to do with the matter; the business of the tribunals was not to prevent women from being ruined by their spiritual fathers, but only to see that the sacrament of penitence was not profaned in such wise as to justify suspicion of the orthodoxy of the confessor. In 1577, inquisitors were warned that it did not suffice for prosecution that confessors had illicit relations with their penitents, or that they solicited in the confessional when there really was no confession and, in 1580 it was expressly stated that they were not to be prosecuted if they said that they did not intend to have their penitents confess.[213] This covered assignations under pretext of confession, to deceive onlookers, which we are told was a frequent custom and, as there were no confessional stalls, and the churches were largely deserted, there was little danger of interruption. It was argued that there was no confession and no sacrament, so there could be no heresy, but the Roman Inquisition, in 1614, decided it to be solicitation, and the brief of Gregory XV, in 1622 settled the question, although it required another brief of Urban VIII, in 1629, to render it authoritative in Spain.[214] This involved the question as to the knowledge which either party might have of the other's intention, opening the door to the endless refinements of antecedent or consequent invincible ignorance, in which the casuists disported themselves.[215]

Even more dubious and fruitful of discussion was the question as to what constituted the solicitation itself. About torpezas or physical indecencies, there could be no rational doubt, though even here the laxity of Probabilism gave scope for arguing them away.[216] It is such things that usually meet us in the trials, in a shape admitting of no debate, but there was a wide range of less incriminating acts, such as words of flattery and endearment, praising the penitent's beauty or telling her that if he were a layman he would marry her. Theoretically, what were known to the moralists as parvitas materiæ-- trifles insufficient for animadversion--were not admitted in solicitation. Pressing the hand, touching the foot, foul expressions and the like were admitted to be subjects for denunciation, but the gradations of such advances are infinite, and the elaborate discussions in some of the works on the subject are examples of perverted ingenuity, apparently directed to teach libidinous priests how to gratify sensuality without incurring risk.[217] The question of lewd and filthy talk was an especially puzzling one, for the confidences of the confessional presuppose a licence on subjects usually forbidden between the sexes, which may readily be abused by a brutal or foul-minded priest, and it is impossible to frame a definition which in practice shall rigidly differentiate moral instruction from heedless pruriency or deliberate corruption. How difficult it is to draw the line in such matters is indicated by a case before the Valencia tribunal in 1786. A nun of the convent of Santa Clara in Játiva complained of the indecent and unnecessary questions repeatedly put to her in confession by the Observantine Fray Vicente González. Under the advice of the definitor of the Order she empowered him to denounce González to the Inquisition. Then the regular confessor of the convent pronounced that the questions were necessary and proper, and persuaded the definitor to write to the tribunal to that effect.[218]

DOUBTFUL QUESTIONS

There were other intricate questions arising from human perversity. A Cunha tells us that the more probable opinion affirms the guilt of a confessor who acts as a pimp with his penitent for the benefit of another, and also in the more frequent case in which he solicits the penitent to serve as procuress for him with her daughter or a friend. De Sousa, however draws a distinction and asserts positively that, in the former case, he is liable under the papal briefs and, in the latter, he is not, nor is he if he tries to seduce a woman who is confessing to another priest.[219] Then there was a nice question as to priests without faculties to hear confessions, or who were under suspension or excommunication, on which the doctors were evenly divided.[220] Distantly akin to this were cases in which laymen would secrete themselves in confessionals and listen to confessions, whether from prurient motives, or through jealousy, or to obtain opportunities for seduction. If they carried deceit to the point of conferring absolution, they incurred serious penalties, as we shall see hereafter; if they merely solicited the penitent, the weight of authority is that there is no sacrament and no liability to the papal briefs.[221]

There was another phase of the subject on which the doctors were hopelessly divided--what was known as passive solicitation, where the woman was the tempter. This case, we are told, was rare, and we can readily believe it, although there are not wanting zealous defenders of the cloth who assert that in the majority of cases the penitent is really the guilty party. The earliest allusion to the matter is by Páramo, in 1598, whose treatment of it shows that as yet there had been no formal decision; if the confessor resists, he says, he should denounce the woman; if he yields, he should denounce both her and himself, though perhaps it would be best to consult the pope.[222] As regards the confessor, the authorities differ irreconcileably, but they are virtually unanimous in holding that, as the woman is not mentioned in the papal briefs, she is not subject to the Inquisition.[223] Yet, notwithstanding the absence of papal authority, we happen to find María Izquierda prosecuted for this offence, in 1715, by the Valencia tribunal and, in 1772 Antonia Coquis, wife of Bruno Vidal, by that of Madrid.[224]

It will be seen that solicitation subject to inquisitorial action was so purely technical an offence, and one so difficult of precise definition, that it offered many doubtful points affording ample opportunity of evasion by the adroit. Gregory XV had sought to be precise and explicit, but the ingenuity of casuists and evildoers continued to find exceptions and, in 1661, the Roman Inquisition rendered sixteen decisions on disputed points, but its ingenuity was baffled by so intricate a subject, and it was obliged to leave some matters rather darkened than illuminated.[225] Then it was pointed out that the papal briefs were silent as to handing love-letters to penitents during confession and, as everything not specifically prohibited was held to be licit, this was assumed to be allowable, until Alexander VII stamped the proposition as erroneous.[226] After this the perverted ingenuity of the casuists had free scope until, in 1741, Benedict XIV, in the solemn bull Sacramentum Poenitentiæ, deplored that human wickedness was perverting to the destruction of souls that which God had instituted for their salvation. He renewed and confirmed the brief of Gregory XV, and added to its definitions all attempts in the confessional to lead penitents astray by signs, nods, touching, indecent words and writings, whether to be read there or subsequently. In eloquent words he warned all those in authority to see that the wandering sheep, endeavoring to re-enter the fold, should not be abandoned to the cruel beasts seeking their destruction, and he branded the sacrilegious seducers as ministers of Satan, rather than of Christ.[227] Still, it was only the technical heresy and not morality that was considered, and illicit relations between spiritual father and daughter, outside of the confessional, were left unpunished as before.

ABSOLUTION OF ACCOMPLICE

At the same time he endeavored to suppress the most flagrant abuse connected with solicitation--an abuse which, more than anything else, smoothed the path for the seducer--the absolution of the woman by her partner in guilt. Alexander VII, in 1665, had only gone so far as to condemn the proposition that this absolution relieved her from the obligation of denouncing her seducer--a proposition which proves how audacious were the laxer moralists of the period who asserted it.[228] Benedict now formally prohibited the guilty confessor from hearing the confession of his accomplice, except on the death-bed when no other confessor could be had; he deprived him of the power of granting absolution, which consequently was invalid, and the attempt to do so imposed ipso facto excommunication, strictly reserved to the Holy See.[229] As this excommunication suspended all the functions of the priest until removal, its observance would have gone far to check any abuse that was not incurable, but neither priest nor penitent paid to it the slightest attention. It is impossible to trace, in the business of the Spanish Inquisition, any result from Benedict's well-meant legislation. Trials for solicitation continued as numerous as ever, and the only difference observable is that, in the second half of the eighteenth century, the sentences almost invariably assume that the culprit has incurred excommunication for absolving his accomplice; that, until he obtains absolution from this, he must abstain from using his functions, that he must consult his conscience as to his ministrations hitherto while under this irregularity, and that his penitents must be discreetly warned to repeat their confessions which, having been made to him, were invalid. This continued to the end and is a feature in the case of Fray Josef Montero, the last one sentenced by the Córdova tribunal, April 24, 1819.[230]

MORALITY DISREGARDED

It is no wonder that confessors endeavored to evade the technical definitions of the papal briefs for, if they could do so, no matter how heinous was their guilt there was practically no penalty. Juan Sánchez asserts that a priest who has commerce with his penitent is not obliged to specify the fact when making confession, for it is not incest and there is no papal prohibition of it.[231] All authorities, from that time to this, tell us that he can obtain absolution from any confessor, for it is not a reserved case, which shows the universal benignity of the bishops and the popes, who have the power of reserving to themselves the absolution of what sins they please.[232] It is easy to understand, therefore, how, in the trials, the inquisitors bent their energies to obtain definite evidence as to the exact location and time of the acts of solicitation, and how the accused sought to prove, not his innocence, but his dexterity in evading the definitions of the papal decrees. A suggestive example is the case of Doctor Pedro Mendizabal, cura of the parish of Santa Ana in the City of Mexico. He was denounced, June 21, 1809, by Doña María Guadalupe Rezeiro, by command of her confessor, when she stated that, in January, 1807, she made to him a general confession, too long to be finished in one day. On returning to his church to complete it, she was told to go up to his room, when he said he was too busy to listen to her. She retired but, on her way down stairs, his servant recalled her and, on entering his apartment, he threw his arms around her, professed ardent love and promised to support her if she would become his mistress, which she refused. As he had thus eluded the definitions of Benedict XIV, four calificadores out of six reported that he was not technically guilty of solicitation. The denunciation was filed away and, in 1817, there came another, of which he had warning in order that he might spontaneously accuse himself, as he did. It was from an attractive young girl of 17, and investigation developed four more cases of girls of whom he was confessor. Abundant evidence showed habitual indecent liberties--hugging, kissing, sitting in his lap, in presence of their families or even in public resorts. He had been ordered out of two houses and, on appeal to the archbishop, he had been forbidden to confess one of the girls who was a boarder in a convent. The distraction of the mother of the first accuser, endeavoring to save her daughter from one whose authority as a priest overawed her, is very touching and suggestive. Yet in all this there was no proof of anything in the act of confession--as one of the calificadores piously remarked, "God, in his goodness, preserved him from this." Two calificadores argued at much length that he was not guilty of solicitation; then two others proved that he was guilty, and finally two more laboriously demonstrated that the first pair were correct. This is the last document in the case. It is dated November 3, 1819, and, as the Inquisition was suppressed in June, 1820, and as there is no endorsement on the record showing that the case was concluded, Mendizabal undoubtedly escaped to continue his corrupting career, especially as he had four out of six calificadores in his favor.[233]

The technicalities, which eliminated morality from consideration, resulted in curious contrasts. In November 1762, Fray Clemente de Cartagena went to Toledo to assist in the profession of his neice Gerónima, in the Bernardine convent, where he already had a sister. He and his sister were in the confessional near the altar, when some duty called her away and she told Gerónima to go to her uncle. She seated herself in the confessional, while he occupied the penitent's place outside and, in an affectionate talk, he asked her to kiss him. The next day he said to her that he had forgotten at the moment that they were in the confessional; this made no impression on her, until she heard the nuns talking about the exceeding delicacy of such matters, and she consulted Fray Fernando de San Josef, who ordered her to denounce her uncle. This she did in writing, and Fray Fernando conveyed it to the tribunal, which duly took up the case. We shall see that prosecutions required two distinct and separate denunciations; inquiries, according to custom, were made of all the other tribunals; fortunately for Fray Clemente nothing was found against him and the case was suspended, but if there had been, or if subsequently he chanced to draw upon himself a denunciation, the innocent kiss to his neice would count as though he had deliberately seduced a penitent.[234] It was the spot and not the nature of the act that was decisive.

Against this may be set the case of Cristóbal Ximeno, parish priest of Manzanera, a brute who was in the habit of violating the young girls of his church, who came to his house for examination in the Doctrina Cristiana, as a preparation for communion at marriage, until mothers would not trust their daughters there alone. They were his penitents, but the outrage was not in the confessional and he had nothing to fear under the papal decrees. At length, however, he made himself liable to the Inquisition by pretending to confess Pasquala Torres, at her marriage, without absolving her and then, when administering communion to her and her bridegroom, dropping the host into the ciborium--a sacrilege for which he was duly punished by the Valencia tribunal.[235] So complete, indeed, is the dissociation of morals and solicitation, that some doctors hold that, when a priest is confessing a sick woman, if she falls into delirium or stupor, he can violate her without exposing himself to denunciation. It is satisfactory, however, to be told that the weight of authority is opposed to this opinion.[236]

FLAGELLATION

Yet there was one species of abuse of the confessional, not contemplated in the papal briefs, which the Spanish Inquisition, by a somewhat forced construction, classed with solicitation. This, which was known as flagellation, consisted in imposing penance of the discipline and administering it on the spot, or letting the penitent administer it herself, in either case requiring her to disrobe and expose herself to a greater or less degree. Sometimes this was mingled with the debased mystic ardor, of which we have seen examples above, leading both parties to expose themselves and lash one another. The earliest case that I have met of this occurred in 1606, at Nájera, when María Escudero, a widow aged 40, testified that she had long confessed to the Franciscan Fray Diego de Burgos. They exchanged vows of obedience to each other; he would visit her in her house when they would discipline each other with exposure almost complete, under agreement that their eyes should be kept closed. Then he introduced a pious exercise still more indecent, but he was always scrupulously correct in the confessional. She chanced to make a general confession to another priest who refused absolution unless she would denounce Fray Diego. The case was evidently novel and dragged on until 1609, when it reached the Suprema, which submitted the matter to two calificadores. One opined that the acts savored of the heresy of the Adamites and Alumbrados; the other attributed it merely to imprudent simplicity and ignorance. Apparently there was no precedent for guidance and the case seems to have been suspended.[237] A parallel case, with a different ending, was one in which there were a number of women concerned and the practices were foul almost beyond belief. The priest was an ignorant and simple man who, by the advice of another confessor, came with the women to denounce themselves. He was sentenced to rigid reclusion in a convent, where he died after giving a most edifying example, and the women were not prosecuted, as they were mostly barefooted Carmelites and Capuchins.[238]

The flagelante soon came to be recognized as an offender akin to the solicitor, and was held to be subject to the papal briefs. The old inquisitor, who relates the last case, and writers like de Sousa and Alberghini, all speak of stripping penitents and disciplining them as a species of solicitation, to be visited with the same penalties.[239] As a rule, in fact, it was regarded as rendering the offence more serious, for it inferred more than the technical suspicion of heresy, especially after Molinism had deepened the guilt of Illuminism, and we find allusions to hereges flagelantes. Cases become frequent in the records and we even, in 1730, find a Fray Domingo Calvo spontaneously denouncing himself to the Madrid tribunal for having caused himself to be flagellated, showing to what means perverted sexual instincts resorted for gratification.[240]

The extent to which these practices were sometimes carried is indicated in the trial, in 1795, of Padre Paulino Vicente Arevalo, priest of Yepes, as "solicitante y flagelante." He confessed to the most flagrant indecencies committed in this manner, with his female penitents, among whom were nine pupils or sisters of the Bernardine convent. Sometimes he made them discipline themselves in his presence and, as the scourge had to be applied to the peccant parts, he had choice of such exposure as he desired, an opportunity of which he admitted availing himself. The record is discreetly mute as to worse excesses but, as six of his penitents were required to repeat to another confessor all the confessions specified in the evidence, it follows that sins must have been committed for which he absolved them.

For this perversion of so many young lives he was only sentenced to a year's reclusion in a monastery, thirty days' spiritual exercises, deprivation of the faculty of confession, perpetual exile from Yepes and eight years' exile from some other places--penalties which, although severe under the mild inquisitorial standard, were wholly inadequate to his offences.[241]

A considerable portion of the cases in the later years of the Inquisition are characterized as "solicitante y flagelante" and many of them illustrate the easy transition from Illuminism to solicitation. As early as 1651 we meet the case of the Dominican Fray Gerónimo de las Herreras, condemned by the Toledo tribunal to deprivation of the faculty of confession and three years' reclusion in a convent, as an "alumbrado y solicitante," convicted of repeated practices of obscenity with many women. When Molinism came to the front, those who taught it with its debauching consequences were more severely dealt with, as in the case of Buenaventura Frutos, cura of Mocejon, who, in 1722, was pronounced by the Toledo tribunal to be a formal heretic and dogmatizer, a contumacious solicitor and seducer. As such his sentence was read with open doors, he appeared in a sanbenito de dos aspas, was reconciled, verbally degraded and recluded irremissibly for life in a convent where, for two years he was shut up in a cell, under instruction.[242] Similar cases continued to occur occasionally, but more numerous in the later period were those in which solicitation is conjoined with mala doctrina, showing that the evil teaching was of a less dangerous character than fully developed Molinism--a mere soothing of the conscience of the penitent with assurances that what her confessor desired was not mortal sin--but even this was regarded as increasing the suspicion of heresy and requiring severer punishment.[243]

PROCEDURE

It is perhaps not without interest to note the advanced age to which some of these soliciting confessors retained the ardor which impelled them to the offence. Cases of septuagenarians are by no means rare. The Dominican, Fray Antonio de Aragon, sentenced, July 24, 1734, at Toledo, was 78 and the Observantine, Fray Miguel Granado, denounced, in 1786, to the Cuenca tribunal, was 80. In the former case the punishment was mitigated in consideration of his years, though a less sympathizing court would have heightened its rigor, in view of the evil which such a sinner must have wrought during so prolonged a career.[244]

***

When, in 1561, the Inquisition obtained jurisdiction over solicitation, it had no precedents on which to frame its procedure or to regulate the penalties. The episcopal courts had been inert and merciful, and the fact that the offence had been transferred from them inferred that the new jurisdiction was expected to be vigorous and rigorous. Its first care, however, was to preserve secrecy and avert scandal, so that no layman should be admitted to knowledge of clerical delinquencies. The earliest utterance is a carta acordada of 1562, prescribing that, when the denunciation affords conclusive evidence, it shall be considered by the inquisitors and Ordinary, without calling in the usual consultors, and the arrest shall be made with the utmost circumspection; the accused is to be admitted to bail; when the case is concluded, if he is a fraile he is to be confined in his convent with orders not to preach or hear confessions, or to have active and passive voice; if he is a secular priest, he is to be confined somewhere else than where the offence was committed, he is not to exercise his functions and the final disposition of the case is to rest with the Suprema.[245] In 1572, consultors were admitted to examine the evidence before arrest, but they were to be exclusively clerics, and the result was to be submitted to the Suprema before action. It made little difference that the heinousness of the offence was emphasized, and the necessity of exemplary punishment, when the culprit was treated with this exceptional tenderness.[246] In 1600, even the Ordinary was excluded from the preliminary deliberations and the Suprema was to be consulted before any action was taken.[247] The same precautions as to publicity were to be observed with regard to the sentences, which were to be read in the audience-chamber with closed doors, the only witnesses present being a prescribed number of the brethren of the culprit--members of his Order if he was a fraile, or curas and rectors, if a secular priest.[248] The care taken to avert attention from these delinquencies is illustrated in the case of Fray Antonio de la Portería, in 1818; he was resident in the convent of Mondoñedo, and the guardian was ordered to send him on some pretext to the house of the Order at Santiago, where he was duly tried.[249]

***

Even greater favoritism was manifested in the matter of evidence. We have seen that, in ordinary trials, while two witnesses were required as to each fact yet, in practice, a single witness sufficed, not only for arrest but for torture and that the testimony of the vilest persons was welcomed without discrimination. In solicitation, it was self-evident that there could be but one witness to each specific act, so that perforce the tribunals were instructed that they must be content with "singular" witnesses. A single denunciation however, did not suffice for arrest, but in 1571, and again in 1576, they were allowed to deliberate on it and consult the Suprema. Even this was thought to be too harsh and, in 1577, the rule was adopted that there must be two separate and independent denunciations before arrest and trial--a rule fraught, as we shall see, with far-reaching consequences for, when it was so difficult to induce women to accuse their seducers, innumerable culprits escaped because two of their victims did not happen to act independently.[250] Similar exceptional consideration was shown with regard to the character of the witnesses, repeated instructions being issued that this was to be carefully investigated, and the results be noted upon the record and reported to the Suprema, so that due weight be given to it, both in ordering arrest and apportioning penalties--precautions eminently commendable, but deplorably lacking in trials for other offences.[251] Justification for this solicitude was sought in the customary monkish abuse of women in general. It was a misfortune that their evidence was to be received at all but, from the nature of the crime, this was unavoidable, and Páramo tells us that by nature they are lying, deceitful, perjurers, crafty, changeable, frail, mutable and corruptible--a daily curse, the gate of the devil, the tail of the scorpion, a whitened sepulchre, an incurable sore, but they are the only witnesses to be had and two of them, if of good character, must suffice for full proof.[252] Such tirades show the different temper in which inquisitors approached the consideration of these cases and those of Jews or Protestants.

After arrest the culprit could be committed to the secret prison, but this was exceptional, the custom being to remand regulars to houses of their Order, and to admit seculars to bail, with the city as prison, in a manner to attract as little attention as possible. The trial took the usual course, interrogation being made as to intention and belief in the sacrament of penitence, on which inquisitorial jurisdiction was based. Of course all heretical tendencies were disclaimed, but, in the possible case of error and pertinacity, there was provision for confinement in the secret prison with sequestration of property and seizure of papers.[253]

In the Spanish Inquisition, solicitation uncomplicated by Illuminism or Molinism, inferred only light suspicion of heresy, requiring merely abjuration de levi. Consequently the accused was not exposed to torture. It is true that, academically speaking, though he could not be tortured as to intention and belief, he might be subjected to it if he denied facts, but in practice it was never employed, although the formal accusation contained the otrosi demanding it.[254] Yet, when there was mala doctrina or Illuminism torture was employed without scruple, as in the case, in 1725, of Manuel Madrigal, in Toledo, accused as "solicitante, Molinista y flagelante."[255] In the Roman Inquisition, however, after the brief of Gregory XV, the suspicion of heresy was vehement, the abjuration was de vehementi and there was no exception to the general rule of torturing on intention. The testimony of one woman of good character, supported by indications such as the evil repute of the confessor, or that of two women unsupported, sufficed. In every way Rome treated the offence with less charity than did Spain.[256]

The instructions as to the examination of accusers offer a strong contrast to the negligence habitual in trials for formal heresy, of which the penalties were so much more severe. Tribunals were warned that it required special attention and the utmost exactitude; the woman must declare precisely the spot and the time, whether confession was real or simulated, and she must repeat in full detail the words and acts of the confessor without omission. If any one was near enough to see or to hear, she must state who it was; if she had spoken to any one, the name must be given, and the inquisitor was urged to exercise his ingenuity according to the circumstances of the case. If she had subsequently confessed to the same priest, she must give her reasons and state whether he had absolved her. Special inquiry was to be made as to any cause of enmity on her part or that of her kindred; whether she had heard of his doing the same with other women; what she thought or knew as to his character, and whether any other confessor had told her that she was not bound to denounce him.[257] All these were salutary precautions which, if general and not exceptional, would have prevented much injustice.

TWO DENUNCIATIONS REQUIRED

This instruction would appear to require that, in case of consent, the witness should be forced to reveal her shame. Protection from this would seem necessary to overcome reluctance to make denunciation, and the Roman Inquisition, by decree of July 25, 1624, ruled that neither the woman nor the accused was to be questioned as to this and, if the information was volunteered, it was to be omitted from the record, while confessors were ordered to assure penitents that no such inquiries would be made.[258] If such a rule existed in Spain, it was not observed until near the end, for the records of trials show that the examination was pushed to the last point, and the results were fully set forth in the proceedings. As late as the middle of the eighteenth century, instructions to commissioners taking testimony in these cases require them to obtain all details as to words and acts and to write them out fully and distinctly, no matter how obscene they may be.[259] Soon after this, however, occurs the first intimation as to reticence that I have met, in instructions to a commissioner, January 27, 1759, as to taking testimony from a nun, in which he is told to notify her that, if she volunteers to relate her own ruin, this is not to be stated or included in the testimony.[260] Subsequently this became the rule, as appears by instructions in 1816 and 1819.[261]

The most important discrimination in favor of these delinquents was the requirement of two independent denunciations to justify arrest and trial. This was not reached without some hesitation. The earliest formal instructions that we have on the subject are embodied in a letter to the tribunal of Sardinia, in 1574, when forwarding to it the brief of Pius IV. As the crime is understood to be very prevalent in the island, the inquisitor is ordered to prosecute it with rigor, according to the procedure in cases of heresy, no exception being alluded to as respects single denunciations.[262] Instructions to the tribunal of Peru, about the same time, specify that a single witness suffices for prosecution and that Indian women can be admitted.[263] Then, as we have seen, there is an inclination in favor of the accused, in a carta acordada of March 2, 1576, ordering single accusations to be received, but the Suprema is to be consulted before taking action. This tendency increased, and fuller instructions to Sardinia, in 1577, require two witnesses with conclusive evidence as a condition precedent to arrest.[264] This was repeated in general instructions issued in 1580 and, after some variations, it remained an absolute rule until the end.[265] Even this was regarded by churchmen as too harsh. A Cunha holds that, while two witnesses may suffice for prosecution, there should be at least four for conviction, and he grows eloquent in pointing out the dignity of the priest, the scandal to the Church and the exultation of the heretic. De Sousa likewise considers two witnesses insufficient for conviction, though, if they are of exemplary character, their evidence may justify some moderate penalty.[266]

It is probable that, for awhile, practice was not uniform in all tribunals. In that of Valladolid, in 1621 and 1622, there are several cases in which arrest was voted on the evidence of a single witness and these votes were confirmed by the Suprema.[267] On the other hand, about 1640, an inquisitor tells us that, when the accused denies, conviction requires the evidence of three witnesses whom he has been unable to disable for enmity, low rank of life, or doubtful repute. Some authors, he adds, insist that four are necessary, but he admits that, when there are two whose characters stand thorough investigation and there are supporting indications, conviction may follow.[268] It is impossible not to recognize the charitable motives that prompted this reluctance to punish.

The requirement thus established of two independent denunciations threw serious impediments in the way of suppressing a crime in which it was so notoriously difficult to find accusers. The routine gradually established was, when a denunciation was received, to search the records for a previous one. If none were found, letters were addressed to all the other tribunals requesting a similar examination of their registers and, if this was unsuccessful, the denunciation was filed away to await the chances of another accuser presenting herself, thus giving the accused, if guilty, the opportunity of continuing his profligate career, and leading the woman to believe that the case was too trivial to deserve the attention of the Inquisition. These long intervals of impunity illustrate the difficulty of obtaining denunciations, and the preponderant chances of escape, when prosecution was thus obstructed.

Numberless cases show how prolonged was often this period of immunity in a career of crime, to say nothing of the yet more frequent instances where the second denunciation never came. Thus at Valencia, on September 22, 1734, María Theresa Terrasa accused Fray Agustin Solves of having taken her, after confession and communion, to a room back of the altar and committed violence on her. This was laid aside for fourteen years when, on November 12, 1748, Sor Vitoria Julian, of the convent of San Julian, appeared and denounced him for having, some fifteen years before, solicited her some twenty times in the confessional of the convent of which he was the regular confessor, though she had not understood until now the obligation of denunciation. He had meanwhile been removed to the convent of Villajoiosa and had doubtless profited fully by the interval thus afforded.[269] This is by no means an extreme instance. In the list of soliciting confessors, kept by the Madrid tribunal, there occurs, in 1772, the name of Fray Andrés Izquierdo as accused in Valladolid, with a reference back to the years 1751 and 1752. Fray Bartolomé de Montijo appears as denounced in 1740 and again in 1776. Fray Fernando López, ex-provincial of the Escuelas pías, was denounced in 1780 for tampering with the children under his charge, and again in 1795, when he was tried and exiled. The Jesuit Juan Francisco Nieto, was denounced in Toledo in 1708 and again in 1731 in Madrid. Fray Joseph de San Juan was accused in Toledo in 1732 and in Granada in 1772. Fray Pedro de la Madre de Dios was denounced in Barcelona in 1722 and again in 1744. Even two denunciations, in many cases, did not suffice to put an end to these corrupting careers, and it required three or four. Fray Alonso de Arroya was denounced in 1768, 1788 and 1803; Fray Francisco de la Asuncion Torquemada in 1735, 1770 and 1776; Domingo Galindo, rector of Nules, in 1790, 1792, and 1795; Fray Francisco Escriva in 1769, 1775, 1786 and 1787; and Padre Feliciano Martínez, S. J., in 1767, 1771, 1784 and 1800. It is scarce worth while to multiply instances of which the records furnish an abundant supply.[270]

As the majority of offenders were frailes, who had no settled residence, it became necessary, in order to meet the exceptional requirement of two denunciations, to establish communication between the several tribunals. This was felt as early as 1601, when each one was ordered to send to all the rest, information as to solicitantes, whose cases had been suspended without prosecution. This seems to have received scant obedience, while cases of solicitation were constantly becoming a more important portion of inquisitorial duty, leading to a more comprehensive effort in 1647. The tribunals were required to search their records for thirty years back and make out lists of those charged with solicitation with all necessary details; copies of these lists were to be sent to the Suprema and to all other tribunals, and every year the new cases were to be similarly circulated. A complete alphabetical list of the whole was to be compiled and copies were to be furnished to all tribunals making application.[271] If this was obeyed at the time, it must soon have fallen into desuetude, for the custom became universal, when a denunciation was received, of addressing all the sister tribunals with the inquiry as to whether the name of the accused appeared on their records. To facilitate these frequent researches, in compiling the Libras Vocandorum and other registers, a separate volume was reserved for solicitation.[272]

***

When all impediments were overcome and conviction was reached, the penalties inflicted were singularly disproportionate to the gravity of the offence, especially when compared with the severity exercised on those whose guilt consisted in putting on clean linen on Saturdays and avoiding the use of pork. The earliest definition as to punishment occurs in the Sardinia instructions of 1577, where the prescriptions embody the general features of the policy pursued to the end, including the secrecy preserved by reading the sentence in the audience-chamber. The penalties, it is stated, are customarily arbitrary, varying with the character, degree and frequency of the offence but, in all cases, there must be abjuration de levi and perpetual deprivation of the faculty of administering the sacrament of penitence; as to the other sacraments and preaching, or reclusion or exile, it is discretional. For religious there may be discipline in the chapters of their convents, while a notary reads the sentence or, in atrocious cases, a discipline in the audience-chamber; there may also be other penances, such as reclusion and suspension or deprivation of sacerdotal functions, deprivation of active and passive voice, being last in choir and refectory, and penance for heavy sin, discipline, prayers etc. For secular priests, besides the general penalties, there may be reclusion, deprivation or suspension of functions and benefice, fines, secret disciplines, fasts and prayers.[273]

PUNISHMENT

How these general rules were reduced to practice, at this period, may be gathered from a few examples in Toledo, all of whom had of course the regular abjuration de levi and reprimand. In 1578 the Carmelite, Fray Agustin de Cervera, against whom there were ten witnesses, was sentenced to perpetual deprivation of confession, reclusion for a year in a convent of his Order, where he was to receive a discipline, and Friday fasting on bread and water. The Dominican Fray Domingo de Revisto, against whom there were forty-nine witnesses, besides others who came after the conclusion of the case, was perpetually deprived of confessing and recluded in a desert convent for ten years, during which, for a year, he was deprived of active and passive voice, of preaching and of saying mass. In 1581, Pedro de Villalobos, acting cura of Halía, had many witnesses as to his acts in the confessional and an infinite number as to his general licentiousness, for he kept a concubine, had debauched two sisters and their aunt, and committed much else of the same kind. These latter sins were outside of inquisitorial jurisdiction; for the solicitation he was exiled from Halía for three years, of which the first was to be passed in a monastery with suspension from celebrating, he was perpetually suspended from confessing, and was fined in fifteen thousand maravedís. Fray Juan Romero was accused by five women; he admitted using words of endearment, but innocently, as he claimed to be impotent. Either the claim or the fact seems to have been regarded as an aggravation, for he was deprived of confessing and was recluded for ten years, without active and passive voice, to be last in choir and refectory, with a monthly discipline during the first year, a discipline in the audience-chamber and one in the convent of San Pablo while his sentence was read.[274]

These examples will suffice to show the spirit in which aggravated cases were treated. Those of less gravity had concessions in the variable factors, but the deprivation of confessing was perpetual. About 1600, Miguel Calvo summarizes the practice, with a distinct inclination towards greater severity, and adds that, when the culprit has solicited men, the penalties are to be increased.[275] On the other hand, in 1611, a Cunha pleads for moderation, and warns the inquisitor not to drive the culprit to despair, while de Sousa endeavors to argue away the stern penalties prescribed by Gregory XV, and repeats the warning as to despair.[276]

It was wholly superfluous to plead for leniency. The Spanish Inquisition paid no attention to Gregory's brief, although, in 1629, it ordered the tribunals to follow its prescriptions, for it even began to show an increased tendency towards benignity. The severest sentence I have met at this period concerned a peculiarly scandalous case before the tribunal of Valladolid where, in 1625, the Trinitarian Fray Juan de Ramírez was accused by five youths and one woman, and besides he had once celebrated mass without confessing. He was verbally degraded, deprived perpetually of confessing and condemned to ten years of reclusion, lifelong exile from Burgos and a circular discipline in his convent. This was justice tempered with mercy, but there was much mercy and little justice, in 1637, in the case of the Franciscan Fray Alonso del Valle before the same tribunal. He was accused by two sisters of his Order; there was a vote in discordia and the Suprema ordered suspension of the case, but, before this could be done, there supervened two more witnesses with evidence of the foulest character. The result was a sentence April 14, 1638, of deprivation of confessing women, one year's reclusion and four years of exile from Toro and Astorga. Equally fortunate was the Dominican Fray Juan Gómez, accused by two women, with one of whom, for fifteen years, he had illicit relations in the chapels used for confession. Some sisters of his Order likewise denounced him and, for all this he was sentenced, February 4, 1638, to be deprived of confessing women and to Friday fasting for six months. Even greater was the benignity shown, in 1642, to the Licenciate Morales, cura of Robadillo, against whom there were two accusers. The vote of the consulta de fe on the sumaria was not unanimous, when the Suprema cut the affair short by ordering suspension, with a private reprimand of the accused in the apartments of the inquisitor.[277]

Evidently the Inquisition was beginning to regard the offence with a compassionate eye, and it would be superfluous to adduce more cases of its tenderness. Still the regular scheme of punishments was nominally held in force, and is duly recapitulated by an old inquisitor about 1640, who includes fines for secular priests and adds that the galleys might be inflicted, and that those who relapsed deserved them. Abjuration de vehementi was never imposed and, although the papal constitution permitted relaxation, this was never used, though it is well that there is a faculty for it in extreme cases.[278] Even the fines here alluded to were not heavy. Another authority of about the same date says that, if the priest is rich, he may be mulcted in from six to ten thousand maravedís.[279] The heaviest pecuniary penalty that I have met was imposed, in 1744, on Fernández Puyalon, cura of Ciempozuelos, who was fined in half his property, but here solicitation was complicated with heretical propositions, which, as we have seen, greatly enhanced guilt.[280]

As regards the galleys, I have met with but one case of their employment--that of the Licentiate Lorenzo de Eldora, assistant cura in Torre de Beleña, tried in Toledo in 1691. He had already been punished for the same offence in Granada, and had relapsed, which explains the severity of the sentence suspending him from orders and banishing him from a number of places for ten years, of which the first five were to be spent in the galleys.[281] That this punishment was reserved for relapse may be inferred from a case which, about the same time, was occupying the Barcelona tribunal and which certainly deserved it. The Mercenarian Padre Estevan Ramoneda was accused in 1690, but it was not until 1694 that a second denunciation enabled action to be taken. After many evasions, in ignorance of the exact charge, he confessed to much more than was required. Since entering a convent, in 1660, as a boy of fifteen, his life had been one of sexual abominations, almost warranting the belief that the monasteries of the time were outposts of Sodom. The number of women whose testimony was obtained was only eight, but among these were some with whom extraordinary obscenities were practised in church. He had no defence to offer and, in his sentence, September 11, 1696, all reference to his unnatural crimes of all kinds was carefully omitted. He was deprived of confession, had a circular discipline in his convent, and was recluded for four years in the house of N. Señora del Olivar, from which he was allowed to return in October 1700.[282] This was considered sufficient punishment for a brute whose life had been spent in corrupting men, women and beasts.

There is one feature in these cases which shows how great was the dread of scandal. We frequently find details of the worst excesses committed in the churches. According to the canon law (Cap. 5, Extra, v, xvi) a church thus polluted required to be reconciled, but there is no trace in any of the records of the observance of this rule. It was presumably for the purpose of averting knowledge of such disgraceful occurrences that casuists discovered that pollution occurred only when the act was public and not occult.[283]

***

It was a favorite device, when a confessor had reason to fear that a denunciation was impending, for him to denounce himself, in the expectation of merciful treatment. Roman practice encouraged this by conferring virtual immunity in such cases, as was experienced by the Minim Hilario Caone of Besançon, who fled from Spain, in 1653, and presented himself before the Roman Inquisition, stating that for ten years he had heard confessions in the church of San Francisco de Paula in Seville, and that he had come in post to confess that he had solicited in confession some forty women, mostly with success. When questioned as to belief and intention, he answered satisfactorily and was only sentenced to abjure de vehementi, to visit the seven privileged altars of St. Peter's, and for three years to recite weekly the chaplet of the Virgin. This was not exceptional mercy for, in the same year, an equivalent sentence was pronounced on Vincenzo Barzi, who similarly denounced himself, and the existing rule is to impose only spiritual penance on the self-accuser, with advice to avoid in future those whom he has solicited.[284]

SELF-DENUNCIATION

The Spanish Inquisition, at least at first, was not so lenient and it followed its rule with espontaneados of examining for confirmation those whom the delinquent named as the objects of his solicitations. In the early cases there is little difference in the sentences between those who denounced themselves and those who were accused. In 1582, the Franciscan Fray Sebastian de Hontoria accused himself to the Toledo tribunal for having, as vicar of a nunnery, corrupted several of the nuns under peculiarly aggravating circumstances. On examination they confirmed his confession, and he was sentenced to a circular discipline in the convent of San Juan de los Reyes, to be deprived of confessing, and reclusion in a convent for ten years, without active or passive voice and being last in choir and refectory.[285] He had confessed fully and freely. In another case, in 1589, before the same tribunal, the Franciscan Fray Marcos de Latançon, in accusing himself, suppressed the worst features of his offence. He confessed that, at Orche, he had handled indecently some five or six unmarried and perhaps six or eight married women, but averred that this was without any licentious feeling or intention to induce them to sin. Five of the girls were examined, whose concurrent testimony showed that the confessions were heard in a chamber in which there was a bed. As each one entered he locked the door; when the confession was half through he would interrupt it with the foulest indecencies and violence, after which the confession was resumed and absolution was granted. For this profanation of the sacrament the sentence was the same as in the last case, except that the reclusion was for only four years.[286]

So long as the practice of examining the woman was continued, self-denunciation always had the advantage that they would very frequently, in defence of their honor, deny everything. The result of this, and the prevailing tendency towards leniency, are indicated in rules expressed about 1640, which tell us that, if one witness has already testified against the culprit, self-denunciation ensures a lighter penalty; there is no imprisonment and it is customary to deprive him of confessing women. If he accuses himself before there is any evidence against him, and if the women are numerous and they confirm his statements, the case proceeds to deprivation of confessing; if they deny, the case is suspended, with a warning to him. If there is but one and the case is not grave, he is merely reprimanded.[287]

The custom of examining the women compromised by the self-accuser gradually grew obsolete, doubtless because they mostly protected themselves from exposure by denial. Thus, in 1707, in the Madrid tribunal, when Padre Pablo Delgado, provost of the Casa del Espiritu Santo, accused himself, there seems to have been no examination of the women and his case was promptly suspended, with a monition to abstain for six months from confessing women.[288] So, in the case of the Observantine Fray Gabriel Pantoja, who denounced himself, May 8, 1720, to the Toledo tribunal, for offences committed during the previous ten years, which show him to have lost no opportunity of seducing women, in the confessional or out of it, and of promising absolution if they would yield to his desires, the absence of his name from the record of autos particulares shows that none of the women were examined and that no action was deemed necessary.[289] Indeed, what chiefly impresses one, in a series of these cases, is the matter of fact way in which every body--priests, penitents and inquisitors--seems to take it for granted that such things were a matter of course and that the confessor should be in pursuit of every woman who came before him. So, in a letter of the Mexican tribunal, May 13, 1719, to its commissioner, in the case of Fray Antonio Domínguez, who had denounced himself, the instructions are that the culprit is to be exhorted to abstain in future and to sunder an illicit connection with a daughter of confession; he is to be absolved sacramentally which, as the rule in all cases of self-denunciation, is to be made known to all confessors in the district "for the solace and comfort of their souls"--thus assuming them to be all guilty of the same offence.[290]

INDIFFERENCE

Still, practice as yet was not uniform. In 1740, the Recollect Fray Joseph Rives accused himself before the Valencia tribunal, when the evidence of two women was taken, showing the beastliness to which such men resorted to inflame the passions of their penitents. A formal trial resulted, ending in his deprivation of confession and three years' exile from Valencia and the scenes of his excesses.[291] This was probably one of the latest cases in which an espontaneado suffered. A writer shortly afterwards complains of the uncertainty of practice, as the Suprema constantly issued varying decisions under conditions precisely similar, but he states the rule to be that, when a priest accuses himself, the registers are searched and, if nothing is found of record against him, he is discharged with a charitable warning, and a recommendation to abstain from the confessional save when necessary to avert scandal.[292] Complete immunity soon followed for self-accusation. In 1780 the Suprema seems to have desired to introduce uniformity, and enquired of the tribunals whether they were accustomed to make espontaneados abjure and then absolve them, or whether they suspended the cases, to which Valencia replied that the custom was to suspend, without abjuration or absolution, unless there was complication of mala doctrina.[293] When self-denunciation thus secured immunity it naturally was frequent. In a list of a hundred and eight cases in Madrid, between 1670 and 1772, thirty-two, or thirty per cent., are espontaneados.[294]

In fact, during the later period, the whole matter seems to have excited but a languid interest, and to have been treated commonly with indifference. We meet with instances in which accusations are pigeon-holed without even making the prescribed inquiries of other tribunals, or cases are suspended without examining the accuser.[295] So relaxed was discipline that when, in 1806, the Franciscan Fray Francisco de Paula Lozano had been deprived by Córdova of the faculty of confessing, and not only disregarded the inhibition but complicated his offence by opening a letter from the tribunal of Granada to the cura of Salar, he was tried by Granada and merely reprimanded with a warning of what would happen to him if he persisted in his evil courses.[296]

***

It would be interesting sociologically if complete statistics could be compiled, from the time when jurisdiction was conferred on the Inquisition, but this is impossible, for there are only a few fragmentary sources of the earlier period, although for the eighteenth century there are satisfactory materials in the special registers kept of this class of cases. In no case, however, do they furnish a standard by which to estimate the frequency of the crime, for the difficulty of inducing women to accuse left the great majority of cases buried in secrecy, in addition to which a marked feature of the records is the disproportion between the accusations and the trials, owing principally to the impediment arising from the requirement of at least two accusations, so that the trials and sentences are comparatively few in number. The working of this is exhibited, as early as 1597, in a report by Inquisitor Heredia of Barcelona of a visitation of part of his district, in which ten cases of solicitation were brought before him. Of these seven are noted as suspended in consequence of there being but one witness, another is suspended because the offender had been already tried and punished, leaving but two in which arrest and trial were ordered. In the visitation the whole number of cases was eighty-eight and the only offences more numerous than solicitation were unnatural lusts, of which there were fifteen, propositions which furnished twelve, the assertion that marriage is better than celibacy which furnished eleven, while blasphemy was on an equality with ten. All, or nearly all, of these latter classes doubtless led to prosecutions, while solicitation resulted in only two trials.[297]

STATISTICS

Llorente explains the discrepancy between the accusations and the convictions by misconstruction put on the interrogations of confessors, leading simple-hearted nuns to imagine themselves solicited.[298] This implies eagerness on the part of women to bring such accusations when, as we have seen, the main difficulty was to induce them to denounce, by threats of excommunication and refusal of absolution; in the majority of cases it was done only by order of a subsequent confessor, and this frequently five, ten, or more years after the occurrence. The fact is that only a small portion of offenders were denounced, and of these but a fraction were brought to trial. So far moreover from the evidence being only the excited imaginations of young girls, it rarely happened that a case reached trial without resulting in conviction--the preliminaries were too carefully guarded, and the dread of scandal too vivid, to permit the arrest of a priest against whom the evidence was not conclusive.

The number of cases pushed to sentence was therefore not large. The Toledo record, from 1575 to 1610, only furnishes fifty-two in a total of eleven hundred and thirty-four of all kinds.[299] In the later period, when the activity of the tribunals had greatly slackened, solicitation formed a much larger proportion of their business.[300] We have a record of all cases despatched in Toledo, from 1648 to 1794, in which those for solicitation amount to only sixty-eight. This seems but few and yet, when we compare this total with that of other offences, in which there were no special impediments to prosecution, it becomes surprisingly large, for there were but sixty-two cases of bigamy, thirty-seven of blasphemy, seventy-four of propositions and one hundred of sorcery and divination. Between 1705 and 1714, the whole number of sentences was but twenty-six and of these eight were for solicitation, while between 1757 and 1763 it contributed six cases out of a total of eight.[301]

When we turn to the number of accusations we find them unexpectedly large. The registers of solicitations, kept during the final century of the Inquisition, afford trustworthy statistics showing that, from 1723 to the final suppression in 1820, the total number of cases entered amounts to thirty-seven hundred and seventy-five. Of these, it is worthy of note that the secular clergy only furnished nine hundred and eighty-one, leaving for the regulars twenty-seven hundred and ninety-four, or nearly three-quarters. Partly this is explicable by the greater popularity of the regulars as confessors but, to a greater extent, by the opportunities of the beneficed priests, who were usually well off, to gratify their passions without incurring the dangers of polluting the confessional.[302] One noteworthy fact is the large proportion of those occupying prominent positions as Provincials, Guardians, Ministers, Priors, Comendadores, Visitadores, Superiors, Rectors, Lectors, and the like, whose titles appear in the registers with a frequency greater than their mere numbers would seem to justify.

**

In 1797, Tavira, then Bishop of Osma and subsequently of Salamanca, assumed that the crime of solicitation had greatly increased and was increasing, which he attributed partly to the influence of Illuminism and Molinism, but still more to its cognizance having been taken from the bishops and the requirement by the Inquisition of two denunciations before prosecution.[303] That the latter provision conferred practical immunity on many culprits is self-evident, but this was probably less effective than would have been the habitual indifference and leniency of the spiritual courts, their dread of scandal and the inevitable disgrace which deterred women from appearing in their public proceedings. There is practically no reason for supposing that the crime was either more or less prevalent, at the close of the eighteenth century, than it had been ever since, in the thirteenth, auricular confession was made obligatory, or than it has been since the nineteenth century opened. The strain of the confessional is too great for average human nature, and the most that the Church can do, in its most recent regulations, is to keep these lapses of the flesh from the knowledge of the faithful.[304]

CHAPTER VII - PROPOSITIONS

DELATION HABITUAL

Although the Spanish Inquisition was founded for the suppression of crypto-Judaism, it promptly vindicated its jurisdiction over all aberrations from the faith. There were, at the time, no other formal heresies in Spain, but the people at large were not universally versed in all the niceties of theology, and the supineness of the spiritual courts permitted a licence of speech in which the trained theologian could discern potentialities of error. All this the Inquisition undertook to correct and ultimately, under the general denomination of "Propositions," there developed an extensive field of action, which towards the end became the principal function of the institution. Reckless or thoughtless expressions, uttered in anger or in jest, or through ignorance or carelessness, gave to pious zeal or to malice the opportunity of secret denunciation, which in time impressed upon every Spaniard the necessity of caution, and left its mark upon the national character. As we have seen, the closest family ties did not release from the obligation of accusation, and every individual lived in an atmosphere of suspicion, surrounded by possible spies of his own household.[305] Men of the highest standing for learning or piety, moreover, were exposed to the torture of prolonged prosecution and possible ruin, for words spoken or written to which an heretical intent could be ascribed, in relation to the obscurest points of theology, and thus the development of the Spanish intellect was arrested at the time when it promised to become dominant in Europe. From every point of view, therefore, the miscellaneous offences, grouped under the general term of Propositions, was by no means the least noteworthy subject of inquisitorial activity.[306]

How soon began the espionage, which eventually brought every man under its baneful influence, is seen in the case of Juan de Zamora, condemned in the Saragossa auto of February 10, 1488, to perpetual prison, because at Medina, in chatting with some casual aquaintances, he was said to have spoken disrespectfully of the Eucharist and to have denied the real presence, while, in the auto of May 10, 1489, Juan de Enbun, a notary, was penanced for saying that he cared more for ten florins than for God.[307] Even more significant of the danger overhanging every man was the case of Diego de Uceda, before the Toledo tribunal, in 1494, on the very serious charges of having said that the Eucharist was only bread, that so villanous a crew as the Jews could not have put Christ to death, and that he ate meat on fast-days. He explained that, some six or eight years before, at Fuensalida, a priest in celebrating found the wafer broken and angrily cast it on the floor, ordering the sacristan to bring him another; the people were scandalized and Diego sought to quiet them by explaining that the wafer before consecration was only bread. The next charge arose from a remark in a discussion on an exuberant sermon on the Passion. As for the third, he proved that he was a devout Catholic, punctual in all observance, with a special devotion to St. Gregory, to whose intercession he attributed his relief from a chronic trouble of stomach and liver, that had forced him at one time to eat meat on fast-days. He lay in the secret prison for six months, with sequestration of property, and was finally sentenced to compurgation, which he performed with the Count of Fuensalida and two priests as his compurgators, but had he not been a man of standing and influence he might have been burnt as an impenitent heretic.[308] There was no prescription of time for heresy, and trivial matters occurring years before might thus at any moment be brought up, when they had faded from the memory of all but those who had a grudge to satisfy.

The ever-present danger impending over every man is well illustrated by the case of Alvaro de Montalvan, a septuagenarian, in 1525. Returning to Madrid, after a day's pleasure excursion in the country, Alonso Rúiz, a priest, who was of the party, took occasion to moralize on the troubles of life, in comparison with the prospects of future bliss. Alvaro (who subsequently pleaded that he was in his cups) remarked that we know what we have here but know nothing of the future. Some six months later, one of the party, in his Easter confession, chanced to mention this, and was instructed to denounce Alvaro. He was arrested and, on searching the records, it was found that, nearly forty years before, in 1486, during a term of grace, he had confessed to some Jewish observances without intention, and was discharged without reconciliation or penance. On this new charge he was made to confess intention and was sentenced, October 18, 1525, to reconciliation, confiscation and perpetual prison, the latter being commuted, November 27, 1527, to confinement in his own house.[309]

TRIVIALITIES

There was scarce anything, however innocently spoken, that might not be tortured into a censurable sense and as, in so wide and vague a region, no formal rules could be enunciated to restrain inquisitorial zeal, it afforded ample opportunity for oppression and cruelty, especially before the tribunals were thoroughly subordinated to the Suprema. The occasional visitations by an inspector might reveal abuses but could not prevent them. That of de Soto Salazar at Barcelona affords ample evidence of the recklessness with which inquisitors exercised their power. In 1564 we hear of a physician, Maestre Pla, prosecuted for saying that his wife was so exhausted that she looked like a crucifix dead with hunger. Juan Garaver, a swineherd, was forced to appear in an auto with a mitre, followed by scourging, for saying that if he had money and enough to eat, the devil might take his soul-- which the Suprema decided to belong to episcopal and not to inquisitorial cognizance. It rebuked the tribunal sharply for relaxing Guillen Berberia Guacho for a single proposition, without calling in learned men to persuade and advise him, especially as one of the witnesses stated that he uttered the words in French. Clemensa Paresa was fined ten ducats and penanced for saying "You see me well enough off in this world and you will not see me punished in the other," and Juana Seralvis, for the same utterance was condemned to public penance. Badia, priest of Falset, was fined twenty ducats, with spiritual penances, for saying that he would not forgive God. Juan Canalvero was fined six ducats and penanced for saying that he would cheat his father or God in buying or selling. There were many other similar cases, in some of which the Suprema ordered the fines to be returned and the names to be stricken from the registers.[310]

The very triviality of these cases illustrates the atmosphere of suspense and distrust in which the Spanish population existed, nor can their full import be realized unless we remember that, slight as the penalties may seem, they were the least part of the punishment, for penancing by the Inquisition was fatal to limpieza. How readily a man's career could thus be ruined by rivals or enemies is seen in the case of the Dominican Alonso de los Raelos in the Canaries. In 1568 some assertions of his respecting purgatory attracted attention, but led to no formal trial, because he did not deny its existence, and theologians are not agreed as to its exact locality and character. Some years later, there were feuds in the Order, due to an attempt to erect the Canaries into a separate province, when the prior, Blas de Merino, who hoped to become provincial, and who regarded Fray Alonso as a possible rival, accused him to the tribunal for this proposition. He was thrown into prison and, in 1572, was sentenced to penance and reclusion, thus rendering him ineligible.[311]

We have seen in the previous chapter the penalties regarded as sufficient for the crime of seduction in the confessional, and a comparison between these and the punishments inflicted for utterances in the heat of discussion and indicative of no settled tendency to heresy, reveal the very curious standard of ethics prevalent at the period. In 1571, a priest named Miguel Lidueña de Osorio was accused in Valencia of having said that the bishops at the Council of Trent deserved to be burnt, because they assumed to be popes, and moreover that St. Anne was deserving of higher honor than St. Joaquin. For this he was required to abjure de vehementi, he was suspended from orders, recluded for six years and banished perpetually from Valencia.[312] It was not often that flagrant cases of solicitation were visited with such severity.

RULES OF PROCEDURE

The infinite varieties and intangible nature of the offence rendered impossible the formulation of hard and fast rules for the tribunals, which were thus left to their discretion in a matter which was constantly forming a larger portion of inquisitorial business. The space devoted to it by Rojas, in his little book, indicates its growing importance, and he tells us that he was led to treat it thus at length because so many of the accused admit the facts, while denying belief and intention, and he had seen such diametrically opposite modes of treatment and punishment adopted in different tribunals. He is emphatic in insisting on the allowance to be made for the ignorance and rusticity of most of the culprits, and he points out that, in view of the restrictions on the defence, the inquisitor should be especially careful to give weight to whatever could be alleged in favor of the accused, whether he were ignorant and rude, or learned and subtle. The manner and occasion of the utterance ought to be carefully considered, as well as the nativity of the speaker, if he comes from lands where heresy flourishes. How much depended on the temper of the tribunal is exhibited in a case in which a man, going to hear mass and finding that it was over, said "faith alone suffices" and was prosecuted for the remark. Rojas decided that he was not to be held as asserting that faith without works suffices, which would be heretical, for doubtful words are to be interpreted according to circumstances, but a more zealous or less conscientious inquisitor could readily have convicted him. For ordinary cases, he tells us, the accused should rarely be confined in the secret prison; the abjuration may be de levi or de vehementi according to circumstances, and the extraordinary punishment should be scourging or fines.[313]

As the Suprema gradually assumed control over the tribunals, there grew up certain more or less recognized rules of procedure. Thus, if there was evidence of heretical utterances, and the accused confessed them but denied intention, he was to be tortured; if this brought confession of intention, he was to be reconciled with confiscation in a public auto as a formal heretic; if he overcame the torture he had to abjure de vehementi in an auto, with scourging, vergüenza, exile etc., according to his station and the character of the propositions. This, we are told, was merciful, for the common opinion of the doctors was that, if the propositions were formally heretical, the offender should be relaxed, in spite of his denying intention. Mercy was carried even further for, if ignorance was alleged with probable justification, the accused was not tortured nor condemned as a heretic, but abjured de levi, with discretional penalties. There was moreover, as we have seen, a vast range of propositions in which heresy was only inferential, characterized as scandalous, offensive to pious ears etc., for which abjuration de levi was considered sufficient, with spiritual penances.[314]

In this enumeration of penalties there is no allusion to fines, which, however, were by no means neglected. In 1579, for instance, the Bachiller Montesinos, in defending an adulteress, put in an argument of cynical ingenuity to prove that she had committed no sin. This was transmitted to the Toledo tribunal, whose calificadores found in it four heretical propositions besides a citation from St. Paul amounting to heretical blasphemy. Montesinos threw himself on the mercy of the tribunal, wept and wrung his hands, protested that he must have been out of his senses, owing to old age, and offered every excuse that he could suggest. He escaped with abjuration de levi, six months' suspension from his functions as an advocate, and a fine of eight thousand maravedís. Many similar cases could be cited from the Toledo record, but two more will suffice. In 1582, the Bachiller Pablo Hernández denounced himself for having, in the heat of discussion, been led on to say that in canonizations the pope had to rely upon witnesses who might be false and therefore it was not necessary to believe that all so canonized were saints. He was sentenced to abjure de levi, to pay six thousand maravedís, and to have his sentence read in his parish church while he heard mass. From this he appealed to the Suprema, which remitted the humiliation in church, but thriftily increased the fine to twenty thousand maravedís. In 1604 the tribunal had a richer prize, in an old German named Giraldo Paris, a resident of Madrid who seems to have been a dabbler in alchemy. He was accused of saying that the Old Testament was a fable, that St. Job was an alchemist, the Christian faith was a matter of opinion and much more of the same kind. The evidence must have been flimsy for, serious as were these charges, there was discordia on the question of arresting him, and it required an order from the Suprema before he was confined in the secret prison. He gradually confessed the truth of the charges, but was not sentenced to reconciliation, escaping with absolution de vehementi, a year's reclusion in a monastery, the surrender of all books and papers dealing with alchemy and quintessences, and a fine of three thousand ducats. The general impression produced by a group of these cases is that scourging was reserved for those too poor to pay a moderate fine, and that fines were scaled rather upon the ability of the culprit than on the degree of his guilt.[315] In determining penalties, however, it was advised that considerable weight in extenuation should be allowed for drunkenness, and for the readiness and frankness of the culprit in confessing, as well as for his ignorance or simplicity.[316]

MARRIAGE BETTER THAN CELIBACY

There were two special propositions, which were so widely held and came so repeatedly before the tribunals that they almost form a special class. One of these was the assertion that the married state is as good as or better than that of celibacy as prescribed for clerics and religious. That this was plainly heretical could not be doubted after the anathema of the Council of Trent in 1563, and its prevalence is a noteworthy fact.[317] In the Toledo record, from 1575 to 1610, there are thirty cases of this: in strictness, as the assertion of a doctrine contrary to the teachings of the Church, and condemned as heretical, it should have been visited with reconciliation, or at least with abjuration de vehementi and heavy penalties, but, as the heresy was one of Tridentine definition and a novelty, it was mercifully treated with abjuration de levi and usually with a moderate fine or vergüenza, or even with less. Extreme leniency was shown to Sebastian Vallejo, in 1581, who had declared that if he had a hundred daughters he would not make nuns of them, in view of the licentiousness of the frailes, for those in the convents were as lecherous as those outside; no parent should put his children in religion until they were of full age and, as to marriage, he advanced the customary argument that it was established by God, while monachism was the work of the saints. He came to denounce himself and pleaded drunkenness in extenuation, which probably explains his escape with a reprimand. Soon after this María de Orduña was treated with equal mercy, on denouncing herself for the same offence, the reason alleged being that she was a very simple-minded woman.[318] As the offence was thus lightly regarded, it follows that torture was not permitted in the prosecution.[319] The error was difficult of eradication. In 1623 a writer calls attention to the number of cases still coming before the tribunals, and suggests for its repression that the sentences be read in the churches of the offenders, so that a knowledge of the erroneous character of the assertion should be disseminated.[320] Some twenty years later it still was sufficiently frequent to be treated as a separate class, though we are told that it was visited with less severity than of old, as it presumably arose from ignorance and was not to be considered as a heresy.[321] This is remarkable in view of the ease with which it might have been regarded as Lutheran.

A still more frequent proposition, which gave much trouble to eradicate, was that fornication between unmarried folk is not a mortal sin. Although the theologians held that this assertion in itself was a mortal sin,[322] there was really in it nothing that savored of heresy, and its cognizance by the Inquisition was an arbitrary extension of jurisdiction without justification. Perhaps there was some confused conception that it was derived from the Moors whose sexual laxity was well known, but the usual argument offered in its defence, by those who entertained it, was the toleration by the State of public women and of brothels, whence the inference was natural that it could not be a mortal sin.

FORNICATION NOT SINFUL

It seems to have been between 1550 and 1560 that the Inquisition commenced its efforts to suppress this popular error. The earliest record of its action that I have met occurs in the great Seville auto of September 24, 1559, where there were no less than twelve cases, of whom eight abjured de levi, one de vehementi, six were paraded in vergüenza, four were scourged with a hundred lashes (of whom one was a woman) and two heard mass as penitents.[323] The requirement of abjuration shows that suspicion of heresy was already attributed to the proposition, but this as yet was not universally accepted for, in 1561, the Suprema wrote to the tribunal of Calahorra that Pedro Cestero, whom it had penanced for this offence, ought to have been prosecuted as a heretic, for it would seem to be heresy.[324] Thus heresy was injected into it and we speedily find it to be a leading source of business in the Castilian tribunals. Seville was notably active. In the auto of October 28, 1562, there were nineteen cases.[325] In that of May 13, 1565, out of seventy-five penitents, twenty-five were for this proposition. The punishments were severe. All abjured de levi and appeared in their shirts with halter and candle; all but one were gagged; fourteen were scourged with an aggregate of nineteen hundred lashes; five were paraded in vergüenza, two were fined in two hundred ducats apiece, and two others in a thousand maravedís each; six were exiled and one was forbidden to leave Seville without permission. Besides these there was one man who had a hundred lashes for saying that there was no sin in keeping a mistress, and three women were penanced for saying the same of living in concubinage, of whom two had a hundred lashes apiece and the third was paraded in vergüenza. Two men appeared for saying that keeping a mistress was better than marriage, of whom one had the infliction of the gag. To these we may add two who held that marriage was better than the celibacy of the frailes, and we have a total of thirty-three cases, or nearly one-half of all in the auto, for errors concerning the relations of the sexes.[326]

Active as was this work it did not satisfy the Suprema which, in a carta acordada of November 23, 1573, speaks of the prevalence of the offence as indicated in the reports of autos, and the little progress thus far made in its suppression; greater vigor was therefore ordered and, in future, all delinquents were to be prosecuted as heretics. This was followed by another, October 2, 1574, ordering the proposition to be included in the Edict of Faith, and yet another December 2^{d}, of the same year, repeating the complaint of its frequency and the little improvement accomplished. It was apparently an error of ignorance and, to remedy this, a special edict was ordered to be published everywhere, declaring it to be a heresy condemned by the Church, and that all uttering and believing it would be punished as heretics; all preachers moreover were to be instructed to warn and admonish the people from the pulpits.[327]

All this was wholesome, and yet it is difficult to understand this ardent zeal for the morals of the laity, when compared with the slackness as to solicitation. Be this as it may, the activity of the tribunals under this stimulus was rewarded with an abundant harvest of culprits. We chance to hear of eight cases in the auto of 1579 at Llerena and of five at Cuenca in 1585.[328] A more effective showing is that of the Toledo record from 1575 to 1610, in which the number of cases is two hundred and sixty-four--by far the largest aggregate of any one offence, the Judaizers only amounting to a hundred and seventy-four and the Moriscos to a hundred and ninety.[329] These statistics comprehend only the tribunals of the crown of Castile; those at hand for the kingdoms of Aragon are scanty but, from such as are accessible, it would appear probable either that there was less energy or a much smaller number of culprits. The only cases that I have happened to meet are two in a Saragossa auto of June 6, 1585, while, in a Valencia list for the five years 1598-1602, comprising in all three hundred and ninety-two cases, there are but four of this offence and not a single one in the reports for the three years 1604-6.[330]

Notwithstanding the characterization of the offence as heresy, torture was not to be employed in the trial, although confinement in the secret prison and sequestration were permitted.[331] The energy and severity with which it was prosecuted virtually suppressed it in time. In 1623 a writer speaks of it as less common than formerly and, in a list of the cases tried at Toledo, commencing in 1648, the first one of this offence occurs in 1650, the next in 1665 and the third in 1693. Thenceforth it may be said practically to disappear from the tribunals, although as late as 1792, Don Ambrosio Pérez, beneficed priest of Candamas was tried for it in Saragossa and in 1818 there was a case in Valencia.[332] Thus the Inquisition succeeded in suppressing the expression of the opinion though, as it took no action against the sin, its influence on the side of morality was inappreciable.

INTELLECTUAL REPRESSION

A reference to the cases of propositions tried by the Toledo tribunal between 1575 and 1610 (see Vol. II, p. 552) will indicate the very miscellaneous character of the utterances for which its interposition was invoked. These involved culprits of all classes of society and as, for the most part, they concerned theological questions of more or less obscurity, this method of enforcing purity of faith frequently brought under animadversion the foremost intellects of Spain and rendered the Inquisition the instrument through which rivals or enemies could mar the careers of those in whom lay the only hope of intellectual progress and development. What between its censorship and the minute supervision, which exposed to prosecution every thought or expression in which theological malevolence could detect lurking tendencies to error, the Spanish thinker found his path beset with danger. Safety lay only in the well-beaten track of accepted conventionality and, while Europe, in the seventeenth and eighteenth centuries, was passing through a period of evolution, Spanish intellect became atrophied. The splendid promise of the sixteenth century was blasted by the steady repression of all originality and progress, and Spain, from the foremost of the nations, became the last.

The minuteness of the captious criticism which exposed the most eminent men to the horrors of inquisitorial prosecution can best be understood by two or three cases. Of these perhaps the most notable is that of the Augustinian Fray Luis de Leon, who was not only one of the most eminent theologians of his day, and who was unsurpassed as a preacher, but who ranks as a Castilian classic in both prose and poetry.[333] It is so suggestive of inquisitorial procedure in such matters that it is worthy of examination in some detail.

To a brilliant intellect Luis de Leon united a personal activity which led him to take a prominent part in the feverish life of the schools, not only in disputations but in the frequent rivalries and competitions, through which professorial vacancies were filled, for in Salamanca the professors were elected for terms of four years by the students of the faculty to which the chair belonged, after a disputation between the candidates. In these he had abundant opportunities of making enemies for, at the age of 34, he had been elected to the chair of Thomas Aquinas, from which he passed to that of Durandus. These opportunities he largely improved, if we may trust his characterizations of the numerous opponents whom he sought to disable as witnesses in the course of his trial. Even in his own Order he had enemies, owing to his active and influential participation in its internal politics.

Theological disputes are rarely wanting in rancor, no matter how minute may be the points at issue. In Salamanca, not only were there frequent disputations but, as the leading school of theology, questions were frequently submitted to it by the Suprema on which conferences and congregations were held, leading to interminable wrangles. Azpilcueta tells us that this disputatious mania led the participants to uphold what was false, for the purpose of exhibiting their dexterity, not only misleading their auditors but often blinding themselves to the truth, and Luis de Leon himself says that the warmth of debate sometimes carried them beyond the bounds of reason, and so confused them that they could scarce recall what they themselves had said. One of his witnesses, Fray Juan de Guevara, corroborates this with the remark that Maestro Leon de Castro (Luis de Leon's chief accuser) sometimes might not understand what was said, but this happened to all theologians when heated in the disputations.[334]

A fairer field for inquisitorial intervention could scarce be devised and, from one point of view, its restraint of this dialectic ardor might not be amiss, but its influence on intellectual development was deplorable, when it made every man feel that he stood on the brink of an abyss into which, at any moment, he might be precipitated. Nor was such dread uncalled for; while Luis de Leon was on trial, three other Salamanca professors were in the same predicament--Antonio Gudiel, Gaspar de Grajal and Martin Martínez, while yet another, Dr. Barrientos, was released just prior to the arrest of Luis. Denunciation was an easy recourse for a defeated disputant; an incautious utterance in heated debate, imperfectly understood, or distorted in remembrance, furnished the means. Even lectures in the ordinary courses contributed their share, when zealous students disagreed with their teachers or made mistakes in their hasty notes.

LUIS DE LEON

The two prime movers in the prosecution of Fray Luis were Leon de Castro and Bartolomé de Medina. De Castro was an elderly man, a jubilado professor of Grammar, who had frequent wordy encounters with Fray Luis, usually to his discomfiture.

He had based great hopes on a Commentary on Isaiah, the publication of which was delayed by the Suprema requiring him to submit it to examination; he had to spend some months at the court before he could obtain permission for its sale, and then it proved a failure, entailing on him a loss of a thousand ducats--all of which he attributed to Fray Luis, who happened at the time to be in Madrid. Bartolomé de Medina was a younger man, ambitiously working his way upward, and meeting several rebuffs from Fray Luis, which accentuated the traditional hostility between the Dominicans and Augustinians, to which they respectively belonged. They were habitually opposed in the disputations, but it seems somewhat eccentric to find Medina accusing Luis and his friends Grajal and Martínez of introducing novelties and innovations, seeing that his own reputation is chiefly based on his invention of the greatest novelty of the period--the Probabilism which revolutionized the ethical teaching of the Church and gave rise to the new science of Moral Theology.[335]

It was not difficult for these enmities to find means of gratification. Robert Stephen's edition of the Latin Bible, with the notes of François Vatable, had involved that printer in endless disputes with the Sorbonne, which accused him of having hereticated the comments of the thoroughly orthodox editor. In 1555, the University of Salamanca undertook its correction, but the result did not satisfy the sensitiveness of Spanish theology, and the edition was forbidden in the Index of 1559. Yet the work was wanted in Spain and, at command of the Suprema, in 1569, the university undertook the task anew. Numerous congregations were held, in which every point was hotly disputed. Medina, who had not yet attained his master's degree, took no part in the meetings, but Leon de Castro and Fray Luis had many passages at arms. De Castro accused him of scant respect for the Vulgate text of the Bible, and of preferring the authority of the Hebrew and Greek originals. He stigmatized Luis, who was of converso descent, of being a Jew and a Judaizer and, on one occasion, declared that he ought to be burnt. In truth the question of the Vulgate was one of importance. The new heresies were largely based on the assumption of its imperfection, and sought to prove this by reference to the originals. Scholastic theology rested on the Vulgate and, in self-defence, the Council of Trent, in 1546, had declared that it was to be received as authentic in all public lectures, disputations, preaching and expositions, and that no one should dare to reject it under any pretext.[336] Yet it was notorious that, in the course of ages, the text had become corrupt; the Tridentine fathers included in their decree a demand for a perfected edition, but the labor was great and was not concluded until 1592, when the Clementine text was issued, with thousands of emendations. Meanwhile to question its accuracy was to venture on dangerous ground and to invite the interposition of the Inquisition. As one of the calificadores, during Fray Luis's trial, asserted "Catholic doctors affirm that now the Hebrew and Greek are to be emended by the Vulgate, as the purer and more truthful text. To emend the Vulgate by the Hebrew and Greek is exactly what the heretics seek to do. It is to destroy the means of confuting them and to give them the opportunity of free interpretation."[337] Fray Luis not only did this in debate but, in a lecture on the subject four years before, he had maintained the accuracy of the Hebrew text, contending that St. Jerome the translator was not inspired, nor were the words dictated by the Holy Ghost, and moreover that the Tridentine decree in no way affirmed such verbal inspiration.[338]

On another point he was also vulnerable. Ten or eleven years previously, at the request of Doña Isabel de Osorio, a nun in the convent of Santo Spirito, he had made a Castilian version of the Song of Solomon, with an exposition. This he had reclaimed from her but, during an absence, Fray Diego de Leon, who was in charge of his cell, found it and made a copy, which was largely transcribed and circulated. At a time when vernacular versions were so rigidly proscribed this was, at the least, a hazardous proceeding and Bartolomé de Medina heightened the indiscretion by charging that, in his exposition, he represented the work as an amatory dialogue between the daughter of Pharaoh and Solomon.

***

In December 1571, de Castro and Medina presented formal denunciations of Fray Luis, Grajal and Martínez, to the Salamanca commissioner of the Valladolid tribunal, charging them with denying the authority of the Vulgate and preferring the interpretations of the rabbis to those of the fathers, while the circulation of Canticles in the vernacular was not forgotten. Other accusers, including students, joined in the attack, making thirteen in all, with a formidable body of denunciations. Grajal was soon afterwards arrested and Fray Luis, warned of the impending danger, presented himself, March 6, 1572, to Diego González, the former inquisitor of Carranza, then on a visitation at Salamanca, with a copy of his lecture on the Vulgate and the propositions drawn from it, and also his work on Canticles. He asked to have them examined and professed entire submission to the Church, with readiness to withdraw or revoke anything that might be found in the slightest degree objectionable.[339]

In any other land, this would have sufficed. The inculpated works would have been expurgated or forbidden, if necessary. Luis would have retracted any expressions regarded as erroneous, and the matter would have ended without damage to the faith. Under the Inquisition, however, the utterance of objectionable propositions was a crime to be punished, and the submission of the criminal only saved him from the penalties of pertinacious heresy. On March 26th the warrant for the arrest of Fray Luis was issued and, on the 27th he was receipted for by the alcaide of the secret prison of Valladolid. He was treated with unusual consideration, in view of his infirmities and delicate health for, on his petition, he was allowed a scourge, a pointless knife to cut his food, a candle and snuffers and some books.[340] The trial proceeded at first with unusual speed. By May 15th the fiscal presented the formal accusation, in which Fray Luis was charged with asserting that the Vulgate contained many falsities and that a better version could be made; with decrying the Septuagint and preferring Vatable and rabbis and Jews to the saints as expositors of Scripture; with stating that the Council of Trent had not made the Vulgate a matter of faith and that, in the Old Testament, there was no promise of eternal life; with approving a doctrine that inferred justification by faith, and that mere mortal sin destroyed faith; with circulating an exposition of Canticles explaining them as a love-poem from Solomon to his wife--all of which was legitimately based on the miscellaneous evidence of the adverse witnesses.[341] This, as required, Fray Luis answered on the spot, article by article, attributing the charges to the malice of his enemies, denying some and explaining others clearly and frankly.

It was a special favor that he was at once provided with counsel and allowed to arrange his defence--a favor which brought upon the tribunal a rebuke from the Suprema, January 13, 1573, as contrary to the estilo, which must be followed, no matter what might be the supplications of the accused. Fray Luis identified many of the witnesses--out of nineteen he recognized eight--and he drew up six series of interrogatories, mostly designed to prove his allegations of mortal enmity. Of these the inquisitors threw out three as "impertinent" and the answers to the others were, to a considerable extent, unsatisfactory, as was almost inevitable under a system which made the accused grope blindly in seeking evidence. As time wore on in this necessarily dilatory business, Fray Luis grew impatient at the stagnation which seemed to preclude all progress, not being aware that in reality it had been expedited irregularly.[342]

It would be wearisome to follow in detail the proceedings which dragged their slow length along. Additional witnesses came forward, whose depositions had to go through the usual formalities; Fray Luis presented numberless papers as points occurred to him; he defended himself brilliantly and, through the course of the trial there were few of the customary prolonged intervals, for his nervous impatience kept him constantly plying the tribunal with arguments and appeals which it received with its habitual impassiveness. At length, after two years, early in March, 1574, it decided that there was no ground for suspicion against him in the thirty articles drawn from the testimony of the witnesses, while he could not be prosecuted criminally on the seventeen propositions extracted from his lecture on the Vulgate, seeing that he had spontaneously presented them and submitted himself to the Church. The fiscal, however, appealed from this to the Suprema and his appeal must have been successful, for the trial took a fresh start.[343]

***

After some intermediate proceedings, Fray Luis, on April 1st was told to select patrones theólogos to assist in his defence. He at once named Dr. Sebastian Pérez, professor in the royal college which Philip II had founded at Párraces, in connection with San Lorenzo del Escorial, and two days later he added other names.

In place of accepting them the tribunal endeavored to compel him to take men of whom he knew nothing and who, in reality, were the calificadores who had already condemned his propositions. The struggle continued until, on August 3d, the Suprema wrote that he could have Pérez, but his limpieza must first be proved and Philip's consent to his absence be obtained. We have seen how prolonged, costly and anxious were investigations into limpieza and, as Fray Luis remarked, this was to grant and to refuse in the same breath. At last, after endless discussions, in October he despairingly accepted Dr. Mancio, a Dominican and a leading professor of theology at Salamanca. Mancio came in October, again towards the end of December, and finally on March 30, 1575, while Fray Luis meanwhile was eating his heart in despair. At length, on April 7th Mancio approved of Fray Luis's defence, declaring that he had satisfied all the articles, both the series of seventeen and that of thirty, which had been proved against him or which he had admitted having uttered.[344]

If Fray Luis imagined that this twelve months' work to which such importance had been attributed, had improved his prospects, he was speedily undeceived. We hear nothing more of Dr. Mancio or of his approval. The propositions, with the defence, were submitted again to three calificadores (men who had been urged upon him as patrones) and it illustrates the uncertainties of theology and the hair-splitting subtilties in which the doctors delighted, that not only were the original seventeen articles declared to be heretical for the most part, but five new ones, quite as bad, were discovered in the defence which had elicited Dr. Mancio's approval, and these five thenceforth formed a third category of errors figuring in the proceedings.[345] It is not easy for us to comprehend the religious conceptions which placed men's lives and liberties and reputation at the hazard of dialectics in which the most orthodox theologians were at variance.

When Fray Luis was informed that five new heretical propositions had sprouted from the hydra-heads of the old ones, he was dismayed. Sick and exhausted, the prospects of ultimate release from his interminable trial seemed to grow more and more remote. Arguments and discussions continued and were protracted. New calificadores were called in, who debated and opined and presented written conclusions on all three series of propositions. It would be useless to follow in detail these scholastic exercises, of which the chief interest is to show how, in these infinitesimal points, one set of theologians could differ from another and how completely the enmity of the two chief witnesses, Leon de Castro and Bartolomé de Medina, was ignored. Thus wore away the rest of the year 1575 and the first half of 1576. There was no reason why the case might not be continued indefinitely on the same lines, but the inquisitors seem to have felt at last that an end must be reached, and a consulta de fe was finally held, in which Dr. Frechilla, one of the calificadores who had condemned the propositions, represented the episcopal Ordinary.[346]

The case illustrates one incident of these protracted trials. During its course it had been heard by seven inquisitors, of whom Guijano de Mercado was the only one who served from the commencement to the end, and his colleague in the consulta, Andrés de Alava, had appeared in it only in November, 1575, and had not been present in any audiences after December. There was, moreover, an unusual feature in the presence of a member of the Suprema, Francisco de Menchaca, indicating perhaps that the case was regarded as one of more than ordinary importance. There were five consultors, Luis Tello Maldonado, Pedro de Castro, Francisco Albornoz, Juan de Ibarra and Hernando Niño, but the two latter fell sick, when the examination of the voluminous testimony was half completed, and took no further part in the proceedings.

***

On the final decision, September 18, 1576, Menchaca, Alava, Tello and Albornoz voted for torture on the intention, including the propositions which the theologians had declared that Fray Luis had satisfied, after which another consulta should be held. They humanely added that it should be moderate in view of the debility of the accused. Those better acquainted with the case, Guijano and Frechilla, were more lenient. They voted for a reprimand, after which, in a general assembly of professors and students, Fray Luis should read a declaration, drawn up by the calificadores, pronouncing the propositions to be ambiguous, suspicious and likely to cause scandal. Moreover his Augustinian superior was to be told, extra-judicially, to order him privately to employ his studies in other directions and to abstain from teaching in the schools. The vernacular version of Canticles was to be suppressed, if the inquisitor-general and Suprema saw fit.[347] Comparatively mild as this sentence might seem, it gratified to the full the vindictiveness of his enemies--it humiliated him utterly and destroyed his career.

As there was discordia the case necessarily reverted to the Suprema, which seems to have recognized that both votes assumed the nullity of the laborious trifling, by which the calificadores had found dangerous heresies in his acknowledged propositions. Discussion must have been prolonged however, for the final sentence was not rendered until December 7th. This fully acquitted Fray Luis of all the charges, but ordered a reprimand in the audience-chamber and a warning to treat such matters in future with great circumspection, so that no scandal or errors should arise. The Suprema could scarce say less, if the whole dismal farce, of nearly five years, was not to be admitted as wholly unjustifiable, and it enclosed the sentence in a letter instructing the tribunal to order Fray Luis to preserve profound silence and to avoid dissension with those whom he suspected of testifying against him. It was probably on December 15th that the sentence was read and the reprimand administered. Fray Luis took the necessary oaths, he made the promises required, and was discharged as innocent after an incarceration, incomunicado, which had lasted for four years, eight months and nineteen days. His requests were granted for a certificate de no obstancia and for an order on the paymaster of the schools to pay him his professorial salary from the date of his arrest to the expiration of his quadrennial term.[348]

During this prolonged imprisonment, Fray Luis seems to have been treated with unusual consideration. He was allowed to send for all the books needed for his defence and for study--even for recreation, for we find him, July 6, 1575, asking for the prose works of Bembo, for a Pindar in Greek and Latin and for a copy of Sophocles.[349] He relieved the distractions of his defence and the anxieties of his position by the composition of his De los Nombres de Christo, which has remained a classic. Yet these were but slender alleviations of the hardships and despairing tedium of his prison cell. On March

12, 1575, he is begging for the sacraments; though he is no heretic, he says, he has been deprived of them for three years. This petition was forwarded to the Suprema, which replied by drily telling the tribunal to complete the cases of Fray Luis, Grajal and Martínez as soon as opportunity would permit.[350] At an audience of August 20th, of the same year, when remanded to his cell, he paused to represent that, as the inquisitors well knew, he was very sick with fever; there was no one in his cell to take care of him, save a fellow-prisoner, a young boy who was simple; one day he fainted through hunger, as there was no one to give him food, and he asked whether a fraile of his Order could be admitted to assist him and to aid him to die, unless they wished him to die alone in his cell. This was not refused but, as the condition was imposed that the companion should as usual share his imprisonment to the end, the request was in vain. Then, on September 12th, in his reply to the five propositions suddenly sprung upon him, he feelingly referred to the years of prison and the sufferings caused by the absence of comforts in his weakness and sickness, as a torture long and cruel enough to purge all suspicions.[351] Even more pitiful was a petition to the Suprema in November of the same year--"I supplicate your most illustrious body, by Jesus Christ, on my giving ample security, to order me to be placed in one of the convents of this city, even in that of San Pablo (Dominican), in any way that it may please you, until sentence is rendered, so that if, during this time, God should call me, which I greatly fear, in view of my much trouble and feeble health, I may die as a Christian among religious persons, aided by their prayers and receiving the sacraments, and not as an infidel, alone in prison with a Moor at my bed-side. And since the rancor of my enemies and my own sins have deprived me of all that is desirable in life, may the Christian piety of your most illustrious body give me this consolation in death, for I ask nothing more."[352] It is perhaps needless to say that this touching appeal did not even receive an answer.

***

After the term of his professorship had expired, about March 1, 1573, his special enemy, Bartolomé de Medina, was elected in his place and was promoted, in August 1576, to the leading chair in theology, while Fray García del Castillo succeeded to that of Durandus. On Fray Luis's return, he was warmly and honorably received in an assembly of the Senate, convoked for the purpose, where the Commissioner of the Inquisition declared that the Holy Office had ordered his restoration to honor and to his professorship. Luis however refused to disturb Castillo and, in January 1577, an extraordinary chair on the Scriptures was created for him. The next year, on the chair of moral philosophy falling vacant, he obtained it and subsequently he became regular professor of Scripture--one of the highest positions in the University. His colleague Grajal had been less fortunate, having perished in prison before the termination of his trial.[353]

Fray Luis's mental vigor was unimpaired, although his delicate frame never wholly recovered from the effects of his long imprisonment. Such an experience of the dangers attendant on the discussions of the schools might seem sufficient to dampen his disputatious ardor, but in a theology, which sought to reduce to hard and fast lines all the secrets of the unknown spiritual world, there was risk of heresy in every speculation. In an acto of the University, held January 20, 1582, the debate widened into a discussion upon predestination and free-will, in which Fray Luis and Fray Domingo de Guzman were bitterly opposed to each other. It was continued in another theological Act the next week; the students became excited and called upon Father Bañez to repress these novelties, which he did in a lecture declaring that the views of Fray Luis savored of Pelagianism. The latter was angered and the next day, in an assembly of all the faculties, the question under debate was: If God confers equal and sufficing grace on two men, nothing else interfering, can one be converted and the other reject the aid? The discussion between Fray Luis and Bañez was hot, and the excitement increased. Then on January 27th there was another assembly which wrangled over the intricate questions involved in prevenient aid and human coöperation.[354]

This was the commencement of the long debate De Auxiliis, between Jesuits and Dominicans, which lasted for a century, until both sides were silenced by the Holy See, without either being able to claim the victory. Fray Luis had excited many enmities--though not as many as he was in the habit of claiming--and the occasion was favorable for striking at him and at those whom he supported. Fray Juan de Santa Cruz drew up an account of the discussions, with a censure of the erroneous and heretical propositions defended; it was not a personal denunciation of any one, but he declared that the agitation and disquiet of the schools demanded a settlement by the Inquisition. This he presented, February 5th, at Valladolid, to the inquisitor, Juan de Arrese and, from the marginal notes, it appears that, besides Fray Luis, two Jesuits and a Benedictine were marked for prosecution. In March, Inquisitor Arrese came to Salamanca on a mission to suppress astrology and took the opportunity to gather testimony on the scholastic quarrel. Various witnesses, some of them Augustinians, came forward spontaneously with evidence, and the Mercenarian, Francisco Zumel presented a series of propositions, purporting to be drawn from a lecture by Fray Luis on predestination, of which the worst was that Christ on the cross was destitute of God and was provoked to sin. Zumel was a bitter enemy of Luis, who had defeated him, four years before, in competition for the chair of moral philosophy; both had their partizans and their quarrels were the cause of much trouble.[355]

***

Fray Luis's experience of the Inquisition naturally led him to seek exculpation. Three times he appeared voluntarily before Arrese and made verbal and written statements, in which he rendered an account of his share in the debates. He admitted that he had defended a position opposite to what he had previously taught, which was not without a certain temerity, as differing from the ordinary language of the schools, and not proper for public debate, as it was delicate, difficult of comprehension and liable to lead the hearers into error. He protested that he had not intended to offend Catholic doctrine and, if he had said anything inconsiderately, he submitted it to the censure and correction of the holy tribunal. He also laid much stress on the notorious hatred of the Dominicans towards him, and the manner in which they lost no opportunity of decrying his doctrine, his person and his morals.[356]

Inquisitor Arrese returned to Valladolid with the evidence, after which there was pause before the case of Fray Luis was taken up. There would seem to have been some hesitation concerning it, for the Suprema took the unusual step of summoning him before it, from which he excused himself on the plea of illness and forwarded a physician's certificate in justification. The next document in the case is a letter of August 3d, from the Suprema to the tribunal, calling for the papers in the cases of the Salamanca theologians, with its opinion concerning them. In its reply the tribunal said that Fray Luis had confessed to everything testified against him, submitting himself to correction, and conceding that what he had said was not devoid of temerity; he had evidently spoken with passion and after the debate had begged pardon of Domingo de Guzman for telling him that what he advocated was Lutheran heresy. In view of all this the tribunal proposed to call him before it and examine him when, if nothing further resulted, he should be gravely reprimanded and, as the school of Salamanca was gravely excited and, as some Augustinians were boasting that his utterances had been accepted by the tribunal as true, he should be required publicly to read in his chair a declaration drawn up for him censuring the propositions, and also to declare that he had spoken wrongly when he had characterized the opposite as heresy.[357]

This would have been a profound humiliation for the proud and domineering theologian, but again Quiroga seems to have interposed to save him. There is a blank in the records for eighteen months, explicable by the affair being in the hands of the Suprema. What occurred during the interval is unknown, but the outcome appears in the final act of the trial, February 3, 1584, at Toledo. There Fray Luis stood before Inquisitor-general Quiroga who reprimanded and admonished him charitably not in future to defend, publicly or privately, the propositions which he had admitted were not devoid of temerity, adding a warning that otherwise he would be prosecuted with all the rigor of the law, to all of which Fray Luis promised obedience.[358] That he had in no way lost the respect of his fellows is seen in his election to the Provincialate of the Augustinian Order, in 1591, shortly before his death.

In addition to their exhibiting the attitude of the Inquisition towards the most distinguished intellects of the period, these two trials of Fray Luis illustrate its arbitrary methods, operating as it did in secret. His fault, if fault there was, was the same in both cases--the enunciation of opinions on which the most learned doctors differed. In both cases he denounced himself, freely confessed what he had spoken or written, and submitted himself unreservedly to the judgement of the church. In the first case he was arrested; he endured nearly five years of incarceration and only escaped torture or the ruin of his career through the kindly interposition of Quiroga. In the second, there was no arrest, the case was decided on the sumaria, or suspended, and although Quiroga probably again intervened, it was only to save the accused from a humiliation which would have gratified malevolence. Judged by its own standard, the Inquisition abused its powers--either, in one case, by unpardonable severity or in the other by excessive moderation, but it was responsible to no one and had no public opinion to dread.

FRANCISCO SANCHEZ

Just as the case of Fray Luis was ending, prosecution was commenced against another Salamanca professor, of equal or even greater distinction. As a man of pure letters, no one at the time was the peer of Francisco Sánchez, known as el Brocense, from his birth-place, las Brozas. Vainglorious, quarrelsome, caustic and reckless of speech, he made numerous enemies, but probably he would have escaped the Inquisition had he confined himself to his chair of grammar and rhetoric. He delighted however in paradoxes, and he held himself so immeasurably superior to the theologians, and was so confident in the accuracy of his own varied learning, that he could not restrain himself from ridiculing their pretensions, from exposing the errors of pious legends and denouncing some of the grosser popular superstitions, thus rendering himself liable to inquisitorial animadversion, whenever malice or zeal might call the attention of the tribunal to his eccentricities. He flattered himself that he did not meddle with articles of faith, but he failed to realize how elastic were the boundaries of faith, and that, in attacking vulgar errors, he might be regarded as undermining the foundations of the Church. Scandal was a convenient word which bridged over the line between the profane and the sacred.[359]

His habitual intemperance of speech was stimulated by a custom in the Salamanca lecture-rooms of students handing up questions for the lecturer to answer, and it would appear that malicious pleasure was felt in thus provoking him to exhibit his well-known idiosyncrasies. It was an occasion of this kind that prompted the first denunciation, January 7, 1584, by Juan Fernández, a priest attending the lectures. Others followed, and the character of his utterances appears in the propositions submitted to the calificadores:--That Christ was not circumcised by St. Simeon but by his mother the Virgin.--That there ought to be no images and, but for apparent imitation of the heretics, they would have been abolished.--That those were fools who, at the procession of Corpus Christi, knelt in the streets to adore the images, for only Christ and his cross were to be adored.--Only saints in heaven were to be adored and not images, which were but wood and plaster.--Christ was not born in a stable, but in a house where the Virgin was staying.--That the eleven thousand virgins were only eleven.--Doubts whether the Three Kings were kings, as Scripture speaks only of Magi.--That the Magian kings did not come at Christ's birth, but two years after, and found him playing with a ball.--That theologians know nothing.--That many Dominicans thought the faith was based on St. Thomas Aquinas; this was not so and he did not care a ---- for St. Thomas.--When asked why St. Lucia was painted without eyes, he said that she had not torn them out, but she was reckoned the patron saint of eyes from her name--Lucia a lucere.

That these free-spoken propositions should be duly characterized by the calificadores as heretical, rash, erroneous, insulting and so forth was a matter of course and, on May 18th, the consulta de fe voted for imprisonment in the secret prison with sequestration, subject to confirmation by the Suprema. The latter delayed action until August 29th and then manifested unusual consideration for the eccentricities of Sánchez, which were doubtless well known. He was merely to be summoned before the tribunal, to be closely examined and to be severely reprimanded, with a warning to give no further occasion for scandal, as otherwise he would be treated with all rigor.[360]

His first audience was held on September 24th. There is a refreshing and characteristic frankness in his reply to the customary question whether he knew the cause of his summons. He supposed it was because, about Christmas-time, in his lecture-room, he was asked why St. Lucia was painted with her eyes on a dish and why she was patron saint of eyes, when he replied that she was not such a fool as to tear out her eyes to give them to others; the vulgar believed many things that had no authority save that of painters, and it was on account of her name that she was patron saint of eyes. Then, he added, some days later he was asked why he talked against what the Church holds; this angered him and he told them they were great fools who did not know what the Church is; they must think that sacristans and painters are the Church; he would be speaking against the Church if he spoke against the Fathers and Councils. If they saw eleven thousand virgins painted in a picture, they would think that there were eleven thousand, but in an ancient calendar there was only undecim M. virgines--there were ten martyrs and Ursula made the eleventh. Then, some three years ago, the Circumcision was represented in the cathedral of Salamanca, where appeared the Virgin, Simeon and the child Jesus. He said to many of those present that it was a pity such impertinences were permitted in Salamanca; that the Virgin did not go to the temple until the forty days were expired, and no priest was required for the circumcision, for it is rather believed that the Virgin performed it in her own house. He mentioned various other criticisms which he had made on pictures, such as the Last Supper, where Christ and the apostles should be represented on triclinia, and the Sacrifice of Abraham where Isaac should be a man of 25. For this all he was called in Salamanca a rash and audacious man, and he supposed this was the cause of his summons; if there was more, let him know it and he would obey the Church; if in what he had said he had caused scandal, he was ready to retract and to submit to the Church.[361]

***

This fearless frankness was preserved in the examination that followed on the charges not explained in his avowal. When asked whether he knew these things to be heretical and if his intention was to oppose the Church, he replied that in the form of the charges he held them to be heretical, but he had uttered them only in the way he stated, with the intention of a good Christian and for the instruction of others, but, if he had erred, he begged mercy with penance, and was ready to make whatever amends were required. His confessions were duly submitted to calificadores who reported, reasonably enough, that he denied some, explained others and left others as they were, but that as a whole he deserved to be reprimanded and punished, because he exceeded his functions without discretion and, if not restrained, he would come to utter manifold errors and heresies. Under ordinary routine his punishment would have been exemplary, but the tribunal was controlled by the instructions of the Suprema and, on September 28th, he was duly reprimanded and warned to abstain in future from such utterances, for they would be visited with rigorous punishment. He promised to do this and was dismissed.[362]

With any one else this narrow escape, which shows the strong disinclination to deal harshly with him, would have ensured lasting caution, and even on Sánchez it seems to have imposed restraint for some years. The impression, however, wore away and the irrepressible desire to manifest his contempt for theology and theologians, and to display the superior accuracy of his wide learning, gradually overcame prudence. In 1588, he printed a little volume entitled De erroribus nonnullis Porphyrii et aliorum which, when subsequently examined by calificadores, was said to prove that the author was insolent, audacious and bitter, as were all grammarians and Erasmists; that, if its conclusions were true, we might burn all the theology and philosophy taught by the schoolmen, from the Master of Sentences to Caietano, and by all the universities, from Salamanca to Bologna. Another of his works bore the expressive title of Paradoxos de Theulugia, which went to two editions and was censured as requiring expurgation. Theology seems to have had for him the fatal fascination of the candle for the moth and, with his temperament, he could not touch it without involving himself in trouble. He gradually resumed his free speech and repeated his old assertions which he had promised to suppress, and to these he added new ones, such as approving the remark of a canon of Salamanca that he who spoke ill of Erasmus was a fraile or an ass, adding that, if there were no frailes in the world, none of the works of Erasmus would have been forbidden. From 1593 to 1595, Dr. Rosales, the commissioner at Salamanca, repeatedly forwarded to the Valladolid tribunal reports and evidence as to his relapse in these evil ways, and urged that he should be summoned and corrected and told not to meddle with theology but to confine himself to his grammar, for he knew nothing else.[363]

The tribunal had these various charges submitted to calificadores, who duly characterized them in fitting terms, but it took no action until May 18, 1596, when it commissioned Rosales to put in shape the informations against Sánchez. Rosales was replaced by Francisco Gasca de Salazar, who was instructed, September 17th, to finish the matter without delay. He returned the papers as completed, September 29th, adding that Sánchez was so frank that he said these things publicly, as a man unconscious of error and, if examined, would tell the truth and give his reasons; he did not seem to err with pertinacity but like the grammarians, who usually deal in paradoxes, for which reason Gasca said that he had taken no notice of them.[364]

***

Probably some restraint exercised by the Suprema explains why, after these preparations, four years were allowed to pass without action. If so, this restraint was suddenly removed, for there is no evidence that any fresh imprudences on the part of Sánchez stimulated the tribunal when, September 25, 1600, it took a vote that, in view of the previous warning and continued repetition of the same propositions and additional ones, and especially of the De Erroribus Porphyrii and other books suspect in doctrine, he should be summoned to the tribunal and a house be assigned to him as a prison, while all his books and papers should be seized. The Suprema confirmed this; on October 20th the summons was issued and, on November 20th, the books and papers were forwarded. On November 10th Sánchez appeared before the tribunal and, with kindly consideration, the house of his son, Dr. Lorenzo Sánchez, a physician residing in Valladolid, was assigned as his prison. Three audiences were held, on November 13th, 16th, and 22d, in which he said that, if he had uttered or done anything contrary to the faith, he was ready to confess it and reduce himself to the unity of the Church. As the charges were not as yet made known to him, he tried to explain various matters which were not contained in them, such as denying free-will, as holding the opinion that Magdalen was not the sister of Lazarus, and that Judas did not hang himself.[365]

No more audiences were held. The next document is a petition, dated November 30th, in which Sánchez set forth that he was mortally sick and given over by the physicians; that he had through life been a good Christian, believing all that the Holy Roman Church believes, and now, at the hour of death, he protested that he died in and for that belief. If, having labored for sixty years in teaching at Salamanca and elsewhere, he had said or was accused of saying anything against the holy Catholic faith, which he denied, if yet by error of the tongue it was so, he repented and begged of the Inquisition pardon and penance in the name of God. When taking pen in hand he had always recommended himself to God and, if in his MSS. there should be found anything ill-sounding, he desired it stricken out and, if there were useful things, he asked the Inquisition to permit their printing, as he left no other property to his children, and also that his enemies and rivals might be confounded. Finally, as he was in prison, by order of the Inquisition, he supplicated that he might have honorable burial, suitable to his position, and that the University of Salamanca be ordered to render him the customary honors.[366]

Thus closed, in sorrow and humiliation, the career of one of the most illustrious men of letters that Spain has produced. Under the existing system the Inquisition could do no otherwise than it had done, and its treatment of him had been of unexampled forbearance. That forbearance, however, seems to have ceased with his death. The records are imperfect, and we have no knowledge of the course of his trial which, as usual, was prosecuted to the end, but the outcome apparently was unfavorable. On December 11th the calificadores who examined his papers made an unexpectedly moderate report.

There was a certain amount of minute and captious verbal criticism, but the summing up was that he seemed somewhat free in his expositions of Scripture, attaching himself too much to human learning and departing too readily from received opinions, but he was easily excusable as these were private studies and mostly unfinished, so that his final opinions could not be assumed.[367]

Notwithstanding this, his dying requests were not granted. The interment was private and without funeral honors. As regards the University of Salamanca, Dr. Lorenzo Sánchez reported, on December 22d, that his father had many enemies there, that there was much excitement and scandal, and it was proposed not to render him the customary honors, to the great injury of his children's honor, wherefore he petitioned for orders to pay the honors and also the salary for the time of his detention. To this supplication no attention was paid, and the same indifference was shown when, long afterwards, on June 25, 1624, another son, Juan Sánchez, a canon of Salamanca, represented that malicious persons asserted that his father had died in the secret prison, wherefore he petitioned for a certificate that his father had not been imprisoned in either the secret or public prison, and that no sentence had been rendered against him. The influence of all this on the fortunes of his descendants can readily be estimated. As for the MSS. which had occupied the dying man's thoughts, the final judgement passed upon them left little to be delivered to the children.[368]

JOSEPH DE SIGUENZA

Another contemporaneous case is worthy of mention if only because the Geronimite Joseph de Sigüenza has customarily been included among the victims of the Inquisition, in place of which he sought its jurisdiction in order to protect himself against the machinations of his brethren. At an early age he had entered the Order, where his talents and varied learning gained him rapid advancement. When the Escorial was completed, Philip II sent for him to preach the first sermon in the church of San Lorenzo; since then he had preached oftener than any one else and many of the gentlemen and ladies of the court had selected him as their confessor. Philip placed him in charge of the royal archives and of the sagrarios and reliquaries of the two libraries, which brought him into frequent communication with the king, and he had utilized this to cause appointments and dismissals, and to institute reforms in the college of Párraces. This caused jealousy and enmity, and Diego de Yepes, the prior of his convent of San Lorenzo, endeavored to procure his removal. Then he incurred the hostility of the prior of the college, Cristóbal de Zafra, who was a florid preacher. In a sermon before the king on the previous Nativity of the Virgin (September 8th) he had said that the Minotaur was Christ and the Labyrinth was the Gospel and Ariadne was Our Lady and the child she bore to Theseus was faith, and if any one desired to enter the Labyrinth he must pray to the Virgin for her child. Such sermons were the fashion, and Diego de Yepes eclipsed this, on January 1st, when he told his audience that when Delilah had exhausted Samson she removed him from her and delivered him to the Philistines, so when the Virgin had exhausted God she removed him and placed him in the manger, with other equally filthy topics. Fray Joseph sought to repress this style of preaching, insisting that it should be confined to expositions of the Evangel and moral instruction, which gained him enemies among those whose eccentricities and bad taste he reproved. Another source of enmity was that he was entrusted with the selection of students to attend the lectures on Hebrew of Arias Montano, when he came to San Lorenzo, which angered those who were omitted. A formidable cabal was formed for his ruin; careful watch was kept on his utterances in unguarded moments and in the pulpit, and it was not difficult to collect propositions which, when exaggerated or distorted, might furnish material for prosecution.

It was safer to trust to a prejudiced court within the Order than to the Inquisition. A visitation of the convent and college was ordered, with instructions to withdraw the licence of any preacher or confessor found to be insufficient. The visitors came on April 13, 1592 and reported on the 17th. The frailes were examined separately and secretly and, of twenty-two, all but one offered objections to opinions uttered by Fray Joseph. From their testimony was extracted a series of nineteen propositions, most of them utterly trivial. He was accused of decrying scholastic theology, of holding that preaching should be based on the bare Scriptures, of exaggerated praise of Arias Montano at the expense of other expounders of Holy Writ, of advising a fraile to study Scripture in place of books of devotion and much else of the same nature. The frailes had learned the processes of the Inquisition; they submitted these propositions for qualification to Gutiérrez Mantilla, the chief professor of theology in the college, who rendered three opinions, varying in tone, but the final one declared that some of the propositions inclined to Lutheranism and Wickliffitism and others to Judaism. Moreover, on May 18th he wrote to the king, announcing the discovery of a dangerous heresy in the college of San Lorenzo which, if not checked at the outset, might bring upon Spain the dangers developed in other lands. It had spread among the students, some of whom, by the vigilance of the prior, were already in the Inquisition of Toledo, and he begged Philip to urge on the prior unrelaxing efforts to avert the evil.

All this had been done in secret, but enough reached the ears of Fray Joseph to convince him of the ruin impending at the hands of his brethren. Such matters belonged exclusively to the jurisdiction of the Inquisition and they could not prevent his appealing to that tribunal, in which he lost no time. On April 23d he presented himself at Toledo, with a letter from his prior, Diego de Yepes, stating that he was learned, able and a prior of the Order, but that some of his expressions in preaching and conversation had created scandal, in consequence of which he had been tried by visitors; this trial Yepes was ready to submit to the tribunal, and he asked that Fray Joseph be treated with its customary benignity. With this Fray Joseph handed in a written statement, containing what he had been able to gather as to the accusations, and submitting himself to the judgement of the Inquisition, both in correcting what was wrong and in accepting whatever punishment might be imposed.

The tribunal sent for the papers of the trial and assigned to him the convent of la Sisla as a prison, which he was not to leave without permission under the customary penalties. This confinement, however, was scarce more than nominal for, on May 14th, he represented that the king and court were at San Lorenzo, and his absence would be a great dishonor to him, wherefore he asked to have, by return of his messenger, permission to go there, which was immediately granted. Subsequently he was allowed the unusual favor of consulting with his counsel at the latter's house and, on October 21st, he asked licence to return to San Lorenzo for a month, because he was suffering from fever and his physician stated that his life was at risk at la Sisla--a request which was doubtless granted. The contrast is marked between his treatment and that of Luis de Leon.

THEOLOGICAL TRIVIALITIES

Meanwhile the trial was in progress with all customary formalities. The propositions were submitted to calificadores and, on July 30th, the fiscal presented the accusation, denouncing him as an apostate heretic and excommunicated perjurer, demanding his relaxation and asking that he be tortured as often as necessary. He duly went through the examinations on the accusation and publication of evidence, and presented eight witnesses, who testified to his distinguished reputation for learning, piety and orthodoxy, also that Fray Cristóbal de Zafra was noted for bringing fables and poetry into his sermons, and that Fray Justo de Soto, who had accused him of saying that Jews and Turks could be saved, was an ignoramus, knowing little of grammar and nothing of theology.

It was not until October 22d that was held the consulta de fe, which voted unanimously for acquittal; the Suprema confirmed the sentence, on January 25, 1593, when Fray Joseph was probably absent, for it was nearly a month before he appeared, on February 19th to hear it read. At his request a copy of it was given to him and thus ended a case in which the Inquisition was the protector of innocence against fraternal malignity.[369]

***

The extent to which Spanish intellect wasted itself in interminable controversies over the infinitely little, and the dangers to which all men were exposed who exercised the slightest originality, are illustrated in the case of Padre Alonso Romero, S. J., lector, of theology in the Jesuit college of Valladolid. For a proposition concerning the intricate question whether a man violates the law of fasting by eating nothing on a fast-day, his fellow-Jesuit, Fernando de la Bastida, with a number of students, denounced him to the Inquisition, August 29, 1614. The main proposition, and a number of others, on which it was based, or which were deduced from it, were pronounced by the calificadores, or at least by some of them, to be false, scandalous, rash and approximating to error. No less than seventeen witnesses were examined against him and when, on January 9, 1615, he presented himself, he admitted uttering the proposition, but said that he had consulted many learned men and the principal universities and he offered in defence the signatures of many Jesuits and of professors of Salamanca, Alcalá and Valladolid, to the effect that it was not subject to theological censure. The case proceeded to a vote in discordia, October 15th, when the Suprema ordered his confinement in a Jesuit house, that he should cease lecturing, and that the papers in his cell should be examined. On October 29th, while he was detained in the audience-chamber, his keys were taken and his papers were seized, although during this audience he stated that, when he found that many learned men condemned his proposition, he had retracted it publicly and had defended the opposite, which he offered to do again. To the ordinary mind this would appear to render further proceedings superfluous, but the assumed injury inflicted on the faith demanded reparation, and the case went on.

Thirty-three propositions, dependent on the first one, were submitted to calificadores and condemned as before, while nineteen others, extracted from his papers, were explained by him and dropped. Drearily and slowly the proceedings dragged along. On March 3, 1616, the accusation was presented, but it was not until June 6, 1619, that the publication of evidence was reached. Yet the case seems still to have been in the preliminary stage for on July 10th the Suprema ordered that the propositions, which had now grown to fifty-seven in number, should be submitted to calificadores and on their report the tribunal should decide whether to transfer him to the secret prison. It waited more than six months before it reached a decision, February 5, 1620, to make no change but, when the Suprema learned this, it ordered him to the prison of familiars, which was done on August 12th. Then, on the 18th, he selected patrones to advise him and, on September 25th, he presented the interrogatories for the witnesses in defence. On May 12, 1621, he was informed that all that he had required had been done for him. On July 5th the consulta de fe voted that he should be warned and required to retract the proposition respecting fasting and those derived from it--which he had already done spontaneously six years before; as for the others, he was acquitted. The Suprema took nearly a year to consider this and did not confirm it until June 2, 1622, when the trial ended with the reading of the sentence on June 30th.[370] All this reads like a travesty and might well be the subject of ridicule were it not for the serious import on a nation's destiny of a system under which eight years of a man's life could be consumed on a matter which the outcome showed to be so frivolous, to say nothing of the indefinite number of calificadores and officials whose energies were wasted on this solemn trifling.

THE PULPIT

Preachers were as liable as professors to prosecution for their utterances, and Spanish pulpit eloquence, as we have seen it illustrated in the case of Fray Joseph de Sigüenza, afforded ample field for censure. The auditor who took exception to anything heard in a sermon had only to denounce the speaker and, if the proposition was exceptionable, prosecution followed. Thus, in 1580, Fray Juan de Toledo, a Geronimite of the convent of Madrid, was denounced to the Toledo tribunal for having, in a sermon before Philip II, asserted that the royal power was so absolute that the king could take his vassals' property and their sons and daughters to use at his pleasure. Possibly this exuberance of loyalty might have escaped animadversion, had not the preacher called attention to the enormous revenues of the bishops, squandered on their kindred, and urged that the king and pope should unite to reduce them to apostolic poverty. On trial he admitted his remarks in a somewhat less offensive form; he attempted to disable the witnesses and presented evidence of good character without much success. The consulta de fe voted in discordia, and the Suprema sentenced him to abjure de levi, to recant, in the pulpit on a feast-day, the propositions, in a formula drawn up for him, to be recluded in a convent for two years, to be suspended from preaching for five years, and to perform certain spiritual penances.[371]

The severity of this sentence shows how little ceremony there was in restraining the eccentricities of the Spanish pulpit, even when it would be difficult to discern where suspicion of heresy came in. The formula of retraction prescribed rendered the humiliation of the ceremony most bitter. There were forms suited for the different characters of propositions, but all bore the essential feature that the culprit in the pulpit admitted having uttered the condemned expression; that the inquisitors had ordered him to retract it; that he recognized that it ought to be retracted and, as an obedient son of the Church and in fulfilment of the command, he declared, of his own free will, that he had uttered a proposition heretical and contrary to express passages of Holy Writ and, as such, he retracted and unsaid it and confessed that he did not understand it when he said it nor, for lack of knowledge, did he understand the evil contained in it, nor did he believe it in its heretical sense, nor understand that it was heresy and, as he had spoken evil and given occasion to be justly suspected that he said it in an heretical sense, he was grieved and begged pardon of God and the holy Roman Catholic Church, and begged pardon and mercy of the Holy Office. A notary with a copy followed his words and, if the performance was correct, made an official attestation of the fact.[372]

Instances of this sharp censorship of pulpit eloquence were by no means rare. Thus in the single tribunal of Toledo, after Madrid had been separated from it, Fray Juan de Navarrete, Franciscan Guardian of Talavera, was sentenced, December 19, 1656, for an heretical proposition in a sermon, to make a retraction. On April 21, 1657, Fray Diego Osorio, regent of studies in the Augustinian convent of Toledo, was required to retract, was suspended for two years from preaching and was banished for the same period from Madrid and Mascaraque. On April 23, 1659, the Mercenarian, Maestro Lucas de Lozoya, Definidor General of his Order and synodal judge of the province, was condemned to retract, was suspended from preaching for two years and was exiled from Madrid and Toledo. Similar sentences were pronounced July 14, 1660, on the Trinitarian Jacinto José Suchet, and August 31st on the Franciscan Juan de Teran. The Trinitarian, Juan de Rojas Becerro, December 24, 1660, was allowed to retract in the audience-chamber, but was suspended and banished for one year. Juan Rodríguez Coronel, S. J., on June 28, 1664, was suspended and banished for two years, but was not required to retract. These instances will suffice to indicate the frequency of these prosecutions and the manner in which such cases were treated. They offer a curious contrast to the mercy shown, January 31, 1665, to Sebastian Bravo de Buiza, assistant cura of Fresno la Fuente, who was only reprimanded and required to explain in the pulpit the most offensive proposition that the Virgin was a sinner and died in sin.[373]

This last case suggests that favoritism sometimes intervened to shield culprits and this would seem to be confirmed by the leniency shown, in 1696, to Fray Francisco Esquerrer. He was the leading Observantine preacher and theologian in Valencia and teacher of theology in the convent of San

Francisco in Játiva. It was an episode in the quarrel between Dominicans and Franciscans over the Immaculate Conception, when, November 13, 1695, the Dominican Fray Juan Gascon denounced him to the Valencia tribunal for having defended at Játiva, October 9, 1693, the proposition that Christ, in the three days of his death, was sacramented alive in the heart of the Virgin; that he who should die in defence of the Immaculate Conception would die a martyr, for it was a point of faith settled by Scripture, by the Council of Trent, by the Apostolic Council of Jerusalem and by the cult of the Church. Gascon had denounced this at the time, but the tribunal had taken no notice of it, and he now repeated the charge, adding that Esquerrer, preaching in 1693 at Olleria, had held it to be a point of faith that the adoration of latria was due to St. Francis; in the same year at Játiva he preached that Christ owed more to St. Antony of Padua than St. Antony owed to Christ. Also, when preaching about an image known as the Virgin of Salvation, he said that she was rather the Mother of Salvation than the Mother of Christ. Then, on August 28, 1695, preaching to the Augustinians of Játiva, he proved logically that the wisdom of St. Augustin was greater than the wisdom of the Logos and, on November 6, 1695, to the Franciscans of Játiva, he declared that the Immaculate Conception had been made a point of faith by Alexander VII and Innocent XI. Then the tribunal at last was spurred to action; it gathered evidence and procured from the calificadores a definition that some of the propositions were blasphemous, others heretical and others ill-sounding. Early in 1696 Esquerrer was thrown into the secret prison; he endeavored to explain away the propositions; the trial proceeded with unwonted celerity and, on September 9th, the case was suspended with merely the usual reprimand and the suppression of the propositions of October 9, 1693.[374] Apparently the Inquisition was content to have the people fed upon such doctrines.

It was probably less to favoritism than to indolence that we may attribute the outcome of the case of the Minim, Fray N. Serra, lector in the Barcelona convent of S. Francesco de Paula. On St. Barbara's day, December 4, 1721, he preached a sermon in which, among various other ineptitudes, he said that St. Barbara was a virgin and yet pregnant, and that Christ was the fourth person of the Trinity. An artillery regiment in quarters had been taken to the church and, in the evening, some of the officers, visiting Doña Bernarda Vueltaflores, amused themselves by repeating his grotesque utterances. A week later she chanced to mention the matter to Fray Antonio de la Concepcion and he, for the discharge of his conscience, carried the tale to the tribunal. Doña Bernarda was sent for, told what she remembered and furnished the names of the witnesses. They were summoned and gave their evidence. The fiscal fussed over it, said that he had only two concurrent witnesses, and wanted others of the audience looked up and examined, which was not done. The registers were searched, but no former complaints against Fray Serra were found. Then the fiscal asked that all the other tribunals of Spain be written to, which was postponed. On April 22, 1722 he had the propositions submitted to calificadores, five of whom unanimously pronounced that the one relating to Christ was formally heretical and the others scandalous and irreverent, rendering the culprit vehemently suspect and of little sense. Then ensued a pause until 1726, when in July replies were received from all the tribunals that they had nothing against Fray Serra. Then followed another pause, until June 27, 1728, when the inquisitors resolved that the case should be suspended after consulting the Suprema, which assented with the mild rebuke that, as the sumaria had been formed in 1721, it should have been acted upon at once, in place of waiting until 1728.[375]

***

Cognizance of the more or less trivial utterances of individuals continued to the last and formed an increasing portion of inquisitorial business as Judaism gradually disappeared. How the people were still taught to keep a watch over their fellows is exhibited in the case of Manuel Ribes, of Valencia, in 1798. He was a boy only nine years of age, attending a primary school, who was denounced by a fellow-pupil for an heretical expression. That the case was seriously considered is inferable from the fact that it was suspended, not dismissed, and remained of record against the child in case of future offences. How keen, moreover, was the inquisitorial eye to discern peril to the faith, is visible in the prosecution at Murcia, in 1801, of Don Ramon Rubin de Celis y Noriega, a dignitary of the cathedral of Cartagena and rector of the conciliar seminary, for a proposition concealed in his printed plan for instruction in Latin.[376]

RELIGION AND POLITICS

Under such impulses it is not a matter for surprise that, in this later period "propositions" furnished half the business of the tribunals. In the register compiled in Valencia of all the cases tried in Spain, after 1780 until the suppression of the Inquisition in 1820, the aggregate is 6569 cases, out of which 3026, or not far from one-half, are designated as for propositions. Of these latter 748 are noted as suspended or laid aside in Valencia, leaving 2278 carried on through trial. Of the 3543 cases for other offences, 1469, as we have seen, were for solicitation, leaving only 2074 as the total number for the miscellaneous business of the tribunals. Those accused for propositions represent every sphere of life, but a larger portion than of old belong to the educated classes--clerics, professional men, officers of the army, municipal officials, professors in colleges and the like.[377]

That this class of business should increase was natural in view of the infiltration of the irreligious philosophy and liberal ideas of the later eighteenth century, which escaped the censorship and watchfulness at the ports. The Napoleonic war poured a flood of this upon the land, traversed in almost every part by armies, whether hostile like the French or heretic allies like the English. After the Restoration, the duty of the Inquisition was largely the extirpation of these seeds of evil in a political as well as a spiritual sense, and propositions antipoliticas, as we shall see, were as freely subject to its jurisdiction as the irreligiosas. The punishments inflicted were not usually severe, but the trial itself was a sufficient penalty, for the accused was thrown into the secret prison during the dilatory progress of his case, his property was embargoed and his career was ruined, while in most cases he was subsequently kept under strict surveillance, for which the inquisitorial organization furnished special facilities.

As a typical case it will suffice to allude to that of two merchants of Cádiz, Julian Borrego and Miguel Villaviciosa, sentenced in 1818 by the Seville tribunal, for "propositions and blasphemies," to abjure de vehementi and to ten years' exile from Cádiz, Seville and Madrid, including service in a presidio. In consideration, it is said, of the extraordinarily long imprisonment which they had endured, the service of the former was only to be four years in Ceuta and of the latter six years in Melilla. As was so frequently the case at this time, the Suprema interposed in favor of leniency and reduced the term to presidio for both to two years. They were married men; the trial and sentence virtually meant ruin, and probably influence was exerted in their behalf for, after six months, the Suprema allowed them to return to Spain to support their families.[378]

What was the precise nature of the propositions the record does not inform us, but, had the offence been political, it is improbable that this mercy would have been shown. If it were religious, it may have been the deliberate expression of erroneous belief, or a hasty ejaculation called forth by an ebullition of wrath for, as of old the Inquisition took cognizance of everything and, in its awe-inspiring fashion, undertook to discipline the manners as well as the faith of the people. In 1819, the sentence of Bartolomé López of Córdova, for propositions, warns him on the consequences of his unbridled passion for gambling and lust, which had caused his offence, and, in another case, the culprit's inconsiderate utterances are ascribed to his quarrels with his wife, with whom he is urged to reconcile himself.[379]

***

Thus to the last the Inquisition, in small things as in great, sought to control the thoughts and the speech of all men and to make every Spaniard feel that he was at the mercy of an invisible power which, at any moment, might call him to account and might blast him for life.

CHAPTER VIII - SORCERY AND OCCULT ARTS

Man's effort to supplement the limitations of his powers by the assistance of spiritual agencies, and to obtain foreknowledge of the future, dates from the earliest ages and is characteristic of all races. When this is attempted through the formulas of an established religion it is regarded as an act of piety; when through the invocation of fallen gods, or of the ministers of the Evil Principle, or through a perverted use of sacred rites, it is the subject of the severest animadversion of the law-giver. When it assumes to use mysterious secrets of nature, it has at times been regarded as harmless, and at others it has been classed with sorcery, and the effort to suppress it has been based, not on its being a deceit, but a crime.

When the Roman domination in Spain was overthrown by the Wisigoths, the Barbarians brought with them their ancestral superstitions, to be superadded to the ancient Ligurian beliefs and the more recent Christianized paganism. The more current objectionable practices are indicated by the repressive laws of successive Wisigothic monarchs, and it illustrates the imperishable nature of superstitions that under their generalizations can be classed most of the devices that have endured the incessant warfare of the Church and the legislator for a thousand years. The Wisigothic ordinances were carried, with little change, into the Fuero Juzgo, or Romance version of the code, but their moderation was displeasing to Ramiro I, who, in 943, prescribed burning for magicians and sorcerers and is said to have inflicted the penalty in numerous instances.[380] It is not probable that this severity was permanent for, as a rule, medieval legislation was singularly lenient to these offences, although, about the middle of the thirteenth century, Jacobo de las Leyes, in a work addressed to Alfonso X, classes among the worst offenders those who slay men by enchantment.[381]

Alfonso himself, in the Partidas, treated magic and divination as arts not involving heresy, to be rewarded or punished as they were used for good or for evil.[382] In no land were they more widely developed or more firmly implanted in popular belief, for Spain not only preserved the older errors of Wisigothic times but had superadded those brought by the Moors and had acquired others from the large Jewish population. The fatalism of Islam was a fruitful source of devices for winning foreknowledge. The astrologer and the diviner, so far from being objects of persecution, were held in high honor among the Moors, and their arts were publicly taught as essential to the general welfare. In the great school of Córdova there were two masters who taught astrology, three of necromancy, pyromancy and geomancy, and one of the ars notoria. Seven thousand seven hundred Arabic writers are enumerated on the interpretation of dreams, and as many on goetic magic, while the use of amulets as preservatives from evil was universal.[383] Spain was the classic land of magic whither, during the middle ages, resorted for instruction from all Europe those who sought knowledge of its mysteries, and the works on the occult arts, which were circulated everywhere, bore for the most part, whether truly or falsely, the names of Arabic authors.

MEDIEVAL TOLERATION

Long after these pursuits had fallen elsewhere under the ban of the Church, the medieval spirit of toleration continued in Spain. Until the fourteenth century was drawing to an end, astrology, we are told, was in general vogue among the upper classes, while the lower placed full confidence in the wandering mountebanks who overspread the land--mostly Moorish or Jewish women--who plied their trade under the multifarious names of saludadores, ensalmadores, cantadores, entendederas, adivinas and ajodadores, earning a livelihood by their various arts of telling fortunes, preserving harvests and cattle, curing disease, protecting from the evil eye, and exciting love or hatred.[384] So little blame attached to these pursuits that Miguel de Urrea, Bishop of Tarazona from 1309 to 1316, was popularly known as el Nigromántico, and his portrait in the episcopal palace of Tarazona had an inscription describing him as a most skilful necromancer, who even deluded the devil with his own arts.[385]

The Church, however, did not share in this tolerant spirit and was preparing to treat these practices with severity. There is comparative mildness, in 1317, in the definition of its policy by Astesanus, the leading canonist of his time who, after reciting the ferocious imperial legislation, adds that the canons impose for these arts a penance of forty days; if the offender refuses to perform this he should, if a layman, be excommunicated and, if a cleric, be confined in a monastery. If he persists in his evil ways, he should, if a slave be scourged and, if a freeman, be imprisoned. Bishops should expel from their dioceses all such persons and, in some places, this is laudably accompanied with curtailing their garments and their hair. Yet the uncertainty still prevailing is indicated by the differences among the doctors as to whether priests incurred irregularity who misused in magic rites the Eucharist, the chrism and holy water, or who baptized figurines to work evil on the parties represented, and in this doubt Astesanus counsels obtaining a dispensation as the safest plan.[386]

All doubts as to such questions were promptly settled. Pope John XXII divided his restless activity between persecuting the Spiritual Franciscans, warring with the Visconti, combating Ludwig of Bavaria and creating a wholesome horror of sorcery in all its forms. Imagining that conspirators were seeking his life through magic arts, he ordered special inquisitors appointed for their extermination and urged the regular appointees to active persecution. In various bulls, and particularly one known as Super illius specula, issued about 1326, he expressed his grief at the rapid increase of the invocation and adoration of demons throughout Christendom, and ordered all who availed themselves of such services to be publicly anathematized as heretics and to be duly punished, while all books on the subject were to be burnt. The faithful were warned not to enter into compacts with hell, or to confine demons in mirrors and rings so as to foretell the future, and all who disobeyed were threatened with the penalties of heresy.[387] Thus the Church asserted authoritatively the truth of the powers claimed by sorcerers--the first of a long series of similar utterances which did more, perhaps, than aught else to stimulate belief and foster the development of the evil. The prosperity of the sorcerer was based on popular credulity, and the deterrent influence of prospective punishment weighed little against the assurance that he could in reality perform the service for which he was paid.

There was no Inquisition in Castile, and the repression of these unhallowed arts rested with the secular power, which was irresponsive to the papal commands. The Partidas, with their quasi approval of magic, were formally confirmed, by the Córtes of 1348, as the law of the land, and remained the basis of its jurisprudence. Yet the new impulse from Rome commenced soon afterwards to make itself felt. About 1370 a law of Enrique III declared guilty of heresy and subject to its penalties all who consulted diviners.[388] In this the injection of heresy is significant of the source of the new policy, reflected further in a law of Juan I, in 1387, which asserts that all diviners and sorcerers and astrologers, and those who believe in them, are heretics to be punished as provided in the Partidas, laymen by the royal officials and clerics by their prelates.[389] That these laws accomplished little is indicated by the increasing severity of the pragmática of April 9, 1414, which ordered all royal and local judges, under pain of loss of office and one-third confiscation, to put to death all sorcerers, while those who harbored them were to be banished and the pragmática itself was to be read monthly in the market-places so that no one could pretend ignorance.[390] Even the Mudéjares assimilated themselves in this to their Christian conquerors, threatening the practice of sorcery with death, and warning all to avoid divination and augury and astrology. This accomplished little, however, and, after their enforced conversion, the Moriscos continued to enjoy the reputation of masters of the black arts.[391]

INQUISITORIAL JURISDICTION

In the kingdoms of Aragon the secular power seems to have been negligent, and the duty reverted to the episcopate, which was for the most part indifferent. It was not wholly so, however, for, in 1372, Pedro Clasquerin, Archbishop of Tarragona, ordered an investigation of his province by testes synodales, and among the matters to be inquired into was whether there were sorcerers. Even Inquisitor Eymerich appears to consider it as in no way the business of the Holy Office, when he seeks to impress upon all bishops the duty of searching for such enemies of Christ, and of punishing them with all severity.[392]

In Castile, while all the arts of sorcery were reckoned heretical, jurisdiction over them remained secular, even after the establishment of the Inquisition although, among Isabella's good qualities, is enumerated her exceeding abhorrence of diviners and sorcerers and all practitioners of similar arts.[393] There was evidently no thought of diverting the Inquisition from its labors among the New Christians, when a royal decree of 1500 ordered all corregidors and justicias to investigate as to the existence in their districts of diviners and such persons, who were to be arrested and punished if laymen, while if clerics they were to be handed over to their prelates for due castigation.[394]

The question of jurisdiction, in fact, was a difficult one, which required prolonged debate to settle. It is true that, in 1511, a case in Saragossa shows the Inquisition exercising it, but a discussion to which this gave rise indicates that as yet it was a novelty. Some necromancers were condemned by the tribunal and the inquisitors asked whether confiscation followed. Inquisitor-general Enguera decided in the affirmative, but referred to Ferdinand for confirmation. The king instructed the archbishop to assemble the inquisitors and some impartial lawyers to discuss the question and report to him; their conclusion was in favor of the crown and not till then did he order the receiver to sequestrate and take possession of the property, which was considerable. The fact that it had not been sequestrated indicates that there had been no precedent to guide the tribunal.[395] Soon after this, in Catalonia, there came a demand for the more effective jurisdiction of the Inquisition, in order to repress sorcery. When the Concordia of 1512 was arranged, one of the petitions of the Córtes was that it should put into execution the bull Super illius specula of John XXII, and that the king should procure from the pope the confirmation of the bull. There was no objection to this, and Leo X accordingly revived the bull and ordered its enforcement in Aragon.[396] It must have been immediately after this that the Edict of Faith, in the Aragonese kingdoms, required the denunciation of sorcery, for, in the Sicilian instructions of 1515, issued to allay popular discontent, it was provided that this clause should only be operative when the sorcery was heretical.[397] Convictions, however, were few, at least in Aragon, for after those of 1511 there were no relaxations for sorcery until February 28, 1528, when Fray Miguel Calvo was burnt; the next case was that of Mossen Juan Omella, March 13, 1537, and no further relaxations occur in the list which extends to 1574.[398]

Castile followed the example of Aragon, and Archbishop Manrique (1523-1538) added to the Edict of Faith six clauses, giving in full detail the practices of magic, sorcery and divination.[399] Yet, as late as 1539, Ciruelo seems to regard the crime as subject wholly to secular jurisdiction, for he warns sovereigns that, as they hold the place of God on earth, they should have more zeal for the honor of God than for their own, and should chastise these offenders accordingly, being certain that they would be held to strict account for their negligence.[400]

PACT WITH THE DEMON

The question, in fact, was a somewhat intricate one, admitting of nice discussion. In 1257, not long after the founding of the Old Inquisition, Alexander IV was asked whether it ought to take cognizance of divination and sorcery, when he replied that it must not be diverted from its proper duties and must leave such offenders to their regular judges, unless there was manifest heresy involved, a decision which was repeated more than once and was finally embodied in the canon law by Boniface VIII.[401] There was no definition, however, as to what constituted heresy in these matters, until the sweeping declaration of John XXII that all were heretical, but in this there was a clear inference that his bulls were directed solely to malignant magic working through the invocation and adoration of demons. This, however, comprised but a small portion of the vast array of superstitious observances, on which theological subtilty exhausted its dialectics. Many of these were perfectly harmless, such as the simple charms of the wise-women for the cure of disease. Others were pseudo-scientific, like the Cabala, the Ars Notoria and the Ars Paulina, by which universal knowledge was attained through certain formulas. Others again taught spells, innocent in themselves, to protect harvests from insect plagues and cattle from murrain. There were infinite gradations, leading up to the invocation and adoration of demons, besides the multiplied resources of the diviner in palmistry, hydromancy, crystallomancy and the rest-- oneiroscopy, or dream-expounding, being a special stumbling-block, in view of its scriptural warrant. To define where heresy began and ended in these, to decide between presumable knowledge of the secrets of nature and resort to evil spirits, was no easy matter, and by common consent the decision turned upon whether there was a pact, express or implied, with the demon. This only created the necessity of a new definition as to what constituted pact and, in 1398, the University of Paris sought to settle this by declaring that there was an implied pact in all superstitious observances, of which the result could not reasonably be expected from God or from nature.[402] This marked a distinct advance in the conception of heretical sorcery, but it still left open the question as to what might or might not be reasonable expectation, and it was merely an opinion, albeit of the most authoritative theological body in Europe.

Discussion continued as lively as ever. In 1492, Bernardo Basin, a learned canon of Saragossa, considered it necessary to prove by logic that all pact with the demon, implicit or explicit, if not heresy was yet to be treated as heresy.[403] In 1494, the Repertorium Inquisitorum in quoting the canon law, that sorcery must savor of heresy to give jurisdiction of the Inquisition, still admits that there is no little difficulty in defining what is meant by savoring of heresy, while even at the close of the sixteenth century Peña tells us that no question excited more frequent debate.[404] It is true that, in 1451, Nicholas V had conferred on Hugues le Noir, Inquisitor of France, cognizance of divination, even when not heretical, but this had been a special provision, long since forgotten.[405]

The tendency, however, was irresistible to extend the definition of heretical sorcery, and to bring everything under the Inquisition. In 1552 Bishop Simancas argues that the demon introduces himself into all superstitious practices and charms, even without the intention of the man; he admits that many jurists argue that it is uncertain whether divinations and sorceries savor of manifest heresy, and therefore inquisitors have not cognizance of them, but the contrary is accepted by law, reason and custom, for it is a well-known rule that, when there is a doubt whether a judge has jurisdiction, the jurisdiction is his, and this matter is not exceptional; inquisitors can proceed against all guilty of these offences as suspect of heresy and this is received in practice.[406] Yet in practice these conclusions were reached tentatively. In 1537 Doctor Giron de Loaysa, reporting the results of a visitation of the Toledo tribunal, says that he has examined many processes for sorcery and desires instructions, for there are a number which are more foul and filthy than heretical; and even as late as 1568 the Suprema, in acting on the Barcelona visitation of de Soto Salazar, reproves Inquisitor Mexia for inflicting a fine of ten ducats and spiritual penances on Perebona Nat, for having used charms and uttered certain words over a sick woman; such cases, it says, do not pertain to the Inquisition, and in future he must leave all such matters to the Ordinary, to whom they belong.[407]

INFERENTIAL HERESY

The tribunals evidently were less doubtful than the Suprema as to their powers. Among the practitioners who speculated on popular credulity there were some called zahories, who claimed a special gift of being able to see beneath the surface when it was not covered with blue cloth, and who were employed to discover springs of water, veins of metal, buried treasure and corpses, as well as aposthumes and other internal diseases. There was no pretence of magic in this but, in 1567, Juan de Mateba, a boy of 14, who claimed among other gifts to be a zahori, was sentenced by the Saragossa tribunal to fifty lashes in the prison, to six years' reclusion in a convent under instruction, and subsequently to a year's exile, together with prohibition, under pain of two hundred lashes through the streets, to cure by conjurations, or to claim that he has grace to effect cures, to divine the future, or to see corpses and other things under the earth.[408]

Whatever doubts existed rapidly disappeared. It would be difficult to see where the heresy lay which earned, from the Saragossa tribunal, in 1585, a public scourging for Gracia Melero, because she kept the finger of a man who had been hanged, together with a piece of the halter, thinking that they would bring her good luck.[409] In fact, by this time the omnipresent demon was held accountable for everything. A case exciting considerable attention in 1588 was that of Elvira de Cespedes, tried by the tribunal of Toledo, who, as a slave-girl at the age of 16, was married to Cristóval Lombardo of Jaen and bore to him a son, still living at Seville. Subsequently at San Lucar she fell in love with her mistress and seduced her, as well as many other women. Running away, she assumed male attire and, during the rebellion of Granada served as a soldier in the company of Don Luis Ponce. In Madrid she worked in a hospital, obtained a certificate as a surgeon and practised the profession. At Yepes she offered marriage to a girl, but the absence of beard and her effeminate appearance caused her sex to be questioned; she was medically examined, pronounced to be a man and the Vicar of Madrid granted a licence under which the marriage was solemnized. Doubts, however, still continued; she was denounced to the magistrates of Ocaña, who arrested her and handed her over to the Inquisition. In the course of her trial she was duly examined by physicians, who declared her to be a woman and that her career could only be explained by the arts of the demon. This explanation satisfied all doubts; she was sentenced to appear in an auto, to abjure de levi, to receive two hundred lashes and to serve in a hospital ten years without pay. In this the tribunal was merciful, for hermaphrodites customarily had a harsher measure of justice.[410]

CONFIRMATION OF BELIEF

It is thus easy to understand how the definition of pact by the University of Paris came to be so extended as to cover every possible act that might be classed as superstitious--all the old women's cures and all the traditional usages and beliefs that had accumulated through credulous generations trained to place confidence in unintelligible phrases and meaningless actions--for any result greater than could naturally be produced, if not attributable to God was perforce ascribed to pact with the demon. Torreblanca thus assures us that, in the cure of disease, pact is to be inferred when nothing, either natural or supernatural, is employed, but only words, secretly or openly uttered, a touch, a breathing, or a simple cloth which has no virtue in itself. So it is with prayers and verbal formulas approved by the Church, but used for purposes other than those for which they were framed, or even exorcisms or conjurations against disease and tempests and caterpillars and drought, employed without the rites prescribed by the Church, or by those who have not the Order of Exorcists. There is pact in the use of idle prayers, as to stop bleeding with In sanguine Adæ orta est mors, or Sanguis mane in te ut sanguis Christi mansit in se; or of false ones, as for head-ache Virgo Maria Jordanum transivit et tunc S. Stephanus ei obviavit; or of absurd ones as the old Danatadaries, or the more modern Abrach Haymon etc., or that inscribed on bread Irivni Teherioni etc.; or that against the bite of mad dogs, Hax, Pax, Max. Suspect of pact are pious and holy prayers, in which some extraneous or unknown sign is introduced, written and hung on the neck, or anything by the wearing of which protection is expected from sudden death or imprisonment or the gallows: also the use of natural objects which, by their nature are not fitted for the expected results, or which are inefficient of themselves and are supposed to derive virtue from words employed, or are applied with prayers and observances not prescribed by the Church and, finally, all cures of disease which physicians cannot explain.[411] Moreover, theologians decided that in sorcery there was no parvitas materiæ, or triviality, which redeemed it from being a mortal sin.[412]

Thus all wise-women and charlatans became subject to the jurisdiction of the Inquisition, and no richer field for the folklorist can be found than in their numerous trials, where all the details of their petty devices and spells and charms are reported at length. There was the corresponding duty imposed on it to exterminate all popular superstitions throughout the land, and possibly it might have had a measure of success in this if it could have treated these practitioners as impostors. Unfortunately its jurisdiction over them was based on the reality of their exercising demonic powers, and their persecution only tended to confirm popular belief in the efficacy of their ministrations, while the public reading of their sentences con meritos spread abroad the knowledge of their powers and formulas.

If aught was lacking to strengthen belief in sorcery and divination it was furnished, in 1585, by Sixtus V, in his solemn bull Coeli et Terræ. In this he denounced astrology and all other species of divination, all magic incantations, the invocation and consultation of demons, the abuse of the sacraments, the pretended imprisonment of demons in rings, mirrors and vials, the obtaining of responses from demoniacs or lymphatic or fanatic women; he commanded all prelates and bishops and inquisitors diligently to prosecute and punish all who were guilty of these illicit divinations, sorceries, superstitions, magic, incantations and other detestable wickedness, even though hitherto they had no faculty to do so, and the rules of the Tridentine Index, prohibiting all works on divination and magic were to be strictly enforced.[413] The Spanish Inquisition, as we have seen, had long before exercised all the faculties conferred by the bull, and it is difficult to understand why, in 1595, it obtained for the first time, in the commission issued to Inquisitor-general Manrique de Lara, a clause covering all who practised these diabolical arts, and all who believed and employed them--a clause retained in all subsequent commissions.[414] The Inquisition, in fact, had not welcomed the bull, possibly in fear of claims based on it of cumulative episcopal jurisdiction. It did not allow it to be published in Spain until 1612 when, for some reason, a Romance version was printed and sent to all the tribunals with orders for its publication and enforcement, leading subsequent writers to attribute to it the cognizance of these matters by the Inquisition.[415]

EXCLUSIVE JURISDICTION

Not only had the Inquisition, as we have seen, exercised jurisdiction over sorcery, but as usual it claimed this to be exclusive and warned off all trespassers. As a matter of form it conceded that non-heretical sorcery was mixti fori--was subject to either the secular or spiritual court which first commenced action[416]--but non-heretical sorcery had become non-existent, and the Inquisition was as resolute in maintaining its exclusive claims in this as in all else. It mattered little that, in 1598, the Córtes petitioned for the total abolition of all kinds of sorcery, divination, auguries and enchantments, and that Philip II responded by ordering the revival and enforcement of the ferocious law of 1414 inflicting severe penalties on secular judges who did not put sorcerers to death.[417] If this produced any effect, which is doubtful, it was but temporary. Already, in 1594, we find the Toledo tribunal compelling the corregidor to surrender Isabel de Soto, after he had pronounced sentence. Her offences had been the giving of love-powders, which she asserted were holy and need not be confessed; curing a child with a parchment inscribed with crosses, and using certain divinations to bring a man from the Indies--all harmless enough frauds, for which she was sentenced to abjure de levi, to hear mass in the audience-chamber and to undergo six years of exile. This severity, however, was mercy itself in comparison with the corregidor's sentence, which had been scourging and perpetual exile.[418]

This assertion of exclusive cognizance continued. In 1648, Ana Andrés was undergoing prosecution in both the secular and episcopal courts, when the Valladolid tribunal claimed her, took her and tried and sentenced her.[419] In 1659, Pedro Martínez Ruvio, Archbishop of Palermo, issued an edict in which he proposed to enforce a brief of Gregory XV, in 1623, directed against sorcerers. The Suprema promptly presented to Philip IV a consulta, representing that simple superstitions were justiciable by bishops but, where there was even light suspicion of heresy, the Inquisition had exclusive cognizance. It could inhibit him with censures it said, but a royal order prohibiting him from proceeding with so prejudicial an innovation was preferable as less demonstrative, and there can be no doubt that Philip signed whatever letters the Suprema laid before him.[420]

When dealing with the common run of officials, the Inquisition enforced its claims with its customary peremptory aggressiveness. In 1701, the Valencia tribunal learned that the paheres, or local officials of Tortosa, were trying for sorcery Jusepa Zorita, Francisca Caset and a girl. On November 30th they were ordered to cease proceedings under pain of excommunication and five hundred ducats for each official concerned, while Pedro Martin Aycart, archdeacon of the cathedral, was commissioned, in case of disobedience, to post them on the church doors as excommunicated, and to take possession of the accused in the royal prison and hold them until further orders. There was some delay and, on January 4, 1702, the authorities of Tortosa were served with a demand, under the same penalties, to surrender the prisoners and the papers to Aycart, with notification that prosecution would follow refusal.

This was effectual; the prisoners were surrendered and were duly tried by the tribunal.[421]

***

Perhaps the most emphatic assertion of the authority of the Inquisition is to be seen in its treatment of astrology. All divination which pretended to reveal the future had long been regarded as heretical, on account of its denial of human free-will and its assertion of fate. This applied especially to astrology, with its array of horoscopes and its assumption that the destinies of men were ruled by the stars. It was on this ground that Pietro d'Abano, the greatest physician of his time, was prosecuted and only escaped condemnation by opportunely dying, in 1316, in Padua, and Cecco d'Ascoli, the foremost astrologer of the age, was burnt alive in Florence, in 1327. In spite of these examples, the profession of astrology continued to flourish unchecked, and astrologers were indispensable officials in the courts of princes and prelates. Theologians and canonists persevered in its condemnation. Ciruelo, while admitting that the study of the influence of the stars on the weather and on persons is lawful, like the practice of medicine, holds that foretelling from them what they cannot foreshadow can only be done by the aid of the demon, and all who practise this should be punished as half-necromancers.[422] Simancas classes astrology with all other methods of divination, which he attributes to the operation of the demon, and those who make everything depend upon the stars are perfected heretics.[423] These condemnations however were purely academical; the old prohibitions had become obsolete; belief in the science was almost universal; it was not only openly practised but openly taught, and there is significance in the fact that, in the Index of 1559, while there are general prohibitions of all books on necromancy and divination by lots, there is none of those on astrology, which must have been numerous, and only two obscure works on nativities are forbidden.[424] Indeed, one of the petitions of the Córtes of 1570 represents that in consequence of physicians not studying astrology many failed in their cures, wherefore the king was asked to order that in the universities no one should be graduated as a physician who was not a bachiller in astrology, to which the royal reply was that the Council would consult the universities and determine what was fitting.[425]

ASTROLOGY

It therefore manifests no little determination of purpose that, before Sixtus V, in his bull of 1585, had ordered the suppression of astrology by the Inquisition, the Suprema, in 1582, attacked it in its stronghold, the University of Salamanca, sending thither in March the Valladolid inquisitor, Juan de Arrese, with an edict condemning all the practices of the so-called science. In a letter of the 10th, Arrese says that he had been there for eight days, without having had an opportunity of publishing the edict, but he expects to do so the next day. Then, on the 20th, he reports that he is obtaining the first results and is overwhelmed with them; there are many who teach judicial astrology, both genethliacal, in casting nativities, and in answering all questions put to them, and they excuse themselves by saying that they only teach what is in the books that are permitted. Those inculpated under the edict are so numerous that it would be an infinite affair to punish them, and to overlook them would be worse, for they expect to be allowed to continue. Meanwhile he has taken testimony as to some and has suspended others till he receives orders, to which the reply was to go on taking testimony and report the results. Then, on March 31st he writes that he is still gathering evidence against the teachers of astrology, among whom are some who treat of invocation of demons and necromancy, especially Diego Pérez de Messa, who had been banished for other offences by the maestre escuela and is in hiding, but Arrese had ordered his arrest. Then, on April 24th, Arrese forwards a declaration drawn up by Maestre Muñoz, professor of astrology, for such action as the Suprema may please to take. At the same time he says that all those occupied in making astrological predictions excuse themselves on the ground that, under the statutes of the university, this is ordered to be taught; he suggests that the Suprema shall prohibit teaching from such books, and also judicial astrology, except as regards weather, but there are also indications of magic, about which he promises further information.[426] The documents before me fail to state what action the Suprema took with the professors and teachers, but that this was the condition in the foremost Spanish seat of learning indicates the magnitude of the task of eradicating beliefs so widely spread and so firmly established. That it forthwith suppressed the public teaching of astrology is indicated by the Prohibitory Index, which appeared the following year, 1583. This proscribed all books and writings that treat of the science of predicting the future by the stars, and it forbade all persons from forming forecasts as to matters dependent on free-will or fortune. Yet it conceded the influence of the stars by permitting the astrology which pertained to the weather and the general events of the world, agriculture, navigation and medicine, and also that which indicated at birth the inclinations and bodily qualities of the infant.[427]

This half-hearted condemnation was not calculated to overthrow the belief of ages, and astrology maintained its hold on popular credulity. It is said that, on the birth of Philip IV, in 1605, Philip III consulted the celebrated Argoli, master of astrology in Padua, as to his son's horoscope, and was told that the stars threatened the child with so many disasters that he would certainly die in misery if he had not for his inheritance the wide dominions of Spain--a prophecy which seems to have been suggested by the event.[428] However this may be, the Inquisition maintained its position and was active in prosecuting the practitioners of the science as a means of divination. An experienced writer, about 1640, states that, since 1612, astrologers had been rigorously punished. Judicial astrology was permitted only in so far as it related to commerce, agriculture and medicine. The casting of horoscopes to predict the future, especially with regard to the death of individuals--a frequent practice, productive of much evil--was punishable by appearance in a public auto, abjuration de levi, exile and fine proportioned to the means of the delinquent, while even further severity was due to its employment for the detection of thieves and finding things lost.[429] A clause was introduced, in the Edicts of Faith, requiring the denunciation of all engaged in such practices, with a careful accumulation of details that reveals how wide was the sphere of influence ascribed to the stars.[430]

PROCEDURE

The severity visited upon astrologers shows the determination of the Inquisition, and its estimate of the difficulty of the task. Ecclesiastics, as we have seen, except when relaxed, were spared appearance in public autos in order to avert scandal, but astrology was made an exception and the penalties were extreme. Thus, in the Toledo auto of October 7, 1663, there appeared Don Pedro Zacome Pramosellas, arch-priest of Brimano (Cremona) sentenced to abjure de levi and perpetual banishment from Spain, after three years of galley-service, besides prohibition to practice astrology or to read books on the subject. So, in the Toledo auto of October 30, 1667, the Licentiate Pedro López Camarena Montesinos, a beneficed priest of San Lorenzo of Valencia, for judicial astrology and searching for treasures, was condemned to abjure de levi, to four years in an African presidio, followed by six years' exile from Madrid and Toledo, suspension from Orders and deprivation of all ecclesiastical revenues.[431] This severity, doubtless, did much to aid advancing intelligence in outgrowing the ancient beliefs but, as late as 1796, we find Fray Miguel Alberola, a lay-brother of San Pedro de Alcántara, prosecuted in Valencia for using the "wheel of Beda"--evidently the Petosiris, a device by which the motions of the moon were used in place of the multitudinous and complex details of the stars and planets.[432]

***

Procedure in cases of sorcery had little to distinguish it from that in ordinary heresy, except that, as a rule, torture was not employed. One authority, indeed, tells that, although in Italy torture was used in cases of heretical sorcery, it was never used in Spain, but another assumes that in certain cases it was at the discretion of the tribunal.[433] That this discretion was used is seen in the Mexican case of Isabel de Montoya, a wretched old woman, in 1652, who freely confessed to numerous devices for procuring money--charms and philtres and conjurations. In addition to this was the evidence of her dupes, as to her stories of her relations with the demon, which required elucidation. She was tortured without extracting further confessions and then was sentenced to a hundred lashes, three years' service in a hospital and perpetual exile from Puebla.[434]

As pact with the demon was the basis of inquisitorial jurisdiction over sorcery, it was important to obtain from the accused admission of its existence. To this end, in 1655, the Suprema issued special instructions as to examination in all cases dependent on pact--instructions which reveal implicit belief in the reality of the powers claimed for sorcery. The accused was to be asked if the prayers, remedies and other things employed produced the expected results wholly or partially, and as they had not the natural virtues to effect this, what was the cause of the result. When, in the prayers or conjurations, certain demons were invoked, was it to make them appear and speak and in what mode or form. Whether the invocation was in virtue of a pact, express or tacit, with the demon and, if so, in what way had it been made. Whether the demon sometimes appeared in consequence of the prayers or conjurations and, if so, in what figure or guise, and what he said or did. With what faith or belief they did these things and framed the remedies, and whether it was with the intention and hope that the desired effect should be produced, and with the belief that they would attain it, and whether they held this for certain--with other similar interrogatories, suited for particular cases.[435]

PUNISHMENT

Based on these instructions a curious series of formulas was drawn up, adapted to all the different classes of offenders. As a sample of these we may take the one used in the examination of Zahories, who assumed to have a natural gift to see under the surface of the earth, involving no heresy, so that they were subject to the Inquisition only through an arbitrary assumption that their work must necessarily require the aid of the demon, in which there was no parvitas materioe, and that it was a mortal sin to employ them. The Zahori is to be asked whether it is true that he can see clearly and distinctly what is hidden under the earth and to what distance his vision penetrates; whether this power is confined to buried treasure, or extends to other things; at what age and on what occasion he first recognized the possession of this power; whether it is continuous, or stronger at times than at others; whether he has exerted this power and has found it effective; whether he has thus obtained treasures and, if so, of what kind or amount; who assisted him and whether the treasures were divided and what then happened; whether to reach the treasure, either in preparation or at the time of raising it, anything else was done, such as masses, prayers, conjurations, fumigations, invocations of saints or of other unknown names, or use was made of holy water, blessed palms, lights, genuflections, reading from a book or paper or other similar means; whether some treasures are more difficult to obtain than others and, if so, from what cause, such as enchantment; whether Zahories have any sign by which this power is recognized, and whether they recognize each other; in what principally does this power consist; whether money has been paid to him for pointing out a place where treasure was hidden and, if so, where he received it and what was the spot designated.[436] We can readily see how apt would be such an interrogatory, followed up by a trained examiner, to lead to admissions justifying implied pact, especially as there was a craze for finding buried treasure, and a wide-spread belief that stores of it were hidden underground, awaiting the coming of Antichrist, and guarded by demons, who must be placated or subdued before the gold could be secured.

In all this it is evident that the inquisitor, if conscientious, must himself have been firmly convinced of the truth that all the arts of sorcery, simple as many of them were, were based on demonic aid. Yet the occasional use of the term embustero shows that it was sometimes recognized that there was imposture as well as pact. Thus, in the Córdova auto of December 21, 1627, three women appeared, Ana de Jodar, sentenced to two hundred lashes in Córdova and one hundred in Villanueva del Arzobispo, with six years of exile; María de San Leon, to a hundred lashes and four years of exile and Francisca Méndez to vergüenza and exile. Now all these were declared to be sorceresses, invokers of demons with whom they had pacts, and their feats, as detailed in the sentences, showed them to be adepts and yet they were all stigmatized in addition as embusteras.[437] So, in the Saragossa auto of June 6, 1723, Sebastian Gómez is described as supersticioso y embustero, though his sentence of two hundred lashes and perpetual service in a hospital with shackles on his feet shows that his offence was not regarded as mere imposture.[438]

***

Severe as may seem some of the sentences alluded to, there is no question that, in most cases, the delinquents were fortunate in having the Inquisition as a judge rather than the secular courts, which everywhere showed themselves merciless where sorcery was concerned. We have seen the demand, in 1598, for the revival of the savage law of 1414, and this rigor had the support not only of popular opinion but of the learned. Ciruelo taught that all vain superstitions and sorcery were inventions of the devil, wherefore those who learned and practised them were disciples of the devil and enemies of God. There was no distinction between classes of offenders; all were to be persecuted with unsparing rigor. Thieves, he argued were properly hanged or beheaded, because every thief is presumed to be a homicide, and much more should it thus be with every sorcerer, as his efforts were directed rather against persons than property.[439] Torreblanca tells us that Huss and Wickliffe and Luther and almost all heretics contend against the punishment of sorcerers, but this is heretical, detestable and scandalous, and all orthodox authorities teach that they should be unsparingly put to death and be persecuted by both the spiritual and temporal swords.[440] It is well to bear in mind this consensus of opinion when considering the practice of the Inquisition. In the tribunals there was nothing to control the discretion of the judges save the Suprema, and that discretion showed itself in a leniency difficult to understand, more often than in undue harshness, and even their harshness was less to be dreaded than the mercy of the secular law. The systematic writers lay down the rule that, if the culprit confesses to pact with the demon, he is presumably an apostate; if he begs mercy he is to be admitted to reconciliation in an auto, with confiscation and a hundred lashes or vergüenza; if he is not an apostate, the reconciliation is modified to abjuration de levi and the scourging to vergüenza.[441] These rules, however, were not observed; reconciliation was exceedingly rare, abjuration de vehementi was unusual, abjuration de levi almost universal, and the tribunals exercised wide discretion in the infliction of the most diverse penalties.

A few cases will illustrate how completely the temper of the tribunal influenced the sentences. In 1604, Valencia seems to have had exceptionally lenient inquisitors. Alonso Verlango, desiring to compromise a suit, hired a woman to perform the conjuration of the ampolletas or vials, placing in them wine, sulphur and other things, and throwing them into the fire, with the adjuration that as they burnt so might the hearts of men come to an agreement. There was also the conjuration of the oranges, cutting nine of them and placing in them oil, soap, salt and other things, with the formula that, as oil gives flavor, so might it be with the men; also driving a nail into each and saying that the nails were driven into their hearts. In both of these conjurations were invoked Bersabu, Satanas and other demons, the great and the crippled, along with St. Peter, St. Paul and other saints. There was also a long conjuration with a virgin child by which one could learn whatever was desired. Verlango himself, moreover, used conjurations to discover treasures and possessed the Dream-book of Solomon, "Vaquerio" and Cardan de Proprietatibus Rerum. For all this he escaped with a reprimand and hearing mass in the audience chamber, abjuration de levi and two years of exile. Another case was that of Fray Miguel Rexaque, a priest of the Order of Montesa, who denounced himself for going with an Italian fraile, a virgin girl and some others, to discover treasure. They dug a hole; the Italian with an olive wand made a circle, in which was lighted a blessed candle; incense was burnt and the angels were summoned to drive away the demons guarding the treasure for the coming of Antichrist, and there was also a response from a demon obtained by the girl looking into a mirror. When the papers were submitted to the Suprema it ordered Rexaque to be reprimanded and the case to be suspended, while the girls who officiated had only a year's exile and some spiritual penances. More serious was the ease of Francois Difor, a French priest, and Francisco Juseria, a student, for it involved sacrilege. They sought the advice of an adept, who told them to baptize three coins with certain names and the coins when paid out would return to their purses. Difor solemnly baptized three pesos; Juseria spent them for fritters and pastry, but they did not come back. Under instructions of a confessor, they denounced themselves; they were duly tried and sentenced to abjure de levi, to be severely reprimanded and to perform some slight spiritual penances.[442]

Valladolid furnishes similar examples of leniency. In 1629, Isabel García, a married woman, under trial confessed that to regain a lover she had invoked the demon, who appeared in human shape, when she entered into explicit pact with him and performed various other sorceries, yet she was sentenced only to abjure de levi and to four years' exile from Valladolid and Astudilla. The next year Gabriel de Arroya, under pressure from a confessor, denounced himself and stated that, carried away by the passion of gambling, he had, during the last seven years, gone five times into the open fields, and invoked the demon to give him money for stakes, promising in return to devote his first child to the demon and offering to sign with his blood a pact to that effect. It is true that the demon never appeared, nor did he get money that seemed to come from such a source. In the consulta de fe, some of the members pronounced him to be vehemently suspect, others lightly, but it was finally voted to suspend the case without sentence and to reprimand him in the audience-chamber.[443]

***

There is contrast between these and some cases, in 1641, gathered in by a Valladolid inquisitor during a visitation in Astorga. Eight old men and women curanderos, whose offences consisted in superstitious cures of the most harmless character, were arrested and brought to Valladolid, where they were confined for months in the secret prison, to be finally sentenced to more or less prolonged exile, their simple ministrations being characterized as implicit pact with the demon. On the other hand, the Licentiate Pelayo de Ravanal, cura of Anicio, who charged twenty-three reales for blessing and ineffectually sprinkling with holy water a herd of sick cattle, and who failed in a superstitious cure of a husband and wife, was not arrested but was privately summoned and reprimanded in the apartments of the senior inquisitor. There were also two cases of loberos--practitioners whose speciality consisted in preserving sheep from wolves. One was Macias Pérez, a shepherd of Medina del Campo, accused by ten witnesses of having the wolves at his command, and using them to injure whom he pleased; five testified that he had threatened them with the wolves and that consequently many of their sheep had been destroyed. The other, Juan Gutiérrez of Baradilla, speculated on his neighbors, who gave him grain, kids, sheep etc., to preserve their flocks. The calificadores held this to be implicit pact but, although both were arrested, both escaped with reprimands.[444] The same moderation was exhibited by the tribunal of Toledo, in a curious case, in 1659. Juan Severino de San Pablo, of Wilna in Lithuania, was living as a hermit in the Sierra Morena. He had a skull which he had laboriously inlaid with silver images; this he exhibited and gave certificates as cures for tertian fevers. After his trial had been carried to the accusation, it was suspended; he was severely reprimanded and threatened with a hundred lashes for relapse; the skull was buried in consecrated ground, but not until the silver had been carefully removed and given to the receiver in part settlement for the culprit's maintenance in prison.[445]

There are two colonial cases which illustrate the capricious character of these judgements. In 1760, at Lima, a Guinea negro slave named Manuel Galiano, aged 70, was tried as a curandero. Several cases were in evidence in which he had cured swellings that had baffled the faculty, by making a small incision, inserting a hollow cane and sucking out blood, which would be accompanied with maggots, scorpions, lizards, snakes and the like, after which he would apply certain crushed herbs. It was decided that this inferred pact with the demon; he was arrested and freely admitted the cures, explaining that he hid the animals in the cane and blew them forth as though they had been drawn from the swelling; he had pronounced the patients to be bewitched and received four or five pesos for the cure; he had also pretended to give a charm to another slave. The case was simple enough but the trial was prolonged for three years, during which he lay in prison, to be finally sentenced to appear in an auto, with the insignia of sorcery and a halter, to vergüenza and to five years (counted from the time of his arrest) of service in a hospital.[446]

In wholesome contrast to this was a similar case in Mexico, in 1794. Juana Martínez was an Indian aged 40, married to a mulatto. She made her livelihood as a curandera, using a decoction of the root of a plant known as palo de Texer or Peyote, which she gathered with invocation of the Trinity and three signs of the cross--ceremonies which she repeated when administering the remedy--and she said that her patients ejected, from mouth and nose, insects, flies etc., which was a sign that they had been bewitched. She also had an image of the Virgin, which she kept in a little reliquary and declared that it performed miracles. In short, she was an accomplished embustera, and she richly earned the designation in the accusation of a simulator of miracles. Mariano de la Piedra Palacio, cura and ecclesiastical judge of their village, Temasunchale, arrested the pair and sequestrated their little property. By active threats of scourging he elicited a confession that she had invoked the devil who appeared and taught her the art, and that she operated by his power. It was a clear case of sorcery and he handed them over to the Inquisition. The long journey to Mexico was performed handcuffed and they were consigned to the secret prison, July 22. A little skilful pressure brought Juana to admit that both the miracles of the Virgin and the insects voided by her patients were impostures. The fiscal chanced to be somewhat of a rationalist and, on August 4th he presented a report of a character not usual in the Inquisition.

He pointed out that the consummate ignorance of Cura Mariano had already caused these poor creatures sufficient suffering in tearing them from their home, defaming them, arresting them obstreperously and sending them to the prison of the tribunal without reason or justice. It was he who was to blame, for their ignorance was attributable to him, whose duty it was to instruct them. Assuming then that there was no legal basis for prosecution and that their lies were sufficiently punished by what they had endured, the fiscal suggested their discharge, with orders to abstain in future from cures and miracles, under pain of rigorous punishment, while the cura was to be warned to avoid future meddling with what pertained to the Inquisition. He should also be told to restore to them the mare and colt which he had unlawfully embargoed, to send at his own cost proper persons to conduct the prisoners comfortably home, and moreover that he and his vicars must see to the proper instruction of his flock. The tribunal was not prepared to rise to this height of justice, but it discharged the prisoners and notified Mariano to return to them the mare and colt and whatever else he had seized, without charging for their keep, and further to present himself to the tribunal on his first visit to the capital.[447]

PERSISTENT BELIEF

Yet, notwithstanding the sanity of the conclusions reached in this case, there was no surrender of belief in the reality of sorcery and of demonic influence. Far more effective for the suppression of sorcerers was the position assumed, in 1774, by the Inquisition of Portugal under the guidance of Pombal. In its reformed regulations it takes the ground that malignant spirits cannot, through pacts with sorcerers and magicians, change the immutable laws of Nature established by God for the preservation of the world; that the theological argument of cases in which God permits such spirits to torment men has no application to legislature or law. Those who believe that there are arts which teach how, by invocations of demons, or imprecations, or signs, to work the wonders ascribed to sorcerers, fall into the absurdity of ascribing to the demon attributes belonging solely to God. Thus the two pacts, implicit and explicit, are equally incredible and there is no proof of them in the trials which for two centuries have been conducted by the Inquisition, save the unsupported confessions of the accused. From this it is deduced that all sorceries, divinations and witchcraft are manifest impostures, and the practical instructions, based on these premises, are that offenders are not to be convicted of heresy but of imposture, deceit and superstition, all of which is to be pointed out in the sentence, without giving the details as formerly. The penalties imposed are severe--scourging, the galleys and presidio, while if any one defends himself by asserting that these practices are legitimate, that a pact can be made with the demon, and that his operations are effective, he is to be confined, without more ado, in the Hospital Real de Todo os Santos--the insane hospital.[448]

The Spanish Inquisition was too orthodox to accept so rationalistic a view of sorcery, and continued to prosecute it as a reality. In 1787, Madrid was excited by an auto in which an impostor named Coxo was sentenced to two hundred lashes and ten years of presidio. He had thrived by selling philtres to provoke love, formed indecently of the bones and skin of a man and a woman, for which he had numerous customers, including ladies of quality. The affair abounded in lascivious details, which, when inscribed on the insignia hung in the church caused no little scandal.[449] In 1800, Diego Garrigo, a boy of 13, was prosecuted by the Seville tribunal for superstitious cures when, probably on account of his tender years, he escaped with a warning.[450] In 1807 the trial in Valencia of Rosa Conejos shows how the insatiable credulity of the vulgar was fed by the inexhaustible ingenuity of the impostor. She had been giving instructions as to charms by which supernatural powers could be gained, for the character of which a single example will suffice. After 11 o'clock at night, place on the fire a vessel full of oil; when it boils, throw in a living cat and put on the lid; at the stroke of midnight remove it and inside the skull of the cat will be found a little bone, which will render the person carrying it invisible and enable him to do whatever he pleases; the bone will ask "What do you want?" but if carried across running water it will lose its virtue.[451]

Under the Restoration, cases become less numerous than of old, but there is no change in the attitude of the Inquisition. In 1818, for instance, the Suprema on February 12th, ordered the arrest and imprisonment, by the Seville tribunal, of Ana Barbero, for superstition, blasphemy and pact with the demon and, for these offences, she was sentenced, October 15th, to abjuration de levi, spiritual exercises, six years of exile and two hundred lashes--the latter being humanely commuted by the Suprema to eight years' reclusion in a reformatory for loose women. The same tribunal ordered, June 17th, Francisca Romero to be thrown in the secret prison, with embargo of property, as a superstitious curandera and a year later, June 18, 1819, we find her sentenced to the ordinary penalties of exile and two hundred lashes, the latter of which were mercifully omitted by the Suprema.[452] Belief in the virtues of the consecrated wafer was as lively as ever and prosecutions were frequent for retaining it, as that of Doña Antonia de la Torre, in 1815, by the Granada tribunal, for taking repeated communions in a day, retaining the forms and converting them to an evil use.[453] Treasure-seeking was not forgotten. In 1816 the Santiago tribunal discovered a book of conjurations for the purpose, which was promptly prohibited by edict, all copies were to be seized, investigation was ordered into popular beliefs and Fray Juan Cuntin y Duran was prosecuted for using the conjurations. This probably led to the discovery, in 1817, at Tudela of a similar MS. work which the Suprema ordered to be suppressed.[454]

***

It is easy to understand that the prosecution of sorcery constituted a not inconsiderable portion of the duties of the Inquisition, at least during the later stages of its career. Cases were comparatively few as long as only serious matters were held to fall within its jurisdiction but, with the extended definition of pact, they increased considerably and, as the business of prosecuting Moriscos and Judaizers declined, its energies were more largely directed to the wise-women and the sharpers who found a precarious livelihood in the vulgar superstitions pervading the community. Thus, in the Toledo record, from 1575 to 1610, out of a total of 1172 cases, there are only eighteen of sorcery, or a trifle over one and a half per cent., while, in the same tribunal from 1648 to 1794 there are a hundred out of a total of 1205, or about eight and one-third per cent.[455] Occasionally they furnish the chief part of the business of a tribunal. In the Valencia auto of July 1, 1725, fifteen of the eighteen penitents were sorcerers and, in that of Córdova, December 5, 1745, there were five out of eight.[456] A record of the business of all the tribunals, from 1780 to the suppression in 1820, furnishes a total of four hundred and sixty-nine cases of which a hundred and sixteen may be classed as maleficent and three hundred and fifty-three as merely superstitious.[457]

Belief in the powers of sorcery had been too strongly inculcated to disappear with the cessation of persecution. A modern writer assures us that all the old superstitions flourish as vigorously as ever-- conjurations and formulas to cure or to kill, to foretell the future, to create love or hatred, to render men impotent and women barren, to destroy the flocks and herds and harvests, to bring tempests and hail-storms. The wise-woman is as potent as of yore in her control of the forces of nature and the passions of man, and the profession is as well filled and as well paid as in the sixteenth century.[458] We can readily believe this when Padre Cappa, S. J., in his defence of the Inquisition, gravely assures us that communications and compacts with the demon are incontestable and are as frequent as formerly.[459]

***

We have still to consider a further development of the belief in the malignant power of the demon working through human instruments, in which the Inquisition of Spain rendered a service of no little magnitude.

CHAPTER IX - WITCHCRAFT

The culmination of sorcery was witchcraft and yet it was not the same. In it there is no longer talk of pact with the demon, express or tacit, to obtain certain results, with the expectation of washing out the sin in the confessional and thus cheating the devil. The witch has abandoned Christianity, has renounced her baptism, has worshipped Satan as her God, has surrendered herself to him, body and soul, and exists only to be his instrument in working the evil to her fellow-creatures, which he cannot accomplish without a human agent. That such a being should excite universal detestation was inevitable, and that no effort should be spared for her extermination was the plainest duty of legislator and judge. There are no pages of European history more filled with horror than those which record the witch-madness of three centuries, from the fifteenth to the eighteenth. No land was more exposed to the contagion of this insanity than Spain where, for more than a hundred years, it was constantly threatening to break forth. That it was repressed and rendered comparatively harmless was due to the wisdom and firmness of the Inquisition.

THE SABBAT

This witch-madness was essentially a disease of the imagination, created and stimulated by the persecution of witchcraft. Whereever the inquisitor or civil magistrate went to destroy it by fire, a harvest of witches sprang up around his footsteps. If some old crone repaid ill-treatment with a curse, and the cow of the offender chanced to die or his child to fall sick, she was marked as a witch; the judge had no difficulty in compelling such confession as he desired and in obtaining a goodly list of accomplices; everyone who had met with ill-luck hurried forward with his suspicions and accusations. Every prosecution widened the circle, until nearly the whole population might become involved, to be followed by executions numbered, not by the score but by the hundred, in blind obedience to the scriptural injunction "Thou shalt not suffer a witch to live." All destructive elemental disturbances--droughts or flood, tempests or hail-storms, famine or pestilence--were ascribed to witchcraft, and victims were sought, as though to offer propitiatory holocausts to the infernal gods or expiatory sacrifices to the Creator.

Belief in witchcraft was of comparatively recent origin, dating from the middle of the fourteenth century. Malignant sorcery had been known before, but the distinctive feature of the Sabbat first makes its appearance at this period--the midnight gathering to which the devotees of Satan were carried through the air, where they renounced Christ and worshipped their master, in the shape usually of a goat, but sometimes in that of a handsome or hideous man; where they feasted and danced and indulged in promiscuous intercourse, accommodating demons serving as incubi or succubi, and were conveyed back home, where other demons, assuming their shape, had protected their absence from observation.[460]

The development of this myth would seem ascribable to the increasing rigor of persecution towards the end of the fourteenth century, when, as we have seen, the University of Paris formulated the theory that pact with Satan was inherent in all magic, leading judges, in their eager exploration of cases brought before them, to connect this assumed pact with an old belief of night-riders through the air, who swept along in gathering hosts. With the methods in use, the judge or the inquisitor would have little difficulty in finding what he sought. When once such a belief was disseminated by trials and executions, the accused would seek to escape endless torture by framing confessions in accordance with leading questions and thus a tolerably coherent, though sometimes discordant, formula was developed, to which witches in every land were expected to conform. That this was a new development is shown by the demonologists of the fifteenth century--Nider and Jaquerius, Sprenger and Bernardo da Como--treating witches as a new sect, unknown before that age, and to this Innocent VIII impliedly gave the sanction of the Holy See in his well-known bull, Summis desiderantes, in 1484. This rapidly growing belief in the power of witchcraft and the duty of its extermination were stimulated by nearly every pope for almost a hundred years--by Eugenius IV in 1437 and 1445, by Calixtus III in 1457, by Pius II in 1459, and, after the special utterance of Innocent VIII, by Alexander VI in 1494, by Julius II, by Leo X in 1521, by Adrian VI, in 1523 and by Clement VII in 1524.[461]

While, for the most part, the so-called confessions of witches under trial were the result of the torture so unsparingly employed, there can be little doubt that at least a portion were truthful accounts of illusions really entertained. Even as the trances and visions of the mystics, such as Santa Teresa and the

Venerable María de Agreda, are attributable to auto-hypnotism and auto-suggestion so, when the details of the Sabbat were thoroughly established and became as much a part of popular belief as the glories seen in mystic ecstasy, it is easy to understand how certain temperaments, seeking escape from the sordid miseries of laborious poverty, might acquire the power of inducing trances in which the transport to the meeting-place, the devil-worship and the sensual delights that followed, were impressed upon the imagination as realities. The demonographers give us ample accounts of experiments in which the suspected witch was thrown into a trance by the inunction of her ointment and, on awaking, gave a detailed account of her attendance on the Sabbat and of what she did and saw there. This should be borne in mind when following the long debate between those who upheld the reality of the Sabbat and those who argued that it was generally or always a delusion.

***

To appreciate the attitude of the Spanish Inquisition in this debate the origin of the myth must be understood. The flying by night of female sorcerers to places of assemblage was an ancient belief, entertained by Hindus, Jews and the classical nations. This was handed down through the middle ages, but was regarded by the Church as a relic of paganism to be suppressed. There was an utterance, not later than the ninth century, which denounced as an error, induced by the devil, the popular belief that wicked women ride through the air at night under the leadership of Diana and Herodias, wherefore priests everywhere were commanded to disabuse the faithful and to teach that those who professed to take part in these nocturnal excursions were deluded by dreams inspired by the demon, so that he who believed in their reality entertained the faith of the devil and not that of God. This utterance was ascribed to an otherwise unknown Council of Anquira; it passed through all the collections of canons-- Regino, Burchard and Ivo--found a place finally in the authoritative Decretum of Gratian, where it became known to canonists as the canon Episcopi.[462]

When, therefore, in the fifteenth century, there was formulated the perfected theory of the witches' Sabbat, it had to struggle for existence. No theologian stood higher than St. Antonino, Archbishop of Florence, yet in his instructions to confessors, he requires them to ascertain from penitents whether they believe that women can be transformed into cats, can fly by night and suck the blood of children, all of which he says is impossible, and to believe it is folly. Nor was he alone in this, for similar instructions are given by Angelo da Chivasso and Bartolommeo de Chaimis in their authoritative manuals.[463] The new school could only meet the definitions of the can. Episcopi by asserting that witchcraft was the product of a new sect, more pernicious than all former inventions of the demon. This brought on a warm discussion between lawyers like Ponzinibio on the one side and papal theologians on the other, such as Silvester Prierias, Master of the Sacred Palace and his successor Bartolommeo Spina, and the authority of the Holy See triumphed over scepticism.

Spain, in the fifteenth century, lay somewhat out of the currents of European thought, and the new doctrine as to the Sabbat found only gradual acceptance there. Alfonso Tostado, Bishop of Avila, the most learned Spanish theologian of the time, in 1436, treats the Sabbat as a delusion caused by the inunction of drugs, but subsequently he argues away the can. Episcopi and says that the truth is proved by innumerable cases and by the judicial penalties inflicted.[464] Even so bigoted and credulous a writer as Alonso de Espina treats it as a delusion wrought by the demon to whom the witch has given herself and so does Cardinal Torquemada, in his Commentary on the Decretum.[465] Martin de Arles, Canon of Pampeluna, speaks of the Broxæ who flourished principally in the Basque provinces, north of the Pyrenees; the belief in them he treats as a false opinion and quotes the can. Episcopi as authoritatively proving it to be a delusion. At the same time he admits that sorcerers can ligature married folk, can injure men and devastate their fields and harvests, which are works of the demon operating through them.[466] Bernardo Basin, of Saragossa, who had studied in Paris, took a middle ground; the Council of Anquira is not authoritative, in some cases there may be illusions sent by the demon, in others the Sabbat is a reality.[467] In 1494, the Repertorium Inquisitorum recognizes the existence of witches, who were popularly known as Xorguinas; it quotes the essential portion of the can. Episcopi in answer to the question whether they are justiciable by the Inquisition, adding that such a belief is an illusion wrought by the demon but, although it is folly, it is infidelity worse than paganism, and can be prosecuted as heresy.[468] The Inquisition itself could have no doubt as to its powers; if the Sabbat was true, the witch was an apostate; if a delusion, she was a heretic and in either case subject to its jurisdiction.

DOUBT AND INQUIRY

This reference to Xorguinas shows that witches were already well known in Spain, and we can assume from subsequent developments that their principal seat was in the mountainous districts along the Pyrenees, penetrating perhaps from France and favored by the ignorance of the population, its sparseness and poverty.[469] The earliest case, however, that I have met of prosecution by the Inquisition was in 1498, when Gracia la Valle was burnt in Saragossa. This was followed in 1499 by the burning of María, wife of García Biesa and, in January 1500, by that of three women, Nanavina, Estefabrita and Marieta, wife of Aznar Pérez. There was an interval then until 1512, when there were two victims, Martina Gen and María de Arbués. There was no other in Saragossa until 1522, when Sancha de Arbués suffered, and the last one in the record is Catalina de Joan Díez, in 1535.[470] Persecution would seem to be more active in Biscay, for Llorente quotes from a contemporary MS. a statement that in 1507 there were burnt there more than thirty witches, leading Martin de Arles y Andosilla to write a learned treatise on the subject, printed in Paris in 1517.[471] It would seem that, in 1517, there was a persecution on foot in Catalonia, for the Barcelona inquisitors were ordered to visit the mountainous districts, especially in the diocese of Urgel, to publish edicts against the witches and to prosecute them with all rigor.[472] Doubtless there were other developments of which no trace has reached us, and there was every prospect that Spain would be the seat of an epidemic of witchcraft which, if fostered by persecution, would rival the devastation commencing throughout the rest of Europe.

The time had scarce come for a change of policy, but there is a manifestation of a spirit of doubt and inquiry, very different from the unreasoning ferocity prevalent elsewhere. Arnaldo Albertino tells that, in 1521, at Saragossa, by command of Cardinal Adrian, he was called in consultation by the Suprema, over two cases, when he pronounced the Sabbat to be a delusion.[473] Possibly one of these cases may have been the woman who, we have seen, was burnt at Saragossa in 1522, but the effect of such a discussion is visible, in this same year 1522, in an Edict of Grace addressed to the witches of Jaca and Ribagorza, granting them six months in which to come forward and confess their offences.[474] Considering that, about this time, Leo X and Adrian VI were vigorously promoting the massacre by wholesale of witches in the Lombardo-Venitian valleys, and resenting any interference with the operation of the inquisitors, such action on the part of the Suprema is of marked significance.

It evidently felt the matter to be one requiring the most careful consideration and, on the outbreak of a witch-craze in Navarre, stimulated by the secular authorities, it assembled, in 1526, a "congregation" in Granada, laid the papers before it and asked its examination of the whole subject, which was condensed into six questions, going to the root of the matter: 1. Whether witches really commit the crimes confessed, or whether they are deluded. 2. Whether, if these crimes are really committed, the culprits are to be reconciled and imprisoned, or to be delivered to the secular arm. 3. Whether, if they deceive and do not commit these things, they are to be similarly punished, or otherwise. 4. Whether the cognizance of these crimes pertains to the Inquisition and if so, whether this is fitting. 5. Whether the accused are to be judged on their confessions without further evidence and to be condemned to the ordinary punishment. 6. What will be a wholesome remedy to extirpate the pest of these witches.[475] The mere submission to rational discussion of such a series of questions shows a desire to reach a just method of treatment, wholly at variance with practice elsewhere, when legislators and judges were solely occupied with devising schemes to fight the devil with his own weapons and to convict, per fas et nefas, the unfortunates who chanced to incur suspicion.[476]

***

The ten members of the congregation were all men of consideration and included the Licentiate Valdés, in whom we may recognize the future inquisitor-general. On the first question, as to reality or delusion, the vote stood six to four in favor of reality, Valdés being one of the minority and explaining that he regarded the proofs of the accusations as insufficient, and desired inquisitors to be instructed to make greater efforts at verification. The second question was of the highest importance. For ordinary heresy, confession and repentance ensured exemption from the stake but, in the eagerness to punish witchcraft, when a witch confessed it was customary to abandon her, either formally or informally, to be punished by the secular authorities for the crimes assumed to be proved against her--usually sucking the blood of children or encompassing the death of adults. Obedience to the Scriptural injunction of not suffering a witch to live was general.[477] On this point there was wide variety of opinion, but the majority decided that, when culprits were admitted to reconciliation, they were not to be remitted to the secular judges, to be punished for homicides, for such homicides might be illusory, and there was no proof beyond their confessions; after they had completed the penance assigned to them, if the secular judges chose to try them for homicide, the Inquisition could not interfere. This decision was adopted in practice and, some years later, was cited in justification of protecting convicted witches from the secular courts.

ACTIVE PERSECUTION

On the third question, votes were too much divided for any definite result. On the fourth there was substantial affirmative agreement. On the fifth, five voted that confession sufficed, but Valdés limited its sufficiency to the minor inflictions of exile, vergüenza and scourging. With regard to the final question, as to remedial measures, it is worthy of remark that only three suggested greater activity and severity of the Inquisition; nearly all favored sending preachers to instruct and enlighten the ignorant population; two proposed reforming the regular clergy, and one the secular beneficed clergy; several thought well of building churches or monasteries on the spots where the Sabbats were held; one recommended an edict promising release from confiscation for those who would come forward within a specified time, and two voted that the Inquisition should give material aid to the poorer suspects, in order to relieve them from temptation. Valdés further presented detailed instructions for inquisitors, the most important of which were that the statements of witches implicating other parties were not to be accepted as satisfactory evidence, and that, when accused to the Inquisition, it should be ascertained whether they had already been tortured by the secular judges.[478] Halting as these deliberations may seem, they manifest gleams of wholesome scepticism and an honest desire to reach the truth, when elsewhere throughout Christendom such questions were regarded as beyond discussion. Yet for awhile the Suprema was not prepared to allow these opinions to influence action. In 1527 there was an outbreak of witchcraft in Navarre, the treatment of which by Inquisitor Avellaneda he reports in a letter written, in response to an inquiry from Iñigo de Velasco, Constable of Castile. Witchcraft, he declared, was the worst evil of the time; he had written to the king and twice to the Suprema urging a remedy, but neither at court nor on the spot was there any one who understood its cure. For six months he had been laboring in the mountains, where, by the help of God, he had discovered many witches. In a raid on the valley of Salazar he had captured a number and brought them to Pampeluna where, with the regent and members of the Royal Council and other doctors and lawyers, the whole subject was discussed; it was agreed that witches could be carried through the air to the Sabbat, and that they committed the crimes ascribed to them--principally, it would seem, on the strength of an experiment which he had tried with one of his prisoners. On a Friday at midnight he allowed her to anoint herself with the magic unguent which they used; she opened a window overhanging a precipice, where a cat would be dashed to pieces, and invoked the demon who came and deposited her safely on the ground--to be recaptured on Monday with seven others, three leagues away. These were all executed, after which he prosecuted his researches and discovered three places of assemblage--one in the valley of Salazar, with two hundred and fifty members, of whom he had captured sixty, another with eighty members in another valley and a third near Roncesvalles with over two hundred. Fifty had been executed and he hoped, with the favor of God to despatch twenty more. He had discovered that which, if proper assistance were given to him, would redound to the great service of God and benefit to the Republic for, without God's mercy, the evil would grow and the life of no one would be safe. To gratify the curiosity of the constable, Avellaneda proceeded to give a detailed account of the wonders and wickedness of the Sabbat and the evils wrought by witches. In spite of all his efforts the demon urged them on to still greater crimes by showing them phantoms of those who had been executed, pretending that he had resuscitated them and would resuscitate all who might be put to death. This evil, he concludes, is general throughout the world. If the constable wishes to ascertain whether there are witches in his district, he has only to observe whether the grain is withered while in bloom, or the acorns fail in the mountains, or there are children smothered, for wherever these things occur, there are witches.[479] Altogether, Avellaneda affords a typical illustration of the manner in which witchcraft was created and spread by the witch-finders.

There is no reason to suppose that Avellaneda was reproved for the exuberance of his zeal, for his policy was continued in 1528, when the witch epidemic was extending to Biscay, and the civil authorities were arresting and trying offenders. More eager to assert the jurisdiction of the Inquisition than to adopt the conclusions of the congregation, on February 22, 1528, Inquisitor-general Manrique ordered Sancho de Carranza de Miranda, Inquisitor of Calahorra, to go thither with full powers to investigate, try and sentence, even to relaxation, the witches who are reported to have abandoned the faith, offered themselves to the devil and wrought much evil in killing infants and ruining the harvests. He is to demand from the civil authorities all who have been arrested and the papers concerning their cases, for this is a matter pertaining to the Inquisition. A thorough inquest is to be made in all infected places, and edicts are to be published summoning within a given time and under such penalties as he sees fit, all culprits to come forward and all cognizant of such offences to denounce them.[480] There is in this no injunction of prudence and caution, no requirement that the cases are to be submitted for confirmation to the Calahorra tribunal; Carranza is provided with a fiscal and a notary, so that he can execute speedy justice and the Edict of Grace is replaced by an Edict of Faith.

It is not until 1530 that we find evidence that the discussion of 1526 was producing a change in the view taken of witchcraft and of the methods of its repression. A carta acordada, addressed to all the tribunals, enjoined special caution in all witchcraft cases, as it was a very delicate matter to handle, and this was followed by another manifesting a healthy scepticism and desire to repress popular superstition, for it stated that the ensalmadores, who cured diseases by charms, asserted that all sickness was caused by witches, wherefore they were to be asked what they meant and why they said so.[481]

ZEAL RESTRAINED

The practical position assumed by this time may be gathered from a letter of December 11, 1530, from the Suprema to the Royal Council of Navarre, when a fresh outbreak of the witch-craze had, as usual, brought dissension between the tribunal and the secular courts, for the latter refused to acknowledge the exclusive jurisdiction of the Inquisition, and complained of its delays and the leniency of its sentences, in comparison with the speedy and unsparing action demanded by popular clamor. The Suprema now, in reply to the complaints of the Royal Council against the Calahorra tribunal, replied that this matter of the witches was not new; on a previous occasion there had been the same altercation; some of the cases which had caused the most complaint had been brought to the court and had, by order of the emperor, been examined by learned men when, after much debate, it was ordered that the prisoners should be delivered to the inquisitors who, after examining them, should try those pertaining to their jurisdiction and surrender the others. There was much doubt felt as to the verification of the crimes alleged, and the Suprema deplored the executions by the secular courts, for the cases were not so clear as had been supposed. In view of all this, inquisitors were enjoined to use caution and moderation, for there is so much ambiguity in these cases that it seems impossible for human reason to reach the truth. When the same questions had arisen elsewhere, the Suprema had ordered the inquisitors to act with the greatest circumspection, for these matters were most delicate and perilous, and some inexperienced judges had been deceived in treating them. The Suprema therefore deprecated a competencia; it entreated the Royal Council to hand all cases over to the tribunal, which would return those not subject to its jurisdiction, and the inquisitors would be ordered to remove the censures and fines--which shows that the quarrel had been pushed to extremes.[482] There was equal determination in resisting the claims of the episcopal courts to jurisdiction. In 1531 the Saragossa tribunal complains of the intrusion of the Bishop of San Angelo, who had refused to surrender a prisoner and had invited the tribunal to join him in prosecuting witches in places under his jurisdiction. To him the Suprema accordingly wrote, asserting the exclusive cognizance of the Inquisition and requiring him to deliver to the tribunal any prisoners whom he had arrested.[483]

The cautious and sceptical attitude assumed by the Suprema was all the more creditable because the leading authorities of the period were firm in their conviction of the reality of witchcraft. Arnaldo Albertino, himself an inquisitor who, in 1521, had deemed the Sabbat an illusion, writing about 1535, says that since then, on mature consideration, he had reached the opposite opinion; he now accepts all the horrors and crimes ascribed to witches and argues away the can. Episcopi. Alfonso de Castro, another writer of the highest distinction at this time, gives full credence to the most extravagant stories of the Sabbat, and he disposes of the can. Episcopi by asserting that it referred to an entirely different sect.[484]

Notwithstanding all this, the Suprema pursued its course in restraining the cruel zeal of the tribunals. The craze was spreading in Catalonia, where it required the Barcelona tribunal to submit to it for confirmation all sentences in these cases. In 1537, it returned, July 11th, a number of sentences, with its decisions as to each, and instructions as to the future. The tribunal was chafing under the unaccustomed restriction, and the fiscal was scandalized at the solicitude displayed for the friendless wretches who, everywhere but in Spain, were deprived of the most ordinary safeguards against injustice, but the imperturbable Suprema maintained its temperate wisdom. The utmost care, it said, was to be exercised to verify all testimony and to avoid conviction when this was insufficient. Arrests had been made on the mere reputation of being witches, for which the inquisitors were reproved and told that they must arrest no one on such grounds, nor on the testimony of accomplices, nor must those who denied their guilt be condemned as negativos. When any one confessed to being present at the killing of children or damage to harvests, verification must be sought as to the death of the children at that time, and of what disease, and whether the crops had been injured. When such verification was made, arrests could follow and, if the character of the case and of the accused required it, torture could be employed.[485] It will be noted how much more scrupulous was the care enjoined in these cases than in those of Moriscos and Judaizers, and the limitation on the use of torture is especially observable, as that was the universal resort in witchcraft throughout Europe.

***

It was difficult to enforce these rules in Barcelona. The result of the visitation of Francisco Vaca was a long series of rebukes, in 1550, largely concerning the procedure in witch cases and eventually leading to the dismissal of Inquisitor Sarmiento, although his offences were simply what was regarded, everywhere but in Spain, as the plain duty of those engaged in a direct contest with Satan, represented by his instrument the witch. Sarmiento is told that he made arrests without sufficient proofs and accepted the evidence taken by secular officials without verifying it, as required by the practice of the Inquisition, and, whereas the Suprema ordered certain precautions taken before concluding cases, he concluded them without doing so, and subjected parties to reconciliation and scourging that were not included in the sentence. Although the Suprema had ordered all sentences of relaxation to be submitted to it, he had relaxed seven persons as witches, in disregard of this, and when repeatedly commanded to present himself, he had never done so. Then the fiscal was taken to task because he had been present at the examination of witches, conducting the interrogation himself, putting leading questions, telling them what to confess and assuring them that this was not like a secular court, where those who confessed were executed. In the case of Juana, daughter of Benedita de Burgosera, he told her that she was a witch, that her mother had made her a witch and had taken her to the Bach de Viterna, and he detailed to her the murders committed by her mother. In witch cases he caused arrests without presenting clamosas or submitting evidence, but when he learned that a visitor was coming he fabricated and inserted them in the papers. In this the notary del secreto was his accomplice besides taking part in the examinations, bullying the accused and making them confess what was wanted by threats and suggestions. The alcaide of the prison had allowed one of the prisoners, who endeavored to save himself by accusing others, to enter the cells and persuade the prisoners to confess and not to revoke; the alcaide had also urged the women to confess, telling them that they were guilty and promising them release if they would confess and, when taking back to his cell a man who had revoked his confession, he so threatened the poor wretch that he returned and withdrew his revocation.[486] Elsewhere than in Spain such methods of securing confession were the veriest commonplaces in witch trials.

Meanwhile the chronic witchcraft troubles in Navarre had called forth, in 1538, a series of enlightened instructions to Inquisitor Valdeolitas, who was sent with a special commission. He was told to pay no attention to the popular demand that all witches should be burnt, but to exercise the utmost discretion, for it was a most delicate matter, in which deception was easy. He was not to confiscate but could impose fines to pay salaries. He was to explain to the more intelligent of the people that the destruction of harvests was due to the weather or to a visitation of God, for it happened where there were no witches, while the accusations of homicide required the most careful verification. The Malleus Maleficarum--that Bible of the witch-finder--was not to be believed in everything, for the writer was liable to be deceived like every one else. The demands of the corregidores for the surrender of penitents, to be subsequently punished for their crimes, were not to be granted, under the decision of the congregation of 1526. Then, a year later, October 27, 1539, the Calahorra tribunal was notified that the Royal Council of Navarre had agreed to surrender thirty-four prisoners; one of the inquisitors was to go to Pampeluna to examine the cases; those pertaining to the Inquisition were to be tried in strict conformity with the instructions and the rest were to be left with the civil authorities.[487]

In the instructions to Valdeolitas there is a phrase of peculiar interest, prescribing special caution with regard to the dreams of the witches when they sally forth to the Sabbat, as these are very deceitful. This, so far as I have observed, is the earliest official admission of the view taken in the can. Episcopi that the midnight flights were illusions. We have seen how this was denied by Albertino and de Castro. Ciruelo admits that there are two ways in which the Xorguina attends the Sabbat, one by personally flying, and the other by anointing herself and falling into a stupor, when she is spiritually conveyed, but both are the work of the demon and he admits of no distinction in the punishment.[488] Bishop Simancas, also an inquisitor, has no doubt as to the bodily transportation of the witch to the Sabbat; he admits that most jurists hold to the theory of illusion, as expressed in the can. Episcopi, but theologians, he says, are unanimous in maintaining the reality; he argues that the can. Episcopi does not refer to witches, and that stupor with illusions is much more difficult to comprehend than the truth of the Sabbat.[489]

***

With such a consensus of opinion as to the truth of the Sabbat, or Aquelarre as it came to be called (from a Biscayan word signifying "field of the goat") it is not surprising that the Suprema advanced slowly in designating it as an illusion, although practically its instructions assumed that no reliance was to be placed on the multitudinous testimony of its existence, of the foul horrors enacted there and of the presence there of other votaries of Satan. A curious case, occurring at a somewhat later period, may be alluded to here as showing the conclusion reached on the subject, and as throwing light on the auto-suggestion and hypnotic state which lay at the bottom of the Sabbat, although its connection is merely with the carnal indulgence that formed a prominent feature of the nocturnal assemblies. In 1584 Anastasia Soriana, aged 28, wife of a peasant, denounced herself to the Murcia tribunal for having long maintained carnal relations with a demon. The tribunal wisely regarded the matter as an illusion and dismissed the case without action. Twelve years later, in 1596, she presented herself to the tribunal of Toledo, with the same self-accusation and again, after due deliberation, she was discharged, although in any other land it would have gone hard with her.⁴⁹⁰

Meanwhile the Suprema continued the good work of protecting so-called witches from the cruelty of the secular courts and of restraining the intemperate zeal of its own tribunals. The craze, in 1551, had extended to Galicia, where at the time there was no Inquisition. Many arrests had been made and trials were in progress by the magistrates, when a cédula of August 27th, evidently drawn up by the Suprema for the signature of Prince Philip, addressed to all officials, informed them that the matter of witchcraft was a very delicate one in which many judges had been deceived, wherefore, by the advice of the inquisitor-general, he ordered that all the testimony should be sent to the Suprema for its action, pending which the accused were to be kept under guard without proceeding further with their cases or with others of the same nature.⁴⁹¹ Then, in September, 1555, the Suprema forwarded to the Logroño tribunal two memorials from some towns in Guipúzcoa, with an expression of its sorrow that so many persons should have been so suddenly arrested, for, from the testimony at hand and former experience, it thought that there was little basis for such action, and that wrong might be inflicted on many innocent persons. The evidence must be rigidly examined and, if it proved false, the prisoners must be discharged and the witnesses punished; if there was ground for prosecution, the trials might proceed, but the sentences must be submitted for confirmation and no more arrests be made without forwarding the testimony and awaiting orders. Six months later, in March, 1556, the Suprema concluded that the cases had not been substantiated; more careful preliminary investigations were essential for, in so doubtful a matter, greater caution was needed than in other cases.⁴⁹²

The secular authorities were restive under the deprivation of their jurisdiction over the crimes imputed to the witches; they continued to assert their claims, and the question came up for formal decision in 1575. The high court of Navarre had caused the arrest of a number of women and was trying them, when the Logroño tribunal, in the customary dictatorial fashion with threats of penalties, issued a summons to deliver all the prisoners and papers. This was duly read, November 24th, to the alcaldes, while sitting in court, to which they replied that the parties had been arrested under information that they had killed children and infants, that the women had had carnal intercourse with goats, and had killed cattle and injured harvests and vineyards with poisons and powders, and had carried off many children at night from their beds, while stupefying the adults with powders, of all of which as alcaldes they were the lawful judges. Therefore they appealed to the inquisitor-general against the penalties threatened and promised that, if the prisoners had committed heresy, they would be remitted to the inquisitors after undergoing punishment according to law. Finally they complained of the disrespect shown them and asked for a competencia.

MODERATION

The alcaldes further sent a memorial to the king, setting forth their claims to jurisdiction for crimes other than heresy, protesting against the assumption of the inquisitors to be sole judges of what pertained to them, to inhibit proceedings in the interim, and to interfere with the death-penalty which the alcaldes might decree. The royal court also petitioned the king in the same sense, adding that the prisoners spoke a dialect unintelligible to the inquisitors and that, if the cases were transferred, the king would lose the confiscations, which promised to be large. All this proved vain. A letter of the Suprema to the tribunal, in 1576, informs it that the alcaldes had been ordered to surrender all the prisoners and the papers in the cases.⁴⁹³ While this matter was in progress, a similar controversy arose about numerous witches in Santander, for a letter of January 10, 1576, instructs the Logroño tribunal that it can proceed against them for anything savoring of heresy, requiring the secular judges meanwhile to suspend proceedings; the facts are to be carefully verified and everything is to be submitted to the Suprema.⁴⁹⁴

The use made by the tribunals of the jurisdiction thus secured for them, under the cautions so sedulously inculcated, may be gathered from a case in the Toledo tribunal, in 1591, which further shows that witchcraft was not wholly confined to the mountainous districts of the east and north. The vicar of Alcalá had arrested three women of Cazar, Catalina Matheo, Joana Izquierda, and Olalla Sobrina. During the previous four years there had been four or five deaths of children; among the villagers, the three women had the reputation of witches, and sixteen witnesses testified to that effect. The vicar tortured them and obtained from Catalina a confession that, some four or five years before, Olalla asked her whether she would like to become a witch and have carnal intercourse with the demon. Then Joana one night invited her to her house where she found Olalla; the demon came in the shape of a goat, they danced together and after some details unnecessary to repeat, Olalla anointed the joints of her fingers and toes, they stripped themselves and flew through the air to a house which they entered by a window; placing somniferous herbs under the pillows of the parents, they choked to death a female infant, burning its back and breaking its arms. The noise aroused the parents and they flew with the goat back to Olalla's house. All this she ratified after due interval and repeated when confronted with Olalla, who had been tortured without confessing and who denied Catalina's story. As for Joana, she had likewise overcome the torture, but she had told the wife of the gaoler that one night some fifteen witches, male and female, had forcibly anointed her and carried her to a field where they danced, Catalina being one of the leaders and Olalla a follower. This she repeated to the vicar, adding stories of being present when the children were killed, but taking no part in it, after which she duly ratified the whole. At this stage the vicar transferred his prisoners to the tribunal. Catalina, at her first audience, begged mercy for the false witness which, through torture, she had borne against herself and the others. Sixteen witnesses testified to the deaths of the children, and she was sentenced to torture, when, before being stripped, her resolution gave way and she repeated and ratified the confession made to the vicar. Joana asserted that her confession to the vicar had been made through fear of torture and she overcame torture without confessing, as likewise did Olalla. The outcome was that Catalina was sentenced to appear in an auto with the insignia of a witch, to abjure de levi, to be scourged with two hundred lashes, and to be recluded at the discretion of the tribunal. The other two were merely to appear in the auto and to abjure de levi, without further penance. This was not strictly logical, but anywhere else than in Spain, all three would have been tortured until they satisfied their judges, and would then have been burnt after denouncing numerous accomplices and starting a witchcraft panic. As it was, the Toledo tribunal had no more witchcraft cases up to the end of the record in 1610.[495]

THE LOGROÑO AUTO OF 1610

The tribunal of Barcelona was more rational in 1597. In a report to the Suprema of a visitation made by Inquisitor Diego Fernández de Heredia, there occur the entries of Ana Ferrera, widow and Gilaberta, widow, both of Villafranca, accused by many witnesses of being reputed as witches and of killing many animals and infants, in revenge for little annoyances. Also, Francisco Cicar, of Bellney, near Villafranca, numerously accused as a wizard using incantations, telling where lost animals could be found, enchanting them so that wolves could not harm them, and killing the cattle of those who offended him. Here was the nucleus of a whole aquelarre for Villafranca, but all these cases are marked on the margin of the report as suspended, and nothing came of them.[496] The Logroño tribunal also showed its good sense, in 1602, when a young woman of 25, named Francisca Buytran, of Alegria, accused herself in much detail, before Don Juan Ramírez, of witchcraft, including attendance at the aquelarre. She was brought before the tribunal, which dropped the whole matter as being destitute of truth; again the magistrates sent it back, asking that it be revived and prosecuted and, when this was refused, they scourged her in Alegria as an impostor who defamed her neighbors.[497]

Yet it was reserved for this same tribunal to give occasion to an agitation resulting in a clearer understanding than had hitherto been reached of the nature of the witch-craze, and rendering it impossible for the future that Spain should be disgraced by the judicial murders, or rather massacres, which elsewhere blacken the annals of the seventeenth century. One of the customary panics arose in Navarre. The secular authorities were prompt and zealous; they made many arrests, they extorted confessions and hastily executed their victims, apparently to forestall the Inquisition. The tribunal reported to the Suprema, which ordered one of the inquisitors to make a visitation of the infected district. Juan Valle de Alvarado accordingly spent several months in Cigarramundi and its vicinity, where he gathered evidence inculpating more than two hundred and eighty persons of having apostatized to the demon, besides multitudes of children, who were becoming witches, but who were yet too young for prosecution. The leaders and those who had wrought the most evil, to the number of forty, were seized and brought before the tribunal. By June 8, 1610, it was ready to hold the consulta de fe, consisting of the three inquisitors, Alonso Becerra, Juan Valle de Alvarado and Alonso de Salazar Frias, with the episcopal Ordinary and four consultors. In his vote, Salazar analyzed the testimony and showed its flimsy and inconclusive character; he seems to have had no scruples as to the reality of witchcraft, but he desired more competent proof, while his colleagues apparently had no misgivings.[498]

This was not the only retrograde step. For seventy-five years the Suprema had consistently repressed the ardor of persecution and had favored, without absolutely asserting, the theory of illusion, but its membership was constantly changing and it now seems to have had a majority of blind believers. On August 3d it presented to Philip III a consulta relating, with profound grief, the conditions in the mountains of Navarre and the steps already taken. Since then further reports showed that the demon was busier than ever in misleading these poor ignorant folk, and the evil had increased so that there now were more than twenty aquelarres to which they gather, and the evil was still spreading; the people were greatly afflicted with the damages endured, and parents who saw their children misled were so desperate that they wanted to put them to death. An Edict of Grace was published, but the demon so blinded them that few took advantage of it, and these speedily relapsed. The progress of the infection was such that the powerful hand of the king was absolutely required for its rigorous repression, and the popular ignorance was so dense that orders should be issued to the Archbishop of Burgos and the Bishops of Calahorra, Pampeluna and Tarazona, whose dioceses were concerned, and to the Provincials of the Religious Orders, to send pious and learned men to instruct the people, while the vigilance would not be lacking of the inquisitors, who would shrink from no labor.[499] The Suprema evidently regarded the emergency as most serious, calling for united effort to withstand the victorious onslaught of the demon. It had wholly forgotten the wholesome caution which it had inculcated so sedulously since 1530 and there was imminent danger that Spain would be swept into the European current of witch-extermination.

Whether the pleasure-loving king organized the projected preaching crusade we do not know, but he was sufficiently impressed to promise that he would honor with his presence the coming auto de fe, which was fixed for November 7th. Something distracted his attention and, at the last moment, it was announced that important affairs would prevent his attendance. The disappointed inquisitors, on November 1st, wrote to the Suprema expressing their regret and reporting that there would be thirty-one persons in the auto, besides a large number of prisoners whose trials were under way.

***

Thus far twenty-two aquelarres had been discovered, and the accused were so numerous that the special favor of heaven would be necessary to overcome the evil. Accompanying this was a letter to the king, enclosing two of the sentences con méritos, to enlighten him as to the ravages of the devil among his subjects. This sect of witches, they said, was of old date in the Pyrenees, and had of late spread over the whole region; the inquisitors were devoting their lives to its suppression; they were fighting the devil at close quarters, and they hoped to excite the royal zeal to lend the Inquisition efficient support. These letters bore the signature of Salazar as well as those of his colleagues.[500]

Great preparations had been made to render the auto impressive. Crowds assembled from a distance, and it was reckoned that in the processions there were a thousand familiars and officials. Two days were required for the solemnities and on the second day, to finish the work between dawn and sunset, many of the sentences had to be curtailed for, as usual, they were con meritos, with full details of the abominations of the aquelarres and the crimes of the culprits. All the grotesque obscenities, which the foul imaginations of the accused could invent to satisfy their prosecutors, were given at length, and doubtless impressed the gaping multitudes with the horror and detestation desired. One novelty in the sensual delights of the aquelarre was that the feast was usually composed of decaying corpses, which the witches dug up and conveyed there--especially those of their kindred, so that the father sometimes ate the son and the son the father--and it was stated that male flesh had a higher flavor than female. There were also the usual stories of the destruction of harvests by means of powders, of sucking the blood of infants, of bringing sickness and death by poisons so subtile that a single touch, in a pretended caress, would work its end. When the demon reproached them with slackness in evil-doing, two sisters, María Presona and María Joanto, agreed to kill the son and the daughter of the other, aged 8 and 9, and they did so with the powders. It was natural that a population, placing full credence in the existence of malignity armed with these powers, should be merciless in the resolve for its extermination. Yet the auto, in its absolute outcome, could scarce be classed with the murderous exhibitions to which the Spaniard had grown accustomed. In all there were fifty-three culprits, of whom but twenty-nine were witches of either sex. Of these there were eleven relaxed--five, who had died in prison, in effigy with their bones, and five negativos who had not been induced to confess. There was but one relaxation of a buen confitente, María Zozaya, whose terrible confession overshot the mark, as it showed her to be a dogmatizer. Even under this excitement the Inquisition maintained its rule not to execute those who confessed and repented; under any other jurisdiction the eighteen who were reconciled would have been burnt, and of these apparently only five were scourged.[501]

Merciful as was this, the effect of the auto was to cause a revulsion of feeling among the more intelligent. When the local magistrates were proceeding as usual to arrest suspects, the alcaldes of the Royal Court of Navarre, early in 1611, interposed by arresting them in turn for exceeding their powers and prosecuted them to punishment. This incensed the Logroño tribunal which, on May 17th, addressed an energetic protest to the viceroy; the action of the local authorities had been of the utmost service, not only in sending culprits to the Inquisition, but in leading to many spontaneous self-accusations; this had now all ceased, and those who had confessed were beginning to retract; the tribunal had relied upon the court for aid in exterminating this accursed race and now it was protecting them. Possibly the tribunal may also have invoked the authority of the Suprema but, if so, it can have found no sympathy, for there also had there been a change of heart and a return to the old policy. On March 26th it had ordered the publication of an Edict of Grace, which Salazar was deputed to carry with him on a visitation to the infected districts and, after some delay, he started with it, May 22d, on a mission destined to open his eyes and put a permanent end to the danger of witchcraft epidemics in Spain.[502]

PEDRO DE VALENCIA

To this a contribution of some weight, though by no means so influential as has been reckoned, was made by Pedro de Valencia, a disciple of Arias Montano, and one of the most learned men of his time. At the request of Inquisitor-general Sandoval y Rojas, he composed an elaborate "discourse" on witchcraft, addressed to Sandoval under date of April 20th. In this, after premising the great grief and compassion with which he had read the relations of the auto of the previous November, he proceeds to discuss three hypotheses. The first is rationalistic; there is no demon, the aquelarres are assemblages for sensual indulgence, to which the members go on foot, and the presiding demon is a man disguised. The second is illusion, produced by a pact with the demon, who gives to the witch an ointment throwing her into a stupor during which she imagines all that is related of the aquelarres, whence it follows that the evidence of the witch as to those whom she has seen there is not to be accepted. The destruction of cattle and harvests is the work of the demon, or may be accomplished by poisons. The third supposition, believed by the vulgar, in conformity with the evidence and confessions, is the most prodigious and horrible of all, and against this he brings his strongest arguments in full detail. Pedro does not express any positive conclusion of his own, but his reasoning all tends to support the second hypothesis--of stupor and illusion produced by the demonic ointment, and from this he deduces the result that witches are by no means innocent. They delight in the crimes which they believe themselves to commit, and desire to persevere in their apostasy from God and their servitude to the devil. Men sometimes become heretics through ignorance and mistaken zeal, but these seek the devil in all his hideousness for the purpose of partaking in foul and unhallowed pleasures. They merit any punishment that can be inflicted on them, for such rotten limbs should be lopped off, and the cancer be extirpated with fire and blood. Their conspiracies to kill and the crimes which they commit and the injuries inflicted on their neighbors, before and after these dreams deserve all this and greater rigor.

This virtual equalization of criminality in illusive and actual witchcraft was not likely to be of benefit to so-called witches, but there was wisdom in the caution which Pedro urged on judges, to assure themselves of the reality of alleged crimes and not, through preconceived views, to so direct their interrogatories as to lead ignorant, foolish, crazy or demoniac persons, like the witnesses and the accused in these cases, to testify or to confess to extravagances, because they see that it is expected and hope to gain the favor of those holding the power of life or death. Similar stories were told of the early Christians and, in view of all this, and the utter legal insufficiency of the witnesses, the whole tissue of evidence and confessions vanishes into smoke. Amid all these deceits, the prudence of the judge should seek the true and the probable, rather than monstrous fictions for, if he desires to find the latter, he will be fully satisfied by the miserable lying women before him--disciples, by their own confession, of the father of lies.[503]

The inconsistencies in this discourse suggest that probably Pedro had stronger convictions than he deemed it wise to express. It is possible that Inquisitor Salazar may have read the paper and have been somewhat influenced by it, when he started in May on the visitation which proved to be the turning-point in the history of Spanish witchcraft, but we have seen that, in the consulta de fe of the previous June 10th, his attention had already been aroused by the contradictions and unsatisfactory character of the evidence on which the tribunal was accustomed to act and, when once his mind was directed to investigating the problems thus suggested, the close acquaintance with facts afforded by the visitation enabled him to reach conclusions vastly more definite than any which his predecessors ventured to form.

ALONSO DE SALAZAR FRIAS

He started, as we have seen, on May 22, 1611, with the Edict of Grace; his work was thoroughly conscientious and he did not return until January 10, 1612, after which he employed himself, until March 24th, in drawing up his report to the Suprema, which was accompanied with the original papers, amounting to more than five thousand folios. It will be remembered that an Edict of Grace was published in 1610 with little or no result. In contrast with this, showing the effect of a different spirit in its administration, Salazar received eighteen hundred and two applicants, of whom thirteen hundred and eighty-four were children of from twelve to fourteen years of age and, besides these, there were eighty-one who revoked confessions previously made. All applicants for reconciliation made full confessions of misdeeds, after kindly warning of the obligation to tell the truth and the danger of committing perjury, and were promised secrecy to relieve them of fear. The enormous mass of evidence thus collected Salazar carefully analyzed and presented under four heads--I, the manner in which witches go to the aquelarre, remain and return; II, the things they do and endure; III, the external proofs of these things; IV, the evidence resulting for the punishment of the guilty. The first two of these present a curious medley of marvels, such as holding aquelarres in the sea without being wet, and the testimony of three women that, after intercourse with the demon, in a few hours they gave birth to large toads; but we need not dwell on these feats of imaginative invention. The importance of the report lies in the last two sections.

Many instances are given to prove the illusory character of cases in which the penitent truthfully believed what she confessed. María de Echaverria, aged 80, one of the relapsed, made copious confessions, with abundant tears and heart-felt grief, seeking to save her soul through the Inquisition. Without her consent, she said, she was every night--even the preceding one--carried to the aquelarre, awaking during the transit and returning awake. No one saw her in going and coming, even her daughter, a witch of the same aquelarre, sleeping in the same bed. All the frailes present at her confession had a long discussion with her and the conviction was unanimous that what this good woman said of her witchcraft was a dream. Catalina de Sastrearena declared that, while she was waiting to be reconciled, she was suddenly carried to the aquelarre, but her companions said that they were talking to her during the time when she claimed to be absent. The mother of María de Tamborin testified to the girl telling her of going to the aquelarre, so she maintained close watch on her and kept a hand on her but was unaware of her absence. Physical examination, in several instances, showed that girls were virgins who had confessed to intercourse with demons. Many boys testified that, when Salazar went to San Esteban, there was a great aquelarre held, but his two secretaries happened that night to be on the spot indicated and they saw nothing. Thirty-six persons were examined as to the localities of nine aquelarres, but some said they did not know and others contradicted what they had confessed, so that none of the nine could be identified. As for the broths and unguents and powders so often described as used for flying to the aquelarres and working evil, nothing whatever could be learned. Twenty ollas had been brought forward during the visitation, but investigation showed them all to be frauds, for physicians and apothecaries used the materials on animals without producing the slightest injury. From all this Salazar concludes that the matters confessed were delusions of the demon, and the accusations against accomplices were likewise induced by the demon. No testimony could be had from those not accomplices and he holds it a great marvel that, in a thing reputed to be of so wide an extent, there should be no external evidence accessible.[504]

Equally destructive to credibility, he says, were the threats and violence employed to extort confessions. One stated that he was burned with blazing coals and it inspires horror even to imagine how they were thus forced to pervert the truth. Sometimes the father or husband or brother would combine with the magistrate or the commissioner of the Inquisition. Thus all were forced to confess and to bear witness against their neighbors, so that it seems marvellous that any one escaped. The groundlessness of the whole was further exemplified by the fact that many who applied importunately to be admitted as witches to reconciliation were unable to confess anything requiring it. The belief was general that no one was safe who did not come forward and take the benefit of the edict, so that some invented confessions, while others admitted that they had nothing to confess, but all wanted certificates, for one of the violences committed had been to deny the sacraments to all reputed to be witches or testified against, and when they applied to Salazar their greatest anxiety was to obtain certificates entitling them to the sacraments.

***

As for the eighty-one who revoked their confessions, Salazar is sure that they did so to relieve their consciences. At first he refused to receive their revocations in compliance with the views of his colleagues, but he had subsequently orders from the Suprema to admit them. There would have been many more had it been generally understood that they could do so with safety; it was individual action on the part of each, for every care was taken not to let it be known who revoked, and some of them said that they must revoke if they had to burn for it, as they had wrongfully accused others. One especially distressing case was that of Marquita de Jaurri, an old woman who had been reconciled at Logroño. She returned home with her conscience heavily burthened about those whom she had unjustly inculpated and, at her daughter's instance, she applied to her confessor. He ordered her to revoke her confession before Phelipe Díaz, the commissioner of Maeztu, but he rejected her with insult, telling her that she would have to be burnt for maliciously revoking what she had truthfully confessed, whereupon in a few days she drowned herself. It will be remembered (Vol. II, p. 582) that revocation of confession was held to prove impenitence, punishable by relaxation.

Salazar adds that the value of the evidence was still further diminished by the command of the demon to accuse the innocent and exonerate the guilty, and by the fact that bribes were given in order to have enemies prosecuted. In Vera, each of several boys accused about two hundred accomplices and, in Fuenterrabia a beggar boy of 12 accused a hundred and forty-seven. Besides those who revoked there were many who asked to have stricken out the names of those whom they had falsely accused so that, in all, there were sixteen hundred and seventy-two persons known as having had false witness borne against them, so that, when there were this many acknowledged perjuries, there could be little faith placed in the other accusations. The cause of the wide-extended and profound popular belief in the reality of witchcraft he ascribes solely to the auto de fe of Logroño, the Edict of Faith and the sending of an inquisitor through the district, which had caused such apprehension that there was no fainting-fit, no death and no accident that was not attributed to witchcraft. Fray Domingo de Velasco of San Sebastian, after preaching the Edict, told Salazar that for four months there had not been a natural tempest or hailstorm, but all had been the work of witches, yet when questioned he had no evidence save the gossip of the streets. Sailors exaggerated these reports and they were fomented by the knaves known as santigueadores, who professed to know the witches and sold charms and spells to counteract them.

In summing up the results of his experience Salazar declares that "Considering the above with all the Christian attention in my power, I have not found even indications from which to infer that a single act of witchcraft has really occurred, whether as to going to aquelarres, being present at them, inflicting injuries, or other of the asserted facts. This enlightenment has greatly strengthened my former suspicions that the evidence of accomplices, without external proof from other parties, is insufficient to justify even arrest. Moreover, my experience leads to the conviction that, of those availing themselves of the Edict of Grace, three-quarters and more have accused themselves and their accomplices falsely. I further believe that they would freely come to the Inquisition to revoke their confessions, if they thought that they would be received kindly without punishment, for I fear that my efforts to induce this have not been properly made known, and I further fear that, in my absence, the commissioners whom, by your command, I have ordered to do the same, do not act with due fidelity, but, with increasing zeal are discovering every hour more witches and aquelarres, in the same way as before.

"I also feel certain that, under present conditions, there is no need of fresh edicts or the prolongation of those existing, but rather that, in the diseased state of the public mind, every agitation of the matter is harmful and increases the evil. I deduce the importance of silence and reserve from the experience that there were neither witches nor bewitched until they were talked and written about. This impressed me recently at Olague, near Pampeluna, where those who confessed stated that the matter started there after Fray Domingo de Sardo came there to preach about these things. So, when I went to Valderro, near Roncesvalles, to reconcile some who had confessed, when about to return the alcaldes begged me to go to the Valle de Ahescoa, two leagues distant, not that any witchcraft had been discovered there, but only that it might be honored equally with the other. I only sent there the Edict of Grace and, eight days after its publication, I learned that already there were boys confessing. After receiving the report of a commissioner whom I deputed, I sent from Azpeitia to the Prior of San Sebastian of Urdax to absolve them with Secretary Peralta. This quieted them but, since my return to Logroño the tribunal has been asked to remedy the affliction of new evils and witchcrafts, all originating from the above."

HUMANE INSTRUCTIONS

Salazar's colleagues did not agree with him and attempted to answer his reasoning, but the Suprema was convinced. It followed his advice in imposing silence on the past, while the Court of Navarre continued to prosecute and punish the local officials whose superserviceable zeal had occasioned so much misery. A second visitation was made in 1613 and we find Salazar urging a third one to cover the remaining portion of the infected region, and pointing out the peace which reigned in the district that he had visited. His next step was to draw up a series of suggestions covering the policy of the Inquisition with regard to witchcraft, covering both amends for the past and future action. It would scarce seem that he would venture to do this without orders, but the paper purports to be volunteered in view of the urgent necessity of the matter. Be this as it may, the suggestions were the basis of an elaborate instruction, issued by the Suprema August 31, 1614, which remained the permanent policy of the Inquisition. It adopted nearly every suggestion of Salazar's, often in his very words, and is an enduring monument to his calm good sense, which saved his country from the devastation of the witch-madness then ravaging the rest of Europe.

These instructions consist of thirty-two articles and commence by stating that the Suprema, after careful consideration of all the documents, fully recognized the grave wrong committed in obscuring the truth in a matter so difficult of proof, and it sent the following articles, both for the verification of future cases and in reparation of the past.

This is followed by a series of regulations pointing out in detail the external evidence which must be sought in every case, both as to attendance on the aquelarres and the murder of children, the killing of cattle, and the damage of harvests, and no one was to be arrested without strict observance of these precautions. There is careful abstention from denial of the powers attributed to witches, but the whole tenor is that of scepticism, and preachers were ordered to make the people understand that the destruction of harvests is sent for our sins, or is caused by the weather, and that it is a grievous error to imagine that such things and sickness, which are customary throughout the world, are caused by witches. The powers of commissioners were strictly limited to taking depositions and ascertaining whether these could be verified by external evidence. When witnesses or accused came to make revocations, whether before or after sentence, they were to be kindly received and permitted to discharge their consciences, free from the fear so commonly entertained, that they would be punished for revoking [as we have seen was the case in other crimes], and this was to be communicated to the commissioners, who were to forward all revocations received. Those who spontaneously denounced themselves were to be asked whether, in the day-time, they had persevered in the renunciation of God and adoration of the demon; if they admitted having done so, they were to be reconciled but, in view of the doubt and deceit surrounding the matter, this reconciliation was not to entail confiscation or liability to the penalties of relapse, the latter being discretional with the tribunal after consulting the Suprema, and further the Suprema was to be consulted before action taken against those confessing to relapse. Those who denied perseverance in apostasy were to be absolved ad cautelam and reconciled by commissioners, in the same way as foreign heretics applying for conversion. In view of the doubts and difficulties concerning witchcraft, no action was to be taken save by unanimous vote of all the inquisitors, followed by consultation with the Suprema. All pending cases were to be suspended, without disqualification for office. On all evidence, the violence or torture used in procuring it was to be noted, so that its credibility could be estimated; when a vote was taken, unless it was for suspension, the case was to be submitted to the Suprema. All cases were to be dropped of those dying during their pendency, without disability of their descendants. As regarded the auto de fe of 1610, the sanbenitos of those relaxed or reconciled were never to be hung in the churches, their property was not to be confiscated; an itemized statement of it and of the fines levied, with an account of the expenses, was to be submitted to the Suprema, and this was to be noted in the records of their cases, so that they should not be liable in case of relapse, nor should their descendants be disabled for office, nor should those be disqualified who had since then been penanced with abjuration.

DELUSION RECOGNIZED

Having thus provided reparation for the past and caution for the future, the Suprema sought to protect reputed witches from the inordinate zeal of the local authorities and to vindicate its exclusive jurisdiction. The commissioners were to be summoned, one by one, and made to understand the grief and just resentment of the Holy Office at the violence of the alcaldes and others towards those reported to be witches. They were to publish this and let it be known that, as the High Court of Navarre had undertaken to punish these intermeddlers, it would be permitted to do so, but that in future the Inquisition would adopt rigorous measures to chastise all who intruded on its jurisdiction, as perturbers and impeders of the Holy Office. Confessors were instructed to require all who were guilty of defaming others to denounce themselves to the tribunal, for the discharge of their conscience and the restoration to honor of the injured, and priests were notified not to refuse the sacraments to those reputed as witches, while commissioners were warned to confine themselves to their instructions and to act with all moderation.[505]

In this admirable paper we cannot help applauding especially the moral courage evinced in making reparation for the Logroño auto, which must have had the sanction of the Suprema. The whole witch epidemic of Navarre and the Provinces of Biscay was evidently regarded as a delusion but, in view of the attitude of the Church for the last two centuries, this could not be openly proclaimed and the wisest course was adopted to repress, as far as possible, popular fanaticism, and to protect its victims for the future. The superstition was too inveterate to be easily eradicated, but the effort to protect its victims was not abandoned. There is the formula of an edict, dated 162-(the year left blank to be filled in) issued by Salazar, now senior inquisitor, and his colleagues, reciting that the prosecutions for many years had given them ample experience of the grave evils and obscuration of the truth, resulting from the threats and violence offered to those who confessed or were suspected of witchcraft, as many persons, under pretext of kinship to the suspect, or to the persons said to be injured, endeavor to force them to confess publicly as to themselves and others, wherefore all persons were ordered to abstain from threats or inducements, so that every one might have free access to the tribunal and its commissioners, under penalty of rigorous punishment according to the circumstances of the offence.[506] It is inferable from this, that the people, distrusting the leniency of the Inquisition, discouraged application to it, and sought rather to obtain satisfaction extra-judicially.

PERSISTENT DELUSION

The virtual supervision assumed by the Suprema over all cases of witchcraft was exercised with a moderation which must have been greatly discouraging to believers. Under this impulsion, the tribunals became exceedingly lenient, frequently exercising the power left to them of suspending cases. One that is exceedingly significant occurred at Valladolid, in 1622. At the instance of her confessor, Casilda de Pabanes, a girl of 19, from Villamiel, near Burgos, presented herself and confessed that, at Christmas 1615 (when she was 12 or 13 years old) she was sick in bed with a fever, and her parents had gone to mass, leaving the house locked up. Suddenly a neighbor, a widow named Marina Vela, appeared at her bed-side and, with threats of killing her, forced her to rise and dress and accompany her to a hermitage in the vicinage, where they found a tall, naked man, dark and with horns like a bull, who welcomed them and made them strip to their shifts, with an exchange of indecent kisses. Then they dressed and returned; although the house doors were locked they entered, and she was again in bed before her parents came back. Then followed long details of other similar adventures, in which the presiding demon usually wore the form of a goat. He made her renounce God and wrote with her blood her name on a paper; she was provided with an incubus demon whom she could summon by breaking a stick; with Marina she entered houses at night, killing children with powders or by sucking their fingers. There is no allusion to the aquelarre, but all other features of witchcraft are minutely detailed. By Marina's advice, she pretended to be possessed, and was taken to San Toribio de Liebara to be exorcised by Fray Gonzalo de San Millan, to whom she confessed. The inquisitors examined and cross-examined her closely, without her varying in her story; they sought, without success, for evidence of illusion or fantasy, but, on investigation it was found that she was really sick of a fever at Christmas, 1615, and that subsequently she seemed to tremble and be as one possessed. Confirmatory statements were procured from the frailes, and evidently in accordance with the instructions, all means were exhausted of testing her confession. In any other land this victim of hysteric auto-suggestion would have been, if not burnt, at least made an exhibition that would have spread the craze, but the tribunal, after carrying the case through the preliminary stages, voted to suspend it without rendering sentence and to reconcile and absolve her in the audience chamber without confiscation.[507] The same policy was followed in the few other cases brought before the tribunal. María de Melgar of Osorno, who died during trial, was given Christian burial in 1637; in 1640, it suspended the case of María Sanz of Trigueros, against whom there was testimony of witchcraft and, in 1641, it discharged with a reprimand María Alfonsa de la Torre, accused of killing cattle, although a witness swore to seeing her at midnight riding on a stick over a rye-field, with a noise as though accompanied by a multitude of demons.[508]

When we compare these cases with the penalties inflicted at the period on vulgar sorceresses and poor old curanderas, for implied pact, it is evident that the Inquisition had reached the conclusion that witchcraft was virtually a delusion, or that incriminating testimony was perjured. This could not be openly published; the belief was of too long standing and too firmly asserted by the Church to be pronounced false; witchcraft was still a crime to be punished when proved but, under the regulations, proof was becoming impossible and confessions were regarded as illusions.

It was difficult for the conservatives to abandon their cherished beliefs, and the can. Episcopi remained a bone of contention. Torreblanca has no inklings of doubt; to him the aquelarre and all its obscene horrors are a reality; the witch is to be burnt, not for illusions but for acts, as the Church has decreed in so many constitutions.[509] His book was duly licensed by the Council of Castile in 1613, but some censor presented a learned criticism of it, calling especial attention to this point, citing the can. Episcopi and the experience of the Inquisition, and arguing that the feats attributed to witches transcended the powers of the demon. This was so effective that the licence was withdrawn. Then Torreblanca produced a verbose and discursive "Defensa," in which he argued that the can. Episcopi was apocryphal; he showed that the Church had always punished such malefactors with death, so that either his critic or the Church must err, and the Church cannot, for it is illuminated by God.[510] This was successful, his licence was restored in 1615 and his work saw the light in 1618. Jofreu in his notes to Ciruelo's "Reprovacion," defends the can. Episcopi, but finds in it three kinds of witches--those who renounce God and seek the aid of the devil, those who are superstitious and know that their illusions are the work of the evil spirit, and those who are deceived by them--and the witches of today are the same, whence he argues in favor of caution and a policy of clemency.[511] Alberghini, about 1640, admits that the aquelarre is a phantasm, but he holds that none the less are witches apostates from God and devil-worshippers, and he seems to think it still an open question whether those who kill by sorcery are to be relaxed, even if they truly repent and are converted.[512] About the same time, all that an old inquisitor will grant is that, even if there is illusion in the aquelarre, the witch ratifies all that is done there, when awake, dwelling on it with pleasure and anointing herself for the purpose, but he concedes that the deceits of the devil render necessary stronger evidence than in other crimes and that, as he represents in the aquelarre phantoms of innocent persons, the testimony of accomplices must be fortified with other proofs.[513] Nearly the same ground was taken, in 1650, by Padre Diego Tello, S. J., as calificador in the case of an unlucky monomaniac on trial by the Granada tribunal, whom he sought to prove responsible by showing that the witches who fly with Diana and Herodias, as in the can. Episcopi, had free-will, rendering them culpable for their commerce with the demon.[514] Even as late as towards the close of the seventeenth century, a systematic writer holds it as certain that witches renounce the faith, adore the demon and enter into a pact with him and, if this can be proved by confession or witnesses, they are to be punished as heretics with the regular penalties.[515]

VIRTUAL DISAPPEARANCE

Yet the Inquisition imperturbably pursued its way. It did not deny the existence of witchcraft, or modify the penalties of the crime but, as we have seen, it practically rendered proof impossible, thus discouraging formal accusations, while its prohibition of preliminary proceedings by its commissioners and by the local officials, secular and ecclesiastical, was effectual in preventing the outbreak of witchcraft epidemics. So far as the records before me show, cases became very few after the Logroño experience of 1610. Scattering ones occur occasionally, such as those alluded to above but, in the Valladolid record from which they are derived, embracing in all six hundred and sixty-seven cases between 1622 and 1662, there are but five of witchcraft, of which the latest is in 1641.[516] In Toledo, from 1648 to 1794, there is not a single one, nor is there one among the nine hundred and sixty-two cases in the sixty-four autos celebrated by all the tribunals of Spain between 1721 and 1727.[517] It was not that popular belief was eradicated, for this is ineradicable and still exists among all nations, but its deadly effects were prevented. Some fragmentary papers show that, from 1728 to 1735, there was a tolerably active investigation, in Valencia and Castellon de la Plana, into cases of mingled sorcery and witchcraft. There was evidence as to the use of ointments by which persons could transport themselves through the air and pass through walls, and as to people being bewitched and rendered sick, showing that the superstition had as firm a hold as ever on the lower classes.[518] In 1765, at Callosa de Ensarria (Alicante) when some young children disappeared, it was attributed to Angela Piera who had the reputation of a witch, able to fly to Tortosa and back, and who was supposed to have killed them for her incantations.[519] These scattering cases become rarer with time. In a record of all the operations of the Spanish tribunals, from 1780 to 1820, there are but four. In 1781, Isabel Cascar of Malpica was accused as a witch to the tribunal of Saragossa. In 1791, at Barcelona, María Vidal y Decardó of Tamarit, a widow aged 45, accused herself of express pact with the demon, of carnal intercourse with him, of presence four times a week at the aquelarres, where she adored him as a God, and of having trampled on a consecrated host and flung it on a dung-hill--a case which forcibly recalls that of Casilda de Pabanes, in 1622, as an illustration of the hypnotic illusions which aided so greatly in the dissemination of the belief. The latest cases are two, occurring in 1815, of which details are lacking except that they were not brought to trial.[520]

Thus the belief, so persistently affirmed by the Church, continued to exist among theologians. Even one so learned as Fray Maestro Alvarado, in 1813, when defending the Inquisition against the Córtes of Cádiz, told the deputies that Cervantes was better authority in favor of the belief than they were against it, and he instanced a recent case in Llerena, where two women in a church, and in sight of all the people, were carried through the air by demons.[521] Still, so long as the belief was academical and did not lead to the stake, it was comparatively harmless, and the Inquisition deserves full credit for depriving it of its power for evil.

THE ROMAN INQUISITION

In this, there is a remarkable coincidence between the Holy Offices of Spain and of Rome, although the latter was somewhat tardy in the good work. After the organization of the Congregation, in 1542, by Paul III., there was a considerable interval before it asserted exclusive jurisdiction over witchcraft. It is true that, in 1582, in the papal city of Avignon, it relaxed to the secular arm eighteen witches in a single sentence,[522] but the next year, 1583, when the people of the Val Mesolcina found themselves ruined by the numerous witches among them, they applied for relief not to the Inquisition but to their archbishop, San Carlo Borromeo. After a preliminary investigation he came with a group of learned theologians and so worked on the consciences of the culprits that he won nearly all to repentance--more than a hundred and fifty are said to have confessed and abjured at one time. There were, however, twelve pertinacious ones, including the Provost of Roveredo; he was degraded from Orders and all were duly burnt--they of course being negativos who refused to admit their guilt.[523] The Inquisition, in fact, was willing to share its jurisdiction with the bishops, but not with the secular courts, with which, in 1588 and 1589 we find it in controversy. It contended that, as witchcraft infers apostasy, its cognizance is ecclesiastical, residing either in the bishop or the Inquisition, and further that, when a civil court has commenced a prosecution, the inquisitor has the right to inspect the proceedings and decide as to whether or not the case belongs to him. Various decisions and instructions from this time until 1603 indicate the line of action. The jurisdiction is only spiritual, for the heresy and apostasy, and takes no count of alleged murders or other crimes; the penalty is therefore merely penance, usually scourging, and inquisitors are told not to exile witches to places where they were not known, but to settle them where they could be kept under watch. That this leniency did not satisfy the people was shown at Gubbio, in 1633, where a woman undergoing the scourge was set upon by the populace and stoned to death. Nor was the Inquisition itself always consistent for, in 1641, the tribunal of Milan relaxed Anna María Pamolea to the secular arm for witchcraft and homicide.[524]

When murders were charged, the rule was that, if a secular court had commenced prosecution, the culprit was returned to it for due punishment, after the spiritual offence had been penanced but, if the Inquisition had been the first to act, it was not to abandon its penitent to the secular arm, except in case of relapse. The practical working of this is seen in a case at Padua, in 1629, where three witches, imprisoned in the public gaol, were handed over to the tribunal, which made them abjure formally, and then returned them, when the magistrates burnt them. That there was considerable scepticism as to the truth of the Sabbat may be assumed from the rule that the evidence of witches about persons seen in these assemblies was not to be received to the prejudice of such persons, as it is all held to be an illusion.[525]

This scepticism increased and there was a desire to train the people to disbelief, as appears from a highly creditable act in 1631. The Inquisitor of Novara reported that his vicar in "Vallis Vigelli" had commenced proceedings for witchcraft against a woman, when she hanged herself in prison, and he asked instructions whether to continue the prosecution against the corpse or whether she had been strangled by the demon or other witches; also whether he should proceed against a girl and her accomplices who had confessed extra-judicially to have been at the Sabbat. In reply the Congregation ordered him to send the proceedings in the case of the suicide and also the deposition of the girl; meanwhile he was to remove the vicar and replace him with a proper person and take pains himself, by means of the parish priests, to instruct the people as to the fallacies of witchcraft. The same spirit was manifested, in 1641, when an affirmative answer was given to the Inquisitor of Mantua, who asked whether he should prosecute those who beat and insulted witches on the pretext of their being witches.[526] The Congregation, however, did not place on the Index the Compendium Maleficarum of Fray Francesco María Guaccio (2^{d} Edition, Milan, 1626) which taught all the beliefs concerning witches and was adorned with wood cuts representing them as riding on demons through the air and worshipping Satan in the Sabbat.

***

What renders the leniency of the Congregation especially remarkable is that it was in contravention of a decree of Gregory XV, in 1623, sharpening the penalties of those entering into compacts with the demon; if they caused death by sorcery they were to be relaxed to the secular arm, even for a first offence, while, for causing impotence, or infirmity, or injury to harvests or cattle, they were to be imprisoned for life.[527] Without, of course, venturing formally to mitigate the harshness of these penalties, the Congregation could at least elude them practically, by interposing difficulties in the way of conviction, and this it did, in 1657, in a series of instructions to inquisitors. Full belief in the reality of witchcraft was assumed, but there was a hideous enumeration of the abuses through which so many innocent women were condemned. The mode of procedure prescribed was based largely on the Spanish instructions of 1614, and special stress was laid upon moderation in the use of torture, which was never to be employed until all the papers in the case had been submitted to the Congregation and its assent had been obtained, while common fame was not to be considered an indication justifying arrest. The injunction of 1593, which prohibited accepting testimony as to those seen in the Sabbat, was renewed for the reason that these assemblages were mostly an illusion and justice did not demand prosecution of those recognized through illusion.[528]

While thus there was no concession in principle, in practice the persecution of witchcraft became much less deadly. A manual, dating about 1700, states that in these cases the Inquisition is accustomed to move slowly and with the greatest circumspection, for the indications are generally indirect and the corpus delicti most difficult to prove. If the evidence is strong, torture is employed both for the fact and the intention; if apostasy is confessed, formal abjuration is required; if it or evil belief is denied, the abjuration is de vehementi; the accomplices are prosecuted, but not those named as seen in the Sabbat, on account of the illusions of the demon. Relaxation is the penalty for heretical sorcery causing death, but the difficulty of proving this is very great.[529]

Thus gradually the worst features of witch persecution disappeared in Italy, while yet belief in the reality of witchcraft was untouched. As late as 1743, Benedict XIV manifests complete acceptance of it, when discussing the nice question whether a witch, terrified by threats and blows, commits a fresh sin by transferring to an ox the deadly spell which she has cast upon the son of the man who beat her. He concludes that she is guilty of a fresh sin, while the father is excusable, for he presumably does not know that she has to have recourse to the demon to effect the transfer, and his only object is to save his son. Moreover Benedict, in his great work on canonization, not only admits the common opinion as to incubi and succubi, but he does not deny that in some way such unions may result in offspring.[530] In fact, the supreme authority of the modern Catholic Church, St. Alphonso Liguori, repeats without disapproval the common opinion of the doctors, that witches are transported through the air and that the theory of illusion is very pernicious to the Church, as it relieves them from the punishment prescribed for them.[531]

PERSISTENT BELIEF

Thus the two lands in Christendom, in which the Inquisition was thoroughly organized, escaped the worst horrors of the witch-craze. The service rendered, especially by the Spanish Holy Office, in arresting the development of the epidemics so constantly reappearing, can only be estimated by considering the ravages in other lands where Protestants, who had not the excuse of obedience to papal authority, were as ruthless as Catholics in the deadly work. Did space permit, it would be interesting to trace the development and decline of the madness throughout Europe, but it must suffice to allude to Nicholas Remy, a witch-judge in Lorraine, who boasts that his work on the subject is based on about nine hundred cases executed within fifteen years,[532] and to the estimate that the total number in Germany, during the seventeenth century, was a hundred thousand.[533] In these, burning alive was often considered an insufficient penalty, and the victims were torn with hot pincers or roasted over slow fires. France was less a prey to the delusion than Germany, but, in 1609, Henry IV sent a commission to cleanse the Pays de Labour of witches, which, in the hurried work of four months, burnt nearly a hundred, including several priests, and was obliged to leave its task uncompleted, for the land was full of them; two thousand children were transported to the aquellares almost every night and the assemblages consisted of a hundred thousand, though some of these were phantoms.[534] For Great Britain the total estimate of victims is thirty thousand, of whom about a fourth may be credited to Scotland.[535] When, in 1775, Sir William Blackstone could deliberately write "To deny the possibility, nay, actual existence, of witchcraft and sorcery is at once flatly to contradict the revealed word of God.... and the thing itself is a truth to which every nation in the world hath in its turn borne testimony,"[536] we cannot judge the Inquisition harshly for maintaining to the last its existence in theory, while refusing to reduce that theory to practice.

NOTE.--*Since this chapter was in type, the indefatigable Don Manuel Serrano y Sanz has printed in the Revista de Archivos (Nov.-Dic. de 1906) the second discourse by Pedro de Valencia on the Auto de fe of Logroño. In this he states that in the previous one he had only had opportunity for a cursory glance at the proceedings of the auto, and had taken into consideration exceptional cases which God may have permitted of old. Now that he had thoroughly examined the confessions of the culprits he proceeds to give in much detail the monstrosities which they relate and concludes with a brief expression of the convictions resulting therefrom. This is that the aquelarre has nothing supernatural about it, such as flying through the air and the presidency of the demon in the shape of a goat. It is merely a nocturnal assemblage on foot of men and women to gratify disorderly appetites, inflamed perhaps by the instigation of the devil, and that their confessions are fictions invented to cover their wickedness. From this he concludes that they should be held not as confessing but as denying--which, under the inquisitorial code, would expose them to the fiery death of the negativo impenitente. He is careful, moreover, not to discredit the poisonings and the inunctions to cause sleep and dreams. Unfortunately the paper is not dated; it may have been seen by Salazar Frias, but if so it exercised no influence on him, as appears from the different conclusion reached in his report. Señor Serrano y Sanz states that in 1900 he printed the first discourse of Pedro de Valencia in the Revista de Extremadura.*

CHAPTER X - POLITICAL ACTIVITY

DEVELOPMENT OF ABSOLUTISM

Joseph de Maistre, in his profound ignorance of the Inquisition, started the theory that it was a mere political agency.[537] Apologists, like Hefele, Gams, Hergenrother and others, have eagerly elaborated this idea in order to relieve the Church from responsibility for its misdeeds, wholly overlooking the deeper disgrace involved in the assumption that for three centuries the Holy See assented to such misuse of delegated papal authority, and stimulated it with appropriations from ecclesiastical revenues.[538] They base their arguments on the difference between the Old and the New Inquisition--the former consisting of inquisitors selected by Dominican or Franciscan Provincials, and the latter organized with its inquisitor-general and supreme council, appointed by or with consent of the sovereign, so that its whole corps was virtually composed of state officials[539]--forgetting that their authority consisted of apostolical faculties, delegated by the popes and exercised without restraint through their recognition by the State. Ranke falls into the same error and so do Maurenbrecher and some other Protestant historians, apparently in an overstrained effort at impartiality and without investigation of the facts.[540] In the Catholic reaction since the time of Hefele, the most advanced writers of that faith no longer seek to apologize for the Inquisition, and to put forward royal predominance to relieve it from responsibility. They rightly represent it as an ecclesiastical tribunal which discharged the duty of preserving the religious purity for which it was created.[541]

The synchronism of the development of the Inquisition and of absolutism in Spain renders seductive the theory that the one was the product of the other, but this is wholly fallacious. Nowhere in the transformation of the State does the Inquisition appear as a factor. Isabella, as we have seen, laid the foundations of monarchism when she subdued the anarchy pervading Castile by the vigorous assertion and extension of the royal jurisdiction. Ferdinand eliminated some of the most troublesome elements of feudal power when he incorporated in the crown the masterships of the great Military Orders. The restiveness of the nobles under the unaccustomed restraint manifested itself when, in 1506, they flocked to Philip and Juana, had the Inquisition been a political force, Ferdinand would have used it, for Inquisitor-general Deza was devoted to him, in place of which he suspended it. After the death of Philip I, during the retirement of Juana and the absence of Ferdinand, the nobles attempted to reassert themselves but, when he returned, the severe punishment of the Marquis of Priego, the great Duke of Medina Sidonia, Don Pedro Giron and others, was a severe blow to feudalism, redoubled, after Ferdinand's death, when Ximenes as governor raised a standing army and crushed the rebellion of the Girons and their allies, punishing them with the destruction of the town of Villadefrades. What remained of feudalism disappeared under the steady policy of Charles V and Philip II, in keeping the great nobles aloof from the higher offices of state, and employing them in military service abroad or in vice-royalties, until they became mere courtiers, wasting their substance in adding to the splendor of the throne. In all this there is no trace of the Inquisition, nor is there in the rise and suppression of the Comunidades, which destroyed the privileges of the communes, and left the crown supreme. The comuneros had no grievance against the Inquisition, nor had it any share in their defeat and punishment, although Charles V applied to Leo X for special briefs empowering it to act and one was granted, commissioning Cardinal Adrian to try and punish ecclesiastics concerned in the movement.[542] Even when Acuña, Bishop of Zamora, was prosecuted, as we have seen, the Inquisition was not charged with the work, as Ranke mistakenly asserts. The revolt arose from the coercive measures applied by Charles to the Córtes of 1518 and 1520, by which he reduced to impotence the only representative and deliberative body of the nation. Thus the last obstacle to autocracy was swept away, and thenceforth royalty was supreme. The process was a normal development, such as accompanied the downfall of feudalism throughout Europe and, from first to last, it accomplished itself without aid or opposition on the part of the Inquisition.

Much has been made of the saying attributed to Philip II, that he kept his dominions in peace with four old ecclesiastics, and the Suprema was fond of referring to this, when putting forth claims for its services, but it meant nothing except that the Inquisition maintained religious unity, which, in that age and in view of the troubles in France, the Netherlands and Germany, was not unnaturally regarded as the sole guarantee of internal quiet--in fact, the Suprema, when quoting the remark, in 1704, says expressly that Philip uttered it in reference to the turbulence of the Huguenots.[543] That Philip himself did not regard the Inquisition as a political instrument sufficiently appears in his private and confidential instructions of May 7, 1595, to Gerónimo Manrique de Lara, when appointing him inquisitor-general; his anxiety is solely for the faith and there is not the slightest intimation that political service would be expected.[544]

IRREGULAR FUNCTIONS

Yet the average statesman has few scruples in employing any agency at hand to effect his purposes, and to this the Spanish monarchs were no exception. When it suited them to use the Inquisition they did so but, in view of their control over it, their employment of it was singularly infrequent, prior to the advent of the Bourbon dynasty. In the Old Inquisition, with which writers like Hefele endeavor to establish a contrast in this matter, Philip the Fair used it to destroy the Templars, the Regent Bedford to burn Joan of Arc, and Alexander VI to rid himself of Savonarola--three cases to which no parallels exist in the annals of the Spanish Holy Office. The nearest approach to them is to be found in the trials of Carranza, Antonio Pérez and Villanueva. In the first and last of these, as we have seen, inquisitors-general instituted action for their own purposes and the monarchs were brought in to their support. The case of Antonio Pérez will be discussed presently and need not be further referred to here.

Still, a tribunal, whose undefined powers and secrecy of action fitted it so perfectly for use as a political agent, could scarce exist for centuries without occasionally being called upon, and the only legitimate source of surprise is that it was so rarely employed and that the objects for its intervention were usually so trivial. Ferdinand occasionally found it a convenience in settling questions outside of its regular functions, as when Marco Pellegrin appealed to him in a dispute with the authorities of his city and Ferdinand wrote, August 31, 1501, to the inquisitor of the place, charging him to examine the question and do justice, for which he gave him full royal power. So when, in 1500, complaints reached him from Valencia of injustice in the assessments for a servicio, he ordered the papers to be submitted to the inquisitor who was to report to him, and, in 1501, he called for a report from the inquisitor of Lérida as to the necessity of certain repairs to the castle.[545] When, in 1498, he was endeavoring to carry out in Aragon the reform of the Conventual Franciscans, which Ximenes had undertaken in Castile, and they had obtained papal briefs restraining him, he applied to the pope to revoke the letters and meanwhile obtained others from the nuncio, which he transmitted to the tribunal of Saragossa with instructions to act promptly. The inquisitors carried on the reform much to his satisfaction and, when the frailes got the public authorities to protect them, he instructed the inquisitors to represent that they were acting under apostolic authority, that there was no violation of the liberties of the kingdom, that they were salaried by the king, not only for the Inquisition but for whatever duties he might assign to them; they were therefore public officers and, if the Saragossa authorities should endeavor to create scandal, they would be duly punished. This distinction between inquisitorial and non-inquisitorial functions, however did not prevent him, when occasion required, from enforcing outside operations with inquisitorial authority. In 1502, when prosecuting, in the same way, the Franciscan reform in Sardinia and the Bishop of Ocaña, in virtue of a surreptitious papal letter, released from the castle of Fasar the Franciscan vicar, Ferdinand wrote with much indignation to him and to the governor of Cabo de Lugador; it was great audacity to intervene, in a matter concerning the Inquisition, without consulting him or the inquisitor-general; the prisoner must be recaptured forthwith and be held until the inquisitor and reformador apostolico comes.[546]

This indicates the dangerous tendency to extend inquisitorial activity beyond its original limits, and it is remarkable that a monarch entertaining these conceptions and engaged in the struggle with feudalism should not have frequently sought the assistance of the Holy Office. The only definite case that I have met with of its political use occurred in 1507, when Cæsar Borgia escaped from the castle of Medina del Campo to Navarre, and was made commander of his army by Jean d'Albret, whose sister Charlotte he had married. Ferdinand vainly endeavored to obtain his surrender and then caused a prosecution to be brought against him in the Inquisition for heretical blasphemy and suspicion of atheism and materialism. As Cæsar came to his death, March 12, 1507, while besieging the castle of Viana, which held out for Luis de Beaumont, and the prosecution was abandoned, we can only conjecture what the outcome might have been.[547] Navarre was also the scene of a trivial political use of the Inquisition in 1516, when, as we have seen (Vol. I, p. 227) it was instructed to ascertain the names of those friendly to Jean d'Albret.

Henry Charles Lea, LL.D.

ANTONIO PEREZ

There was evidently a purpose to use the Inquisition against the revolt of the Germanía of Valencia, when a brief of October 11, 1520, was obtained from Leo X, granting to Cardinal Adrian faculties to proceed against all persons conspiring against public peace. No use seems to have been made of this, but the Valencia tribunal had an opportunity of making itself felt towards the end of the disturbances. After Vicente Peris, the leader of the Agermanados was killed in a tumult, March 3, 1522, a mysterious individual, known as el Encubierto, and variously described as a hermit from Castile and as a Jew from Gibraltar, presented himself as the avenger of Peris and became the spiritual chief of those who kept up the revolt in Játiva and Alcira. He assumed to be a prophet and the envoy of God, which brought him under the ordinary jurisdiction of the Holy Office, and it made record of the heresies uttered by him in a sermon preached at Játiva, March 23d. He organized a conspiracy in Valencia, but one of the accomplices, named Juan Martin, was betrayed and was seized, by the Inquisition. El Encubierto was assassinated, May 18th, at Burjasot, and his head was cut off; the corpse was brought to Valencia, where the inquisitors had it dragged through the streets on the way to the tribunal. He was condemned as a heretic, the headless body was relaxed and burnt and the head was set over one of the gateways.[548] The action of the Inquisition had no influence on the course of affairs, but it manifests the readiness of the tribunal to assert itself as a political force.

The fable that the Inquisition was invoked to accomplish the death of Don Carlos, in 1568, has been sufficiently disproved to call for no attention here. There is probably, however, more truth in the statement that, about the same time, Philip II, in promotion of his designs on the remnants of Navarre, caused Inquisitor-general Espinosa to collect testimony as to the notorious heresy of Jeanne d'Albret and her children, and formed with the Guises a plot to abduct and deliver her to the tribunal of Saragossa, but the secret was not kept and the attempt was abandoned.[549] Perhaps, also, we may class with political service the utilization by Philip of the Inquisition to supply him with galley-slaves.

The most prominent instance of the employment of the Inquisition in a matter of State was in the case of Antonio Pérez. Its dramatic character attracted the attention of all Europe; the mystery underlying it has never been completely dispelled, and its resultant effect upon the institutions of Aragon invests it with an importance justifying examination in some detail.

Antonio Pérez was the brilliant and able favorite of Philip II, who in 1571 succeeded his patron, Ruy Gómez, Prince of Eboli, in acquiring his master's fullest confidence and becoming the most powerful subject in Spain. In 1573, the Venitian envoy Badoero describes him as a most accomplished man, whose courtesy and attractive manners soothed the sensibilities of those provoked by the delays and penuriousness of the king, while his dexterity and ability promised soon to make him the principal minister. At the same time, he was a man of pleasure and the magnificence of his daily life was the admiration of his countrymen.[550] He found his fate in the widow of his patron, the Princess of Eboli. Sprung from the noble house of Mendoza, she was proud, vindictive and passionate, unflinching in the gratification of her desires and reckless as to the means. Whether Philip II had been her lover, and if so whether he was favored or rejected, is a disputed question, which we need not discuss; it suffices that Pérez, who had a devoted wife in Juana Coello, became enamoured of her mature charms and a slave to her imperious will.

***

Don John of Austria had been sent to the Netherlands on the desperate task of pacifying them, and had been left without resources. Much to the king's displeasure, he sent, in July, 1577, his secretary, Juan de Escobedo, to Madrid to urge the necessity of supplying funds. Escobedo was thoroughly honest, but rugged and uncourtly, and the vigor of his representations increased the royal ill-humor. Pérez had for some time been secretly fanning the king's suspicions of his half-brother's designs, even to the point, it is said, of mistranslating cypher despatches. He represented Escobedo as an emissary sent to perfect Don Juan's plans, including a descent upon Santander and raising Castile in revolt. Convinced that Escobedo must be put out of the way, Philip ordered Pérez to procure his death. If Pérez felt any scruple as to this, it was removed by the fact that Escobedo, who was a retainer of the house of Mendoza, discovered the relations between the princess and the favorite; he remonstrated with freedom and threatened to inform the king. His doom was sealed and, after two ineffectual attempts at poison, bravos were hired who assassinated him in the street on the night of March 31, 1578, and were rewarded with commissions in the army of Italy.

Suspicion fell on Pérez, whose fellow-secretary and bitter enemy, Mateo Vázquez, reported the rumors to the king. The princess in her wrath threatened that Vázquez should share the fate of Escobedo; the court was divided into factions which Philip vainly sought to pacify. He was bound in honor to protect his instrument, and repeatedly assured him that he was in no danger, but, whether he was beginning to realize that he had been unpardonably deceived, or was prompted by jealousy of the relations between Pérez and the princess, he at length was willing to sacrifice his secretary as an escape from a situation that was becoming impossible. Some one to replace him was required; Cardinal Granvelle, then living in retirement in Rome, was sent for; he arrived at the Escorial, July 29, 1579, and, on the preceding night Pérez and the princess were arrested in Madrid. She was carried to the castle of Pinto and was kept in strict confinement until February 1581, when she was allowed to return to her palace at Pastrana, when her extravagant freaks caused her affairs to be placed in charge of a commission, leading to her virtual imprisonment until her death, February 2, 1592.

Pérez, meanwhile, had undergone various vicissitudes of imprisonment, more or less harsh. In May, 1582, Philip ordered an investigation into the different branches of administration, directed principally against Pérez. This resulted in showing that he had habitually sold the royal favor and, in January, 1585, he was condemned to two years' imprisonment in the castle of Turruegano, to ten years' exile from the court, and to refund 12,224,739 maravedís, of which 7,371,098 went to the fisc and the balance to the heirs of Ruy Gómez, in restitution of presents given to him by the princess. The family of the murdered Escobedo had been vainly clamoring for justice. Philip had shrunk from being compromised in the affair, but now that Pérez was thoroughly disgraced, if the documents proving his own complicity could be secured, Pérez could safely be sacrificed to justice. His wife, Juana Coello, was imprisoned and threatened with starvation unless she would surrender his papers; she resisted heroically until a note from Pérez, which he says was written with his blood, permitted her to do so, but he had, with his usual foresight, abstracted from them in advance and placed in safety what he deemed necessary for his justification.

In the summer of 1585, Philip permitted the Escobedo kindred to commence the prosecution. Antonio Enríquez, the page of Pérez, who had arranged the assassination, gave full testimony, but the conteste, or corroboration by another witness was lacking. The affair dragged on, until, September 28, 1589, Pedro Escobedo, son of the victim, abandoned it for the sum of twenty thousand ducats and pardoned his father's murderers. Philip's rancor, however, had deepened with time, and the prosecution was continued. Pérez was tortured, February 22, 1590, when, at the eighth turn of the cordeles, his resolution gave way; he confessed the crime at the royal command and stated the reasons which had moved the king to order the murder. Soon after this he took to his bed and was reported to be dangerously sick; his wife, early in April, was admitted to attend him and, on the 20th, by a side-door, of which he had procured a false key and from which the bolts had been removed, he escaped at night. Friends with horses were in waiting and he took the road to Aragon. He was of Aragonese descent, so that he could claim the fueros and the court of the Justicia, which, as we have seen, sat in judgement between the sovereign and his subjects.

Aragon, at the moment, was especially excited in defence of its privileges, among which was the claim that none but an Aragonese could serve as viceroy. Philip was contesting this and had sent the Count of Almenara to conduct a suit on the question before the court of the Justicia. Almenara earned general ill-will by assuming superiority over all the local officials; the Count of Sástago, then viceroy, resisted his pretensions and was removed and replaced by Andrés Ximeno, Bishop of Teruel, a timid and irresolute man; so great became Almenara's unpopularity that a nearly successful attempt was made to burn at night the house which he occupied; there was a spirit of turbulence abroad, peculiarly favorable to Pérez, who came to claim the protection of the fueros as a faithful servant, whom his king was endeavoring to destroy, in reward of his fidelity.

***

Philip's wrath was boundless. His first impulse was to wreak vengeance on the helpless wife and children, who were thrown into prison, where they lay for nine years until after their persecutor had gone to his last account. Orders were at once despatched to seize the fugitive, dead or alive, before he should cross the Ebro, and so swift were the pursuers that they reached Calatayud, where he made his first halt, only ten hours after him. He threw himself into the Dominican convent for asylum, while his faithful friend, Gil de Mesa, who had accompanied him, hurried forward to Saragossa and claimed for him the manifestacion which secured for him the jurisdiction of the Justicia. Alonso Celdran, lieutenant of the governor, rushed to Calatayud and, after some difficulty, forcibly removed Pérez from the convent, but the veguero of the Justicia came with letters of manifestacion and obliged him to surrender his prey. Nobles and gentlemen flocked to Calatayud, and Pérez was conducted to Saragossa in a veritable triumphal procession, where he was received by the populace as though he were a king and was safely lodged in the cárcel de los manifestados. Then commenced the curious spectacle of a duel to the death between the disgraced fugitive and the whole power of the greatest monarch of Christendom, giving us an enlarged respect for the fueros of Aragon to see that the monarch was helpless until he invoked the overriding powers of the Inquisition, under the pretext that his thirst for vengeance was a matter of faith.

Had the political utility of the Inquisition been the customary expedient that has been asserted, recourse would have been had to it at once. As soon as the flight of Pérez became known, a special junta had been formed in Madrid to manage the affair, and there Juan de Gurrea, Governor of Aragon, familiar with the institutions of his native land, advised that the Inquisition be at once invoked, but there was repugnance to do this and it was resolved to rely on the regular process of law. Philip presented a formal accusation to the court of the Justicia alleging that Pérez had had Escobedo killed, falsely using the king's name; that he had betrayed the king by divulging state secrets and altering despatches, and that he had fled. The documents were sent to Almenara, who pushed the prosecution, while Pérez endeavored to convince the king that it would be better to allow the matter to drop and permit him to live in obscurity rather than to bring the compromising documents to light, as there was no secrecy in Aragonese procedure. He wrote in this sense to Fray Diego de Chaves, the royal confessor, and he sent, by the Prior of Gotor, copies of the papers to Philip, who gave the prior two or three audiences, read the papers and then, on July 1st, published a sentence condemning Pérez to be hanged and beheaded, with confiscation. At the same time instructions were sent to Almenara to push the prosecution and to find some means to seize Pérez and convey him to Castile.

Pérez had already drawn up a memorial replying to the charges, in which he observed considerable reticence. Now he threw off all reserve and prepared another, fortified with documents exposing Philip's share in the tragedy, and representing himself as undergoing ten years of persecution in reward for faithful service. Philip asked Batista de Lanuza, a lieutenant of the Justicia, to send him a copy of the memorial with his opinion as to the result. Lanuza in reply said he expected an acquittal, whereupon Philip withdrew the prosecution on the grounds that it would reveal matters not proper for publication, declaring at the same time that Pérez had committed crimes as great as any subject could and he reserved the right to prosecute him elsewhere. The Justicia, however, continued the case which resulted in acquittal. Then an accusation was brought that Pérez had poisoned his astrologer, Pedro de la Hera, and his servant Rodrigo de Morgado, but these charges were easily refuted and again he was acquitted. Then an attempt was made under an Aragonese law permitting inquisitio or inquest, in accusations of officials by the king, and he was prosecuted for misfeasance in office, but he proved that he had served Philip as King of Castile, not of Aragon, and that he had already been tried and punished for the alleged offences, so this also failed. The principal object of these successive actions was to prevent his discharge from prison, but they had the effect of heightening the popular enthusiasm for Pérez, whose cause became identified with the preservation of the fueros.

As a last resort, when all legal processes were exhausted, recourse was had to the Inquisition. For this some charge involving the faith was necessary and the first suggestion was an assumed attempted flight to the heretics of Béarn. A safer base of operations, however, was devised by Almenara, who won over by bribery an old servant, Diego Bustamente and a teacher named Juan de Basante in whom Pérez had the fullest confidence. In explosions of despairing wrath, they said, he had uttered expressions indicating disbelief in God and blasphemous rebellion against His will. We have seen how much of inquisitorial activity was directed against more or less trivial ejaculations of the kind, and it was strictly in rule to act upon such denunciations. It mattered little on what grounds the Holy Office might obtain possession of him; once in its hands, he would be conveyed, openly or secretly, to Castile, where his fate was certain and, before the dreaded words "a matter of faith" all barriers were vain.

***

Inquisitor Medrano put the testimony in proper shape and forwarded it to the Suprema. Philip ordered that Fray Diego de Chaves should be the sole calificador and he, within twenty-four hours, pronounced the expressions to be heretical. On the strength of this, Inquisitor-general Quiroga and the Suprema, on May 21, 1591, issued orders for the arrest of Pérez and his confinement in the secret prison for trial.

This was hurried to Saragossa, where it was received on the 23d, and on the 24th, the three inquisitors, Medrano, Mendoza and Morejon, issued a warrant of arrest, which was presented at the prison of Manifestacion and was refused obedience. The tribunal then sent, between 9 and 10 A.M., to the lieutenants of the Justicia a mandate, under the customary penalties, requiring the surrender in spite of the pretended right of manifestacion, which was abolished in matters of faith. This could not be evaded and the officials of the Justicia were sent to the prison with orders to deliver Pérez to the alguazil of the tribunal. He was put in a coach and driven to the Aljafería, a short distance beyond the gates, where the Inquisition had its seat.

Two servants of Pérez carried the news to Diego de Heredia and Gil de Mesa, who assembled their friends and sallied into the streets, with the cry, Contrafuero! Viva la libertad y ayuda a la libertad!--the cry which, under the law, could only be raised by order of the Justicia and which, as we have seen, summoned every citizen to come in arms and defend the liberty of the land. The tocsin of the cathedral was tolled and the city rose. Under the leadership of nobles and gentlemen, a part of the mob rushed to the dwelling of the hated Almenara. The Justicia, Juan de Lanuza, with his two sons and his officials, endeavored to protect him, but the door was battered in; he refused to fly, but allowed himself to be conducted to prison, on the promise of the mob to spare his life, but he was attacked on the way and, when the prison was reached, it was with injuries of which he died within a fortnight.

The other section of the populace hastened to the Aljafería and demanded the restoration of Pérez and of his friend Francisco Majorini, who had been included in the prosecution and surrender. Don Pedro de Sesé is said to have brought four hundred loads of wood with which to burn the castle in case of refusal, and the situation was menacing in the extreme. The Viceroy Bishop of Teruel came and urged the inquisitors to compliance. The Archbishop Bobadilla wrote three notes, in increasing desperation--his palace and that of the Justicia would be burnt that night if Pérez were not given up. For five hours the inquisitors resisted this pressure, but finally they yielded, though even then they safeguarded their authority with an order that Pérez's place of confinement should be changed from the secret prison to that of the manifestados. At 5 P.M. the prisoners were delivered to the Counts of Aranda and Morata, with a protest that the trial would be continued. Pérez was conveyed back in a coach to his former prison; the people could not see him and were not satisfied until the viceroy made him stand up and show himself, when they shouted that he must appear at a window thrice daily to prove that no wrong was done him in violation of their liberties and fueros.

There was a tradition that Queen Isabella had once expressed a wish that Aragon would revolt, so that an end could be put to the fueros which limited the royal power. Such an opportunity had now come and Philip was not a sovereign to neglect it. Cabrera relates that, when he lay sick at Ateca and the Count of Chinchon brought him the news, he rose at once from bed, had himself dressed and commenced sending despatches in all directions, ordering the levy of troops. He also wrote to the towns of Aragon and to the nobles, protesting that he meant no violation of their privileges, and the answers encouraged him greatly, for they condemned the troubles at Saragossa and proffered their services. The Inquisition, moreover had opened to it an enlarged field of operations, for which it had abundant justification. Already, on June 4th, the Council of Aragon presented a consulta, calling attention to the impeding of its action, in the threatening of the inquisitors and the killing of a servant of one of them; they should therefore commence to take testimony and arrest the culprits, one by one, who should be relaxed; in such a matter of faith the nobles could not plead privilege and there could be no manifestaciones and firmas.

**

Work to this end was commenced at once in Madrid. Anton de Almunia, who had testified against Pérez, had fled thither with a tale of the threats uttered against him to force him to revoke his evidence. This was a crime against the Inquisition and Pedro Pacheco, Inquisitor of Aragon, was deputed to take his deposition; the investigation widened; all the refugees from Aragon and enemies of Pérez were heard and it was shown that the instigators of the troubles aimed at transferring Aragon to France or to found a republic, and in this were implicated the Diputados of the kingdom, the jurados of Saragossa and the gentlemen who favored Pérez, including the Duke of Villahermosa, who was the head of Aragonese nobility and the Count of Aranda, the richest and most powerful noble. Even Inquisitor Morejon, who had not been as zealous as his colleagues, was laid under suspicion. As a preparation for the impending struggle, the Saragossa tribunal, under orders from Madrid, published, on June 29th, in all the churches, an edict embodying the savage bull Si de Protegendis of Pius V, concerning impeders of the Inquisition, in virtue of which all persons were called upon to aid it, not only in the matter of Pérez but of all others. This created intense excitement; an armed mob assembled in the plaza of the cathedral and discussed whether they were included in the papal censures and if so what remedies should be tried to preserve their liberties, while multitudes sought their confessors and asked to be absolved from the ipso facto excommunication incurred. The Diputados complained to the king and to Quiroga of this stirring up of trouble, when every effort was required to maintain quiet, but they only received from the king a reply thanking them for their zeal for peace.

Pérez and his friends meanwhile were busy in provoking excitement by addresses and pasquinades in prose and verse, stigmatizing their opponents and urging vigilance in defence of the fueros. He also petitioned the Zalmedina to investigate the methods by which Almenara and Medrano had gathered evidence against him, and the testimony thus obtained as to bribes, promises and threats had large influence on public opinion. When the results, however, were sent to Philip by the Diputados, he merely replied that he had not read them, for the whole was invalid because witnesses before the Inquisition could only be impugned in it; Pérez must be returned to the tribunal before anything else could have attention. The papers however were carefully preserved, for the mere investigation was a grave offence against the Inquisition, which was subsequently charged against its authors. The Inquisition judged all men and was to be judged by none and, in the sacredness which shielded it, any attempt to examine its methods was a crime.

As the summer drew to a close, the cooler-headed citizens became anxious for an accommodation.

Conferences were held with jurists and it was recognized that the position was untenable, that Pérez must be surrendered and an understanding was reached with the inquisitors as to certain unimportant conditions which avoided the appearance of complete abandonment. The aspect of the populace, however, was threatening, and the nobles brought their retainers to the city to enforce order. Philip had no objection to the delays which enabled him to collect his forces at Agreda, on the Castilian border, and September 24th was named for the delivery of Pérez as a solemn public act. He was fully alive to the danger and resolved on escape; a file was furnished to him with which during three nights he worked at his window bars. A few hours more would have set him free when he was betrayed by his false friend Juan Basante, who still retained his confidence and was to share his flight. He was transferred to a stronger cell, where he was kept incomunicado, with a guard of thirty arquebusiers, watching him day and night.

On September 22d died the Justicia, Juan de Lanuza, an old and experienced man, succeeded by his son of the same name, who was but 27 years of age, universally beloved on account of his many good qualities, but untried and lacking in influence. Great preparations were made for the surrender on the 24th. The gates were closed, troops were posted, the streets from the prison to the Aljafería were patrolled by cavalry, and death was threatened for the slightest disturbance. Complicated formalities were observed when the mandate for the delivery of Pérez and Majorini was presented to the court of the Justicia by Lanceman de Sola, secretary of the tribunal. Under guard of arquebusiers a procession was formed of officials and dignitaries, who on reaching the market-place bestowed themselves in the overlooking windows. The prison was entered, Pérez and Majorini were produced, shackles were placed on them and they were formally surrendered to Lanceman de Sola. The coaches to convey them were brought up and they were descending the stairs when the roar of a multitude outside brought a pause.

***

The friends of Pérez had not been idle. The gentlemen who still adhered to him had brought their retainers to the city; propagandism had been active and a majority of the arquebusiers declared themselves ready to die in defence of the fueros. The streets were filled with clamorous crowds; already during the march of the procession, stones had been thrown and now, under the leadership of Diego de Heredia and Gil de Mesa, the market-place was attacked on several sides. Some of the guards were slain, others fled and others joined the assailants. The plaza was strewn with some thirty dead and numerous wounded; the governor's horse was shot and he escaped to a house which was promptly set on fire; the notables at the windows broke out a way to escape by the rear and hurried off amid the insults of the people. Inside the prison the officials saved themselves by flight over the roof, except a lieutenant of the Justicia who made Pérez show himself at a window to calm the mob, which sent up shouts of joy and commenced to break in the doors, when he was delivered to them through a postern. He was carried in triumph to the house of Diego de Heredia and then Majorini was remembered. He was sent for; the prison was found abandoned and he was set free.

Pérez mounted a horse and, accompanied by Gil de Mesa and Francisco de Ayerbe, with a couple of servitors, fled to the mountains, reaching Alagon that night and Tauste the next day, where he rested five days in the house of Francisco de Ayerbe. The agents of the Inquisition tracked him and came near seizing him; when, finding escape to France blocked, he returned secretly to Saragossa, by the advice of Martin de Lanuza, in whose house he was secreted, while directing the course of affairs. The city had been in a state of chaos, the magistrates not daring to show themselves, but through his counsels comparative tranquility was restored under Diego de Heredia. He set to work to organize Aragon, Catalonia and Valencia in opposition to Castile, with a view of forming a republic under the protection of France, but his efforts met with no practical response.

Aragon itself was lukewarm. The assembling of an army at Agreda under Alonso Vargas, a distinguished captain, with the pretext of an expedition to France, gave warning that revolt would be crushed with a heavy hand and both sides sought the support of the kingdom at large. In Saragossa the fuero prohibiting the introduction of foreign troops was invoked, and the new Justicia, Juan de Lanuza, was summoned by the Diputados to call the kingdom to arms to resist the contrafuero. He did so with a proclamation, October 31st, ordering the towns and nobles to send their quotas to Saragossa on November 5th, but the course of affairs at Saragossa had been watched with disfavor. Jaca responded with protestations and not with men; Daroca sent thirty musketeers; Bielsa, Puertolas and Gistain furnished two hundred men who turned back after reaching Barbastro. There were disturbances at Teruel which only resulted in the punishment subsequently inflicted on the leaders. The other towns united in a letter to the Justicia, declaring Philip to be the defender of the fueros and those who resisted him to be the violators, and the same ground was taken by the nobles and gentry outside of Saragossa. Villahermosa and Aranda had remained in the city by Philip's orders, and were forced to serve on the council of war which was formed, but they were regarded with suspicion and were insulted and menaced.

This practical abandonment produced profound discouragement and the gates were locked to prevent desertions, but all who could left the city. The leaders, however were too deeply compromised to withdraw and, in their irritation, they provoked quarrels and discord. To give an air of legality to resistance the leadership of the Justicia was essential, and they summoned Juan de Lanuza to take the field with the municipal forces. He and the Diputado Juan de Luna established relations with Villahermosa and Aranda and all four agreed to escape on the occasion of a review to be held on November 7th, but when Lanuza ordered a gate to be opened and the review to be held outside the walls, there was a cry of treason. Villahermosa and Aranda succeeded in escaping and took refuge in Epila, a fortified town belonging to Aranda, but Lanuza and Luna were pulled from their horses and were with difficulty rescued alive.

Bruised as he was, however, Lanuza was forced, the next day, to take the field at the head of four hundred men, the rest of the forces following the next day, and with a so-called army of two thousand he advanced to Utebo, to contest the advance of Vargas, who had crossed the border November 7th with a well-equipped force of twelve thousand foot and two thousand horse, supported by sufficient artillery. A messenger from Vargas offering terms gave him an opportunity of escape and, accompanied by Luna, he sought the refuge of Epila. When the news of this spread through the camp the little army disbanded and Vargas, on November 12th, presented himself before the Aljafería, to the great joy of the inquisitors. The viceroy and officials came forth to welcome him, and he made a triumphal entry into the city. The plaza of the cathedral was made a place d'armes, heavy guards were posted, cannon commanded the streets and the soldiers were billeted on the citizens. The working classes had abandoned the town and there were more than fifteen hundred vacant houses.

***

Pérez had been watching the wreck of his schemes of vengeance, and, not caring to share in the ruin that he had wrought, he sought to save himself. Martin de Lanuza escorted him to a gate and had it opened for him and, on the 10th, two days before the arrival of Vargas, he took the road to Sallent, on the French frontier. The next day Don Martin offered to the Diputados to die for the city if they proposed to defend it, but, as they did not, he suggested that the gates be opened and that all who desired be allowed to depart. This was done and, in the exodus that followed, he betook himself to the mountains in order to save Pérez.

Resistance had ceased, but there was still some apprehension as to what was known as the Junta of Epila, where Lanuza had invited a conference to consult as to the best means of preserving the fueros. Such fears were superfluous. Villahermosa and Aranda, at the earnest request of Vargas, returned to Saragossa; Luna went into hiding and Lanuza retired to his lands at Badallur, subsequently coming to Saragossa and resuming his functions as Justicia. Vargas conducted himself with great adroitness, receiving most graciously deputations from the towns, inviting absentees to return and assuring every one that the fueros would be respected. Then, on November 28th came the Marquis of Lombay, as special royal commissioner, with letters assuring the preservation of the fueros and clemency for culprits. He was received with great distinction and was hailed as an Angel de Paz; all was thought to be settled peacefully and the refugees returned. Vargas and Lombay urged Philip to issue a general pardon with specified exceptions, to limit the Inquisition to matters absolutely its own, to assemble the Córtes under his own presidency and they even suggested Aranda as the new viceroy.

Suddenly this dream of pacification was dispelled. Without communicating his resolve to any one, Philip sent, by a secret messenger, an order written in his own hand and not countersigned, to arrest the Justicia at once "and let me know of his death as soon as of his arrest." He was to be beheaded, his estates confiscated and his castles and houses razed to the ground. Villahermosa and Aranda were likewise to be arrested and to be sent to Castile.

Vargas felt acutely his position in being thus forced to belie his promises of clemency, but he was a soldier, trained to obey orders. Lombay was indignant at the use made of him and asked to be relieved, a request promptly granted for the court had no further need of him. Vargas lost no time in executing the royal commands. The next morning, December 19th, at 11 o'clock, Lanuza was arrested as he and his lieutenant were on their way to mass, prior to opening their court. Villahermosa and Aranda were enticed to Vargas's quarters on a pretext; he detained them in friendly conversation until word was brought of Lanuza's arrest, when he dismissed them and they were arrested as they left him. In three hours they were placed in coaches, each with two captains charged not to lose sight of them. Four companies of horse and a thousand infantry guarded them to the border, after which two companies of foot conducted them, Villahermosa to the castle of Burgos and Aranda to the Mota of Medina del Campo. Both died in prison.

The early light of the next dawn showed a black scaffold erected in the market-place; the troops were under arms and cannon guarded the approaches. The citizens shut themselves up in their houses and there were none present but the soldiery who, we are told, although Castilians, shed tears over the fate of Lanuza, whose brief three months of office had brought him to such end. The executioner struck off his head while he was reciting a hymn to the Virgin and he was honorably buried, in the tomb of his ancestors in the church of San Felipe, the bier being borne on the shoulders of high officers of the Castilian army.

This unexpected blow aroused indescribable terror throughout Aragon, and the impression caused by the revelation of the hidden purposes of the king was intensified by his granting to the Governor a commission authorizing him to punish the notoriously guilty without regard to the fueros. Under this there followed arrests and executions of those compromised in the troubles, especially of those concerned in the death of Almenara, including many men of rank, who were generally regarded as innocent, or at most as lightly culpable. No one felt himself safe, and the sense of insecurity was heightened by the razing of the houses of the victims--the palace of the Lanuzas, one of the most conspicuous in Saragossa, and those of Diego de Heredia, Martin de Lanuza, Pedro de Bolea, Manuel Don Lope and others--the ruins made in the principal streets symbolizing to the people the destruction of their liberties. Nor was the Inquisition remiss in vindicating its insulted dignity. The inquisitors had been changed and the tribunal now consisted of Pedro Zamora, Velarde de la Concha and Juan Moriz de Salazar, who fully realized the work expected of them. They filled the prisons of the Aljafería with men of all classes, who had taken part in obstructing the action of the Holy Office, though they subsequently, under orders from Philip, delivered to Vargas certain of their prisoners who were marked for execution for offences outside of inquisitorial jurisdiction.

***

Satisfied with the impression thus made, Philip now took measures to calm the agitation. He withdrew the special commission of the Governor of Aragon and promised to the accused a regular trial by an impartial Aragonese judge. Then, on January 17, 1592, there was solemnly proclaimed in Saragossa a general pardon, in which the king dwelt on his love for Aragon and on his clemency, but also on his duty to enforce justice and uphold the Inquisition. There were certain classes excepted from the benefit of the amnesty, which, when subsequently applied to individuals, amounted to 196, whom every one was ordered by proclamation to capture wherever found. The promised impartial judge was appointed in the person of Doctor Miguel Lanz, whose ignorance and cruelty were the cause of bitter complaints.

It was part of Philip's tranquilizing policy that the Inquisition should issue simultaneously an edict of pardon, with exceptions like his own. The two classes of culprits were largely distinct, and the tension of the public mind could not be relieved until the extent of both should be known. With this view, when drawing up his own proclamation, he ordered the Suprema to do the same, but he encountered resistance. The Inquisition was playing for its own hand. It had not only to avenge insults endured but it was resolved to make the most of the opportunity to break down the obstinate resistance in Aragon to its arbitrary proceedings. The Suprema was therefore indisposed to accede to Philip's wishes and, in a consulta of January 2d, it asked for delay. To this Philip replied, in his own handwriting, that the postponement would prevent the desired restoration of confidence and, where there were so many involved, it sufficed to punish those most guilty. He was about to publish his own pardon and he charged the Suprema to do the same on its part with all despatch.

Considerations such as these had no weight with the Suprema, which calmly disregarded the king's wishes. The silence of the Inquisition kept alive popular anxiety and, on March 3d, Philip renewed his urgency. The pardon should be such as to give satisfaction to the people, relieving from infamy those comprehended in it who should come and confess spontaneously. Proceedings could be taken against those arrested and fugitives, who could be summoned by edicts, and the pardon could be general, excepting the prisoners and those cited and to be cited in contumacy, without giving names, but all this he left to the Suprema to do what it deemed best for the authority of the Holy Office.

Philip evidently shrank from too positive insistence, and the Suprema on various pretexts continued to postpone the pardon. In answer to renewed urgency, it presented a consulta, April 29th, reporting its operations, according to which the tribunal of Saragossa had recently voted the arrest of a hundred and seventy-six persons; it had already seventy-four in its prisons, and it contemplated the prosecution of three hundred--which explains the reluctance to issue a general pardon. This was so contrary to the policy of the king that he replied by suggesting the liberation on bail of those whose offences admitted of it, and suspending arrest in cases that might reasonably be condoned. He made no allusion, this time, to a general pardon and the Inquisition carried its point. Without issuing a pardon, on October 20th it celebrated an auto de fe with more than eighty culprits, of whom all were impeders of its free action, except a few Moriscos and a bigamist. Six were relaxed, ostensibly as guilty of homicide in the disturbances of September 24, 1591, and the rest were penanced, mostly by exile from Aragon, although some were sent to the galleys, among whom was Manuel Don Lope. The procession at the auto was closed with the effigy of Pérez, condemned to the flames in a sentence which, we are told, recited a million of arrogant and ill-sounding propositions against God and the king, his affection for Vandoma (Henry IV), treasons committed in his office of Secretary, strong indications of sodomy, his flight to France, his listening to preachers and taking communion with Huguenots, sufficient to prove him a Huguenot, with presumption that all his actions had been directed to that end and to destroy the Inquisition, as he was a descendant of Jews and great-grandson of Aubon Pérez, a Jew who relapsed after conversion, was burnt and his sanbenito was hanging in the church of Calatayud. The sentence was relaxation, with disabilities of descendants.

***

On the day of the auto Philip was at Rioja, on his way to Tarazona, where the Córtes which had been called had been sitting and had nearly finished its labors. As the Inquisition had still withheld its general pardon, he again insisted that it be put into shape and sent to him, in order that everything might be concluded before he reached Tarazona. Still unsatiated and procrastinating, the Suprema replied with the names of eleven persons, whom it characterized as principal leaders of the tumults and asked him to give such instructions as he pleased. He responded that he would delay answering till he reached Tarazona and could survey the aspect of matters there. Some days later he wrote asking that the propriety of issuing the pardon should be discussed, as also the form which it should have. Thereupon the Suprema sent him a form, with a letter to the inquisitors which he could forward, at the same time stating that there were objections. The royal pardon was unconditional and took effect of itself, but the Inquisition was not so easily satisfied and required that all who availed themselves of its mercy should make personal application and submission. The papal decree Si de protegendis inflicted an ipso facto anathema on all who obstructed in any way the action of the Holy Office, and this censure had to be removed, wherefore the proposed formula required that all applicants for pardon should seek relief from the censures, those present within two months, and the absent within four, but the Suprema added that publication should be preceded by edicts against seven specified persons and others notoriously guilty who could not be named without violating the secrecy of the Inquisition. Even this the Suprema felt to be too great a concession, and the next day it forwarded another consulta, saying that it had received from the Saragossa tribunal the names of some parties notoriously and deeply inculpated; there was evidence of their guilt in the tribunal and it had commenced action against them with edicts. This was submitted to the king so that he could order the inquisitors to commence before publishing the pardon, in order that the parties might be excepted. Philip disregarded this last effort of the Inquisition to maintain its hold on those who had offended it. Without further correspondence he sent the pardon to Saragossa with orders for its publication, which was done with great solemnity, November 23d, when more than five hundred penitents presented themselves.

Meanwhile the Córtes had been employed in modifying the institutions of Aragon to meet the wishes of the king. While resolved thus to take full advantage of the opportunity, he was shrewd enough to see that such a settlement to be enduring must be in conformity with the fueros. While his army still overawed the land he therefore convoked the Córtes, which met at Tarazona, June 15, 1592. According to rule, he should have presided over it, but he desired not to enter Aragon until the trials and executions under Dr. Miguel Lanz should be completed, and, though he left Madrid May 30th, he took the circuitous route by way of Valladolid, and his leisurely journey was interrupted by attacks of gout. After some difficulty, the Córtes accepted the presidency of Archbishop Bobadilla, and modified the immemorial rule requiring unanimity in each of the four brazos or chambers. The way being thus cleared, and still further smoothed by a lavish distribution of "graces," it was merely a work of time to obtain the adoption of a carefully devised series of fueros which, without changing the form of Aragonese institutions, removed the limitations on the royal power which had so long been the peculiar boast of the kingdom. The changes were too numerous for recapitulation here in full; some of them were beneficial in facilitating the punishment of crime, but the most important from the monarch's stand-point were those which established his right to appoint viceroys who were not Aragonese; which placed in his hands the nomination and dismissal of the Justicia and the nomination of his lieutenants, with preponderance in the machinery for hearing complaints against the latter; which took from the Diputados the power of convoking the cities and citizens, which limited the amount that they could spend, and which transferred from them to the crown control over the rural police; which prohibited raising the cry of "libertad" under penalties extending even to death; which provided punishment for offences against royal officials; which established extradition for crime between Castile and Aragon; which required the royal licence for the printing of books, and which deprived the lands of the nobles, secular and ecclesiastical, of the right of asylum for criminals. Thus the Justicia and his court, which had been the pride of the land, became in fact, if not in name a royal court; the Diputados, who had been the executive of the popular will, were deprived of all dangerous exercise of authority, the barriers against the encroachments of arbitrary power were removed, and all this had been accomplished through the representatives of the people, apparently of their own volition.

When, early in December, Philip at Tarazona held the solio in which he confirmed the acts of the Córtes, he followed it with a general pardon, liberating all those prosecuted by Dr. Lanz, except the jurists and lieutenants of the Justicia, who had counselled resistance and who were punished with exile. Cosme Pariente, an unlucky poet, was sent to the galleys as the author of the pasquinades which had stimulated revolt, and there was another significant exception. Philip's inextinguishable hatred of his favorite still kept in prison Juana Coello and her seven children, the youngest of whom was born in captivity. Thus they languished for nine years until their gaoler had passed away. Philip III signalized the first year of his reign with pardoning those excepted in his father's edicts and, in April 1599, Juana was set free. She hesitated to leave her children, the eldest of whom was in her twentieth year, but she finally did so to labor for their release, which she accomplished in the following August. The friends of Pérez sought to have him included in the royal mercy, but were told that his offence was a matter of the Inquisition with which the king could not interfere.

Before relieving Aragon of his army, Philip caused the Aljafería to be fortified and lodged there a garrison of two hundred men to keep the turbulent city in check. To this the inquisitors objected strongly, and asked to be transferred to some other habitation, but he refused, as their protection served as an excuse for the garrison. They never grew reconciled to their unwelcome guests and, in 1617 and again in 1618, we find them complaining that the soldiers exercised control over the castle and that their audacious pretensions diminished greatly the popular respect due to the Holy Office.[551] Their remonstrances were unheeded until, in 1626, Philip IV, as a special favor transferred the garrison to Jaca.

Pérez and his friends had succeeded in reaching Béarn, where they were welcomed by the governess, Catherine, sister of Henry IV. Imagining that a small force would raise the Aragonese in defence of their liberties, they persuaded Henry to try the experiment, to be followed, in case of success, by an army of fifteen or twenty thousand men, to wrench from Spain Aragon, Catalonia and Valencia, and form a republic under French protection. In February, 1592, therefore, some fifteen hundred or two thousand Béarnese, under the leadership of Martin Lanuza, Gil de Mesa, Manuel Don Lope, and Diego de Heredia attempted an invasion, but the Aragonese rose against them. Embarrassed by the deep snows in the mountains, they attempted to retreat but were vigorously attacked and most of them were taken prisoners, including Dionisio Pérez, Francisco de Ayerbe and Diego de Heredia. Vargas liberated the Béarnese, but the refugees were sent to Saragossa, where they expiated their treason on the scaffold.

In spite of this misadventure, Pérez was warmly welcomed and was pensioned by Henry IV, as a personage of importance, a statesman versed in all the arts of Spanish diplomacy. The peace of Vervins, however, in 1598 reduced him to insignificance. Age and infirmities overtook him and his adventurous existence terminated in misery, November 3, 1611, when he manifested every sign of fervent Catholicism. After his death, Juana Coello and his children undertook the vindication of his memory and solicited to be heard in his defence. It was not, however, until January 22, 1613 that the Suprema presented to Philip III a consulta recommending that the widow and children should be heard by the Saragossa tribunal. Sentences rendered in absentia, as we have seen, were never regarded as conclusive, but the tribunal was unforgiving. It interposed delays and then, on March 16, 1615, it rendered an adverse judgement. This the Suprema refused to confirm and, after an obstinate resistance, the tribunal, on June 19th was forced to utter a sentence absolving the memory and fame of Antonio Pérez, declaring the limpieza of his blood and pronouncing that his descendants were under no disabilities. Nothing, however, was said about removing the confiscation of his property, probably because this had been decreed both by the secular sentence of July 17, 1590 and by the inquisitorial one of October 20, 1592.[552]

OCCASIONAL CASES

Thus in this, the most prominent instance of inquisitorial political intervention, the Holy Office was invoked only as a last resort, when all other methods had failed, and, when it was called in, so far from being the obsequious instrument of the royal will, it resolutely sought to advance its own interests with little regard for the policy of the monarch.

Yet the impression made at the time is reflected in the report of the Venetian envoy, Agostino Nano, in 1598, when he says that the king can be termed the head of the Inquisition, for he appoints the inquisitors and officials. He uses it to hold in check his subjects and to punish them with the secrecy and severity of its procedure, when he cannot do so with the ordinary secular authority of the Royal Council. The Inquisition and the Royal Council mutually help each other in matters of state for the king's service.[553] This was a not unnatural conclusion to draw from a case of this nature, but the royal power, by this time, was too securely intrenched to require such aid. It was only the peculiar features of the Aragonese fueros that called for the invention of a charge of heresy in a political matter. The

Inquisition, as a rule, considered it no part of its duties to uphold the royal power for, in 1604, we find it sentencing Bartolomé Pérez to a severe reprimand, a fine of ten thousand maravedís and a year's exile for saying that obedience to the king came before that due to the pope and to the Church.[554] Thus the mere denial of the superiority of the spiritual power over the temporal was a crime.

Sporadic cases occurred in which special considerations called for the aid of the Inquisition, but they were not numerous and were apt to be directed against ecclesiastics, whose privilege exempted them from the secular courts. Such was that of the Jesuit, Juan de Mariana, distinguished in many ways, but especially by his classical History of Spain. He had served the Inquisition well as a censor of books, but in his Tractatus septem, published anonymously at Cologne, in 1609, in an essay on the debased Spanish coinage, the freedom with which he reprobated its evils and spoke of the malfeasance of officials gave great offence to the royal favorite Lerma and his creatures. Had Mariana been a layman there would have been no trouble in punishing him severely, but to reach the Jesuit Philip invoked the papal nuncio Caraffa and the Toledo tribunal took a hand. The whole proceeding was irregular and the pope was asked to render sentence, but, after a year's imprisonment, Mariana was liberated, without an imputation on his character, and he died, in 1624, full of years and honor, at the age of 87.[555]

It is true that, when the Barcelona tribunal was battling to maintain its pretensions against the Córtes of Catalonia, it represented, in 1632, in a memorial of Philip IV, among its other claims to consideration, the secret services often rendered in obtaining information and in the arrest of powerful persons, which could not otherwise be so well accomplished. Its thorough organization, no doubt, occasionally enabled it to be of use in this manner, and there was no scruple in calling upon it for such work, as in 1666, when Don Pedro de Sossa, the farmer of the tax of millones, in Seville, absconded with a large sum of money and was understood to be making his way to France, the Suprema wrote to Barcelona and doubtless to other tribunals at the ports and frontier districts, with a description of his person and an order to arrest him and embargo his property.[556]

The prosecutions of the two fallen favorites, Rodrigo Calderon, in 1621 and Olivares, in 1645, were not state affairs but intrigues, to prevent their return to favor and were rendered unnecessary, in the one case by the decapitation of Calderon and in the other by the death of Olivares.[557] The secrecy of the Inquisition and its methods of procedure rendered it a peculiarly favorable instrumentality for such manoeuvres, as was seen in the Villanueva case, as well as for the gratification of private malice, and it was doubtless frequently so abused, but this has no bearing on its use as a political agency.

THE WAR OF SUCCESSION

With the advent of the Bourbon dynasty there was a change. In the governmental theory of Louis XIV the Church was part of the State and subject to the dictation of the monarch. In the desperate struggle of the War of Succession, the advisers of the young Philip V had no hesitation in employing all the resources within reach and the Inquisition was expected to play its part. At an early period of the conflict, the Suprema sent orders to the tribunals to enjoin earnestly, on all their officials, fidelity to the king, who thus had the benefit of a well-distributed army of missionaries in every quarter of the land.[558] It was easy, as we have seen, for inquisitorial logic to stretch the elastic definition of heresy in any desired direction, and lack of loyalty to Philip was made to come within its boundaries. In an edict of October 9, 1706, the Suprema pointed out that Clement XI had threatened punishment for all priests who faltered in their devotion to the king, yet notwithstanding this there were some who in the confessional urged penitents to disobedience and relieved them from the obligation of their oath of allegiance. This was a manifest abuse of the sacrament and, as it was the duty of the Inquisition to maintain the purity of the faith and prevent the evil resulting from a doctrine so pernicious, all penitents so solicited were ordered, within nine days, to denounce their confessors, under pain of excommunication and other discretional penalties.[559]

The Inquisition, during the war, was especially serviceable in dealing with ecclesiastics, who were beyond the reach of secular and military courts, and this in cases where there was no pretence of heresy. The events of 1706--the capture and loss of Madrid by the Allies and the revolutions in Valencia and Catalonia--occasioned a number of trials for high treason. The Suprema was still in Burgos when Philip V informed Inquisitor-general Vidal Marin that he had ordered the arrest of Juan Fernando Frias, a cleric, who was to be delivered to the Inquisition at Burgos, to be tried for high treason, with all speed. The Suprema replied, August 13th, that it had placed Frias in safe custody, incomunicado; the inquisitor-general had commissioned the Prior of Santa María de Palacio de Logroño to serve on the tribunal, and there should be the least possible delay in the verification and punishment of the offence. It assured the king that he could rely on the promptest fulfilment of his wishes and of the vindicta publica, for the Apostolic jurisdiction of the Suprema extended to the infliction of the death-penalty.[560] In its loyal zeal it took no thought of irregularity. Indeed, the Suprema seems to have issued commissions to tribunals to act in such cases. In 1707, Isidro de Balmaseda, Inquisitor of Valencia, signs himself as "Inquisidor y Juez Apostólico contra los eclesiasticos difidentes," in the case of Fray Peregrin Gueralt, lay-brother of the Servite convent of Quarto, whom the testimony showed to be an adherent of the Archduke Charles, industriously carrying intelligence to the Allies and, on his return, spreading false reports, to the disturbance of men's minds. In this trial the formality of a clamosa by the fiscal was omitted; the inquisitors had the testimony taken and on receiving it ordered the arrest of Gueralt without submitting it to calificadores.[561]

From this time forward the Inquisition was at the service of the State whenever it was required to suppress opinions that were regarded as dangerous though, when its interests clashed with those of the crown, the cases of Macanaz and Belando show that it could still assert its aggressive independence. As the century wore on, however, it became more and more subservient. A writer about 1750, while regretting that it did not repress the Probabilism of the fashionable Moral Theology, gives it hearty praise for its political utility; it is not only, he says, engaged in preserving the purity of the faith, but, in an ingenious way, it maintains the peace of the State and the subordination due to the king and the magistracy. In his wars Philip V made use occasionally of its tribunals in difficult conjunctures with happy results and therefore he honored and distinguished it throughout his reign.[562]

UNDER THE RESTORATION

Thus, as its original functions declined, a new career was opened. We have seen how its censorship was utilized to prevent the incursion of modern liberalism, and its procedure was similarly employed against individuals. With the outbreak of the French Revolution, its vigilance was directed especially against the propagation of the dangerous doctrines of popular liberty, and any expression of sympathy with events beyond the Pyrenees was sufficient to justify prosecution. As early as 1790, Jacques Jorda, a Frenchman, was tried by the Barcelona tribunal for propositions antagonistic to the spiritual and temporal authorities, and prosecutions for such offences continued to be frequent. In 1794, during the war with the French Republic, even so important a personage as Don Antonio Ricardo, general-in-chief of the army in Roussillon, was on trial by the tribunal of Madrid for utterances in sympathy with occurrences in France and, at the same time, his secretary, Don Josef del Borque, was undergoing a similar experience in the Logroño tribunal.[563] War carried on in such fashion could not fail to be disastrous.

This prostitution of an ecclesiastical tribunal to temporal purposes was one of the reasons given by the Córtes of Cádiz for its abolition. Even its chief defender, Fray Maestro Alvarado, could not deny the accusation, but, he turned the tables by ascribing the fault to the Jansenists, to whom the orthodox attributed all the evils of the time. It was they, he argued who mingled religion and politics, and set the State above the Church.[564] He did not live to see the refutation of his dialectics, when Ultramontanism triumphed in the Restoration, and the political functions of the Inquisition became still more prominent. In 1814, a copy of the treaty of July 30th with Louis XVIII was sent to the tribunals in order that they might enforce the clauses appertaining to them, and when, in 1815, the news of Napoleon's return from Elba was received, King Fernando, by an order of April 8th, included the tribunals of the Inquisition in the instructions given to the military and ecclesiastical authorities to keep watch on the frontier against surprises, and to guard in the interior against the artifices and seductions of the disaffected.[565] In fact, we may say, the chief work expected of the Inquisition was that of the haute police, for which its organization rendered it especially fitted. April 8, 1817 we find it notified that the refugees, General Renovales and Colonel Peon, accomplices in the attempted rising of Juan Diaz Porlier in Galicia, were hovering on the Portuguese border. The tribunal of Santiago (Galicia) was therefore to put itself in communication with that of Coimbra, it was to devise means for their capture and, through its commissioners and familiars, find out what was on foot, for the security of the throne and of the altar required of the Holy Office extreme vigilance under existing circumstances. The inquisitor-general forwarded this to Galicia with orders to execute it "at once, at once, at once" and, not content with this, instructions were sent to the tribunals of Murcia, Córdova, Saragossa and Barcelona, all of which responded with promises of the utmost activity and of watchfulness over reactionaries.[566] So, in 1818 the Logroño tribunal reported that its commissioner at Hernani (Guipúzcoa) reported that he had heard a person utter the proposition "La nacion es soberana." To this the Suprema replied that this was a matter of high importance and might lead to great results. Llano must make a formal denunciation with all details; also he must declare why he suspected Don Joseph Joaquin de Mariategui, and how he knows of his journey to France and England and his relations with the refugees there--all of which must be done with the utmost caution and speed and the results be reported.[567]

It is scarce worth while to multiply trivial details like these to indicate how efficient a political agency the Inquisition had become under the Restoration. Its activity in this direction continued until the end and when, in the Revolution of 1820 at Seville, on March 10th, the doors of the secret prison were thrown open, the three prisoners liberated were political.[568]

Besides these direct political services, the Inquisition was sometimes called upon by the State to aid in enforcing secular laws, when the civil organization found itself unequal to the duty. The most conspicuous instance of this is found in the somewhat incongruous matter of preventing the export of horses.

EXPORTATION OF HORSES

From a very early period this was regarded with great jealousy. From the twelfth century onward, the Córtes of Leon and Castile, in their petitions, constantly asked that the prohibition should be enforced and, at those of Burgos in 1338, Alfonso XI decreed death and confiscation for it, even if the offenders were hidalgos, a ferocious provision which was renewed by Ferdinand and Isabella in 1499.[569] Aragon, which lay between Castile and France, suffered from this embargo. The Córtes of Monzon, in 1528, petitioned Charles V for the pardon of certain citizens who had drawn horses from Castile and were condemned to death and other penalties, to which Charles replied that he would not pardon those who had carried horses to France; as for those who had merely taken them to Aragon, if they could be pointed out, he would grant them pardon. Another complaint of the Córtes indicates the rigid methods adopted to prevent evasions. If an Aragonese went to Castile on business, he was allowed to remain ninety days; if he exceeded the limit, on his return his horse was seized at the frontier, even though at the same place by which he had entered.[570] Severe as were these measures, they were ineffective. Contraband trade of all kinds flourished in the wild mountain districts along the French frontier, and the prohibition respecting a beast of burden, which transported itself, was notoriously difficult of enforcement.

In 1552, we find the Suprema ordering the Saragossa tribunal to prosecute and punish one of its commissioners in the mountains of Jaca, accused of passing horses to France, but this was evidently due to the fact that the offender was entitled to the fuero of the Inquisition.[571] There was as yet no ingenious attribution of suspicion of heresy to this contraband trade and, when in 1564, the Córtes of Monzon prohibited the exportation of horses and mares from Aragon, the only reason alleged was their scarcity in the kingdom.[572] The third Lateran Council, however, in 1179, had denounced excommunication and severe penalties on all who furnished the infidel with warlike material, and this had been carried into the Corpus Juris; Nicholas IV had specifically included horses and had sharpened the penalties; Boniface VIII, in 1299, had placed the offence under the jurisdiction of the Holy Office, and had ordered all inquisitors to make vigilant inquest in their districts, and the prohibition was repeated in the annual bulls In coena Domini.[573] The south of France, and especially the contiguous territory of Béarn, had become interpenetrated with heresy and a colorable pretext was afforded of invoking the aid of the Inquisition to suppress the contraband traffic.

***

This was first confided, in 1573, to the tribunal of Saragossa, by a commission empowering it to act in the premises. It accordingly inserted in the Edict of Faith a clause requiring the denunciation of all who sold arms or horses to infidels, heretics, or Lutherans, or who passed, or assisted to pass, them to Lutheran lands. This brought in numerous denunciations but, as there were no means of knowing what became of the horses after they passed the border, the tribunal was powerless to prosecute and so reported to the Suprema. It replied, August 25, 1573, that further provision was necessary; assuming that Béarn was inhabited by heretics under heretic rulers, the tribunal could proceed against and punish, as fautors of heretics, those who bought or sold or passed horses to Béarn, even when it did not appear that they had been sold to heretics, and it was urged to be active in the matter. The edict was therefore modified to include, as fautors of heretics, all concerned in passing horses to Béarn; it was sent, with a secretary, to all the principal fairs where horses were sold, to be published in the church, with notice that the commissioner would receive any one who desired to unburden his conscience. Exportation was forbidden, unless the owner was known and would give security that the horses were not to be taken to Béarn, or else would present himself with his horses before the inquisitors within a designated time, so that note could be taken of the animals and an account be required as to their destination. Another device, which proved effective, was to register all the horses at the fairs, with descriptions and the names of the owners, who were required to keep an account of all sales and purchasers. This however, applied only to natives; as for Frenchmen and Béarnais, any horses that they had were seized without ceremony; if the owner was a Frenchman, the horses would be kept, awaiting instructions from the Suprema; if a Béarnais, he was seized with his horses and prosecuted, as being included in the Edict. Spaniards found with horses going towards France or Béarn, were treated like Frenchmen--the horses were sold to pay expenses and, if any balance was left, it was handed to the receiver. Pains, moreover were taken to find who made a trade of passing horses to France; they were arrested on some pretext and thrown into prison; if evidence were found against them, they were prosecuted; if not, after detention they were released under bail, because, as the inquisitors said, there was no penalty expressed in the Edict or in the laws of the kingdom. In view of the risk that the parties might apply for a firma or manifestacion, the Suprema was asked for further instructions, when it replied, July 1, 1574, that the prosecutions were to be conducted as in cases of heresy, the accused be required to give their genealogies and then, if recourse was had to manifestacion, it was to be met with an assertion that the case was a matter of faith. Yet the fraudulent character of this assumption is revealed in the admission that the secular magistrates could prosecute for the offence.[574]

Thus the zeal and activity of the Inquisition, working through its disregard of all laws, and its methods of procedure, virtually placed under its control the whole trade of the kingdom in horse-flesh. Encouraged by this, the Saragossa tribunal sought a still further extension of jurisdiction and, in 1576, it reported to the Suprema great activity in the exportation to France, Béarn and Gascony of arquebuses, powder, sheet iron for cuirasses and other warlike material, and it suggested an edict concerning that trade similar to that respecting horses. To this the Suprema assented, with the caution that it must be understood that these arms and munitions were intended for heretics.[575] The difficulty inherent in this probably prevented action, for I have met with no case of its enforcement.

It will be observed that the Saragossa tribunal pointed out that there was no penalty defined by law for the offence. This omission was rectified in the Córtes of Tarazona, in 1592, which deprived of what was known as the via privilegiata a long list of crimes, including that of passing horses and munitions of war to Béarn and France, with the addition that it could be punished with the death-penalty.[576]

A decision of the Suprema, rendered to the Barcelona tribunal in 1582, was to the effect that, if horses were taken to France, it must be ascertained whether they were for heretics in order to justify prosecution by the Inquisition, but, if to Béarn, that alone sufficed.[577] In time this nice distinction was abandoned, although the fiction was maintained that it was a matter of faith. About 1640, an inquisitor informs us that it was customary to punish those who exported horses or warlike material to France, even though there were no evidence that they were for heretics, for the act was very prejudicial. The accused was generally confined in the secret prison, the trial was conducted as one of faith, and was voted upon in a regular consulta de fe, including the episcopal Ordinary. Unless the case was light, the culprit appeared in a public auto. If he belonged to the lower classes, he was sometimes scourged; if of higher estate, he suffered exile and a fine, together with forfeiture of the horse or, if it had been passed successfully, he paid double its value. In the case of a Benedictine abbot, who had passed one or two horses to France, the Suprema fined him in six hundred ducats and suspended him from his functions for a year. Sometimes the sentence included disability for public office for both the culprit and his descendants.[578]

Oddly enough, in the case of Antonio Pérez this matter emerges for a moment in a manner significant of the uses to which it could be put. In the Spring of 1591, when it was desirable to suppress Diego de Heredia, Inquisitor-general Quiroga wrote, March 20th to the Saragossa tribunal, that he was suspected of passing horses to France. By April 4th, the tribunal was taking testimony to show that, a year or two before, he had sold two horses to a Frenchman for three hundred and sixty libras and that they were to be taken to France. There had been no secrecy in the transaction and further evidence was obtained that Heredia brought horses from Castile to Saragossa, whence they were taken to the mountains and were seen no more.[579] The events of May 24th, however, rendered further researches in this direction superfluous.

When this peculiar inquisitorial function was abandoned, does not clearly appear. In 1667 the Barcelona tribunal prosecuted Eudaldo Penstevan Bonguero for exporting horses to France. Already it would seem that the cognizance of the offence had become obsolete for, in 1664 the Suprema had called in question the competence of the tribunal to deal with it, when it replied, July 23d, that it held a papal brief conferring the faculty. The Suprema asked for an authentic copy of this or of the instructions empowering it to act, but neither was forthcoming and, on November 11, 1667, the Suprema again asked for them in order to decide the case of Bonguero.[580] We should probably not err in considering this to mark the last attempt to enforce a jurisdiction so foreign to the real objects of the Holy Office.

COINAGE

A still more eccentric invocation of the terror felt for the Inquisition, when the secular machinery failed to accomplish its purpose, occurred when the debasement of the coinage threw Spanish finance into inextricable confusion. The miserable vellon tokens were forced into circulation at rates enormously beyond their intrinsic value, and statesmen exhausted their ingenuity in devising clumsy expedients to arrest their inevitable depreciation--punishments of all kinds to keep down the premium on silver, and laws of maximum to regulate prices, from shirts to house-rent. The rude coinage, mostly battered and worn, was easily counterfeited, and there was large profit in manufacturing it abroad and flooding Spain with it at its fictitious valuation. Sanguinary laws were enacted to counteract this temptation, and the offence was punishable, like heresy, with burning, confiscation and the disabilities of descendants. To render this more effective, it was declared to be a case for the Inquisition and, like the exportation of horses, there was an attempt to disguise it as a matter of faith. A carta acordada of February 6, 1627, informed the tribunals that it fell within their jurisdiction if any heretic or fautor of heretics imported vellon money for the purpose of exporting gold or silver or other munitions of war, thus weakening the forces of the king, and all such offences belonged exclusively to the Inquisition. But when this was done by Catholics, for the sake of gain, the jurisdiction belonged exclusively to the king and as such he granted it cumulatively to the Inquisition, with the caution that, in competencias, censures were not to be employed. A papal brief confirming this was expected and meanwhile such prosecutions were to be conducted as matters of faith. It is not likely that Urban VIII condescended to authorize such misuse of the power delegated to the Inquisition for, in little more than a year, Philip IV revoked this action and confined the cognizance of the offence to the secular courts.[581]

***

If, as we have seen, the Inquisition was not a political machine of the importance that has been imagined, this was not through any lack of willingness on its part to be so employed. When its services were wanted, they were at the command of the State and if this rarely occurred under the Hapsburg princes, it was because they were not needed.

CHAPTER XI - JANSENISM

Jansenism is a convenient term wherewith to stigmatize as heresy whatever is displeasing to Ultramontanism, whether in Church or State, and it served as a pretext for the continued existence of the Inquisition, after the older aberrations were exterminated. As a concrete heresy, however, it defies accurate theological definition. It took its rise in the interminable disputes over the insoluble questions of predestination, grace and free will, as settled by St. Augustin and the Second Council of Orange, and accepted by the Church, till the use made of predestination by Calvin forced a modification by the Council of Trent, and the daring Jesuit, Luis de Molina, revived the problem. Then the discussion became a trial of strength between the rising Company of Jesus and its elder rivals, the Augustinians and Dominicans, when Clement VIII vainly imposed silence on the disputants. Cornelis Jansen, Bishop of Ypres, sought to vindicate St. Augustin in his work entitled "Augustinus," around which the controversy raged, until the Jesuits won a victory, in 1653, by procuring the condemnation of the famous Five Propositions, drawn from the work--a condemnation to which the followers of Jansen assented, while denying that he had taught them.[582]

NATURE OF THE HERESY

Another contest, of which we shall see the results, was waged over the writings of Cardinal Henry Noris, in which the Jesuits suffered defeat. He was also an Augustinian and professor of ecclesiastical history at Pisa, who busied himself in vindicating the doctrines of St. Augustin. Two of his works, the Historia Pelagiana and the Dissertatio de Quinta Synodo OEcumenica, were accused, before publication, of Baianism and Jansenism; the MSS. were ordered to Rome and were carefully examined by revisers, who pronounced them orthodox and licence to print was granted. When published, interpolations in the press were charged and disproved. Noris was called to Rome as chief of the Vatican Library by Innocent XI and, as this was regarded as a step to the cardinalate, fresh accusations of Jansenism were brought against him. His promotion was deferred; eight theologians were set to work upon his books; their favorable report was confirmed by the Congregation of the Inquisition, and Innocent appointed him one of its consultors. Attacks on him continued, which he answered in five dissertations, printed in 1685, when Innocent gave him a cardinal's hat and made him member of several important congregations, including that of the Inquisition, in which he served with distinction, until his death in 1704.[583]

France, however, was the principal seat of Jansenism, where the impalpable doctrinal points involved, after the decision of 1653, were obscured by more living issues. The Jansenists represented the more austere and puritanical portion of the clergy, as opposed to the supporters of the relaxed morality of Probabilism, of which the Jesuits were the foremost advocates--an aspect of the controversy which has been immortalized by Pascal. Besides, as Rome had decided against Jansen, those who had defended him were naturally led to minimize the authority of the Holy See, to disregard its condemnatory utterances as subreptitious, to assert the supremacy of general councils, and to exalt the independence and privileges of the Gallican Church, which, since the time of St. Louis, in the thirteenth century, had steadily resisted the encroachments of the papacy. There was a reinfusion of theology in the quarrel, when the Jesuits procured the condemnation, in the Bull Unigenitus, of Quesnel's views on sufficing contrition and inchoate charity, but this was only another incident in the struggle between rigorism and laxism.

While Jansenism thus was denounced as a heresy, it really was concerned much less with faith than with discipline and morals, and every one hostile to Probabilism, Jesuitism and Ultramontanism was stigmatized as a Jansenist. Louis XIV and Madame de Maintenon, who had persecuted the original Jansenists, were of the sect, because of their enforcement of the royal prerogative; Bossuet was suspected of Jansenism for his defence of the Declaration of the Gallican clergy, in 1682, against the Ultramontane doctrines of the papal power; Cardinal Aguirre was a Jansenist, because he opposed the laxity of Probabilism, and so was even the Jesuit General, Tirso González, because he wrote a book to prove that the Jesuits were not all laxists. When, under the protection of Leopold, Grand-duke of Tuscany, Bishop Scipione de'Ricci, in his Council of Pistoja, in 1786, sought, without papal authority, to effect an internal reformation of his Church, he was a Jansenist and, after his protector had been transferred to the imperial throne, Pius VI, in 1794, had the satisfaction of condemning, in the bull

Auctorem fidei, no less than eighty-five errors of the Council, mostly Jansenistic. In France the clergy were, for the most part, attached to Gallicanism and were largely rigorist, so practically Jansenism flourished and made itself felt in such measures as the expulsion of the Jesuits. The ex-Jesuit Bolgeni took his revenge by writing a book to prove that the Jacobinism of the Revolution was merely Jansenism in action. In fact, the Civil Constitution of the Clergy of 1790 was clearly Jansenistic because, without meddling with dogma, it embodied the democratic development of Gallicanism.

STRUGGLE IN FLANDERS

Spain paid little attention to the theological controversy over Jansen, though his works and those of his followers were duly condemned by the Inquisition.[584] It is a curious illustration of this indifference that when the great bibliographer, Nicolás Antonio, in defending Prudentius against the attack of Hincmar of Reims, pronounced as good Catholic doctrine the assertion of Prudentius that the blood of Christ was shed only for believers and not for unbelievers, this, which is virtually the same as the fifth of the condemned propositions of Jansen, escaped attention. The book was printed in Rome at the expense of Cardinal Aguirre; the Spanish Inquisition took no note of it in the Indexes of 1707 and 1747 and the passage is retained in the edition of 1788, produced under the auspices of Carlos III.[585] Yet Spain could not keep wholly out of the quarrel, for its Flemish provinces were a hot-bed of Jansenism which could not be eradicated from the University of Louvain. In 1649 Doctor Rescht, as the representative of the University and of its great protector Engelbert Dubois, Archbishop of Malines, came to Madrid, where he printed and circulated a memorial against the bull of Urban VIII and the Archduke Leopold so insulting to both that the Inquisition suppressed it, by a decree of September 13, 1650.[586] This did not cool the ardor of the Flemish followers of Jansen and, in 1656, Alexander VII felt obliged to address Don John of Austria, then Governor of the Low Countries, with an urgent exhortation to suppress the propagation of the condemned errors.[587]

The struggle continued and, soon after 1690, Carlos II was induced to issue an order that all Jansenists and Rigorists and other innovators should be dismissed and excluded from all offices and preferment, secular and ecclesiastical. Under this decree some of the prominent Jansenists were deprived and exiled, among them five doctors of Louvain--Gummare Huygens, E. van Geet, G. Baerts, R. Backz and Willem van den Enden. The persecuted sect appealed to Rome and procured from Innocent XII a brief of February 6, 1694, addressed to the bishops, forbidding that any one should be defamed for Jansenism on vague charges, or be excluded from any spiritual function or office unless convicted, in the regular order of justice, of having merited a punishment so severe. This trammeled episcopal action, for it was represented that the bishops could not be expected to undergo the expense and the labor of regular trials requiring absolute proof and subject to legal cavils, but it did not affect the secular arm and the Elector of Bavaria, then Governor of Flanders, reiterated in October and November 1695, to the Councils of the Provinces and the University, the repeated royal orders to exclude from all ecclesiastical dignities and secular employment those suspected of Jansenism and Rigorism. Then, on March 1, 1696, Carlos modified his decrees in a manner to embolden the schismatics, who seem to have had abundant popular and official support. We hear of a writing in defence of the Catholic party being publicly burnt by the executioner in Brussels, in front of the palace and, on January 29, 1698, the people of Brussels went tumultuously to the Archbishop of Malines, Ferdinand de Berlo de Brus, demanding that he should withdraw his opposition to N. van Eesbeke, who had been appointed by the chapter of the church of Sainte Gudule as their parish priest. This condition of affairs led the Jesuit General González to address a memorial to Carlos warning him that this spirit unless suppressed would lead to the ruin of religion and the destruction of his dominions, and supplicating, in terms much less respectful than Spanish custom required, that he should represent to the pope the dangerous consequences of the papal brief, that he should punish those who procured it as well as the authors of a memorial presented to Carlos in 1696 and that he should order the Flemish bishops to disregard the pretexts put forward as to vague accusations. The Jesuits overshot the mark in this insolent interference, and the memorial was suppressed by the Spanish Inquisition, in a decree of September 28, 1698, as insulting to the authorities, secular and ecclesiastical, of Flanders.[588]

QUARREL OVER CARDINAL NORIS

Spain, though with less success than France, had long been struggling to emancipate itself from papal control, and it is a curious paradox that its most resolute assertion of political Jansenism arose from an attempt to discredit doctrinal Jansenism. Jesuit influence had gradually dominated the Inquisition and, as we have seen, Cardinal Noris was the special object of Jesuit hatred. When, in 1721, the Augustinian Manso published at Valladolid his "S. Augustinus de Virtutibus Infidelium," the work was condemned and suppressed in 1723, while virulent attacks on him by Jesuits, in both Latin and the vernacular, were allowed free circulation.[589] The culmination came when the Jesuit Padre Rábago, confessor of Fernando VI, controlled the weak and irresolute inquisitor-general Pérez de Prado y Cuesta, bringing about an anomalous condition in which the Inquisition defied the Holy See, the so-called Jansenists became the warmest defenders of papal authority, and the Jesuits asserted the supremacy of the regalías.

When Prado y Cuesta assumed his office, in September, 1747, it was announced that the Suprema had a new Index Expurgatorius in an advanced state of preparation by the Jesuits Casani and Carrasco. The printing was nearly finished, when the 1744 edition of the Bibliothèque Janseniste of the Jesuit Dominique de Colonia reached Madrid. This was substantially a polemical work, a catalogue of writers and books opposed to Jesuitism, and the Jesuits conceived the brilliant idea of printing it as an appendix to the Index, and thus suppressing at one blow all antagonistic literature. Some trifling omissions were made but, when the Index appeared, it contained Noris's Historia Pelagiana and Dissertatio. There were many other equally orthodox books, but these became the storm-centre as they had been repeatedly and formally approved by the Holy See, after special examination. Appeal was made to Benedict XIV, who addressed, July 31, 1748, to Prado y Cuesta a brief in which he recited the investigations into Noris's books and pointed out that all questions concerning them had been finally settled by the solemn judgement of Rome, so that it was not lawful for the Spanish Inquisition to reopen the question, and much less to condemn the books. He could not patiently endure the injury thus without reason inflicted on Noris and he admonished Prado y Cuesta to find means to avert discord between Spain and Rome.[590]

The inquisitor-general adopted the favorite inquisitorial device of evasion. He replied that he had found the Index nearly printed when he assumed office; he had endeavored to have it issued without his name, but this was impossible; he had not known that Noris's name was in it until the Augustinians complained, and he dwelt on the difficulty of making a change, especially in view of the grave reasons for which the books had been included. This correspondence was strictly secret, but the brief had been shown in Rome to the Augustinian procurador-general, who sent a copy to Madrid, where it was busily transcribed and circulated throughout the land, creating a tremendous sensation. Prado y Cuesta, addressed, September 16, 1748, a bitter complaint to Benedict, dwelling on the indiscretion of allowing such matters to be gossiped on the streets, and of affording such comfort to the heretics. The Jesuit party openly proclaimed the independence of the Spanish Inquisition in such matters, and asserted that its honor was at stake. Padre Rábago undertook to manage the king and induced him to inform the pope that he would not permit any invasion of the privileges of the Inquisition.

The affair dragged on. Portocarrero, the ambassador to Rome, hurried to Spain and came to a compromise with Prado y Cuesta, but Rábago, who would agree to nothing but the submission of the Holy See, persuaded Fernando to hold firm and the affair became a struggle between the regalías and the papal supremacy, in which Noris was merely an incident. Fernando wrote, July 1, 1749, to Benedict, stating plainly that he would not permit his rights and those of the Inquisition to be impaired. It was of no importance whether the faithful in Spain could or could not read the works of Noris, but it was of supreme importance to him to remove the discord excited among his subjects. Benedict replied moderately and the king relented in so far as to offer a compromise, which would have closed the matter had it not become doubly embroiled by a papal decree of September 24th condemning Colonia's Bibliothèque Janseniste, thus putting on the Roman Index a considerable section of the Spanish. In a letter to the Spanish agent in Rome, Rábago threatened in retaliation that the king would not only prohibit the works of Noris but the Roman Index itself. Still more audacious were the instructions which he sent to Portocarrero. Of these there were two sets, one long and argumentative, the other briefer, to be used only in case of necessity. It insolently asserted that the papal eagerness in defence of Noris was a new argument against infallibility; that Popes Liberius and Honorius, for suspicions no graver, had been anathematized by a synod, and it would be humiliating to his Holiness if the same should happen to him. Portocarrero was a trained diplomatist but, in an audience of November 26, 1749, he handed to Benedict a copy of this portentous document, translated into choice Italian, and the next day he wrote cheerfully to Rábago that he thought it would end the affair; the pope was displeased but, knowing his character, this need cause no alarm.

***

Benedict seems to have passed over in dignified silence this indecent threat that he might be anathematized for heresy, but the breach was wider than ever. In the Spring of 1750 the affair was taken out of the hands of Portocarrero and was confided to Manuel Ventura Figueroa, an auditor of the Rota, who skilfully induced Benedict to drop the matter, while with equal skill and unlimited bribery he negotiated the Concordat of 1753, which virtually gave to the crown the patronage of the Spanish Church. Then, in 1755, came the dismissal of Rábago, for his share in exciting the resistance of the Jesuits of Paraguay to the treaty of 1750 transferring that colony to Portugal. He was succeeded as confessor by Manuel Quintano Bonifaz who, in that same year, had become inquisitor-general on the death of Prado y Cuesta. Benedict had never ceased to claim the fulfilment of an offer once made by Fernando to remove Noris's name from the Index and, in 1757 he urged the king to afford him that satisfaction, before his death, in return for the many favors bestowed.

Jesuit influence was no longer supreme, and Fernando ordered an investigation. The documents were collected and were submitted to Bonifaz who, in December, presented a consulta, dwelling upon the care habitually bestowed by the Inquisition before condemning the most insignificant book while, in this case, Casani and Carrasco had included in the Index the works of Noris, without any preliminary examination and without the knowledge of the inquisitor-general, which was a foul abuse of the confidence reposed in them. Noris's book had been printed in Spain in 1698, dedicated to Inquisitor-general Rocaberti, and had undisputed circulation until these two padres discovered in it traces of Jansenism. Bonifaz therefore concluded that the pope had just cause of complaint and that the royal promise should be fulfilled. Accordingly, on January 28, 1758, an edict was issued, reciting the prohibition and ending with "But, having since considered the matter with the mature and serious reflection befitting its importance, we order the removal of the said work from the Index, and declare that both it and its most eminent author remain in the same repute and honor as before." For this the good old pope expressed his gratification in warm terms to Fernando.[591]

This may be assumed as the last struggle over what were conceived to be the doctrinal errors of Jansenism, and subsequent persecution was directed against it as the opponent of Ultramontanism and Jesuitism, and as the supporter of the royal prerogative. There had been, under Philip II, a strong tendency in the Spanish Church to the Gallicanism which became known as Jansenism. In 1598 Agostino Zani, the Venetian envoy, says that the Spanish clergy depend on the king first and then on the pope; there was talk of separation from the Holy See and forming under Toledo a national Church in imitation of the Gallican.[592] The Concordat of 1753, which concentrated patronage in the crown, could only strengthen this dependence of the clergy, while the second half of the eighteenth century witnessed an ominous tendency throughout Europe to throw off subjection to Rome. The celebrated work of "Febronius,"[593] in 1763, boldly attacked the papal autocracy, and encouraged the assertion of the regalías; the claims of the Holy See, in both spiritual and temporal matters, were called in question with a freedom unknown since the great councils of the fifteenth century, while the reforms of Joseph II and of his brother Leopold of Tuscany and the "Punctation" of the Congress of Ems were disquieting manifestations of the spirit of revolt. It was convenient to stigmatize this spirit as heresy under the name of Jansenism, which thenceforth became the object of the bitterest papal animadversion.

ITS DEVELOPMENT

Fray Miguélez informs us that Bonifaz, for his share in the vindication of Noris, was reproached with Jansenism, and that thenceforth the Inquisition became a mere instrument in the hands of a court bitterly hostile to Rome; that instead of being a terrible repressor of heresy, it was the defender of the regalías and persecutor of Ultramontanism--in other words, that it was Jansenist--and that it was used in an attempt to lay the foundations in Spain of a schismatic Church like that of Utrecht.[594] This was not the case, but as Jansenism was now merely a doctrinal misnomer for a principle, partly political and partly disciplinary, the Inquisition had a narrow and difficult path to tread. Carlos III was fully convinced of the extent of the regalías; he was involved in constant struggles with the Roman court, and had little hesitation in dictating to the Inquisition. It did not dare to interfere with the royal prerogatives but, in so far as it could, it favored Ultramontanism by persecuting those against whom it could formulate charges under the guise of Jansenism.

The ministers of Carlos III, who survived into the earlier years of Carlos IV, were animated with this spirit of revolt and there was an active propaganda. The book of Febronius was secretly printed in Madrid and was largely circulated for, although condemned, the Inquisition was compelled prudently to close its eyes.[595] The acts of the Synod of Pistoja were translated into Spanish and persistent efforts were made to obtain licence for their publication, until Pius VI intervened with a letter to the king and frustrated the attempt.[596] When the bull Auctorem fidei, condemning, in 1794, the errors of the synod, reached Spain the Council of Castile reported against its admission.[597] The University of Salamanca was regarded as a Jansenist hot-bed. Jovellanos tells us that all who were trained there were Port-Royalists of the Pistoja sect; the works of Opstraet, Zuola and Tamburini were in everybody's hands; more than three thousand copies were in circulation before the edict of prohibition appeared, and then only a single volume was surrendered.[598] We hear of the Marquis of Roda, one of the most influential ministers of Carlos III, uttering warm praises of Port-Royal and of the great men connected with it.[599] Naturally episcopal vacancies were filled with bishops of the same persuasion and one of them, Joseph Clíment of Barcelona, had trouble with the Inquisition for lauding the schismatic Church of Utrecht. In 1792, Agustin Abad y la Sierra, Bishop of Barbastro, was denounced to the Saragossa tribunal as a Jansenist who favored the French Revolution, but soon afterwards his brother Manuel was appointed inquisitor-general and the prosecution was suspended, but, when the latter, in 1794, was ordered by Carlos IV to resign, he was immediately denounced in his turn.[600]

The Inquisition, in fact, could not but be opposed to Jansenism, for one of the objects of the Jansenistic movement was the restoration of episcopal rights and privileges, so seriously curtailed by the Holy Office, and the remodelling of its organization was regarded as essential to the overthrow of Ultramontanism.[601] The Jesuits were therefore inevitably the allies of the Inquisition; they had conceived a strong hostility to Carlos III who, since his accession in 1759, had diminished their influence by dismissing from office those who were devoted to them. Their disaffection culminated in the tumults and disturbances of April 1766, which spread through the kingdom from Guipúzcoa to Andalusia, and humiliated Carlos to the last degree. These were evidently the result of concerted action, intelligently directed and supported by ample funds, working on popular discontent caused by scarcity and high prices. Prolonged investigation convinced the king that the Company of Jesus was responsible for the troubles, thus explaining the rigor with which the expulsion was executed in 1767, and the implacable determination of Carlos in demanding of Clement XIII and Clement XIV the suppression of the Order.[602]

REACTION

The elimination of the Jesuits was a triumph for so-called Jansenism. It left the educational system of Spain in confusion, and advantage was taken of this to reconstruct it on lines which should train the rising generation in Gallican ideas as to the relations of Church and State, and should replace medievalism by modern science.[603] Yet the Inquisition continued the struggle, and its jealous watchfulness is indicated when, in 1773, some chance expressions of a student led to the denunciation, to the Barcelona tribunal, of the teaching of the great Catalan University of Cervera, as infected with Baianism and Jansenism, in conformity to the Théologie de Lyon, a book condemned in Rome for its Gallican principles--a denunciation which was duly followed by the prosecution of one of the professors, a Dominican named Pier.[604]

A reaction in the policy of the court came with the rise to power of the infamous royal favorite Godoy. By a decree of October 19, 1797, Carlos IV permitted the repatriation of the survivors among the Jesuits expelled in 1767. The occupation of the papal states by Napoleon had deprived them of their Bolognese refuge, and they found themselves ill at ease in the Ligurian Republic to which they had gone. They were therefore compassionately allowed to return, under precautions that should scatter them where they should not trouble the public peace, but they speedily made their influence felt, and were busy in denouncing to the Inquisition as Jansenists all who did not share their blind devotion to the Holy See.[605] Still more threatening was the reception, in 1800, of the bull Auctorem fidei, brought about by the influence of Godoy, and enforced by a royal decree of December 10th, charging the bishops to punish all opinions contrary to the definitions of the bull, while the Inquisition was ordered to suppress all writings in support of the condemned propositions, and the king promised to employ all the power given to him by God to enforce these commands. The triumph of Ultramontanism was complete, and Godoy richly earned the grotesquely incongruous title bestowed on him, by Pius VI, of Pillar of the Faith.[606]

The charge was one easy to bring, and the intelligent classes in Spain were kept in a state of unrest and apprehension. An illustrative case was that of two brothers, Gerónimo and Antonio de la Cuesta, one penitentiary and the other archdeacon in the church of Avila. They incurred the enmity of their bishop, Rafael de Muzquiz, confessor of Queen María Luisa de Parma: he organized a formidable conspiracy against them and they were denounced as Jansenists, in 1801, to the tribunal of Valladolid. Muzquiz was promoted to the archiepiscopal see of Compostela, but there was no slackening in the energy of the prosecution. Antonio escaped to Paris but Gerónimo was thrown into the secret prison, where he lay for five years. In spite of the mass of testimony accumulated against him, he was acquitted by the tribunal, but the Suprema refused to accept the decision and removed the inquisitors. The brothers had powerful friends at court, who prevailed on Carlos to intervene, when he had all the papers submitted to him and decided the case himself--an assumption of royal jurisdiction for which it would be difficult to find a precedent. By royal decrees of May 7, 1806, he ordered that the Valladolid inquisitors should be in no way prejudiced by their removal but should be capable of promotion. Gerónimo was restored to his dignity in the church of Avila, with ceremonies galling to his adversaries;

he was to receive all the arrears of his prebend; his trial and imprisonment were not to inflict any disability on him or his kindred, and his name was to be erased from the record so that no trace of it should remain. The papers in the case against the fugitive brother Antonio were to be sealed up and delivered to the Secretaria de Gracia y Justicia. Heavy fines moreover were levied on all concerned in the prosecution, to defray the expenses of the trial, and any excess was to be paid to Gerónimo. They amounted in all to 11,455 ducats, assessed upon twenty-one persons, all clerics except one or two officials and, in addition to these, there were nine regulars--Carmelites, Benedictines, Franciscans and Dominicans--who were banished for thirty leagues around Madrid and royal residences. Two of them were calificadores and one a notary of a commissioner, who were incapacitated for their functions.[607]

DISAPPEARANCE

Archbishop Muzquiz did not wholly escape. Gerónimo's defence placed him in the position of a calumniator and, in his efforts at extrication, he accused the inquisitors of Valladolid and the Inquisitor-general Arce y Reynoso of partiality. This exposed him to prosecution under the bull Si de protegendis; his episcopal dignity protected him from arrest, but he was fined in eight thousand ducats and the Bishop of Valladolid who, when canon of Avila, had joined in the conspiracy, was fined in four thousand. They would not have escaped so easily but for the influence with Godoy of a lady who was popularly reputed to have received a million of reales for her services.[608]

***

As we have seen, in Jansenism the doctrinal points involved were of interest only to the sublimated theologian and they were virtually lost to view at an early period. Being thus incapable of precise theological definition, it was a favorite weapon for the gratification of enmity, as it could be charged against all opponents of whatever character. Even as the French Jacobins were stigmatized as Jansenists, so those Spaniards who submitted to the "intrusive" government of Joseph Bonapart were classed as Jansenists, and so were their most active antagonists, the liberal members of the Córtes of Cadiz.[609] The fact is that the French Revolution, which orthodox writers represent as the triumph of Jansenism, was, in reality, its death-blow, for in that cataclysm disappeared the powerful and well-organized hierarchy which alone could struggle within the Church against the advance of Ultramontanism and its attendant Probabilism.

We hear little of Jansenism under the Restoration, though it is sometimes included subordinately in the charges of anti-political opinions. The bitterness still felt towards it, however, is well expressed by Vélez, Archbishop of Santiago, as late as 1825, when he ignorantly declares that Jansen caused the rebellion of the Low Countries against Spain in the Assembly of 1633, while his disciples, uniting in Bourg-Fontaine and Portugal, conspired against the lives of all princes. Jansen supported the doctrines of the Calvinists and Lutherans against the faith and his followers promulgated the greatest errors against the Church and its discipline.[610]

Henry Charles Lea, LL.D.

CHAPTER XII - FREE-MASONRY

Few subjects have been so fertile as Free-Masonry in the growth of legend and myth. If we may believe some of its over-enthusiastic members, the Archangel Michael was the Grand Master of the earliest Masonic lodge; the builders of the Tower of Babel were wicked Masons and those who held aloof from the impious work were Free-Masons. Others trace its origin to Lamech and others again tell us that the first Grand Lodge in England was founded by St. Alban in 287. Its adversaries are equally extravagant; if we may trust them it is the precursor of Antichrist and a survival of Manicheism; it is supreme in European cabinets and directs the policy of the civilized world in opposition to the Church. Every pope in the nineteenth century fulminated his anathema against it. The Abbé Davin assures us that Jansenism is the masterpiece of the powers of evil and that it has become, in the form of Masonry, the most formidable of secret societies, organized for the destruction of the Christian Monarchy.[611] There are zealous Spanish Masons who assure us that the Comunidades of Castile and the Germanía of Valencia were the work of Masons; that Agustin and Pedro Cazalla and the other victims of the auto of May 21, 1559 were Masons, and that the unfortunate Don Carlos was a victim to Masonry.[612]

PROHIBITED BY ROME

Descending to the sobriety of fact, Masonry emerges into the light of history in 1717, when Dr. Desaguliers, Anthony Sayer, George Payne and a few others formed, in London, an organization based on toleration, benevolence and good-fellowship. Its growth was slow and its first appearance in Spain was in 1726, when the London lodge granted a charter for one in Gibraltar. Lord Wharton is said to have founded one in Madrid, in 1727, and soon afterwards another was organized in Cádiz. These were primarily for the benefit of English residents, although doubtless natives were eligible to membership. As yet it was not under the ban of the Church, but its introduction in Tuscany led the Grand-duke Gian Gastone to prohibit it. His speedy death (July 9, 1737), caused his edict to be neglected; the clergy represented the matter to Clement XII, who sent to Florence an inquisitor; he made a number of arrests, but the parties were set at liberty by the new Grand-duke, Francis of Lorraine, who declared himself the patron of the Order and participated in the organization of several lodges.[613] Clement sustained his inquisitor and issued, April 28, 1738, his bull In eminenti, calling attention to the oath-bound secrecy of the lodges, which was just cause for suspicion, as their object would not be concealed if it were not evil, leading to their prohibition in many states. Wherefore, in view of the grave consequences threatened to public tranquility and the salvation of souls, he forbade the faithful to favor them or to join them under pain of ipso facto excommunication, removable only by the Holy See. Prelates, superiors, Ordinaries and inquisitors were ordered to inquire against and prosecute all transgressors and to punish them condignly as vehemently suspect of heresy, for all of which he granted full powers.[614] Thus the only accusation brought against Masonry was its secrecy, but this sufficed for the creation of a new heresy, furnishing to the Inquisition a fresh subject for its activity.

The nature of the condign punishment thus threatened was left to the discretion of the local tribunals, but a standard was furnished by an edict of the Cardinal Secretary of State, January 14, 1739, pronouncing irremissible pain of death, not only on all members but on all who should tempt others to join the Order, or should rent a house to it or favor it in any other way. The only victim of this savage decree is said to have been a Frenchman who wrote a book on Masonry; it is true that, in this same year, 1739, the Inquisition in Florence tortured a Mason named Crudeli, and kept him in prison for a considerable time, but the death-penalty was a matter for the secular authorities and in Florence these were not under control. Indeed, when the Inquisition offered pardon for self-denunciation, and a hundred crowns for information, and made several arrests, the Grand-duke interposed and liberated the prisoners.[615] Even when the arch-impostor Cagliostro, in 1789, ventured to found a lodge in Rome and was tried by the Inquisition, the sentence, rendered April 7, 1791, recited that, although he had incurred the death-penalty, it was mercifully commuted to imprisonment for life.[616] He was accordingly imprisoned in the castle of San Leone where he is supposed to have died in 1795.

The Parlement of Paris refused to register the bull of 1738 and when, in 1750, the jubilee attracted crowds of pilgrims to Rome, so many had to seek relief from the excommunication incurred under it that Benedict XIV was led to revive it, May 18, 1751, in his constitution Providas, pointing out moreover the injury to the purity of the faith arising from the association of men of different beliefs, and invoking the aid of all Catholic princes to enforce the decrees of the Holy See.[617] When thus, without provocation, Rome declared war to the knife against the new organization, it naturally became hostile to Rome, and when its membership was forbidden to the faithful, it was necessarily confined to those who were either indifferent or antagonistic to the Roman faith.

PERSECUTION

While the papal commands were ignored in France, they had been eagerly welcomed in Spain. The bull In eminenti received the royal exequatur and the Inquisitor-general Orbe y Larreategui published it in an edict, October 11, 1738, pointing out that the Inquisition had exclusive jurisdiction in the matter. He promised to prosecute with the utmost severity all disobedience to the bull, and called for denunciations, within six days, of all infractions, under pain of excommunication and of two hundred ducats. The edict was to be read in the churches and to be affixed to their portals, thus giving an effective advertisement to the new institution by conveying a knowledge of its existence to a population thus far happily ignorant.[618]

The Inquisition, however, was not allowed long to enjoy the exclusive jurisdiction claimed, for Philip V, in 1740, issued an edict under which, we are told, a number of Masons were sent to the galleys, while the Inquisition vindicated its rights by breaking up a lodge in Madrid and punishing its members.[619] There was thus established a cumulative jurisdiction which continued, for State autocracy and Church autocracy were alike jealous of a secret organization of unknown strength which, in troublous times, might become dangerous. Fernando VI manifested this by a pragmática of July 2, 1751, in which he forbade the formation of lodges under pain of the royal indignation and punishment at the royal discretion; all judges were required to report delinquents, and all commanders of armies and fleets to dismiss with dishonor any culprits discovered in the service. That, in spite of these repressive measures, Free-Masonry was spreading, may be assumed from the publication, about this time, of two editions of a little book against it, in which this decree is embodied.[620] Padre Feyjoo assisted in advertising the Order by devoting to it a letter in which, with gentle satire, he treated it as a hobgoblin, imposing on public credulity with false pretences, although there might be evil spirits among the harmless ones.[621]

The Inquisition meanwhile was not idle, though it did not imitate the severity of the papal government or of the royal edicts. In 1744 the Madrid tribunal sentenced, to abjuration de levi and banishment from Spain, Don Francisco Aurion de Roscobel, canon of Quintanar, for Free-Masonry; in 1756 the same tribunal prescribed reconciliation for Domingo de Otas and, in 1757, a Frenchman named Tournon escaped with a year's detention and banishment from Spain, although, by endeavoring to induce his employees to join the Order, he was reckoned as a dogmatizer.[622] Another case about the same time reveals a strange indifference, possibly attributable to hesitation in attacking a dependent of a powerful minister. A priest named Joachin Pareja presented himself, April 19, 1746, to the Toledo tribunal and related that when, in 1742, he accompanied the Infante Phelipe to Italy, he lay for some months in Antibes, where he made the acquaintance of Antonio de Rosellon, gentleman of the chamber to the Marquis of la Ensenada, who talked freely to him about Free-Masonry, of which he was a member. He had but recently learned that Free-Masons were an infernal sect, condemned by a papal bull, and he had made haste to denounce Rosellon. No action was taken for eighteen months when, on October 13, 1747, the tribunal asked the Madrid inquisitors to examine Rosellon, after consulting the Suprema. The Suprema promptly scolded it for its remissness and ordered it to make inquiry of other tribunals; the customary interrogations were sent around with negative results and, on January 8, 1748, the fiscal reported accordingly; there was but one witness and therefore he recommended suspension, which was duly voted. Some twenty months passed away when suddenly, September 7, 1751, the Suprema recurred to the matter and wrote to Toledo demanding a report. Toledo waited for more than a month and then, on October 16th, replied that it referred the whole affair to the Madrid tribunal as Pareja and Rosellon were both in that city.[623] This probably ended the case.

POLITICAL ACTIVITY

Free-Masonry was growing and extending itself throughout influential circles. In 1760 the Gran Logia española was organized and independence of London was established; in 1780 this was changed to a Grand Orient, symbolical Masonry being subordinated to the Scottish Rite. In this we are told that such men as Aranda, Campomanes, Rodríguez, Nava del Rio, Salazar y Valle, Jovellanos, the Duke of Alva, the Marquis of Valdelirias, the Count of Montijo and others were active; that the ministers of Carlos III were mostly Masons and that to them was attributable the energetic action against Jesuitism and Ultramontanism.[624] To what extent this is true, it would be impossible to speak positively, but unquestionably Masonry afforded a refuge for the modern spirit in which to develop itself against the oppressive Obscurantism of the Inquisition.

A disturbing element was furnished by Cagliostro who, in his two visits to Spain, founded the lodge España, in competition with the Grand Orient. This attracted the more adventurous spirits and grew to be revolutionary in character. It was the centre of the foolish republican conspiracy of 1796, known as the conspiracy of San Blas, from the day selected for the outbreak. Arms were collected in the lodge, but the plot was betrayed to the police; three of the leaders were condemned to death but, at the intercession of the French ambassador, the sentence was commuted to imprisonment for life. The chiefs were deported to Laguayra where they captured the sympathies of their guards and were enabled to escape. In 1797 they organized a fresh conspiracy in Caraccas, but it was discovered and six of those implicated were executed.[625]

In the troubled times that followed, the revolutionary section of Masonry naturally developed, at the expense of the conservative. There is probably truth in the assertion that the French occupation was assisted by the organization of the independent lodges under Miguel de Azanza, one of the ministers of Carlos IV, who was grand master. The ensuing war was favorable to the growth of the Order. The French armies sought to establish lodges in order to popularize the "intrusive" government, while the English forces on their side did the same, and the Spanish troops were honeycombed with the trincheras, or intrenchments, as these military lodges were called.

With the downfall of Napoleon and liberation of the papacy, Pius VII made haste to repeat the denunciation of Masonry. He issued, August 15, 1814, a decree against its infernal conventicles, subversive of thrones and religion. He lamented that, in the disturbances of recent years, the salutary edicts of his predecessors had been forgotten and that Masonry had spread everywhere. To their spiritual penalties he added temporal punishments--sharp corporal affliction, with heavy fines and confiscation, and he offered rewards for informers. This decree was approved by Fernando VII and was embodied in an edict of the Inquisition, January 2, 1815, offering a Term of Grace of fifteen days, during which penitents would be received and after which the full rigor of the laws, secular and canonical, would be enforced. Apparently the result was inconsiderable for, on February 10th, the term was extended until Pentecost (May 14th) and inviolable secrecy was promised.[626] Fernando had not waited for this but had already prohibited Masonry under the penalties attaching to crimes of the first order against the State and, in pursuance of this, on September 14, 1814, twenty-five arrests had been made for suspicion of membership.[627]

UNDER THE RESTORATION

Thus, as before, there was cumulative jurisdiction over Masonry. The time had passed for competencias between the Inquisition and the royal courts; it was too closely identified with the State to indulge in quarrels, but still there was jealous susceptibility and self-assertion. As early as 1815 this showed itself in the prosecution of Diego Dilicado, parish priest of San Jorje in Coruña, because he had reported the existence there of a lodge to the public authorities and not to the Inquisition.[628] Several cases, in 1817, show that when a culprit was tried and sentenced by the royal courts, the Inquisition insisted on superadding a prosecution and punishment of its own. Thus when Jean Rost, a Frenchman, was sent to the presidio of Ceuta by the chancellery of Granada, the Seville tribunal also tried him and ordered his confinement in the prison of the presidio, at the same time demanding from the chancellery the Masonic title and insignia of the prisoner and whatever else appertained to the jurisdiction of the Inquisition.[629] The Madrid tribunal, May 8, 1817, sentenced Albert Leclerc, a Frenchman, for Free-Masonry; he had already been tried and convicted by the royal court and a courteous note was addressed, as in other similar cases, to the Alcalde de Casa y Corte, to have him brought to the secret prison, for the performance of spiritual exercises under a confessor commissioned to instruct him in the errors of Masonry, and to absolve him from the censures incurred, after which he would be returned to the alcalde for the execution of his sentence of banishment. So, in July 1817, the Santiago tribunal collected evidence against Manuel Llorente, sergeant of Grenadiers, and the Suprema directed that, as soon as the secular trial was finished, he was to be imprisoned again and tried by the tribunal.[630]

For this punctiliousness there was the excuse that the papal decrees rendered Masonry an ecclesiastical crime involving excommunication, of which the temporal courts could take no cognizance. This duplication of punishment may possibly explain the extreme variation in the severity of the penalties inflicted. In 1818 the Madrid tribunal sentenced Antonio Catalá, captain in the volunteer regiment of Barbastro, to a very moderate punishment, alleging as a reason his prolonged imprisonment and ill-health. The Suprema sent back the sentence for revision, when the abjuration was changed from de levi to de vehementi. Then the Suprema took the matter into its own hands and condemned him to be reduced to the ranks for four years' service in the regiment of Ceuta, which was nearly equivalent to four years of presidio. On the other hand, in 1819, the sentence was confirmed of Martin de Bernardo, which was merely to abjuration de levi, absolution ad cautelam, a month's reclusion and spiritual penances. Greater severity might surely have been shown in the case of the priest, Vicente Perdiguera, commissioner of the Toledo tribunal, when, in 1817, the Madrid tribunal suggested that, in view of his notorious Free-Masonry and irregular conduct, he should be deprived of his office and insignia and of the fuero of the Inquisition. To this the Suprema assented and with this he escaped.[631]

It casts doubt upon the reported extent of Free-Masonry that, in spite of the vigilance of the Inquisition, the number of cases was so small. From 1780 to 1815 they amount in all only to nineteen. Then, in 1816, there is a sudden increase to twenty-five; in 1817 there are fourteen, in 1818 nine and in 1819 seven.[632] Possibly there may have been others tried by the civil or military courts, which escaped inquisitorial action, but, in view of its jealous care of its jurisdiction, these cannot have been numerous.

Yet all authorities of the period agree that, under the Restoration, Masonry flourished and spread, especially in the army; that it was the efficient source of the many plots which disturbed Fernando's equanimity, and that the revolution of 1820 was its work, backed by the widespread popular discontent aroused by the oppression and inefficiency of his rule. When, in January, 1820, the movement was started by the troops destined for America, in their cantonments near Cádiz, there was a lodge in every regiment. Riego, who led the revolt, was a Mason, and so was the Count of la Bisbal who ensured its success when, at Ocaña, whither he had been sent to command the troops gathered for its suppression, he caused them to proclaim the Constitution. At Santiago, the first act of the revolutionaries was to sack the Inquisition and to liberate the Count of Montijo, grand master of the Masonic organizations, who lay in the secret prison.[633]

We shall have occasion hereafter to see the ruinous part played by Free-Masonry, and its offshoot the Comuneros, during the brief constitutional epoch from 1820 to 1823. With the restoration of absolutism the Comuneros disappeared and Masons became the object of persecution far severer than that of the Inquisition. They were subjected to the military commissions set up everywhere throughout Spain, and those who would not come forward and denounce themselves were declared, by an order of October 9, 1824, to be punishable with death and confiscation.[634]

CHAPTER XIII - PHILOSOPHISM

In the earlier period, Spanish orthodoxy seems to have been little troubled with free-thinking, nor, when this was encountered, does it seem to have been visited with the same vindictiveness as Protestantism. From a temporal point of view, it was less dangerous, and the denial of God was an offence less than the denial of papal supremacy. In an auto at Toledo, November 8, 1654, there appeared Don Francisco de Vega Vinero, characterized as "herege apostata, ateista," who escaped with reconciliation, confiscation, ten years of prison and three years of exile from Toledo, Madrid and Renedo.[635] The intellectual movement of the eighteenth century in France, however, could not but awake an echo in Spain, despite the severity of censorship, and the quarantine at the ports. There was a steady infiltration of liberalism, political and spiritual; Spaniards of culture who travelled, or who were sent abroad on missions, returned with enlarged horizons of thought, and could not but compare the backwardness of their native land with the activity, for good or for evil, of the other European nations. The more the writings of the fashionable philosophers of France were denounced, the greater became the curiosity to examine them. A reactionary writer tells us that the works of Filangieri, Rousseau, Mably, Condillac, Pereira, Febronius (Hontheim) and Scipione de'Ricci had full circulation in the universities and colleges. Some professors taught many of their principles, the students were infected and this moral pestilence extended rapidly without attracting due attention.[636] The Abbé Clément found, in 1768, that one of the obstacles to the success of his Jansenizing mission was the secret tolerance and indifferentism; it was difficult to believe how great were the evidences of incredulity, united with all the externals of devotion, even under the oppression of habitual dread of the severity of the Inquisition.[637] Thus, in the latter half of the eighteenth century, the decadent activity of the Holy Office found a new heresy to combat, which it styled Philosophism or Naturalism.

The leading ministers of Carlos III, such as Aranda, Campomanes, Roda and Floridablanca, were shrewdly suspected of sympathy with these dangerous speculations, but the time had passed when the Marquis of Villanueva could be arrested and prosecuted without the assent of the king. It was safer to make examples of men not thus protected but yet sufficiently conspicuous to serve as warnings. Such a case was that of Dr. Luis Castellanos, health-officer of the port of Cádiz--a free-thinker calling himself a philosopher, an agnostic who professed to know nothing of God and who probably was indiscreet in airing his opinions. On his trial by the Seville tribunal he at first denied, but subsequently he confessed and begged for mercy. On June 30, 1776, an auto with open doors was held in the chapel of the castle of Triana, at which were present, doubtless by invitation that could not be declined, the Duke of Medina Celi, the Count of Torrejon and innumerable other distinguished personages, at which Castellanos was sentenced to abjuration and confiscation, to wear a sanbenito de dos aspas and to serve for ten years in the hospital of the presidio of Oran--a severity which emphasizes the dread inspired by this negation of opinion.[638]

PABLO OLAVIDE

Contemporary with this was a case of more far-reaching influence. Pablo Olavide, a young lawyer of Lima and judge in the Audiencia, distinguished himself in the terrible earthquake of 1746 and was made custodian of the treasures dug from the ruins. After satisfying those who could prove their claims, he employed the remainder in building a church and a theatre. There were disappointed claimants who carried their complaints to Madrid. Olavide was summoned thither, disbarred, condemned to pay various sums and imprisoned. His health failing, he was allowed to go to Leganes, where he contracted marriage with Isabel de los Rios, whose two successive husbands had left her large fortunes. He was remarkably intelligent, brilliant in society, and, with the aid of his wife's money, he speedily acquired prominent social position. He travelled and in France he formed relations with Voltaire and Rousseau, with whom he maintained correspondence. Aranda, who secretly sympathized with him in this, was then at the height of his power and became his warm friend, seeking to use his abilities in the projects on foot to elevate Spain from its condition of poverty and misery.

Practical statesmen had long recognized as a serious evil the baldios, or extensive and numerous tracts of uncultivated land, useless for all purposes except as pasturage for the migratory flocks of the Mesta, that powerful combination of sheep-owners who had secured legislation restricting all cultivation that interfered with their privileges. As early as 1749 the Marquis of la Ensenada had entertained projects of introducing colonies of foreigners to occupy these idle lands; in 1766 the idea was revived and Nuevas Poblaciones, as they were called, were established in various places. A contract was made to bring six thousand German and Swiss Catholics and establish them on the southern slope of the Sierra Morena, along the main road from Madrid to Cádiz--a wild and rugged country, the haunt of highway robbers. Campomanes drew up the plan, under which establishments of the religious Orders were absolutely prohibited; the settlers were to have pastors of their own race; all spiritual affairs were to be in the hands of the parish priests, subject to episcopal jurisdiction, and the dreaded Mesta was not allowed to intrude. Olavide was appointed superintendent of the colony, and was also made assistente, or governor of Seville.

He threw himself into the project with enthusiasm, labored with intelligent activity, overcame the initial difficulties and for some years success seemed assured. Gradually however trouble arose with the Capuchin friars who had accompanied the colonists as their priests. Friar Romuald of Freiburg, the prefect of the group, was a disturbing element, involved in quarrels with the episcopal officials; friction sprang up between him and Olavide, which developed into hatred, and the Inquisition furnished ready means for gratifying malevolence. In September, 1775, Romuald presented a formal denunciation of the Superintendent as an atheist and materialist, who was in correspondence with Voltaire and Rousseau, who read prohibited books, denied the miracles, and held that non-Catholics could be saved. Ample details were furnished of his irreligious walk and conversation, some of which indicate the points on which quarrels had arisen--not resorting to prayer and good works to avert calamities, forbidding the ringing of bells in tempests, wanting corpses buried in cemeteries rather than in churches, and defending the Copernican system condemned by the Church. Olavide's protector, Aranda, had fallen from power in 1773 and the opportunity was not to be lost by the Inquisition of striking at a man, conspicuous enough to serve as a terrifying example, and yet who, as a "kinless loon," had no influential family behind him. Besides, the whole scheme of the Poblaciones had aroused the hostility of two influential classes--the friars whose establishments were excluded and the Mesta whose flocks were not allowed to ravage the fields.

***

It shows the decadence of the Inquisition that the royal permission to prosecute was sought and obtained. Olavide was summoned to court, towards the end of 1775, on a pretext; after some delay he realized the situation and sought the protection of Manuel de Roda, then minister of Gracia y Justicia, who was too vulnerable himself to compromise his own safety, and who merely wrote to Inquisitor-general Beltran a note speaking favorably of Olavide. The Madrid tribunal moved with deliberation, for it was not until November 14, 1776, that Olavide was arrested. For two years he disappeared from human sight. Seventy-two witnesses were examined, and the fiscal accumulated a formidable array of a hundred and sixty-six heretical propositions. He admitted imprudent talk, while denying all lapse from the faith, but he confessed enough for the inquisitors to assume that he secretly cherished the opinions of the fashionable philosophy, and his condemnation was inevitable. We are told that a public auto was desired, in order to emphasize the warning, but it was felt that the occasion scarce justified such a solemnity, and the Roman Inquisition was consulted which suggested that the purpose would be answered by a private auto with a huge number of spectators. It was held, November 24, 1778, in the audience-chamber, after inviting--invitations equivalent to commands--Campomanes and numerous prominent nobles, statesmen and others who had been connected with Olavide, or were suspected of philosophism, so that when he was brought in he found himself surrounded by his friends assembled to witness his humiliation. For three hours he listened to the long-drawn recital of all the heretical propositions proved against him by the witnesses, to which he responded by ejaculating "I never have lost the faith although the fiscal says so." Then followed the sentence, pronouncing him a convicted heretic, a rotten member of the Church, and condemning him to reconciliation, confiscation, and banishment for ever for forty leagues from Madrid and all royal residences, the kingdoms of Lima, Andalusia and the colonies of the Sierra Morena, to reclusion for eight years in a convent and to the customary disabilities for himself and his descendants to the fifth generation. This tremendous severity so overcame him that he fell senseless to the floor. A distant convent at Gerona was selected for his confinement; in 1780, on the plea of ill-health, he was allowed to visit a watering-place, from which he escaped to France, not without, it is said, the secret connivance of the court, although, when his extradition was demanded, he sought safety in Geneva. With the outbreak of the Revolution he returned to France, where he narrowly escaped the guillotine; adversity brought a change of heart and, in 1798, he published anonymously at Valencia his "El Evangelio en Triunfo, ó História de un Filósofo disengañado," which had an enormous circulation and so impressed Inquisitor-general Lorenzana that he was allowed to return to Spain. He was offered restoration to his positions, but he was disillusioned with the world; he retired to Baeza, devoting himself to good works and dying in 1804.[639]

The Inquisition had not miscalculated the salutary influence of the example. Don Felipe

Samaniego, Archdeacon of Pampeluna, Knight of Santiago and member of the Royal Council, was one of those constrained to be present, and was so frightened that the next day he denounced himself to the tribunal as a reader of prohibited books, of which he presented a long list. This, he said, had led him to religious doubt but, on serious reflection, he had resolved to adhere firmly to the Catholic faith and he asked to be absolved ad cautelam. He was turned to account by being required to submit a sworn statement as to where and how he had procured the books, how long he had held these views, who had taught him, with whom had he discussed these matters, and who had refuted or accepted his opinions. This brought out a detailed confession compromising almost all the learned and enlightened men of the court--Aranda, Floridablanca, Campomanes, O'Reilly, Lacy, the Duke of Almodovar and many others of high position. Prosecutions were instituted against them all, but the testimony of a single witness was insufficient and the power of those implicated was so great that the tribunal was content to let the cases remain in suspense.[640]

Offenders less conspicuous were less fortunate, and numerous cases attested the resolve of the Inquisition to crush out the new ideas. It was merciful to Benito Bails, a professor of mathematics and author of a series of text-books long in use, for a niece was allowed to enter with him the secret prison and take care of him, as he was aged and crippled in all his limbs. Before the publication of evidence he confessed to having entertained doubts as to the existence of God and as to immortality, but that solitude and reflection had removed them, and that he was ready to abjure and accept penance. As reclusion in a convent would have deprived him of the care of his neice, his house was charitably assigned to him as a prison, with various spiritual penances.[641] A more suggestive case was that of Doctor Gregorio de Vicente, professor of philosophy in the University of Valladolid, for certain theses in which were discovered twenty propositions savoring of "naturalism," and for a sermon in which he argued that true religion consisted in the practice of virtue and not in external observance. For eight years he lay in the secret prison, but it chanced that he had an uncle who was an inquisitor of Santiago, whose influence induced the Valladolid tribunal at length, in 1801, to pronounce him insane, while condemning his propositions. On his release, however, he gave such evidence of sanity that the tribunal felt obliged to arrest him again and repeat his trial. This time a year of incarceration sufficed; he abjured his errors publicly and accepted certain penances.[642]

CONSERVATISM AND PROGRESS

A case which excited much attention was that of D. Ramon de Salas, a prominent man of letters and professor in Salamanca, imprisoned in 1796, on the charge of entertaining the errors of Voltaire, Rousseau and other exponents of the new philosophy. He admitted that he had read their works, but only for the purpose of confuting them, which he had done publicly and in writing. The accounts which have reached us of his trial differ irreconcileably, but it appears that the prosecution was the result of private enmity on the part of men high in office, and that Salas had powerful protectors who induced Carlos IV to evoke the case, after he had been condemned. This invasion of inquisitorial jurisdiction led to resistance on the part of Inquisitor-general Lorenzana, which caused Queen María Luisa to exclaim to him "It is you, hypocrite, and the like of you who cause the revolutions of Europe." Not only was the sentence annulled and Salas was liberated, but a royal order was obtained that in future no arrest should be made without previously consulting the king. This was duly drawn up, but Vallejo, Archbishop of Santiago and President of the Council of Castile, one of the enemies of Salas, had sufficient influence with Godoy to procure its withdrawal.[643]

This case illustrates the struggle on foot between the forces of conservatism and progress, in which the Inquisition, as the protagonist of the former, was not always successful. The propagators of the new ideas were difficult to silence. Even under Carlos III, we are told that in 1785-6 there appeared in Saragossa essays scandalizing to the faithful, for they sought to establish that celibacy is prejudicial to the State, that vows of religion should be postponed to the age of 24, that the Church had customs detrimental to the State and that its abuses and superstitions should be suppressed. Apparently the Inquisition took no steps to vindicate the faith, and when Fray Diego de Cádiz, at the request of many ecclesiastics, preached against these subversive propositions, he was obliged to fly and even then he was pursued by the wrath of the innovators.[644] Under the anomalous government of Carlos IV, constant changes in the ministry and the fluctuating whims of his favorite Godoy, who liked to pose as the patron of letters and enlightenment, in turns repressed the Inquisition and gave it free rein. A prominent personage of the time was the Count Francisco Cabarrús, a French adventurer who founded the Bank of San Carlos and alternated, like other statesmen of the period, between guiding the destinies of the nation and a dungeon. After his imprisonment in the castle of Batres, he relieved his mind in 1792 and 1793 of the thoughts which had accumulated there, in three letters to Jovellanos, developing in verbose rhetoric the ideas of Rousseau and the contrat social. Education, he argued, should be universal, but it should be purely secular, and the clergy should not be allowed to meddle with it, religious training being left to parents and parish priests. In colleges the studies should be directed to fitting youth for actual life; the existing universities were sewers of humanity, whose scholastic theology and teaching of jurisprudence were equally destructive to the human race. The numbers of the clergy were enormously excessive, constituting a running sore and a body subversive of all the principles of morals and statesmanship. There should be stimulated a holy and virtuous indignation against all the absurd and apocryphal devotions which pervert reason, destroy virtue and cause heathendom to ridicule Christianity.[645] For much less than this many a man, like Olavide, had suffered bitterly but, in 1795, Cabarrús prefaced these letters with one addressed to Godoy himself as "mi amigo" and, secure in the protection of the all-powerful favorite, he was beyond the reach of the Inquisition, showing how uncertain were its functions during the disastrous period when absolutism was in the hands of a frivolous courtier.

***

The feelings of the orthodox towards these innovators are comprehensively expressed by Fray Francisco Alvarado, the leading champion of conservatism against the Córtes of 1810. "These philosophers" he says, "have come to disrupt our union, to disturb our peace, to embarrass our defence, to distract our attention, to corrupt our fidelity, to overturn our State, to seize our fortunes, to degrade our reason, to abolish our religion, to--what shall I say?--to make our free cities a hell where nothing but blasphemies are heard and where there is little lacking to replace order with sempiternal horror."[646] Virulent as is this objurgation, it is but the natural expression of the passions excited by the struggle in progress, which each side felt to be a combat to the death. A moderated philosophism, as we shall see, triumphed in the Córtes of 1810-13 and, although there has followed nearly a century of vicissitudes, some of them sanguinary, it has, at least established its right to existence. The Inquisition was not mistaken in recognizing it, from the first, as its most dangerous enemy--the embodiment of the modern spirit, destined, for better or worse, finally to supplant medievalism.

CHAPTER XIV - BIGAMY

From an early period the Church assumed jurisdiction over marriage, derived from the function of the priest for its due celebration, and when, in the twelfth century, matrimony was erected into a sacrament, its control became absolute. Monogamy was a distinguishing feature of Christianity, and marriage was declared to be insoluble. The sacrament could be enjoyed but once during the life of both spouses, and its repetition was invalid, all of which naturally came within the province of the episcopal courts. The infraction of the ecclesiastical law, however, considered as an offence against society, was subject to secular penal statutes and, under the Partidas, it was punishable with relegation to an island for five years and confiscation for the benefit of children, to which penalties Juan I, in the Córtes of Briviesca, in 1387, added branding in the face.[647] In 1532, the Córtes of Segovia petitioned to have it made a capital offence, which Charles V refused, but added half confiscation and, in 1548, the Córtes of Valladolid substituted the galleys, the term for which Philip II, in 1566, defined as ten years, with public vergüenza.[648]

RESISTANCE IN CATALONIA

Thus there was ample provision for the trial and punishment of the offence by the spiritual and secular authorities, and there was no necessity for the assumption of jurisdiction by the Inquisition. Presumably it obtained a foothold through the laxity of the marriage tie among Moors and Jews, so that bigamy, like abstinence from pork and wine and change of linen on Saturday, created suspicion of heresy. This showed itself first in Aragon. As early as 1486, the Saragossa tribunal burnt in effigy the fugitive Dionis Ginot, a notary, for marrying a second wife during the lifetime of the first, and a number of other cases followed in which bigamy is conjoined with Judaic practices. For simple bigamy the penalty seems to have been perpetual prison, the punishment indicated for two culprits in the auto of February 10, 1488.[649] It also involved confiscation, for a letter of Ferdinand, October 22, 1502, to his receiver at Saragossa, orders him to deliver to certain parties ninety-four head of cattle confiscated on the bigamist Dornan Morrell.[650] In some way bigamy was construed as heresy for, in the Barcelona auto of February 3, 1503, Pere de Sentillana was required to abjure for marrying two wives, and in that of July 2, of the same year, Pere Ubach abjured for marrying in Rhodes and in Barcelona.[651]

This was one of the grievances of the Catalans, which they thought to remove in the Concordia of 1512, where it was agreed that bigamists, male and female, should be tried by the Ordinaries and not by the Inquisition, but they unwarily allowed the insertion of a provision "unless they believe erroneously as to the sacrament of matrimony or are suspect in the faith."[652] As this practically left it to the discretion of the inquisitors, Inquisitor-general Mercader, in his Instructions of 1514, was safe in telling the tribunals that they were not to try cases of bigamy unless there was presumption of erroneous belief as to the sacrament, and this was the answer sent, in 1515, to the Sicilians, when they made complaint of inquisitorial abuses.[653] Leo X, when, in 1516, confirming the Concordia of 1512, in the bull Pastoralis officii, was careful to make the same reservation,[654] but in this, as in everything else ostensibly gained by the Concordia, the subjects of the crown of Aragon found themselves deceived and when the Córtes, about 1530, complained that the inquisitors assumed jurisdiction over bigamy, the curt answer was that they observed the provisions of the law.[655]

A case occurring in 1513 suggests ample justification for this struggle to prevent the Inquisition from acquiring cognizance of bigamy. In 1477, Don Jorje de Bardaxí betrothed himself by words de præsenti to Leonor Olzina but, learning that she was pregnant or had borne a child, he never married her in the face of the Church or consummated the marriage. He remained single, but she, in 1497, married Antonio Ferrer. In some way the Saragossa tribunal got wind of the betrothal twenty years previous and prosecuted her in 1513. In her defence she alleged that Bardaxí had previously been married to Doña Juana de Luna, whereupon the tribunal commenced proceedings against him for the betrothal in 1477 and would have thrown him into the secret prison had he not been too infirm. He was a man of consideration and appealed for protection to Ferdinand, who ordered that he should not be arrested, that every care be taken to eliminate perjured testimony and that, on conclusion of the case, the papers be sent to Inquisitor-general Mercader.[656] The result is unknown, but Bardaxí was at least exposed to the terrors of an inquisitorial trial on a vague assertion of an indiscretion committed thirty-six years before.

Whether there was any formal opposition in Castile it would be impossible to say. There was a decided assertion of episcopal jurisdiction in the Council of Seville, held in 1512 by Archbishop Deza, the former inquisitor-general, which imposed a fine of two thousand maravedís on bigamists, in addition to the penalties provided by law; long absence of a missing spouse was not to be accepted as an excuse, and the death must be notorious or be duly proved before the Ordinary, before he could permit a second marriage.[657] Still, there was no special reclamation on the subject by the Córtes of Valladolid in 1518, nor any provision in the reform attempted through the Chancellor Jean le Sauvage. As in Aragon, the question turned theoretically upon the presumable heresy of the bigamist. About 1534, Arnaldo Albertino devoted an elaborate discussion to the matter,[658] but all this was academical rather than practical. In 1537, Dr. Giron de Loaysa, in his inspection of Toledo, reported that he had found everywhere many bigamists; they were so numerous that the inquisitors prosecuted them without distinction as to belief, and he suggested that special orders should be accordingly issued as the offence was so evil and so frequent.[659] This would have been superfluous. Simancas admits that, if the culprit says that he knew that he could not have two wives and thus did not err in the faith, it would seem that the Inquisition was estopped from proceeding, but custom has prevailed, though it would appear wiser to leave them to the episcopal courts. In a later work, however, he says that the Inquisition prosecutes them as thinking wrongly of the sacrament and impiously abusing it.[660] Thus it became settled, and otherwise the Inquisition would have been obliged to abandon its jurisdiction, for about 1640 an experienced inquisitor tells us that the accused never admitted heresy, but always professed consciousness of guilt. He was always asked whether he regarded a bigamous marriage as lawful and, if he answered in the affirmative, he was to be punished as a heretic.[661]

To keep up this fiction, the formal accusation by the fiscal asserted heresy or at least suspicion, at first in a simple form but subsequently with much amplification, stigmatizing the accused as an apostate heretic, or at least gravely suspect in the faith, for "thinking ill of the holy sacrament of matrimony and its institution and adopting the error of the heretics against the prohibition of polygamy."[662] With the same view he was always required to abjure for suspicion of heresy, in the earlier time de vehementi, but later de levi.[663] The flimsiness of the pretext, however, is exposed by the fact that, in the Suprema, bigamy cases were always considered in the afternoon sessions, at which assisted the two lay members of the Council of Castile, and where public pleas and other secular matters were discussed.[664] Still, when the jurisdiction once was acquired, it was asserted to be exclusive and was defended with customary aggressiveness. The civil magistrates were unwilling to surrender their immemorial cognizance of the crime, and assumed that it was mixti fori, leading to frequent collisions. The tenacity with which these contests were conducted is illustrated in a Sardinia case, in 1658, where the royal court arrested Miquel Fiori for bigamy. When the inquisitors heard of this, they demanded the accused and the papers but, three hours after the demand was made, Fiori was paraded through the streets of Cagliari, receiving two hundred lashes, and was sent to the galleys. The indignant tribunal refused conference and competencia, and promptly excommunicated the veguer and his assessor. Then the quarrel was transferred to Madrid, where the Suprema and the Council of Aragon alternately for two years pelted the king with consultas, the former assuming that the crime was purely one of faith and that the jurisdiction of the Inquisition was exclusive; there could be no competencia, because the inquisitor-general was the sole judge of what constituted cases of faith. In October, 1659, the king ordered the excommunication of his judges to be lifted; the Suprema replied that it had commanded this in the previous February, but the inquisitors had given reasons for not obeying; it had repeated the order in August and presumed that it had been complied with, but it had not been and, in November the king reiterated his commands. He decided, however, as usual, in favor of the Inquisition, and the judges were summoned to surrender the prisoner and the papers, but they replied that Fiori had escaped from the galleys and that the papers had been sent to Spain. The Suprema regarded this as an evasion and the utmost it would do was to suspend the excommunications for six months at a time, especially as the offending judges refused to present themselves before the tribunal and beg for absolution.[665]

PENALTIES

The time-honored episcopal jurisdiction over bigamy was treated with similar imperiousness. In 1650 the Suprema ordered the Valencia tribunal to demand from the Ordinary the case of Joana Arais, charged with bigamy, because it was a matter of faith, pertaining exclusively to the Inquisition. So, in 1658, when the Bishop of Salamanca arrested Domingo Moreno on the same charge, as soon as the Valladolid inquisitors heard of it, they claimed and obtained and tried him.[666] Yet, notwithstanding this, the episcopal authority over the sacrament of matrimony was acknowledged and, in all sentences, there was a clause referring to the Ordinary the question as to the validity of the marriages.

The Roman Inquisition was less aggressive than the Spanish for, while it claimed jurisdiction, it was willing that bigamy should be regarded as mixti fori between the secular, the spiritual and the inquisitorial tribunals. If the civil magistrate was the first to take action he could carry a case to its conclusion, and punish the delinquent according to the municipal law, but the episcopal Ordinary, or the inquisitor, ought to demand the culprit for examination as to his belief in the sacrament and then, after making him abjure and imposing appropriate penance, return him to the secular court.[667] Offenders were treated with somewhat greater severity than in Spain. The abjuration was always de vehementi and torture was freely employed for intention. The penalty was the galleys—five years in ordinary cases and seven or more when justified by circumstances.[668]

In Spain, as we have seen, the secular laws provided penalties, but these were disregarded by the Inquisition, when it secured exclusive jurisdiction, and in practice the tribunals exercised a wide discretion. Ordinarily men were punished with one or two hundred lashes and from three to five years of galleys at the oar, though those of gentle blood were exempt from scourging and were sent to presidios or to military service in the galleys.[669] The Seville auto of May 13, 1565, may be taken as an example, where there were fourteen bigamists. Ten of them were scourged with an aggregate of seventeen hundred lashes, and five, in addition, were sent to the galleys, with an aggregate of twenty-nine years. A woman had two hundred lashes, with prohibition to leave Seville for ten years, and two others were paraded in vergüenza. The heaviest punishment was that of the Bachiller Cristóbal de Ordaz, a physician, who was fined in two hundred ducats, provided that this did not exceed half his property, he suffered two hundred lashes and was sent to the galleys for six years irremissibly, after which he was banished for life, with a threat of perpetual galleys in case of infraction.[670]

Full allowance was made for extenuating circumstances. If husband or wife had been absent for years and reasonable effort had been made to ascertain their fate, or false news of death had been received, the accused was acquitted or the penalty reduced.[671] This is illustrated in the case of Anton de Cueba, a peasant of Cienpozuelos, before the Toledo tribunal in 1606. Both his wives were of his native place. He left it for awhile and on his return found his first wife absent. Then news came of her death in the hospital of Anton Martin in Madrid. He went there and verified it, returning with a certificate, on the strength of which and of public notoriety, four years afterwards, a licence for a second marriage was granted. Then the first wife returned and he was placed on trial. All this was carefully verified and the case was suspended.[672] There can, indeed, be little doubt that honestly misguided bigamists fared better at the hands of the Inquisition than they would have done in the secular courts, while the thorough organization of the tribunals enabled it to collect evidence throughout the land, whether for severity or mercy, in a manner impossible to either the civil or episcopal authorities. Its unwearied perseverance was sometimes severely taxed in the case of soldiers, removed from post to post, and is fairly illustrated in that of Joseph Antonio Ferro, a private in the regiment of Castile, accused, in 1763, to the Barcelona tribunal. His corps shifted its quarters and he was transferred to the regiment del Rey; his movements were followed up for years, the tribunals of Barcelona, Seville and Valladolid were successively employed on the case and, in 1769, that of Madrid was charged with its conduct.[673]

JURISDICTION DISPUTED

Discretion could be used to sharpen as well as to mitigate penalties, as may be seen in the case of the most accomplished bigamist in the records, Antonio ----, who appeared in the Valladolid auto of October 4, 1579. He confessed promptly and freely that within ten years he had married fifteen wives. It was the profession by which he earned a livelihood, for he wandered through the land marrying and running away with whatever he could secure. He must have been a most plausible scamp, for his favorite device was to personate some one who had disappeared, after gathering information sufficient to enable him to maintain the deception. This plan he repeated eleven times, in some cases establishing claims to considerable property. His sentence was to appear in the auto with a mitre bearing the insignia of all the fifteen marriages (usually the figure of a woman for each), two hundred lashes and the galleys for life. In view of the latter clause it seemed slightly superfluous to remit to the Ordinary, as usual, the question as to which of the women he should live with.[674]

***

As the eighteenth century advanced, the inquisitorial claim to exclusive jurisdiction was called in question. In the New Granadan case of Alberto Maldonado, of Santafé de Bogotá, the alcalde resisted the interference of the Inquisition with his prosecution of the culprit; the matter was brought before the royal Audiencia, which decided in favor of the tribunal, on grounds of expediency. Appeal was made to the home government, resulting in a decree, February 18, 1754, to the effect that bigamy was mixti fori and that cognizance belonged to the jurisdiction taking first action. Against this the Suprema presented a consulta, March 18th, but to no purpose. The decree was enclosed to all viceroys in a royal cédula, commanding that, in no case, should a competencia be admitted, for no custom could prevail against the regalías, without the royal consent. If the Inquisition desired to take action for the suspicion of heresy involved, it could do so after the culprit had served out the punishment imposed by the royal courts.[675]

The Inquisition was irrepressible and, in spite of these positive commands, a competencia arose in New Granada, which induced Carlos III to reconsider the questions. Consultas were called for and were presented, by the Suprema in April, 1765, and by the Council of Indies in April, 1766, resulting in a decree of July 21, 1766, by which Carlos restored the exclusive jurisdiction of the Inquisition. This was sent to the viceroys, September 8th and we find it ordered to be duly obeyed in Mexico by the Marquis de Croix, February 26, 1767.[676] Carlos soon saw reason to change his views. The Auditor de la Guerra had tried and sentenced an invalid soldier, when the Inquisition interposed and demanded the papers. This aroused him to a sense of the incongruity of the position, and he ordered the Royal Council to consider the matter. It presented a unanimous report, January 10, 1770, in conformity with which he decreed, February 5th, that the case belonged exclusively to the Auditoria de la Guerra. He utilized the occasion, moreover, by adding that he had ordered the inquisitor-general to instruct inquisitors that, in cases of this kind, they must observe the laws of the kingdom and not embarrass the royal judges in matters appertaining to them, but must limit the use of their faculties strictly to heresy and apostasy and not dishonor the royal vassals by arrests without manifest preliminary proof. All the royal tribunals were ordered to try and punish bigamists, according to the laws and to be zealous in preventing any contravention of the decree.[677]

This was a bitter rebuke, sullenly resented by the Inquisition. There were many pending cases in the tribunals and they forthwith suspended proceedings. This led to a royal letter of September 30, 1771, in which authority was granted to proceed with all cases not on trial in the royal courts, and all that might be denounced to the Inquisition, but subject to the condition that, when the culprit was not reo de fe, through belief that bigamy is lawful, sentence should not be rendered or punishment be inflicted but that the case should then be handed over to the courts having jurisdiction.[678]

JURISDICTION DIVIDED

Although this conceded only the power of trying without convicting, it was an entering wedge, which the Suprema lost no time in turning to advantage, by stimulating denunciations and making the people believe that it still held jurisdiction. In the Edict of Faith for 1772, therefore, bigamy was included, with the cautious formula "so that the Holy Office may prevent the offences against God committed in this crime."[679] The royal decree was sent around to the tribunals, with instructions that, when denunciations were received, care was to be taken to see that the accused was not on trial elsewhere. In that case he was to be regularly tried and convicted and made to appear in an auto particular, with the insignia of bigamy and double-knotted halter indicating scourging; he was to be made to abjure and be remanded to prison for two or three weeks of penance and then be handed over to the secular court, so that his subsequent punishment might have the appearance of being merely the execution of a sentence by the tribunal.[680]

While these devices doubtless had the effect designed, the offensive decree of 1770 remained in force and was a standing humiliation which the Suprema strove earnestly to remove. In 1777 it presented a memorial representing that the decree was printed and sold and published in the journals, causing infinite prejudice to religion and giving immense impulse to profligacy and infidelity. It debarred the Inquisition from acting in any cases save those of heresy and apostasy, and even in these it could make no arrests unless guilt was conclusively proved. Since that year, it says, how many have abandoned themselves to solicitation, sorcery and other crimes, believing themselves secure from the Inquisition! How many have allowed themselves to utter propositions impious or heretical, believing that, even when denounced, they could not be arrested until their offences were fully proved--a thing which could rarely or never happen! It is in vain that the Inquisition publishes its yearly Edict of Faith; the impression produced by the cédula is uneffaced and it ought to be called in and suppressed.[681]

This appeal led to a royal declaration of September 6, 1777, to the effect that the cédula of 1770 did not impede the jurisdiction of the Inquisition in cases of which cognizance was reserved to it. As to bigamy, the offence was partitioned between three jurisdictions; the deceit of the woman and the injury of offspring were subjected to the secular courts; the validity or invalidity of the marriage, to the episcopal courts; and heresy as to the sacrament, when it existed, to the Inquisition. The three jurisdictions should coöperate, by each imposing the penalties belonging to it and delivering the culprit from one to another in order that his offences might be verified.[682] This subdivision of a crime into three was too clumsily scientific to be reduced to practice. In appearance it only defined the existing method, but in a shape which enabled the Inquisition to encroach on the secular jurisdiction. As early as 1781, we find that the bigamist, after trial, was handed over to the royal court with a certificate designating him not merely as a convict but expressing the punishment of exile and presidio, thus showing that the tribunal presumed to sentence him to temporal as well as to spiritual penance. In 1791 a case indicates that it even went further, for the Toledo tribunal held an auto particular for Gabriel Delgado, in which his sentence was read, prescribing not only abjuration de levi and spiritual penance, but exile for eight years from Toledo, Madrid and royal residences. The only difference between this and the practice of a century earlier, was a clause that his person was to be delivered to the secular justice.[683]

NUMBER OF CASES

Under the Restoration the Inquisition assumed full jurisdiction over bigamy; the tribunal sentenced the culprit as of old, usually to scourging and presidio or exile, and the Suprema, in confirming the sentence, ordered the scourging omitted on some pretext. Nothing was said about handing the culprit over to the secular courts. They might, if they saw fit, exercise cumulative jurisdiction, and entertain cases that came to them, but, after they rendered judgement, the Inquisition tried the culprits over again and modified the sentence at its pleasure, either to increase or diminish the penalties. Thus, in 1818, the Granada criminal court sentenced Eusebio Reulin to six years of presidio of which one was to be in Africa. Then the tribunal took hold of him, adding spiritual penances and perpetual exile from certain places, and increasing the presidio to ten years, but, when this went for confirmation to the Suprema, it cut down the exile to eight years and the presidio to two. The sentence of the criminal court was treated with the utmost contempt. An exception to this seems to have been made when the army was concerned. In 1817, Eladio de Aragon was tried by the Madrid tribunal and convicted of having three wives; his sentence comprised only abjuration and spiritual penances, after the performance of which he was to be handed over to the captain-general with a copy of his sentence and a recommendation to mercy, in view of his long imprisonment, his confession and the hopes entertained of his amendment.[684] Evidently, in dealing with the army, the Inquisition felt constrained to obey the laws.

***

Bigamy formed a portion by no means inconsiderable of the current business of the Inquisition. In the Toledo record, from 1575 to 1610, the number of cases is fifty-four, ranking next to those of Moriscos. In the same tribunal, from 1648 to 1794, there were sixty-two cases, being next in number to solicitation. In the sixty-four autos held in Spain from 1721 to 1727, there were thirty-four cases, the only crimes exceeding this being Judaism and sorcery. In the later period, owing doubtless to the interference of the secular jurisdiction and the decadence of the Inquisition, the number falls off, the total in all tribunals from 1780 to 1820 being one hundred and five.[685]

CHAPTER XV - BLASPHEMY

Blasphemy is a somewhat elastic term but, for our purpose, it may, in a general way, be defined as imprecation derogatory or insulting to the Divinity. Punished with lapidation under the Levitical law, it was, during the Middle Ages, the subject of infinite legislation, both on the part of secular and ecclesiastical lawgivers, and savage punishments, such as boring the tongue with a hot wire, were frequently imposed. Enrique IV, in 1462, prescribed cutting out the tongue, together with scourging or banishment and, in 1476, Ferdinand and Isabella confirmed this.[686] Jurisdiction over blasphemy was cumulative, belonging both to the secular and spiritual courts, and was also within the cognizance of the Old Inquisition, provided it was heretical, but the distinction between non-heretical and heretical was not easy. Eymerich tells us that imprecations reviling God or the Virgin, or expressing ingratitude to him, are simple blasphemy with which the Inquisition has no concern; to give it cognizance there must be a denial of some article of faith, and the repetition of this definition by the Repertorium in 1494 shows that this continued to be accepted as the rule in practice.[687]

MUST BE HERETICAL

The Spanish Inquisition, at its inception, thus found itself possessed of jurisdiction and, in Aragon at least, where the institution had the tradition of centuries, there was no hesitation in exercising it, immediately after the reorganization. In the Saragossa auto of December 17, 1486, there appeared a Christian punished for blasphemy, his tongue being pierced with a stick, and a Jew with a bridle in his mouth, a mitre and a straw espuerta. In this field, as in so many others, inquisitorial zeal outran discretion; there was little attention paid to the distinction between heretical and non-heretical and, in the Instructions of 1500, inquisitors were told that they made arrests for trifling matters, not directly heretical, as for words uttered in anger that were blasphemy and not heresy; in future, no one was to be arrested for such things and, if there was doubt, the inquisitor-general was to be consulted.[688] This warning was all the more needed, as the secular courts were not ready to abandon their jurisdiction, for a pragmática of Ferdinand and Isabella, in 1502, provides lashes, prison and other penalties for blasphemies so evidently heretical as descreo de Dios (I disbelieve in God).[689] The bishops likewise continued to assert control, for the Council of Seville, in 1512, under ex-Inquisitor-general Deza, imposed a fine of three gold florins and imprisonment at discretion on clerics, while for laymen, in addition to the legal penalties, the ecclesiastical judge was directed to prosecute for swearing, blasphemy, or insults to God, the Virgin and the saints.[690]

The caution enjoined in the Instructions of 1500 was lost on the inquisitors and their abuse of power, in this respect, suggested one of the complaints of the Córtes of Monzon, in 1510. In the Concordia of 1512 it was provided that they should not have cognizance of blasphemy, unless it manifestly savored of heresy, such as denying the existence of God or his omnipotence. Inquisitor-general Mercader embodied this in his Instructions of 1514, and Leo X confirmed it, in 1516, in his bull Pastoralis officii.[691] The Aragonese Suprema accepted this and, in the Edict of Faith of 1515, it was specially stated that denunciation of blasphemy was not required, except when it was contrary to articles of faith.[692] As we have seen in bigamy, however, no attention was paid to this and, among the grievances of the Córtes about 1530, there is complaint that the Inquisition threw into prison orthodox persons for blasphemy and for words merely uttered in the heat of passion, to which the imperturbable inquisitor-general replied that the inquisitors acted only in accordance with the law and, if parties had been aggrieved, let their names be given, when due provision would be made.[693]

These troubles were by no means confined to Aragon. In Castile a royal pragmática of 1515 recites a supplication to the king asking that inquisitors should not have cognizance of blasphemy, wherefore it was ordered that they should only hear cases which they could and ought to hear, and a special charge was given to the inquisitor-general not to permit them to do otherwise, and to provide that abuses, if such there were, should cease.[694] This ambiguous utterance naturally produced no effect and, in 1534, the Córtes of Madrid represented forcibly the hardship that a blasphemy, uttered in the excitement of gambling or in the passion of a quarrel, should expose a man, noble and of pure blood, to arrest by the Inquisition, when, as the cause was not known, the whole lineage suffered infamy. They asked, therefore, that the offence should be remanded exclusively to the secular courts, which should punish it rigorously. To this Charles evasively replied that the judges would execute the laws and the inquisitors would not exceed their powers, and he contented himself with reissuing the pragmática of 1515.[695]

It is easy to appreciate the feelings underlying these remonstrances, for there was no function of the Inquisition which brought it more fully in contact with the mass of the Old Christian population, thoroughly orthodox at heart, strict in observance, proud of purity of blood, and dreading nothing so much as the nota incurred by the slightest suspicion of heresy. The Spaniard was choleric, and not especially nice in his choice of words when moved by wrath; gambling was an almost universal passion and, in all lands and ages, nothing has been more provocative of ejaculations and expletives than the vicissitudes of cards and dice. What, to women in the humbler walks of life, were the prosecutions for sorcery, those for blasphemy were to men of all ranks. Trivial as this portion of inquisitorial activity may seem to us, we may feel sure that in no other way was the influence of the Holy Office more keenly felt or more dreaded by that great body of the nation which zealously welcomed its persecution of the Jewish and Moorish New Christians.

DEFINITION DIFFICULT

It is true that, in theory, the jurisdiction of the Inquisition was confined to heretical blasphemy and, if the older definitions were observed, only a moderate self-restraint was required for the most inveterate gambler or hot-headed ruffler to keep on the safe side, but definitions were malleable and could be moulded to suit the temper or the aggressiveness of a tribunal anxious for business and for fines. The doctors found it no easier to agree upon the delimitation of heretical blasphemy than upon the thousand other questions suggested by Moral Theology. It was easy to say in general terms that heretical blasphemy consisted in affirming or denying of God that which the faith requires to be denied or affirmed, or in attributing to the creature that which pertains solely to the Creator, but when it came to applying these abstract principles in the concrete, there was apt to be discordance, and it is easy to imagine how ample a field for casuistry was afforded by the variety, vigor and picturesqueness of the blasphemy of the southern races.

As a rule, the Suprema was inclined to check the readiness of the tribunals to discover heresy in expletives which were, it is true, blasphemous, irreverent and indecent, but not indicative of lack of faith. There was a class of these, which seem to have been in the mouth of every one, ineradicable by the most severe legislation, such as "Mal grado aya Dios" (May it spite God), "Pese á Dios" (May God regret) "Reniego á Dios" (I renounce God), "Descreo de Dios" (I disbelieve in God) etc., for which Ferdinand and Isabella, in their laws of 1492 and 1502, provided penalties ranging from a month's imprisonment for a first offence, to piercing the tongue for a third and, in 1525, Charles V added "Por vida de Dios" (By God's life) to the list. In 1566, Philip II in his desire for naval recruits, added ten years of galleys to the penalties for blasphemy and six years of galleys to the tongue-piercing for the third offence, as provided by his predecessors.[696] When these offences were so fully covered by secular law, the Suprema deemed it unnecessary that the tribunals should be diverted from their legitimate functions to take cognizance of them. In 1537, Dr. Giron de Loaysa, in his visitation of Toledo, writes for instructions concerning these expletives. He regards them as heretical, but he understands that the Suprema does not wish the tribunals to take action on them, as they are so common and there are already judges enough for them.[697] It was probably in response to this that, in the same year 1537, the Suprema decided that utterances such as these were not within its jurisdiction, because they were conditional, being merely explosions of wrath or disappointment, a decision which it repeated in 1547; it had already, in 1535, construed the Instructions of 1500 as implying that sudden ejaculations of anger were to be handed over to the episcopal courts and, in 1560, it included "por vida de Dios" among non-heretical blasphemies. In 1567, however, among the charges against Estevan Pueyo, in Valencia, is included his exclaiming "pese á Dios" and the tendency of inquisitors to widen the definition is seen in the rebuke by the Suprema of Inquisitor Moral because, in San Sebastian, he had punished for sayings such as "God cannot do me more harm" and "in this world you will not see me suffer," unless, indeed, it sagely observes, the last expression is used with disbelief in the final Judgement.[698]

This latter remark illustrates the ingenious casuistry with which heresy could be discovered whenever desirable, of which we have already seen an example in the case of Antonio Pérez, for one of the charges against him was his swearing that, if God the Father interfered with his defence, he would cut off his nose, in which Fray Diego de Chaves found savor of the heresy of the Vaudois who attributed human members to God. It is possible that the successful employment against Pérez of the jurisdiction over blasphemy may have led to a more liberal definition of heresy for, in the seventeenth century, we find a consensus of opinion that such expletives as "reniego de Dios" or "de la fee" or "de la crisma" or "de Nuestra Señora" or "descreo de Dios" were heretical. Whether this applied to renouncing St. Peter, St. Paul and other saints was a more doubtful question on which the doctors differed. There were even strict constructionists who held that to call God all-wise or all-beautiful, as a lover might address his mistress, was blasphemy. In Sicily, the exclamation "Sanctus Diabolus" was usually admitted to be heretical, but it was not prosecuted because it was so universally used that it was more convenient to class it as simple blasphemy.[699] It will readily be seen how elusive were the questions arising from the variegated ingenuity of blasphemers, and what scope there was for the indulgence of temperamental idiosyncracies among inquisitors.

CUMULATIVE JURISDICTION

In the region so full of doubt, where there were three claimants of jurisdiction--the secular, the spiritual and the inquisitorial--much clashing might naturally be expected, but I have not met with any competencias with the royal courts arising from this source.[700] In his anxiety to suppress blasphemy, Philip IV in 1639 assembled a junta to consider whether the jurisdiction of the Inquisition could not be enlarged, so that it could punish the utterance of a single "por vida," when the outcome of its deliberations was a comprehensive decree punishing all swearing, save in judicial procedures, with a graduated scale of penalties, and those addicted to the habit were incapacitated for holding office under the State. Of course this was ineffective and, in 1655 and 1656 he ordered the rigid infliction of the punishment in order to disarm the divine indignation manifested in the public misfortunes.[701]

Neither did the episcopal courts surrender their jurisdiction, and it proves the ineradicable character of the offence that it continued to flourish in spite of persecution by all three. A case illustrative of their cumulative action, and of the susceptibility of Spanish piety, was that of Diego Cabeza, of Manzanal de la Puente who, about 1620, in quarrelling with a man, said that he did not know what God was about when he made him. The local magistrate, Francisco Prieto, exacted of him a fine of forty ducats, by threatening to denounce him to the Inquisition, but the episcopal court heard of the matter, arrested, tried and punished him. Then, some ten years later, in 1630, he was denounced to the Valladolid tribunal; the calificadores duly pondered over his utterance and pronounced it to be an heretical blasphemy, but, when the inquisitors learned that it was ten years old, and that he had already been punished by the episcopal Ordinary, they wisely suspended the case.[702]

Presumably it was the worst cases of blasphemy that came before the Inquisition and, as a rule, its moderation offers a favorable contrast to the savage ferocity of secular legislation. It is true that, as suspicion of heresy was inferred, the accused was thrown in the secret prison which, in itself, was a severe infliction, but torture was not employed. The penalties prescribed were abjuration de levi, appearance in an auto, gagging, scourging and galleys, according to the gravity of the offence, while frailes were recluded in convents of their own Orders.[703] These, however, were reserved for aggravated cases of habitual blasphemy by offenders of low degree; nobles and gentlemen had their sentences read in the audience-chamber, were excused from abjuration, and were recluded in a monastery for some months. Outbreaks of passion, in quarrels or gambling and even drunkenness, were held to entitle the accused to acquittal, or to merely nominal penalties. A writer of about 1640, indeed, assumes as a rule that the culprit was only reprimanded in the audience-chamber, without abjuration, except in very scandalous cases, deserving of scourging and the galleys, but even in these such punishments were no longer inflicted. There was no sequestration of property, and repetition of the offence was not regarded as relapse.[704] A later writer, however, holds that such heretical blasphemies as "reniego de Dios," "descreo de Dios" and the like are punishable with vergüenza or a hundred lashes.[705]

NUMBER OF CASES

It may be assumed, in fact, that there was a wide discretion in these matters. We have seen the severity with which the wild outbursts of rage of Antonio Pérez were treated, yet, in 1624, a young soldier who, when put in the stocks, exclaimed "I renounce God and the saints; devils why don't you come and carry me off?" when duly tried with all formality by the Valladolid tribunal, was discharged with a reprimand and without a sentence. So, in 1630, two girls in the Dominican convent of Valladolid, on being confined in a room by the prioress, in a burst of rage repeatedly renounced God and the saints. Naturally on trial they expressed extreme repentance and were discharged with a reprimand.[706] This wise moderation did not exclude severity, when the case seemed to demand it. In 1669, Antonio del Hero, for heretical blasphemy "en grado superlativo" was sentenced in Toledo to appear in the auto of April 7th, to abjure de levi, to hear mass as a penitent, to receive a hundred lashes and to serve three years in the galleys.[707]

***

Considering the prevalence of the vice and the energetic efforts for its suppression, the number of cases in the Inquisition is less than might be expected. In the Toledo record, from 1575 to 1610, there are only forty-six. In that of the same tribunal from 1648 to 1794, the number is but thirty-seven. In all the tribunals, from 1780 to 1820 the total is one hundred and forty-seven. It is evident that, in this matter, the activity of the Inquisition diminished greatly as time wore on, whether from an increase in popular reverence or from a growing disinclination to denounce the offence.

CHAPTER XVI - MISCELLANEOUS BUSINESS

In the undefined and widely extending jurisdiction of the Inquisition there were a number of matters, more or less connected with the faith, of which it assumed cognizance. Their cursory consideration is indispensable and they can more conveniently be grouped together.

MARRIAGE IN ORDERS

The celibacy enjoined on the Catholic clergy includes the seculars, from the subdiaconate upwards, and the regulars who are bound by the three vows of chastity, poverty and obedience. Even degradation from orders does not remove the disability, as the indelible character impressed in ordination remains.[708] Strict as has been the enforcement of the canons, since the twelfth century, the weakness of the flesh has, at all times, led to occasional infractions of the rule, punishable with degradation, reclusion in a monastery and other penalties. Whether the offence was justiciable by the Inquisition was, in the earlier period, the subject of debate, some authors holding that, if the marriage was public, it implied heretical error, bringing it under inquisitorial jurisdiction, but that, if it was secret, this showed that there was no intellectual misbelief, making the offender guilty only of violating the law and subjecting him, if secular, to the spiritual courts, and if regular, to the prelates of his Order.[709]

***

The Reformation, which sanctioned clerical marriage, introduced a new and controlling factor that in time altered the situation. Yet, for a considerable period there was a powerful movement, especially among German Catholics, to relax the prohibition in the hope of effecting a reunion. The question was regarded as open for discussion, as a matter merely of discipline; Arnaldo Albertino argues that the pope can dispense for marriage in orders, and instances the dispensation granted by Alexander VI to his son Cæsar Borgia, then a cardinal-deacon, to marry the heiress of Valentinois.[710] The reactionary influences which controlled the Council of Trent changed all this when, in 1563, it made clerical celibacy a matter of faith, rendering priestly marriage unquestionably thenceforth heretical.[711]

The Inquisition, however, did not wait for this to assume jurisdiction, though it seems not to have acted until after the outbreak of the Reformation had rendered clerical celibacy a subject of discussion. The earliest case that I have met is that of Miguel Gómez, a priest of Saragossa, sentenced, for marrying in orders, by the Toledo tribunal in 1529, when the peculiar punishment would seem to show that it was a novelty for which no precedent existed. He was exhibited for three days on a ladder at the portal of the cathedral, in his shirt and drawers, with his hands tied, his feet chained and a mitre on his head, after which he was deprived for life of sacerdotal functions and banished forever from the province. Toledo had no other case until 1562, when it had to deal with the somewhat complicated offence of Fray Juan Ramírez, who entered a religious order while married, but twice left it and returned again, during which performances he married two wives.[712] That jurisdiction depended wholly on the sacrament is seen in the case of Juan Carrillo, alias Fray Juan Ortiz, a Franciscan denounced, in 1596, to the Toledo tribunal by his prelate, Fray Juan de Ovando, for apostasy and living with a woman reputed to be his wife. Investigation showed that she was merely his concubine, so the case was suspended, and he was remanded to Ovando to be dealt with under the rules of the Order.[713]

PERSONATION OF PRIESTHOOD

After the offence had clearly been made heresy by the Council of Trent, the terrifying formula of accusation by the fiscal describes the offender as unworthy of mercy, to be deprived of all ecclesiastical privilege, to be degraded from his orders and to be relaxed to the secular arm, to which was added the otrosi demanding the free use of torture.[714] In practice, however, there was the widest discretion. It is true that writers speak of appearance in public auto or degradation and reclusion in a monastery for a few years, or a similar term of galley service, but there seems to have been no rule.[715] Indeed, it is not easy to understand how an offence so uniform in its nature should have been visited with penalties so diverse. In 1597, Francisco Agustin, an Augustinian of Barcelona, married in Toledo, sought to defend himself on the plea that he had entered the Order under compulsion in order to escape his debts; his sentence was appearance in an auto, abjuration de levi and imprisonment for life in the convent where he had made profession.[716] In 1629, Fray Lorenzo de Avalle, a Benedictine priest, accused himself to the Valladolid tribunal of having married and lived for eight years as a musician in Aragon. Notwithstanding his self-denunciation, he was sentenced to verbal degradation and to four years' detention in a monastery, where he was to undergo a circular discipline, while the woman was notified that she was free to marry again.[717] In strong contrast with this was the case of Juan Alonso Palacios, a married Jesuit, before the Toledo tribunal in 1659, who, though not an esponianeado, escaped with a reprimand and four years of reclusion. Then, in 1664, Fray Juan de Ayala, a Mercenarian priest, was, by the same tribunal, suspended perpetually from his functions and recluded for three years in a convent with one year's Friday fasting and some spiritual penance. Again, in 1675, the same tribunal condemned Gerónimo de Morales, a married subdeacon, to five years in the galleys, three more of exile and disqualification for orders.[718] Five years of galleys, with three more of exile and deprivation of functions and benefices, was the portion of Don Cristóval de Zabiati, alias Don Juan Baptista de Verganza, priest of Talavera de la Reina, who appeared in the great Madrid auto of 1680.[719] In 1700 the Toledo tribunal had to deal with a case characterized as "con circonstancias gravísimas," so that we may regard the sentence as representing the extremity of punishment for the offence. The culprit was not required to appear in an auto, but his sentence was read in the audience-chamber, in the presence of twenty-four ecclesiastics. It prescribed abjuration de levi, perpetual deprivation of functions, perpetual confinement in a convent cell, to be left only for choir and refectory, in which he was to have the last place, to fasting for four years, on bread and water on Fridays and vigils, and to a circular discipline when taken to the convent. The details of his career are not given, but there is a suggestion of material for a picaresque novel, as the culprit was a Dominican, Fray Tomas Juster, who had been a calificador of the Inquisition and a preacher of the king, and who enjoyed the multifarious aliases of Don Juan de San Feliú Cisneros, Don Vicente de Ochaita and Don Juan de Ibarrola.[720] It is somewhat remarkable that degradation appears so rarely to be resorted to.

The offence seems to have been by no means frequent. In the Toledo reports from 1575 to 1610, there are only the two cases referred to above, and, in the record of the same tribunal from 1648 to 1794 the number is only ten. From 1780 to 1820 the combined records of all the tribunals show only six cases.[721]

***

The veneration with which the sacraments are regarded, and the supreme importance ascribed to them as a means of salvation, render it indispensable that they should be guarded with the utmost solicitude. Not only is their validity essential to those who seek them, but any fraud in their dispensation is sacrilege, which, in the case of the mass, may plunge all worshippers present into the sin of idolatry. With the exception of baptism, they can be administered only by those in full priest's orders, and the pretence to do so by men unqualified is a wrong, not only to the faithful who are deceived, but to the Creator who has established them for the solace and salvation of His creatures.[722]

The fees attaching to the confection and bestowal of the sacraments are a valuable privilege of the priesthood, and the temptation was great for graceless laymen or clerics in the lower orders to simulate the possession of the requisite faculties, and to betray the unsuspecting into accepting from their hands the worthless simulacra. In the venality of the fourteenth century this would seem not to have been regarded as an especially grave offence for, in the tax-roll of Benedict XII, the official fee for absolution for pretending to be a priest, hearing confessions and granting absolution, is only six grossi or about three-quarters of a florin.[723] After the outbreak of the Reformation it was regarded as a more serious matter. Paul IV, in briefs of May 20, 1557, and February 17, 1559, defined the offence as subject to the Inquisition, and to be punished by relaxation, even when there was not relapse.[724] Sixtus V felt compelled to reissue the brief of Paul, and Clement VIII, in 1601, confirmed the acts of his predecessors, authorizing prosecution by either the Inquisition or the episcopal Ordinary. This was applicable only to culprits who had reached the age of 25, but Urban VIII, in 1627, reduced the limit to 20.[725]

***

This repetition of legislation shows the stubbornness of the evil and the papal determination to suppress it. Even complicity was sternly punished for, in 1619, a layman assisting a celebrant, whom he knew to be unqualified, was tortured for intention, made to abjure de vehementi, to serve five years in the galleys, and was perpetually suspended from assisting at mass.[726] Cardinal Scaglia, however, states that when the offence was committed through thoughtlessness, relaxation was commuted to ten years of galleys,[727] but there was no hesitation in inflicting the full penalty in appropriate cases. As late as July

18, 1711, Domenico Spallacino, a hardened offender, who had lived for five years by celebrating mass in Rome, Loreto and other places, was relaxed and condemned to be hanged and burned; he was duly hanged in the Piazza di Campo de'Fiori, the body was fastened to an iron stake on a pile of wood and was reduced to ashes, which were gathered up and buried.[728]

In Spain the matter was treated less seriously. The Inquisition at first did not regard itself as having jurisdiction unless there were misbelief as to the sacraments. A carta acordada of January 31, 1533, instructs the tribunals that, in these cases, the culprit is to be asked whether he thought himself possessed of the power, or whether he had anywhere heard it so asserted as an opinion, and what was his intention; if he acknowledges no erroneous belief, the matter does not concern the Inquisition and, he is to be handed over to the magistrate. The briefs of Paul IV were not admitted in Spain, and the matter slumbered until 1574 when, on January 13th, the Suprema addressed to the tribunals a circular inquiry, asking whether there had been any prosecutions for this offence; if so, on what grounds was the jurisdiction based, what form of procedure was followed, and what penalty was inflicted; also opinions were asked as to how such cases should be treated.[729] Evidently no attention had as yet been paid to the question; the replies showed that there was no general policy, and a brief of August 17th, of the same year, was obtained from Gregory XIII reciting that in Spain there were conflicting opinions whether the Inquisition had or had not jurisdiction, wherefore he granted to it exclusive cognizance, and forbade the episcopal courts from entertaining such cases.[730] This the Suprema sent, November 26th, to all the tribunals with orders to prosecute in such cases, and to introduce a corresponding clause in the Edict of Faith.[731]

It is evident that the Spanish Inquisition did not share the horror felt in Rome for such offences, and this is manifested in the comparative moderation of the penalties inflicted. About 1650, a Spaniard in Rome, writing to a friend at home, and comparing the severity of the Italian Inquisition with the mildness of the Spanish, instances the Roman torture of bigamists and soliciting confessors, the longer terms of galleys for the former, and the implacable relaxation of those who celebrate mass without ordination.[732] There was no such ferocity in Spain. No time had been lost in assuming the jurisdiction and already, in 1575, there was a culprit in a Toledo auto--Fray Alonso García, a Franciscan--who had celebrated mass and heard confessions, and whose sentence was merely abjuration de levi and four years' galley service. The most complete discretion was exercised and the penalties varied in the same tribunal according to the circumstances of the case and the temper of the inquisitors. Thus in Toledo, in 1578, Pero Joan Queito, a student, who carried forged certificates and had confessed many persons, absolving them and imposing penance, appeared in an auto, with halter and candle, abjured de levi, and had two hundred lashes and three years of galleys. In the same year a Frenchman named Pierre Saletas, accused of having for twenty years heard confessions and celebrated mass on forged certificates, was tortured without confessing and was banished the kingdom for four years and forbidden to administer sacraments without genuine certificates. In 1600, Balthasar Rodríguez, a deacon, appeared in an auto, abjured de levi, was suspended for ten years from the exercise of his orders, with perpetual disability for promotion, and had six years of galleys. In the same year the Mercenarian, Fray Gregorio de Palacios, was spared appearance in an auto, but abjured de levi, had fifty lashes and was recluded for three years in a monastery of his Order.[733] In 1622, at Valladolid, the Franciscan deacon, Fray Juan Tapia, for celebrating mass, was merely ordered to keep his convent as a prison and to present himself when summoned. Somewhat greater severity was shown to Fray Antonio Frechado, a Trinitarian subdeacon, who for publicly hearing confessions was required to abjure de levi, was suspended from his functions for two years, during which he was recluded in his convent, was disabled for promotion and had some spiritual penance.[734]

***

It would be useless to multiply examples of this diversified moderation. I have met with but one case in which the papal prescription of relaxation was obeyed and this occurred in Mexico, in 1606, when Fernando Rodríguez de Castro, a mulatto, was relaxed for administering sacraments without ordination, but this was no precedent for, in the great auto of 1648, Gaspar de los Reyes was sentenced to two hundred lashes and the galleys for life and Martin de Villavicencio Salazar to the same scourging and five years of galleys.[735]

The systematic writers assure us that the papal decrees were not received in Spain, and that the punishment varied with the nature of the case, consisting usually of scourging, unless the offender was a fraile, the galleys, exile, reclusion, degradation, suspension of functions, etc., varied at the discretion of the tribunal and that, in cases of minor culpability, it could be commuted for money. Relaxation was kept in view only for some error in faith persistently held--a purely academical supposition, although the culprit was exhaustively examined as to his belief in the necessity of priestly orders to the validity of sacraments.[736] That ecclesiastics between themselves in reality attached but little importance to the offence may be inferred from the case of the Mercenarian Fray Pedro de la Presentacion, who celebrated mass when only in subdeacon's orders. The Toledo tribunal condemned him, June 16, 1662, to three years of galleys. The superior of his Order at once interceded for him and, in September, the Suprema commuted the penalty to three years' reclusion in a convent, with three years' subsequent exile from Daimiel, Toledo and Madrid. When only ten months of the term had expired the Provincial of Castile applied for the remission of the remainder, but in vain and, when two years had passed the effort was renewed.[737] Evidently the good frailes recked little of the idolatry into which he had plunged all who were present at his ministration.

As the eighteenth century advanced a still more lenient view seems to have obtained. In 1749 the case of Fray Juan de Santa Rosa, a Franciscan deacon, was an aggravated one, for he had administered the sacraments of baptism, the Eucharist, penitence and matrimony, but the Toledo tribunal only declared him "irregular" for promotion, suspended him from the diaconate for two years and imposed fifteen days of spiritual penance. No special expectation of amendment earned this benignity, for his Provincial was instructed to send him to a convent, from which he was not to go out alone, so as not to expose him to relapse.[738]

Under the Restoration there was leniency difficult to understand. The sentence of the Dominican Fray Tomas García by the Cuenca tribunal, November 14, 1816, for celebrating mass without priests' orders, was that the commissioner of Villaescusa was to reprimand him in presence of the superior of his convent, pointing out the severe penalties provided by the papal decrees and prescribing spiritual penances for a year, besides informing the prelate that he could not ascend to full orders. This was confirmed by the Suprema, with the addition that he be transferred to a house of stricter observance. December 11th of the same year, Angel Sampayo, a married layman of Campo Ramiro (Lugo) was convicted of celebrating mass. The Suprema alludes to his atentato horrible, but merely orders him to be reprimanded and sent back to his home, where the parish priest and his father are to keep watch over him.[739]

***

In connection with this subject it may be mentioned that the Inquisition also took cognizance of a class of cases, alluded to above under Solicitation, in which laymen managed to hear confessions of women, not with a view to administer the sacrament of penitence, but through jealousy, or for the opportunity of asking indecent questions, or in the hope of listening to prurient details. These cases were by no means infrequent. In 1785, there were three before the tribunal of Valencia; in 1793, one in Murcia; in 1796, Joseph Herranz was prosecuted in Madrid for doing this in order to hear his wife's confession. The same year there was a case in Seville; in 1797, one in Barcelona and, in 1807, Miguel Domínguez, sacristan of San Miguel de Niebla, pretended to be a Capuchin with the object to listening to the confession of a woman.[740] With what severity such cases were treated, I have not been able to ascertain.

PERSONATION OF OFFICIALS

In the universal dread inspired by the Holy Office, the temptation was great to personate its agents, and to extort money as the price of forbearance, for no one ventured to question the authority or acts of any stranger who presented himself as an official.

The opportunities thus afforded were speedily recognized and utilized. As early as 1487, at Saragossa, a special auto was held, April 1st, at which appeared a cleric who had pretended to be an inquisitor and as such had made an arrest. The penalty inflicted is not recorded, but evidently the opportunity was taken to make an impressive warning[741].

The systematic writers assume that in these cases there should be careful consideration of the injury inflicted, for the pretender may deserve exemplary punishment. The usual offence is asserting that there are accusations and that he will save the accused from prosecution; for this he must refund the money received, appear in an auto and suffer two hundred lashes and five years of galley service. If the imposture is assumed only to escape from some trouble and causing no damage, there is some penalty of fine or exile; if there has been only an assertion of official position, the penalty is very light and secret.[742] Other authorities tell us that, if the culprit is of a low class, he has two hundred lashes and four years of galleys, more or less according to the gravity of the offence; if he is a noble or rich, he is fined one or two thousand ducats and serves for two or three years, without pay, as a gentleman in the galleys, or against the Moors or heretics[743]. Evidently in an offence which varied so much in motive and result, much was necessarily left to the discretion of the tribunal and a few cases will serve to indicate the different methods of operating and the deterrent penalties inflicted.

***

In the Seville auto of September 24, 1559, there were three cases of personation. Alonso de Hontiveros, for pretending to be a familiar and endeavoring to make arrests for the purpose of extortion, appeared with halter and gag and was sent to Xeres his place of residence to receive a hundred lashes; Juan de Aragon, of Málaga, for the same offence, was spared the gag, but wore a mitre and had a scourging at Málaga and another where his offence was committed, besides two years of exile, while his accomplice, Francisco Prieto, received the same sentence, with the substitution of vergüenza for scourging[744]. On the other hand, at Toledo, in 1581, Francisco de la Bastida was visited with the utmost rigor. He represented himself as an alguazil, carrying a vara de justicia and using the name of the inquisitor-general. He would summon the alcades and other officials to render assistance, which was freely given without question; he would make arrests, carry his prisoners to some distance, take their money, leave them in charge of some local familiar and disappear. In this way he moved from Fuente de Enzina to Almaden and Madrid, and thence to Saragossa where he was arrested. He confessed freely at once and was condemned to relaxation, by virtue of a special brief obtained from Gregory XIII, but the Suprema, with doubtful mercy, commuted this to six hundred lashes--two hundred each in Toledo, Almaden and Fuente de Enzina--and the galleys irremissibly for life[745]. Zapata relates what is evidently the exploit which brought to a close the promising career of this enterprising knave. At Almagro, he says, the agent of the Fuggers of Augsburg was Juan Xelder, a man highly esteemed and reputed to be of great wealth. Suddenly a stranger appeared, with the vara of an alguazil of the Inquisition, who sought out two familiars and commanded them to assist him in making an arrest. Proceeding to Xelder's house he made the arrest, locked him up in a room and consoled the frightened family by assuring them of the customary mercy of the Inquisition. He then summoned a notary and placed all the property of the prisoner under sequestration, except two thousand ducats which he said he had orders to take for the expenses of the trial. The whole town was thrown into commotion, but no one dared to ask for papers, or authority, or identification. Xelder was placed in a carriage, with strict orders that no one should exchange a word with him; the familiars were required to accompany it to the next halting place, where they and the carriage were dismissed with handsome gratuities and the stranger confided Xelder to the care of a familiar of high standing, with orders to guard him carefully, incomunicado, while he would proceed to Toledo and send instructions. Ten days passed when the familiar, growing tired of the expense, made inquiries and ascertaining the facts released the prisoner. Meanwhile the impostor, fearing to carry the gold, deposited it with a banker and took a bill of exchange on Saragossa, so that he was readily tracked and arrested when he presented the bill for payment. The secular court claimed him, but the Inquisition asserted its jurisdiction--fortunately, Zapata says, for the culprit, for the offence was capital and he escaped with scourging and the galleys[746].

Another method of speculation on the fears and hopes of the defenceless appears in the case of Gerónimo Roche, son of the secretary of the University of Lérida. He pretended to be an official, to have much influence with the tribunal, and to hold faculties to remit four sanbenitos and to appoint four familiars. He approached a Morisca who, with her three daughters, had been reconciled, and offered to relieve her of her sanbenito for two hundred ducats, and those of her three daughters if one of them would abandon herself to him. He was forbidden the house but he persisted in writing letters of mingled threats and love. For this he appeared in the Saragossa auto of June 6, 1585, where he was sentenced to vergüenza and eight years in the galleys, being spared the scourging in consideration of his father[747].

There appears to have been a very lenient view taken, in 1582, by the Toledo tribunal, of the case of Pedro Moreno, a sacristan, who pretended to be a familiar and as such visited the hospital and asked the inmates whether they had confessed, when he arrested and carried off those who had not. It was in evidence also that, on seeing two men quarrelling in a church, he arrested one in the name of the Inquisition. There does not seem to have been a pecuniary motive in these eccentricities, and he escaped with a reprimand and banishment for a year[748]. Another motive, which was regarded with a lenient eye, was assuming official position in order to enjoy the exemptions and privileges of the Inquisition. Thus when Jayme Corvellana of Barcelona in this manner bluffed off the officers of justice who came to his house to seize some salt, Inquisitor Padilla imposed on him a fine of fifty ducats and some spiritual penance, and was rebuked by the Suprema for inflicting so heavy a penalty for so trifling a cause--"en causas tan livianas."[749]

Personation was by no means uncommon, but I am convinced that Llorente is mistaken when he says that there rarely was an auto in which some one was not punished for this offence. In the Toledo record from 1575 to 1610, the number of cases is only thirteen and, in the same tribunal, from 1648 to 1794, they amount only to four.[750]

The principal interest in these cases is the evidence which they afford of the terror inspired by the Inquisition, the very name of which seemed to paralyze, so that no one, whether magistrate or individual, dared to question the authority of any impostor who assumed to represent it, and this same terror doubtless is the reason why this apparently facile method of trading on popular fear was not more frequently exploited. It required more than common nerve to incur the risk of inquisitorial vengeance.

Somewhat akin to this was the levying of blackmail by threats of denunciation. No doubt there was a good deal of this, in which the victims prudently suffered in silence, rather than to draw upon themselves the attention of the dreaded tribunal. It was a matter of which the Inquisition took cognizance, but the only case which I have happened to meet is that of Pedro Jacome Pramoseltes, who was sentenced by the Toledo tribunal, in 1666, to three years of galley-service for astrology and had his term extended to five for attempts at extortion in this manner.[751]

DEMONIACAL POSSESSION

That evil spirits can take possession of a human being, deprive him of his free-will and subject him to extreme bodily and mental suffering, is a belief handed down from ancient times and still largely held as a matter of faith. That relief can be had by the ministrations of an exorcist, duly authorized by admission into one of the lower orders of the priesthood, is a corresponding belief, and formulas without number have been prepared to enable him to exercise his power over the demon. There is no heresy involved in either the possession or the exorcism and, under normal conditions, there was no call for interference by the Inquisition, but when, for any reason, such interference was desired, there was little trouble in finding pretext for its jurisdiction. We have seen (Vol. II, p. 135) the active measures taken, in 1628, with the nuns of San Placido, whose demoniacally inspired revelations were somewhat revolutionary. Greater self-denial was exhibited by the Valladolid tribunal in a contemporaneous case, when a Jesuit confessor reported to it that Doña Felippa and Doña Aña de Mercado, Bernardino nuns in Santo Espíritu of Olmeda, made gestures and other irreverent acts in confession and communion, which caused scandal, and he thought proceeded from demoniacal possession. The tribunal felt doubts as to its jurisdiction and consulted the Suprema, which submitted the matter to a calificador of high attainments. Prolonged investigations were made, other nuns were examined, and it was in evidence that the two inculpated were women of exceptional virtue and piety who had prayed to God to test them with afflictions. The case dragged on for more than ten years, resulting in the conviction that it was undoubtedly one of possession, for which the nuns were free from blame, and finally, April 16, 1630, the Suprema ordered its suspension[752]. Wherever there was the faintest suspicion of heresy, the Inquisition could assert jurisdiction.

This involved the question of the responsibility of the demoniac for his utterances, which was somewhat intricate. In the case of one under trial by the Granada tribunal, in 1650, the learned Jesuit, Padre Diego Tello, who was called in as a calificador, reported, with an immense array of authorities, and after three visits to the accused in the secret prison, that there could be no doubt as to the possession, for he was able to discuss points of theology and other matters far beyond his capacity; he could also speak Latin intelligibly and he quoted Scripture while, as he uttered many heresies, it was evident that the spirit was evil. At the same time he was rational on so many points that he could not be regarded as irresponsible for his heresies. Luther and Zwingli, he added, were notoriously possessed by demons, but they were none the less held responsible for their teachings and it was the uniform practice of the Inquisition so to decide in these cases.[753]

In the hysterical epidemics which form so notable a feature of possession, the Inquisition was apt to be called in and was ready to act, although it would be difficult to determine on what grounds. In 1638 there was such an epidemic in one of the Pyrenean valleys and, on September 24th, Jacinto de Robles, secretary of the Governor of Aragon, reported to the Saragossa tribunal that, on a recent visit to Jaca, he had found, in the Valle de Tena, that there were about sixty endemoniadas and that the malady was spreading. It was attributed to Pedro de Arrecibo and his friend Miguel Guillen, who had been seized by the secular authorities; Guillen had been executed, while Arrecibo's trial was nearly concluded. He had confessed that a Frenchman had given him a paper and some conjurations through which to win women, but it only rendered them possessed--a statement evidently fabricated to satisfy his torturers. It was the demons who had accused these two men, adding that their death would not stay the infection, for there were other accomplices. The women affected were of the best families, their ages ranging from 7 to 18--some were pregnant and others were suckling their infants, for demons were able to produce these results in the virtuous. The Bishop of Jaca and some Jesuits were exhausting their exorcisms, and an inquisitor was badly needed. What function was expected of an inquisitor is not stated, but the Suprema was consulted and, after some delay it appealed to the king. It was ready to send an inquisitor and four frailes, but it had no funds for the expenses of the latter, which would have to be defrayed from some other source. The king gave orders accordingly, but they were not obeyed, and the last we hear of the matter is another consulta of March 28, 1640, in which he was urged to speedy action in view of the great importance of the affair.[754]

***

The intervention of the Inquisition might well be welcomed if it was always as rational and as effective as in an epidemic of the kind which troubled Querétaro (Mexico) in 1691. Two young girls who had suffered themselves to be seduced pretended to be possessed. The Franciscans and Padres Apostólicos took them in hand, exorcising them at night in the churches with the most impressive ceremonies, which spread the contagion, until there were fourteen patients, and the community was thoroughly excited. It would doubtless have extended much further, but fortunately the Dominicans, the Jesuits and the Carmelites, jealous of the rival Orders, pronounced the whole to be an imposture. The two factions denounced each other from the pulpits, the people took sides, and passions grew so hot that severe disturbances were impending. Both factions appealed to the Inquisition, which submitted the matter to calificadores. These decided that the demoniacal possession was fraudulent, and that the blasphemies and sacrilegious acts of the energumens and the violent sermons of the frailes were justiciable by the Inquisition. With great good sense the tribunal issued a decree, January 9, 1692, ordering the cessation of all exorcism and of all discussion, whether in the pulpit or in private. The excitement forthwith died away and the energumens, left to themselves, for the most part recovered their senses. Prosecutions were commenced against four of them and against the Franciscan Fray Mateo de Bonilla, which seem to have been suspended after a few years. One of the girls, however, who had caught the infection, had her nervous system too profoundly impressed for recovery; she continued under the inspection of the Inquisition, gradually sinking into a condition of confirmed hypochondria, until we lose sight of her in 1704.[755]

Cases of imposture were not infrequent. Whether this in itself rendered the impostor liable to prosecution by the Inquisition may be doubted but, in the deception, she was very apt to commit acts or to utter blasphemies which brought her under its jurisdiction. Thus, in 1796, we find the Valencia tribunal prosecuting Benita Gargori, a pretended demoniac, and Francisca Signes, an accomplice, for irreligious actions and utterances.[756]

The exorciser also occasionally laid himself open to inquisitorial animadversion. Thus, in 1749, Fray Jaime Sans, a lay-brother of the Order of San Francisco de Assis, used to visit the sick and pronounce them to be possessed, when he would make the sign of the cross and sprinkle them with holy water. He was denounced to the Barcelona tribunal, which warned him to desist, for he had no power to exorcise, and threatened to proceed against him, whereupon he promised to obey[757]. Exorcists also sometimes abused their opportunities by committing indecencies upon their patients. I have not met with such cases in the Spanish Inquisition, but in this it would doubtless follow the example of the Roman Congregation, which, in 1639, ordered the prosecution of a most flagrant one, reported by the Inquisitor of Bergamo[758].

Considered as a whole, the influence of the Inquisition must have been decidedly beneficial in restraining the development of this disease, for experienced inquisitors recognized that the methods usually adopted only aggravated it. Cardinal Scaglia ([dagger symbol] 1639), in treating of these epidemics among nuns, remarks that the superiors, not content with exorcisms, commence prosecutions, examine witnesses and interrogate the pretended criminals suggestively and absurdly and threaten them with torture, thus extracting whatever confessions they desire and creating still greater disturbance in the convent and the city[759].

INSULTS TO IMAGES

Allusion has already been made to the invasion of episcopal jurisdiction by the assumption of the Inquisition that outrages or insults offered to sacred images fell under its cognizance. For this there was more justification than for some other inferential heresies, for wilful irreverence to the objects of universal cult was reasonably regarded as causing suspicion of erroneous belief, and during the period of active persecution of crypto-Judaism and of Protestantism such offences were readily ascribable to heretical fanaticism.

***

In one instance, at least, the secular magistrates exercised jurisdiction. In December, 1643, Madrid was much excited by a robbery committed on a miracle-working image of Nuestra Señora de la Gracia, when all its jewels, ornaments and vestments were taken, and worst of all, the image was left lying face downwards on the ground. Great efforts were made to detect the perpetrators of the sacrilege, and it was accounted miraculous when they were identified while investigating another robbery. They must have been tried by the criminal judges, for no mention is made of the Inquisition and all three were hanged in March, 1644, in presence of an immense crowd[760].

This was exceptional, and the jurisdiction of the Inquisition was generally admitted. We are told, by a writer of the period, that, when images of the saints are outraged by word or act, if the accused belongs to a nation infected with iconoclastic heresy, and the evidence is sufficient and he denies intention, he must be tortured. Overcoming the torture, without having sufficiently purged the evidence, he can be sentenced to an extraordinary penalty and to abjuration, either de levi or de vehementi: if he confesses both fact and intention and begs for mercy, he is to be reconciled, but if pertinacious he must be relaxed[761]. This however applies to cases of absolute heretics, in which the sacrilege was apt to be merely an aggravating incident, while the great majority of cases consisted of more or less reckless Catholics, whose punishment varied with the circumstances and was rarely vindictive. In the Toledo tribunal, from 1575 to 1610, there were but four cases, which illustrate the general principles of treatment and the extreme susceptibility felt with regard to any irreverence towards sacred objects. The first of these occurs in 1579, when Francisco del Espinar, a boy of 13, was tried for pulling up a wayside cross, playing with it until he broke it and cast the fragments into a vineyard, and then alleging that it was no sin because the cross was not a blessed one. He confessed freely and pleaded that it was not through irreverence, because he was drunk, but he was punished with sixty lashes and two years of exile. The second was in 1595, when Fernando Rodríguez was accused by three witnesses of throwing a stick at a paper image of the Virgin on an altar, tearing it and uttering a filthy jest, but he proved an alibi and the case was suspended. The next was in 1600, when Anton Ruiznieto was punished with abjuration de levi and three years' exile, for maltreating a crucifix and using offensive words to it. The fourth, in 1606, illustrates the circumspection requisite to avoid even the appearance of irreverence, and the danger of denunciation which constantly impended over every one. Isabel de Espinosa was denounced by three witnesses because she had placed on a close-stool, which she kept in her living-room, a painted board on which were representations of Christ and some saints. A neighbor removed it and she replaced it, when the neighbor spoke to her and she changed its place. She was brought from Ocaña to Toledo and a house was assigned to her as a prison. In defence she explained that her mother-in-law had left her some old furniture, which her husband had just brought to the house; among it was this board, black and indistinguishable with age and, without examination, she had put it on the objectionable article, but when this was pointed out to her she had removed it. As she was a simple woman and there was no apparent malice, the case was suspended[762].

In contrast with the severity of the secular courts, as manifested by the Madrid case of 1644 above referred to, and the French case of the Chevalier de La Barre, the Inquisition was singularly merciful. In 1661, Francisco de Abiles, chief auditor of the Priors of St. John, for insults to an image of Christ, was only exiled for two years by the Toledo tribunal, which likewise, in 1689 merely exiled for one year Juan Martin Salvador for stabbing a cross[763]. Perhaps the instance of greatest rigor that I have met was that visited, in 1720, by the Madrid tribunal on a youth named Joseph de la Sarria. While confined in the royal prison he became enraged in gambling and, in his wrath, he threw in the dirt a picture of the Virgin and tore up another, for which he was sentenced to two hundred lashes, five years in the galleys and eight years of exile from Madrid and his native province of Galicia[764].

UNCANONIZED SAINTS

During the active period of the Inquisition, cases of this offence are singularly few. In all the sixty-four autos held in Spain, from 1721 to 1727, there is not a single specific instance serious enough to require appearance in an auto, indicating how universal and deep-seated was the popular reverence for sacred symbols. It is therefore significant of the spiritual and intellectual unrest characterizing the close of the century, that outrages on images became comparatively frequent. In the decade, 1780-1789 inclusive, there were sixteen cases; in that of 1790-1799, thirty-three and, from 1800 to 1810, nineteen, some of them, such as trampling on the cross, indicative of iconoclastic zeal. Under the Restoration, there are but three cases on record.[765]

During this period the spirit of revolt manifested itself in other kindred ways. In 1797, 1798, 1799, 1800 and 1802 there were trials for throwing down and trampling on consecrated wafers. In 1797, in Valencia, Bernardo Amengayl, Ignacio Sánchez, Miguel Escribá and Valentin Duza were prosecuted for exhibitions burlesquing the saints and sacred objects. In 1799, at Seville, Manuel Mirasol was tried for a sacrilegious assault on a priest carrying the sacrament to a sick man. In 1807, Dr. Vicente Peña, priest of Cifuentes was prosecuted in Cuenca for celebrating a burlesque mass and Don Eusebio de la Mota for assisting him.[766] These were surface indications of the hidden currents which were bearing Spain to new destinies, and it is worthy of note that they almost ceased during the brief years of the Inquisition under the Restoration.

***

Akin to the function of preserving images from insult, was the reverent care with which the Inquisition sought to protect the cross from accidental pollution. A carta acordada of September 20, 1629, instructs the tribunals to suppress the custom of painting or placing crosses in recesses of streets or where two walls form an angle, or other unclean places, where they are exposed to filth, while all existing ones are to be removed or erased under discretional penalties. Another carta of April 19, 1689, recites that not only has this not been done, but that the custom of placing crosses in these objectionable places is extending, wherefore the previous orders are reissued, with notice that six days after publication will be allowed, subsequently to which the penalties will be enforced.[767]

***

In the exuberant cult offered to saints, there must be some central and absolute authority to determine claims to sainthood and to preserve the faithful from the superstition of wasting devotion on those who have no power of suffrage. St. Ulric of Augsburg is said to be the first saint whose sanctity was deliberately passed upon by Rome, in 993, and Alexander III, in 1181 definitely forbade the adoration of those who had not been canonized by the Holy See.[768] The assumption of such authority was essential, for the cult of a local saint was profitable to a shrine fortunate enough to possess his remains, and popular enthusiasm was ready at any moment to ascribe sainthood to any devotee who had earned the reputation of especial holiness.

How difficult it was for even the Inquisition to crush this eagerness for new intercessors between God and man, is seen in the disturbances which troubled Valencia for seven years, between 1612 and 1619. After the death of Mosen Francisco Simon, a priest of holy life, there developed a fixed belief that he was a saint in heaven. Chapels and altars were dedicated to him, books were printed filled with the miracles wrought by his intercession, his images were adorned with the nimbus of sanctity, processions and illuminations were organized in his honor, and the question of his right to a place in the calendar became a political as well as a religious one. It was in vain that the Holy See asserted its unquestioned right of decision and ordered the Inquisition to suppress the superstition. Popular excitement reached such height that an attempt was made to murder in the pulpit a secretary of the tribunal, when he endeavored to read the edict; a priest named Ozar was slain for opposing the popular frenzy, and Archbishop Aliaga, for six years after his election in 1612, was unable to perform the visitation of his see, because he would everywhere have met with the unauthorized cult which he could not sanction by partaking. The Suprema did its best by continual consultas to Philip III, asking the aid of the secular arm in suppressing this schismatic devotion, and enable it to publish its condemnatory edicts. Its efforts were neutralized by the Council of Aragon, backed by the all-powerful favorite Lerma, whose marquisate of Denia led him to favor the Valencians. It was doubtless his disgrace, in 1618, which enabled the Suprema to attain its purpose, when an energetic consulta of January 10, 1619, was returned with a decree in the royal autograph to the effect that, if certain five points that had been agreed upon were not executed within a month, the tribunal could be ordered to publish the edicts without further delay.[769]

***

In this case the Inquisition acted under special papal commands, but the growing abuse of the unauthorized cult of supposititious saints led Urban VIII, in 1634, to issue a general decree empowering bishops and inquisitors to repress, with penalties proportioned to the offence, all worship of saints and martyrs not pronounced as such by the Holy See, or relating their miracles in books, or representing them with the nimbus.[770] Under this the Index of Sotomayor, in 1640, and the subsequent ones, ordered the suppression of all images or portraits adorned with the insignia of sanctity, unless the persons represented had been duly beatified or canonized by Rome.[771]

Yet they did not condemn a work issued, in 1636, by a pious priest of Salamanca and Toledo, Francisco Miranda y Paz, urging the cult as a saint of Adam, the father of the human race, and audaciously asking whether this could not be done without the licence of the Roman pontiff.[772] In fact, what the Inquisition did in discharge of this duty is less significant than what it left undone. We have seen (Vol. I, p. 134) that the assumed martyrdom of El Santo Niño de la Guardia was followed by a popular cult of the unknown victim. That cult proved exceedingly lucrative to those who exploited it and has continued to the present day, although Rome could never be induced to sanction it, yet the Inquisition prudently forbore to interfere with it in any way.[773] Similar abstention was observed in the celebrated case of the forgeries known as the Plomos del Sacromonte--inscribed leaden plates, accompanied by bones assumed to be those of the earliest Christian martyrs, exhumed in 1595, on a mountain near Granada. The forgeries were clumsy enough, but they favored the two points dearest to the Spanish heart--the Immaculate Conception of the Virgin and the Spanish apostolate of St. James. They were welcomed with the intensest fervor, a house of secular canons was erected on the spot, which grew wealthy through the offerings of pilgrims, and innumerable miracles attested the sanctity of the relics. Rome refused to admit the authenticity of the plomos without examining them; after a long struggle they were sent there in 1641, and after another protracted contest they were condemned as fabrications, May 6, 1682, by Innocent XI in a special brief. The bones of the so-called martyrs were not specifically condemned as spurious, but they were not accepted as genuine, yet the Index of Vidal

Marin, while printing the condemnation of the plomos and of the books written in their defence, was careful to assert that the prohibition did not include the relics or the veneration paid to them; the Sacromonte is still a place of pilgrimage and, in the Plaza del Triunfo of Granada, there stands a pillar bearing the names and martyrdoms of the saints as recorded in the plomos.[774] Yet, so long as the claims of the martyrs were not allowed by Rome and the only evidence in their favor was condemned as fabricated, this was superstition, and its suppression was the duty of the Inquisition.

While it was empowered to do this by the decree of Urban VIII, it is not easy to see whence Inquisitor-general Arce y Reynoso obtained faculties to authorize the cult of supposititious saints not accepted by the Holy See. The success of the plomos led a learned Jesuit, Roman de la Higuera, and his imitators, to fabricate chronicles of early Christian times, principally designed to stimulate Mariolatry and belief in the Christianization of Spain by St. James. They were long accepted as genuine and, in 1650, Arce y Reynoso ordered the fictitious saints and martyrs who figure in them to be included in litanies as objects of veneration and worship.[775]

Still, the Inquisition asserted to the last its authority under the decree of Urban VIII. So recently as 1818, when Josef de Herrera, an apothecary of Xeres de la Frontera, desired to establish the cult of an engraving of the Trinity, copied from a picture venerated in the cathedral of Mexico, the tribunal of Seville prohibited the effort.[776]

THE IMMACULATE CONCEPTION

The dogma of the Immaculate Conception of the Virgin had a struggle for recognition through six centuries, before it was defined as an article of faith by Pius IX in 1854.[777] In Spain, where popular devotion to the Virgin was especially ardent, it had, in the seventeenth century, become almost universally accepted, except by the Dominicans, whose reverence for their great doctor, St. Thomas Aquinas, bound them to follow him in its denial. In this they had long been fighting a losing battle with their great rivals, the Franciscans, and of late with their still more bitter foes, the Jesuits. Successive popes—Sixtus IV, Paul IV, Paul V and Gregory XV—in vain sought to suppress the disputatious scandals by forbidding public discussion of the subject under severe penalties, and the two latter extended these penalties to those who should publicly assert the Virgin to have been conceived in original sin—but still the Holy See cautiously abstained from declaring the conception to have been immaculate. The enforcement of these penalties was confided to all bishops and inquisitors.

From 1617 to 1656, Philip III and Philip IV made the Immaculate Conception a matter of state policy, by long and earnest efforts with the papacy to decide it affirmatively, and negotiations for combined action were carried on with France, but the Gallican court responded only with pious phrases.[778] That in this the crown was but voicing the wishes of the people was manifested when, in 1636, a man who ventured, in Madrid, to assert that the Virgin was conceived in original sin, was promptly cut down by some passing soldiers, was arrested by the Inquisition, and as soon as his wounds were healed, was thrown into the secret prison for due prosecution under the papal decrees.[779]

The Dominicans and their followers found it hard to observe the discreet silence prescribed by the popes and, in 1661, the Spanish bishops united in earnest request to Alexander VII, representing that persons were still found who publicly denied the Immaculate Conception. Philip IV sent the Bishop of Plasencia to Rome, as a special envoy, to convey this memorial, resulting in the brief Sollicitudo, of December 8, 1661, in which Alexander expressly abstained from defining it as a dogma, but forbade the teaching of the opposite, as well as stigmatizing the opposite as heresy, thus continuing the non-committal policy of his predecessors, to prevent discussions and quarrels without deciding the question. To this end he empowered all prelates and inquisitors to prosecute and punish transgressors severely, no matter what exemptions they might claim, and including even Jesuits. He also placed on the Index all books impugning the Immaculate Conception and likewise those which should tax unbelievers with heresy.[780]

This brief was received with great rejoicings by the upholders of the doctrine, who regarded it as a triumph. In Valencia it was made the occasion of a splendid festival, in which pasquinades on the opponents were plentiful. One, which was greatly applauded, represented a Dominican stretched on a sick-bed and watched by a Jesuit. A Franciscan opening the door enquires "How is the good brother?" to which the Jesuit replies "He is speechless, but he still lives." It was doubtless to the temper thus evinced that we may attribute the suppression by the Suprema of the city's official report of the celebration, the prohibition of one paper and the correction of another.[781]

UNNATURAL CRIME

The brief was promptly transmitted to the tribunals by the Suprema, with orders for its enforcement which show how delicately such explosive material had to be handled. They were cautioned that, when they or their commissioners were present at sermons preached by Dominicans, they must be careful that any action taken was such as not to create scandal. They were not trusted with prosecuting transgressors, but were ordered, beforehand, to transmit to the Suprema the sumarias with the opinions of the calificadores, and to await instructions. Apparently the customary jealousy arose between the episcopal and inquisitorial jurisdictions, for a carta acordada of 1667 calls for information as to whether the Ordinaries concurred in hearing cases, or whether they were treated as belonging exclusively to the Inquisition.[782]

It was impossible to make the angry disputants keep the peace, and the Suprema was busy in condemning and suppressing writings on both sides. In 1663 we find it ordering the seizure at the ports of two books printed in Italy. An edict of January 4, 1664, suppressed fifteen books and tracts, issued in 1662 and 1663, as indecent and irreverent to the Holy See, the Religion of St. Dominic and the Angelic Doctor Aquinas. Another decree, of December 7, 1671, suppressed two books indecently attacking the Dominicans and another of prayers and exercises for the devotion of the Immaculate Conception by the Franciscan Provincial Bonaqua. Books of devotion thus assumed a controversial character, and we can safely assume this to be the cause of an order, in 1679, to seize at Alicante and transmit to the Suprema a box of Dominican breviaries.[783]

I have chanced to meet with but few cases of prosecutions for impugning the Immaculate Conception, but they occurred occasionally. Thus, in 1782, Don Antonio Fornes, a pilot's mate of a naval vessel, was tried in Seville for obstinately denying it and, in 1785, Don Isidro Moreno, a physician, and his son Joaquin, were brought before the Saragossa tribunal for the same offence.[784]

***

Inherited from classical antiquity, unnatural crime was persistent throughout the Middle Ages, in spite of the combined efforts of Church and State. It is true that, with the leniency shown to clerical offenders, the Council of Lateran, in 1179, prescribed for them only degradation or penitential confinement in a monastery, which was carried into the canon law, but secular legislation was more severe and the usual penalty was burning alive.[785] In Spain, in the thirteenth century, the punishment prescribed was castration and lapidation, but, in 1497, Ferdinand and Isabella decreed burning alive and confiscation, irrespective of the station of the culprit. The crime was mixti fori--the law treated it as subject to the secular courts, but it was also ecclesiastical and, in 1451, Nicholas V empowered the Inquisition to deal with it.[786] When the institution was founded in Spain it seems to have assumed cognizance, for we are told that, in 1506, the Seville tribunal made it the subject of a special inquest; there were many arrests and many fugitives, and twelve convicts were duly burnt.[787] Possibly this may have called attention to the incongruity of diverting the Inquisition from its legitimate duties with the New Christians, for a decree of the Suprema, October 18, 1509, assumes that this had already been recognized, and it informs the tribunals that they are not to deal with the crime, as it was not within their jurisdiction.[788] This apparently settled the matter as far as the Castilian kingdoms were concerned.

***

In Aragon it does not appear that the early Inquisition took cognizance of the matter, as is shown by the curious connection of the crime with the rising of the Germanía. In 1519, the city of Valencia was suffering from a pestilence which had driven away most of the nobles and higher officials when, on St. Magdalen's day (June 14th), Fray Luis Castelloli preached an eloquent sermon in which he attributed the pest to the wrath of God excited by the prevalence of the offence. The populace were excited and hunted up four culprits, who confessed and were duly burnt by the justiciary, Hieronimo Farragud, on July 29th. There was a fifth, a baker who wore the tonsure and was delivered to the episcopal court, which sentenced him to vergüenza. This dissatisfied the people who tore him from the spiritual authorities, garroted and burnt him. The governor was summoned, and the leaders of the mob feared punishment. There had been a scare concerning a rumored attack by the Moors, which had led the trades to form military companies; these were further organized, elected a chief and swore confraternity, when, recognizing their strength, they utilized the opportunity of gratifying their hatred of the nobles and the rebellion broke out.[789]

In all this the Inquisition was evidently not thought of as having jurisdiction, but possibly it may have drawn attention to the crime and led to an application to Clement VII for a special brief placing it under inquisitorial jurisdiction. Bleda, however, tells us that, when the Duke of Sessa, ambassador at Rome, made request for such a brief, he gave as a reason that it had been introduced into Spain by the

Moors.[790] Be this as it may, the brief of Clement, February 24, 1524, recites that Sessa had represented the increasing prevalence of the crime and had asked for an appropriate remedy, which the pope proceeded to grant. The form in which it is drawn shows that the matter was regarded as wholly foreign to the regular duties of the Holy Office, for it is addressed, not to the inquisitor-general as usual, but to the individual inquisitors of Aragon, Catalonia and Valencia, and it authorizes them to sub-delegate their powers to whom they please. They are empowered to proceed against all persons, lay or clerical, of whatever rank, either by accusation, denunciation, inquisition, or of their own motion, and to compel the testimony of unwilling witnesses. That the offence was not ecclesiastical or heretical was admitted by the limitation that the trial was to be conducted in accordance with local municipal law, but yet, with singular inconsistency, the episcopal Ordinary was to be called in when rendering sentence.[791] The Barcelona tribunal seems to have questioned, in 1537, whether the brief continued in force, for the Suprema wrote to it July 11th, that there had not been time to decide this positively, but that it might continue to act.[792] Whatever doubts existed were settled in favor of the Inquisition, and the Aragonese tribunals enjoyed the jurisdiction to the end. The Archbishop of Saragossa had complained of being thus deprived of cognizance of these cases, and it was restored to him by a brief of January 16, 1525, but, at the request of Charles V, Pope Clement, July 15, 1530, evoked all pending cases to himself and committed them to the inquisitors, with full power to decide them, in conjunction with the Ordinary.[793]

Castile was never included within the special grant. In answer to some inquiring tribunal, the Suprema replied, November 6, 1534, that the matter did not pertain to the Inquisition, nor was it deemed advisable to procure a brief conferring such power. This was adhered to. In 1575, the Logroño tribunal was informed that it could not prosecute such cases as it had no faculty and, about 1580, the tribunal of Peru was told not to meddle with it in any way, except in cases of solicitation.[794] The Consulta Magna of 1696 states that Philip II, towards the close of his reign, applied to Clement VIII for a brief conferring the power on the Castilian Inquisition, but the pope declined for the reason that the whole attention of the inquisitors should be concentrated on matters of faith.[795]

Majorca, although belonging to the crown of Aragon, was not specifically included in the brief of Clement VII, and never assumed the power. When, in 1644, the commissioner in Iviza reported to Inquisitor Francisco Gregorio about Jaime Gallestria, a cleric denounced for this offence, Gregorio replied that he had no jurisdiction; still the tribunal was accustomed to arrest offenders and hand them over for trial to the secular judges, so he sent a warrant for the arrest of Gallestria, even though he had taken asylum in a church.[796] It is symptomatic that arrest by the Inquisition, for a crime over which it had no jurisdiction, was considered a matter of course.

***

Sicily also belonged to Aragon, but was not included. In 1569 Philip II ordered the death-penalty to be rigidly enforced, without exceptions, and that the informer should receive twenty ounces from the estate of the convict, but this was slackly obeyed by the secular courts and, in the Concordia of 1597, he reserved the crime exclusively to the Inquisition, with the understanding that a papal brief should be applied for, relieving inquisitors from irregularity for relaxing culprits. Application was accordingly made to Clement VIII, but, after Philip's death, the Viceroy Duke of Maqueda and the ambassador, the Duke of Sessa, at the instance of influential Sicilians, urged Clement to refuse, which he not only did but forbade the Inquisition to take cognizance of such cases. The tribunal complained that this deprived it of its jurisdiction over its own officials, to which the reply was that it was not the pope's intention to exonerate them from it. The tribunal therefore continued to punish its own guilty ministers, and the number of cases cited would seem to indicate that the crime was by no means uncommon. The punishments inflicted were comparatively moderate--occasionally imprisonment for life or banishment, perpetual or temporary, from the place of offending, or deprivation of office with heavy fines.[797]

Dr. Martin Real, who tells us this, writing in 1638, further informs us that, throughout Italy, the crime was everywhere treated with a leniency wholly inadequate to its atrocity. The Roman Inquisition, moreover, took no cognizance of it. When, in 1644, some Conventual Franciscans rendered themselves conspicuous by sounding the praises of the practice, the Congregation contented itself with ordering their superiors to proceed against them with severity.[798]

In Portugal, João III had no sooner got his Inquisition into working order than he was seized with the desire to obtain for it jurisdiction over the pecado maao. This he pursued with characteristic obstinacy, while the papacy manifested its customary repugnance. It was not until after his death that Pius IV, in a brief of February 20, 1562, committed the decision to the conscience of Cardinal Henrique, confirming in advance what he might do--but trials were to be conducted according to municipal law. Henrique had no scruples, but, in 1574, he applied to Gregory XIII for confirmation and for using the process for heresy in these cases, when again the pope committed to him the decision and ratified it in advance.[799] In 1640, the Regulations prescribe that the offence is to be tried like heresy, and the punishment is to be either relaxation or scourging and the galleys. In a case occurring in the Lisbon auto of 1723, the sentence was scourging and ten years of galley-service.[800]

***

In their general hostility to the Inquisition, the Aragonese kingdoms objected to this extension of its jurisdiction. There were complaints by the Córtes and, in the various Concordias and settlements, there were concessions secured which gave to the secular judges some participation in the trials. Into the details of these more or less temporary arrangements it is scarce worth while to enter, except to mention that, in the struggle which resulted in the Concordia of 1646, Aragon gained the point that the crime was recognized as mixti fori, to be tried by either the secular court or the Inquisition, according to priority in commencing action, and that familiars were included in this.[801]

The current practice may be gathered from the answers of Valencia and Saragossa, in response to inquiries by the Suprema, in 1573. In Valencia arrest was accompanied by sequestration, but not in Aragon, where the crime did not entail confiscation. In Aragon, when a new inquisitor was inducted, the papal briefs were presented to him and he accepted them, and all sentences commenced by qualifying the inquisitors as juezes comisarios apostolicos para conocer en el crimen de sodomia, showing that this was a special jurisdiction. The routine of procedure in the two tribunals did not vary much; the process was somewhat simpler than in heresy trials, the accused was allowed ample means of defence in counsel, advocates and procurators, witnesses' names were not suppressed, except in Valencia when the accused was of high rank, in which case the Suprema was consulted. After the publication of evidence, the procurator had the right to examine the witnesses. The Concordia of 1568 had provided that convicts should not appear in autos, but in Aragon this was left to the discretion of the tribunal, which generally exhibited them there.[802]

***

These reports make no allusion to the concurrence of secular judges, but the practice may be gathered from a letter of Philip II, March 17, 1575, to the Captain-general of Catalonia, where it appears that, when a convict was relaxed, the royal court demanded to see the papers of the case before pronouncing sentence. This the king pronounced to be wholly wrong and ordered the custom of Valencia and Aragon to be followed--that, when a case was ready for decision, the inquisitors notified the captain-general, who delegated judges to take part in the consulta, after which the sentence was to be executed without further examination.[803]

Torture was freely employed, even on the testimony of a single accomplice. This raised a question in Aragon, where the use of torture was forbidden, as the trials were to be conducted in accordance with municipal law, but the Inquisition replied that the brief of Clement VII had been applied for at the request of the secular judges, who had found themselves unable to convict for lack of torture, and desired, for that reason, the Inquisition to have jurisdiction--the truth of which assertion may well be doubted. In 1636 there was raised a question as to torturing witnesses who revoked, but it was decided in the negative.[804]

Punishment varied with time and place. In Aragon, spontaneous confession was encouraged by simply reprimanding the culprit, warning him and ordering him to confess sacramentally, and this was confirmed by the Suprema, in a decree of August 6, 1600. In Valencia, however, self-denunciation was visited with scourging and galleys and, if testimony of accomplices supervened, with relaxation.[805] For those accused and regularly convicted, the statutory and ordinary punishment was burning. When, in 1577, the Captain-general of Valencia had some hesitation as to his duty, in the case of two culprits relaxed to him by the Inquisition, Philip II ordered him to execute them promptly and, as late as 1647, in an auto at Barcelona, one was garroted and burnt.[806] Yet, on the whole, there seems to have been a disinclination to relax these offenders, who could not escape, as heretics could, by confession and conversion. In 1616 we find the Suprema asking the Valencia tribunal why it had not confiscated the estate of Dr. Pérez, convicted of this crime and, in 1634, it enquires whether there is any fuero prohibiting the pena ordinaria, when guilt has been fully proved and the offender is of full age.[807] About 1640, an experienced inquisitor informs us that, in Saragossa, the penalty for those over 25 was relaxation; for minors, scourging and the galleys, but he adds that this is not observed; he had seen many thus convicted and condemned to relaxation, but the Suprema always commuted the penalty.[808]

Ecclesiastics seem to have been regarded as entitled to especial leniency. In 1684, the Suprema called to account the Valencia tribunal for its benignity, in a case of this kind, when it replied in much detail. Two decrees of Pius V in 1568, it said, had prescribed relaxation, with preliminary degradation, in the case of priests and, in 1574, the tribunal had so treated the case of a subdeacon. Many authorities, however, held that clerics were not to be subjected to the rigor of the law for this offence, and it was the common opinion that incorrigibility was required to justify the ordinary penalty. This had been the practice in Valencia, especially since 1615, when a priest was convicted of a single act and, by order of the Suprema, was sentenced to an extraordinary penalty. This had since been followed in various cases, so that clerics were not relaxed unless incorrigible, and this was defined to be when repeated punishment showed that the Church could not reform them. This argument, moreover, precluded the use of torture which, as the tribunal pointed out, could be used only when the penalty was worse than torture.[809]

***

The case which called forth this explanation affords a very instructive example of the advantage to justice of an open trial, with opportunity of cross-examination. The accused was Fray Manuel Sánchez del Castellar y Arbustan, a distinguished member of the Order of La Merced. The trial had lasted for nearly three years, when the papers were submitted to the Suprema, in August, 1684. There were two accomplice witnesses to consummated acts, others to solicitation, others to lascivious and filthy actions, and others to general foul reputation. Under the ordinary inquisitorial process, condemnation would have been inevitable, but repeated examinations and cross-examinations revealed discrepancies and contradictions and variations, and a knowledge of the witnesses enabled the accused to present evidence of enmities. The conclusion reached by the tribunal was that nearly the whole mass of evidence was the result of a conspiracy, embracing a number of frailes of the convent, incited by jealousy of the honors and position obtained by Sánchez. Still, there was some testimony as to indiscretions, which was not rebutted and, as there had been a great scandal requiring a victim, with customary inquisitorial logic, he was sentenced to four years' exile from Valencia, Orihuela and Madrid, for the first two of which he was deprived of active and passive voice, of confessing and preaching and of all honors in his Order. In this, consideration was given to three years spent in prison, so that, if innocent, he had suffered severely and was sent forth branded with an ineffaceable stigma while, if guilty, he had a penalty far less than his deserts. When the Suprema asked why the two witnesses to complicity were not prosecuted, the tribunal replied that they were regarded as spontaneously confessing, and it was not customary to prosecute in such cases; besides, although their enmity and contradictions invalidated their testimony, these were insufficient to justify prosecution for false-witness.[810] Altogether it was an unpleasant business, which the tribunal evidently desired to despatch with as little damage as possible to the Church.

The tendency towards leniency increased with time, and was shown to laymen as well as to ecclesiastics. In 1717, the Barcelona tribunal sentenced Guillaume Amiel, a Frenchman, to four years of presidio and perpetual banishment from Spain. The Suprema commuted the presidio to a hundred lashes but, when the sentence was read, Amiel protested that his father was a gentleman and that he held a patent as "teniente del Rey Christianisimo," thus claiming exemption from degrading corporal punishment. The proceedings were suspended, and the Suprema was consulted, which omitted the lashes and, on the same account, the boy Ramon Gils, who was the accomplice, was spared the vergüenza to which he had been condemned.[811]

USURY

The most conspicuous case of this nature in the annals of the Inquisition was that of Don Pedro Luis Galceran de Borja, Grand-master of the Order of Montesa. He was not only a grandee of Spain, but was allied to the royal house, he was half-brother to Francisco de Borja, Duke of Grandía and subsequently General of the Jesuits, and was of kin to nearly all the noblest lineages of the land. For his arrest, in 1571, the assent of Philip II was necessary; he was not confined in the secret prison, but had commodious apartments from which, during his trial, he conducted the affairs of the Order. He claimed exemption on the ground of the privileges of the Order, and more than two years were spent in debating the question, though it was pointed out that, while the Trinitarians had even greater privileges, two members professed of that Order had recently been relaxed for the same crime, and Borja was not even a cleric, but a married man with children. The claim was finally disallowed and the trial went slowly on. The evidence reduced itself to two "singular" witnesses, who testified to solicitation and attempt, and to one, Martin de Castro, who testified to consummation and then revoked. Powerful influence from all quarters was brought to bear to save the accused, and in the final consulta de fe there was discordia. Two inquisitors and the Ordinary voted for acquittal. The other inquisitor, who was Juan de Rojas, in a written opinion, called for four years of exile and a heavy fine. The Suprema, after prolonged correspondence with the tribunal, accepted this, but changed the exile to six years of reclusion in his convent of Montesa. Llorente intimates that the inquisitors expected to gain bishoprics, or at least places in the Suprema, and that a bargain was made through which, on Borja's death, the Order of Montesa was incorporated with the crown, as the military Orders of Castile had been under Ferdinand; to this latter some color was lent by Philip's appointment of Borja's natural son to the grand commandership of the Order, from which he rose to the cardinalate. There is an evident allusion to this case in the remark of an Italian traveller in 1593, who, when speaking of the severity of the Inquisition in these matters, illustrates it by the story of a grandee who, for merely throwing his arm around the neck of a page, spent ten years in prison and fifty thousand ducats.[812]

Cases were sufficiently frequent to give the Aragonese tribunals considerable occupation, especially after it was included in the Edict of Faith in 1574, as a crime to be denounced.[813] I have but a few scattering data, but they are suggestive. Thus, in Saragossa, at the auto of June 6, 1585, there were four culprits relaxed.[814] In Catalonia, in 1597, the report, by Inquisitor Heredia, of a visitation through the see of Tarragona and parts of those of Barcelona, Vich and Urgel, contains sixty-eight cases of all kinds and of these fifteen were for this class of offences, though most of them were subsequently suspended.[815] In Valencia, there appeared in the autos from January 1598 to December 1602, twenty-seven of these culprits, of whom seven were frailes.[816] As it was customary to read the sentences con meritos, the populace had an edifying education. From 1780 to 1820, the total number of cases coming before the three tribunals was exactly one hundred.[817]

***

The ecclesiastical definition of usury is not, as we understand the term, an exorbitant charge for the use of money, beyond the legal rate, but any interest or other advantage, however small or indirect, derived from a loan of money or other article. Forbidden by the Old Law, between the Chosen People, and extended under the New to the brotherhood of man, it has been the subject of denunciation continuously from the primitive Church to the most recent times. Ingenuity has been exhausted in devising methods of repression and punishment, only to show how impossible has been the task of warring against human nature and human necessities.

From an early period, usury was regarded as an ecclesiastical sin and crime, subject to spiritual jurisdiction in both the forum internum and forum externum. In 1258 Alexander IV rendered it justiciable by the Inquisition and, at the Council of Vienne, in 1312, the assertion that the taking of interest is not a sin was defined to be a heresy, which the Inquisition was in duty required to prosecute.[818] During the later Middle Ages, when the greater heresies had been largely suppressed, the prosecution of usurers formed a considerable, and the most profitable, portion of inquisitorial activity. It is true that the heresy consisted in denying that usury is a sin, but, as the Repertorium of 1494 explains, the usurer or simonist, who does not affirm or deny but is silent and tacitly believes it not to be a sin to commit usury or simony, is a pertinacious heretic mentally.[819]

***

In Spain, the usurious practices of Jews and Conversos were the principal source of popular hostility, but Jews were not subject to the Inquisition and, in its earlier years, it appears not to have recognized its jurisdiction in this matter over the Conversos, for I have met with no trace, at this period, of action by it against usury, whether in Castile or in Aragon. As regards the latter, indeed, it was impeded by a fuero of the Córtes of Calatayud, in 1461, prohibiting the prosecution of usurers, by both the secular and spiritual courts, and the procuring of faculties for the purpose by the Inquisition. To ensure the observance of this, Juan II was required to swear that he would not obtain any papal rescript or commission authorizing inquisition into usury and that, if such rescript were had, it should not be used but be delivered within a month to the Diputados.[820] It may be assumed that the Inquisition sought relief from this restriction, for Julius II issued a motu proprio, January 14, 1504, reciting the fuero of Calatayud and stating that the usuraria pravitas had so increased that a measure of wheat would be multiplied to twenty-five within three years, chiefly because the Inquisition, in consequence of this fuero, was precluded from the exercise of its lawful jurisdiction. He therefore ordered Inquisitor-general Deza to prosecute all Christian usurers and compel them to desist, by inflicting the penalties prescribed by the general council, while Ferdinand was summoned to aid the inquisitors, and he and his successors were released from any oaths to observe the fuero.[821]

As all commercial and financial transactions at the time were based on interest payment and, as the agriculturist habitually borrowed seed-corn before sowing, to be repaid with increase after harvest, the Inquisition thus had an ample field opened for its operations. That it did not neglect the opportunity is fairly inferable from the opposition excited. It was the subject of one of the most energetic remonstrances of the Córtes of Monzon in 1510, and the Concordia of 1512 bore an article in which Ferdinand promised to obtain from the pope the revocation of the faculties granted to the inquisitors; that he would allow no other grant to be obtained, and that meanwhile he would arrange that no prosecutions should be brought except for open assertion that usury was no sin. For this, as for the other articles, he swore to procure the papal confirmation. Inquisitors were likewise sworn to obey the Concordia and, when Ferdinand was released from his oath by Leo X, in the brief of April 30, 1513, a motu proprio followed, September 2d, to the effect that, as heresy and usury are the most heinous of crimes, to be prosecuted with the sharpest rigor, the inquisitors were released from their oaths and directed to employ the faculties granted by Julius II for the suppression of usury.[822] This serves to explain why, in the compromise embodied in Inquisitor-general Mercader's Instructions of 1514, there is no allusion to usury--the inquisitors were not to be disturbed in the exercise of their functions in this respect.[823] When, however, Leo, in 1516, confirmed the Concordia of 1512, he removed usury from inquisitorial jurisdiction and prohibited its prosecution unless the culprit should hold it not to be a sin.[824]

It has already been seen how completely the Inquisition ignored all these agreements, in spite of royal and papal confirmations. So, when Charles V was obliged, in 1518, at the Córtes of Saragossa, to take the specific and elaborate oath imposed on Juan II, it proved equally futile.[825] Inquisitors continued to exercise jurisdiction, but, in Aragon proper, they were impeded for a time by a brief of Clement VII, January 16, 1525, ordering them to confine themselves in future to heresy--a brief procured by Juan of Austria, Archbishop of Saragossa, who claimed jurisdiction over usury for his own court.[826] This afforded slender relief, for he employed the inquisitorial process and the Córtes of Saragossa, in 1528, adopted a fuero, confirmed by Charles V, reciting that the laws provide for the punishment of usurers by the secular courts, but that the ecclesiastical judges were prosecuting them, wherefore, at the desire of the four brazos, his majesty ordered the ancient laws of the kingdom to be enforced without exception.[827]

So long as the Inquisition was not involved, Charles was indifferent as to how usurers were treated, but, when the Catalans, at the Córtes of Monzon, in the same year, complained of the prosecution of usury by inquisitors and petitioned that it be prevented, he drily answered that the laws should be observed and justice should be done.[828] No greater satisfaction than this could be had when, a few years later, the Córtes of the three kingdoms reiterated the complaint of the prosecutions for usury by the Inquisition, inflicting an ineffaceable stain upon parties and their descendants, even though they were discharged without penance. The reply of the inquisitor-general to this was a simple denial, coupled with the demand that the names of injured parties should be produced.[829]

MORALS

In the absence of documents, it is not easy to understand why the Inquisition suddenly abandoned a jurisdiction for which it had contended so strenuously, but so it was. In 1552, Simancas asserts that inquisitors have no cognizance of questions arising from usury, but must leave them to the Ordinaries, for usurers are not moved by erroneous belief, but by the desire for sordid gains.[830] In this Simancas evidently spoke by authority, for the Suprema, in a carta acordada of March 17, 1554, forbade the tribunals to take cognizance of usury, and the subject disappears from inquisitorial records.[831] The secular and spiritual courts were left to fight the losing battle with industrial and commercial progress, which eventually compelled the recognition of the fact that payment for the usance of money is customarily profitable to both parties.

***

The object of the Inquisition was the preservation of the purity of faith and not the improvement of morals. The view taken of its duties as to the latter is set forth in the comments of the Suprema on the report by de Soto Salazar of his visitation, in 1566, of the Barcelona tribunal. Clement, Abbot of Ripoll, was prosecuted for saying that so great was the mercy of God that he would pardon a sinner who confessed, even though he had not a firm intention to abstain in future, and also for keeping a nun as a mistress. He was fined in four hundred ducats, and was ordered to break off relations with the nun under pain of a thousand ducats. The Suprema sharply reprimanded Inquisitor Padilla for inflicting so heavy a penalty and for exceeding his jurisdiction in prohibiting the unlawful connection. So, when the inquisitors fined Jaime Bocca, an unmarried familiar, in twelve ducats for keeping a married woman as mistress, the Suprema told them that it was none of their business. It is true that in two other cases of familiars, fined in twenty ducats each for keeping mistresses, the comment is simply that the rigor was excessive.[832]

The same principle, as we have seen, was observed in the treatment of solicitation. The question of morals was studiously excluded, as a matter entirely beyond the purview of the Inquisition, and the only point considered was the technical one whether cases came within papal definitions drawn up to safeguard the sacrament of penitence. The same remark applies to the vigorous prosecution of those who held simple fornication to be no sin. There was no attempt to repress the sin itself, for this was beyond the faculties conferred on the Inquisition, but merely to ascertain and punish the mental attitude of the accused.

As time passed on, however, and as the heretics who were the legitimate objects of the Holy Office grew scarce, there arose a tendency to enlarge its sphere of action and to assume the position of acustos morum. This has been seen in the censorship, which, during the later period, came to be applied not only to obscene books but to all manner of works of art that did not accord with the censor's standard of decency.

From this it was an easy step to intervene in the private lives of individuals, in matters wholly apart from its legitimate jurisdiction, of which we find occasional examples in the later period of decadence. Thus, in 1784, Josef Mas was prosecuted in Valencia for singing an improper song at a dance, and in 1791, there is a prosecution of Manuel de Pino for "indecent and irreligious acts." In 1792 the Barcelona tribunal takes the testimony of Ramon Seroles of Lloc, with respect to the scandalous life of the parish priest of that place and his abuse of the holy oils. In 1810 the Valencia tribunal is investigating Rosa Avinent, keeper of a tobacco-shop, for suspicion of maltreating some children in her house. In 1816 the Santiago tribunal sentences Don Miguel Quereyzaeta, a post-office official, to leave the city where he has led a disorderly and scandalous life, and charges him to reconcile himself to his wife and to live with her. In 1819, Don Antonio Clemente de Polar is prosecuted by the Madrid tribunal for propositions and for dressing in such wise as to satisfy the passions and for other excesses.[833]

THE SEAL OF CONFESSION

In these and similar cases, it may be assumed that the parties inculpated richly deserved correction, but this sporadic defence of virtue and punishment of vice was much more likely to encourage the gratification of malice than to elevate the standard of public morals, and the employment of the tremendous machinery of the Inquisition in such matters marks the depth of its fall from its former height. Had its object from the beginning been the purification of morals as well as of religion, possibly the awe which it inspired in all classes might have resulted in some ethical improvement but, during the time of its power, the impression that it produced was that morals were of slender account in comparison with faith and, in the day of its decline, these occasional attempts to extend its jurisdiction could only produce exasperation without amendment.

***

When, in 1216, the fourth Council of Lateran rendered auricular confession imperative, it was essential that the father confessor should be bound to preserve absolute silence as to the sins revealed to him. For a time there were some exceptions admitted, as heresy for instance, but eventually the obligation became universal and the schoolmen exhausted their ingenuity in devising the most extreme cases by which to illustrate the inviolability of what has become known as the seal of confession. Human nature being what it is, and priestly nature being subject to human infirmities, the violation of the seal has, at all times, been a source of anxiety and the object of rigorous punishment, administered to the secular clergy by the spiritual courts, and to the regulars by their superiors. The Roman Inquisition, in the first half-century of its existence, assumed exclusive cognizance of the offence, and demanded that all offenders, whether secular or regular, should be tried by its tribunals, but, in 1609, it abandoned its jurisdiction and left them to their bishops and prelates.[834]

As the heresy involved in betraying the confidence of the penitent was only an inferential error as to the sacrament--an artificial pretext like that devised with regard to solicitation--the Spanish Inquisition did not hold it to be comprised in the general delegation of faculties, but that a special papal commission was requisite. No attempt seems to have been made to obtain this until 1639, when, on October 11th, the Suprema addressed Philip IV a consulta setting forth that numerous denunciations were received by the tribunals against confessors who revealed confessions, and that inquisitors were asking urgently for permission to prosecute such cases as violations of divine, natural and political law, rendering culprits suspect in the faith, this being even more derisory of the sacrament than solicitation. It was notorious that the Ordinaries did not check it among the secular clergy, nor their prelates among the regulars, nor could, in such hands, any remedy be efficacious, because in public trials the witnesses would be bought off or frightened off, and there were no secret prisons to assure the necessary segregation of the accused. The king was therefore asked to procure from the pope, for the Inquisition, exclusive jurisdiction over the offence.[835] The Suprema probably did not exaggerate as to the denunciations received by the tribunals, for, in the minor one of the Canaries, we find it, in 1637, receiving testimony against Diego Artiaga, priest of Hierro, for this offence, in 1643, against Diego Salgado, priest of la Palma and, in 1644 against Fray Matías Pinto of Teneriffe.[836]

There can be no doubt that Philip, as usual, acceded to the request of the Suprema, but Urban VIII seems not to have been responsive. He had a plausible reason for declining, in the fact that the Roman Inquisition had abandoned its jurisdiction over the matter and, at the moment, he was at odds with the Spanish over the question of censorship and of the Plomos del Sacromonte. The offence was never included in the Edict of Faith, but occasionally it is enumerated among the charges against confessors on trial for solicitation, as in the cases of the Franciscan Fray Juan Pachon de Salas, in Mexico in 1712, of the Carmelite Ventura de San Joaquin in 1794, and of Fray Antonio Ortuño in 1807.[837] It was difficult to eradicate belief in the competence of the Inquisition and, as lately as 1808, José Antonio

Alvárez, priest of Horcajo de los Montes, was denounced for this offence to the Toledo tribunal, but the trial was suspended, probably through doubt as to jurisdiction.[838] When the question was brought up squarely, in the case of Doctor Don Francisco Torneo, before the Valencia tribunal, after due discussion it decided, March 28, 1816, that it had no jurisdiction, and the case was accordingly dismissed.[839]

GENERAL UTILITY

The efficient organization of the Inquisition and the dread which it inspired caused it to be invoked in numberless contingencies, most diverse in character and wholly foreign to the objects of its institution. A brief enumeration of a few of these will serve to complete our survey of its activity and, trivial as they may seem, to illustrate how powerful was the influence which it exercised over the social life of Spain.

The value of its services, arising from the indefinite extent of its powers, was recognized early. In 1499, a Benedictine monastery complained to Ferdinand that it had pledged a cross to a certain Pedro de Santa Cruz and could not recover it, as he had placed himself under protection of Dominicans, who claimed exemption from legal processes. Ferdinand thereupon ordered the inquisitors of the city to settle the matter; they neglected it and he wrote again peremptorily, instructing them to seize the cross and do justice between the parties. In April, 1500, the king instructs the Valencia tribunal to recover for Don Ramon López, of the royal guard, two runaway slaves and some plate which they had stolen.[840] Evidently there was no little variety of duties expected of the Holy Office.

In 1518 a nunnery of Clares, in Calatayud, complained that, within ten paces of their house, there had been built a Mercenarian convent of which the inmates were disorderly; the nuns could not walk in their garden without being seen and great scandals were apprehended. Charles V applied to Leo X to have the Mercenarians replaced by Benedictines or Gerónimites and the Inquisition was invoked to assist.[841] Parties sometimes obtained papal briefs to have their suits transferred to the tribunals. In 1548 Doña Aldonza Cerdan did this in a litigation with Don Hernando de la Caballería and, in 1561, Doña Isabel de Francia in a suit with Don Juan de Heredia. In both cases the inquisitors of Saragossa refused to act until Inquisitor-general Valdés ordered them to do so.[842] All inquisitors were not thus self-restrained, for when, about this time, a general command was issued forbidding them to prosecute for perjury committed in other courts, it shows that they had been asked to do so and that some of them, at least, were ready to undertake such business.[843] In 1647, when the prevalence of duelling called for some effective means of repression, among the remedies proposed was that sending a challenge should be made a matter for the Inquisition, on the ground that the infamy accruing to the offender and his descendants would be the most effective discouragement to punctilious gentlemen.[844] The suggestion apparently was not adopted, but it illustrates the readiness to have recourse to the elastic jurisdiction of the Holy Office.

The Jesuits found the Inquisition of much service when, through the favor of Olivares, they were enabled to invoke its intervention in one of their quarrels with the Dominicans. In 1634, Fray Francisco Roales issued a pamphlet against the Society and Dr. Espino, an ex-Carmelite, published two others. They were answered by Padre Salazar and there the matter might have ended, but the Jesuits appealed to Philip IV and to Olivares, who promised satisfaction and ordered the Inquisitor-general Sotomayor (himself a Dominican) to take action, with the significant hint that he would be watched. A royal decree of January 29, 1635, rebuked the Suprema for lack of zeal, and ordered it to act with all diligence and to inflict severe punishment. It responded promptly on February 1st with an edict suppressing the pamphlet of Roales under heavy penalties, but this did not suffice and, on June 30th, it prohibited every one, layman or ecclesiastic, from saying anything in private or in public, derogatory to any religious Order or the members thereof, under exemplary penalties, to be rigorously executed--a decree which had to be repeated in 1643.

On June 27, 1635 the three obnoxious pamphlets were burned with unprecedented ceremony. There was a solemn procession of the officials and familiars, with the standards of the Inquisition, while a mule with carmine velvet trappings bore a chest painted with flames in which were the condemned writings. It traversed the principal streets to the plaza, where a fire was lighted; a herald, with sound of trumpet, proclaimed that the Company of Jesus was relieved of all that had been said against it and that these papers were false, calumnious, impious and scandalous; they were cast by the executioner into the flames and then the box and the procession wended their way solemnly back to the Dominican College of San Tomas. The effect of the demonstration, however, was somewhat marred by the populace believing that the box contained the bones of a misbelieving Jew, and accompanying the procession with shouts of "Death to the dogs!" and other pious ejaculations.

***

Espino was arrested and incarcerated--not for the last time for, in 1643, he boasted that he had been imprisoned fifteen times for his attacks on the Jesuits. Roales was more fortunate; he was a chaplain of Philibert of Savoy; his pamphlet had been printed in Milan and he was safe in Rome, but a printer who had issued an edition in Saragossa was arrested and presumably sent to the galleys, and a Dominican Fray Cañamero, who had circulated the three pamphlets, was ordered to be arrested but seems to have saved himself by flight. Still the irrepressible conflict continued and the Inquisition was kept busy in prosecuting offenders and suppressing obnoxious utterances. It even construed its duty so rigidly that it condemned a memorial of the unfortunate creditors who suffered by the bankruptcy, in 1645, of the Jesuit College of San Hermengildo in Seville, when some three hundred depositors lost four hundred and fifty thousand ducats, and were struggling to rescue the remaining assets from the hands of the Jesuits.[845]

The Granada tribunal did not pause to enquire as to its jurisdiction when, in May 1646, owing to the scarcity of wheat, there were bread-riots and the mob had control of the city. It summoned all the grain-measurers and porters, under pain of excommunication, to appear before it on a matter of importance. By examining them, considerable stores of hidden corn were revealed; the corregidores registered it and the price was fixed at forty-two reales.[846] This was volunteer action but, in 1648, when a pestilence was raging in Valencia, the tribunal was called upon to maintain the quarantine at one of the city gates. The king, on February 1, 1649, notified the Suprema that the pest had ceased in Valencia, but that it was violent at Cádiz, San Lucar and other places, and urged continued vigilance, to which the Suprema replied that it had, since April, done its full duty, but that the municipal officials were very negligent, and it asked him to order them to do their share.[847] Apparently the Inquisition was relied upon for quarantine work. As lately as July 2, 1818, the Suprema wrote to all the tribunals that the plague had appeared at Tangier and threatened Spain with the most terrible of calamities. The king had ordered energetic precautions, in which all branches of the Government must coöperate, and it was no time for hesitation or scruples. The tribunals were therefore instructed to keep watch on the officials of all departments and see that they did their duty and, if they could devise more effective measures, they were invited to make suggestions.[848]

The unlimited interference of the Inquisition with matters pertaining to episcopal supervision is seen in two or three cases tried by the Madrid tribunal. May 5, 1656, it sentenced the priest, Francisco Pérez Lozano, to exile for a year from various places for his share in founding a confraternity with what were called "statutos execrables." February 6, 1688, Juan Moreno de Piedrola, a priest of the Congregation of San Salvador, who proposed to establish a congregation, in the rules of which the tribunal discovered censurable propositions, was ordered to surrender all the papers and not to discuss it in word or writing and was exiled until he should have permission to return, with warning that otherwise he would be prosecuted with the full rigor of the law. As he was not required to abjure even de levi, it shows that there was no suspicion of heresy involved. Then, in 1697, Fray Juan Maldonado, of the Order of San Juan de Dios, had three years of exile for preaching, in the church of his convent at Ciudad Real, a sermon characterized as burlesque and scandalous, though there is no hint of its being in any way heretical.[849]

***

This perpetual intrusion into all manner of affairs, irrespective of heresy rather increased towards the last. In 1788, Antonio López was prosecuted in Valencia for selling rosaries with bones made of clay as relics. In 1789, Andrés Joáñez, a coachman, for a conversation on a superstitious subject. In 1791, the Carmelite Fray Bonifacio de San Pablo, for attempting to print a satirical paper; Josef de la Rosa, in Cordova, for carrying a consecrated wafer in a relic-bag; Vicente Felerit, in Valencia, for a "vain observance." In 1795, Don Miguel Catalá, fiscal in Buñol and Josef Sánchez Masquifa, a scrivener, were prosecuted for using, in drafting testaments, the words "diversos atributos," when alluding to the Trinity. In 1799, Juan Rodríguez, a priest in Santiago, for assisting and performing ceremonies in a mock-marriage. In 1808, Josef Várquez de la Torre, a scrivener of Valencia, for drawing a deed of separation between spouses. In 1818, in Valencia, Vicente Maicas, priest of Cedrillos, for not wanting his parishioners to die in the Franciscan habit.[850] As all these cases presuppose denunciation, they illustrate the popular estimate of the all-embracing powers of the Inquisition and the espionage under which every Spaniard lived.

In fact, there was scarce anything in which the Inquisition did not feel itself authorized to intervene. The latitude with which inquisitors construed their own powers is manifest in their assuming to issue licences to hunt in prohibited places, sometimes for their own benefit and sometimes for that of others. This was an abuse which the Suprema strove to correct by forbidding it in 1527, but it was so persistent that the prohibition had to be repeated in 1530 and again in 1566.[851]

As the Inquisition was supreme within its jurisdiction and claimed the right to define the extent of its powers, there was no one to call it to account for their arbitrary exercise. If any other body in the

State felt that its rights were invaded, the only recourse was to the sovereign and we have seen how, under the Hapsburgs, the crown, with scarce an exception, decided in its favor.

BOOK IX - CONCLUSION

CHAPTER I - DECADENCE AND EXTINCTION

The Inquisition may be said to have reached its apogee under Philip IV. We have had ample opportunity to see how that pious monarch yielded to its aggressiveness, until it became a virtually independent organization within the State, obeying the royal mandates or not, as best suited its convenience, and engaged in almost perpetual controversies with the other branches of the government, while the king, with rare exceptions, submitted to its exigencies. It is true that, in his financial distress, he compelled the restitution of a small part of the confiscations and that he asserted the royal prerogative of making and unmaking inquisitors-general and of appointing members of the Suprema but, when once he had exercised the power, his appointees acted in independence. It would not be easy to imagine a more complete assertion of irresponsible authority than the sudden arrest of Villanueva--of a leading minister in the absence of the sovereign, at a time of the utmost confusion, when nothing would have been risked by delay, save perhaps that the sovereign might have refused assent. Yet not only did Philip condone this but he threw himself into the persecution of his favorite with such ardor that he could scarce restrain himself from risking a rupture with the Holy See in defence of the Holy Office. Under the disastrous regency of Maria Ana of Austria and the reign of Carlos II, the royal authority almost disappeared and, although this gave such men as Nithard and Valladares opportunity to assert still further the independence of the Inquisition, it also enabled Don John of Austria to banish Nithard and the other governmental departments to emulate its disregard of the royal authority. There was an omen of the future when they united, in 1696, in the Junta Magna, to protest against the encroachments of the Inquisition and to demand its withdrawal into its proper limits, although by dextrous management the attempt was baffled.

THE BOURBONS

With the advent of the Bourbon dynasty a new element entered into the political organization of Spain. The absolutism of Louis XIV had embraced the Church as well as the State, and the Gallican theories as to the power of the Holy See were encouraged in order to assure the headship of the crown. It was inevitable that Philip V and his French advisers should entertain very different views as to the relations between the king and the Inquisition from those which had been current for a century. Even at the height of the War of Succession, we have seen how Philip, in the affair of Froilan Díaz, intervened as master and regulated the relations between the inquisitor-general and the Suprema, how he undertook to reform the Inquisition and how, in many ways he curbed its audacity. But for a court intrigue, working through Philip's uxoriousness, Macanaz might have succeeded in his project of rendering the Inquisition wholly subordinate to the crown, and though the vindictiveness of the Holy Office inflicted on him life-long punishment for the attempt, this did not prevent the continued assertion of the royal supremacy, as we have had occasion to see in repeated instances and in many different directions.

PHILIP V

Philip's assertion of the royal prerogative, however, by no means implied any lack of zeal for the faith and, as long as the Inquisition confined itself to its duties of exterminating heresy, it had his cordial support. Frequent allusions have been made above to its renewed activity during the period following the close of the War of Succession. Full statistics are lacking, but in sixty-four autos, between 1721 and 1728, there appeared nine hundred and sixty-two culprits and effigies, of whom one hundred and fifty-one were relaxed.[852] That this met his hearty approbation is manifested by the letter which he addressed, January 14, 1724, to his son Luis, when abdicating in his favor. In this the exhortations breathing a lofty morality are accompanied with earnest injunctions to maintain and protect the Inquisition, as the bulwark of the faith, for to it is attributable the preservation of religion in all its purity in the states of Spain, so that the heresies which have afflicted the other lands of Christendom, causing in them ravages so deplorable and horrible, have never gained a foothold there.[853] Small-pox cut short the reign of Luis to seven months, after which Philip was obliged to resume the weary burden, till death released him, July 9, 1746, and if, during this later portion of his government, the Inquisition was less busy, this may safely be attributed to flagging energies and lack of material and not to any restraint on the part of the sovereign. The punishment which it allowed to inflict on Belando, for the history of his reign of which he and his queen, after careful scrutiny, had accepted the dedication, shows how untrammelled was its exercise of its recognized functions.

Yet Philip unwittingly started the movement that was ultimately to undermine the foundations on which the Inquisition rested. He brought with him from France the conviction that the king should be the patron of letters and learning, and he had the ambition to rule over a people of culture. He aroused the slumbering intellect of Spain by founding the Academies of Language and of History and of Medicine, the Seminary of the Nobles, and the National Library, and he replaced for Catalonia the University of Lérida by that of Cervera. Notwithstanding the vigilance of the censorship, it was impossible that the awakening intelligence of the nation, thus stimulated, should not eagerly grasp at the forbidden fruit of modern philosophism, all the more attractive in that it had to be enjoyed in secret. Fernando VI, from 1746 to 1759, followed his father's example, in encouraging the spread of culture. Carlos III was even more energetic in urging the enlightenment of his subjects, and thus there was gradually formed a public, few in numbers, it is true, but including the statesmen in power, which had lost the old Spanish conception that purity of faith was the first essential, and regarded the Inquisition as an incumbrance, save in so far as it might be used for political ends. The Inquisition still inspired fear, and the case of Olavide shows that these opinions had to be cherished in secret, but the number who entertained them was indicated when the bonds of society were loosened and the national institutions crumbled in the earthquake of the Napoleonic invasion.

Possibly the diffusion of this modern rationalistic spirit, insensibly affecting even those opposed to it, may partly explain the rapidly diminishing activity of the Inquisition. The great tribunal of Toledo, in the fifty-five years, from 1740 to 1794 inclusive, despatched but fifty-seven cases, or an average of but one a year.[854] This cannot be attributed to a lack of culprits, for bigamy, blasphemy, solicitation, sorcery and similar offences, which furnished so large a portion of the penitents of old, were as rife as ever. The fact is, that the officials were becoming indifferent and careless, except in the matter of drawing their salaries. When, on May 22, 1753, the priest Miguel de Alonso García was to be sentenced in the audience-chamber with closed doors and in the presence of the officials, it happened that there were no witnesses of the solemnity because none of the officials were to be found in the secreto.[855]

CARLOS III

The personnel of the Inquisition was visibly deteriorating and consequently forfeiting the respect of the community. There had long been complaint of the insufficiency of the salaries, which had remained stationary while the purchasing power of money had greatly diminished, and there had been no reduction in the official staffs to correspond with the dwindling business. Thus, in spite of the empleomanía characteristic of the nation, and of the privileges and exemptions attached to official position, it became increasingly difficult to fill the offices properly. As early as 1719, the inquisitors of Barcelona complained to the Suprema of the trouble they experienced getting people to serve, on account of lack of desire for the offices and the absence of advantage accruing from them.[856] In 1737 we find that the Toledo tribunal had neither a commissioner nor a notary in Guadalajara, the capital of a province which, in 1787, numbered 112,750 souls.[857] In 1750, a writer deplores that the stipend of eight hundred ducats is insufficient to support the dignity of an inquisitor, so that the inquisitor-general is not always able to make fitting nominations. This necessitates the appointment of calificadores to examine the doctrines brought under review, resulting in the indefinite prolongation of cases, and also in lack of vigilance to suppress the errors perpetually propagated in books; when the calificadores are not paid, they are slow in their work and, to escape paying them, many things which ought to be referred to them are passed over.[858] That the respect felt for the Inquisition should diminish under these circumstances was inevitable and altogether, at this period, it presents the aspect of an institution which had survived the causes of its creation and was hastening to its end. Yet it had exercised too powerful an influence in moulding the Spanish character for it to disappear when its mission was accomplished, and we shall see how violent were the struggles attendant upon its dissolution.

Meanwhile it dragged on its existence under constantly increasing limitations. Fernando VI, it is true, gave it obstinate support in its quarrel with Benedict XIV over the works of Cardinal Noris, but he dealt a severe blow when, in 1751, he deprived of the fuero the officials of the tribunal of Lima. Carlos III, who succeeded in 1759, came from Naples with the highest ideals of royal supremacy, coupled with less respect for ecclesiastical claims than was current in Spain; he surrounded himself with advisers such as Roda, Campomanes, Aranda and Floridablanca, who were more than suspected of leanings to modern philosophism, and his reign of benevolent despotism was marked with a series of measures designed to diminish or abolish the privileges of inquisitorial officials, to repress abuses and to tame arrogance. The complete control which he assumed over its functions is exhibited in the rules imposed, in 1768, on its censorship and, in 1770 and 1777, on its jurisdiction over bigamy, when he ordered it in future to limit its operations to the suppression of heresy and not to embarrass the royal courts. The theory thus developed of the relations between the crown and the Holy Office is formulated in a consulta of the Council of Castile, November 30, 1768: "The king as patron, founder and endower of the Inquisition, possesses over it the rights inherent in all royal patronage.... As father and protector of his vassals, he can and ought to prevent the commission of violence and extortion on their persons, property and reputation, indicating to ecclesiastical judges, even in their exercise of spiritual jurisdiction, the path pointed out by the canons, so that these may be observed. The regalías of protection and of this indubitable patronage have established solidly the authority of the prince, in issuing the instructions which he has deigned to give to the Holy Office acting as an ecclesiastical tribunal."[859] Under such conditions, he was quite content with its existence and, when Roda suggested its suppression and presented various documents to show that this had been discussed under Charles V, Philip II and Philip V, he merely replied "The Spaniards want it and it gives me no trouble."[860] In fact, the time had not arrived for such drastic measures. The Abbé Clément reports a conversation with Aranda, October 29, 1768, in which the count warned him that it was necessary to speak of the Inquisition with great reserve, for people imagined that all religion depended on it; it was, in truth, an obstacle to all improvement, but time would be required to deal with it, and he advised Clément to allude to it only to Roda and Campomanes.[861]

***

With the accession, in 1788, of Carlos IV, there opened for Spain a new and disastrous epoch. Timid, irresolute, indolent, he had fallen completely under the influence of his wife María Luisa, an energetic and self-willed woman. Until 1792 he kept in office Floridablanca, who was succeeded for a short time by Aranda, and then power was grasped by Manuel Godoy, subsequently known as Prince of Peace. Cadet of an obscure family of Badajoz, he had entered the royal body-guard, where he attracted the attention of the queen, whose favored lover he was universally believed to be, as well as the favorite of her husband. He speedily rose to the highest dignities and became omnipotent; although a court intrigue occasioned his dismissal in 1798, he was restored in 1800, remaining arbiter of the destinies of Spain, until the "Tumult of Lackeys," at Aranjuez, in 1808, directed against him, caused the abdication of Carlos in favor of his son Fernando VII. Light-headed, selfish, vain and unscrupulous, he was mainly responsible for the misfortunes which overwhelmed his country and from which it may be said not to have as yet recovered.

ALTERED FUNCTIONS

The outbreak of the French Revolution gave a new importance to the Inquisition. When the seductive theories of the French philosophers were preached as the foundation of practical politics, overturning thrones and threatening monarchical institutions with the doctrines of the social compact, the sovereignty of the people and the universal brotherhood of man, the Holy Office might claim that, as the foundations of social order were based on religion, its labors were essential for the safety of the State, while the State recognized that it was the most available instrumentality for the suppression and exclusion of the heresies of liberty and equality.

In this tumultuous breaking down of the standards of thought and belief, in this emergence of a new order on the ruins of the old, the functions of the Inquisition adapted themselves to the exigencies of the times, in other ways besides the increased sharpness and vigilance of its censorship. I have frequently had occasion above to refer to an alphabetical list of all the persons denounced to the various tribunals, from 1780 to 1820, some five thousand in all, and this, taken as a whole, affords us an insight into the change in the objects of inquisitorial activity. Judaism and Islam and Protestantism no more claim its attention. The Church is no longer threatened by enemies from without; what it has to dread is revolt among its own children. Three-fifths of the denunciations are for "propositions," largely among the cultured classes, including a fair proportion of ecclesiastics. Their precise errors are not stated, but doubtless many were Jansenistic and more were hostile to the claims of the Church Militant and to the absolutism of the monarchy. There is also a large class of cases, virtually unknown a century earlier, significant of a vital change in the intellectual tendencies of the nation, calling for the special vigilance of the Inquisition. Popular indifferentism is revealed in the numerous prosecutions for inobservance or contempt of church observances. Even more noteworthy are those for outrages on images of Christ, the Virgin and the saints, and even for sacrilegious treatment of the Venerable Sacrament. In many other ways was manifested the weakening of the profound and unquestioning veneration which, for three centuries, had been the peculiar boast of the Spanish race. On the other hand it is not a little remarkable that there are very few cases of offences against the Inquisition, for, in all these forty years, there are but nine that can in any way be included in this class.⁸⁶²

At the same time, when we recall the old-time punctilious enforcement of profound respect, it argues no little decline in popular awe when, in 1791, a simple parish priest, Dr. Joseph Gines of Polop (Alicante) dared to address the Valencia tribunal in terms of violent indignation at the conduct of its secretary, Dr. Pasqual Pérez, when on a mission to collect testimony. He tells the tribunal that, if it does not dismiss Pérez it will sink greatly in his estimation, and his whole epistle breathes a spirit of independence and equality wholly impossible at an earlier time.⁸⁶³ It was not without reason that, in 1793, the tribunal, in appealing for increase of salaries, complained of the decline in popular respect for its officials, which it attributed to their meagre pay and the curtailment of their privileges.⁸⁶⁴ How completely the tribunals had lost their former energy is indicated by the abandonment, about this time, as we have seen (Vol. II, p. 98) of the publication of the Edict of Faith, which of old had been so impressively solemnized and had proved at once so fruitful a source of denunciations and so powerful a means of maintaining popular awe.

POLITICAL FUNCTIONS

Coincident with this, and as though the Inquisition felt that it was on trial before the people, there was a marked tendency towards amelioration of procedure, coupled with benignity in treatment of culprits. Allusion has been made above to the introduction of the audiencia de cargos, through which the accused was afforded an opportunity of knowing what was alleged against him, and frequently of clearing himself without the disgrace of arrest and trial. There is a very suggestive instance of merciful consideration, in 1791, in the case of Josef Casals, a weaver, charged before the Barcelona tribunal with the utterance of shocking blasphemies in the church of Santa Catalina. A century earlier he would have been arrested and, on proof of the offence, he would have been sentenced to scourging or the galleys. In place of this Padre Miguel Alberch was instructed to report secretly as to the character of the accused, which he did to the effect that Casals had regular certificates of confession, but was of quick temper and occasionally broke out in curses. Then a commission was issued to Alberch to summon Casals and to represent to him the gravity of his offence and of the punishment incurred, and the mercy shown by the tribunal, which would keep a watch on him.

In pursuance of this the good priest reported that Casals was deeply repentant and desired to be heard in confession, which he had permitted.⁸⁶⁵ The case is trivial, but of such was the bulk of inquisitorial business, and the temper in which it was conducted was of no little import to the people at large.

Partly this may be attributable to the modern softening of manners, partly to a growing sense of insecurity, and partly to the inertia which led the officials to shun all avoidable labor. It was becoming more and more a political machine and neglectful of the objects of its creation. During the inquisitor-generalship of Manuel Abad y la Sierra, from 1792 to 1794, we are told that, in all Spain, there were but sixteen condemnations to public penance. Abad was an enlightened man; he thought of assimilating the inquisitorial procedure to that of other courts of justice, and consulted with Llorente as to the formula for such a reform, but conservatism, however relaxed in practice, was not ready for total abandonment of the old methods. His design became known: he was forced to resign and was relegated to the Benedictine monastery of Sopetran, under a charge, as we have seen of Jansenism.⁸⁶⁶

In fact, an absolute renunciation of the old procedure would have largely deprived the Inquisition of its usefulness in its new political functions, to which its established methods were peculiarly adapted. When, in 1796, a powerful intrigue was formed for the overthrow of Godoy, the Inquisition was naturally selected as the only weapon with which to strike at the favorite. Three friars were found to denounce him, because for eight years he had avoided confession and communion, and because of his scandalous relations with women. Had Inquisitor-general Lorenzana been resolute, Godoy's fate might have been that of Olavide, but he was timid. Archbishop Despuig of Seville and Bishop Muzquiz, then of Avila, who were the leaders of the plot, vainly assured him that Godoy's arrest would insure success; he refused to act except under orders from Pius VI. Despuig then prevailed upon his friend Cardinal Vincenti to induce the pope to write to Lorenzana reproaching him with his indifference to a scandal so hurtful to religion. It chanced that Vincenti's letter, inclosing that of Pius, was intercepted at Genoa by Napoleon who, to ingratiate himself with Godoy, forwarded to him the correspondence. Godoy assured his position and took a mild revenge, which does credit to his sense of humor, by sending Lorenzana, Despuig and Muzquiz into honorable exile as special envoys to condole with the pope on the occupation of his territories by the French.⁸⁶⁷ In fact, Capmany describes the Inquisition of the period as devoted to the unholy work of an Inquisition of State, in order to preserve its imperilled existence, and its ministers as trembling at the sight of the infamous favorite, when they had the honor of joining the crowd of his flatterers.⁸⁶⁸

Inquisitors might reasonably feel anxious as to their position, for projects of reform were in the air. Gaspar Melchor de Jovellanos, the most conspicuous Spaniard of his time for intellectual ability and rectitude, had been exiled from the court, in 1790, and had betaken himself to his native Gijon, where for years he labored in founding the Instituto Asturiense. Desiring to endow it with a library of scientific works, he applied, in 1795, to Lorenzana for licence to import them, but Lorenzana refused on the ground that there were good Spanish writers, rendering recourse to foreigners unnecessary, especially as foreign books had corrupted the professors and students in various universities--a process of reasoning applied to works on physics and mineralogy, which Jovellanos characterized as a monumento de barbarie. The attention thus drawn to his library aroused the suspicions of the commissioner of the Inquisition, Francisco López Gil, priest of Somió, who secretly entered it one day while the owner was taking his siesta. Word was brought to him and he hastened thither, finding Gil examining a volume of Locke. Jovellanos turned him out, telling him that his office rendered him an object of suspicion and forbidding him to enter the building without permission. Gil became a spy and was probably the author of a denunciation which cost Jovellanos years of captivity.[869]

JOVELLANOS

He was suddenly recalled from his exile, November 23, 1797, to assume the position of minister of Gracia y Justicia, where he speedily gave the Inquisition abundant cause to dread him. A competencia had arisen between the Seville tribunal and the episcopal authorities over a confessional which it had ordered to be closed. The matter came before Carlos, who instructed Jovellanos to obtain the opinion of Tavira, Bishop of Osma, which he duly transmitted to the king, February 15, 1798, with a Representation arguing that the time had come to restore to the bishops their old jurisdiction in matters of faith; the object for which the Inquisition was established had been attained; its processes were cumbrous and inefficient, and its members were ignorant. The jurisdiction of the bishops could alone furnish an effective remedy for existing evils--a jurisdiction more natural, more authoritative, more grateful to the people, and fuller of humanity and gentleness, as emanating from the power granted to them by the Holy Ghost, wherefore the authority that had been usurped from them should be restored. Moreover he took into consideration the condition of the Holy See, deprived of its temporalities by the French Republic. Everything, he said, pointed to a fearful schism at the death of Pius VI, in which case each nation must gather itself under its own pastors. The papacy would endeavor to retain the cumbrous and costly organization of the curia, by increasing its exactions, and it would have to be reduced to the functions exercised during the first eight centuries.[870]

Jovellanos was a sincere Catholic, but after utterances so hardy it was not difficult for his enemies to convince the king that he was inclined to heresy and atheism. Godoy had grown alarmed at the ascendancy which he was acquiring over Carlos; his fellow-minister Caballero conspired with the Inquisition, and on August 15th the king signed the dismissal of his minister, whose official life had endured but eight months. A fortnight later a royal carta orden declared it to be his unalterable will that the Holy Office should permanently enjoy its jurisdiction and prerogatives without modification.[871] Jovellanos returned to Gijon where he lived in dignified retirement for two years and a half. His offence however had been too great for pardon and his influence was still dreaded. An anonymous denunciation of the flimsiest character was laid before Carlos, describing him as having abandoned all religion and as being at the head of a highly dangerous party, engaged in schemes for the overthrow of Catholicism and the monarchy. The pusillanimous king adopted the course suggested to him by the secret accuser. Before day-break of March 13, 1801, the house of Jovellanos was surrounded by a troop of horse; he was aroused from sleep, his papers were seized and transmitted to the ministry of State; he was kept in his house incomunicado for twenty-four hours, then thrust into a coach and carried, still incomunicado, across Spain to Barcelona and thence to Majorca, where he lay in prison until the abdication of Carlos, in 1808, and the consequent troubles effected his release.[872]

ATTEMPTED SUPPRESSION

A case nearly parallel was that of Mariano Luis de Urquijo, who followed Jovellanos in the ministry of Gracia y Justicia. He had no cause to love the Inquisition. Among his youthful indiscretions was a translation of Voltaire's Mort de César, which led the Inquisition to make secret investigations, resulting in the conviction that he was dangerously infected with philosophism. He was about to be arrested when Aranda, who recognized his merit, recommended him to the king and, in 1792, he was appointed to a position in Aranda's office. The Inquisition had learned respect for royal officials and substituted for a decree of arrest a summons to an audiencia de cargos, ending in a sentence of light suspicion of sharing philosophic errors, absolution ad cautelam, some secret penances and the suppression of his book, though his name was considerately omitted in the edict of prohibition. His official promotion was rapid and, at the age of thirty, he found himself a minister, employing his power, possibly with more zeal than discretion, in encouraging enlightenment and all humanizing influences. On the death of Pius VI he incurred Ultramontane hostility by inducing the king to sign the decree of September 5, 1799, restoring to the bishops the right of issuing dispensations--a measure which provoked long and bitter discussion. This was followed, as we have seen above (Vol. III, p. 504) October 11th by a sharp rebuke to the Inquisition, ordering it to confine itself to its proper duties and, soon afterwards, he presented to Carlos for signature, a decree suppressing the institution and applying its property to purposes of charity and public utility. This was too bold a measure; the king shrank from the responsibility and Urquijo only succeeded in concentrating upon himself clerical hostility, which was reinforced by the enmity of First Consul Bonaparte, whose policy he had opposed. Godoy, who commenced to fear him as a rival, and who was irritated by some imprudent jests, withdrew his support. A triple prosecution was commenced against him by three inquisitors and he fell in December, 1801. He was sent to Pampeluna, to the cell which had been occupied by Floridablanca, and there he lay for a year or two, deprived of fire, lights, books and writing materials. He was liberated under surveillance; in 1808 he refused to accompany Carlos and Fernando to Bayonne, but he attended the so-called Junta of Notables there, accepted the French domination, served as secretary of State and, with the other Afrancesados, sought refuge in France in 1813, dying in Paris in 1817.[873]

It is evident from all this that the opposition to the Inquisition was gathering strength and boldness, but that its foundations were too deep and solid to be overthrown without an upheaval that should shatter the social fabric. A well-intentioned, but somewhat absurd, attempt was made by Grégoire, Constitutional Bishop of Blois, whose fervent Catholicism, combined with equally fervent liberalism, was of service so essential in piloting the Church of France through the storms of the Revolution. In 1798, he addressed a letter to the Spanish inquisitor-general, urging the suppression of the Inquisition and universal toleration, as a preliminary to the redemption of Spain from despotism, and to enabling it to take its place among the nations which had recovered their rights. This was translated into Spanish and some thousands of copies were circulated; it may have made some secret converts but the only visible result was to elicit several replies. One of these, by Pedro Luis Blanco, told Grégoire, with more or less courtesy, to mind his own business; assured him that, if the Inquisition was suppressed, Spain would remain as intolerant as ever, and asserted that no Spaniard had ever imagined that coercion could be employed to obtain conversion. It was probably this, mingled with some skilful adulation of the king and his ministers, that procured for the author, in 1800, the episcopate of Leon.[874] There was also an anonymous "Discurso historico-legal," evidently by a well-informed inquisitor, probably Riesco of Llerena. It was the most rational history of the Inquisition that had as yet appeared, although it assures us that experience showed that penitents were most grateful for the benevolence shown to them, and that it was a tribunal full of gentleness, the centre of benignity, compassion and mercy, but also of justice.[875]

A third was by Lorenzo Villanueva, a calificador of the Valencia tribunal, whose defence of the reading of Scripture has been alluded to above. It was published under the transparent pseudonym of Lorenzo Astengo, his maternal name. In view of his subsequent career it is not without interest to see his indignation at the advocacy of toleration and his dithyrambic denunciation of the horrors to which philosophism has led in the assertion of human liberty. The first portion of his work is an impassioned and rhetorical defence of persecution, supported by ample learning. Vigorous is his denunciation of the modern theories of philosophism and the rights of man--since original sin, he asks, what rights has man save to slavery, to punishment, to ruin? So he combats at length the doctrine of the sovereignty of the people, which he stigmatizes as a delirium, a dream and a deception. Yet he admits that the Inquisition is not perfect--that it has committed errors through imprudence, through ignorance, through excessive zeal, and through human frailty, and that it has prevented the development of some things which would aid the prosperity of the nation.[876] If, as has been asserted, he expected a bishopric in reward for this, he was disappointed.

POLITICAL UPHEAVAL

Thus, at this period the Inquisition was inert and its very existence seemed to be threatened, but its potentiality of evil was undiminished. It was still an object of terror to all inclined to liberal opinions, and it was regarded by the Conservatives as the bulwark protecting the land from the deluge of modern thought.

Feeble though it might be in appearance we shall see how prolonged and stubborn was the contest required for its final suppression.

THE CORTES

The treaty of Fontainebleau, October 27, 1807, dismembered Portugal, of which Godoy was to have the southern portion, as an independent kingdom, and the King of Etruria (Ferdinand of Parma) the northern portion. Napoleon sent Junot with an army which, accompanied by Spanish troops, speedily overran the land, when Junot issued a decree declaring Portugal annexed to the empire. Simultaneously French armies, under Dupont and Moncey, entered Spain and occupied the strongholds of Pampeluna, Barcelona, Figueras and other places. Murat was sent as commander in chief and took possession of Madrid. The Tumult of Aranjuez drove Godoy from power and, on March 19, 1808, Carlos abdicated in favor of his son, Fernando VII, whose accession was received with enthusiasm by the nation. Beauharnais, the French ambassador at Madrid, and Murat, however, refused to recognize him; Carlos protested to Napoleon that his abdication had been coerced; by various devices, Carlos and his queen, Fernando and his younger brother Don Carlos, were induced to go to Bayonne to lay their respective pretensions before the emperor. There, on May 5, Fernando was obliged to renounce the crown to his father and the latter to transfer it to Napoleon. Carlos and María Luisa were sent to Compiègne and Fernando to Valençay, where he remained until 1814. Meanwhile in Madrid, Murat, under instructions, ordered the Infantes Antonio and Francisco, the remaining members of the royal family, to depart for Bayonne on May 2d. The indignant populace rose, with the aid of a few officers and soldiers and, after a gallant struggle against the veterans of Napoleon, the insurrection was repressed with heavy slaughter, followed by numerous executions. The heroic "Dos de Mayo" was the signal of resistance to the invader and, in a few weeks, Spain was aflame; the desperate six years' War of Liberation was commenced, and the nation showed what a people could do when abandoned by its incapable and cowardly rulers. With a soldier's contempt for an unorganized militia, Napoleon pursued his plans. Joseph was called from Naples to occupy the vacant throne and was acknowledged as king by an Assembly of Notables, convoked at Bayonne in June, which transformed itself into Córtes and adopted a Constitution.

This summary of the situation is necessary to an understanding of the position of the Inquisition. Whatever may have been the views of some of the local tribunals, the central body accepted the intrusive domination and was afrancesado--a term which, to the patriots, became one of the bitterest contempt. The Constitution of Bayonne provided that, in Spanish territories, no religion save Roman Catholicism should be tolerated. Raimundo Ethenard, Dean of the Suprema, was a member of the Córtes and, when he took the oath of allegiance to Joseph, the latter assured him that Spain was fortunate in that the true faith alone was there honored. When the Constitution was under consideration, two members, Pablo Arribas and José Gómez Hermosilla, advocated the suppression of the Inquisition, but Ethenard and his colleagues of the Inquisition, Galarza, Hevia Noriega and Amarillas, successfully opposed it, although they admitted that, in conformity with public opinion, its procedure should be made to conform to that of the spiritual courts in criminal cases.[877]

SUPPRESSION BY NAPOLEON

The Inquisition thus deemed itself safe and earnestly supported the Napoleonic government. After the sanguinary suppression of the Madrid rising on May 2d, it made haste to counteract the impression produced and, on the 6th, the Suprema addressed a circular letter to the tribunals, describing the affair as a scandalous attack by the lowest mob on the troops of a friendly nation, who had given no offence and had observed the strictest order and discipline. Such demonstrations, it said, could only result in turbulence and in destroying the confidence due to the government, which was the only one that could advantageously direct patriotic energies. The tribunals were therefore instructed to impress on their subordinates, and the commissioners and familiars in their districts, the urgent necessity of unanimously contributing to the preservation of public tranquillity. This communication was received by the Valencia tribunal on May 9th and, on the 11th, it was read to the assembled officials, calificadores, notaries and familiars of the city, with exhortations to comply strictly with its commands--action which was doubtless taken by the other tribunals.[878]

The Inquisition thus remained in Madrid under the protection of the French arms, but its freedom of action was curtailed. The Abate Marchena, a fine classical scholar, but revolutionary and tinctured with atheism, had abandoned Spain early in the French Revolution and had barely escaped the guillotine during the Terror. He returned, in 1808, as Murat's secretary, when the Inquisition thought fit to arrest him, but Murat sent a file of grenadiers and forcibly released him.[879] When Napoleon reached Madrid, December 4, 1808, the capitulation granted to the city provided that no religion but Catholicism should be tolerated but, on the same day, he issued a decree which suppressed the Inquisition, as contrary to sovereignty and to civil authority, and confiscated its property to the crown.[880] The Inquisitor Francisco Riesco stated, during the debate in the Córtes of Cádiz, that this sudden decree was motived by the refusal of the members of the Suprema to take the oath of allegiance to the new dynasty, but this is evidently incorrect, as most of them had already done so at Bayonne, and Arce y Reynoso, who resigned his inquisitor-generalship, adhered to the French and accompanied them on the final evacuation. Riesco further asserts that Napoleon ordered them to be imprisoned, but they escaped and scattered to places of safety.[881] The Inquisition was thus left in an anomalous position and without a head, for correspondence with Pius VII was cut off, and neither his acceptance of Arce's resignation nor his delegation of powers to a successor could be had. The Junta Central, which was striving to govern the country, attempted to fill the vacancy with Pedro de Quevedo y Quintano, Bishop of Orense, but he could obtain no papal authorization and made no attempt to act. It was argued that during a vacancy the jurisdiction continued with the Suprema, but this was denied and it remained an open question.[882]

During the period which followed, the tribunals maintained their organization and exercised their functions after a fashion, when not prevented by the French occupation. Thus when the invaders reached Seville, February 1, 1810, the Inquisition was suppressed, but its members took refuge in Ceuta. Valencia remained in operation until the city was captured by Suchet, in 1811, while Barcelona at one time transferred itself to Tarragona. Activity was intermittent and, in the excitement of that stirring time, there was little energy for the prosecution of heresy while, even when the enemy had withdrawn, in many cases the buildings had been ruined. The Valencia record shows that the total number of cases brought before all the tribunals in 1808 was 67; in 1809, 22; in 1810, 17; in 1811, 25; in 1812, 1; in 1813, 6. Probably few of these cases were regularly heard, if we may judge from that of Don Vicente Valdés, captain of volunteers who, in 1810, was denounced to the Valencia tribunal for blasphemous propositions. October 27th it was ordered that, in view of the circumstances, a fitting occasion should be awaited for the audiencia de cargos demanded by the fiscal--a postponement which proved to be protracted for it was not until 1816 that he was tried.[883] Still, where the Inquisition itself was concerned it could act swiftly and effectively. In 1809 the French took possession of Santiago. Felipe Sobrino Taboada, professor of civil law in the university, was acting as police-magistrate and, by order of the director-general of police, he issued a proclamation exhorting the people to lay down their arms and praising the suppression of the Inquisition. When the French retired, the university refused to readmit him to his chair. He obtained a decision of the tribunal of Public Safety of Coruña re-establishing him and then the Inquisition arrested him, without the prescribed preliminary formalities, and kept him for five months in the secret prison. Afterwards he was allowed to keep his house as a prison and, when finally the bounds were enlarged to the province of Galicia, it was with the condition that he would accept no public office.[884]

ASSEMBLING OF THE CORTES

The Junta Central, which had endeavored to govern, amid much opposition from the particularist tendencies of the provincial juntas, retired to Cádiz when the French occupied Andalusia.

On January 1, 1810, it issued a convocation for the assembling of Córtes, and on the 31st it dissolved, after appointing a Regency and imposing on it the duty of convoking the Córtes by March 1st. The Regency delayed until, forced by the pressure of public opinion, on June 18th it published a decree ordering elections where they had not been held, and summoning the deputies to meet in August in Isla de Leon, now San Fernando, near Cádiz. Suffrage was virtually universal and, in the letters of convocation, the nation was called upon to assemble in general Córtes "to establish and improve the fundamental constitution of the monarchy," while the commissions of the delegates empowered them to decide all points contained in the letters and all others, without exception or limitation.[885] The Córtes accordingly assumed the title of Majesty, as embodying the will of the people and occupying the throne of the absent sovereign. When they were opened, September 24th, about a hundred deputies were present, two-thirds of whom were elected by the provinces not occupied by the French armies, and the rest selected in Cádiz from among natives of the unrepresented districts, including the colonies, then more or less in open revolt, while, as the vicissitudes of the war permitted, deputies came straggling in from districts unrepresented at first. As a whole, the body fairly reflected existing public opinion. The Liberals numbered forty-five, and the majority consisted of ecclesiastics, men of the privileged classes and government employees.[886] It was an unavoidably hazardous experiment, this sudden wrenching of Spain from the old moorings and launching it on the tempestuous waters of modern ideas, under the conduct of men without training or experience in self-government. Grave mistakes were inevitable and their constructive work was idealistic and doomed to failure--a failure bound to result in blood and misery. At the moment, however, there were no misgivings and the Córtes were regarded as the salvation of the nation.[887]

The oath administered to the members bound them to maintain Catholicism as the exclusive religion of Spain and to preserve for their beloved monarch Fernando VII all his dominions. Their first act was to adopt a series of five resolutions, offered by an ecclesiastic, Diego Muñoz Torrero, rector of the University of Salamanca, of which one provided that the Regency should be continued as the executive power, on taking an oath recognizing the sovereignty of the nation as embodied in the Córtes and promising obedience to their enactments. Rather than do this, the Regency proposed to break up the Córtes, but the threatening aspect of the people and the army caused a change of heart, and that same night they took the oath, except the implacable conservative Quevedo Bishop of Orense, who resigned both from the Regency and the Córtes. His resignations were accepted but he was forced to take the oath required of all prelates and officials before he was allowed to retire to his diocese. It was evident that the Córtes and the Regency could not pull together; on October 28th, the latter was dismissed, its membership was reduced from five to three and a new Regency was installed with which the Córtes could work in harmony.[888]

THE INQUISITION ASSAILED

After settling relations with the other departments of the State, the first attention of the Córtes was given to the freedom of the press. Two days after the opening session the subject was introduced and referred to a committee; no time was lost, a decree was reported October 8th, and on the 18th, in spite of the reclamations of the opposition, it was passed by a vote of 68 to 32. This was regarded as a preliminary attack on the Inquisition, which was thus deprived by implication of the function of censorship. Some members desired this to be explicitly stated, giving rise to a hot debate in which Inquisitor Riesco, a member of the Córtes, pleaded in vain for some honorable mention of the Holy Office. There was also indignation excited by the provision subjecting prohibition by the bishops to revision by the secular power, which was subversive of the imprescriptible rights of the Church, whose judgements are final.[889] If this was really the first move in a campaign against the Inquisition, it was not unskilful, for it set at liberty the pens which had hitherto been restrained. At once there arose a crowd of pamphleteers and journalists, not only in Cádiz but throughout Spain, who attacked the institution unsparingly, raising a clamor which showed how severe had been the repression. Sturdy defenders were not lacking and the wordy war was vigorously waged. The two most prominent champions on either side were Antonio Puigblanch, who, under the pseudonym of Natanael Jomtob, issued a series of pamphlets, collected under the title of "La Inquisicion sin Máscara" or "The Inquisition unmasked," and Padre Maestro Fray Francisco Alvarado, a Dominican of high repute for learning and eloquence, whose letters under the name of El Filósofo Rancio or Antiquated Philosopher, continued for two years to keep up the struggle against all the innovations of the Liberals.[890]

Puigblanch was no exception to the general rule that those who attacked the Inquisition were careful to profess the highest veneration for the faith and in no way to advocate toleration. His work commences with an eloquent description of religion as the foundation of all civil constitutions and Catholicism as the noblest adornment of enlightenment and liberty, the only question being whether the Inquisition is the fitting institution for its protection. He is careful to maintain to the last his abhorrence of heresy and his desire for its suppression, which he proposes to effect by reviving episcopal jurisdiction under certain limitations.[891] With all this his denunciation of the Inquisition was unsparing, and he had ample store of atrocities with which to justify his attacks, although there was unfairness in attributing to it, in the nineteenth century, the cruelties which had stained its previous career.

Alvarado was a man of extensive learning, but of little claim to the title of philosopher, whether antiquated or modern. Though his methods were not such as to make converts, they were well adapted to stimulate those of his own side, for he was an effective partizan writer, fluent, sarcastic, often coarse, vulgar and vituperative, using assertion for argument and indifferent as to truth. The chief value of his letters is the flood of light which they shed on the conservative attitude of the time, which explains much in the subsequent vicissitudes of Spain. Philosophers, he says, are wolves, robbers and devils, monsters who cannot be regarded without horror, enlighteners who are nothing but ignoramuses and cheats and emissaries sent by hell. To seek to undermine popular confidence in the priesthood he holds to be a crime greater than the crucifixion of Christ. The ferocity of his intolerance shows how little Spanish churchmen had changed since the days of Torquemada. As to the relations of religion and the State, he assumes that the only function of the civil power is to punish him who offends the faith; the Catholic religion is as intolerant as light is of darkness, or as truth is of falsehood, and this intolerance distinguishes it from all religions invented by man. Repeatedly and savagely he proclaims that burning is the proper remedy for unbelief, and he tells his adversaries that, if they wish free thought, they may go to England or to the United States, but in Spain what they had to expect was the quemadero.[892] Such advocacy could only render the Liberals more eager to accomplish their work.

THE CONSTITUTION OF 1812

While this controversy was contributing to the greater enlightenment or obscuration of public opinion, the Córtes were engaged in framing a Constitution. The committee entrusted with this task had a majority of conservatives, including several ecclesiastics, but these were quite willing to circumscribe the royal power, while seeking to extend the privileges of the Church, and all the members signed the project as presented.[893] It commenced by asserting the sovereignty of the nation, which had the exclusive right to establish its fundamental laws, and could never be the patrimony of any person or family, and it affirmed that the religion of the nation was, and always forever would be the Catholic, Apostolic, Roman, the only true one, which the nation protects by wise and just laws, and prohibits the exercise of any other.[894] This apparent concession to intolerance was denounced, when too late, as a trap, for it placed in the hands of the representatives of the nation the power of deciding what the wise and just laws should be for the protection of religion. Be this as it may, the Córtes were resolved that there should be no refusal to accept the new framework of government. In secret session of March 16, 1812, it was decreed that whosoever should refuse to swear to it should be declared an unworthy Spaniard and be driven from Spain, and measures were taken to have it read in every parish church, where the assembled people should swear to obey it and to be faithful to the king. As the French armies were driven back, the Spanish commanders made it their first duty to see this ceremony performed, and where there was opposition, chiefly arising from the priests, force was employed. A priest of the Cádiz cathedral who alluded to it slightingly as a libelo, or little book, was prosecuted, and the irreconcileable Bishop of Orense, who refused to take the oath, was exiled and declared to be an unworthy Spaniard. As a whole, however, it was enthusiastically accepted as the dawn of a new era, though we may well question how many of those who took the oath comprehended the purport of its three hundred and eighty-four articles, covering all the complicated minutiæ of institutions based on an entirely new conception of the relations between the Government and the governed.[895]

It was inevitable that, in the effort to create a new Spain, the fate of the Inquisition should be involved, especially as its disabled condition invited attack. That a struggle was impending had long been evident to all parties, and that this was felt to be decisive as to the character of the future institutions of Spain is seen in the tenacity with which it was fought. The Inquisition was the conservative stronghold, to be defended to the last, after all the outer defences had been abandoned, and the deep roots which it had established are manifested by the tactics required for its overthrow, and by the fact that the contest was the bitterest and the most prolonged in the career of the Córtes, which had so unceremoniously converted Spain from absolutism to liberal constitutionalism.

Some preparation had been made for the struggle by the conservatives. The first Regency had endeavored to reconstitute all the old Councils of the monarchy and, on June 10, 1810, Ethenard, the Dean of the Suprema, addressed to it a memorial requesting it to order the reassembling of the Suprema, to which it responded, August 1st, by issuing such an order. The scattering of the members precluded this, but, when the early acts of the Córtes foreshadowed what was to come, on December 18th, Ethenard and Amarillas asked the new Regency to appoint as a member the fiscal Ibar Navarro and as fiscal the Madrid inquisitor, Galarza, thus enabling the body to resume its functions. As no attention was paid to this, an old member, Alejo Jimenez de Castro, who had been exiled to Murcia by Godoy, was brought from his retreat to Cádiz, so as to have material for a quorum present. The occasion to utilize this offered itself in January, 1811. The freedom of the press enabled Don Manuel Alzaibar to start "La Triple Alianza," a frankly irreligious journal, in the second number of which there appeared an article ridiculing the immortality of the soul and suffrages for the dead. On January 28th advantage was taken of this to ask the Córtes to refer it to the Inquisition for censure, which was carried in spite of opposition. The next day the editors asked that the action be rescinded, leading to a three days' debate in which the Inquisition was denounced as a mysterious, cruel and antichristian tribunal and, for the first time, its suppression was openly advocated. President Dou ruled that the inculpated journal must be passed to the Junta de Censura, for he understood that the Inquisition was not organized, when he was told that there were three members of the Suprema in Cádiz, and that the Seville tribunal was in Ceuta. This raised larger questions and the whole matter was referred to a committee so composed that it was expected to report against re-establishment, but it withheld its report for a long time and meanwhile there were other moves in the game.[896]

SKIRMISHING FOR POSITION

On May 16th, the members of the Suprema notified the Regency that they were prepared to act, in response to which the minister of Gracia y Justicia expressed his surprise that they should meet as a tribunal, without awaiting the decision of the questions submitted to the Córtes, and forbade them from forming a Council until they should have express authorization.[897] The matter was brought before the Córtes and Inquisitor Riesco vainly argued in favor of the Inquisition; his motion was referred to the committee, where it lay buried in spite of repeated calls for a report. The Liberals insisted that a National Council would be a more suitable body for the mature consideration of such questions; their object was solely to gain time, which was fighting on their side, but the idea was seriously entertained, even by the clericals. The committee on the external discipline of the clergy reported, August 22d, in favor of the project, with a list of matters to be submitted to the Council; on August 28th the Córtes ordered it to be convoked, but postponed consideration of the details. Other matters supervened and no further action was taken, which Archbishop Vélez assures us saved Spain from a schism, or at least from a scandal for, under the proposed program, it would have proved a second Synod of Pistoja. In fact, the journals naturally took a lively interest in the matter; thousands of pamphlets, we are told, appeared everywhere, pointing out the abuses and relaxed morals of the clergy and demanding a reform that was assumed to be necessary. It is easy to imagine that the ecclesiastical authorities were willing to let the project drop.[898]

The position of the Liberals was greatly strengthened by the adoption of the Constitution, in March 1812, as was abundantly shown in the next debate on the Inquisition. This was provoked by the publication, in April 1812, of the "Diccionario crítico-burlesco" of Gallardo, librarian of the Córtes, in which all that the mass of the population held sacred was treated with ridicule, neither refined nor witty. It created an immense sensation and was brought before the Córtes, which enabled Riesco, on April 22d, to call for the immediate presentation of the report of the committee on the Inquisition, for which the Córtes had been waiting for more than a year. The committee, in fact, had reached a decision, in July 1811, in favor of the Inquisition, and we are not told why it had been held back, for four members had concurred in it and only Muñoz Torrero had dissented. The report was accordingly presented, re-establishing the Suprema in its functions, with certain limitations as to political action; the debate was hot, but the Liberals had taken precautions to avoid a direct vote on the question. In a decree of March 25th, creating a supreme court of justice, they had introduced an article suppressing the tribunals known by the name of councils, and they pointed out that this embraced the Suprema, which gave abundant opportunity for discussion. Even more important was a decision of the Córtes, adroitly planned for this especial purpose, December 13, 1811, during the discussion on the Constitution, that no propositions bearing on the fundamental law should be admitted to debate without previous examination by the committee on the Constitution, to see that it was not in opposition to the articles thereof. It was notorious that inquisitorial procedure was in direct contravention of the constitutional provisions to secure justice in criminal prosecutions and, after an exciting struggle and a postponement, the report was referred to the committee on the Constitution. The Conservatives were so exasperated that they proposed to dissolve the Córtes, and have a new election under the Constitution, to which the Liberals agreed, except that the new body should meet October 1, 1813, and the existing one should remain in session until then. Archbishop Vélez tells us that the policy of the Liberals was to gain time, for their personal safety was at stake if the Inquisition was re-established, nor does he recognize how monstrous was the admission involved in this, for an institution that could prosecute and punish legislators for their official acts was virtually the despot of the land. Doubtless the deputies felt this, and that the struggle was one for life or death.[899]

The flank of the enemy was thus skilfully turned. The committee on the Constitution was in no haste to report and occupied itself with collecting documentary material from the archives wherever accessible. Its conclusion was that the Inquisition was incompatible with the fundamental law and, on November 13th, it voted on a project for establishing "Tribunales protectores de la fe" in compliance with the constitutional requirements. Finally, on December 8th two reports were presented. That of the minority by Antonio Joaquín Pérez, who had been an inquisitor in Mexico, argued that the abuses of the Inquisition were not inherent; that its procedure conflicted with the Constitution and should therefore be modified accordingly.[900]

DEBATE ON SUPPRESSION

The majority report was a very elaborate document, tracing the treatment of heresy from the earliest times, and pointing out the irreconcileable incompatibility of the Inquisition with the constitutional provisions securing to the citizen the right of open trial and opportunities for defence. It concluded with the draft of a decree "Sobre Tribunales protectores de la fe," in which such caution was deemed necessary that the Inquisition was nowhere mentioned. It appealed to the national pride, by simply reviving a law of the Partidas concerning the prosecution of heretics by bishops, it prescribed the form and procedure of the episcopal tribunals, the punishment by lay judges of those pronounced guilty, and it provided for appeals as well as for the suppression of writings contrary to religion. The reports were duly received and January 4, 1813, was appointed for the opening of debate.[901]

Probably no measure before the Córtes provoked so bitter and prolonged a debate. The Liberals had secured the advantage of position, and the Conservatives felt that the issue involved the whole future relations of Church and State. There was a preliminary skirmish on December 29th, when Sánchez de Ocaña asked for a postponement until the bishops and chapters could be consulted, on the ground that the Church was an independent body.[902] This was voted down and the debate was opened on the designated day, January 4, 1813. The friends of the Inquisition had not been idle; the Church organization was in good working order, and the Córtes were bombarded with memorials from bishops, chapters, ayuntamientos, military officers, towns and provinces, showing how active the canvass had been during the two years in which the subject had been mooted. Yet the Conservatives could only procure, out of the fifty-nine sees existing in Spain, protests from two archbishops and twenty-four bishops, the authorities of three vacant sees, and four chapters of those occupied by the French; while the number from officers of the army was not large, those from towns were but a small fraction of the municipalities, and only two provinces--Alava and Galicia--spoke through their authorities. Muñoz Torrero declared, January 10th, that every mail brought him mountains of letters in favor of the Inquisition and Toreno spoke of the reclamations that came in, showing how the signers of protests had been coerced.[903]

The debate was vigorous and eloquent on both sides but, while it took the widest range, embracing the history of the Church from apostolic times and the career of the Inquisition from the thirteenth century, the parliamentary question in reality turned upon the power of the Córtes to intrude in the sphere of ecclesiastical jurisdiction. After discussion lasting until January 22d on the preliminary propositions, the decree itself was taken up, article by article and strenuously fought over; amendments were presented and accepted or rejected, as they strengthened or weakened the measure, and hot resistance was offered to the clauses allowing appeals from the judgements of the bishops, which the Liberals supported on the ground that all the members who opposed the Inquisition had been denounced throughout Spain as heretics, and the safety of the citizen demanded that episcopal definition of heresy should not be final. The debate was prolonged until February 5th, when the last article was agreed to, and the decree in its final shape did not differ essentially from that proposed by the Committee. There was no formal suppression of the Inquisition; it was simply declared to be incompatible with the Constitution and the law of the Partidas was revived. This latter had been agreed to on January 26th by a vote of 92 to 30, and that date was assumed as determining the extinction of the Inquisition, regulating the disposition of its property. It is not worth while to recapitulate the details of the episcopal tribunals and the provisions for censorship, as the bishops took little interest in the exercise of their restored jurisdiction, though there are traces of their action in one or two cases--that of Joaquin Ramírez, priest of Moscardon and of Doña Antonia de la Torre of Seville.[904] During the seventeen months that elapsed until the re-establishment of the Inquisition, we are told that, although the land was full of Freemasons and other anticatholics, the bishops had no occasion to arrest any one, for no informers or accusers came forward--doubtless because they realized that their names would be known.[905]

THE INQUISITION SUPPRESSED

In the debate several ecclesiastics distinguished themselves by their able advocacy of the measure, among whom were pre-eminent Muñoz Torrero, who had borne a leading part in drafting the decree; Lorenzo Villanueva, who had defended the Inquisition against Bishop Grégoire, and Ruyz Padron, parish priest of Valdeorras in Galicia and formerly of the Canaries. How they fared in consequence we shall see hereafter. On the other side one of the most vehement was Pedro Inguanzo, who was rewarded with the see of Zamora, and ultimately with the archbishopric of Toledo.

The Liberals had won their victory by unexpectedly large majorities, indicating how great had been the advance in public opinion. No measure had created such intensity of feeling on either side; the rejoicing of the Liberals was extravagant, and the anger of the clerical party may be gauged by the declamation of Archbishop Vélez, who is as vehement as though the whole fate of Christianity was at stake--the abomination of desolation, he declares, seemed to have established its throne in the very house of God.[906] The clergy had already been alienated by various measures adverse to their interests-- the appropriation of a portion of the tithes to the support of the armies, the escheating of the property of convents destroyed by the invaders, or having less than twelve inmates, and the abrogation of the Voto de Santiago, a tax on the agriculturists of some provinces based on a fraudulent tradition of a vow made by Ramiro I, when, by the aid of St. James, he won the suppositious victory of Clavijo.[907] The debate on the Inquisition had heightened the reputation of the Córtes as an irreligious body, and it was not wise to inflame still further the hostility of a class wielding such preponderating influence, but the Liberals, intoxicated by their victory, proceeded to render the measure as offensive as possible to the defeated clericals.

On February 5th, after the final vote, the committee on the Constitution was instructed to prepare a manifesto setting forth the reasons for the suppression of the Inquisition which, together with the decree, should be read in all parish churches for three consecutive Sundays, before the offertory of the mass; that in all churches the insignia of those condemned and penanced should be removed, and that a report should be made as to the disposition of the archives of the tribunals. The preparation of the manifesto delayed the publication of the decree until February 22d, for it was a long and wordy document, in which the decadence of Spain was attributed to the abuses of the Inquisition; the ancient laws had therefore been revived, restoring their jurisdiction to the bishops, in whose hands the Catholic faith and its sublime morals would be secure; Religion would flourish, prosperity would return, and perchance this change might some day lead to the religious brotherhood of all the nations.[908]

It was not long before the imprudence of this step manifested itself, for it gave the Church a battle-ground on which to contest, not only the reading of the manifesto but the execution of the decree itself and, if defeated, of occupying the advantageous position of martyrdom. Opposition had for some time been in preparation. As early as December 12, 1812, the six bishops of Lérida, Tortosa, Barcelona, Urgel, Teruel and Pampeluna, in the safe refuge of Majorca, had prepared a manifesto widely circulated in private, representing the Church as outraged in its ministers, oppressed in its immunities, and combated in its doctrines, while the Jansenist members of the Córtes were described as adherents of the Council of Pistoja.[909] No sooner was the decisive vote of February 5th taken than the chapter of the vacant see of Cádiz prepared for a contest over the reading of the decree and manifesto. It had already appointed a committee of three with full powers, and it now instructed the committee to communicate secretly with refugee bishops in Cádiz, and with chapters elsewhere, with a view to common action. Letters were sent to the chapters of Seville, Málaga, Jaen and Córdova, representing that the Cádiz chapter was ready to be the victim, but would be strengthened by the union of others. Seville replied with promises to do the same; the rest more cautiously, for they felt that they were treading on dangerous ground.

RESISTANCE OF THE CLERGY

This dampened somewhat the ardor of the fiery Cádiz chapter and it sought for other support. On February 23d the parish priests and army chaplains of Cádiz were assembled and addressed the chapter at great length. To read the decree and manifesto would be a profanation and a degrading servility. The papal constitutions creating the Inquisition were binding on the consciences of the faithful, until revoked by the same authority, and from this obligation the secular power could not relieve them. To obey would be to incur the risk of a dreadful sacrilege, and the penalties for impeding the Inquisition imposed by Julius III and Sixtus V; it was better to fall into the hands of man than into those of God, and they were ready to endure whatever fate might befall them. This was rank rebellion, slightly moderated by the expression of a desire to learn the opinions of the holy prelates who were in Cádiz. The chapter duly transmitted this address to the prelates--the Bishops of Calahorra, Plasencia, San Marcos de Leon, Sigüenza and Albarracin (Calahorra and San Marcos were deputies in the Córtes and had signed the Constitution)--stating that it entertained the same sentiments and repeated the request for their opinion. The bishops replied cautiously, and in substance advised that representations be made to the Government, which might be induced to modify its decrees.[910]

Time was growing short, for March 7th had been designated as the first Sunday for reading the decree and manifesto. On March 3d a capitular meeting was assembled, in which it was unanimously resolved to obey, but to make use of the provisions which authorize citizens to obey without executing and to represent reverentially the reasons for suspending action until further determination.[911] This was the first step in the development of a somewhat formidable plot which was organizing. On March 5th the papal nuncio, Pedro Gravina, Archbishop of Nicæa, addressed to the Regency a very significant protest against the decree itself. The abolition of the Inquisition, he said, was contrary to the primacy of the Holy See; he protested against this and he asked the Regency to induce the Córtes to suspend its publication and execution until happier times might secure the consent of the pope or of the National Council. On the same day he was guilty of the indiscretion of writing to the Bishop of Jaen and to the chapters of Málaga and Granada, under strict injunctions of secrecy, advising them of the proposed resistance of the Cádiz chapter and inviting their coöperation.[912] The next day, March 6th, the chapter sent to the Regency the address of the priests and chaplains of Cádiz, with a communication setting forth the reasons which not only prevented the execution of the mandate of the Córtes, but imperiously required the secular power to protect the Church and relieve it from an act in contravention of its honor and sanctity. The Chapter, it argued, could not be accused of disobedience for insisting on the spiritual law which was more binding than the temporal.[913]

The Regency evidently was participating in the plot to overthrow the Córtes for the purpose of saving the Inquisition. The legislative and executive branches of the Government had become estranged. There had been dissension in the matter of the suppression of the convents, and an investigation made by the Córtes into the affairs of the Regency had led to a damaging report on February 7th. The Liberals were convinced that it was planning a coup d'état when, on the night of Saturday, March 6th the rumor spread that it had dismissed the Governor of Cádiz, D. Cayetano Valdés, and had replaced him with D. José María Alós. Sunday passed without the reading of the decree and manifesto in the churches and, on Monday, the minister of Gracia y Justicia sent to the Córtes the communications of the chapter to the Regency. A permanent session was at once declared; the Córtes dismissed the regents and replaced them with the three senior members of the Council of State, Cardinal Luis de Bourbon, Archbishop of Toledo, D. Pedro Agar and D. Gabriel Ciscar, who forthwith took the oaths and at 9 P.M. assumed possession of their office, the dismissed regents offering no resistance.[914]

***

Harmony between the legislature and the executive being thus restored, on March 9th the Córtes ordered the Regency to compel obedience. Under threats of measures to be taken, the chapter yielded at 10 P.M. and promised that the next morning, and on the two following Sundays, the decree and manifesto should be duly read. It was obliged to furnish authentic copies of all papers and correspondence, on the basis of which a sharp reprimand was addressed to the Seville chapter and, on April 24th, prosecution was commenced against the Cádiz capitular vicar and the three members of the committee, for treasonable conspiracy. Their temporalities were seized and for six weeks they were imprisoned, incomunicado. The trial dragged on until the restoration of Fernando VII rendered acquittal a matter of course and enabled them, in their defence, to declare that to destroy the Inquisition or to impede its action in matters of faith was the same as prohibiting the jurisdiction of the Roman Pontiff, thus trampling under foot a dogma established by Jesus Christ.[915]

The documents thus obtained showed that Nuncio Gravina had been active in furthering the plot of resistance. Now that it had been crushed, policy would have dictated dropping the matter but, on April 22d, the minister of Gracia y Justicia addressed him a sharp letter, expressing the confidence of the Regency that he would in future observe the limits of his office, as otherwise it would be obliged to exercise all its authority. To this he of course replied defiantly; whenever ecclesiastical matters were concerned he might find himself obliged to follow the same course, and the Regency could do as it pleased. Some further correspondence followed in the same vein and then, after an interval, his passports were sent to him, his temporalities were seized, and he was informed that the frigate Sabina was at his disposal to transport him whither he desired.[916] He declined the proffered frigate and established himself in Portugal, near the border, whence he continued busily to stir up disaffection, assuming that he still retained his functions as nuncio. On July 24th he addressed a protest to the Government and sent a circular to the bishops inviting them to apply to him in cases requiring his aid. This led to a lively controversy, in which the Government charged him with deceit and he retorted by accusing it of falsehood and challenging it to publish the documents.[917]

This was by no means the only trouble excited by the enforced reading of the decree and manifesto. Recalcitrant priests were found in many places, whose cases caused infinite annoyance and bad blood and the Bishop of Oviedo was recluded in a convent for refusing obedience.[918] The Government triumphed, but it was a Pyrrhic victory, multiplying its enemies, heightening its reputation for irreligion, and weakening its influence.[919]

The result was seen in the elections for the new Córtes ordinarias, when the deputies returned were largely reactionary, owing to clerical influence. There were many vacancies, however, which were filled by the old members for the corresponding places, and thus the parties were evenly balanced. The new Córtes met, September 26th and, on November 29th adjourned to meet in Madrid, January 15, 1814; the Regency transferred itself to Madrid, January 5th.[920] By that time the French were virtually expelled from Spain; Wellington was following Soult into France, and Suchet was barely holding his own against Copons in Catalonia.

The return of Fernando el Deseado was evidently at hand and was eagerly expected. The reaction following the prolonged excitement of the war was beginning to be felt. There was widespread misery in the devastated provinces, the relief of which was slow and difficult and was aggravated by a decree of the Córtes requiring those which had been subjugated to pay the arrears of the war contributions. Dissatisfaction with the Córtes was aroused by what were regarded as their sins both of commission and omission--the lowering of the value of French money caused great suffering and trouble; all who had served under the intruso were ejected from office; the parish priests were reinstated in their old cures, which turned into the streets the new incumbents; people began to grumble at the preponderance of the Liberals in the Córtes--in short, there was no lack of subjects of complaint.[921] Exhaustion and poverty, the inevitable consequences of so prolonged and desperate a struggle, produced discontent, and it was natural that those who had guided the nation through its tribulations should be held responsible, while their services should be forgotten. The military also were dissatisfied at finding that, at the close of a successful war, they had not the importance that they considered to be their due, while the clergy were outspoken in opposition and, through two widely circulated journals, "El Procurador de la Nacion y del Rey" and " La Atalaya de la Mancha," attacked the Government furiously.[922]

FERNANDO'S RETURN

During all this period, Fernando's existence at Valençay had been as agreeable as was consistent with his safe-keeping. The only restriction on his movements was a prohibition to ride on horseback; Napoleon is said to have kept him supplied with women to satisfy his strongly developed sensuality, and he manifested his characteristic baseness in letters to his captor congratulating him on his victories and soliciting the honor of a matrimonial alliance with his family. After the battle of Leipzig, Napoleon, striving to save what he could from the wreck, represented to Fernando that the English were seeking to convert Spain into a Jacobin republic; Fernando was ready to agree to any terms and, on December 11, 1813, there was signed what was known as the Treaty of Valençay, under which peace was declared between France and Spain, the English and French troops were to be withdrawn, the Afrancesados, who had taken refuge in France, were to be restored to their property and functions, and Fernando was to make a yearly allowance of 30,000,000 reales to his father and mother.[923]

Fernando sent the Duke of San Carlos with the treaty to Madrid for ratification, instructing him that, if he found the Córtes and Regency infected with Jacobinism, he was to insist on ratification pure and simple; if he found them loyal, he was to say that the king desired ratification, with the understanding that he would subsequently declare it invalid. The treaty excited general indignation. As early as January 1, 1811, the Córtes had decreed that they would recognize no treaty made by the king in captivity, and that he should not be considered free until he was surrounded by his faithful subjects in Córtes. Now the Córtes responded to Fernando's message with a decree of February 2, 1814, reissuing the former one and adding that obedience should not be rendered to him until he should, in the Córtes, take an oath to the Constitution; on his arrival at the frontier this decree was to be handed to him, with a copy of the Constitution that he might read and understand it; he was to follow a route prescribed by the Regency and, on reaching the capital, he was to come directly to the Córtes, take the oath, and the government would then be solemnly made over to him. All this was agreed to with virtual unanimity; it was signed by all the deputies and was published with a manifesto denouncing the treaty and expressing the warmest devotion to the king. The publication aroused general indignation at the treaty and the manifesto elicited universal applause.[924]

To Fernando, trained in the traditions of absolutism, the Treaty of Valençay was vastly preferable to the reception prepared for him, but he uttered no word of dissent when, after Napoleon had liberated him without conditions on March 7th, he was transferred by Suchet, on the banks of the Fluviá, March 24th, to Copons, the Captain-general of Catalonia. He exercised volition however in deviating from the route laid down by the Regency, and made a detour to Saragossa on the road to Valencia, but he preserved absolute silence as to his intentions. Everywhere he was received with delirious enthusiasm; the people idealized him as the symbol of the nationality for which they had struggled through five years of pitiless war, and there were no bounds to their exuberance of loyalty.

THE RESTORATION

To few men has it been given, as to Fernando, to exercise so profound and so lasting an influence on the destinies of a nation. His ancestor, Henry IV, had a harder task when he undertook to impose harmony on compatriots who, for a generation had been savagely cutting each others' throats. Fernando came to a nation which had been unitedly waging war against a foreign enemy. Differences of opinion had grown up, as to the reception or rejection of modern ideas, and parties had been formed representing the principles of conservatism and innovation; mistakes had been made on both sides and bitterness of temper was rising, but a wise and prudent ruler, coming uncommitted to either side and enthusiastically greeted by both, could have exorcised the demon of faction, could have brought about compromise and conciliation, and could have gradually so trained the nation that it could have traversed in peace the inevitable revolution awaiting it. This was not to be. Unfortunately Fernando was one of the basest and most despicable beings that ever disgraced a throne. Cowardly, treacherous, deceitful, selfish, abandoned to low debauchery, controlled by a camarilla of foul and immoral favorites, his sole object was to secure for himself the untrammelled exercise of arbitrary power and to abuse it for sensual gratification. Cruel he was not, in the sense of wanton shedding of blood, but he was callously indifferent to human suffering, and he earned the name of Tigrekan, by which the Liberals came to designate him.[925]

REACTION

When Fernando entered Spain he was naturally undecided as to the immediate attitude to be assumed towards the changes made during his absence, but the enthusiasm of his reception and the influence of the reactionaries who surrounded him emboldened him in the determination to assert his autocracy. Several secret conferences were held during the journey to decide whether he should swear to the Constitution, and the negative opinion prevailed. In fact, to a man of Fernando's character, voluntary obedience to the Constitution was an impossibility. Not only did it declare that sovereignty resided in the nation, with the corresponding right to determine its fundamental laws, but the powers of the crown were limited in many ways; the Córtes reserved the right to exclude unworthy aspirants to the succession, and to set aside the incumbent for any cause rendering him incapable--clauses susceptible of most dangerous interpretation. At this very time, indeed, the Córtes were deliberating on the appropriation to be made to the king for the maintenance of his court, which implied the right to subject him to the most galling conditions.[926]

If anything was needed to induce him to assert the full powers enjoyed by his predecessors it was afforded by a manifesto known as the Representation of the Persians, from an absurd allusion to the ancient Persians in the opening sentence. This was signed by sixty-nine deputies to the Córtes; at much length and with turgid rhetoric it set forth the sufferings inflicted on Spain by the Liberals; it argued that all the acts of the Córtes of Cádiz were null and invalid; it pointed out the limitations on the royal power prescribed by the Constitution, and it asserted that absolute monarchy was recognized as the perfection of government. It did not omit to declare that the Inquisition was indispensable to the maintenance of religion, without which no government could exist; it dwelt on the disorders consequent upon its suppression and it reminded Fernando that, from the time of the Gothic kingdom, intolerance of heresy was the permanent law of the nation. Even if the king should think best to swear to the Constitution, the manifesto protested that it was invalid and that its destructive principles must be submitted to the action of Córtes assembled according to the ancient fashion. This paper, dated April 12th, was drawn up and secretly circulated by Bernardo Moza Reales, who carried it to Valencia and presented it to Fernando, receiving as reward the title of Marquis of Mataflorida.[927]

Fernando reached Valencia April 16th and paused there until May 4th, while secret preparations were made to overthrow the government. The Córtes, unaware of the contemplated treachery, were amusing themselves in arranging the hall for the solemnity of the king's oath and his acknowledgement as sovereign, and took no measures for self-protection. Troops were secretly collected in the vicinity of Madrid, under General Eguia, a violent reactionary, who was made Captain-general of New Castile. On the night of May 10th, when Fernando was nearing the capital, Eguia notified Joaquin Pérez, President of the Córtes, that they were closed; troops took possession of the hall and the archives were sealed, while police-agents were busy making arrests from a list of thirty-eight marked for proscription, including two of the regents, two ministers and all the more prominent liberal deputies.[928] No resistance was encountered and the precedent was established which has proved so disastrous to Spain.

DESPOTISM RE-ESTABLISHED

In the early dawn of the 11th, there was found posted everywhere a royal manifesto dated at Valencia on the 4th. In this, after a rambling summary of antecedent events, Fernando promised to assemble as soon as possible Córtes of the old fashion and, in conjunction with them, to establish solidly whatever was necessary for the good of the kingdom. He hated despotism; the enlightenment and culture of Europe would never permit it, and his predecessors had never been despots. But the Córtes of Cádiz and the existing body were illegal and all their acts were invalid; he did not intend to swear to the Constitution or to the decrees of the Córtes, but he pronounced them all void and of no effect, and any one supporting them in any manner or endeavoring to impede the execution of this manifesto was declared to be guilty of high treason and subject to the death-penalty.[929] It is perhaps needless to say that the promised convocation of Córtes and the salutary legislation never took place. All the modernized institutions framed since 1810 were swept away at a word, the old organization of Government was restored, and Fernando was an absolute despot, disposing at his pleasure of the lives and property of his subjects who had fought so desperately for his restoration.

How he used this power was manifested in the case of the fifty-two prisoners who were arrested at the time of the coup d'état. Nineteen months were spent in endeavoring to have them condemned by tribunals and commissions formed for the purpose, but no crime could be proved that would not equally affect all who had voted with them, many of whom stood in high favor at court. The last tribunal convened for their trial advised Fernando to sentence them in the exercise of his royal omnipotence, and he did so, December 17, 1815, sending them to distant fortresses, African presidios and convents, with strict orders to allow them to see no one and to send or receive no letters.[930] As regards the three specially obnoxious clerical deputies, Villanueva was recluded for six years in the convent of la Salceda, from which we shall see him emerge and again play a brief part on the political stage. Muñoz Torrero was sent to the convent of Erbon, in Galicia. He finally fell into the savage hands of Dom Miguel of Portugal and perished, after severe torture, in 1829.[931] Ruiz de Padron was not on the list of the proscribed; he had not been elected to the new Córtes but was detained by sickness in Cádiz. On his return in May to his parish of Valdeorras, his bishop, Manuel Vicente of Astorga, made a crime of his absence from his cure without episcopal licence and prosecuted him for this and for sustaining in the Córtes projects adverse to religion and the throne. On November 2, 1815, he was sentenced to perpetual reclusion in the desert convent of Cabeza de Alba and, to prevent appeal, the bishop sent the process to the Inquisition of Valladolid. Ruiz appealed to the metropolitan, but the bishop refused to allow the appeal. Then a recurso de fuerza to the Chancellery of Valladolid was tried, which thrice demanded the process before the bishop, to escape exposure in a secular court, allowed the appeal. Finally the metropolitan annulled the proceedings and Ruiz was set at liberty, after four years' imprisonment, broken in health and ruined in fortune. This action probably superseded a prosecution against him for printing his speech in the Córtes against the Inquisition, a prosecution commenced by the Madrid tribunal and transferred to Valladolid.[932]

REORGANIZATION

It was at first thought that the manifesto of May 4th, by invalidating all the acts of the Córtes, in itself re-established the Inquisition. In fact, Seville, its birth-place, had not waited for this and, on May 6th, a popular tumult restored it. The next day its banner, piously preserved by Don Juan García de Negra, a familiar, was solemnly conducted to the castle of Triana by a procession, at the head of which marched Juan Acisla de Vera, coadministrator of the diocese; the Te Deum was sung in the cathedral, the houses were illuminated and splendidly adorned with tapestries.[933] All this was premature, as likewise were the attempts made by some tribunals to reorganize, for the absence of an inquisitor-general and Suprema rendered irregular the transaction of business. Representations were made to the king by Seville and other towns, by the chapter of Valencia, and by bishops, praying him to take action, and the scruples as to the intervention of the civil power in spiritual affairs vanished.[934] Fernando accordingly, by decree of July 21, 1814, recited the appeals made to him and announced that he deemed it fitting that the Holy Office should resume the exercise of its powers, both the ecclesiastical granted by the popes and the royal, bestowed by his predecessors. In both of these the rules in force in 1808 were to be followed, together with the laws issued at sundry times to restrain abuses and curtail privileges.

But, as other reforms might be necessary, he ordered that, as soon as the Suprema should assemble, two of its members, selected by him, and two of the Royal Council should form a junta to investigate the procedure and the methods of censorship and, if they should find anything requiring reform, they should report to him that he might do what was requisite.[935] Even the Córtes could not assert more authoritative domination.

The inquisitor-generalship was filled by the appointment of Francisco Xavier de Mier y Campillo, Bishop of Almería, and the vacancies in the Suprema were supplied. The junta of reform was organized and met and consulted. In 1816 we hear of their being still in session, but we are told that they found nothing requiring amendment.[936]

The Suprema lost no time in getting to work. A circular of August 8th, to the tribunals, enclosed the royal decree and announced that, in virtue of it, the council was that day restored to its authority and functions, which had been interrupted only by the invasion and the so-called Córtes. The tribunals were ordered to proceed, as in former times, with all business that might offer, and the officials were to discharge their accustomed duties, until the Bishop of Almería should receive his bulls. Lists of all officials were to be sent, with statements of their dates of service, and of popular report as to their conduct during the troubles, and whether they had publicly attacked the rights of the sovereign and of the Holy Office. A process of "purification" ensued, investigating the records of all officials, many of whom had bowed to the tempest during the short-lived triumph of Liberalism. April 7, 1815, a circular letter directed that any one who had petitioned the Córtes for the abolition of the Inquisition, or had congratulated them on their action, was no longer to be regarded as in office or entitled to wear the insignia, but considerable tenderness was shown to the erring. Thus Don Manuel Palomino y Lozano, supernumerary secretary of the Madrid tribunal, had signed an address of congratulation to the Córtes, but on his pleading coercion and fear he was allowed to retain office.[937]

Allusion has already been made (Vol. II, p. 445) to the difficulties experienced in re-constituting an institution which, during five years of war, had been exposed to spoliation and destruction, resulting, in some places, in the wrecking of its buildings, the purloining of its movables and the scattering of its papers. Thus, for instance, in September and October 1815, the Logroño tribunal, which had lost its habitation, was negotiating with the Marquis of Monasterio for his house, which he offered rent-free, if it would keep the premises in repair and make the necessary alterations; the Suprema instructed it to secure better terms if it could, and to be very economical with the alterations.[938] As late as 1817 we chance to learn that Santiago and Valladolid had no prisons and, in 1819, that Llerena was in the same plight.[939]

The financial question was even more serious. We have seen how, under Godoy, the tribunals had been obliged to convert all their available securities into Government funds, which of course had become worthless, and how the Córtes, by decree of December 1, 1810, had applied the suppressed prebends to the conduct of the war. It must therefore have been well-nigh starved when suppressed by the Córtes, but there was no disposition to expose individuals to suffering and, when its property was declared to belong to the nation, elaborate provision was made for the payment of salaries and the customary gratifications, though we may safely assume that in the majority of cases, these kindly intentions failed of effect.[940]

FINANCIAL TROUBLES

When re-establishment came the task of gathering the salvage from the wreck of the past six years was most disheartening. The royal decree simply called on the Inquisition to resume its functions and said nothing about its property, the restoration of which was evidently taken for granted, under the manifesto invalidating the acts of the Córtes. There was no disposition, however, on the part of the treasury officials to do this and, in response to a consulta of August 11th, the king, on the 18th, issued an order on them to make over to the tribunals all real estate of every kind that had been absorbed by the treasury, the account of rents to be made up to July 21st and apportioned on that basis. This left personal property out of consideration and a further decree was procured, September 3d, ordering the restoration of everything that had passed into the Caja de Consolidacion, as well as the fruits of the suppressed prebends, balancing the accounts up to July 21st.[941] This was slackly obeyed; the necessities of the tribunals were pressing, and the Suprema presented consultas of October 1st and 23d asking that they should be allowed to collect the revenues, and that restitution should be made of all past collections or, in default of this, that a monthly allowance of eighty thousand reales be made to the Inquisition. To this Fernando replied that the needs of the royal treasury did not permit the repayment of back collections, nor could it meet the proposed monthly allowance, but it was his will that such payments as the General Treasury and the Junta del Crédito Público could spare should be made as a payment on account for the most necessary expenses of the Inquisition. This last was doubtless an empty promise; the royal financiers were determined not to go back of July 21st, and it appears, by a letter of December 16th, that the royal officials were still making collections. The most that the Suprema could accomplish was to procure from the Junta del Crédito Público an order of January 9, 1815, and from the chief of the Treasury one of January 30th, to their subordinates to cease collecting from the property of the Inquisition, under the rigid condition that an account should be kept by the tribunals of their collections, so that whatever they might obtain of arrears due prior to July 21st should enure to the benefit of the Government.[942] In this, however, there was recognized the justice of a claim for the unpaid back salaries of the officials, and elaborate arrangements were made to ascertain and put these in shape, but it was labor lost. The treasury was at too low an ebb, and the claimants for services rendered during the troubled years of war and revolution were too numerous, for the Inquisition to obtain what it demanded.

The Suprema was also diligent in seeking to recover the amounts which the tribunals had been obliged to invest in Government securities, but this was as fruitless as other attempts to save fragments of the wreck. The last we hear of it is in 1819, when the Suprema was still endeavoring to meet the exigencies of the Treasury in framing lists of the dates and numbers of the bonds.[943]

It was difficult to evolve order out of the chaos of destruction, especially where the papers had been scattered, so that evidences of indebtedness and accounts were lost, interfering greatly with efforts to reclaim property. In November, 1814, we find the Valencia tribunal issuing an edict requiring the return of all books and papers and records within fifteen days, under pain of excommunication and two hundred ducats; as to the furniture and other effects, they were to be restored under threat of legal proceedings. Although Valencia had been for two years under French occupation, it seems to have been more prompt than some others in getting its finances into intelligible condition. In November the Suprema calls upon it for a detailed schedule of resources and expenses and, in the latter it is not to omit the contribution required by the Suprema, amounting to 130,896 reales, and meanwhile it is not to pay out anything for salaries or other purposes without awaiting permission. Under this it was allowed, January 21, 1815, to pay salaries up to the end of 1814, and in May to make further payments. Yet in 1816 we find it reduced to seeking a loan wherewith to meet the salaries and a sum of thirteen thousand reales demanded by the Suprema.[944]

The Suprema itself, despite the contributions which it sought to levy from the tribunals, was in a condition of penury so absolute that, on July 3, 1815, it announced that it had no funds wherewith to pay the salaries of its officials or the postage on the official communications from the tribunals, which must therefore in future arrange with the Post-Office to prepay the postage and settle monthly or quarterly. This, however, as it explained August 19th, applied only to what was addressed to it as, under a decree of May 19, 1799, letters to the inquisitor-general and other heads of councils were carried free.[945]

RESUMPTION OF FUNCTIONS

There was gradual improvement, but it was slow. A carta acordada of September 3, 1818, says that the Suprema cannot view with indifference the deplorable financial condition of nearly all the tribunals, whose diminished revenues force them to allow the meagre salaries of their officials to fall into arrears, nor can it close its ears to the clamors of these unfortunates, reduced as they are to the deepest indigence. Seeking for partial remedies, it must insist on the avoidance of all expenses not absolutely indispensable, and the suppression of all superfluous offices. One of these is the notariate of the court of confiscations; when it falls vacant it is not to be filled, and its duties are to be performed by the secretary of sequestrations, whose salary will consequently be raised by fifty ducats. This was a somewhat exiguous conclusion of so solemn an exordium, seeing that the actual work of the tribunals could readily have been performed by less than half the officials who swelled their pay-rolls, but it is not without interest as showing how persistently the old inflated organization was maintained, and was struggling to support itself on the remnants of its once prosperous fortunes. Under such a system, poverty naturally continued to the last. When the Revolution of 1820 broke out, and the Seville tribunal contributed six thousand reales to the committee organized to resist the rising, it had no funds and was obliged to borrow the money on interest. As almost the first act of the successful revolutionists was to suppress the Inquisition, the lenders in this case doubtless found themselves to be involuntary contributors.[946] At this time the Seville tribunal had a force of twenty-eight officials, with a pay-roll of 92,300 reales, while the amount of its work may be gathered from the fact that the revolutionists found only three prisoners to release.[947]

***

Thus amid difficulties and tribulations the tribunals one by one resumed their functions. In October, 1814, Seville was prosecuting Lt. Colonel Lorenzo del Castillo for propositions; Saragossa was receiving the self-denunciation of Mathias Pintado, priest of Bujanuelo, for heregia mista, and Valencia was suspending the sumaria of the Capuchin Fray Pablo de Altea for mala doctrina, while in December Murcia was prosecuting Don Josef de Zayas, a prominent lieutenant-general of the royal army, for Free-Masonry.[948] Business, however, at the first was scanty. In the book of secret votes of the Suprema, there is an interval from December 22, 1814, until February 16, 1815. As the months of 1815 passed on, the breaks grow shorter and, by the summer of 1815, the decrees follow each other closely. Valladolid seems to have been dilatory in getting to work for, although it had three inquisitors drawing salary, no case came up from it until January, 1817, and, from this one it would seem that it had not been in operation until October, 1816.[949]

The prosecution of such a man as Zayas shows that the reorganized Inquisition did not hesitate to grapple with those in high place, and another early case illustrates this still more forcibly. During the French occupation the Duke and Duchess of Sotomayor and the Countess of Mora had obtained possession of the books and indecent pictures accumulated in the Madrid tribunal. Apparently they refused to surrender them; the tribunal prosecuted them and rendered a sentence, subject to the royal permission, that these objects should be seized, but in such a manner as not to attract attention or to provoke resentment. The Suprema confirmed the sentence, ordering its execution by a single inquisitor, accompanied by a secretary, so as to reconcile the respect due to the parties with the secrecy that was essential.[950]

A politic act was the issue of a general pardon for all that had "impiously and scandalously" been uttered and done against the Inquisition under the fatal circumstances of the recent troubles.[951] It could afford to assume this attitude of magnanimity, seeing that the Government was pitilessly avenging it on its most prominent adversaries. When the Government failed in this duty, the Inquisition had no hesitation in nullifying its edict of pardon. We have seen its prosecution of Ruiz de Padron, until it found that the Bishop of Astorga was rendering this superfluous, nor was this by any means an isolated case. In August, 1815, we find the Suprema acting on sumarias from Canaries, in the cases of Mariano

Romero, a priest, for a sonnet against the Inquisition, and of Francisco Guerra for a sonnet and an epitaph of the same character. So, in November, 1815, there is a prosecution of the Duke of Parque Castrillo for congratulating the Córtes on the abolition of the Inquisition and for a general order to the troops, December 2, 1812. His case dragged on until June 10, 1817, when its suspension was ordered.[952]

FERNANDO'S FAVOR

Yet it was not easy to revive the old-time veneration for an institution that had been so buffeted and roughly handled by the press and the Córtes. A couple of cases in Madrid, in 1814, of women in whose shops scandalous pictures and objects were exhibited, would seem to indicate that its commands were not obeyed with alacrity.[953] It was doubtless with a view of overcoming this indifference that Fernando himself assumed the office of an inquisitor, February 3, 1815, when he visited the Suprema, presided over its deliberations and participated in its decisions, examined all the offices and expressed his royal satisfaction with the methods of procedure. By royal permission the Suprema sent its president and three members to return the visit and express its gratitude for a mark of royal favor such as Ferdinand the Catholic nor any of his successors had ever made. A full report was printed in the Gaceta of February 16th, copies of which the Suprema sent to the tribunals with orders to read it to the officials and place it in the archives.[954] With the same purpose, he erected, as we have seen, the Congregation of San Pedro Martir to a knightly Order, with a habit and badge and, on April 6th, the feast of St. Peter Martyr, he presided over the Congregation, with his brothers Carlos and Antonio, wearing the insignia. In communicating this to the tribunals, the Suprema rendered it especially impressive by ordering them to commence the payment of salaries earned since July 21st and to continue it monthly.[955] Noble courtiers doubtless found that assuming office in the Inquisition was an avenue to royal favor, and we speedily see many of them submitting their genealogies for this purpose. The great Duke of Berwick and Alva, Fitzjames Stuart Silva Stolberg y Palafox, thus seeks the office of alguazil mayor of the tribunal of Córdova; the Marquis of Altamira does the same for the position of honorary secretary in that of Madrid, and we happen to hear of the Count of Mazeda, a grandee of the first class, serving as alguazil mayor of the tribunal of Santiago, and the Marquis of Iscar as honorary secretary to the Suprema.[956]

In spite of all this, the Inquisition could not regain its former position. Not only was it not respected but it dared not to enforce respect. Two Edicts of Grace for Free-Masons were issued, January 2d and February 12, 1815, when the Valladolid tribunal sent those for Medina del Campo and its district to its commissioner Victor González to be posted. The vicar-general and Ordinary, Doctor Josef Suárez Talavera, as ecclesiastical judge, demanded that they should pass through his hands, and when they were posted they bore the MS. subscription "Fixese, Doctor Suárez," thus assuming that it was by his permission, and arrogating to himself a jurisdiction superior to that of the Inquisition. When this was reported to the tribunal it ordered González to take them down and replace them with unsullied ones, which he did. Thereupon Suárez sent him word that, but for starting on a journey, he would make him repent and that, had he known of his being in Medina he would have cast him in prison and seen who could get him out. The tribunal meekly swallowed this flagrant insult; it was under instructions to perform no act indicating jurisdiction superior to that of the Ordinaries, so it quietly gathered evidence verifying the facts and sent the papers, September 15th, to the Suprema.[957]

The Inquisition recognized and felt acutely its altered position. In a report to the king on the subject of visitos de navios, made by the Suprema, in 1819, there are repeated confessions of powerlessness; the times are so unfortunate that its regulations fail to effect their object.[958] The same consciousness of weakness is manifest in the conduct of the occasional competencias which still occurred. In such of these as I have had an opportunity of examining there are a studied courtesy and evident desire to avoid giving offence, without wholly abandoning the claims of the Holy Office.

MISGOVERNMENT

To the same cause we may, at least partially, ascribe the marked tendency to mitigation of punishment--except in the case of political offenders--and to avoid all unnecessary hardship and humiliation of culprits. When, in March, 1819, the Madrid tribunal pronounced a severe sentence on Teodoro Bachiller, for propositions, the Suprema moderated it greatly in every way, in order, it said, to make him understand its benignity in taking care of his honor and of the comfort of his family. In January, 1817, Lorenzo Ayllon was tried in Seville for abusing a priest while celebrating mass and endeavoring to snatch away the host--offences for which, of old, he could scarce have escaped the stake, but now he had only absolution ad cautelam, a reprimand, two years of presidio followed by six years of exile, and the Suprema relieved him of the vergüenza which had been included. Even more marked was the case of Diego Blásquez, postmaster of Villanueba de la Serena, who with some others committed the sacrilege of burying a dog with funeral rites. The Llerena tribunal commenced a prosecution and sent the sumaria to the Suprema, which contented itself with ordering a courteous note to be addressed to the secular and ecclesiastical judges, expressing a hope that they would not permit a repetition of such scandals.[959] It would be easy to multiply similar instances, but these will suffice to show how completely, in dealing with offences against the faith, the spirit of the Inquisition had been tamed, and how factitious was the claim that its existence was essential for the preservation of religion, when there were over half a hundred episcopal tribunals perfectly competent to try such offences and perfectly ready to treat them with greater severity.

***

Meanwhile Fernando's reign had continued as it commenced. Under the influence of a camarilla of low-caste and ignoble favorites, who pandered to his vices and enriched themselves by trafficking in offices and in contracts and in justice, his government was a compound of brutality and imbecility, and the affairs of the nation fell into complete disorder. All the abuses that had flourished under Godoy were intensified and coupled with persistent cruel persecution of those designated as Liberals, who filled the gaols through constantly recurring lists of proscriptions. De Martignac, who, as royal commissioner, accompanied the Duke of Angoulême in the invasion of 1823, was a thoroughly well-informed and unprejudiced observer, who after a vigorous description of the misgovernment of Fernando sums up by saying "We can conceive the influence of such a régime on the prosperity of the land, and yet it is difficult to realize the extent of disorder, wretchedness and weakness to which it fell. It was necessary to resort to arbitrary taxes, to exorbitant duties which destroyed commerce, to loans raised without credit. It was impossible to provide for the most pressing necessities of the State; everything was neglected or abandoned; the army was unpaid; the navy, destroyed at Trafalgar, remained in ruins; the administration, destitute of all means of action, did nothing and could do nothing to improve conditions, or even to preserve what there was. From this arose the discontent of the people."[960] It can scarce excite surprise that the crazy enthusiasm of Fernando's welcome in 1814 had evaporated.

THE REVOLUTION OF 1820

During this disastrous period, every year saw an attempt at revolution. In 1814 it was tried at Pampeluna by General Mina, who escaped; in 1815 in Galicia by Porlier, who was executed; in 1816 in Madrid by Richard, who shared the same fate; in 1817 in Catalonia by Lacy, who was shot; in 1818 in Valencia by Vidal, who was put to death. Again in Valencia a plot was formed to break out January 1, 1819, but it was betrayed and thirteen of the conspirators were hanged. O'Donnell, Count of la Bisbal, an able soldier and unscrupulous intriguer, was privy to this, but averted suspicion and was appointed to command an expeditionary force collecting at Cádiz for Buenos Ayres, against the revolted colony. With customary negligence, transports were not provided; the troops lay idle for months, discontent spread and a formidable conspiracy was organized, which counted on la Bisbal's support; he concluded that loyalty was safest and seized the leading plotters, for which he was rewarded with the grand cross of Carlos III., but suspicion arose; he was removed and replaced by the incapable Count of Calderon.

The situation, however, was growing impossible, and revolution was in the air. A portion of the troops were cantoned at las Cabezas de San Juan, a town not far from Cádiz. There, on January 1, 1820, Rafael de Riego, commander of the battalion of Asturias, assembled his men, made an inflammatory harangue, and they all declared for the Constitution. He made a dash for Arcos, where he captured Calderon and three of his generals, effected a junction with the battalions España and Corona, under Colonel Antonio Quiroga, and failed in an attack on Cádiz. Delay and irresolution followed, until January 27th, when Riego, at the head of fifteen hundred men, marched to Algeciras, where he remained until February 7th. Defeated in an attempt on Málaga, he reached Córdova on March 7th, with some five hundred despairing followers. No effort was made to capture them; the garrison and citizens looked on placidly, while Riego refreshed his men and headed for the Sierra Morena; they dropped off during the march and he was left with fifty followers; so far as he was concerned, the movement was a failure.

Henry Charles Lea, LL.D.

REVOLUTION ACCOMPLISHED

Still, its preliminary success had aroused the slumbering elements of discontent. On February 21st revolution broke out at Coruña and spread to Ferrol and Vigo, when the Count of San Roman abandoned Galicia without a struggle. Saragossa followed on March 2d, the captain-general and garrison joining the magistrates and people. When the news reached Barcelona, on March 10th the people rose and sacked the Inquisition, but did no injury to the officials.[961] Within a few days Tarragona, Gerona and Mataró followed the example, the garrisons participating in the movement. In Navarre, Mina's account of the rising shows that there was prearrangement, and that the municipal authorities and military officials were fully in accord. When he reached Pampeluna with a large force, gathered on his way from the border, he found that the revolution had already been peacefully accomplished on March 11th. Meanwhile la Bisbal, seeing that the movement promised success, spared no promises to obtain command of the forces concentrating in la Mancha to put down Riego's rising. He received the appointment and, on reaching Ocaña, he induced the regiment Alejandro to cry "Viva la Constitucion." The revolution was accomplished and was bloodless, save a hideous massacre at Cádiz of the unarmed multitude, perpetrated in cold blood by Don Manuel Freyre.[962]

During the two months of this desultory movement, which prompt action could so readily have suppressed, the court was nerveless and incapable. When the news came of the rising in Galicia, Fernando issued, February 28th, a plaintive appeal, promising amendment. His terror increased as evil tidings came pouring in, and on March 3d he published a decree bewailing the state of the kingdom, and announcing that he had ordered the Council of State to prepare a comprehensive scheme of reform. This was followed, March 6th, by another calling an immediate convocation of Córtes. It was too late; he found himself abandoned by all, even by his Royal Guard, which General Ballesteros reported was planning to retire to Buen Retiro and send a deputation asking him to swear to the Constitution. This was decisive and, on the night of the 7th, he issued another decree announcing his intention to do so. This was received, on the 8th, with popular rejoicings, but, as no further action was taken, an impatient mob, on the 9th, surrounded the palace with seditious cries and threats. The guard was impassive; Fernando was deserted and was absolutely alone when the crowd began to mount the stairs to demand that he should swear to the Constitution, but they were restrained on learning that he had ordered the reassembling of the Ayuntamiento of Madrid as it had existed under the Constitution. Its members were got together and proceeded immediately to the palace, where Fernando received them with warm expressions of affection; he took the required oath of his own free will, and ordered Ballesteros to make the army do the same. A general illumination and bell-ringing for three nights were ordered, and the people dispersed, not, however, without first visiting the Inquisition, releasing the prisoners and scattering the archives. Only two or three prisoners were found and these were political. Rodrigo tells us that the mob wanted them to pose as victims of persecution, but they prudently refused, and a neighboring cobbler was persuaded to exhibit himself as the presiding figure of the celebration.[963]

INQUISITION SUPPRESSED

On the same day, March 9th, Fernando issued a decree abolishing the Inquisition. This bore that, as its existence was incompatible with the Constitution of 1812, for which reason it had, after mature deliberation, been suppressed by the Córtes, and in conformity with the opinion of the Junta this day established, he ordered that, from this day, the Suprema and the Inquisition be suppressed throughout the monarchy, setting at liberty all prisoners confined for political or religious opinions, and transferring, to the bishops in their respective dioceses, their cases to be determined in accordance with the decree of the Córtes.[964] This was followed, March 20th, by a royal order providing for inventories of all property pertaining to the Inquisition, and reviving the decree of February 22, 1813; the Bureau of Public Credit was to take possession of and administer the property, until its destination should be determined by the Córtes shortly to be assembled, while the salaries of officials were to be continued. When the Córtes met, a decree of August 9th included this with other escheated property, to be sold at auction by the Junta nacional de Crédito.[965]

During the slow progress of the Revolution, the Inquisition seems to have been watching events with full consciousness of the fate in store for it if the movement should prove successful. A letter of January 19th, from the Seville tribunal to the Suprema, states that it had delayed the arrests of the Trinitarian, Fray Juan Montes, and of Don Tomás Díaz in consequence, at first of the epidemic, and then of the insurrection, to which the Suprema replied, January 24th, that it left future action to the prudence of the tribunal.[966] Considering how feeble at the time was the demonstration of Riego, this shows that its ultimate consequences were fully apprehended. Still the Inquisition continued at work, but the last case acted upon by the Suprema was its confirmation, February 10th, of a sentence rendered January 28th, by the Toledo tribunal, on Manuel de la Peña Palacios, priest of Ontoba. As the last act of the dreaded Holy Office, after a career of three centuries and a half, it has an interest beyond its inherent trivial character, and it will be found in the Appendix.

At least one liberated prisoner gave expression to his delight at his release. Don Antonio Bernabeu, a priest, had been a member of the Córtes of Cádiz and had been arrested with the others in May, 1814, but seems to have been released in about six months. He was a Jansenist of an extreme type and, in 1813, had printed a pamphlet to prove that the State could seize all ecclesiastical property and reduce the overgrown numbers of the clergy, putting those who were left on moderate salaries. The tract was a terrible indictment of the Church for its greed of accumulation, its neglect of duty and its departure from the old standards in concentrating all power in the pope, which he attributed to the Isidorian Decretals. On his release from prison, December 14, 1814, he hastened to denounce himself for this to the Inquisition and was placed in reclusion. In 1816 he denounced himself a second time for matters at first omitted. The fiscal presented the accusation, April 20, 1817, rather cleverly drawn, for it demanded precise definition of his opinions on the wide range of subjects, in which he charged the Church with deviation from primitive times, and specific proofs of his somewhat vague declamation as to abuses. To satisfy this would require the resources of a large library and years of research, while Bernabeu was confined in a convent and was denied even a copy of his offending pamphlet, besides being exposed to all manner of persecutions by his fellow inmates. His trial was still pending when the decree of March 9th liberated him; he was promptly returned as a deputy to the Córtes of 1820, and he celebrated his release by reprinting his pamphlet, with an account of his sufferings and his answers to the charges of the fiscal.[967]

SUICIDE OF LIBERALISM

It would carry us too far from our subject to recount in detail the extravagancies and follies with which the triumphant Liberals invited the cruel reaction that awaited them. Moderation, perhaps, was scarce to be expected of men, smarting under the persecution of the last six years, and suddenly brought from fortresses and presidios, or from exile, to take charge of the Government, and to frame laws for the nation. That they should in turn persecute their persecutors was natural but impolitic; mutual hatreds were inflamed, and the land was divided into factions between which harmony and forbearance became impossible. The long centuries of despotism and the repression of independent thought and action had rendered the people incapable of the large measure of self-government provided by the Constitution. So-called patriotic societies were rapidly formed--de Lorencini, de San Fernando, la Fontana de Oro, la Cruz de Malta, la Landaburana and others--which in reality were Jacobinical clubs, where the most radical measures were advocated, and the most violent means of effecting them were urged. An unbridled press was busy in adding fuel to the flames and in stimulating the ardor which sought to realize anarchical dreams. Masonry had been busy in preparing the revolution, and with its success Masonry became the avenue to power and place; its lodges multiplied and were rapidly filled. Then, with the progress of advanced ideas, Masonry became too conservative for the exaltados, who left it and established the Comuneros, whose statutes formed a state of revolutionary character within the State. They rivalled the Masons in numbers and influence, and the virulent struggle for supremacy between the two bodies at times paralyzed the Government and neutralized the forces of order. The disorderly element existing in all communities was utilized whenever there was an object to be gained, and mob rule became of frequent occurrence, not only in Madrid but in nearly all the cities. The orders of the Government were obeyed or disregarded as suited the temper of the populace or of its instigators. Officials commissioned as captains-general or governors or magistrates were admitted or rejected; orderly administration was becoming impossible, and everywhere turbulence reigned supreme. Liberalism was committing suicide.

Yet Liberalism had need of its undivided strength to maintain itself against the opposing forces. Fernando, while playing the part of a constitutional king, was constantly plotting to throw off the yoke, and was entertaining secret relations with those who were striving to overthrow the Government. Successive Córtes seemed to take pleasure in exacerbating the hostility of the clergy, whose influence over the mass of the people was unbounded. Much of this legislation was no doubt salutary in itself but, at the moment, it was dangerous, and the blows succeeded each other so rapidly that the sufferers might well regard it as systematic persecution. August 31, 1820, a law organizing the national army exempted from service only such clerics as were actually in holy Orders. One of September 26th subjected all clerics, secular and regular, to secular jurisdiction for offences incurring corporal punishment. Within a week, another decree suppressed a large portion of the monastic Orders, and the Mendicants who were left were subjected to the bishops and consolidated into houses of not less than twelve inmates, and this was followed by other special decrees of suppression. The property of the suppressed houses was applied to the Crédito público and, when Fernando refused his signature, a popular tumult was organized which frightened him into acquiescence. October 26th it was ordered that dispensations for marriage within prohibited degrees should be issued without charge to those applying in forma pauperis, thus cutting off a large source of income. When bands of insurgent royalists began to make their appearance, and were joined or led by priests, the bishops were ordered, April 20, 1821, to report what steps they had taken to punish them and, within eight days, to issue edicts requiring their flocks to obey the law. Then, on June 29th, without papal authority, a contribution of thirty million reales was levied on the clergy and, on the same day, the tithes were reduced one-half, while allowing some compensation in the removal of certain imposts. The clergy, not unnaturally, promoted disaffection, and to check this, decrees of November 1, 1822, authorized the Government, at discretion, to transfer from one place to another all parish priests and ecclesiastics, the cost of maintenance of those thus deported being thrown upon the bishops.[968]

QUARREL WITH THE CHURCH

In fact, the irreconcileable claims of State and Church rendered hostility inevitable. It was impossible for the latter to understand that, when it entered politics and became a political factor, it had to be treated like other political bodies. The theocracy of the middle ages had so long enjoyed power without responsibility that its immunity became part of Latin doctrine. Elsewhere the impracticability of this had been demonstrated, but in Spain the Church has never ceased to struggle for the maintenance of medievalism, or has understood that sedition in the pulpit should not be treated differently from sedition in the tribune. It refused to recognize that self-preservation is the first law of governments as of individuals, and that they cannot allow artificial privileges to work their destruction. The theory of the Liberals was that external ecclesiastical discipline was subject to the civil authority, while internal discipline was reserved to the Church. The Church asserted that in all things it ruled itself, and that any secular interference was a laying of profane hands on the Ark. The gage of battle was virtually thrown by Veremundo Arías, Archbishop of Valencia, who, on October 20, 1820, addressed to the Córtes a long manifesto, upholding all the extreme claims of the Church, and denying the distinction between external and internal discipline. On November 10th he was arrested and, on the 24th, was put on board ship and sent to France. This was the commencement of a persecution in which many bishops suffered. Álvarez de Palma of Granada was set aside and replaced by the liberal Archpriest Vinegas. Uriz y Lafaga of Pampeluna was summoned to Madrid but, on the road, was rescued by royalists and conveyed to France. Blas Beltran of Coria was banished. The Bishop-elect of Santa Marta (Colombia) received his sentence of exile on his death-bed in Plasencia. Cienfuegos of Cádiz had to fly to save his life. Pablo de Sichar of Barcelona fled and remained absent until 1823. Rentería y Reyes of Lérida was carried under guard to Barcelona, narrowly escaped execution, and was detained in Málaga until 1823. Ramon Strauch y Vidal of Vich was imprisoned in Barcelona, then sent to Tarragona and on the road, under a pretext, was made to descend and was shot with his attendant. Others who were exiled were Jaime Creus of Tarragona, Ceruelo de la Fuente of Oviedo, Rafael de Velez of Ceuta and Castillon y Salas of Tarazona.[969] It is true that the worst of these acts were committed by mobs or irresponsible parties in the growing disorders of the times, but they remained unrebuked and unpunished.

A government which thus treated its clergy was not likely to maintain friendly relations with the Holy See. One of the earliest measures of the new government was an act of August 17, 1820, suppressing the Jesuits.[970] Pius VII met this with a letter of September 16th to Fernando, deploring the perils that threatened religion and the Church and reciting the obnoxious measures taken, for which he had ordered his nuncio to make reclamation, but without effect.[971] Relations were not improved when, April 21, 1821, a decree suppressed all payments, whether in money or other equivalent, for papal bulls for archbishops, bishops, matrimonial dispensations and other rescripts, in lieu of which the paltry annual sum of 9000 silver dollars was offered.[972] This was unwise but still more so was the sending to Rome as ambassador of Joaquin Lorenzo Villanueva, towards the close of 1822, when the intervention of the Holy Alliance was impending. At Turin he was met by a papal order forbidding him to come further and asking the ministry to appoint some one else. Evaristo San Miguel, the Secretary of State, insisted; the papal foreign secretary replied that the opinions expressed by Villanueva in the "Cartas de Don Roque Leal" and in the Córtes were such that the Holy See could never receive him. To this the answer was to send to the nuncio his passports with orders to leave Spain. The rupture with Rome was complete and, in the eyes of pious Spaniards, the government had justified the clerical definition of the Constitution as heresy.[973]

The clerical temper thus stimulated is fairly exhibited in a little pamphlet by Padre Miguel Canto, parish priest of Callosa de Segura, celebrating the downfall of Constitutionalism. He is fairly drunk with joy and consigns the Liberals to the bottomless pit for eternity with vigorous delight. That the civil power should dare to assume any control over the externals of the Church fills him with astonishment and rage, all the greater in view of the suffering which it inflicted, especially on the regulars. Canto tells us that the fabric of his church had enjoyed a revenue of four thousand pesos, and that it was reduced to such poverty that he had not wherewith to provide wafers and wine for the sacrament, or oil for the lamps.[974] Yet the resources of the Spanish Church were such that it still had ample funds for political uses. When, in October, 1823, after his release by the French, Fernando travelled from Cádiz to Madrid, he received in voluntary offerings from the chapters of Toledo, Seville, Granada, Jaen and Cuenca, 11,970,000 reales in silver, although the land was in a condition of complete exhaustion.[975]

DEVELOPMENT OF REVOLT

It is not difficult to believe that the pulpit and the confessional were energetically used to inflame and organize the disaffection that rapidly succeeded to the enthusiasm for the Constitution. The new administration was no more efficient than the old. Ministries, hampered with the underhand intrigues of the king, perpetually guarding against eager rivals, and speedily engrossed with suppressing the armed resistance springing up on every hand, had little opportunity of rectifying the abuses which had made Fernando unpopular. To the people at large the only visible result of the revolution was that the Liberals in turn were persecuting the Serviles. The nobles, moreover were alienated by the suppression of Mayorazgos and Vinculaciones, or entails and perpetual charges on lands, a reform which had long been urged by statesmen such as Jovellanos.[976] Willing and receptive listeners to clerical invective were abundant, and movements to overthrow the Government speedily began taking shape. Before the year 1820 was out, in Galicia there was organized a Junta Apostólica and in Burgos there was a crazy conspiracy of some frailes and a general.[977] Soon wandering bands of insurgents sprang up, among whom members of the clergy were conspicuous, as though it was a holy war. Suppressed in one place, they appeared in another, waging a guerrilla warfare like that against Napoleon. The land was torn with faction, and Liberals and Royalists seemed to emulate each other in contributing to its ruin. Early in July, 1822, the royal guards, with the secret connivance of the king, endeavored to gain possession of Madrid; after a sanguinary conflict in the streets they were defeated, when Fernando, from a balcony of his palace, stimulated the nationals in pursuit of the flying wretches. Civil broils are apt to be pitiless, but in Spain they assumed a ferocity not often witnessed elsewhere. If the Royalists in Catalonia massacred in cold blood the garrison of the Seo de Urgel, a Liberal noyade in Coruña despatched fifty-one political prisoners, many of them ecclesiastics and persons of distinction.[978]

The revolt was constantly assuming proportions more alarming, especially in Catalonia, where it had the almost unanimous support of the peasantry. The insurrectionary bands coalesced into a force of five thousand men styling itself the Army of the Faith which, on June 21, 1822, captured the Seo de Urgel and made it their stronghold. There, on August 15th, was organized a royalist Regency, composed of Creus, the exiled Archbishop of Tarragona, the Baron of Eroles, a soldier of some reputation, and the Marquis of Mataflorida. The Counter-revolution thus adopted a public and official character; the Regency assumed to speak for the king, held in durance by the Jacobins--in fact, as early as June 1st he had authorized Mataflorida to organize it, and was in constant communication with it, through one of the officials of the court. It obtained quasi-recognition abroad; it negotiated a loan of 8,000,000 with the Parisian capitalist Ouvrard and, with the support of Pius VII, it opened negotiations with Austria and Russia, offering surrenders of territory in exchange for aid.[979]

Spain was rapidly drifting into anarchy. The Government was too weak to suppress disorder, whether committed by friends or foes. Compromise between the factions was not to be hoped for, and even patriots could see that the only path to order lay through intervention from abroad. That this was impending became more and more evident. The example of Spain had been followed by Naples and Portugal, and then by Piedmont, in forcing on their sovereigns constitutions like that of 1812; the Holy Alliance took the alarm; the Congresses of Troppau in 1820 and of Laybach in 1821 ordered armed intervention, and the new institutions of Naples and Piedmont were readily overthrown. In May, 1821, communications from Russia to Spain, and a Russian circular to the courts of Europe, openly expressed dissatisfaction at the success of armed rebellion, with scarcely veiled threats of action in case the Córtes should prove disobedient to the monarch; and the conflict with the royal guard, in July 1822, gave the foreign ministers in Madrid a pretext for warnings which were diplomatically veiled threats of intervention.[980] Preparations for it were already on foot in France. An epidemic of yellow fever in Barcelona served as an excuse for establishing a cordon sanitaire on the border, gradually strengthened until it became an army of observation and in reality a support for the Catalan insurgents, as Mina found when he conducted a successful campaign which in the beginning of 1823 forced the Regency to take refuge in France.[981]

Henry Charles Lea, LL.D.

INTERVENTION OF THE HOLY ALLIANCE

The Congress of Verona met in the autumn of 1822. The Urgel Regency sent there the Count de España as its representative to urge that Spain should be restored to the condition prior to March 9, 1820; the Government sent no envoy, relying on the friendly aid of England, represented by the Duke of Wellington. Without his knowledge the Allied Powers signed, on November 22d, a secret treaty, in which they declared against the sovereignty of the people, representative government and the freedom of the press, and in favor of the clergy as an instrument for enforcing the passive obedience of the subject; and each signatory pledged itself to a subsidy of twenty millions of francs annually to France, to which was assigned the duty of suppressing these destructive principles in Spain and Portugal, and of restoring the Peninsula to the conditions prior to 1820.[982] Even yet intervention was not certain, for France was not eager for the task, and there were some negotiations looking to modifications of the Constitution, but the Liberals would not listen to such suggestions. Châteaubriand, however, that curious compound of idealism, bombast and vanity, who, as French foreign minister and representative at Verona, takes to himself all the credit for the enterprise, is especially careful to point out that its real object was the restoration of France to the hegemony of the Continent, after the abasement of the Restoration by foreign bayonets--an object which he assumes was fully accomplished.[983]

Early in January, 1823, four notes from the Allies were presented collectively, offering, in more or less offensive fashion, the alternative of a return to absolutism or invasion.[984] These portentous communications were received with the utmost nonchalance. On the night of their reception, Secretary of State San Miguel carried them to the Grand Orient and drew up his replies, in which Fernando is said to have cunningly stimulated defiance to banded Europe. Whatever might be the decision of France, San Miguel said, Spain would tranquilly follow the path of duty and justice; its rule of conduct would be firm adhesion to the Constitution of 1812 and refusal to recognize the right of intervention on any side.[985]

These would be dignified and resolute words in a united nation facing a coalition but, under the circumstances, they were mere idle vaporing. The Government, in fact, was barely able to make head against the insurrection, save in Catalonia. Navarre, Biscay and Aragon were in open civil war, with forces equally balanced. In Murcia, the famous robber Jaime Alfonso was posing as the defender of the faith; in Castile, the Cura Merino and el Rojo de Valderas were levying war; in Andalusia, Zaldivar held his own in spite of repeated defeats; in Toledo and Cuenca, Joaquincillo and the Cura Atanasio were maintaining the rebellion; in Sigüenza the insurrection of Cuesta was organizing and was soon to break out. In short, the whole of Spain was in convulsion.[986]

The only explanation of the attitude of the Liberals is that they were living in a fool's paradise, and seem to have welcomed intervention in the belief that it would kindle national feeling and restore national unity. Hallucination was carried to the point that they anticipated a popular rising like that of 1808, that the forty thousand insurgents in arms would turn against the invader, even that the French troops would abandon their standards for those of Spain, and that England, which had calmly seen the Constitution overthrown in 1814, would provoke a war with all Europe in its defence. They closed their eyes to the fact that, in 1808, the clergy aroused the masses against the French and were now their warmest allies, eager to revenge systematic persecution; that the throne was secretly undermining them, and that they were without resources, for the treasury was exhausted, the army scarce existed save on paper, the magazines were empty, and the party in power was rent into bitterly opposing factions. A kind of delirium seized the deputies when San Miguel on January 9th laid the correspondence before the Córtes, and his replies were clamorously approved without distinction of party.[987]

THE FRENCH INVASION

Yet this effervescence soon subsided. A decisive victory gained by the insurgents at Brihuega, not far from Madrid, on January 24th, threw the capital into a tremor and, on February 16th, the Córtes adopted a decree looking to the transfer of the Government in case of necessity.[988] New Córtes opened their sessions March 1st and their first thought was to place themselves in safety, carrying with them Fernando, both as a hostage and as necessary to the assumption that the government of Spain travelled with them. Resistance on his part postponed the move until March 20th, when the exodus to Seville took place. There they remained until June, when the approach of the French necessitated a further flight and, on the 9th, Cádiz was selected as the place of refuge. This time Fernando resolutely refused to fly from his liberators and, as coercion of the monarch was incompatible with the theory that he was still governing, it was assumed that he was incapacitated by reason of a temporary delirium; he was deposed and a Regency was appointed which ordered the transfer to Cádiz; on the 12th the king and royal family left Seville; the Córtes adjourned to meet in Cádiz June 18th; in four days Fernando was declared to be again in his right mind and the Regency resigned. The spectacle of a flying Government dragging with it a captive king, whom it recognized as still actively reigning, was worse than ludicrous; it gave to Fernando a claim on the sympathy which he had forfeited, and served as an incentive and an excuse for cruel reprisals.[989]

Meanwhile the army of invasion had been gathering on the border under the Duke of Angoulême, nephew of Louis XIV. From Bayonne, on April 2d, he issued a manifesto to the effect that he did not come to make war but to liberate a captive king, to restore the Altar and the Throne, to release the priesthood from exile, and the whole people from a domination that was preparing the destruction of Spain. On April 7th the army crossed the Bidassoa, consisting of 91,000 men, of whom 35,000 were Spanish royalists. Its discipline was perfect and its conduct admirable. Everywhere it was received as a liberator, with cries of "Viva el Rey absoluto, Viva la Religion y la Inquisicion." Resistance was impossible and, although five armies had been organized, none worthy of mention was attempted, except in Catalonia, where the indomitable Mina prolonged the useless struggle until November, and at Cádiz, where the so-called Government was battling for existence. Siege was laid there on June 23d, and was prolonged until October 1st, when Fernando was ceremoniously conveyed to the camp of his French deliverers. Yet, if rhetoric could have repelled the invaders, they would have been glad to escape from the eloquence which accompanied a solemn declaration of war on April 29th, when Flórez Calderon boasted that the breasts of the deputies would make an impenetrable rampart around the constitutional King and his family.[990]

If the French came as pacifiers, they made a mistake in bringing with them a Junta Provisional of four rabid royalists, formally installed at Ozarzun, April 9th. It assumed to be the Government and issued a manifesto rescinding all the acts of the Revolution and restoring the conditions prior to March 7, 1820.[991] It used its authority in such unsparing proscriptions that even the royalists became alarmed and appealed to de Martignac, the royal commissioner accompanying Angoulême, pointing out the evils to be apprehended from such ferocity. Quarrels within the Junta afforded an excuse for superseding it, and Angoulême, on reaching Madrid, empowered the Councils of Castile and Indias to nominate a Regency, at the head of which was the Duke del Infantado. This body, on June 4th, published a manifesto promising to use its power to prevent persecutions and excesses, to maintain internal peace, execute the laws and make the royal power respected.[992]

These were fair words, belied by acts. The whole arrangement had been dictated by secret instructions from Fernando, and proscription and persecution continued as active as ever. The Regency confirmed a measure of the Junta organizing bodies of so-called Royalist Volunteers, whose duties consisted in arresting and imprisoning all whom greed or malevolence might designate as objects of suspicion, in which work they were aided by the mob, always ready for violence and rapine. In Saragossa fifteen hundred persons were dragged to prison by the populace led by priests and frailes. In Navarre, the guerrilla chief known as el Trapense committed revolting excesses. In Madrid and Córdova the gaols were crowded with prisoners. This work went on in most of the towns, as the national forces retreated, the victims being mostly citizens of wealth and position, while the pulpits resounded with exhortations to persecution and extermination and the French troops, in so far as they could, restrained the outrages.[993]

RELEASE OF FERNANDO

Despite his reluctance to interfere, Angoulême felt called upon to put an end to the cruelty and impolicy of these persecutions and, on his way to Cádiz, he issued from Andujar, August 8th, a decree forbidding arrests by the Spanish authorities without authorization from the commandants of the troops of the districts, who were instructed to liberate all political prisoners, and to arrest those who contravened these orders, while all periodicals were subjected to the inspection of the commandants. The foreign ministers, however, protested against this as an invasion of Spanish independence, which emboldened the Regency to remonstrate in a haughty and insolent manner. The Royalist Volunteers of Navarre, in a manifesto of August 20th, were prodigal of insults and menaces to the duke; a memorial addressed to him, August 23d, signed by Eguia and a large number of military chiefs and priests, stigmatized his effort at pacification as an attempt to perpetuate an impious faction, and demanded the restoration of the Inquisition. Wherever there were no French troops the decree was ignored and finally Angoulême, whether instructed by his court or afraid openly to oppose the Regency, issued an explanatory order, which virtually annulled the decree. Evidently there was to be no peace for the distracted land.[994] Even the Regency felt it necessary to disclaim responsibility for the horrors enacting on every hand. August 10th, it ordered the prosecution of the rioters who, at Alcalá, Guadalajara and Torrejon had committed terrible excesses under pretext of avenging the transfer of the king to Cádiz and, on August 13th, it commanded the people to restrain their zeal in making arrests but, while it was powerful to excite passion it was powerless to enforce order.[995]

When, in view of the hopelessness of further resistance at Cádiz, Fernando was informed, September 28th, that he was at liberty to seek the French camp, a tumult arose and a demand for guarantees. He summoned the ministers, telling them that he desired to give assurances and ordering José María Calatrava to draw up a decree declaring of his own free will and, on the faith of his royal word, that he would adopt a form of government assuring the happiness of the nation, the personal security, the property and the civil liberty of Spaniards, with complete oblivion of the past. The amnesty was rendered complete with elaborate details and, when it was presented to him for signature on the 30th, he said that, to remove all doubts, he would make some changes with his own hand, which he accordingly did, rendering some of the clauses clearer and more emphatic.[996] When, on the next day, he was received by Angoulême, he shut himself up with the Duke del Infantado and Victor Damien Saez, his former confessor, whom he appointed universal minister and, before the colloquy was over, there was drawn up and signed a decree of two articles; the first declared null and void all acts since March 7, 1820; the second confirmed the proscriptions of the Junta of Ozarzun and the Regency. Printed copies of this, together with that of the day before, were circulated to the no small perplexity of all concerned. Then General Bourmont, the French commander, learned that Ferdinand had passed secret sentence of death on some prominent liberals there present, whereupon they were conveyed on naval vessels to Gibraltar and saved from his sanguinary vengeance. This was but a foretaste of the wrath to come.[997] Prescriptive and oppressive measures followed each other and the persecution inaugurated by the Regency was sharpened and systematized.

TEN YEARS OF REACTION

The French had already discovered that they had raised a demon whom they could not exorcise. They had restored unconditionally to absolute power a prince who was utterly faithless, whom no promises could bind, who cared only for the gratification of his passions, and who was surrounded by vindictive counsellors, eager for the blood and spoils of their countrymen. The prisons were crowded to repletion and the untamed ferocity of the multitude, stimulated by the pulpit, was let loose upon defenceless victims. It was a scandal in the face of all Europe and was felt acutely. Effort was made to repair the mischief, but with scant success. Fernando, on leaving Cádiz, had written to Louis XVIII, expressing his gratitude, and Louis seized the opportunity, in his reply, to impress on him his own example and that of their ancestor Henry IV, as the only means of bringing peace to a distracted land, warning him that a blind despotism weakened instead of strengthening royal power. Angoulême had manifested his disapprobation of the decree of October 1st, and a coolness arose between him and Fernando, which went on increasing. They parted, October 11th, Angoulême refusing all honors on his homeward journey, and leaving Bourmont in command. The French army was gradually reduced, but the last detachments did not leave Spain until November, 1827.

CHÂTEAUBRIAND'S FAILURE

Secure in this protection, Fernando was deaf to remonstrances. It is true that, when the ambassadors of the powers met him in Seville, under their pressure, he issued a decree, October 22d, holding out expectations of what he would do on reaching Madrid, but promises cost him nothing and these were as futile as those of September 30th. To emphasize the necessity of conciliation, the French cabinet prevailed upon the Russian ambassador, Pozzo di Borgo, to visit Madrid, in the name of the Holy Alliance. He arrived there October 28th and held long conferences with Fernando and Victor Saez, urging clemency and a general amnesty, but he met, in reply, with nothing but vague generalizations.[998]

If the welfare of a nation had not been at stake, the reflections of Châteaubriand on the success of his enterprise, and his correspondence with Talaru, the French ambassador, might well raise a smile. He was disgusted, he said, with having to do with a monarch who would burn his kingdom in a cigar, and he declared that the sovereigns of today seem specially created to destroy a society ready to perish. In Spain, the political sore is the king and it is almost impossible to apply a remedy. At first he assumed that he could dictate a policy, and asserted that he would not tolerate the follies of the king nor allow France to appear as an accomplice in stupidity and fanaticism. Talaru was to speak as a master; if the ministry was not to his mind, he was to have it changed, the threatened withdrawal of the troops being what would force Fernando to listen to reason. He soon found, however, that behind the ministry was the camarilla--the real power that could not be dislodged--and that the clergy was also a body to be reckoned with. Châteaubriand's effervescence wore itself out against the impenetrability to reason and argument of Fernando and his advisers, and his demands shrank to asking for a decree of amnesty--it would be badly framed, he knew, but at least it would have the appearance of doing something. After months of urgency, at last Fernando agreed to it. A fairly liberal scheme was drawn up but, after it had been submitted to the revision of the friends of Don Carlos, of the bishops, of the secret Junta de Estado and of the Council of Castile, its framers could scarce recognize it. While it offered pardon to all participants in the disturbances since 1820 in support of the Constitution, there were fifteen excepted classes, some of them vague and comprehensive. It ordered the discharge of all prisoners not comprised within the exceptions, but this was not obeyed. It ordered the bishops to contribute to bring about union, but few of them did so. It was dated May 1, 1824, but was not published until the 20th, and the interval was employed all over Spain in gathering evidence to bring individuals under the excepted classes, so that they could be arrested simultaneously with the publication of the decree; the prisons were filled with new victims, and the courts were overwhelmed with prosecutions. The courts, moreover, were supplemented with military commissions, whose procedure was informal and summary. The Gaceta de Madrid, between August 24th and October 12, 1824, chronicled 112 executions by shooting or hanging. Whatever scanty favor was shown to Liberals in the decree was more than counterbalanced by another of July 1st, granting pardon for all assaults and injuries committed on them or their property except when murder had resulted.[999] The Royalist Volunteers thus had full licence, and the Liberals were virtually outlawed.

DEMANDS FOR THE INQUISITION

Proscription and persecution were systematized in a manner without precedent, by the compilation of lists of all suspects. During the constitutional period, Fernando had kept a Libro Verde, noting down the names of all who displeased him, thus marking them for future vengeance. On his restoration to power, a secret Junta de Estado, consisting chiefly of ecclesiastics, was formed, whose business it was to gather information against all who were opposed to absolutism. Denunciations were invited from priests and frailes, from enemies and from the lowest class of informers, to whom inviolable secrecy was promised, and all the scandal and false evidence thus accumulated was recorded opposite the name of the party, for use as occasion might require. The list was divided into districts, and copies were sent to the respective intendants of police, who contributed such further names and charges as they could gather from all sources however vile. Thus every man's liberty and property were at the mercy of secret and irresponsible informers. It was a Libro Verde on a scale which the Inquisition itself had never imagined, and the system was more thorough and more dangerous to the innocent than that of the Inquisition.[1000] Such was the condition of Spain during the terrible ten years, from 1823 to 1833, known as the Epocha de Chaperon--Chaperon being the president of the military commission of Madrid and notorious for his cruelty.

One result of this is well set forth in a singularly outspoken representation addressed by Javier de Burgos to Fernando, January 24, 1826. He had been sent to Paris to negotiate a loan, and he ascribes his failure, not so much to the poverty of the land, as to the absence of peace essential to prosperity, and this arose from the successive proscriptions which had desolated Spain. Now, he says, simple police orders deprive of common rights whole classes, and subject them to penalties which in well-ordered countries can be inflicted only by tribunals. Much is said of the league of European bankers against Spanish credit, but this has only been made invincible by the efforts of the six or eight thousand proscribed exiles in England, France and Belgium. A few days ago the journal which represents commerce and industry said "As for Spain, it continues to fall rapidly into barbarism. It is a second Turkey, only more miserable and worse governed." Mexico, Colombia, Peru and Chile obtain loans, even though their independence is not recognized, but Spain cannot get a maravedí.[1001] It is creditable to Fernando that he took this plain-speaking good-naturedly and subsequently gave the writer the cross of Carlos III, but he was impervious to the good advice.

***

The decrees of the Regency and of Fernando, restoring the conditions prior to March 7, 1820, and invalidating all subsequent acts, seemed necessarily to revive the Inquisition. Its officials, however, hesitated to resume their functions without positive orders, and it was known that the French were opposed to its restoration. Numerous petitions for it were made to Angoulême, but he evaded categorical replies, saying that he would procure the liberation of the king and leave him to determine what would best promote the happiness of the nation.[1002] After Fernando's release, felicitations came pouring in, warmly thanking him for his proscriptive measures and among these were many urging that the Inquisition should be set to work. If, at the moment, he desired to meet these wishes, he was restrained by the earnest opposition of the Allies, who especially shrank from the responsibility of resuscitating an institution so universally abhorred. As Châteaubriand wrote to Talaru, December 1st, "We will not permit our victories to be dishonored by proscriptions or that the fires of the Inquisition be raised as altars to our triumphs" and, on December 11th, he declared it to be necessary that the royal confessor should not be an inquisitor.[1003]

Fernando, however, seems already to have questioned whether the Inquisition would really be of service to him politically and, as religion with him was merely a matter of policy, he preferred to let the question slumber, without committing himself. It is related that once, when a bishop of extreme views was urging upon him the utility which the Inquisition had always been to the crown, he walked across the room to a balcony and, looking up at the serene sky, exclaimed "What a cloud! a great storm is coming."[1004] His intentions, however, were indirectly manifested, by a decree of January 1, 1824, which withdrew from the Crédito público the administration of the property of the Inquisition and placed it with the Colector-general de Espolios, who was charged to pay the salaries of all the officials of the tribunals.[1005] This indicated that there was no intention to restore the institution to activity, and to this Fernando adhered, notwithstanding the urgency which continued.

THE INQUISITION DORMANT

In fact, as the reaction established itself, Fernando could not but recognize that he had nothing to gain from the Inquisition and might risk something. His one object was unlimited absolutism. Circumstances had enabled him to attain this to a degree which none of his predecessors had enjoyed. The defeat of the Liberals was so complete, and the servility of the Royalists so great, that he could disregard whatever remnants of the old Spanish institutions had still placed some restraints on the crown. There was no secret made of this. A royal order of October 17, 1824, destroyed at a blow all the municipal self-government of Spain; the Ayuntamientos of the towns were no longer to be elective; those in office were to choose their successors in thirds at a time, and the appointees were subjected to revision by the royal Audiencias while, in the preamble, the object of this was openly stated to be that there should disappear for ever from Spanish soil the most remote idea that sovereignty resided elsewhere than in the royal person, and the people should know that not the slightest alteration would ever be made in the fundamental laws of the monarchy.[1006]

The only claim of the Inquisition to efficiency, greater than that of the police and royal tribunals, was in its delegated faculties from the pope and, to a monarch thus resolved to concentrate in his own hands all power, it was naturally distasteful to employ for political ends foreign authority which, nominally at least, was not under his own control. This objection he might have disregarded, if he had reason to expect from the Inquisition any special service, but such there was not. While there still was law in Spain the Inquisition might be useful as being above the law, but now that law was merely the sic volo, sic jubeo, the Inquisition was superfluous, while its secret procedure was more tardy and cumbrous--perhaps even less certain--than that of the military commissions; and the system described above of lists of suspects with evidence gathered from every source by thousands of informers was far more comprehensive in plan and in detail than anything that the inquisitorial organization had ever attempted.

The Inquisition thus had nothing to offer and, careless as was Fernando of the public opinion of Europe, even he could recognize the wisdom of avoiding the odium of re-establishing an institution so generally condemned. To the victims it made little difference whether their judges were called military commissioners or inquisitors; their offences were justiciable by either, for the pulpits resounded with the doctrine that all Constitutionalists and Liberals were Jansenists and heretics--a doctrine justified by a royal order of May 2, 1824, to the bishops, requiring them to celebrate, in their dioceses, Missions calling the Liberals to repentance.[1007]

Yet there was a lurking Jansenism in this tacit assumption that the regalías enabled the king to prolong at his pleasure that suppression of the Holy Office which, in 1813, had been proved by learned theologians to be in violation of the canons and of the authority of the Holy See. The clerical party was restless and dissatisfied, the more so because, as Fernando's theory of government was to render his own power secure by promoting discord among his followers, he occasionally favored the moderate Royalists against the extremists. The latter were not content even with the prevailing cruel persecution, and longed for one more searching with the Inquisition as its instrument. The secret organization known as the Junta Apostólica, or Angel Exterminador, had cast its eyes upon Don Carlos as a leader who could realize their aspirations, for he was completely under priestly influence and belonged to the extreme faction, besides being heir presumptive in the probable case of Fernando dying without issue. Carlos, however, though not a man of strong character, was strictly honorable and was bound to Fernando with ties of a mutual affection which endured to the end. He was quite content to await the chances of succession, but his wife Francisca of Portugal and her sister the Princess of Beira, widow of the Infante Pedro, were ambitious. His apartments in the royal palace were the centre of intrigues, in which he did not personally participate, while Fernando who, through his spies, was kept informed of them, did not interfere, confiding in his brother's loyalty and his own ability to crush attempts against himself.

A History of the Inquisition of Spain: Volume IV
RISING IN CATALONIA

In 1824 and 1825 there were movements and risings of the extremists in various provinces, which indicated concerted action and were suppressed with more or less facility, except in Catalonia. There the hidden leaders of the conspiracy found a population discontented with what they deemed the lukewarmness of the Government, which they were told was now controlled by Free-Masons. The old members of the Army of the Faith, moreover, deemed themselves insufficiently rewarded for their services, and organized under the name of Agraviados, forming the nucleus of a "Federacion de Realistas puros," more royalist than the king. Towards the end of 1826 there was circulated a manifesto from the Federation urging the necessity of placing Don Carlos on the throne; its organization rapidly extended, and April 1, 1827, was appointed for the rising, which was readily suppressed and a free pardon was granted to the insurgents. The pacification was but temporary. In July, at Manresa, a Junta superior was formed, and in August the tolling of the bells summoned the somatenes or levies en masse to arms, when a portion of the troops joined the insurrection, which was soon supreme in Catalonia. A report made, August 27th, by Dehesa, fiscal of the court of Barcelona, states that the war-cry of the insurgents was "Long live the Inquisition! Death to the Constitution! Death to the negros! Death to the police!" They were told that the rising was by order of the pope and that the king was surrounded by Free-Masons; it was supposed to be the work of the clergy, who desired the re-establishment of the Inquisition, and to make themselves all-powerful by working on the fanaticism of the ignorant mountaineers.[1008]

That the situation was becoming dangerous is manifested by the only kingly act in Fernando's record, for he resolved to visit Catalonia himself, after sending the Count de España there with full powers. He reached Tarragona September 28th, being received everywhere with enthusiasm, though there was an abortive project of abducting him by a large body of Royalist Volunteers assembled as though to do him honor. From Tarragona he issued a proclamation to the effect that those who should not lay down their arms within twenty-four hours must expect no mercy, and that he would deal with their leaders as he saw fit. The secret societies had already issued orders of pacification; organized resistance was abandoned, nine of the chiefs were hanged and the land was speedily at peace. Carlos took no part in the rising, but he knew of the plans and had not opposed them, and the name of Carlists was thereafter used to designate the extreme royalists.[1009]

It is significant that, when Fernando ordered the bishops to exhort their subjects to peace, some of them obeyed, but Pablo de Jesus de Corcuera y Caserta, the prelate of Vich, refused in a letter of October 6th, on the ground that he could not conscientiously do so. Fernando, he said, had not kept his promises; he had assembled a junta to examine all books in circulation, yet poisonous ones, like that of Thomas à Kempis, were allowed to be read; he had ordered the restoration of everything to the conditions prior to March 7, 1820, yet the Inquisition had not been re-established; other royal shortcomings were pointed out and, in the face of all this it was impossible for a bishop not to take part in temporal matters; to preach obedience as required would be to compromise the episcopate and to become the instrument of the enemies of God, nor would it avail anything, for it would be impossible to make the people think otherwise. These outspoken sentiments of the fiery bishop explain much that is saddest in modern Spanish history; he was not punished for them but, when the Count de España came to Vich he summoned the recalcitrant prelate before him and reminded him of the fate of Acuña of Zamora, which might be repeated if it so pleased the Catholic king.[1010]

After this there was no further demand for the restoration of the Inquisition, as Fernando's determination was recognized as unalterable. For awhile however it had not accepted its suppression as final, and it still sought to perform some of its functions in hopes of being again revived. This is demonstrated by the Valencia register, laboriously and faithfully compiled and brought up to the end of 1824, and the same seems to have been done in Madrid for, in a document of 1817, there is an appended note referring to the Madrid register of January 31, 1824. As the salaries were continued, an organization was kept up and a show was made of performing some kind of work. The Valencia register thus contains several cases in which it acted in 1824, though it modestly styles itself "este tribunal eclesiastico" and not "Santo Oficio." Thus Valero Andreu was accused to it of a blasphemous proposition and was duly sentenced. The criminal court of Valencia regarded it as still functioning and, when in trials there came evidence of matters cognizable by the Inquisition, the proofs would be sent to the tribunal which would summon the offender and pass judgement on him, the penalty however being not more than a reprimand. Three cases of this kind are recorded, the latest being July 3, 1824.[1011] We may fairly assume that in some, at least, of the other tribunals, trivial work of this kind was similarly performed.

Henry Charles Lea, LL.D.

REMNANTS OF THE INQUISITION

Some papers connected with a quarrel between the officials of the Majorca tribunal give us an insight into its internal condition in 1830. Its business consisted in the collection of the censos and other sources of revenue. There were many of these--loans to towns and villages as well as to individuals throughout the islands; payments were apt to be tardy and the labor of collection was considerable, frequently involving legal proceedings. The inquisitor had disappeared, although from another document we learn that he was named Francisco Antonio Andraca and that he was drawing his salary elsewhere. The existing head of the tribunal was a juez subdelegado, a representative of the old juez de bienes; there was a treasury and an auditing department with an administrador tesorero, Juan Antonio Togores, who was disabled and represented by his son, José Antonio Togores. The secretary of the secreto was Bartolomé Serra y Bennassar, acting as auditor ad interim, whose clerk was Pedro Mascaro, notary of sequestrations. The only other official was the portero, Sebastian Banza. Togores claims that, when the buildings were destroyed in 1820, he incurred many enmities by efforts to compel restitution of plundered materials--among others a Count of Ayamans was sued for purloining building stone. Togores constructed a wall around the site, and the heaps of stone and tiles still lay scattered there. Outside of the enclosure, a couple of small buildings were erected for offices, with a warehouse below for the storage of the rescued materials. One of the charges against him was that he had used the site of the old garden of the senior inquisitor to raise vegetables and flowers for himself.[1012] There is impressiveness in this glimpse of the old officials clinging to the ruins of what had once been so formidable.

From this quarrel we learn that the central authority of the Inquisition was the General Superintendent of the Property of the Inquisition--apparently a subordinate of the Colector-general de Espolios, to whom the assets were confided by the decree of January 1, 1824. In 1830 this General Superintendent was an old inquisitor, Valentin Zorilla, and he had as fiscal another inquisitor, Vicente Alonso de Verdejo. The Inquisitor-general, Gerónimo Cavillon y Salas, Bishop of Tarazona, was still drawing his salary of 71,491 reales 24 mrs. and did not die until 1835. Of the Suprema there were but two survivors, the Dean Ethenard and Cristobal Bencomo, Archbishop of Heraclea, who by 1833 had disappeared, leaving Ethenard alone. There was still a relator, a private secretary of the inquisitor-general, a keeper of the archives, and four minor officials. All these, however, were mere pensioners. The active organization consisted of the superintendent and his fiscal, with a treasurer and receiver-general ad interim, Don Angel Abad, whose accounts for 1830 show that he had received by drafts drawn upon the several tribunals

Logroño, Madrid, Cuenca and Llerena apparently contributed nothing. The sums credited to America and Canaries were probably old balances. The receipts from prebends must have gone directly to the Superintendent, for the decree of final extinction in 1834 shows that they were still held for the benefit of the Inquisition. There were other sources of revenue, principally from censos, of which the most notable was one of the Count of Altamira, from whom was collected, in 1830, the sum of 272,335 reales 25 mrs., being arrearages that seem to run back to 1818. He was still hereditary alguazil mayor of the Seville tribunal, in which capacity he was receiving a yearly salary of 4411 reales 26 mrs. The Duke of Medinaceli, as alguazil mayor of the Madrid tribunal, was still drawing his yearly stipend of a thousand reales and personally signing monthly receipts. There are scattering entries of payments to officials of various tribunals, showing that they were gradually thinning out, and refugees from the American Inquisitions were kept on the pay-roll.[1013] Such was the moribund condition of the Holy Office on the eve of its extinction.

***

While the Inquisition was thus suspended, the more zealous bishops replaced it with so-called Juntas de fe, based on the same principles, with secrecy of procedure and exercising jurisdiction in the external as well as internal forum. No record of the proceedings of these anomalous tribunals seems to have been preserved except in the case of Valencia, where the archbishopric was held by Simon López, in reward for his defence of the Holy Office in the Córtes de Cádiz. Almost his earliest act on assuming his new dignity, in 1824, was to issue a pastoral confirming the junta de fe, established by his predecessor Veremundo Arias, and empowering it to receive denunciations. He took the presidency with Dr. Miguel Toranza, the former inquisitor of Valencia as his colleague, Dr. Juan Bautista Falcó as fiscal and Dr. José Royo as secretary.[1014]

JUNTAS DE FE

Thus the old tribunal was revived under another name, and it speedily proved that such juntas were more dangerous than those of the Inquisition, as they were not subject to the supervision and control of the Suprema. A poor schoolmaster of Rizaffa, named Cayetano Ripoll, had served in the War of Liberation and had been carried as a prisoner to France, where he became a pervert. He abandoned Christianity for Deism, while at the same time he was a living embodiment of the teachings of Christ, sharing his scanty pittance with the needy, and constantly repeating "Do not unto others what you would not have done unto you." He did not seek to propagate his beliefs, but he was denounced to the Junta by a beata for not taking his scholars to mass, for not making them kneel to the passing viaticum, and for substituting in his school the ejaculation "Praise be to God" instead of "Ave Maria purissima." He was arrested September 29, 1824, and his trial lasted for nearly two years. The testimony confirmed the denunciation and showed that the only religious instruction which he gave his pupils was the Ten Commandments. During his prolonged trial he made no complaints; he shared his meagre prison fare with his fellow-prisoners; he openly avowed his convictions, and the repeated efforts of the theologians to convert him were futile. The sentence bore that the tribunal had consulted with the Junta de Fe and concluded that he be relaxed, as a formal and contumacious heretic, which had been confirmed by the archbishop. There was no hypocritical plea for mercy, and the Sala del Crimen of the Audiencia, to which he was handed over, gave him no hearing or opportunity for defence. Its function was purely ministerial, and he knew nothing of its action until the sentence was announced to him that, within twenty-four hours, he was to be hanged and burnt, but the burning might be figurative by painting flames on a barrel, in which his body should be thrust into unconsecrated ground. He listened to this with the patient resignation that he had exhibited throughout his trial, and his last words on the gibbet, July 26, 1826, were "I die reconciled to God and man."[1015]

This barbarity scandalized all Europe and proved to be the last execution for heresy in Spain. While it gratified the zealots, who were clamoring for the resurrection of the Inquisition, it displeased Fernando, who caused the Audiencia to be notified that the Government recognized no such tribunals as the juntas de fe.[1016] In spite of this rebuke, the episcopal juntas continued to exercise an irregular and irresponsible jurisdiction, until the sufferers sought from the Holy See the protection denied to them at home. Pius VIII listened to their prayer, whether from motives of humanity or of establishing in Spain the jurisdiction which the Inquisition had sought so sedulously to exclude, and, in a constitution of October 5, 1829, he recited the numerous prayers reaching him from those persecuted in Spain for matters of faith, asking that they might have opportunity of appealing from sentences rendered by archbishops and bishops, before being subjected to punishment. To save them from the expenses and delays of appeals to Rome, he empowered the tribunal of the Rota, in the papal nunciature, to hear all appeals in matters of faith, even twice, thrice, four or five times in succession, until three concording sentences should be rendered.[1017] Fernando was less sensitive than his predecessors as to papal encroachments, and he gave this the force of law by a royal order of February 6, 1830.

CRISTINA

QUESTION OF SUCCESSION

The death of Queen Amalia, May 17, 1829, was an abundant source of intrigue, for a fourth marriage of Fernando might prove fruitful and thus destroy the prospects of Don Carlos. The efforts of the Carlists to prevent it were vain and, on December 9th, Fernando married his neice, the Neapolitan princess, María Cristina de Bourbon, whose sister Carlotta was the wife of the Infante Francisco de Paula, the second brother of Fernando. There was soon prospect of an heir to the throne, and the uncertainty as to sex rendered it advisable to determine in advance whether the Salic law excluding females from the succession was in force or not. The ancient Spanish law, as expressed in the Partidas, provided for the succession of a daughter in the absence of sons or of children of a son.[1018] Under this, Spain had seen the glorious reign of Isabella the Catholic and the unfortunate one of Juana la Loca, and female succession, in default of male children, was firmly established in the tradition of the nation until 1713, when María Luisa of Savoy persuaded her husband Philip V to effect a change. Much pressure was required to bring this about, but a pragmática, agreed to by the Córtes, provided that only in the event of the total default of male representatives should the daughters of the last reigning sovereign succeed, according to age, and all laws to the contrary were annulled.[1019]

In 1784 there was talk of revoking this pragmática, but it was postponed until after the accession of Carlos IV, when the Córtes of 1789 petitioned for the revival of the law of the Partidas. The king assented but, to avoid giving offence to reigning houses whose possible claims to the succession were thus cut off, it was kept a profound secret, although filed away in the archives.[1020] This was the position when Fernando, to assure the succession to a possible daughter, by a pragmática of March 29, 1830, ordered that of 1789 to be published and commanded the literal observance of the law of the Partidas.[1021] The proceedings of 1789 were freely denounced as fraudulent by the Carlists, they were confident in the support of two hundred thousand Royalist Volunteers, and they regarded the new pragmática as a reason for more energetic organization.

In due time, on October 10th, a girl was born, known to history as Isabel II. Carlos believed that his rights had been sacrificed and, though he refused to snatch at the sceptre during his brother's lifetime, he assured his partizans that he would not permit his neice to mount the throne. Fernando's health was rapidly giving way under repeated attacks of gout and, on September 17, 1832, his life was despaired of. The prospect was most critical. Propositions were made to Carlos about sharing the government, but he declared that conscience and honor would not permit him to abandon rights given to him at his birth by God. In the perplexity of the situation, Calomarde, who for ten years had been the king's most trusted minister, represented to Cristina the terrors of the inevitable civil war, and the dangers to herself and her children, for she had recently given birth to a second daughter, María Luisa Fernanda. She yielded, Fernando assented and signed a paper annulling the pragmática of 1830, which was read to the assembled ministers on the night of September 18th, under the strictest injunctions of secrecy, but it was treacherously divulged, and copies were posted about the court. Cristina's servants commenced packing her effects for departure and Carlos, in his apartments, was saluted as king.

Fernando however commenced to rally; many nobles offered their lives to Cristina and formed an association to defend the claims of Isabel. Carlotta, who was in Andalusia, hastened to Madrid, reaching it on the 22d and, being of a determined character scolded Cristina and threatened Calomarde--it is even said that she cuffed him in the face, when with ready wit he quoted Calderon--"White hands inflict no disgrace." Fernando agreed to recall the decree, when she obtained the original and the copies and destroyed them. This only led the followers of Carlos to prepare to assert his claims by force, and there was no time to be lost in organizing a party to resist them.[1022]

This necessitated a reversal of the policy of the last ten years, identified with Calomarde--in fact the period was often designated as the Epocha de Calomarde. The ministry was dismissed; Calomarde was banished to his native place, and then was ordered to the citadel of Minorca, but he was concealed in a convent from which he escaped to France. Fernando, on October 6th signed a decree constituting Cristina regent during his illness; the next day she issued a general pardon of all political prisoners and, on the 15th, a general amnesty, including the exiles who were allowed to return, the only exceptions being those who at Seville had voted to replace the king with a regency, and those who had commanded bodies of troops against him, all of whom Fernando obstinately refused to pardon. This complete reversal of policy led to some premature insurrectionary movements by the Carlists, but they were easily suppressed.[1023]

ISABELLA RECOGNIZED

The declaration of September 18th had been destroyed, but it had not been invalidated. To effect this in the most impressive manner an assembly was held on December 31st of all the great officers of the Government, representatives of the grandees, and deputations of the provinces, in which Fernando presented a holograph paper setting forth that advantage had been taken of his desperate illness to threaten him with civil war and induce him to sign a revocation of the pragmatic sanction of March 29, 1830; now, convinced of his inability to alter the immemorial customs of the land, he pronounced the nullity of the declaration which had been snatched from him by surprise. Then he signed and rubricated the paper, all present were asked whether they had understood its purport, and the next day, January 1, 1833, the proceedings of the Córtes of 1789 and their confirmation by Carlos IV were published.[1024]

The next step was the assembling of Córtes to take the oath of allegiance to Isabel, and for this summons were issued April 4th appointing June 20th. Carlos was got out of the way by inducing Dom Miguel of Portugal to invite him, but, when Fernando desired to remove him still further to Italy, a long and very curious correspondence ensued between the brothers, couched in the most affectionate terms, in which Carlos evaded obedience. He was the only absent member of the royal family when the Córtes met, where all, including bishops, grandees, nobles and the procurators of the cities duly took the oath of allegiance. The whole kingdom followed the example, and the Biscayans, under the historic Oak of Guarnica, spontaneously recognized Isabel as the heiress of Biscay. Yet sparks of rebellion manifested themselves in one place after another, and there were symptoms of insubordination in the army, showing that the Carlist organization was at work and was awaiting only the death of Fernando.[1025]

By the beginning of September he was scarce more than a living corpse and on the 29th the end came. The obsequies were held on October 3d, the leaden coffin having a glass plate through which the face could be seen and verified. The Duke of Alagon, as captain of the body-guard, commanded silence and, in a loud voice exclaimed Señor! Señor! Señor! As there was no reply, he added "Since his majesty does not answer, he is truly dead." Despite the leaden coffin, the stench was such that several persons fainted.[1026] It might be said that his malignant influence lasted until the grave covered him--or, perhaps, the truth is more fully expressed by Benito Pérez Galdos: "That king, who deceived his parents, his masters, his friends, his ministers, his partizans, his enemies, his four wives, his people, his allies, all the world in fact, deceived also death, who thought to make us happy in delivering us from such a devil, for he left us his brother and his daughter, who kindled a fearful war, and the legacy of misery and scandal is yet unexhausted."[1027]

DEFINITE EXTINCTION

It is not our province to enter into the horrors of the savage Carlist war, which broke out forthwith and lasted until the Convenio de Vergara in 1839. The rapid sketch which we have given of its antecedents suffices to show how Cristina, in order to make head against the extremists, was perforce obliged to consolidate a party composed of the moderate Royalists and the Liberals, while the progress of events threw her more and more into the arms of the latter. The solemn proclamation of Isabel's succession, October 20th, was accompanied by measures restricting the oppressive powers of the Royalist Volunteers, restoring the laws respecting mayorazgos and other reforms of the Constitutional period. That this process, once begun, should continue with accelerated momentum was inevitable, and also that it should sweep aside the poor remnants of the Inquisition. This was so much a matter of course and, in the comatose condition of the institution, was of importance so slender, that the memoir writers and historians of the period, if they allude to it at all, do so in the briefest and most perfunctory manner. Yet the profound roots which it had struck in the national life, and the hold which it had acquired on popular veneration, are manifested in the fact that the struggle for its extinction had extended over a period of more than twenty years, and required for its consummation a change in the ideals of a majority of the people. The time for this had at last come, and the final dissolution was accomplished with only so much of discussion as to show that the opinions of those called upon to decide were virtually unanimous in principle and only different as to the opportuneness of the measure.

At a meeting of the Consejo de Gobierno, July 9, 1834, there was submitted the project of a decree for the extinction of the Inquisition and the disposition of its property. This was considered, July 11th, when the majority, consisting of the Archbishop of Mexico, the Duke of Bailen, the Marquis of las Amarillas and Don José María Puig, approved of the decree, with some unessential modifications. The minority, consisting of the Marquis of Santa Cruz, the Duke of Medinaceli and Don Francisco Xavier Caro, opposed the article extinguishing the Inquisition, on the ground that it was already extinguished, matters of faith were treated in the episcopal tribunals, and it was inopportune to call public attention to an affair which all the world regarded as settled, while the application of the property ought to be submitted to the approaching Córtes. At the next meeting, held July 13th, a dictamen was adopted, embodying the views of the majority and suggesting certain amendments, of no special moment in principle, which were virtually accepted by the Regency.[1028] No time was lost in making the final draft, which was published July 15th. The preamble recited the desire of the Regency to strengthen the public credit in all ways compatible with justice; that the late king had considered the imprescriptible episcopal jurisdiction and the laws of the land sufficient for the protection of religion; that a decree of January 4, 1834, had committed to the bishops censorship over writings on religion, morals and discipline; that the labors on the criminal code, now completed, established appropriate penalties for assaults on religion, and that the Junta eclesiastica, created by decree of April 22d, was occupied with proposing what was deemed necessary to this end. Therefore the Regent, in order to provide a remedy, in so far as the Real Patronato extended and with the concurrence of the Holy See, as far as this was necessary, after consulting the Council of Government and the ministers, decreed--

Art. I. The tribunal of the Inquisition is declared to be definitely suppressed.

Art. II. Its property is appropriated to the extinction of the public debt.

Art. III. The one hundred and one canonries annexed to the Inquisition are applied to the same object, subject to the royal decree of March 9th last, and for the time expressed in the Apostolic bulls.

Art. IV. The employees who possess prebends or obtain salaried civil offices will have no claim on the funds of the Tribunal.

Art. V. The other employees will receive from the sinking fund the exact salaries corresponding to the classification which they will establish with the Junta eclesiastica.[1029]

Such was the brief and decisive decree which terminated the existence of the institution created by the piety of Isabella and the fanaticism of Torquemada.

Henry Charles Lea, LL.D.

VICISSITUDES OF TOLERATION

There still remained the juntas de fe of the bishops, some, at least, of whom persisted in maintaining them, with the old inquisitorial methods, in spite of the constitution of Pius VIII and the royal decree of February 6, 1830. Their continuance was incompatible with the rapidly increasing anticlerical spirit of the dominant party, and they were prohibited by a decree of July 1, 1835, in which, after alluding to the disregard of the papal and royal utterances, Cristina ordered that they should cease immediately wherever they had been established. The ordinary episcopal courts were required to observe the law of the Partidas, the canons and the common law in all cases of faith and others, of which the extinguished Inquisition had had cognizance, conforming their procedure to that in other ecclesiastical matters and admitting the appeals allowed by law. Cases of solicitation were provided for by a clause providing that, where scandal or offence to morals might ensue, a prudent secrecy should be observed, the hearings to be held with closed doors, in the presence of the accused and his counsel, from whom nothing was to be withheld.[1030] Thus the last trace of inquisitorial procedure was forbidden on Spanish soil.

***

After so many centuries of conscientious intolerance, the lesson of toleration was hard to learn. On August 14, 1836, the Motin de la Granja forced Cristina to proclaim once more the Constitution of 1812, with its prohibition of any religion save Roman Catholicism. This instrument, with all its crudities, was soon found to be unworkable, and the Constitution of 1837 marked an advance, in its simple declaration that the State obligated itself to maintain the cult and ministers of the Catholic religion, which was that of Spaniards. Then came a reaction and, when the Constitution was revised in 1845, the principle of intolerance was reaffirmed. The European disturbances of 1848 strengthened this spirit in the Church, and it found expression in the penal code of 1851, of which Articles, 128, 129, 130 and 131 inflict imprisonment and exile for any attempt to change the religion of Spain, for public worship in other faiths, for apostatizing from Catholicism, or for publishing doctrines in opposition to it.[1031] The Spanish bishops were even encouraged to call for the revival of the Inquisition under their management, but this would have been superfluous.[1032] That the law was quite sufficient for the repression of Protestant propaganda was shown, in 1855 by the long imprisonment and exile of Francisco Ruet at Barcelona. It is true that in 1856, during the brief return of the Liberals to power, a Constitution on a more tolerant basis was framed, but a speedy reaction prevented this from going into effect, and the instrument of 1845 remained in force until the revolution of 1868. Ruet's chief disciple was Manuel Matamoros, who made numerous converts in Málaga, Granada and Seville, but, in 1860, prosecution caused to fly to Barcelona, where he was thrown in gaol and taken back to Granada. Some twenty more were arrested, among whom were his two principal aids José Alhama and Trigo. Matamoros and Alhama were condemned to eight years of presidio and Trigo to four, while similar sentences were pronounced in Seville on Tomas Bordallo and Diego Mesa Santaello. The affair made a sensation throughout Europe; the Evangelical Alliance bestirred itself and a deputation representing nearly every nation assembled in Madrid to intercede for the convicts. The pressure was so great that, on May 20, 1862, the sentence rendered three weeks before was commuted to nine years' of exile, which enabled the Evangelicals, from the safe refuge of Gibraltar, to maintain relations with their secret converts.[1033] That under this reaction the resuscitation of the Inquisition was seriously considered, may be assumed from the publication, in 1859, of a pamphlet containing the speech of Ostolaza, in the Córtes of Cádiz, in favor of the Inquisition, and those of Muñoz Torrero and Toreno against it, with the manifesto of the Córtes, thus contributing to the debate, under the guise of impartiality, the weight of argument against the Holy Office.[1034]

When came the revolution of 1868, the Constituent Córtes, after a vigorous debate, affirmed, May 8, 1869, the principle of religious liberty by the decisive vote of 163 to 40. In the new Constitution, proclaimed June 6th, the free exercise, public and private, of faiths other than Catholicism was guaranteed both to foreigners and Spaniards.[1035] Under this the Código penal reformado, which is still in force, provides penalties of fine and imprisonment for any interference with religious belief, whether by constraint to acts of worship or impeding those of the individual's chosen faith.[1036] Finally, in 1876, still another Constitution, which has endured to the present time, after declaring Roman Catholicism to be the religion of the State, prohibits the molestation of any one for religious opinion or for the exercise of his cult, in so far as Christian morals are respected, but it does not permit public ceremonies other than those of the State religion.[1037]

***

This summary of the vicissitudes in the progress of toleration, since the suppression of the Inquisition, is not foreign to our subject, for it teaches two lessons. One is that the main assaults on the ecclesiastical system of Spain, its members and its temporalities, were committed before toleration was extended to the heretic, for the secularization of church property, the abrogation of tithes and first fruits and the suppression of the regular Orders were chiefly effected by measures adopted between 1835 and 1855. The other is that the slender results of Protestant propagandism, from the days of George Borrow to those of Pastor Fliedner, show how little Catholicism has to fear from such efforts among a people who, if they abandon the faith of their fathers, are much more apt to seek refuge in negation of religion than in heresy. Together they demonstrate that the terrors of the Inquisition were superfluous, and that the injuries which it inflicted on Spain were not compensated by any corresponding benefits, even from the stand-point of the Church.

CHAPTER II - RETROSPECT

PRESENT CONDITION

No modern European nation has endured such vicissitudes of good and evil fortune as the Spanish. From the virtual anarchy of the Castilian kingdoms under Juan II and Enrique IV, the resolute wills of Ferdinand and Isabella evoked order and, by the union with Aragon, the conquest of Granada, Naples and Navarre and the acquisition of the New World, they left Spain in a most commanding position. When, under Charles V, to this were added the Netherlands, the Austrian possessions, Milan and the headship of the Holy Roman Empire, the hegemony of Europe was secured, and the prospect of attaining the universal monarchy seemed sufficiently possible to arouse the fears of Europe. The loss of the Empire and of Austria, awarded to the younger branch of the Hapsburgs, strengthened rather than weakened the inheritance of Philip II, by rendering it less cumbrous and unwieldy, while the acquisition of Portugal unified the Peninsula and the increasing wealth of the Indies promised almost unlimited resources for the extension of his power. Yet this power, so colossal in outward seeming, was already becoming a mere shell, covering emptiness and poverty, for its rulers had exhausted the nation in enterprises beyond its strength and foreign to its interests. Throughout the seventeenth century its downward progress was rapid until, at the death of Carlos II, in 1700, it had reached a depth of misery and helplessness in which it might almost despair of recuperation. Yet its efforts, in the War of Succession, showed that it still possessed a virile nationality; its decadence was arrested, and a slow upward progress was begun, accelerated under the enlightened rule of Carlos III, until, at his death in 1788, it had so far regained its position that, if not yet a power of the first rank, it might not unhopefully look forward to attaining that position. Then followed the weak and disastrous reign of Carlos IV, under the guidance of Godoy, when impotence invited the intrusion of Napoleon, resulting in the manifestation of national energy, which surprised the world in the heroic War of Liberation. After the Restoration in 1814, the land was, for more than half a century the scene of almost unintermittent conflict between antagonistic forces, resulting in the apathy of exhaustion after attaining the form of democratic constitutional monarchy. Yet we are told that absolute monarchy has merely been replaced by absolute Caciquismo or, in American parlance, the rule of the political "boss."[1038] Government, it seems, is exploited purely for the private interest of the office-holding class and the strength of the nation has been wasted, its development has been neglected, until the unexpected feebleness revealed in the war of 1898 led earnest patriots to declare that, if the existing maladministration were to continue, it would be better to seek shelter under England or France, and to put an end to the history of Spain as an independent nation.[1039] This shock to the national consciousness, and the skilful and vigorous agitation to which it gave birth, bear promise of results in the political as well as in the material and industrial development of the land, and we may reasonably hope that a nation, which has suffered so much with fortitude, is entering upon a new career that may make amends for the miseries of the past.

Vicissitudes such as these have their causes, and we cannot conclude this long history of the Inquisition without inquiring what share it and the spirit, which at once created and was stimulated by it, contributed to the misfortunes endured, with few intermissions, by the Spanish people since its organization. These causes are numerous, many of them not directly connected with our subject, but yet to be enumerated in order that undue importance may not be ascribed to the influence of the Inquisition.

***

To begin with, the Spanish monarchy developed into a pure despotism, based on the maxim of the Institutes--quod principi placuit legis habet vigorem--the prince's pleasure has the force of law. All legislative and executive functions were concentrated in the crown; the king issued laws, levied taxes, raised troops, declared war, made peace at his will, and the execution of the Justicia Lanuza, in 1591, without a trial, shows that the lives of his subjects were at his disposal. It was the same with their liberties, as illustrated by the imprisonment, without a hearing, of ministers like Cabarrús, Floridablanca, Jovellanos and Urquijo. For awhile the ancient fueros of the kingdoms of the crown of Aragon served as some restraint in those territories, but Philip V, in 1707 and 1714, took advantage of the War of Succession to declare them forfeited. Under such concentration of authority, the fate of the nation depended on the character and capacity of the monarch. Charles V had unquestioned ability, but his ambitious enterprises, while flattering to the national vanity, not only exhausted the resources of Spain, in quarrels foreign to its interests, but crippled its prosperity by the reckless devices employed to supply his needs. Philip II was a man of very moderate talents, irresolute and procrastinating to that degree that the Venetian envoy Vendramino, in 1595, declared that what would cost another prince ten ducats cost him a hundred, in consequence of his dilatoriness.[1040] His enormous and disjointed empire was too much for his narrow intelligence, and his vast expenditures in defence of Latin Christianity consumed all his resources and kept him in perpetual financial straits. At his death, in 1598, he had nothing to show for the ruin of his country but the gloomy pile of the Escorial and the acquisition of Portugal. Holland was hopelessly lost; his rival, Henry IV, was firmly seated on the throne of a reunited France, and the papacy was alienated. The internal condition of the land is depicted in the despairing complaints of the Córtes of 1594--"The truth, which cannot be questioned, is that the kingdom is totally exhausted. Scarce any man has money or credit, and those who have it do not employ it in trade or for profit, but hoard it to live as sparingly as possible, in hope that it may last them to the end. Thus comes the universal poverty of all classes.... There is not a city or a town but has lost largely in population, as is seen by the multitude of closed and empty houses, and the fall in the rents of the few that are inhabited."[1041]

GOVERNMENT BY FAVORITES

With Philip III we commence the long line of favorites who dominated Spain during the seventeenth century. Well meaning, but weak and incapable, he left everything to the Duke of Lerma, under whose guidance a reckless course of prodigality was followed as though the only trouble was to get rid of surplus revenues. Charles V had cast aside the severe simplicity of the old Castilian court for the stately magnificence of the Burgundian household; his successors followed his example, in spite of the remonstrances of the Córtes, but where Philip II spent on it four hundred thousand ducats a year, Philip III lavished a million and three hundred thousand, while he was begging money of his nobles and prelates and seeking to seize all the plate in the kingdom in order to coin it. He was not alone in this, for the nobility and gentry were consumed with usury and overwhelmed with debt, owing to their extravagance. The Venetian envoy Contarini, in 1605 describes the land as overspread with poverty and general discontent and all the evils attendant upon a corrupt and vicious government, under an indolent king and a rapacious and incapable minister. The worst war, he concludes, that could be made on Spain was to allow it to consume itself in peace under misgovernment, while to attack it would be to arouse the dogged determination of the people. The reports of the Lucchese envoys tell the same story.[1042] Such was the condition when the expulsion of the Moriscos robbed the land of its most productive class.

Matters grew worse when Philip IV ascended the throne, in 1621. Good-natured, affable, indolent and pleasure-loving, his thirty-one unacknowledged natural children, besides the acknowledged one-- the second Don John of Austria--serve to explain why he abandoned the cares of state to his favorite, the Count-Duke Olivares, after whose fall in 1643 his nephew, Don Luis de Haro, succeeded to the post. The official historiographer describes Spain, at his accession, as being in extremity, and the people crushed under their burdens; everything was in disorder, and the condition of the nation so weakened that it could only be deplored and not amended. Yet Philip's first act was to break the truce with Holland and, from that time to the end of his long reign, he was involved in almost continual war. He called together the Córtes and asked for supplies to which they replied by petitioning him to try to stop the general depopulation and find occupation for the people, who were wandering with their families over the country in vain search for work.[1043] Yet Philip, engrossed with his plebeian amours and the pleasures of his court, continued his wars and his extravagance, without giving thought to the misery of his people whom he was crushing with ever new exactions. The courtly festivities were conducted with a magnificence till then unexampled; the carnival festival of 1637 was officially admitted to cost three hundred thousand ducats and was popularly estimated at half a million.[1044] In 1658 the Venetian envoy reports his giving to the son of Don Luis de Haro fifty thousand pesos for skilfully arranging a ballet for the ladies of the court. Every bull-fight cost him sixty thousand reales, and the celebration at the birth of Prince Prosper (who speedily died) involved an expenditure of eight hundred thousand pesos. All this, as the envoy remarks, was extracted from the blood of the miserable people, who were poorer in Spain than anywhere else. The immense resources of the kingdom were absorbed by the rapacity of the ministers or were dissipated by the profuseness of the king.[1045]

RESOURCES AND POSSIBILITIES

In 1665, Carlos II, then but four years of age, succeeded to his father, under the regency of the Queen-dowager Maria Ana of Austria. We have seen how she abandoned affairs to her confessor, the Jesuit Nithard, and when he was dismissed by the efforts of Don John of Austria, in 1669, she replaced him with the worthless favorite Fernando de Valenzuela. Again Don John was called in; Valenzuela was exiled to the Philippines and Don John assumed the reins of government. His limited abilities were unequal to the task; he was driven from power and died soon afterwards in 1679. Carlos had been declared of age in 1675; he was utterly incapable and, though he can scarce be said to have had favorites, under such ministers as the Duke of Medinaceli and the Count of Oropesa, Spain sank deeper in misery and degradation until his death in 1700. The kingdom was reduced to the last extremity, without money, without industry, without means of defence to resist the aggressive wars of Louis XIV, or to defend the colonies from the ravages of buccaneers. The population is said to have shrunk to 5,000,000; in 1586 it had been estimated at 8,000,000 by the Venetian envoy Gradenigo.[1046] Such was the result of two centuries of absolute government, under monarchs not wilfully evil, who merely reigned according to the light vouchsafed them.

Yet it was not so much the extravagance of the court, or the perpetual wars of the Hapsburgs, or the emigration to the colonies, that reduced the population and the power of Spain. The land could have endured all these if its rich resources and vast opportunities had been wisely developed. Lying between two seas and holding Sicily and Naples, it commanded the Atlantic and the Mediterranean; with its wealthy colonies, the source of the precious metals which revolutionized the finances of Europe and furnished the basis for the most profitable commerce that the world had seen, it was invited to become the greatest of maritime states, with a navy and a mercantile marine beyond rivalry, dominating the seas as the Catalans had dominated the Mediterranean in the thirteenth and fourteenth centuries. It was largely secured from hostile aggression by the Pyrenees, and could work out its destinies with little to fear from external enemies. It is true that much of its surface is mountainous, and that large districts suffer from insufficient precipitation, but the Moors had shown what wonders could be wrought by irrigation, and how, by patient labor, even mountain sides could be made to yield their increase. No land could boast a greater variety of agricultural products, including those of semi-tropical and temperate zones which, combined with mineral wealth, should have rendered it self-supporting. All that was needed was steady and intelligent industry, fostered by wise legislation, encouraging production and commerce, and enabling every man to work out his own career with as few artificial impediments as possible, and Spain might be today what she was in the sixteenth century, the leader among civilized nations.

This was not to be. The fatal gift of the Burgundian inheritance distracted the attention of her rulers from the true arena of her expansion in Africa and on the ocean, to distant enterprises wholly foreign to her true interests, while the undeviating determination to enforce unity of faith at home, and to combat heresy elsewhere, led her to drive out her most useful population, and involved her in ruinous expenditures abroad. To extort the means for the furtherance of this policy, industry was strangled with the most burdensome and complicated system of taxation that human folly could devise, the weight of which fell almost exclusively on the oppressed producing classes, who were least able to endure it, while the nobles and gentry and clergy, who held by far the larger portion of Spanish wealth, were exempt.[1047] As taxation was virtually at the discretion of the monarch, imposts were added as the exigencies of extravagance demanded, usually with little thought as to their consequences, until the taxpayer was entangled in a network which crippled him at every step. This moreover was accompanied with regulations to prevent evasions, and to protect the consumer at the expense of the producer, which greatly enhanced the deadly influence of the anomalous and incongruous accumulation of exactions.

OPPRESSIVE TAXATION

All this fell with peculiar weight on agriculture and on the labradores or peasants, on whom ultimately the support and prosperity of the nation depended. When, in 1619, the Royal Council, in obedience to the commands of Philip III, presented an elaborate consulta on the causes of depopulation, it commenced by ascribing this to the grinding and insupportable taxation of the producing taxables, and the exemption of the consuming classes--the mules and cart of the peasant were seized for taxes, he was driven from the land and hid himself in the large cities, or sought a livelihood abroad.[1048] The warning was unheeded and, ten years later, Fray Benito de Peñalosa y Mondragon, while enthusiastically extolling the power and wealth of Spain, describes the condition of the labradores as the poorest, most completely miserable and depressed of all, as though all the other classes had combined and conspired to ruin and destroy them. Their cabins and huts of mud walls are decaying and crumbling, they possess some badly cultivated lands and lean cattle, always hungry for lack of the common pasture, and they are burdened with tributes, mortgages, taxes, censos and many impositions, demands and almsgivings that cannot be escaped. In place of wondering at the depopulation of villages and farms, the wonder is that any remain. Probably most of those who go to the Colonies are labradores and they also flock to the cities, engaging in all kinds of service.[1049]

The process went on without interruption. A century later an experienced financial official tells the same story, in a report to Philip V. The burden of taxation fell upon the poor; all that was unpaid was added to the levy of the succeeding year; a horde of blood-suckers lived by selling out delinquents, when the costs amounted to more than the taxes. Consequently the poor were obliged to sell their property to meet the demands of the tax-gatherer, or to let it be seized and sold, thus becoming beggars and tramps, and every year saw their numbers increase. The peasant, moreover, was subject to special and ruinous restrictions. The tassa or price of his grain was officially determined every year, at a maximum above which he was forbidden to sell it; moreover it could not be exported, nor could it be transported by sea from one province to another to prevent infractions of the prohibition. The result of this was that if the harvest was deficient, grain was secreted and held at exorbitant prices and this infraction of the law was winked at under necessity. The sufferer was the peasant, who had not the means of storing his grain but had to sell it to the wealthy who could withhold it, and thus, whether the harvests were abundant or scanty he fared ill. Thus production was discouraged and diminishing; the producer realized little, while the consumer paid extravagantly, checking both production and consumption. Lands were left uncultivated and labor was unemployed; everything moved in a vicious circle, and the evil was constantly growing. Trade was similarly strangled. The alcavala of 10 per cent. and the cientos of 4 per cent. were levied on every transaction, no matter how often an article changed hands. Manufactures, under this system, had almost disappeared. Spaniards were forced to sell their raw products to foreigners at low prices, for there were no other buyers, and to purchase them back in their finished state at the sellers' prices. The heavy tariff increased the cost to the consumer, while innumerable smugglers enabled the importers to realize the benefit of the duties. The foreigner, moreover, secured all the precious metals of the Indies, for all exports thither were of foreign goods, with which Spaniards could not compete, owing to the excessive imposts and tributes, which doubled the price of everything to the consumer. Yet of the product of these crushing burdens but little reached the treasury, owing to the system of collection, smuggling, and frauds.[1050]

THE MESTA--FORESTRY LAWS

The disabilities thus imposed on agriculture, industry, and trade were greatly aggravated by the absence of means of intercommunication, and it is symptomatic of Spanish policy that the energies of the rulers were concentrated on the suppression of heresy, foreign wars and court festivities to the exclusion of care for internal development. It is true that, under Charles V and Philip II, considerable effort was spent on the water-ways; the Canal Imperial de Aragon was built along the Ebro, as well as the smaller canals of Jarama and Manzanares, and there were improvements in the navigation of the Tagus and Guadalquivir, but these ceased and no attention was paid to the roads which, for the most part were mere caminos de herradura, or mule-tracks. Even as late as 1795, Jovellanos tells us that there was no communication by wagon between the contiguous provinces of Leon and Asturias, so that the wines and wheat of Castile could not bear the expense of mule carriage to the seaboard. In 1761 Carlos III undertook to construct highways from Madrid to Andalusia, Valencia, Catalonia, Galicia, Old Castile, Asturias, Murcia and Extremadura, but in 1795 none of them had reached half-way, and no attention was paid to interprovincial wagon-roads, to enable the miserable peasant to get from village to village, or from market to market, save at the cost of exhausting his cattle and at the risk of losing everything in a mudhole.[1051]

Another intolerable burden on agriculture was the Mesta, or combination of owners of the immense flocks of sheep, which wintered in the lowlands and summered in the mountains. Through privileges dating from the fourteenth century and gradually increased, the provinces, through which the trashumantes or migratory flocks passed, were subjected to serious disabilities. Pasturage could not be broken up for cultivation, its rental was fixed by an unalterable tassa, and a mesteño tenant could not be evicted. All enclosures were forbidden in order that the flocks when migrating might feed without payment on the stubble in the autumn and on the fallow land in the spring, although this privilege was somewhat curtailed in 1788 by permitting the enclosure of orchards, vineyards and plantations. Thus the husbandman was deprived of control over his property and the raising of horses and of stationary herds of cattle and sheep--vastly more important than the trashumantes--was effectually discouraged within the range of the Mesta. Equally short-sighted were the forestry laws, designed to foster the production of lumber, which was greatly needed both for building and shipping. The owner was obliged to get and pay for a permit before he could fell a tree, to obey fixed rules as to pruning, to sell against his will and at a fixed price, to admit inspections and official visits, and to answer for the condition and number of his trees--thus opening the door to unlimited extortion. In short, the freedom of action through which men seek their interests, and thus contribute to the general welfare, was destroyed by the paternalism of an absolute government, which blindly hampered all improvement and checked all individual initiative and ambition.[1052]

This explains the despoblados and baldíos--the depopulated villages and uncultivated lands--which were the despair of the statesmen who discussed the possible regeneration of Spain. According to Zavala, in the circumscription of Badajoz alone, the baldíos amounted to over three hundred square leagues, mostly good farm land, in which the remains of buildings could be traced, but then grown up in copses and thickets, affording refuge to wolves, smugglers and robbers. In Andalusia, Jovellanos tells us that these baldíos were immense; they were less in Extremadura, La Mancha and the two Castiles, while, in the northern provinces, from the Pyrenees to Portugal, the population was denser and the baldíos less frequent and of inferior quality.[1053] We have seen the attempt made by Carlos III to reclaim these districts with the nuevas poblaciones, and how the promising experiment was checked by the Inquisition.

INDOLENCE

As though these blind and irrational policies were insufficient to destroy prosperity, an equally efficient factor was devised in tampering with the coinage. This began tentatively in 1566 by Philip II, in diminishing the alloy of silver in the vellon or copper coinage. In 1602, Philip III, in his financial distress, was bolder and resolutely issued a pure copper coinage with a fictitious value of seven to two, calling forth the protest of Padre Mariana which cost him his prosecution by the Inquisition. In 1605 the Lucchese envoy informs us that the treasury had already reaped a profit of 25,000,000 ducats by this fiat money, of which the marc cost 80 maravedís and had a forced circulation of 280. This was the first of a long series of violent measures continued throughout the seventeenth century, of alternate expansion and contraction. Thus, in 1642 the fictitious legal-tender value was suddenly reduced to one-sixth, followed in 1643 by raising it fourfold, and in 1651 by increasing it still further. In 1652 an attempt was made to demonetize the vellon, June 25th, which was abandoned November 14th. In 1659 the vellon grueso was reduced in value one-half and, in 1660 it was trebled. Attempts were made to regulate prices by decrees of maxima and to prevent or define the inevitable premium on gold and silver, but the unwritten laws of trade were imperative, until at last, in 1718, the real de plata was admitted to be worth twice the real de vellon, a ratio which remained nearly permanent. The largest vellon coin was the cuartillo, or fourth of a real, equivalent to about three cents of American money, which became the standard of value in Spanish trade; the coins were tied in bags of definite amount and these passed from hand to hand, for the precious metals necessarily disappeared, and were rarely seen except in Seville, in spite of the most savage decrees against their exportation.[1054] It would be impossible to exaggerate the disastrous influence on industry and commerce of these perpetual fluctuations of the circulating medium. The relations between debtor and creditor, between producer and consumer, were ever at the mercy of some new decree that might upset all calculations. All transactions, from the purchase of a day's supply of bread to a contract for a cargo of merchandise were mere gambling speculations.

***

These causes of decadence were accentuated by an aversion and contempt for labor, which was recognized as a Spanish characteristic, attributable perhaps to the long war of the Reconquest and the endless civil broils which rendered arms the only fitting career for a Spaniard, and accustomed him to see all useful work performed by those whom he regarded as belonging to inferior races--Jews and Mudéjares. Their expulsion was destructive to all industrial pursuits, but the Old Christian still looked down on the descendants of the Conversos who were to a large extent debarred, by the statutes of Limpieza, from the Spanish resource of living without labor by entering the Church or holding office. The evil effects of this were intensified by constitutional indolence. The Spanish Conquistadores gave memorable examples of indefatigable energy and hardihood, sparing no toil when their imaginations were inflamed with the lust of conquest or the hopes of gold, but they would not work as colonists. One of them, Bernardo de Vargas Machuca, who for thirty years was Governor of Margarita, defends the enslavement of the Indians by candidly saying that Spaniards would not settle on unoccupied land, no matter how healthy or how rich in gold and silver, but would go where there were Indians, even if the land were sterile and unhealthy for, if they had not Indians to work for them, they could not enjoy its products, and its possession would be no benefit.[1055] Nor were the Spaniards of whom he speaks gentlemen adventurers, but were mostly drawn from the humbler classes. It was the same at home. Already, in 1512, Guicciardini, who spent two years in Spain as envoy from Florence, describes Spain as a land rich in natural resources, but sparsely populated and largely undeveloped. The people, he says, are warlike and skilled in arms, but they look upon industry and trade with disdain; artisans and husbandmen will work only under pressure of necessity and then rest in idleness until their earnings are spent.[1056] The Córtes of Valladolid, in 1548, complain that agricultural laborers and mechanics would not come to work before 10 or 11 o'clock, and would break off an hour or two before sunset. A century later, Dormer, the historiographer of Aragon, reproves the indolence of the people, except in Catalonia, for they would not work as was customary in other lands, but only a few hours a day, with perhaps frequent intermissions, and they expected this to provide for them as fully as the incessant labor of other lands.[1057]

EDUCATED IDLENESS

Spanish indolence was a frequent theme with the Venetian envoys who describe Spain as abounding in resources, and able to supply all its needs, but dependent upon foreign nations in consequence of the rooted dislike for labor. As Gianfrancesco Morosini writes, in 1581, the people have little aptitude for any of the mechanic arts, and are most negligent in agriculture, while in manual labor they are so slow and lazy that what anywhere else would be done in a month, here takes four.[1058] The Lucchese envoys, in the next century, tell the same story. There are few Spaniards, they say, except office-holders, who will work; the greater part of the workmen are foreigners, who have made a new Spain, to the great detriment of the old kingdoms. This explains why Spain is only a port through which the precious metals pass; the Spaniards consume only foreign merchandise imported by foreign merchants; among the contractors there is not a single Castilian, and there are more pieces of eight in China than in Spain.[1059] So, in 1687, Luis de Salazar y Castro attributes the decline of the monarchy to its substance flowing out through every pore, and the ultimate cause of this is the lack of energy. "I say it is our indolence, ignorance and want of application ... we attribute to deficient population what is laziness and sloth. Could our torpidity go further than our requiring Frenchmen to makes tiles, to grind knives, to carry water and to knead bread?"[1060] A moralist of the period is excessively severe upon this indolence coupled with reckless extravagance, which he compares with the tireless industry and thrift of the Frenchman.[1061] To this he attributes the poverty of Spain, as we have seen (Vol. III, p. 390) had been done, in 1594, by Francisco de Idiaquez, the secretary of Philip II.

One development of this indisposition to labor is touched upon by the consulta of the Royal Council in 1619, when it alludes to the multiplication of grammar-schools, to which the peasants send their children for a smattering of education, and thus withdraw them from productive industry.[1062] The Córtes of the same year asked for restrictions on this and Navarrete, in his commentary on the consulta, dwells at some length on the evils thence arising, for the sons of peasants flock thither, to gain the exemptions of the learned classes; an infinite number of them fail to reach the priesthood, becoming beggars and vagrants and criminals, while many of those who enter orders are forced to dishonorable practices, the public suffering in consequence from the lack of laborers and artisans.[1063] Protests were in vain and, in 1753, Gregorio Mayans y Siscar still called attention to the crowds of half-educated students who sponged on the community--drones who sucked the honey while they might be of service in driving a plough or handling a musket--a complaint echoed with still greater vigor by Jovellanos in 1795.[1064]

To this tendency may be attributed the frenzied rush for office, to which the suggestive name of empleomanía has been given, burdening the State with a vast superfluity of employees and depriving it of their services in useful production. In 1674 the Lucchese envoy wonders at the revenues, estimated at seventy-five millions, without apparent result, which he ascribes partly to the waste in collecting, the collectors employed numbering two hundred thousand--a manifest exaggeration, but yet suggestive.[1065] About 1740, Macanaz ranks this as the first in his enumeration of the causes of Spain's condition; there are, he says, a thousand employees where forty would suffice, if they were kept at work, and the rest could be set at some useful labor.[1066] The evil still continues, if we may believe modern writers who regard it as one of the serious impediments to prosperity.[1067]

IMPROVEMENT

From the depth of poverty, disorder and humiliation to which Spain had fallen, the process of recuperation under the Bourbons was slow and at first vacillating. Something was accomplished by Philip V, in spite of his continual wars and his melancholy madness, when he had rid himself of such adventurers as Alberoni and Ripperda and gave scope to the practical genius of Patiño.[1068] The upward impulse continued under Fernando VII, while, under Carlos III and his enlightened ministers the progress was rapid. A memorial addressed by Floridablanca to the king, towards the close of his reign, enumerates the reforms and works of utility undertaken during his ministry. There were canals, both for navigation and irrigation, the drainage of marsh lands, the establishment of the nuevas poblaciones, the improvement of roads. The trade to the colonies was thrown open to all the ports instead of being restricted to Seville, with the result that the exports quickly trebled and the customs revenue doubled.

The Banco Nacional was founded and the public credit, which had fallen very low, was speedily restored. Insurance companies were established and other trading associations, which gave life to industry and commerce. The tariff on imports was rendered uniform at all the ports, and its schedules were arranged so as to foster internal development, being light on machinery and raw materials and heavy on articles produced in Spain, not only stimulating industry to the great prosperity of the land, but increasing the customs revenue to a hundred and thirty millions when it had previously never exceeded thirty millions in the most prosperous years. The complicated and burdensome Rentas Provinciales were regulated so as to fall equally on the various provinces and to be easily borne; the Millones were reduced one-half; the formalities of the alcavala were simplified and its percentage greatly reduced, so as to bear lightly on industry, and with the expectation of its abrogation. The numbers of the exempts were diminished. All the mechanic arts were "habilitated," so that nobles engaging in them should not forfeit their nobility, thus taking away the excuse for idleness and vice of those who called themselves noble and refused to work, however poor they might be. Through this policy during the reign of Carlos III, the population of Peninsular Spain increased by a million and a half and, under his guidance it emerged from the Middle Ages and began to take position with modern nations.[1069]

Much as had thus been accomplished, much remained to do, as set forth, in 1795, by Jovellanos in his celebrated "Informe." Unfortunately progress was arrested by the indolent Carlos IV and his favorite Godoy. Then came the Napoleonic wars, and the course of events, as traced in the preceding chapter, was not conducive to improvement. Yet, in all the vicissitudes which Spain has endured since then, if we may trust the growth of population as an index of advancement, the substitution of liberal institutions for absolutism has proved a success and, however real may be the abuses of which the reforming element complains, the present situation is vastly better than the past. The census of 1768 showed a total of 9,309,804; that of 1787, 10,409,879; that of 1799, something over 12,000,000. Then there was a falling off and, in 1822, it was 11,661,980. Yet, in spite of Carlist wars and political troubles, in 1885, it had risen to 17,228,776, and it is now reckoned at 19,000,000 or about double that of the period of Spanish greatness. The fair inference from this is that Spain has a future; that, while much remains to do, much has been accomplished, and that there is progress which, if continued, will restore in great measure her ancient strength, although the enormous growth of modern nations precludes the expectation that she can resume her commanding position.

In addition to these secular causes of Spanish decadence, there remains to be considered another class of no less importance--those arising from clericalism, or the relations of the Church to the State, and its influence on the popular character and tendencies.

The accumulation of lands and wealth by the Church, and especially by the religious Orders, was, from an early time, a source of concern to statesmen and of complaint by the people, for the exemption from the royal jurisdiction, from military service and from taxation, claimed as imprescriptible rights by the Church, weakened the power of the State and threw increased burdens upon the population. Almost all the European nations endeavored to curb this acquisitiveness by laws of which the English Statutes of Mortmain and the French droits d'amortissement may be taken as examples. These acquisitions came from two sources, each abundantly productive--gifts or bequests and purchase. The sinner, unable to redeem in money the canonical penance for his sins impossible to perform, would make over a piece of land and obtain absolution or, if on his death-bed, would bequeath a portion of his estate to be expended in masses for his soul--perhaps founding a capellanía for that purpose, or as provision for a son who would serve as chaplain. So audacious became the demands of the Church on the estates of the dying that, in 1348, the Córtes of Alcalá complained that all the Orders obtained from the royal chancery letters empowering them to examine all testaments, whereupon they claimed all bequests made to uncertain places or persons; also, if there was not a bequest for each Order, those omitted demanded one equal to the largest in the will and they further claimed the whole estates of those who died intestate. If these demands were contested, they wearied the heirs with litigation into a compromise. Alfonso promised to revoke all such letters but the Black Death, which speedily followed, brought an immense accretion of lands for the foundation of anniversaries and chaplaincies, which led to lively reclamations by the Córtes of Valladolid, in 1351.[1070]

THE BURDEN OF THE CHURCH

With wealth thus constantly accumulating, the church or monastery would purchase lands from the laity, and as these became exempt from taxation it could afford to pay more than a secular purchaser. Whatever thus passed into ecclesiastical possession was never alienated; it remained in the grip of the Dead Hand which, by constant accretions, came to hold a large portion of the most desirable lands and thus of the wealth of the kingdom.

It would be tedious to recapitulate the complaints of the Córtes and the devices attempted by legislation from the eleventh century onward to check this growth, which was regarded as threatening the most serious evils to the nation.[1071] Laws were adopted only to be evaded or forgotten, and the process went on. A new element, however, was injected into the struggle when, in 1438, the Córtes of Madrigal made a vigorous representation to Juan II that, if no remedy were applied, all the best lands in the kingdom would belong to the Church, resulting in manifold injury to the people and the crown, to which the feeble king evasively replied that he would apply to the pope.[1072] Hitherto Spanish independence of the papacy had regarded all such questions as subject to national regulation, but this utterance indicated that papal confirmation was beginning to be recognized as necessary in everything that affected the Church. This was not at once admitted, for Juan, in 1447, in response to the Córtes of Valladolid, and by a decree of 1452, imposed a tax of twenty per cent, on all purchases, bequests and donations,[1073] but it gradually established itself and furnished a ready answer to the vigorous representations which, with growing insistence, the Córtes of the sixteenth century made in 1515, 1518, 1523, 1528, 1532, 1534, 1537, 1538, 1542, 1544, 1551 and 1573.[1074] This put all remedy out of the question, for no pope could be expected to set limits to ecclesiastical wealth and influence, from which the curia derived its revenues; and the petitions of the Córtes served only to emphasize the magnitude of the evil and its universal recognition by the people.

It was not only the progressive absorption of wealth and land that was detrimental but the corresponding increase in the numbers of the clergy, regular and secular, who were released from all the duties of the citizen, and whose vows of celibacy aided in accelerating the diminution of the population. The process continued with added vigor, especially after the commencement of the seventeenth century, owing partly to a wave of religious fervor which led to the founding of chapels and convents on a greater scale than ever, and partly to the growing destitution forcing men to seek conventual refuge, where they might at least escape starvation, and inducing parents to give their sons such smattering of education as might enable them to take orders and have at least a chance to secure a livelihood free from the crushing burdens of taxation. The result of this is seen in Fray Bleda's boast, in 1618, that one-fourth of the Christians of Spain were priests, frailes or nuns, and, even though this is obviously an over-estimate, it indicates how great was the task imposed on the producing classes to support in idleness so large a portion of the population.[1075] The increase was largely in the Mendicant Orders, whose systematic begging, that no one dared refuse, was a grievous addition to the tithes and first fruits.

A single instance will illustrate this inordinate growth. Cardinal Mendoza, Archbishop of Toledo, the "third king" under Ferdinand and Isabella, stubbornly refused to allow convents to be founded in his province, saying that there were already many that were injurious to the people obliged to sustain them, but this ceased with his death in 1495. His biographer, Doctor Pedro de Salazar, penitentiary of the cathedral, tells us that the city of Toledo held a privilege from Alfonso X prohibiting the erection of convents there. At that time there were six, but in 1625, when he wrote, these had been enlarged and numerous others had been founded, so that they then occupied more than fifty royal and noble houses and more than six hundred smaller ones. The disastrous influence of this on the prosperity of the place is self-evident and Salazar regards this portentous development of ecclesiasticism as the chief cause of the decline in the population of Spain, which he estimates at twenty-five per cent.[1076]

***

The consulta of the Council of Castile, in 1619, naturally included in its enumeration of the causes of national distress the foundation of so many religious houses, which were filled with those attracted, not by vocation but by a life of idleness, while their lands were exempt from taxation.[1077] In a similar mood, the Córtes, assembled by Philip IV on his accession, made a forcible and somewhat rhetorical representation, asking for measures to restrain the multiplication of foundations and the purchases of land, which not only diminished the alcavalas but, in a few years, would exempt all real estate from the royal jurisdiction and accumulate all taxation on the miserable poor, thus destroying the population of the provinces, for it was evident that, if the clergy continued to increase as it was doing, the villages would be without inhabitants, the fields without laborers, the sea without mariners and the arts without craftsmen; commerce would be extinct and, marriage being despised, the world would not last for a century.[1078]

At the earnest request of the kingdom, which represented that it could not support these idle multitudes or furnish soldiers for war, Urban VIII, in 1634, granted a bull reforming the religious Orders and suppressing some of the Barefooted ones, but the opposing influences were too strong and it was ineffective.[1079] In 1677 the matter was again debated, including the excessive numbers of the secular clergy, but action was postponed until there was a better prospect of results. The recognized evils were too serious to remain thus pigeon-holed, and an attempt was again made in 1691, the feebleness of which demonstrates how completely the Church dominated the State and could not be reformed without its own consent. The king deplored the multiplication of convents, and the consequent relaxation of discipline, and the pope was to be asked for authority to appoint visitors with full powers. The excessive increase of the secular priesthood, he said, was the cause of numerous disorders, to cure which the pope was to be applied to for faculties enabling bishops and abbots to reduce their numbers, so that all incumbents could live decently. The clergy in minor orders were so numerous that their exemption from the royal jurisdiction and the public burdens was a grievous injury to the laity and the bishops were asked to limit their ordination. The absorption of lands by the Church was an evil which had puzzled the wisest heads in all ages; many states had adopted laws regulating this, but he hesitated to have recourse to such measures until statistics could be gathered, and it could be decided how to reduce the numbers of the secular clergy.[1080] In short, the Church was an Old Man of the Sea, strangling the State, which lacked power to rid itself of its oppressor.

With the advent of the Bourbons there was less tendency to this hopelessness and, in 1713, the plain-spoken Macanaz, in a report to the king, presented a terrible picture of the misery and impoverishment resulting from the overgrown numbers and wealth of the clergy.[1081] Yet, short of revolution, effective remedy was impossible, and Philip V contented himself with a decree expressing regret that, without papal assent or a concordat, he could not afford general relief to his vassals. While awaiting this, however, he severely characterized the frauds of confessors in inducing the dying to impoverish their heirs. Such testators were declared not to be of free will, their bequests were invalid and scriveners drawing them were threatened with condign punishment.[1082]

Much of this evil would have been averted had the salutary reforms prescribed by the Council of Trent been enforced,[1083] but they had been a dead letter, at least in Spain. In 1723, however, Philip induced the Spanish bishops to supplicate Innocent XIII on the subject, resulting in a constitution in which he embodied at great length the Tridentine decrees as to restricting ordinations and the number of religious in convents.[1084] It was a tribute to the capacious learning rather than to the consistency of Macanaz that the Regular Orders employed him to draw up a memorial to the king, protesting against the enforcement of the papal decree, in which he lavished praises on them, and argued vigorously against any restriction on numbers beyond the capacity of support.[1085] This, however, was but a lawyer's argument for a client and did not prevent him, in memorials to Philip V, about 1740 and to Fernando VI, in 1746, from expressing his true opinions as to the evils which were a main cause of Spanish distress-- more than half the land held in mortmain and exempt from public burdens, and the immense number of those who, in place of being good laborers were bad priests, wandering around as beggars to the scandal of religion, while the overgrown religious Orders were useless consumers, living on the rest of the nation.[1086]

***

In negotiating the Concordat of 1737, Philip obtained with difficulty a concession subjecting to taxation future acquisitions, but it was impossible of enforcement and repeated decrees by him, in 1745, by Fernando VII in 1756 and by Carlos III in 1760 and 1763, only attest the powerlessness of the State when dealing with the Church. In 1795 Godoy dallied with a project of secularizing Church property to meet the expenses of the disastrous war with France, but was obliged to abandon the project and only imposed a tax of fifteen per cent, on new acquisitions.[1087] It was inevitable that the Córtes of Cádiz and the constitutional Government of 1820-3 should partially carry out what Spanish publicists for centuries had demanded, and should earn the bitterest clerical hostility.

As a matter of course the wealth of so numerous, powerful and worldly a Church was enormous. As early as 1563 Paolo Tiepolo states that the clergy possessed little less than one half the total revenues of Spain. He rates the income of the Archbishop of Toledo at 150,000 ducats, and in addition the church of Toledo had 300,000.[1088] Exemption from public burdens gave ample opportunity of increase and, at the end of the eighteenth century, the archbishop was estimated as enjoying an income of half a million dollars.[1089] Navarrete, in 1624 regards as one of the leading causes of the hatred entertained for the Church by the laity, the contrast between its affluence and the general poverty,[1090] nor is this unlikely for, during the worst periods of national disaster, the Church seems always to have enjoyed superabundant resources. As its income, other than the produce of its lands, was largely derived from tithes, it necessarily varied, from year to year, but was always enormous. In 1653, we find Plasencia spoken of as one of the four most lucrative bishoprics in Spain, with an income of 40,000 ducats, but that there were years in which it had been worth 80,000--and this at a time when the State was virtually bankrupt, the currency in frightful disorder, commerce and industry prostrate, and the whole land steeped in poverty.[1091] Against this, it is true, must be set the habit of the monarch in calling upon the bishops, as well as on the nobles, for contributions, as we have seen in the case of Valdés; thus Cardinal Quiroga, when Archbishop of Toledo, from 1577 to 1594, is said to have given to Philip II an aggregate of a million and a half of ducats.[1092] There were also certain papal grants to the crown on the revenues of the clergy at large, known as the subsidio and the excusado which, in 1573, were reckoned at 575,000 crowns a year and in 1658 at something over two million ducats.[1093]

***

It betrays a consciousness of overgrown wealth that all knowledge of its amount was carefully concealed. In 1741, Benedict XIV granted to Philip V eight per cent. of the revenues of the clergy, regular and secular, for that year. The collection of this in Granada was delegated, with full coercive powers, to the Archdeacon Juan Bautista Simoni who, after Easter 1742, issued an edict requiring all incumbents, within ten days, to render sworn statements of their property and income. This aroused intense excitement. Under one pretext or another all, from the archbishop down, endeavored to escape the revelation of their wealth; there were meetings held and open threats were made of a cessatio a divinis if the measure was insisted on. A compromise was offered of payment of a double servicio, which was assumed to be equivalent to eight per cent., but they refused absolutely to make a return of property and income. Simoni seems to have been sincerely desirous of executing his unpleasant duty with as little friction as possible but, in reporting this repugnance to make sworn statements, he does not hesitate to say that its object was to prevent the king from learning that about three fourths of all the property in Spain was in the hands of the clergy, secular and regular, and especially of the Carthusians, Jesuits, Geronimites and Dominicans. It proved to be impossible to compel the archbishop to make the return, and finally it was compromised by taking the average of a valuation made during five years of a vacancy, 1728-32, which resulted in estimating the revenues of the see at about 39,000 ducats-- evidently an undervaluation, although Granada was reckoned as the poorest of the five Castilian archbishoprics.[1094]

All this wealth and splendor was drawn, in its ultimate source, from the labor of the husbandman and the administration of the sacraments, casting a grievous burden on the industry of the land and counting for much in the general impoverishment. When the little development of Protestantism in 1558 excited so much dread, it was assumed as a matter of course that the people would welcome a reform that would bring relief from the burdens of the church establishment. Jovellanos asks what is left of the ancient glory of Castile save the skeletons of its cities, once populous and full of workshops and stores, and now filled with churches, convents and hospitals, which survive the misery that they have caused.[1095] So, in 1820, the learned Canon Francisco Martínez Marina, in indicating the measures necessary to restore prosperity, says that the first one is to reduce the wealth of the clergy for the benefit of agriculture and the poor and oppressed peasant, and to abolish forever the unjust and insupportable tribute of the tithe, a tribute unknown to Spain before the twelfth century, a tribute which directly prevents the progress of agriculture and one of those which have inflicted the greatest misery on the husbandman.[1096]

A clergy thus worldly, and so far removed from apostolic poverty, was not apt to be devoted to its duties, or to set an example of morality to its subjects. A project, drawn up by a Spanish bishop, of matters to be urged on the Council of Lateran in 1512, affords a glimpse into the deplorable condition of the Church which was so deeply concerned with the salvation of the Marranos and Moriscos. Few among the laity observed the prescribed fasts and feasts, and even the Easter communion was neglected. The priests were negligent and, even in cathedrals, it was sometimes difficult to have divine service performed. Among the clergy, from bishops to the lower orders, concubinage was universal and shameless, while simony ruled everywhere.[1097] The provisions of the Council of Seville in 1512, and of Coria in 1537, indicate the vicious and degraded character of the priesthood and the impossibility of restraining their habitual concubinage.[1098] Alphonso de Castro argues that if it were not for the protection of God it would be difficult to preserve religion in view of the unworthiness of the priests and their wickedness. It is known to all, he says, that the contempt felt for them arises first from their excessive numbers, secondly from their ignorance and lastly from their flagitious lives.[1099] Archbishop Carranza is emphatic in reproving the negligence of the clerics, who were so indifferent to their duty that they abandoned their churches and might as well be non-existent, in addition to which were their evil and scandalous lives and the abuse of their wealth.[1100]

CLERICAL DEMORALIZATION

This is confirmed by Inquisitor-general Valdés who states that when, in 1546, he assumed the archbishopric of Seville, he found the clergy and the dignitaries of his cathedral thoroughly demoralized. They had no shame in their children and grandchildren; their women lived with them openly, as though married, and accompanied them to church, and many of them kept public gaming tables in their houses, which were resorts of disorderly characters. If we may believe him, he resolutely undertook a reform and effected it at great labor and expense, owing to appeals and suits in Rome and in Granada and in the Royal Council and before apostolic judges. Then Francisco de Erasso, a favorite of Charles V, obtained a canonry and joined those who desired to return to their former dissolute life, against which, in 1556, he appeals to Philip II for protection.[1101] The lower ranks of the clergy were no better, if we may believe the synod of Orihuela, in 1600, which asserts that their concubinage was the cause of the animosity of the people against them,[1102] and we have seen, when treating of Solicitation, how frequent was the advantage taken of the opportunities of the confessional.

There were few prelates as conscientious as Valdés represents himself. Alfonso de Castro attributes the existence of heresy to their negligence; they were so slothful that they paid no attention to their duties; those who did otherwise were so rare that they were like jewels among pebbles.[1103] The Venitian envoy, Giovanni Soranzo is less cautious in his utterance, for he describes them as living luxuriously and squandering their revenues on splendid establishments; few of them were without children, in whom they took no shame and for whose advancement they employed every means.[1104] At the other end of the scale were the clerks in the lower orders, immersed in secular affairs, who took the tonsure in order to enjoy the protection from justice afforded by the Church. These were the despair of those responsible for public order. Fernando de Aragon, Viceroy of Valencia, complains, August 21, 1544, of the impossibility of enforcing justice owing to the zeal with which the church authorities protected the tonsure, whether right or wrong. The officials of the archbishops, he says, have been debased and ignorant men; whose sole aim has been to save criminals from the punishment of their crimes. He is encouraged to hope for better things from the appointment as archbishop of San Tomas de Vilanova, and the latter follows, September 8th, with allusions to his own sufferings in consequence of his efforts to remedy this condition, which is an offence to justice and to God and a great damage to the people.[1105]

FANATICAL INTOLERANCE

A Church composed of such elements was not fitted to exercise for good the enormous influence which it enjoyed over public affairs, not only in shaping the policy of the kingdom but in directing the national tendencies. The theory was still the medieval one--that the ecclesiastical power is the sun and the royal power the moon, which derives its light from the sun.[1106] To its influence, as represented by Torquemada, was due the expulsion of the Jews; by Ximenes, the enforced conversion of the Moors; by Espinosa, the rebellion of Granada; by Juan de Ribera and his fellows, the expulsion of the Moriscos. In the royal councils, which formed a bureaucracy, prelates held leading and often dominant positions, and their subordinates were largely drawn from clerical ranks. In 1602 a proposition to increase the schools of artillery was referred to a junta presided over by the royal confessor, which reported that the expense could not be afforded; the schools came to be under the charge of Jesuits and frailes and speedily dwindled to nothing.[1107] The position of royal confessor was one of the highest political importance. Under Charles V he participated in all deliberations and had a preponderating influence.[1108] Under Philip II, his confessor Fray Diego de Chaves, played a leading part in the tragedy of Antonio Pérez. Fray Caspar de Toledo, confessor of Philip III boasted that, whenever he told the king that a thing must be done under pain of mortal sin or that it was sinful, he was obeyed without discussion.[1109] The Regent María Ana of Austria was completely under the domination of her confessor Nithard, and the letters to him of Clement XI, on European politics, indicate that be was the real ruler.[1110] The substitution of Froilan Díaz for Fray Pedro Matilla, as confessor of Carlos II, was the only step necessary to effect a revolution in the government and, when Díaz fled to Rome, he was reclaimed as a fugitive chief minister of state. We have seen under Philip V the power wielded by his confessors Daubenton and Robinet, and the part played by Rábago under Fernando VI. What thus ruled the court was perpetually at work in every parish and every family, where the pulpit and the confessional exercised an incalculable influence. What the Spaniard became was what the Church wished him to be. Clericalism thus, for good or for evil, was a leading factor in controlling the destinies of Spain, in exhausting its resources, in moulding the character of its people, and the Inquisition was its crowning work.

Under such influences, the toleration which had been so marked a feature of the medieval period gradually gave place to a fanaticism finding its expression in the Inquisition and inflamed into greater fierceness by the existence and reaction of that institution. There can be no question as to the sincere devoutness of Charles V, according to the unanimous testimony of the Venetian envoys, who describe his punctual discharge of all religious observances and who state that the surest avenue to his favor was the manifestation of earnest zeal for religion.[1111] Shortly before his death, he expressed deep regret that he had not executed Luther at Worms, in spite of his pledged safe-conduct, for he ought to have forfeited his word in order to avenge the offence to God. In his will, executed in 1554 at Brussels, he charged Philip II in the most earnest manner to favor in all ways the Inquisition, because of the many and great offences to God which it prevents or punishes and, in the codicil of September 9, 1558, dictated on his death-bed, his first thought is to repeat the injunction and to urge his son, by the obedience due to a father, to prosecute heresy, rigorously, unsparingly and relentlessly.[1112] Philip II needed no such exhortations. From his earliest youth he had breathed an atmosphere surcharged by the conflict with heresy; he had been taught that a sovereign's highest duty to God and man was to enforce unity of faith, not only as a paramount religious obligation, but because it was an axiom of the statesmanship of the time that, in no other way, could the peace of a kingdom be preserved. There is no reason to doubt his perfect sincerity when, in 1568, the Archduke Charles came to Spain, as the representative of the German princes, to urge an accommodation with the Netherlands, and Philip, besides his formal reply, gave the archduke secret instructions to tell the emperor that no human influence, or considerations of state, or all that the whole world could say or do, would make him vary a hair's breadth from the course which he had adopted and intended to pursue in this matter of religion, throughout all his dominions; that he would listen to no advice with regard to it, and would take ill any that might be offered. At the same time he wrote to Chantonnay, his ambassador at Vienna, that what he was doing in the Netherlands was for their advantage and the preservation of the Catholic faith, and that he would make no change in his policy, if it involved risking all his possessions and if the whole world should fall upon his head. So, in 1574, the instructions to the commissioners sent to Breda to confer with the deputies of William the Silent, were to declare emphatically that he would suffer no one to live under his throne who was not completely a Catholic.[1113] Philip was merely translating into practice the teachings of the Church and won its unstinted admiration. Cardinal Pallavicini contrasts the vacillating persecution in France with his sanguinary rigor, which was not only grateful to heaven but propitious to his kingdom, thus saved by salutary blood-letting.[1114]

***

It was natural that Philip, in his will, executed March 7, 1594, should reiterate to his son and successor the injunctions which he had received from his father. The Inquisition was to be the object of special favor, even greater than in the past, for the times were perilous and full of so many errors in the faith.[1115] Philip III had not energy enough to be an active persecutor and if, under the guidance of Lerma, he expelled the Moriscos, under the same tutelage he made peace with England in 1605 and a truce with Holland in 1609, to the disgust of the pious who could not understand any dealings with heretics. Yet he was a most religious prince, who spent hours every day in his devotions and in examining his conscience, and who set a shining example by the frequency with which he sought confession and communion.[1116]

It was a matter of course that he should, in his will, leave to his successor the customary instructions to foster the Inquisition. As to Philip IV, we have seen abundant instances of his subservience to it, during his half-century of reign, and of his readiness to subordinate to it all other interests. He showed his consistency in this when, at the dictation of the Suprema, he incurred a war with England through his refusal to sign a treaty forbidding the persecution of Englishmen in Spain on account of their religion[1117] and, in his will, executed in 1665, he laid the customary injunctions on his successor to aid and favor the Inquisition, adding an exhortation to honor and defend the clergy in all their exemptions and immunities, and earnestly to labor for the reformation of the religious Orders.[1118]

Carlos II was a nonentity who need not be considered and, with the Bourbons, we enter on the dawn of a new era, in which fanaticism no longer dominates the policy of the State. It is true that Philip V, when abdicating, in 1724, enjoined on his son Luis the preservation of the faith through the instrumentality of the Inquisition as fervently as any of his predecessors and that, during the first third of the century, there was a fierce recrudescence of inquisitorial activity, but we have seen how the spirit of the age gradually made itself felt and, although the duty of exterminating heresy was still admitted in theory, in practice its enforcement was greatly mitigated.

It is difficult for us, in the indifferentism of the twentieth century, to realize or to understand the violence of the passions excited by questions of faith, dissociated from all temporal interests, and their influence on a people so emotional as the Spaniards and so apt, as they tell us themselves, to be swayed by imagination rather than by reason. We have seen (Vol. III, p. 284) the whole kingdom of Portugal thrown into excitement by the theft of a pyx with a consecrated host and that only the opportune discovery of the culprit saved all the New Christians from expulsion. It might seem to us a very trivial affair that, on the eve of Good Friday, 1640, there was posted, in the chapter-house of Granada, a placard ridiculing the Christian religion, praising the Mosaic Law, and blaspheming the purity of the Virgin, but it produced the greatest excitement throughout Spain. Special services were held in all the churches to appease the insulted deity and to discover the malefactor. He was detected, in the person of a hermit of the Santa Imagen del Triunfo, who was arrested, and Inquisitor Rodezno deemed it advisable to break the inviolable secrecy of the Inquisition in order to calm the public agitation, by letting the people know that the culprit had been discovered and convicted. Learned doctors improved the occasion by printing dissertations in which it was proved that he must be burnt alive, if no death more atrocious could be invented to suit the crime.[1119] The fanatical hatred of heresy per se, thus sedulously inculcated and engrained in the moral fibre of every Spaniard is seen in the statutes of Limpieza, which closed the avenues to distinction to the descendants of Conversos and of those who had been penanced by the Inquisition, so that even arrest and imprisonment for a trivial offence inflicted, according to popular prejudice, an indelible stigma on a family. We have seen to what insane extent this was carried and what evil it wrought in the social organization, but more prolific in evil was the habit of thought by which it was engendered and which it intensified.

SUPERFICIAL DEVOUTNESS

Yet practically the religion which was so sensitive as to purity of faith was of a very superficial character. External observances were strictly enforced, and the Inquisition was ever on the watch to punish any irreverence in act or word, yet Alfonso de Castro tells us that, in the mountainous provinces, such as Asturias, Galicia and elsewhere, the word of God was so rarely preached to the people that they observed many pagan rites and many superstitions.[1120] To labor on Sunday or feast-day was a serious offence, involving suspicion of heresy, yet Carranza says that more offences against God were committed on Sundays than in all the week-days combined; those who went to mass mostly spent the time in business or in talking or sleeping; those who did not go, gratified their vanity or their appetites; the ancient Jews used to say that, on their feast-days, the demons left the cities for refuge in the mountain caves, but now it would seem that on week-days the demons avoided the people who were busy with their labors and, on feast-days, came trooping joyfully from the deserts, for then they find the doors open to all kinds of vices.[1121]

Paolo Tiepolo, in 1563, observes that, in all external signs of religion, the Spaniards are exceedingly devout, but he doubts whether the interior corresponds; the clergy live as they choose, without any one reprehending them, and he is scandalized by the buffooneries and burlesques performed in the churches on feast-days.[1122] The churches, in fact, seem to have been places for everything save devotion. Azpilcueta describes the profane observances during divine service, the inattention of the priests, the processions of masks and demons, the banquets and feastings, and other disgraceful profanations, so that there are few of the faithful who do not sin in church, and few who do not utter idle, vain, foul, evil or profane words; in hot weather, the coolness of the churches made them favorite lounging-places for both sexes, including monks and nuns, and much that was indecent occurred; they were moreover places for the transaction of business, and more bargaining took place there than in the markets.[1123] This was not a mere passing custom. A century later Francisco Santos pictures for us a church crowded with so-called worshippers, where the services could scarce be heard for the noise; beggars crying for alms and wrangling among themselves; two men quarrelling fiercely and on the point of drawing their swords; a group of young gallants chattering and maltreating a poor man who had chanced to touch them in passing; people leaving one mass that had commenced to follow a priest, who had the reputation of greater despatch in his sacred functions; in a chapel a bevy of fair ladies drinking chocolate, discussing fashions and waited on by their admirers--all is worldly and the religious observance is the merest pretext.[1124] This irreverence was shared by the priests. A brief of Urban VIII, January 30, 1642, recites complaints from the dean and chapter of Seville concerning the use of tobacco in the churches, both in smoking and snuffing, even by priests while celebrating mass, and of their profanation of the sacred cloths by using them and staining them with tobacco, wherefore he decrees excommunication latæ sententiæ for the use of the weed within the sacred precincts.[1125] It is evident that the Inquisition, while enforcing conformity as to dogma and outward observance, failed to inspire genuine respect for religion.

RESULTS OF INTOLERANCE

It will thus be seen how little really was gained for religion by the spirit of fierce intolerance largely responsible for the material causes of decadence which we have passed rapidly in review. The irrational resolve to enforce unity of faith at every cost spurred Ferdinand and Isabella to burn and pauperize those among their subjects who were most economically valuable, to expel those who could not be reduced to conformity and to institute a system of confiscation of which we have seen the destructive influence on industry and on the credit on which commerce and industry depend, while the application of this to the condemnation of the dead not only brought misery on innocent descendants but unsettled titles and involved all transactions in insecurity. This sanctified the ambition of Charles V with the halo of religion. This was the motive which underlay the suicidal policy of Philip II, leading to the endless wars with the Netherlands, to the rebellion of Granada and to the wasteful support of the Ligue. This was at the bottom of the Morisco disaffection, culminating in the expulsion of 1610, just after Philip III had practically accepted the loss of Holland by the truce of 1609. The land was robbed of its most industrious classes, it was drained of its bravest soldiers, its trade and productiveness were fatally crippled, and it was reduced to the lowest term of financial exhaustion, all for the greater glory of God, and in the belief that it was avenging offences to God. To meet the exigencies arising from this, and from the thoughtless extravagance of the monarchs, the labor, on which rested the resources of the State, was crushed to earth and subjected to burdens that defeated their own ends, for they drove the producer in despair from the soil. Productive industry and commerce, enfeebled by the expulsions, were so handicapped that they dwindled almost to extinction and passed virtually into the hands of foreigners, who dealt under the mask of testas ferrias--of Spaniards who lent their names to the real principals, for the most part the very heretics whom Spain had exhausted herself to destroy. Trade and credit were hampered, not only through the vitiation of the currency but through the ever-impending risk of sequestration and confiscation, and the impediments of the censorship as developed in the visitas de navios. The blindness and inefficiency of the Government intensified in every way the evils created by its mistaken policy but, at the root of all, lay the prolonged and relentless determination to enforce conformity, at a time when the industrial and commericial era was opening, which was to bring wealth and power to the nations wise enough and liberal enough to avail themselves of its opportunities--opportunities which Spain was invited virtually to monopolize through its control of the trade of the Indies and the production of the precious metals. There is melancholy truth in the boast of Doctor Pedro Peralta Barnuevo, in his relation of the Lima auto of 1733, that the determination to enforce unity of faith at all costs had rendered Spain rather a church than a monarchy, and her kings protectors of the faith rather than sovereigns. She was a temple, in which the altars were cities and the oblations were men, and she despised the prosperity of the State in comparison with devotion to religion.[1126]

Isabella and her Hapsburg descendants were but obeying the dictates of conscience and executing the laws of the Church, when they sought to suppress heresy and apostasy by force, and they might well deem it both duty and good policy at a time when it was universally taught that unity of faith was the surest guarantee of the happiness and prosperity of nations. Spain, with accustomed thoroughness, carried out this theory for three centuries to a reductio ad absurdum, through the Inquisition, organized, armed and equipped to the last point of possible perfection for its work. The elaborate arguments of its latest defender only show that it cannot be defended without also defending the whole policy of the House of Hapsburg, which wrought such misery and degradation.[1127] It was the essential part of a system and, as such, it contributed its full share to the ruin of Spain.

INFLUENCE ON THE PEOPLE

That occasionally even an inquisitor could have a glimmer of the truth appears from a very remarkable memorial addressed to Philip IV by a member of the Suprema, with regard to the Portuguese Jews. He states that they consider the rigor of the Inquisition as a blessing, since it drives them from Spain to other lands, where they can enjoy their religion and acquire prosperity. He wishes to prevent this exodus, which is depriving Spain of population and wealth and exposing it to peril, and to win back those who have expatriated themselves, to which end he proposes greatly to soften inquisitorial severity in regard to confiscation, imprisonment and the wearing of the sanbenito, except in the case of hardened impenitents. He would welcome them back and, even if their Catholicism were merely external, he argues that their children would become good Catholics, even as has proved to be the case with the descendants of the Castilian Jews. Indeed, he goes so far as to urge that foreigners in general should be encouraged to bring their capital to Spain, to settle and be naturalized, to marry Spanish wives and thus minister to the wealth and prosperity of the land.[1128] The worldly wisdom of this was too oppugnant to the prejudices of the time, which clamored, as we have seen, for extermination and isolation, and its sagacious counsels were unheeded. The Judaizers were driven forth, to aid in building up Holland with their wealth and intelligence, and Spain, in ever deepening poverty, continued to cherish the ideals which she had embodied in the Inquisition.

There was one service the performance of which it was never tired of claiming for itself and is still claimed for it by its advocates--that in the sixteenth and seventeenth centuries it preserved Spain from the religious wars which desolated France and Germany. This service may well be called in question, for the temperament and training of the Spanish nation render ludicrous the assumption that a couple of hundred heretics, among whom but half a dozen had the spirit of martyrdom for their faith, could cause such spread of dissidence as to endanger peace; yet even should we admit this service, its method, in causing intellectual torpor and segregating the nation from all influences from abroad, only postponed the inevitable, while intensifying the disturbance when the change should come from medievalism to modernism. The nineteenth century bore, in an aggravated form, the brunt which should have fallen on the sixteenth. When the spirit of the Revolution broke in, it found a population sedulously trained to passive obedience to the State and submissiveness to the Church. It had been so long taught, by theocratic absolutism, that it must not think or reason for itself, that it had lost the power of reasoning on the great problems of life. It was without reverence for law, for it was accustomed to see the arbitrary will of an absolute sovereign override the law, and it was without experience to choose between the sober realities of responsible government and the glittering promises of ardent idealists. Yet the Revolution passed away leaving matters as they were before. The habit of unquestioning submission, inherited through generations, has become so fixed a part of the national character that, as we are told, the people fail to recognize that they are as completely under bondage to Caciquism as erstwhile they were to monarchy--that in fact the nation is still in its infancy and is unfit to govern itself.[1129]

As in temporal, so it has been in the spiritual field. In the turmoil of the Revolution the Inquisition died a natural death, but the Church filled the vacancy. It had grown so accustomed to the acceptance, on all hands, of its divine mission, it had so long enjoyed unassailable wealth and power, that it could not adapt itself to the necessities of the new situation and, when it could not rely upon the brute force of the State, it called into play the popular passions which it had fostered. As an irreconcileable, it provoked the attacks made on its overgrown wealth and numbers; it was uncompromising and would listen to no adjustment, for it claimed the full benefit of the canon law under which it was exempted from all interference by the State; its attitude was of immovable hostility to the new order of things, and it suffered the rough handling that inevitably resulted, courting martyrdom rather than tamely to permit profane hands to be laid upon the ark. It has thus continued to be an unassimilable element in the political situation, its policy directed from Rome and the vast influence of its perfect organization employed to retard rather than to stimulate progress in good government and material prosperity.[1130] What may be the outcome of the pending struggle between Church and State, aroused by the recognition of civil marriage, it is too early to predict.

INDIFFERENCE TO MORALS

Thus the conclusion that may be drawn from our review of the causes underlying the misfortunes of Spain is that what may fairly be attributable to the Inquisition is its service as the official instrument of the intolerance that led to such grave results, and its influence on the Spanish character in intensifying that intolerance into a national characteristic, while benumbing the Spanish intellect until it may be said for a time to have almost ceased to think. The objects for which it was so shrewdly and so carefully organized were effectually attained and, in the eyes of experienced statesmen, at the time of its fullest development, it was the bulwark of the faith. In 1573, Leonardo Donato reflects the prevailing view in governmental circles when he speaks of its authority and severity as absolutely necessary, for the number of the New Christians was everywhere so great, recently baptized with God knows what disposition, and with ancestral memories still vivid, that, if it were not for the incessant watch kept over them by the Inquisition, there would be great danger that Spain would lose her religion. In 1581, Gioan Francesco Morosini declares that, although the Spaniards were in appearance the most devout and Catholic of nations, yet, what between the Jews, Moriscos and heretics, Spain would be more infected than Germany or England if it were not for the fear inspired by the severity of the Inquisition; and the same views are expressed by Giambattista Confalonieri in 1591, and by the Lucchese envoy Damiano Bernardini, in 1602.[1131] Yet the faith, thus sedulously preserved at such fearful cost, was largely, as we have seen, one of exterior observance, without corresponding internal piety, ready to burst into flame for the maintenance of a dogma like the Immaculate Conception, and to earn heaven by paying for masses and anniversaries and chaplaincies, but not to labor for it by purity of life and self-abnegation, or by obeying the divine command to earn its bread by the sweat of its brow. The natural result of this, when brought face to face with modern conditions, is that Cánovas del Castillo, in a debate in the Córtes of 1869, declared with sorrow that Spain, of all nations, was the one most indifferent to religion, and a recent author asserts that there would be no hazard in affirming the Spaniards to be the most irreligious, indifferent, and practically atheist people in Europe.[1132]

In fact, the dissociation of religion from morals--the incongruous connection of ardent zeal for dogma with laxity of life--was stimulated by the Inquisition. As we have seen, it paid no attention to morals and thus taught the lesson that they were unimportant in comparison with accuracy of belief. No matter how dissolute was the conduct of the confessor with his spiritual daughters, he was safe so long as he did not commit a technical transgression inferring suspicion of misbelief as to the sacrament, and even when he neglected these precautions we have seen how benignant was the treatment extended to him. It is true that, towards the end of the sixteenth century, the Inquisition showed remarkable ardor in prosecuting those who gave utterance to the common opinion that there was no sin in simple fornication between the unmarried, and that in large measure it suppressed the utterance, but, as it punished only the utterance and not the sin, this did nothing to advance morality. The same may be said of its ignorant destruction of works of art which it regarded as indecent and the occasional prohibition of a book or play that evoked its disapprobation. In the absence of more serious work a few cases may be found of its undertaking to vindicate morals, but they are too rare for us to attribute to them any motive save a desire to intermeddle. The advancement of morality in fact was no part of its functions as a bulwark of the faith; rather, indeed, it aided in disseminating corruption by its custom of reading at the autos de fe sentences con méritos of which the details were an effective popular education in vice.[1133] The result is seen in the seventeenth century, when the only heretics were the scattered and persecuted Portuguese, and yet there has probably never existed a society more abandoned to corruption--so abandoned, indeed, that even the sense of shame was lost. Padre Corella was no rigorist but, towards the close of the century, he draws a hideous picture of social conditions; everywhere, he says, is vice and crime, lust and cruelty, fraud and rapine, in the seats of trade, in the halls of justice, in the family, in the court, in the churches, while the clergy, if possible, are worse than the laity. Philip IV, who so religiously supported the Inquisition, was not only notorious for his licentiousness, but amused himself with scandalously sacrilegious comedies and farces in his palace theatre, where the scenes and persons of Scripture were made subjects of ridicule, and this style passed into popular literature and rhymes which escaped the censure.[1134]

CONTEMPT FOR LAW

Spanish theology, which was supreme in the sixteenth and early seventeenth centuries, made only one real contribution--the invention of Probabilism by Bartolomé de Medina in his commentaries on Aquinas in 1577. On this was founded the new science of Moral Theology, devoted to evading the penalties of sin, and to applying to the decrees of God the favorite Spanish device for eluding those of the king, by obeying and not executing. Escobar, held up to an infamous immortality by Pascal, merely compiled what he found in theologians of the highest authority and, when the laxity of the Jesuit Moya's Opusculum called forth a papal prohibition in 1666, repeated in 1680, the Spanish Inquisition asserted its independence by refusing to put the work on the Index.[1135] The practical influence of all this is described in a memorial of nine Spanish bishops, in 1717, to Clement XI, against the Consultas Morales of the Capuchin Martin de Torricella, in which they state that Probabilism had undermined all morality and all obedience to divine, municipal and canon law, and that multitudes lived disorderly lives under appeal to probabilistic casuistry, for so-called probable opinions could be had to justify whatever men desired to do.[1136]

If the power of the Inquisition thus was withheld when it might have been exerted with benefit to society, it was actively employed, under the later Hapsburgs, to loosen the bonds of social order and stimulate contempt for law. To it was largely attributable the virtual anarchy of Spain, during the seventeenth century, arising from the numerous competing jurisdictions and the contempt felt for the royal officials. This found its origin in the insolent audacity with which the Inquisition enforced its claims to jurisdiction. When the royal officials were excommunicated, arrested and imprisoned without scruple, and the highest courts were treated with contempt and contumely, respect for law and its ministers was fatally weakened. That the other privileged jurisdictions--the Cruzada, the spiritual, and the military--should follow the example was inevitable, and the social condition of Spain became deplorable.[1137] In 1677, the Council of Castile represented to Carlos II the evils thus inflicted on the people by the two chief offenders, the Inquisition and the Cruzada, the most oppressive form of which was the abuse of excommunication for matters purely secular. The Council had endeavored to remedy this, but its authority had been suspended and it was powerless to protect the vassals of the crown. Carlos feebly replied that, although he could deprive them of the royal jurisdiction which they abused, yet he deemed it better not to do so, and he contented himself with prohibiting the use of censures in temporal matters--a prohibition which of course was disregarded.[1138] In the very next year Carlos was made to feel his powerlessness in the face of the arrogant superiority asserted by the Inquisition.

When, in 1678, the raid on the whole trading community of Majorca gave promise of immense confiscations, Carlos prudently ordered, May 30th, the viceroy to look after the safety of the sequestrations. The viceroy thereupon asked for inventories or statements and, on their refusal, made threats of taking further measures. The tribunal reported to the Suprema which instructed the inquisitors to defend their jurisdiction by censures and, if necessary, by a cessatio a divinis, when, if this did not suffice, they were to entrust their prisoners to the bishop and sail for Spain, reporting to the pope. After despatching this defiant and revolutionary missive, the Suprema, on August 8th, condescended to inform the king of it in the form of a stinging rebuke. The request of the viceroy, it said, was an unexampled assault on religion and the Holy See, and also a profanation of the most venerable sacredness of the Inquisition; sequestrated property was ecclesiastical property until confiscated, and to allow a layman to control it would be subversive of all law, as well as a violation of the secrecy of the Inquisition. Carlos humbly apologized; he had not meant to show distrust and would punish the viceroy if he had exceeded his instructions, but he complained that, without notice to him, the inquisitors should have been ordered to leave Majorca, and thus cause irreparable evils. The Suprema, in reply, followed up its advantage. The abandonment of Majorca by the inquisitors would be a less evil than violating the secrecy of the Inquisition; the viceroy should have positive orders to keep his hands off, and the king ought to have consulted it before issuing such instructions; this would have prevented all trouble, for the operations of the Inquisition were so special and peculiar that even his superior intelligence could not understand them without explanations.[1139] This insolence accomplished its purpose; Carlos was effectually snubbed, and we have seen how small was the share of the spoils eventually doled out to him.

DOMINATION

The Inquisition, in fact, was virtually an independent power in the state, which asserted itself after the vigorous personality of Ferdinand had been forgotten. Its aspiration to dominate the land was revealed in the projected Order of Santa María de la Espada blanca which Philip II was shrewd enough to crush while yet there was time, but the measure of independence which it had already attained was seen when the Córtes of the kingdoms of Aragon sought to get the signature of the inquisitor-general, as well as of the king, to the concessions which they secured, and when the Inquisition ignored the royal agreements, even to the point of deliberately contravening them in the matter of confiscations. It was manifested, in the affair of Antonio Pérez, when Philip II was obliged to call it to his assistance, and it followed its own interests in disregard of the royal policy. So, in the long struggle with Bilbao over the visitas de navios, it virtually set at defiance both the crown and all the authorities of Biscay. If it helped the monarchy in the struggle with Rome over the regalías, when it had thus secured its independence of the papal Inquisition it had no scruple in turning its powers of censorship against the royal prerogative. But for the advent of the Bourbon dynasty, it might reasonably have looked forward to becoming eventually dominant, for it combined legislative and executive functions, temporal and spiritual jurisdiction, and asserted, like the Church, the right to define the limits of its own powers. Its whole career, indeed, shows how baseless is the modern theory that it was an instrument of the State in establishing the autocracy of the monarch. If the fallacy of this requires further proof it is sufficiently demonstrated, even under the first of the Bourbons, by the fate of Macanaz, whom it dismissed from power and condemned to a life of poverty and exile because, in the service of the king, he endeavored to render it what Ranke and Gams fancy it to have been. It is true that, in its period of decadence, it joined forces with the crown to withstand the inroad of free thought, which was equally threatening to both, and that it employed its expiring power to suppress political as well as spiritual heresy, but in this it was fighting its own battle as much as that of the monarchy on which it depended for existence.

***

Defenders of the Inquisition, in the controversy over its suppression and since then, have relied largely on the assertion that, during its existence, no voice was raised against it, that all organs of public opinion and all writers praised it, as the protector of religion, and as extremely careful to administer exact justice. So far from this being the case, we have seen its own admissions (Vol. I, p. 538) of the hearty hatred felt for it and its officials, and we have heard the complaints of the Córtes of Valladolid in 1518 and 1523, of Coruña in 1520 and of Madrid in 1575, besides the ceaseless struggles of Aragon and Catalonia, whose Córtes had not been reduced to servility. What was its reputation throughout Europe may be gauged by the fact that, in 1535, when João III was endeavoring to have an Inquisition of his own in Portugal, and there was talk of referring the subject to the general council then expected shortly to assemble, his ambassador at Rome, Martinho, Archbishop of Funchal, warned him that, if the matter was broached in the council, it would result in abolishing the Inquisition of Spain.[1140] In Spain, its reputation is to be gathered from the unbiased reports of the Venetian envoys, who lauded its services in the suppression of heresy, and to whom, as practical statesmen, it was an object of wonder and admiration, as a machine perfectly devised to keep the people in abject subjection. In these reports it is observable that, while all are emphatic as to its rigor, not one hazards approval of its justice. The envoys were profoundly impressed by the universal awe which it inspired. As early as 1525, Gasparo Contarini tells us that every one trembled before it, for its severity and the dread entertained for it were greater even than for the Council of Ten. In 1557, Federico Badoero speaks of the terror caused by its pitiless procedure. In 1563, Paolo Tiepolo, after dwelling on the secrecy and unsparing rigor of its judgements, says that every one shudders at its very name, as it has supreme authority over the property, life, honor and even the souls of men. Two years later Giovanni Soranzo speaks of the great fear inspired by it, for its authority transcends incomparably that of the king. In 1567, Antonio Tiepolo echoes these assertions, and all agree in their comments on the influence of the mysterious secrecy of its operation and the relentless severity of its action.[1141]

HABITUAL SELF-RESTRAINT

It scarce needs this testimony to explain why no unfavorable opinion of the Inquisition is to be expected of Spaniards during its existence, except by those who spoke as mandatories of the people in the Córtes or high officials in contests over competencias. Terror rendered silence imperative, and secrecy made ignorance universal. The discharged prisoner was sworn to reveal nothing of what he had endured and any complaint of injustice subjected him to prosecution. Criticism was held to be impeding its action and was a crime subject to condign punishment. Writers had ever to keep in view its censorship, with the certainty that any ill-judged word would ensure the suppression of a book, and any attempt at self-justification would lead to worse consequences, as Belando found when a petition to be heard cost him life-long imprisonment and prohibition to use the pen. When, in the yearly Edict of Faith, every one was required, under pain of excommunication, to denounce any impeding, direct or indirect, of the tribunal, or any criticism of the justice of its operation, restraint became universal and habitual and, in the instinct of self-preservation, men would naturally seek to teach themselves and their children not even to think ill of the Inquisition lest, in some unguarded moment, a chance utterance might lead to prosecution and infamy. The popular refran, Con el Rey y la Inquisicion, chiton!--Silence as to the king and the Inquisition--reveals to us better than a world of argument, the result of this repression through generations, and its efficiency is seen in the fact that in Toledo, from 1648 to 1794, there was but a single trial for speaking ill of the Holy Office. Such training bore its fruits when autocracy broke down under the Revolution and the experiment of self-government was essayed.

The Spaniard was taught not alone to repress his opinions as to the Inquisition but to keep a guard on his tongue under all circumstances, not only in public but in the sacred confidence of his own family, for the duty of denunciation applied to husband and father, to wife and children. Even as early as 1534, the orthodox Juan Luis Vives complained to Erasmus that in those difficult times it was dangerous either to speak or to keep silent.[1142] The cautious Mariana tells us that the most grievous oppression caused by the introduction of the Inquisition was the deprivation of freedom of speech, which some persons regarded as a servitude worse than death.[1143] We have seen how seriously were treated even the most trivial and careless expressions, which could be tortured into disregard of some theological tenet or disrespect for some church observance, and it behooved every one to be on his guard at all times and in all places. The yearly Edict of Faith kept the terror of the Inquisition constantly before every man and was perhaps the most efficient device ever invented to subject a population to the fear of an ever-impending danger. No other nation ever lived through centuries under a moral oppression so complete, so minute and so all-pervading.

That the Inquisition inspired a dread greater than that felt for the royal authority is illustrated by a curious instance, in which it was utilized for good in subduing a lawless community. In 1588, Lupus Martin de Govilla, Inquisitor of Barcelona, in a visitation came to Montblanch, where no inquisitor had been for many years. He found it a populous town, torn by factions so bitter that men were slain in the streets, battles were fought in the plaza, and women at their windows were shot with arquebuses. After publishing the Edict of Faith he discovered that witnesses were afraid to come to him through the streets and, regarding this as a contempt of the Inquisition, he issued a proclamation forbidding the carrying of arquebuses and cross-bows, and his order was obeyed. He made an example of one offender by requiring him to hear mass as a penitent, banishing him and confiscating his arquebus, which quieted the people, so that the Inquisition could be carried on. Then a murder occurred, and the regidors procured from the viceroy full powers for him to pacify the town; by general agreement all placed themselves under the jurisdiction of the Inquisition, as there was no safety under the royal, and they gave thanks to God that peace was restored, and that men could move around without arms. Govilla went to Poblet, when news was brought him of another murder; he returned and imprisoned and penanced those guilty, who complained to the viceroy, but the Audiencia, after examination dismissed the complaint, and this strange jurisdiction of the Inquisition seems to have continued for some ten years.[1144]

STATISTICS OF VICTIMS

Before dismissing the impression produced by the severity of the Inquisition it will not be amiss to attempt some conjecture as to the totality of its operations, especially as regards the burnings, which naturally affected more profoundly the imagination. There is no question that the number of these has been greatly exaggerated in popular belief, an exaggeration to which Llorente has largely contributed by his absurd method of computation, on an arbitrary assumption of a certain annual average for each tribunal in successive periods. It is impossible now to reconstruct the statistics of the Inquisition, especially during its early activity, but some general conclusions can be formed from the details accessible as to a few tribunals.

The burnings without doubt were numerous during the first few years, through the unregulated ardor of inquisitors, little versed in the canon law, who seem to have condemned right and left, on flimsy evidence, and without allowing their victims the benefit of applying for reconciliation, for, while there might be numerous negativos, there certainly were few pertinacious impenitents. The discretion allowed to them to judge as to the genuineness of conversion gave a dangerous power, which was doubtless abused by zealots, and the principle that imperfect confession was conclusive of impenitence added many to the list of victims, while the wholesale reconciliations under the Edicts of Grace afforded an abundant harvest to be garnered under the rule condemning relapse. In the early years, moreover, the absent and the dead contributed with their effigies largely to the terrible solemnities of the quemadero.

Modern writers vary irreconcileably in their estimates, influenced more largely by subjective considerations than by the imperfect statistics at their command. Rodrigo coolly asserts as a positive fact that those who perished in Spain at the stake for heresy did not amount to 400 and that these were voluntary victims, who refused to retract their errors.[1145] Father Gams reckons 2000 for the period up to the death of Isabella, in 1504, and as many more from that date up to 1758.[1146] On the other hand, Llorente calculates that, up to the end of Torquemada's activity, there had been condemned 105,294 persons, of whom 8800 were burnt alive, 6500 in effigy and 90,004 exposed to public penance, while, up to 1524, the grand totals amounted to 14,344, 9372 and 195,937.[1147] Even these figures are exceeded by Amador de los Rios, who is not usually given to exaggeration. He assumes that, up to 1525, when the Moriscos commenced to suffer as heretics, the number of those burnt alive amounted to 28,540, of those burnt in effigy to 16,520 and those penanced to 303,847, making a total of 348,907 condemnations for Judaism.[1148] Don Melgares Marin, whose familiarity with the documents is incontestable, tells us that, in Castile, during 1481, more than 20,000 were reconciled under Edicts of Grace, more than 3000 were penanced with the sanbenito, and more than 4000 were burnt, but he adduces no authorities in support of the estimate.[1149]

***

The only contemporary who gives us figures for the whole of Spain is Hernando de Pulgar, secretary of Queen Isabella. His official position gave him facilities for obtaining information, and his scarcely veiled dislike for the Inquisition was not likely to lead to underrating its activity. He states at 15,000 those who had come in under Edicts of Grace, and at 2000 those who were burnt, besides the dead whose bones were exhumed in great quantities; the number of penitents he does not estimate. Unluckily, he gives no date but, as his Chronicle ends in 1490, we may assume that to be the term comprised.[1150] With some variations his figures were adopted by subsequent writers.[1151] Bernáldez only makes the general statement that throughout Spain an infinite number were burnt and condemned and reconciled and imprisoned, and of those reconciled many relapsed and were burnt.[1152]

Imperfect as are the records, we may endeavor to test these various estimates by such evidence as is at hand respecting a few of the tribunals. In this we may commence with Seville, which was unquestionably the most active. The Inquisition had started there, as the centre of crypto-Judaism; it was the most populous city of Castile, with nearly half a million of inhabitants, and its unrivalled commercial activity rendered it peculiarly attractive to the Conversos, while Isabella's Andalusian decree of expulsion must have largely increased the number of pseudo-proselytes. In 1524, there was placed over the gateway of the castle of Triana, occupied by the tribunal, an inscription of which the purport is not entirely clear, but signifying that, up to that time, it had caused the abjuration of more than 20,000 heretics and had burnt nearly 1000 obstinate ones.[1153] This is probably an understatement, if we are to believe Bernáldez, who asserts that in eight years, from the founding of the Seville tribunal up to 1488, it had burnt in person more than 700 heretics, besides many effigies of fugitives and an infinite number of bones; those reconciled during the same period he estimates at 5000.[1154] Still its activity must soon have greatly diminished for, in 1502, Antoine de Lalaing, visiting the Castle of Triana, describes it as containing more than twenty heretic prisoners which he evidently regards as a large number, but which would argue a very moderate amount of persecution in view of the leisurely procedure that was becoming usual.[1155] There is therefore an apparent tendency to exaggerate the achievements of the Holy Office in the statement of its secretary Zurita, some half-century or more later, that in Seville alone, up to the year 1520, there were more than 4000 culprits burnt and more than 30,000 reconciled and penanced, besides the numerous fugitives, and he adds that an author, very diligent in the matter, affirms these figures to be exceedingly defective and that, in the archbishopric of Seville alone, there were condemned as Judaizing heretics, more than a hundred thousand persons, including those reconciled.[1156] Cardinal Contarini, when Venetian envoy in 1525, was evidently misled by this tendency to amplification, when he describes the Inquisition as having made a slaughter of the New Christians impossible to exaggerate.[1157]

***

Unfortunately no authentic records have seen the light by which to test the accuracy of these varying estimates of the activity of the most destructive tribunal during the early period. It is otherwise with several of those that ranked next to it in importance. For the province of Toledo, as we have seen, the first tribunal was established at Ciudad Real where, in its two years of existence, it relaxed in person 47 and in effigy 98.[1158] Transferred to Toledo, in 1485, its operations at first were energetic, but they diminished greatly towards the end of the century until, in 1501, it had a spasmodic period of activity through the discovery of "La Moça de Herrera" (Vol. I, p. 186) a young Jewish prophetess, to whose numerous believers no mercy was shown, for those who had been reconciled thus incurred the penalty of relapse. The total operations of the Toledo tribunal, from its origin in 1485 until 1501, amount to 250 relaxed in person, over 500 in effigy, about 200 imprisoned and 5200 reconciled under Edicts of Grace. Of the personally relaxed, nearly half, or 117, were followers of the prophetess, leaving only 139 ordinary Judaizers and, of those imprisoned, about 140 may be accounted for in the same way.[1159] Saragossa was reckoned as one of the most deadly tribunals in Spain--indeed, Llorente remarks that if he had taken it and Toledo as the basis of his calculations, he would have tripled the number of victims.[1160] For this we have the details of the sixty-five autos, held from 1485 to 1502, furnished by the record printed in the Appendix to Volume I. Summarized, this gives the totals of 119 burnt alive, 5 quartered, beheaded or strangled prior to burning, 3 bodies burnt, 29 effigies burnt and 458 penanced, or an aggregate of 614.[1161] The Libro Verde de Aragon, moreover, gives us an official list of the residents of Saragossa burnt, from 1483 to 1574, in summarizing which it appears that, during these ninety-two years, the total of relaxations in person was 125 and in effigy 77, including seven witches, three sorcerers and four Protestants. Tabulation by years emphasizes the diminution of activity after the close of the fifteenth century.[1162]

Barcelona is another important tribunal of which we have accurate statistics during its early years, furnished by the royal archivist, Pere Miguel Carbonell. From its foundation to the end of Torquemada's career, in 1498, there were thirty-one autos celebrated in Barcelona, Tarragona, Lérida, Gerona, Perpignan, Vich, Elne and Balaguer. In these the totals are only 10 strangled and burnt, 13 burnt alive, 15 dead and 430 burnt in effigy, 1 reconciled in effigy, 116 penanced with prison and 304 reconciled for spontaneous confession.[1163]

Valencia, of all the tribunals, was the one which best maintained its activity throughout the sixteenth century, owing to the dense Morisco population. We have a list of all persons imprisoned for heresy, from the beginning in 1485 up to 1592 inclusive, amounting in all to 3104, of whom 530 were contributed by the last four years, 1589-92, when the persecution of the Moriscos was particularly active. There is also an alphabetical list of persons relaxed, from the beginning until 1593, unfortunately imperfect and ending with the letter N, but, by adding twenty-five per cent. we can obtain a reasonably close approximation to the total. The list as we have it gives 515 relaxations in person and 383 in effigy, or, with the addition of twenty-five per cent., 643 of the former and 479 of the latter, being nearly an average of six per annum of the former and four and a half of the latter.[1164]

Valladolid had the most extensive territory of all the tribunals, but it comprised the northern provinces, where the New Christians were comparatively few. It was not organized for work until 1488, making its first arrest on September 29th of that year, and holding its first auto on June 19, 1489, when, after nine months' work on new ground, there were but eighteen relaxations in person and four in effigy. The next auto recorded did not occur until January 5, 1492, when the relaxations in person numbered thirty-two and in effigy two.[1165] This, while sufficiently cruel, indicates that the victims in the northern provinces bore but a small proportion to those in the southern.

***

At the other extremity of Spain was the little tribunal of Majorca, which acquired a sudden and sinister reputation by the occurrences of 1678 and 1691. It started in 1488 and for some years was fairly active, lapsing in time into virtual torpor, as far as persecution was concerned, so that, including its autos of 1678 and 1691, the whole aggregate of its work for over two centuries amounted to 139 relaxations in person, 482 in effigy and 637 reconciliations, in addition to 338 reconciled under Edicts of Grace in 1488 and 1491.[1166]

In the later periods there are records which enable us to reach a fairly accurate computation of the activity of some at least of the tribunals. A few of these I have had the opportunity of consulting and the researches of future students will doubtless in time compile tolerably complete statistics for the second and third centuries of the Inquisition, after the Suprema had compelled the tribunals to render periodical reports.

CONSCIENTIOUS CRUELTY

We have those of Toledo, from 1575 to 1610, not wholly complete, for the auto of 1595 is omitted, and the MS. breaks off at the commencement of that of 1610. Toledo, at the time, was the most important tribunal in Spain, for it included Madrid, yet during these thirty-five years the relaxations amount to only eleven in person and fifteen in effigy, so that, allowing for the omissions, there may have been one in person every three years and one in effigy every two years, while the various penances number in all nine hundred and four.[1167] Small as are these results they continued to diminish. For the same tribunal we have a record extending from 1648 to 1794 and, during this century and a half, there were only eight relaxations in person and sixty-three in effigy, the latest execution occurring in 1738. This gives us an average of one of the former every eighteen years and one of the latter every two years and a quarter. In addition, there were a thousand and ninety-four penanced in various ways.[1168] It is true that, about 1650, a separate tribunal was erected in Madrid, but a list of relaxations there, from its foundation up to 1754, when relaxation had virtually become obsolete, gives us only an aggregate of nineteen in person and sixteen in effigy, or one in every five years of the former and in six years of the latter.[1169] During the height of the renewed persecution of Judaizers in the eighteenth century, in the whole of the sixty-four autos celebrated throughout Spain from 1721 to 1727, the total number of relaxations was seventy-seven in person and seventy-four in effigy, making an average of about eleven a year of each class--a grim record enough, but vastly less than has been popularly accepted.[1170] Nor must it be forgotten that, in the vast majority of cases, the victim was mercifully strangled before the fire was set. We have seen how very small was the proportion of impenitents who persevered to the last and refused to earn the garrote by professing conversion.

The material at hand as yet is evidently insufficient to justify even a guess at the ghastly total. Yet, after all, it is not a matter of as much moment, as seems to have been imagined, to determine how many human beings the Inquisition consigned to the stake, how many bones it exhumed, how many effigies it burnt, how many penitents it threw into prison or sent to the galleys, how many orphans its confiscations cast penniless on the world. The story is terrible enough without reducing it to figures. Its awful significance lies in the fact that men were found who conscientiously did this, to the utmost of their ability, in the name of the gospel of peace and of Him who came to teach the brotherhood of man. It is enough to know that the inquisitors used their utmost efforts to stamp out what they deemed heresy, and the tale of their victims is not the gauge of their cruelty but of the number of heretics whom they could discover. Save when pride or cupidity or ambition may have been the impelling motive, the men are not to be blamed, but the teaching which gave them such a conception of the duty so relentlessly performed, and framed a system of procedure which shrouded their acts in darkness and deprived the accused of his legitimate means of defence. The good Cura de los Palacios was evidently a kindly natured man, but he declares that the fires lighted by the Inquisition shall burn to the very heart of the wood, until all Judaizers are slain and not one remains, even to their children if infected with the same leprosy.[1171]

In the hurried work of the early period there was no effort made to induce the conversion that would save the accused from the stake, but, in later times, the persistent labor bestowed on the condemned, during the three days prior to the auto, is evidence that the tribunals did not act through thirst of blood and that they were sincerely desirous to save both the body and soul of the heretic, in the same spirit that torture was sometimes piously administered in order to confirm the sufferer in the faith. Still, at times, there was doubtless a certain pride in affording to the populace the spectacle of a relaxation and thus demonstrating the authority of the Holy Office. That the public should relish the entertainment thus provided was natural, both from the inherent attraction which the sight of suffering has for a certain class of minds, and from the assiduous teaching that heresy was to be exterminated and that the slaying of a heretic was an acceptable offering to God. The Inquisitor Lorenzo Flores relates that, at the great Valladolid auto of 1609, where there were seventy penitents, many of them reconciled or sentenced to abjuration de vehementi, the people murmured because the one condemned to relaxation had professed conversion in time and had thus escaped the stake, and there were many complaints that the auto was not worth the expense of coming to see. He adds that, at Toledo, where there was no one relaxed, the people declared that the auto was a failure.[1172]

A History of the Inquisition of Spain: Volume IV
PROFITABLE PERSECUTION

There is something terrible in the fierce exultation which fanaticism experienced in the agonies of the misbeliever. Padre Garau, in his account of the Mallorquin auto of May 6, 1691, gloats with an exuberance, which he knew would be shared by his readers, on the agonies of the three impenitents who were burnt alive. As the flames reached them they struggled desperately to free themselves from the iron ring which clasped them to the stake. Rafael Benito Terongi succeeded in releasing himself but to no purpose, for he fell sideways into the fire. His sister Cathalina, who had boasted that she would cast herself into the flames, when they began to lick her, shrieked to be set free. Rafael Valls, who had professed stoical insensibility, stood motionless as a statue so long as only the smoke reached him, but, when the flames attacked him, he bent and twisted and writhed till he could no more; he was as fat as a sucking-pig and burnt internally, so that, after the flames left him, he continued burning like a hot coal and, bursting open, his entrails fell out like those of Judas. Thus burning alive they died, to burn forever in hell.[1173] Such were the lessons which the Church inculcated and such was the training which it gave to Spain, so that the auto de fe came to be regarded as a spectacular religious entertainment on the occasion of a royal visit, or in honor of the marriage of princes. Incidental to this was the cruel perpetuation of ancestral disgrace by the display of sanbenitos in churches, which Philip II rightly reckoned as the severest of inflictions. It intensified the terror inspired by the tribunal which, with a word, could consign a whole lineage to infamy. It kept alive and vigorous the horror of heresy and was aggravated by the statutes of Limpieza.

I hesitate to impugn the motives of those who were active in these terrible "triumphs of the faith," as they were fondly termed and, as stated above, the efforts to induce conversion show that there was no absolute thirst of blood, yet it is impossible, in reviewing the career of the Inquisition, not to recognize how powerful an adjunct to fanaticism was the profitableness of persecution. Had the Holy Office been a source of expense instead of income, we may reasonably doubt whether the ardor of Ferdinand and Isabella would have sufficed for its introduction, and it certainly would have had but a comparatively short and inactive career. We have seen how closely Ferdinand watched its expenditures and endeavored to keep down its cost, while enjoying the results of its productiveness, and how grudgingly the crown ministered to its necessities when aid was unavoidable. We have seen moreover how eagerly the Inquisition itself grasped at all sources of gain, how it was stimulated to convict its victims by the prospect of their confiscations, and how fines and penances were scaled, not by the guilt of the culprits but by its necessities; how jealously it guarded its receipts, and how little it recked of deception and mendacity when there was attempt to investigate its finances. After all is said, the Inquisition was an institution with a double duty--the destruction of heresy and the raising of money to encompass that destruction--and there are not wanting indications that the latter tended to supersede, or at least to obscure, the former. We may well question the purity of zeal which provided punishments and disabilities for heresy and at the same time chaffered over the market price of commutations and dispensations through which those penalties could be evaded. Not only confiscation but pecuniary penance and fines were a source of revenue provocative of continual abuse, and the rage for Limpieza provided abundant opportunities for extortion. The filthy odor of gain pervades all the active period of the Inquisition, and its comparative inactivity during its later career may perhaps be attributed as much to the absence of wealthy heretics as to the diminishing spirit of intolerance.

***

Various ingenious theories have been framed to relieve the Inquisition of responsibility for the remarkable eclipse of Spanish intellectual progress after the sixteenth century.[1174] It is one of the interesting problems in the history of literature that Spain, whose brilliant achievements throughout the Reformation period promised to make her as dominant in the world of letters as in military and naval enterprise, should, within the space of a couple of generations, have become the most uncultured land in Christendom, without a public to encourage learning and genius, and without learning and genius to stimulate a public. For this there must have been a cause and no other adequate one than the Inquisition has been discovered to account for this occultation.

Henry Charles Lea, LL.D.

INTELLECTUAL TORPIDITY

Indeed, but for the effort to argue it away, it would seem superfluous to insist that a system of severe repression of thought, by all the instrumentalities of Inquisition and State, is an ample explanation of the decadence of Spanish learning and literature, especially when coupled with the obstacles thrown around printing and publication by their combined censorship. The tribulations of Luis de Leon and Francisco Sánchez illustrate the dangers to which independent thinkers were exposed; the great printing-house of Portonares was ruined by the exigencies of the Inquisition in the matter of the Vatable Bible. All a priori considerations cast the responsibility on the censorship of thought, whether printed or expressed verbally in what were known as "propositions," and the burden of proof is thrown upon those who deny it. Their reliance is on the fact that Isabella stimulated the development of Spanish culture and, at the same time, established the Inquisition, which thus was in existence for more than a century before the decadence became marked. This is quite easily explicable. The Inquisition was founded to extirpate Jewish and Moorish apostasy; in this it long had ample work without developing its evil capacity in the direction of censorship, save in such a sporadic instance as Diego Deza's prosecution, in 1504, of the foremost scholar of his time, Elío Antonio de Nebrija, for venturing to correct the errors of the Vulgate for the Complutensian Polyglot, in the service of Ximenez who protected him and, when inquisitor-general, allowed him to resume his labors.[1175] With the advent of Lutheranism there gradually commenced the search for errors; crude Indexes of condemned books were compiled, reading and investigation became restricted; the pragmática of 1559 forbade education at foreign seats of learning and an elaborate system was gradually organized for protecting Spain from intellectual intercourse with other lands, while at home every phrase that could be construed in an objectionable sense was condemned. For awhile the men whose training had been free from these trammels persisted, in spite of persecution more or less severe, but they gradually died out and had no successors. In 1601 Mariana explained that he translated his History from the original Latin because there were few who understood that language; such learning brought neither honor nor profit and he feared the unskilfulness of those who threatened to undertake the task.[1176] It is true, however, that Latin was widely studied as essential to gaining place in Church or State, but to the neglect of everything else. Fray Peñalosa y Mondragon, in 1629, while boasting of the thirty-two universities and four thousand Latin schools and of Spanish pre-eminence in the supreme science of theology, for which there were infinite rewards, admits that there were none for the other sciences and arts, which were not regarded with favor or estimated as formerly.[1177] The intellectual energy of the nation, diverted from more serious channels, continued through another period to exhibit itself in the lighter fields of literature, where the names of Cervantes, Lope de Vega, Tirso de Molina, Calderon de la Barca, Quevedo de Villegas and others show of what Spanish intellect was still capable if it were allowed free play. Even these however passed away and had no successors in the growing intellectual torpor created by obscurantist censorship, and a dreary blank followed which even the stimulation attempted by Philip V could not relieve.

INFLUENCE FOR EVIL

To produce and preserve this torpor, by repressing all dangerous intellectuality, Spain was carefully kept out of the current of European progress. In other lands the debates of the Reformation forced Catholics as well as Protestants to investigations and speculations shocking to Spanish conservatism. The human mind was enabled to cast off the shackles of the Dark Ages, and was led to investigate the laws of nature and the relations of man to the universe and to God. From all this bustling intellectual movement Spain was carefully secluded. Short-sighted opportunism, seeing the turmoil which agitated France and England and Germany, might bless the institution which preserved the Peninsula in peaceful stagnation, but the price paid for torpidity was fearfully extravagant, for Spain became an intellectual nonentity. Even the great theologians and mystics disappeared from the field which they had made their own, and were succeeded by a race of probabilistic casuists, who sought only to promote and to justify self-indulgence. How intellectual progress fared under these influences may be estimated by a single instance. When, in England, Halley was investigating the periodicity of the comet which bears his name, in Spain learned professors of the universities of Salamanca and Saragossa were publishing tracts to reassure the frightened people, by proving that the dreadful portent boded evil only to the wicked--to the Turk and the heretic.[1178] The perfect success of the Inquisition in its work is manifested in the contrast between the eighteenth and the early sixteenth century, as illustrated by the statement of Juan Antonio Mayans y Siscar, that a cartload of the precious MSS. bestowed by Ximenes on his University of Alcalá was sold to the fire-works maker Torrecilla, for a display in honor of Philip V, and that several other similar collections had shared the same fate.[1179] Even after half a century of Bourbon effort to revitalize the dormant intellect of Spain, Father Rábago, the royal confessor, grudged the money spent on historiographers and academies; it was a pure gift, he says, for it yields no fruits.[1180]

In fact, the awakening from intellectual stupor was slow, for Dom Clemencin tells us that there was less printing in Spain at the commencement of the nineteenth century than there had been in the fifteenth under Isabella.[1181]

It is impossible not to conclude that the Inquisition paralyzed both the intellectual and the economic development of Spain and it is scarce reasonable for Valera to complain that, when Spain was aroused from its mental marasmus, it was to receive a foreign and not to revive a native culture.[1182]

That science and art and literature should thus be submerged was a national misfortune, but even more to be deplored were the indirect consequences. Material progress became impossible, industry languished, and the inability to meet foreign competition assisted the mistaken internal policy of the government in prolonging and intensifying the poverty of the people. Nor was this the chief of the evils that sprung from keeping the mind of the nation in leading-strings, from repressing thought and from excluding foreign ideas, for the people were thus rendered absolutely unfitted to meet the inevitable change that came with the Revolution. To this, in large measure, may be attributed the sufferings through which Spain has passed in the transition from absolutism to modern conditions.

***

We have thus followed the career of the Spanish Inquisition from its foundation to its suppression; we have examined its methods and its acts and have sought to appraise its influence and its share in the misfortunes which overwhelmed the nation. The conclusion can scarce be avoided that its work was almost wholly evil and that, through its reflex action, the persecutors suffered along with the persecuted. Yet who can blame Isabella or Torquemada or the Hapsburg princes for their share in originating and maintaining this disastrous instrument of wrong? The Church had taught for centuries that implicit acceptance of its dogmas and blind obedience to its commands were the only avenues to salvation; that heresy was treason to God, its extermination the highest service to God and the highest duty to man. This grew to be the universal belief and, when Protestant sects framed their several confessions, each one was so supremely confident of possessing the secret of the Divine Being and his dealings with his creatures that all shared the zeal to serve God in the same cruel fashion.

Spanish Inquisition was only a more perfect and a more lasting institution than the others were able to fashion--as regards witchcraft, indeed, a more humane and rational one, for no one can appreciate the service which in this matter it rendered to Spain who has not realized the horrors of the witchcraft trials in which Catholic and Protestant Europe rivalled each other. The spirit among all was the same, and none are entitled to cast the first stone, unless we except the humble and despised Moravian Brethren and the disciples of George Fox. The faggots of Miguel Servet bear witness to the stern resolve of Calvinism. Lutheranism has its roll-call of victims. Anglicanism, under Edward VI, in 1550 undertook to organize an Inquisition on the Spanish pattern, which burnt Joan of Kent for Arianism, and the writ De hæretico comburendo was not abolished until 1676.[1183] Much as we may abhor and deplore this cruelty, we must acquit the actors of moral responsibility, for they but acted in the conscientious belief that they were serving the Creator and his creatures. The real responsibility can be traced to distant ages, to St. Augustin and St. Leo the Great and the fathers, who deduced, from the doctrine of exclusive salvation, that the obstinate dissident is to be put to death, not only in punishment for his sin but to save the faithful from infection. This hideous teaching, crystallized into a practical system, came, in the course of centuries, to be an essential feature of the religion which it distorted so utterly from the love and charity inculcated by the Founder. To dispute it was a heresy subjecting the disputant to the penalties of heresy, and not to enforce it was to misuse the powers entrusted by God to rulers for the purpose of establishing his kingdom on earth.

RETRIBUTION

In Spain, under peculiar conditions, this resolve to enforce unity of belief, in the conviction that it was essential to human happiness here and hereafter, led to the framing of a system of so-called justice more iniquitous than has been evolved by the cruellest despotism; which placed the lives, the fortunes and the honor, not only of individuals but of their posterity, in the hands of those who could commit wrong without responsibility; which tempted human frailty to indulge its passions and its greed without restraint, and which subjected the population to a blind and unreasoning tyranny, against which the slightest murmur of complaint was a crime. The procedure which left the fate of the accused virtually in the hands of his judges was rendered doubly vicious by the inviolable secrecy in which it was enveloped--a secrecy which invited injustice by shielding its perpetrators and enabling them to make a parade of benignant righteousness. It was the crowning iniquity of the Inquisition that it thus afforded to the evil-minded the amplest opportunity of wrong-doing. History affords no parallel to such a skilfully organized system, working relentlessly through centuries.

The inquisitors were men, not demons or angels, and when injustice and oppression were rife in the secular courts it would be folly not to expect them in the impenetrable recesses of the Holy Office. If we have occasionally met with instances of kindliness and genuine desire to do right, we have incidentally encountered the opposite too often for us to doubt its frequency. That the rulers of the Inquisition recognized the danger of this and sought to diminish it by moral influences is evident from the admirable prayer the utterance of which, by a carta acordada of April 13, 1600, was ordered daily after mass at the opening of the morning session. This implored the Holy Spirit to fill their hearts and guide their judgements, so that they might not be misled by ignorance or favor, or be corrupted by gifts or acceptance of persons; that their decisions might be in unison with His will, so that in the end they might earn eternal reward by well-doing.[1184] Yet we might feel more confidence in the sincerity of this attempt to curb by moral influence the evil tendencies fostered by the system if there had been stern repression and punishment of official wrong-doing, instead of the habitual mercy which served as an encouragement.

After all, the great lesson taught by the history of the Inquisition is that the attempt of man to control the conscience of his fellows reacts upon himself; he may inflict misery but, in due time, that misery recoils on him or on his descendants and the full penalty is exacted with interest. Never has the attempt been made so thoroughly, so continuously or with such means of success as in Spain, and never has the consequent retribution been so palpable and so severe. The sins of the fathers have been visited on the children and the end is not yet. A corollary to this is that the unity of faith, which was the ideal of statesman and churchman alike in the sixteenth century, is fatal to the healthful spirit of competition through which progress, moral and material, is fostered. Improvement was impossible so long as the Holy See held a monopoly of salvation and, however deplorable were the hatred and strife developed by the rivalry which followed the Reformation, it yet was of inestimable benefit in raising the moral standards of both sides, in breaking down the stubbornness of conservatism and in rendering development possible. Terrible as were the wars of religion which followed the Lutheran revolt, yet were they better than the stagnation preserved in Spain through the efforts of the Inquisition. So long as human nature remains what it is, so long as the average man requires stimulation from without as well as from within, so long as progress is the reward only of earnest endeavor, we must recognize that rivalry is the condition precedent of advancement and that competition in good works is the most beneficent sphere of human activity.

APPENDIX

I. ABJURATION OF JOSEPH FERNANDEZ DE TORO, BISHOP OF OVIEDO

(Bulario de la Orden de Santiago, Libro V, fol. 150)

Ego Joseph Fernandez de Toro, olim episcopus Ovetensis, coram Sanctissimo in Christo Patre et Domino nostro Domino Clemente Divina Providentia papa undecimo humiliter genuflexus vobis E^{mis} et R^{mis} DD. cardinalibus contra hæreticam pravitatem Generalibus Inquisitoribus ei assistentibus, sacrosancta Dei Evangelia coram me posita manibus tangens, sciens neminem salvum fieri posse extra illam fidem quam tenet, credit, profitetur ac docet Sancta Catholica et Apostolica Romana Ecclesia contra quam fateor et doleo me graviter errasse quia tenui et docui respective errores et hæreses formales ac dogmata contra veritatem ejusdem S. Ecclesiæ, et præcipue quia tenui et credidi quod non peccaverim nec peccare fecerim ex speciali Providentia Dei in quibusdam actibus turpibus a me habitis cum foeminis. Quod concussiones et corporis tremores cum pollutione sequuta attribuendi essent operationi Dæmonis ideoque absque peccato essent. Quod actus exteriores amplexuum, osculorum aliarumque operationum inhonestarum essent supernaturales in causa, adeoque a Deo et a Jesu procederent. Quod prædicta oscula et amplexus essent immunes a motu libidinis et essent motiva maximæ humiliationis ex supposita unione cum Deo. Quod facta turpia cum foemina complici procederent ex redundantia amoris erga Jesum adeoque a parte inferiore procederent et ex motu ipsius Jesu impellerentur. Quod stante supposita tam mea quam foeminæ complicis unione cum Deo, posset utriusque status componi una simul cum exterioribus actibus peccaminosis omnesque impulsus quos in eandam foeminam habebam, Dei et Jesu essent impulsus. Quod pessima doctrina a me insinuata Dei esset doctrina. Quod a Deo haberem donum discretionis, spirituum impulsus et illustrationes ad agnoscendum spiritualem animæ statum, ipsaque spirituum discretio ac doctrinarum cognitio, esset lux mihi a Deo infusa, essem super omnes illustratus, ideoque essem omnibus superior. Quod facta turpia a me habita cum foemina complici essent exercitium et martyrium a Deo missum ad utriusque humiliationem et purificationem. Quod deosculando et amplectendo foeminam complicem in me adesset Jesus ipseque Jesus mediante me ita ageret et loqueretur. Quod stante dicta supposita unione cum Deo ab ipso motæ essent potentiæ meæ, memoria, intellectus et voluntas, ipseque Deus esset meus intellectus, memoria, voluntas et spiritus idque esset idem, ac tres distinctæ personæ, una Majestas et unus Deus, et alias credidi propositiones et dogmata mihi in processu contestata; quæ quidem propositiones tanquam temerariæ, erroneæ, scandalosæ, Christianæ disciplinæ relaxativæ, male sonantes, periculosæ, præsumptuosæ, errori proximæ, abusivæ verborum Sacræ Scripturæ, injuriosæ in Sanctos, insanæ, sacrilegæ, hæresim sapientes, de hæresi suspectæ, impiæ, blasphemæ, coincidentes cum propositionibus Molinos et hæreticæ respective censuratæ et qualificatæ fuerunt. Nunc de prædictis erroribus et hæresibus dolens, certus de veritate fidei Catholicæ, corde sincero ac fide non ficta abjuro, detestor, maledico, anathematizo et respective retracto omnes supradictos errores et hæreses, quos et quas tenui et credidi, et promitto ac juro me nunc toto corde absque ulla hæsitatione credere et in futurum firmiter crediturum quicquid tenet, credit, prædicat, profitetur ac docet eadem S. Catholica Ecclesia, et abjuro, detestor, maledico et anathematizo non solum supradictos errores et hæreses verumetiam generaliter omnem alium errorem dietæ sanctæ Ecclesiæ contrarium, omnemque aliam hæresim et promitto et juro me neque corde neque voce neque scripto unquam recessurum quacunque occasione sive prætextu a sancta fide Catholica nec crediturum vel edocturum aliquem errorem eidem contrarium seu aliquam hæresim. Promitto etiam me integre adimpleturum omnes et singulas poenitentias mihi a Sanctitate vestra impositas sive imponendas et si unquam alicui ex dictis meis promissionibus et juramentis (quod Deus avertat) contravenero me subjicio omnibus poenis a sacris canonibus aliisque constitutionibus generalibus et particularibus contra hujusmodi delinquentes inflictis et promulgatis. Sic me Deus adjuvet et illius sancta Evangelia quæ propriis manibus tango. Ego Joseph Fernandez de Toro supradictus abjuravi, juravi, promisi et me obligavi ut supra et in fidem veritatis præsentem schedulam meæ abjurationis propria mea manu subscripsi eamque recitavi de verbo ad verbum. Romæ, in palatio Quirinali hac die, 17 Julii, 1719.--Ego Joseph Fernandez de Toro Episcopus abjuravi ut supra manu propria.

II. ABSTRACT OF THE CASE OF CATALINA MATHEO IN 1591

(Relacion de las causas despachadas en el auto de la fee que se celebro en la Inquisicion de Toledo, Domingo de la SS^{ma} Trinidad, nueve dias de Junio, 1591 años.--Königl. Universitäts Bibliothek of Halle, Yc, 20, T. I.)

Catalina Matheo, viuda, vezina del Cazar, de edad de cinquenta años fue presa por el vicario de Alcala con diez y seis testigos de que en la dicha villa de quatro años a esta parte abian muerto quatro o cinco criaturas de muertes violentas que era imposible averlas hecho sino bruxas, y de que la dicha Catalina Matheo y Olalla Sobrina y Joana Yzquierda eran tenidas por tales publicas, y specialmente la dicha Matheo. Hizòle proceso y diòle tormento y en el la dicha Catalina Matheo dixò que era berdad, que podria aber quatro o cinco años que Olalla Sobrina la abia dicho si queria ser bruxa, ofreciendole que el Demonio tendria con ella aceso torpe y que era buen officio. Y que una noche por medio de la dicha Joana Yzquierda la abia llamado a su casa adonde estando todas tres abia entrado el demonio en figura de cabron, y hablando aparte primero con las dichas Olalla y Joana las abia abraçado y despues a la dicha Matheo, porque ellas le abian dicho que tambien ella queria ser bruxa, y que el dicho Demonio le abia pedido alguna cosa de su cuerpo, y ella le abia ofrecido una uña de un dedo del medio de la mano derecha, y que por regozijo del concierto abian bailado con el dicho cabron y el se abia echado carnalmente con todas tres en presencia de todas. Y que aquella noche la dicha Olalla la abia untado las coiunturas de los dedos de pies y manos y en compañia del dicho cabron abian ydo a una casa y llebando unas brosas en una teja abian entrado por una ventana a las doze de la noche y echando sueno a los padres con unas dormideras y otras yerbas puestas debaxo de la almohada, les abian sacado una niña de la cama y apretandola por las arcas la abian ahogado, y encendido lumbre con lo que llebaban, y la quemaron las partes traseras, y quebrantando los braços, y que al ruido abian despertado los dichos padres, y ellas se abian buelto con el dicho cabron por el ayre a casa de la dicha Olalla, adonde se abian bestido y ydo cada una a su casa, y que a la yda y buelta yban por el ayre desnudas, y diziendo de viga (?) con la yra de Sancta Maria. Y que de alli a pocos dias el dicho cabron abia ydo una noche a casa de la dicha Matheo y hallandola acostada la abia forçado y tenido cuenta carnal con ella, diziendo en esto algunas particularidades y lo mesmo abia tenido otras diez o doze noches, y en los dichos quatro años otras vezes a menudo, y lo mesmo abia hecho en las carceles del dicho vicario. Y que a cabo de algunos pocos dias en casa de la dicha Olalla le abia dado un cuchillo y con el se abia cortado la uña que le abia mandado y se la abia entregado. Y otras noches untandose en casa de la dicha Olalla y en compañia de lo dicho cabron abian ydo a otra casa y ahogado un niño y arrancadole sus berguenzas, y despues a otras dos casas en diferentes noches y ahogado otras dos criaturas. Y que una sola vez abia inbocado al demonio diziendole Demonio ven a mi llamado y mandado. Y pasadas las oras del derecho se ratifico en la dicha confesion, y el dicho vicario hiço acareacion de la dicha Catalina Matheo con la dicha Olalla y en su presencia la dicha Matheo le dixo todo lo arriba dicho, afirmandose en ello, y la otra negandolo. Y en este estado remitio a la dicha Matheo a este S^{to} Off° al qual aviendo sido trayda presa en la primera audiencia que con ella se tubo dixo que pedia misericordia del grave pecado que havia hecho en lebantarse a si y las dichas Olalla y Yzquierda lo que dellas avia dicho y de si confessado ante el dicho vicario lo qual avia dicho por miedo del tormento. Y abiendose examinados diez y seis testigos en el Cazar consto ser verdad que los dichos niños abian sido muertos y se hallaron de la misma manera y forma muertos y maltratados que la sobredicha Matheo lo abia confessado. Y aviendose substanciado su processo fue puesta a question de tormento, y abiendose pronunciado la sentencia y abaxadola a la camara para executarse antes de desnudarse abiendo sido amonestada dixo ser berdad todo lo que abia dicho antel vicario de Alcala, y en efecto lo refirio en substancia, aunque en algunas circonstancias mudo alguna cossa, asegurando mucho ser berdad ansi en la manera del confesar como del jurarlo, y pasadas las oras del derecho se ratifico en sus confesiones, y en otras audiencias que con ella se tubieron despues dixo lo mesmo, negando saber de que fuesen hechos los dichos inguentos ni aber tenido otro pacto tacito ni expresso con el Demonio mas de que abia dicho, y dixo las causas que avia tenido de bengarse de los padres en la muerte de sus hijos que son las mesmas que los padres testificaron, por donde sospechaban que ellas se los obiesen muerto. Y subtenciose su causa y votose auto con coroça, levi, doçiento açotes y reclusa por el tiempo que pareciere.

III. LETTER OF THE SUPREMA ON THE TUMULT OF MAY 2, 1808

(Archivo histórico nacional, Inquisicion de Valencia, Cartas del Consejo, Legajo 17, No. 3, fol. 31)

Las fatales resultas que se ban experimentado en esta Corte el dia 2 del corriente por el alboroto escandaloso del bajo Pueblo contra las tropas del Emperador de los Franceses hacen necesaria la vigilancia mas activa y esmerada de todas las autoridades y cuerpos respetables de la Nacion para evitar que se repitan iguales excesos y mantener en todos los pueblos la tranquilidad y sosiego que exige su propio interes no menos que la hospitalidad y atencion debida á los oficiales y soldados de una nacion amiga que á ninguno ofenden y han dado hasta ahora las mayores pruebas de buen orden y disciplina, castigando con rigor á los que se propasan ó maltratan á los Españoles en su persona ó bienes. Es bien presumible que la malevolencia ó la ignorancia haian seducido á los incautos y sencillos para empeñarles en el desorden revolucionario so color de patriotismo y amor al Soberano, y corresponde por lo mismo á la ilustracion y zelo de los entendidos el desimpresionarles de un error tan prejudicial, haciendoles conocer que semejantes movimientos tumultuarios lejos de producir los efectos propios del amor y lealtad bien dirigidos, solo sirven para poner la Patria en convulsion, rompiendo los vinculos de subordinacion en que esta afianzada la salud de los Pueblos, apagando los sentimientos de humanidad y destruyendo la confianza que se debe tener en el Gobierno, que es el unico á quien toca dirigir y dar impulso con uniformidad y con provecho del valor y á los esfuerzos del patriotismo. Estas verdades de tanta importancia ninguno puede persuadirlas mejor que los Ministros de la Religion de Jesu Cristo, que toda respira paz y fraternidad entre los hombres igualmente que sumision, respeto y obediencia á las autoridades; y como los individuos y Dependientes del Santo Oficio deban ser y han sido siempre los primeros en dar exemplo de Ministros de paz y que procuran la paz, hemos creydo, Señores, conveniente y muy propio de la obligacion de nuestro Ministerio el dirigiros la presente carta para que enterados de su contexto y penetrados de la urgente necesidad de concurrir unanimemente á la conservacion de la tranquilidad publica la hagais entender á los subalternos de ese Tribunal y á los Comisarios y Familiares del Distrito, á fin de que todos y cada uno contribuir (sic) por su parte con quanto zelo, actividad y prudencia les fuere posible á tan interesante objeto. Tendreislo entendido, y del recibo de esta dareis el correspondiente aviso. Dios os guarde. Madrid 6 de Maio de 1808.--Dr. D. Gab^{l} Nevia y Noriega.--D. Raimundo Eltenhard y Salinas.--Fr. Man^{l} de San Joseph.--Rubricado. Recibida en 9 de Mayo de 1808.--SS. Bertran, Laso, Acedo, Encina.--Executese como S. A. lo manda. Rubrica. Valencia.

Certifico el infrascrito Secretario del Secreto del Santo Oficio de la Inquisicion de Valencia que en el dia once del mes de Mayo del año mil ochociento y ocho, estando en su audiencia de la mañana los S^{res} Inquisidores Dr. D. Mathias Bertran, Licen^{do} D. Nicolas Rodriguez Laso, Dr. D. Pablo Acedo Rico y Dr. D. Fran^{co} de la Encina, entraron en ella los Ministros, Calificadores, Titulados, Notarios y Familiares que viven en esta ciudad, á los quales, precedida convocacion para este fin, se les leyó esta carta de los Señores del Consejo de S. M. de la Santa y General Inquisicion y en seguida se les exortó por el Señor Inquisidor Decano á su mas exacto cumplimiento. Y para que lo susodicho conste doy la presente Certificacion que firmo en la Camara del Secreto de la Inquisicion de Valencia, en el dia 11 del mes de Mayo de 1808.--D. Man^{l} Fuster y Bertran, Secretario. Rubricado.

IV. DECREE OF FERNANDO VII, SEPTEMBER 9, 1814, RESTORING THE PROPERTY OR THE INQUISITION.

(Archivo de Simancas, Inquisicion, Libro 559).

Exc^{mo} Señor:--Por Real decreto de veintiuno de Julio ultimo, se sirvio S. Magestad mandar restablecer en todos sus dominios el Santo Oficio de la Inquisicion al pie y estado en que se hallaba el año de mil ochocientos ocho y que para la subsistencia y decoro de los Ministros y demas empleados de sus tribunales se restituyesen toda clase de bienes y efectos pertenecientes á su dotacion, como son frutos, creditos, reditos de censos, vales y caudales que se hallan impuestos en la Caja de consolidacion, asi como de los rendimientos de las canongias perpetuamente anejas al Santo Officio afectas por Brebes apostolicos.

Comunicado este Real decreto al supremo Consejo de Inquisicion para su observancia consulto á S. Magestad lo que en su razon tubo por combeniente al cabal cumplimiento de las piadosas Reales intenciones, manifestando al propio tiempo los ruinosos y destruidos que se hallaban los edificios destinados al tribunal del Santo Oficio, estravio de sus papelea mas interesantes, ya de causas de fe, ya de la Hacienda del Real fisco que fueron presa de los executores de los decretos de abolicion de los tribunales de Inquisicion. Enterado S. Magestad de todo y deseoso de llevar á debido efecto su citado Real Decreto de veinteuno de Julio ha resuelto se pongan desde luego sin demora ni detencion alguna á disposicion de los tesoreros de los respectivos tribunales de Inquisicion todas las fincas y efectos de qualquiera clase que sean pertinecientes al tribunal y que en este concepto hayan sido secuestrados, confiscados, detenidos ó aplicados á lo que se llama hacienda publica ó Nacional, devolviendo todos los titulos de propiedad y legitimacion de creditos que hubiesen recebido y cortando la cuenta el dia veinteuno de Julio del presente año den razon de las personas obligadas al pago de sus arrendamientos y obligaciones con expression de sus cantidades y procedencias.

De orden del Rey lo comunico á V. E. para su inteligencia y puntual cumplimiento, y á fin de que esta real resolucion la haga circular á los Gobernadores, Intendentes, Directores del credito publico ó sugetos encargados de la Real recaudacion de intereses en los Pueblos de sus distritos. Dios guarde á V. E. muchos años. Madrid, 3 de Setiembre de 1814.

Sr Virrey y Capitan General de etc.

V. DECREE OF SUPPRESSION, MARCH 9, 1820

(Miraflores, Documentos á los qué se hace referencia en los Apuntes histórico-criticos, I, 93.--Rodrigo, Historia Verdadera, III, 494)

Considerando que es incompatible la existencia del Tribunal de la Inquisicion con la constitucion de la Monarquia Española promulgada en Cádiz en 1812 y que por esta razon lo suprimieron las Córtes generales y estraordinarias por decreto de 22 de Febrero de 1813, previa una madura y larga discusion: oida la opinion de la Junta formada por decreto de este dia, y conformandome con su parecer, he venido en mandar que desde hoy quede suprimido el referido Tribunal en toda la Monarquia y por consecuencia el Consejo de la Suprema Inquisicion, poniendose inmediatamente en libertad á todos los presos que estén en sus cárceles por opiniones políticas ó religiosas, pasandose á los Reverendos Obispos las causas de estos últimos en sus respectivas Diócesis para que las sustancien y determinen con arreglo en todo al espresado decreto de las Córtes estraordinarias. Tendréislo entendido y dispondréis lo conveniente á su cumplimiento. Palacio, 9 de Marzo de 1820. Esta rubricado. Al Secretario de Gracia y Justicia.

VI. THE LAST VOTE OF THE SUPREME COUNCIL, FEBRUARY 10, 1820

(Libro de Votos Secretos, Archivo de Simancas, Inquisicion, Libro 890)

Toledo.--Don Manuel de la Peña Palacios.

En el consejo á 10 de Febrero de 1820. Señores Hevia, Ettenhard, Amarilla, Galarza, Martinez, Beramendi, Prado.--Hagan justicia como lo tienen acordado.

Voto del Tribunal. En el Santo Oficio de Toledo en 29 dias del mes de Enero de 1820, estando en la audiencia de su mañana el Señor Inquisidor Doctor Don José Francisco Bordujo y Rivas (que asiste solo) haviendo visto esta causa contra Don Manuel de la Peña Palacios, Presbitero Cura que fué del lugar de Ontoba y actualmente de Torrejon del Rey en este arzobispado por delitos de proposiciones y propagar doctrinas peligrosas contrarias al sentir de la Iglesia: Dixo, Que su voto y parecer es que á este reo á puerta cerrada en la sala de Audiencia y a presencia del Secretario de la causa se le reprenda amoneste y conmine por las proposiciones propaladas ya en sus sermones ya en sus conversaciones familiares; se le absuelva ad cautelam y por quince dias se le exercite spiritualmente en el convento de Padres Carmelitas Descalzos de esta Ciudad al cargo de Director que se le señale; se le advierta que por ahora le trata el Tribunal con toda conmiseracion y clemencia por haverselo implorado en las audiencias que con él se han tenido y por esperar su total enmienda en el modo irregular con que hasta aqui se ha conducido con sus Feligreses y se estará á la mira de su conducta y operaciones; y antes de executarse se remita á S. A. con todos los expedientes que han precedido para su aprobacion; y lo rubricó de que certifico. Está rubricado.--D. Domingo Sanchez Fijon, Secretario.

VII. DICTAMEN OF THE CONSEJO DE GOBIERNO ON THE DECREE EXTINGUISHING THE INQUISITION

(Archivo de Alcalá Ministerio de Estado, Legajo 906, n. 88)

Señor Secretario de Estado y del Despacho de Gracia y Justicia.

Exmo Señor: He recibido el oficio de V. E. de 9 del presente con el proyecto de decreto en que se declara suprimido el Tribunal de la Inquisicion, se adjudican sus bienes y rentas á la estincion de la deuda publica y se fija la suerte de los dependientes del Tribunal, cuyo proyecto remite V. E. de Real orden al Consejo por que lo examine y esponga su dictamen.

Enterado de todo y despues de una detenida discusion ha acordado el Consejo manifieste á V. E. que reconoce la conveniencia de coadyubar al sostenimiento del credito del Estado por cuantos medios esten al alcance del Gobierno y reconoce asi mismo que los bienes de la Inquisicion (suprimida á lo menos de hecho por el Rey difunto que nunca permitió que restableciese) podran proporcionar algun ausilio á la caja de amortization sin agravio de nadie, pues en el proyecto de Decreto se establece el conveniente para asegurar á los empleados del Tribunal las asignaciones que les correspondan segun sus circunstancias y clasificaciones.

Por estas consideraciones no halla reparo el Consejo en que S. M. apruebe en lo substancial el proyecto de Decreto aunque en su dictamen podrian hacerse en el las siguientes modificaciones.

1ª En la parte del preambulo donde hablando de la autoridad Pontificia se usa de la espresion: Primado de la Iglesia universal, cree el consejo que podria seguirse el uso constante de designar dicha autoridad Pontificia con el nombre de Santa Sede ó Sumo Pontifice; no porque el Consejo desconozca la propiedad del titulo de Primado de la Iglesia universal con arreglo á los sacros canones, sino porque en materia de denominaciones y fórmulas es siempre preferible el uso de las establecidas y mas comunes que inovarlas, porque puede darse lugar à que se crea que la inovacion envuelva algun designio que la malignidad interpreta segun su antojo.

2ª Cuando en el Artº 1º se dice que se declara suprimido el Tribuno de la Inquisicion podra darse motivo á que se infiera por esta espresion que el Gobierno lo había creido subsistente hasta el dia de derecho: cuya idea no parece enteramente exacta, pues el Señor Don Fernando 7º resistiendo siempre á las gestiones de alcunas corporaciones para su restablecimiento, y habiendo restituido á los Arzobispos y Obispos el conocimiento sobre las causas de fe que les corresponde por derecho comun dió bastante á entender que su Real animo estaba decidido á la estincion de la Inquisicion aunque por ciertas consideraciones no la hubiere pronunciado mas esplicitamente, cree pues el Consejo preferible que en dicho articulo se haga algun mencion de lo hecho por el difunto Rey sobre esta materia, á que aparezca dicha estincion como un acto de la Regencia en su totalidad: Y si no juzga S. M. que haya necesidad de ello, por lo menos el Consejo cree que al espresado articulo combendra añadir la palabra definitivamente, para que diga se declara suprimido definitivamente el Tribunal de la Inquisicion.

3º El consejo entiende que en la actualidad convendria suprimir enteramente el Artº 4º por el que se autoriza al Señor Secretario del Despacho de Hacienda para la pronta enagenacion de las fincas: pues habiendose vendido muchas de ellas en tiempo del Gobierno constitucional, y no siendo posible todavia hacer distincion alguna entre las que se enagenaron y las que no se enagenaron en dicha época hasta que las Córtes examinen la grave cuestion relativa á los compradores de bienes nacionales, podria darse motivo á que se sospechase que se decidia este punto general por el presente Decreto de una manera indirecta, mandando vender todos los bienes de la Inquisicion indistintamente y sin hacer diferencia alguna entre los enagenados y los non enagenados. Parece pues que por ahora combiene limitarse á lo que se previene en el Artº 2º aplicando la masa de los bienes de la Inquisicion á la estincion de la deuda publica sin mas esplicacion.

4º El artº 6º en que se ordena que los sueldos de los empleados del Tribunal se paguen del Tesoro público, cree el Consejo que podria modificarse mandando que este pago se hiciese por la caja de Amortizacion pues no parece justo imponer este nuebo gravamen al Real Tesoro cuando nada es mas natural que satisfacer el gravamen vitalicio que pesa sobre los bienes y rentas del Tribunal por el mismo establecimiento adonde han á ingresar sus productos. Esto no ofrecerá inconveniente aun despues que se vendan todas las fincas que pertenecian á la Inquisicion, pues siempre quedarán las ciento y una Canongias de que habla el Artº 3º del proyecto que no son susceptibles de enagenacion, y con cuyo producto habrá mas que lo suficiente para pagar a los cesantes del ramo cuyo número se hallará muy reducido por los que han fallecido ó pasado á otros destinos desde el año de 1823 hasta el dia, y se reducira todabia mas por las disposiciones de los Art^{os} 5º y 6º del mismo proyecto de Decreto.

Lo que por acuerdo del Consejo digo á V. E. en contestacion á su citado oficio con devolucion del Proyecto.

Dios etc. Madrid, 13 de Julio de 1834. El Conde de Ofalía.

VIII. DECREE OF JULY 15, 1834, ABOLISHING THE INQUISITION

(Printed by Castillo y Ayensa, Negociaciones con Roma, Madrid, 1859. Tom. I, Append, p. 165)

Deseando aumentar el crédito público de la Nacion por todos los medios compatibles con los principios de justicia: teniendo en consideracion que mi augusto Esposo (Q. E. E. G.) creyó bastante eficaz al sostenimiento de la Religion del Estado la nativa é imprescriptible autoridad de los muy RR. Arzobispos y RR. Obispos, protegida cual corresponde por las leyes de la Monarquia: que mi Real decreto de 4 de Enero próximo pasado ha dejado en manos de dichos Prelados la censura de los escritos concernientes á la fe, á la moral y disciplina, para que se conserve ileso tan precioso depósito: que están ya concluidos los trabajos del Código criminal en que se establecen las convenientes penas contra los que intenten vulnerar el respeto debido á nuestra Santa Religion; y que la Junta eclesiástica, creada por mi Real decreto de 22 de Abril se ocupa de proponer cuanto juzgue conducente á tan importante fin, para que provea yo de remedio hasta donde alcance el Real Patronato, y con la concurrencia de la Santa Sede en cuanto menester fucre: en nombre de mi excelsa Hija Doña Isabel II, oido el Concejo de Gobierno y el de Ministros, he venido en mandar lo siguiente: Articolo Iº. Se declara suprimido definitivamente el Tribunal de la Inquisicion. 2º Los predios rústicos y urbanos, censos ú otros bienes con que le habia dotado la piedad soberana ó cuya adquisicion le proporcionó por medio de leyes dictadas para su proteccion, se adjudican á la extincion de la Deuda pública. 3º Las ciento una canongias que estaban agregadas á la Inquisicion se aplican al mismo objeto, con sujecion á mi Real decreto de 9 de Marzo último y por el tiempo que expresan las Bulas apostólicas sobre la materia. 4º Los empleados de dicho Tribunal y sus dependencias que posean prebendas eclesiásticas ú obtengan cargos civiles de cualquiera clase con sueldo, no tendrán derecho á percibir el que les correspondia sobre los fondos del mismo Tribunal, cuando servian en él sus destinos. 5º Todos los demas empleados, mientras no se les proporcione otra colocacion, percibirán exactamente de la Caja de Amortizacion el sueldo que les corresponda, segun clasificacion que solicitarán ante la Junta creada al efecto. Tendréislo entendido y dispondreis lo necesario á su cumplimiento. En San Ildefonso á 15 de Julio de 1834.--A. D. Nicolás María Garelly.

IX. PRAYER RECITED DAILY AT OPENING OF MORNING SESSION

(Biblioteca nacional, Seccion de MSS. D, 122, fol. 1)

Adsumus Domine, Sancte Spiritus, adsumus quidem peccati immanitate detenti, sed in nomine tuo specialiter aggregati. Veni ad nos, adesto nobis, dignari illabi cordibus nostris; doce nos quid agamus, quo gradiamus; ostende quid officere debeamus ut, te auxiliante, tibi in omnibus placere valeamus. Esto salus et suggestor et effector judiciorum nostrorum, qui solus cum Deo patre et ejus Filio nomen possides gloriosum. Non nos patiaris perturbatores esse justitiæ qui summam diligis æquitatem, ut in sinistrum nos ignorantia non trahat, non favor infectat, non acceptio muneris vel personæ corrumpat, sed junge nos tibi efficaciter solius tuæ gratiæ dono ut simus in te unum et in nullo deviemus a vero quatenus in nomine tuo collecti, sic in cunctis teneamus cum moderamine pietatis justitiæque ut hic a te in nullo dissentiat sententia nostra, ut in futuro pro bene gestis consequamur premia sempiterna. Amen.

FOOTNOTES:

1. I have considered this subject at greater length in "Chapters from the Religious History of Spain," but the views there expressed have been somewhat modified by access to additional documents.
2. II. Corinth. xii, 2-4.
3. Est hodie soror apud nos revelationum charismata sortita quas in ecclesia inter Dominica solemnia per ecstasin in spiritu patitur; conversatur cum angelis, aliquando etiam cum Domino, et vidit et audit sacramenta et quorumdam corda dignoscit et medicinas desiderantibus submittit.--De Anima, cap. ix.
4. Rufini Aquileiensis Historia Monachorum, passim.--Vitæ Patrum, Lib. III, c. 141.
5. Chapeavilli Gestt. Pontiff. Leodiens., II, 256-7.
6. Treatises of Richard Rolle, VIII, pp. 14-15 (Early English Text Society).
7. Basnage in Canisii Thes. Monum. Ecclesiæ, IV, 366-7.
8. Johann. PP. XXII, Bull. In agro dominico (Ripoll. Bullar. Ord. Prædic. VII, 57).
9. S. Cypriani Epist. iv ad Pomponium.--Concil. Antioch. (Harduin Concil. I, 198).--Lactant. Divin. Institt. VI, xix.

This test of continence was tried by St. Aldhelm (Girald. Cambrens. Gemm. Eccles., Dist. II, cap. xv) and was practised by the followers of Segarelli and Dolcino (Bern. Guidonis Practica, Ed. Douais, p. 260).

10. Clementin. Lib. V, Tit. iii, cap. 3.
11. Abecedario spiritual, P. III, Trat. xiii, cap. 3, fol. 122 (Burgos, 1544).
12. Subida del Monte Carmelo, III, 38.
13. De la Oracion y Meditacion, II, ii.
14. De Oratione et Meditatione, cap. lv.--Cf. S. Pedro de Alcántara, De la Oracion II, iv.
15. Archivo de Simancas, Sala 40, Lib. IV, fol. 231(see Vol. III, p. 570).
16. R. S. Victor Benjaminis Minoris, c. lxxxi.--S. Th. Aquin. Summæ Sec., Sec. Q. clxxv, Art. 1.
17. Joh. Gersoni. Tract. de Distinct. verar. Visionum a falsis (Opp. Ed. 1494, T. I, xix. L).
18. B. Juan de Avila, Audi Filia et vide, cap. li-lv.
19. Arbiol, Disengaños misticos, Lib. III, cap. xv (1707).
20. Amort de Revelationibus etc. P. I, pp. 259-68 (Aug. Vindel. 1744).
21. Abecedario spiritual, P. III, Trat. vi, cap. 2, fol. 52.--Cf. Molinos, Guida, Lib III, cap. xvii, n. 163-4.
22. Melgares Marin, Procedimientos de la Inquisicion, II, 88(Madrid, 1886).
23. Proceso contra Hieron. de la M. de Dios (MSS. of Library of Univ. of Halle, Yc, 20, T. VII).
24. Eymerici Director. P. II, Q. ix, n. 5.--Repertor. Inquisit. s. vv Beatæ, Begardæ, Beguinæ, Hæresis, Hæretici, etc.
25. Abecedario spiritual, P. III, Trat. xxi, cap. 4, fol. 204.--Menendez y Pelayo, Heterodoxos, II, 526.
26. Pet. Mart. Angler. Epistt. 428, 431.
27. D. Manuel Serrano y Sans (Revista de Archivos etc., Enero, 1903, p. 2).
28. See the trial of Alcaraz, epitomized by D. Manuel Serrano y Sana, in the Revista de Archivos, Enero, 1903, pp. 1-16; Febrero, pp. 127, 130 sqq.
29. S. Bonaventuræ de Puritate Conscientiæ, cap. 14.
30. Don M. Serrano y Sans has published (Boletín, XLI, 105-37) the principal features and documents of this trial. He states that much of the testimony is utterly unfit for transcription.
31. Bulario de la Orden de Santiago, Lib. III, fol. 133.
32. This account of Francisco Ortiz is derived from the skilful analysis of his trial by Eduard Böhmer in his "Franzisca Hernandez und Frai Franzisco Ortiz" (Leipzig, 1865).
33. Melgares Marin, Procedimientos de la Inquisicion, II, 94-5.
34. Juan and María were uncle and aunt of the Cazallas who suffered for Protestantism.
35. Melgares Marin, op. cit., II, 74-88.
36. Ibidem, pp. 147-53.
37. Archivo, hist. nacional, Inq. de Toledo, Leg. III, u. 46.--Cf. Schäfer, II, 119.
38. MS. penes me.

39. Diálogo de Mercurio y Caron, cap. lxv.
40. So much has been said about this prosecution of Loyola that Padre Fidel Fita has performed a service in printing the documents of the case in the Boletin, XXXIII, 431-57.
41. Caballero, Vida de Melchor Cano, pp. 549-50, 557-9, 568-9, 572-7, 582-3, 592-3, 598, 601.
42. Salazar de Mendoza, Vida de Carranza, cap. xxxiii.

The first of these undoubtedly is found in the Comentarios (P. III, Obra iii, cap. 3), but it was perfectly admissible doctrine at the period. Aspilcueta, who was no mystic, tells us, in 1577, that prayer is worthless unless uttered in lively faith and ardent charity; innumerable priests are consigned to purgatory or to hell on account of their prayers, each one of which is at least a venial sin.--De Oratione, cap. viii.

It illustrates the progress of the movement against mysticism that the Index of Zapata, in 1632 (p. 980) orders a passage in Don Quixote to be borrado in which this is expressed much less offensively-- "Las obras de Charidad que se hasen tibia y floxamente no tienen merito ni valen nada."

43. Reusch, Die Indices, pp. 237, 438.
44. V. de la Fuente, Escritos de S. Teresa, I, 3-4, 557; II, 439-40, 557, 568, 571.--Index of Sotomayor, 1640, p. 529.--Indice Ultimo, p. 118.
45. José de Jesus María, Vida de San Juan de la Cruz (Escritos de S. Teresa, II, 511-14).
46. Index of Sandoval, 1612, p. 379 (Ed. Genevæ, 1620).
47. Reusch, Die Indices, p. 224.
48. Caballero, Vida de Melchor Cano, p. 597.--Barrantes, Aparato para la Historia de Extremadura, II, 346-7.--Giovanni da Capugnano, Vida del P. Luigi Granata.--Theiner, Annal. Eccles., III, 361.--Palafox y Mendoza, Obras, VII, 65.
49. Alfonso Rodríguez, Ejercicio de la Perfeccion, P. I, Trat. v, cap. 7, 12.
50. Ribadeneira, Vit. S. Ig. Loyolæ, Lib. v, cap. 10.
51. Alegambe, Bibl. Scriptt. Soc. Jesu, p. 136.--Nieremberg, Honor del Gran Patriarca San Ignacio, p. 513.--L. de la Puente, Guia Spirituale, P. II, Trat. 1, cap. 15, n. 3; cap. 18, n. 2 (Roma, 1628).--De Backer, III, 639-53.
52. Archivo de Simancas, Inq., Lib. 76, fol. 343.
53. Caballero, op. cit., p. 526.--Cf p. 359.
54. Fray Alonso's Memorial, from which the subsequent details are drawn, has been printed by Don Miguel Mir in the Revista de Archivas for Aug.-Sept., 1903; Jan., 1904; Aug.-Sept., 1904; June, 1905; July, 1905; and Aug.-Sept., 1905.
55. Barrantes, Aparato para la Historia de Extremadura, II, 332-47.
56. Biblioteca nacional, MSS., S. 151, fol. 54-67.--Barrantes, op. cit., II, 329, 347-57.--Miscelanea de Zapata (Memorial hist. español, XI, 75).--Cipriano de Valera, Dos Tratados (Reformistas antig. españoles, p. 272).--Dorado, Compendio histórico de Salamanca, p. 423.

In 1576 Alonso González Carmena was tried at Toledo for saying that the only object of the Inquisition was to get money, and instancing a wealthy damsel of Llerena recently arrested as an Alumbrado. He probably considered his assertions verified by having to pay a fine of 4000 maravedís, in addition to six months' exile.--MSS. of Library of Univ. of Halle, Yc, 20, T. I.

57. Páramo, p. 302.
58. Archivo de Simancas, Inq., Lib. 939, fol. 108; Lib 979, fol. 30.--The details of the Edict are derived from a copy published in Mexico, July 17, 1579, which I owe to the kindness of the late General Don Riva Palacio. In the Edict published at the opening of the Mexican Inquisition, Nov. 3, 1571, there is no allusion to the subject. See Appendix to Vol. II, p. 587.
59. Páramo, pp. 302, 681-2, 688-9, 854.
60. MSS. of Library of Univ. of Halle, Yc, 20, T. I.
61. MSS. of Library of Univ. of Halle, Yc, 20, T. VII.
62. Archivo de Simancas, Inq., Leg. 552, fol. 1.
63. Mística Teología, Lib. II, cap. 1, 4, 5, 6.
64. Menéndez y Pelayo, II, 547-8.--MSS. of Bodleian Library, Arch S, 130.
65. Barrantes, Aparato, II, 363.
66. Barrantes, op. cit., II, 364-70. Thia copy is somewhat imperfect; a better one is in the Bibliothèque nationale, fonds Dupuy, 673, fol. 181.

Malvasia (Cathologus omnium Hæresum et Conciliorum, Romæ, 1661, p. 269) gives a list of fifty Illuminist errors from this edict of Pacheco. Cf. Bernino, Historia di tutte l'Heresie, IV, 613 (Venezia, 1717).

67. Archivo de Simancas, Inq., Lib. 927, fol. 475.

This bold protest seems to have called attention to Portocarrero's ability for, in 1624, we find him appointed Inquisitor of Majorca and writing a book in defence of the Inquisition against the royal jurisdiction.

68. Barrantes, op. cit., II, 363, 371-2.

69. MSS. of Bodleian Library, Arch S, 130.

70. MSS. of Bodleian Library, Arch Seld. A., Subt. 11; Arch Seld. 130.

71. Llorente, Hist. crit., cap. xxxviii, n. 5.--Llorente's statement is confirmed by the account in Bernino's Historia di tutte l'Heresie, IV, 613. See also Terzago, Theologia historico-mystica, p. 6 (Venetiis, 1764).

72. Bibl. nacional, MSS., V, 377, cap. xxi.

73. Cartas de Jesuitas (Mem. hist. español, XIII, 122, 150-62, 165, 173, 175, 177-80, 184, 205-7, 214, 222, 245, 267, 324, 435, 528, 543, 547; XIV, 12, 21, 47; XV, 80; XIX, 383).--Pellicer, Avisos históricos (Semanario erúdito, XXXIII, 99, 168).--Index of Vidal Marin, 1707, II, 19.--Archivo hist. nacional, Inq. de Valencia, Leg. 1, n. 6, fol. 591.--Decret. authent. Sacræ Congr. Indulgentt. n. 4, 14.

74. Vida, pp. 6, 10, 275 (Ed. 1784).

75. Various biographies of her have been written by Moran de Butron, Pietro del Spirito Santo, P. Gijon y Leon, P. Gius. Boero and Juan del Castillo, of some of which repeated editions have appeared.

76. Pellicer, Avisos históricos (Semanario erúdito, XXXIII, 171).

77. Ochoa, Epistolario español, II, 81.

78. Vita Yen. Mariæ de Agreda, §§ 4, 6, 8, 13, 38.--Præfat. ad Lib. I, Vitæ B. Virginis.

79. Archivo de Simancas, Inq. Leg. 1465, fol. 101.--Index Libb. prohib. Innoc. PP. XI, p. 167; Append. p. 41.--Reusch, Der Index, II, 253.--Mendham, Literary Policy of the Church of Rome, pp. 272-4 (London, 1830).--Phelippeaux, Relation de l'Origine etc. du Quietisme, I, 178-83 (s. l. 1732).

80. D'Argentré, Collect. Judic. de novis Erroribus, III, I, 156.

81. Analecta Franciscana, I, 92.--Reusch, Der Index, II, 256.--Amort de Revelationibus, P. II, p. 226.

82. Index Clementis PP. XI, p. 292.--Index Bened. PP. XIV, 1744, p. 313. It is significant of the resultant dubious position of the books that Caetano Marcecales, in his Enchiridium mysticum (Veronæ, 1766), while giving two lists of mystic works, one permitted and the other prohibited, wholly omits the writings of María de Agreda.

83. Archivo hist. nacional, Inq. de Toledo, Leg. 1.--Biblioteca Casanatense, MS. X. v, 27, fol. 235.

84. Bordoni Sacrum Tribunal Judicum, p. 508 (Romæ, 1648).--Ign. Lupi Bergomens. Nova Lux in Edictum S. Inquisit. (Bergomi, 1648).

85. Reusch, Der Index, II, 610-11.

86. Scaglia, Prattica per le cause del Sant' Officio, cap. 25 (MS. penes me). There are copies in the Bibliothèque nationale, fonds italien, 139; in the Royal Library of Munich, Cod. Ital. 598, and in the Municipal Library of Piacenza.

87. Bernino, Historia di tutte l'Heresie, IV, 712 (Venezia, 1717.)

88. Royal Library of Munich, Cod. Ital. 185, pp. 1-7.--Library of the Seminario della Curia arcivescovile di Firenze, Chiese, Spogli, Vol. I, pp. 407 aqq.--Modesto Rastrelli. Fatti attinenti all' Inquisizione, pp. 173-77 (Venezia, 1782).--Cf. Cantù, Eretici d'Italia, III, 336.

89. Biblioteca del R. Archivio di Stato in Roma, Miscellanea MS., pp. 577-630.--Royal Library of Munich, Cod. Itat. 185, pp. 13-26.--L'Ambasciata di Romolo a Romani, p. 689 (Colon. 1676).--Collect. Decret. S. Congr. S. Officii, p. 7 (MS. penes me).--Cantù, op. cit., III, 330.

90. MSS. of Ambrosian Library of Milan, H, S, VI, 29, fol. 140.

91. Bernino, Historia di tutte l'Heresie, IV, 722-6.--MSS. of Ambrosian Library, H, S, VI, 29, fol. 14. This latter is a considerable body of documents from which are derived the facts that follow.

92. Ambrosian MSS. ubi sup. fol. 111, 113, 117, 119, 121, 135, 137, 138.

93. Ibidem, fol. 58, 61, 66, 80, 83, 86.

94. Ambrosian MSS. ubi sup., fol. 18, 22, 24, 34, 38, 39, 40, 41, 42, 43, 44, 45, 49, 50, 51, 53, 54, 61, 81, 91.

95. Ibidem, fol. 44, 54, 66, 81.

96. Ambrosian MSS. ubi sup., fol. 65, 82, 113, 117, 119.

97. Guida spirituale, Lib. I, n. 128.--"Non parlando, non pensando, non desiderando, si giunge al perfetto silenzio mistico, nel quale Iddio parla con l'anima e a lei si communica e le insegna nel più intimo fondo la più perfetta e alta sapienza."

Cf. Osuna, Abecedario spiritual, P. III, Trat. xxi, Cap. 3, fol. 203.--Santa Teresa, Libro de las Revelaciones.--San Juan de la Cruz, Subida del Monte Carmelo, II, vii.

98. Guida, Lib. I, n. 68-70.

99. Guida, Lib. III, n. 3, 40.

100. Biblioteca Casanatense, MS. X, v, 27, fol. 231 sqq.

101. Reusch, Der Index, II, 612-14. Of these controversial works I have been able to examine only Segneri's Lettera and the Clavis Aurea. The chief impression made by these polemics is the elusiveness of these mystic dreams when an attempt is made at rigid definition and differentiation.

102. Biblioteca Casanatense, MS. X, IV, 39, fol. 19sqq.

103. Bernino, op. cit., IV, 726.

104. Biblioteca Casanatense, MSS. X, VII, 46, fol. 289 sqq. This is an account of the affair by one evidently in position to have accurate knowledge of details.

105. Archivo histórico nacional, Inq. de Valencia, Legajo 1, n. 4, fol. 164.--Archivo de Simancas, Inq., Legajo 1465, fol. 101.

106. Archivo hist. nacional, Inq. de Valencia, Legajo 12, n. 1, fol. 106.

107. Trois lettres touchant l'Etat present d'Italie, pp. 90-120 (Cologne, 1688)

These nineteen errors are here printed with their confutations, but without indication of date or of the authority under which they were prepared. They are also contained, with a different series of confutations, in the mass of papers concerning the Pelagini, in the Ambrosian Library, H, S., VI, 29, fol. 28.

This also contains (fol. 30) a series of instructions for detecting the Quietist heresy, consisting of a list of forty-three errors. Some of these set forth so concisely the leading tenets ascribed, with tolerable accuracy, to the Quietists, that they are worth presenting here.

21. They seek to annihilate the memory, the intellect and the will; to remember nothing, to understand nothing, to desire nothing, and they say that when they have thus emptied themselves they are refilled by God.

22. They say that God operates in their souls without coöperation; that their spirit is identified with God, so that they are purely passive, surrendering their freewill to God who takes possession of it.

23. Thus such souls are preserved from even venial sins of advertence and, if they commit some inadvertently they are not imputed.

24. Also some proceed to claim impeccability, because they cannot sin when God operates in them without their participation.

25. If these souls commit sinful acts, they say it is through the violence of the demon, with the permission of God, for their torment and purgation.

28. Examination of conscience to ascertain if there has been consent to such acts is not expedient, for it distracts introversion and disturbs the quiet of the soul.

108. Bibl. Casanatense MSS., X, VII, 45, fol. 289.

I cannot but regard this as a truthful report. It accords with the briefer abstract in the final sentence, which distinguishes between the articles proved by witnesses and denied by Molinos and those which he admitted. Reusch (Der Index, II, 617-18) states that the sentence has been printed in the Analecta Juris Pontificii, 6, 1653, and in the Appendix to Francke's translation of the Guida Spirituale, published in 1687. I have a copy from the Royal Library of Munich, Cod. Ital. 185, and there is one in the Bibliothèque nationale, fonds italien, 138, which also contains the 263 articles drawn from his correspondence, with his answers.

109. D'Argentré, Collect. judic. de novis Erroribus, III, II, 357-62.

110. The account of the atto di fede is derived from the MS. Casanatense, X, VII, 45, and a relation printed by Laemmer, Meletematum Romanorum Mantissa, pp. 407 sqq., who also prints (pp. 412-22) the sentence of Pedro Peña.

The contemporary printed sources of the whole affair are Trois Lettres touchant l'Etat present d'Italie, Cologne, 1688; Recueil de diverses pièces concernant le Quietisme et les Quietistes, Amsterdam, 1688, and Bernino, Historia di tutte l'Heresie, IV, 711 sqq. The concise account by Reusch (Der Index, II, 611 sqq.) is written with his accustomed thoroughness and careful use of all accessible sources. John Bigelow's "Molinos the Quietist" (New York, 1882) is a popular narrative which rejects the charges of immorality. See also Heppe, Geschichte der quietistischen Mystik, pp. 110 sqq., 260 sqq. (Berlin, 1875).

111. Innocentii PP. XI, Bull. Coelestis Pastor (Bullar. X, 212).

112. Reusch, Der Index, II, 618.--Index Innoc. XI, Append, pp. 7, 28, 45, 47 (Romæ, 1702).

113. MSS. of Ambrosian Library, H. S. VI, 29, fol. 67 sqq.

114. Bernino, op. cit., IV, 727-8.

115. Royal Library of Munich, Cod. Ital. 209, fol. 67 sqq.--Cf. Phelippeaux, Relation du Quietisme, II, 117, 154.

116. Laemmer, op. cit., p. 427.--Heppe, Geschichte der quietistischen Mystik, p. 445.

117. Mongitore, L'Atto pubblico di Fede celebrato à 6 Aprile, 1724 (Palermo 1724).

118. See the extracts from S. François de Sales collected by Fénelon, in his Fifth Letter.--OEuvres, II, 95-98 (Paris, 1838).

119. Noack, Die christliche Mystic, II, 236 (Königsberg, 1853).

120. Heppe, op. cit., p. 88.

121. Abomination des Abominations des fausses Devotions de ce Tems divisées, en Trois, la premiere des Illuminez; la seconde des nouveaux Adamites; la troisieme des Spirituels à la mode, p. 88 (Paris, 1632).

122. Bossuet, who read her autobiography in MS. tells us of this tympanitic condition and the splitting of her garments (De Quietismo, ap. Laemmer, op. cit., p. 423). In the printed life, this special

feature is omitted, but the passage has every appearance of curtailment (II, 33, cf. 234; III, 9).

123. Bossuet's side in this controversy is elaborately set forth in Phelippeaux's posthumous "Relation de l'Origine, du Progrès et de la Condemnation du Quiétisme," 2 vols., 1732 (s. l.). Also in Bossuet's "Relation sur le Quiétisme" and subsequent controversial writings, Paris, 1698. Madame Guyon's statements are contained in "La Vie de Madame J. M. B. de la Mothe Guion, écrite por Elle-même," 3 vols. Cologne, 1720. She is defended in the "Lettres de M. xxx (Abbé de la Blatterie) à un Ami au sujet de la Relation du Quiétisme," 1733 (s. l.). Fénelon's writings on the subject are in his OEuvres, T. II, Paris, 1838.

Comprehensive accounts may be found in Matter, "Le Mysticisme en France au temps de Fénelon," Paris, 1865 and Heppe, "Geschichte der quietistischen Mystik in der katholischen Kirche," Berlin, 1865.

124. Compendio de la asombrosa Vida del gran Siervo de Dios, Fr. Juan Joseph de la Cruz, pp. 276 sqq. (Madrid, 1790).

125. Archivo hist. nacional, Inq. de Valencia, Leg. 1, n. 4, fol. 164.

126. Bulario de la Orden de Santiago, Lib. V, fol. 103; Lib. III de copias, fol. 703, 704.--Archivo hist. nacional, Inq. de Valencia, Leg. 12, n. 4, fol. 124.

127. MSS. of Archivo municipal de Sevilla, Seccion especial, Siglo XVIII, Letra A, Tomo IV, n. 48-49.--These are relations of the auto, one of which I have printed in "Chapters from the Religious History of Spain."

128. Relacion hist. de la Judería de Sevilla, pp. 99-103.

129. Archivo municipal de Sevilla, loc. cit., n. 52.

130. Matute y Luquin, p. 211.

131. Possadas, Triumphos de la Castidad contra la Luxuria diabolica de Molinos, Córdova, 1698. This is a second edition; a third appeared in Madrid, in 1775.

132. Archivo hist. nacional, Inq. de Valencia, Leg. 2, n. 15; Leg. 12, n. 2, fol. 126.

133. MSS. of Library of Univ. of Halle, Yc, 20, T. XI.

134. Matute y Luquin, pp. 216-23.

135. Index of Vidal Marin, 1707, II, 195.

136. Bulario de la Orden de Santiago, Lib. V, fol. 141, 144, 146, 150.--Archivo de Simancas, Inq. Legajos 418, 419 (números antiguos).--See Appendix for the abjuration, which summarizes the errors.

137. Archivo de Simancas, Inq., Lib. 876, fol. 153.--Llorente (Hist. crít. Cap. XLII, n. 15) places this case under Carlos III.

138. Llorente, Hist. crít., cap. XL, art. ii, n. 1-14.

139. There is an allusion to this edict in the Relacion de la Causa contra Don Pedro Fernández Ybarraran (MSS. of David Fergusson Esq.).

140. Proceso contra Fray Eusebio de Villaroja (MSS. of David Fergusson Esq.).

141. Lib. XIII de Cartas, fol. 192 (MSS. of Am. Philosophical Society).

142. Archivo hist. nacional, Inq. de Toledo, Leg. 1.

143. Ibidem, Inq. de Valencia, Leg. 100.

144. Archivo de Simancas, Inq., Lib. 890, fol. 82.

145. Ibidem, Lib. 890.--Matute y Luquin, p. 296.

146. Archivo hist. nacional, Inq. de Toledo, Leg. 114, n. 18.

147. Bibl. nationale de France, fonds espagnol 354, fol. 248-69.--Llorente, Hist. crít., cap. XVI, art. iv.--Miscelanea de Zapata (Mem. hist. español, XI, 70).--Cipriano de Valera, Dos Tratados, p. 480 (Reformistas antiguos españoles).--Ribadeneira, Vit. Ign. Loyolæ, Lib. V, cap. 10.--Luigi de Granata, Vita di Giovanni d'Avila, p. 143 (Romæ, 1746).--Matute y Luquin, p. 18.--Simancæ de Cath. Institt. Tit. XXI, n. 24.

A French translation of the sentence and confession has been printed by M. Campan, in the appendix to the Mémoires de Francisco de Enzinas.

148. Godoy Alcántara, Historia de los falsos Cronicones, p. 2.--Cf. V. de la Fuente, Hist. ecles., III, 255.

149. Relatione del Miracolo delle Stimmate, venute nuovamente ad una Monacha dell' Ordine di S. Domenico, in Portogallo, nella Città di Lisbona.--Bologna, 1584.--Printed also in Rome and in Verona.

150. Cipriano de Valera, Enjambre de falsos Milagros, pp. 564, sqq. Usoz y Rio, in his notes to this reprint, in his Reformistas antiguos, says that Valera's versions are faithfully made from "Les grands Miracles et les Tressainctes Plaies advenuz à la R. Mère Prieure du Monastiere de l'Anonciade." A Paris par Jean Bressant, 1586.

151. Cipriano de Valera, pp. 575-80.--Páramo, pp. 233-4, 302-4.

In 1650, Padre Diego Tello, S. J., in an opinion given to the Granada tribunal alludes to the political objects of Sor María's imposturas, as though it was a well-known fact.--MSS. of Library of Univ. of Halle, Yc, 17.

152. Archivo de Simancas, Inq., Lib. 939, fol. 700.
153. Ibidem, Inq. de Toledo, Leg. 113, n. 6.
154. Cartas de Jesuitas (Mem. hist. español, XIII, 49, 51).
155. Bibl. nacional, MSS., D, 111, fol. 127.
156. MSS. of Bodleian Library, Arch. S., 130.--Bibl. nacional, MSS., V, 377, cap. XXI, § 7.
157. Cartas de Jesuitas (op. cit., XIII, 42, 51, 457).--Archivo de Simancas, Inq., Leg. 552, fol. 17.
158. Bibl. nacional, MSS., V, 377, cap. xxi, § 5.
159. Archivo hist. nacional, Inq. de Toledo, Leg. 1.
160. Bibl. nacional, MSS., D, 118, fol. 405, n. 66.
161. Olmo, Relacion, pp. 201-3, 240.
162. MSS. of Library of Univ. of Halle, Yc, 20, T. XI.--Archivo hist. nacional, Inq. de Toledo, Leg. 1.
163. Royal Library of Berlin, Qt. 9548.
164. Archivo hist. nacional, Inq. de Toledo, Leg. 1.
165. Menéndez y Pelayo, III, 405.--MSS. of Archivo municipal de Sevilla, Seccion especial, Siglo XVIII, Letra A, T. 4, n. 56.--Cartas del Filósofo rancio. II, 495 (Madrid, 1824).
166. Archivo hist. nacional, Inq. de Valencia, Leg. 100.
167. Llorente, Hist. crít., cap. XLIII, art. iv, n. 1.--Archivo hist. nacional, Inq. de Toledo, Leg. 115, n. 25; Inq. de Valencia, Leg. 100.

By edict of June 23, 1805, all writings in which credit of any kind was given to the favors which the beata pretended to have received from heaven were absolutely prohibited.--Suplemento al Indice expurgatorio, p. 25 (Madrid, 1805).

168. Llorente, loc. cit., n. 2.--Archivo, hist. nacional, Inq. de Valencia, Leg. 100.
169. Extracto de la Causa seguida á Sor Patrocinio (Madrid, 1865).
170. Revista Cristiana, Marzo-Abril, 1891 (Madrid).

Spain is by no means the only seat of these manifestations. In 1848 there was at Niederbronn, near Strassburg, a bride of Christ named Elizabeth Eppinger who, though denied the supreme favor of the stigmata, had trances and visions and the gift of prophecy. She founded the Order of Filles du Redempteur, over which she presided as Soeur Alphonse.--Abbé Busson, Lettres sur l'Extatique de Niederbronn (Besançon, 1849-53).

The grace of the stigmata is likewise not uncommon. About 1825 there flourished Katharine Emmerich, the nun of Dülmen, and contemporary with her were three girls in Tyrol, Maria von Mörl, Domenica Lazzari and Crescenzia Nicklutsch, all of whom enjoyed also the customary visions and ecstasies. The learned Joseph Görres was one of the believing pilgrims who put on record his experiences. At the same time Provence boasted of a similar beata, Madame Miollis, known as the stigmatisée du Var, at Villecroze.--Die Tyrolen ekstasischen Jungfrauen (Regensburg, 1843).--Nicolas, L'extatique et les stigmatisées du Tyrol (Paris, 1844).--Boré, Les stigmatisées du Tyrol, 2e. Ed. (Paris, 1846).

The more recent case of Louise Lateau, in Belgium, is well known. All this, however, is trivial in comparison with the development of stigmatisation among the followers of Pierre-Michel Vintras, in France. In 1850 it was reckoned that no less than three hundred were favored with this distinguishing mark of divine approval.--André, Affaire Rose Tamisier, p. 5 (Carpentras, 1851).

171. S. Th. Aquin. Summæ Suppl. Q. VIII, art. 4.--Astesani Summæ, Lib. V, Tit. xiii, Q. 2.--Summa Sylvestrina s. v. CONFESSOR, I, §§ 10-11.
172. Guidonis de Monte Rocherii Manip. Curator. P. II, Tract, iii, cap. 9.
173. S. Antonini Summæ, P. III, Tit. xiv, cap. 19, § 8.
174. S. Th. Aquin. in IV Sentt., Dist. XIX, Q. 1, art. 3.--Joh. Friburgens. Summæ Confessor., Lib. III, Tit. xxxiv, Q. 65.
175. Burriel, Vidas de los Arzobispos de Toledo (Bibl. nacional, MSS. Ff, 194, fol. 9).
176. Concil. Valentin, ann. 1565, Tit. ii, cap. 17 (Aguirre, V, 417).--C. Mediolanensis I, ann. 1565, cap. 6 (Harduin. X, 653).--C. Provin. Mediolanens. IV, ann. 1576 (Acta Eccles. Mediolanens. I, 146).--Rituale Roman., Tit. iii, cap. 1.
177. MSS. of David Fergusson, Esq.--Archivo de Simancas, Inq., Sala 39, Leg. 4, fol. 34, 55, 81.--Archivo hist. nacional, Inq. de Valencia, Leg. 9, n. 2, fol. 236, 237.--Bibl. nacional, MSS., PV, fol. C, 17, n. 38.
178. Archivo hist. nacional, Inq. de Valencia, Leg. 16, n. 6, fol. 9.
179. Gratiani Decret. Caus. xxx, q. i, can. 8, 9, 10.--Constitt. R. Poore, cap. 9 (Harduin. VII, 91).
180. Salcedo, Practica criminalis canonica, p. 276 (Compluti, 1587).

For an instructive sketch of Ghiberti by Miss M. A. Tucker, see English Hist. Review, Jan.-July, 1903.

181. Archivo hist. nacional, Inq. de Toledo, Leg. 233, n. 100.
182. Archivo hist. nacional, Inq. de Toledo, Leg. 231, n. 71.

183. Archivo de Simancas, Inq., Lib. 939, fol. 374.
184. Pauli PP. IV Bull. Cum sicut nuper, 16 Apr., 1559 (Bullar. Roman. II, 48).
185. Páramo, p. 880.
186. Pii PP. IV, Const. 51, Pastoris æterni, 1 Apr. 1562. It is perhaps suggestive that in the Luxemburg Bullarium (III, 71) the omission of the word non completely reverses the purport of the brief. It will be found correctly printed in Cherubini's edition.
187. Páramo, p. 881.
188. Pauli PP. V, Const. Cum sicut nuper, 16 Sept. 1608 (Trimarchi de Confessario abutente etc. Tractat., pp. 7, 10.--Genuæ, 1636).--Archivo de Simancas, Inq., Leg. 1465. fol. 16.
189. Trimarchi, pp. 10, 11.
190. Bullar. Roman. III, 484.--Trimarchi, pp. 14-18.
191. Archivo hist. nacional, Inq. de Valencia, Lib. VIII de autos, Leg. 2, fol. 114.
192. Ant. de Sousa, Opusc. circa Constit. Pauli V, Tract. I, cap. 20.
193. Archivo de Simancas, Inq., Lib. 939, fol. 371.--Archivo hist. nacional, ubi sup.
194. Archivo de Simancas, Inq., Lib. 940, fol. 212; Gracia y Justicia, Inq., Leg. 631, fol. 27.
195. MSS. of Bodleian Library, Arch, S, 130.
196. Archivo hist. nacional, Inq. de Valencia, Leg. 1, n. 6, fol. 274, 393.--Archivo de Simancas, Inq., Leg. 1465, fol. 16.

The clause concerning solicitation in the Edict of Faith, published at Valencia, Feb. 24, 1630, shows this and also the devices used to elude the technical definition of the offence. "Or, whether any confessor or confessors, clerics or religious of whatever station pre-eminence or condition, in the act of confession or immediately before or after it, or with occasion or appearance of confession, although there is no opportunity and no confession may have followed, but in the confessional or any place where confessions are made, or which is destined for that purpose, when the impression is produced that confession is being made or heard, have solicited or attempted to solicit any one, inducing or provoking them to foul and indecent acts, whether between the penitent and confessor or others, or have held indecent and illicit conversation with them. And we exhort and order all confessors to admonish their penitents, whom they understand to have been solicited, of the obligation to denounce the solicitors to this Holy Office, which has exclusive cognizance of this crime."--Archivo hist. nacional, Inq. de Valencia, Lib. 7 de Autos, Leg. 2, fol. 114.

197. Archivo hist. nacional, Inq. de Valencia, Lib. 7 de Autos, Leg. 2, fol. 114.
198. "Cuyo conocimiento pertenece al Santo Oficio de la Inquisition, sin embargo del Breve de la Santidad de Gregorio XV expedido en treinta de Agusto de 1622 años, por declaracion suya, para las Inquisiciones de los Reynos de su Magestad, toca privativamente el castigo de este delito al Santo Oficio y no á los obispos ni á sus vicarios, provisores ni ordinarios."--Bibl. nacional, MSS., D, 118, p. 148.
199. Archivo de Simancas, Inq., Lib. 28, fol. 246; Lib. 890.
200. Ibidem, Lib. 939, fol. 107; Lib. 942, fol. 23, 31; Leg. 1465, fol. 16.--It is scarce worth while to refer to the wild story of Gonzáles de Móntes (Inquis. hist. artes detectæ, p. 185) that in Seville this brought in so many denunciations that twenty secretaries and as many inquisitors were unable to take them down within the thirty days allowed and that four prolongations of the time were required.
201. Bibl. nacional, MSS., D, 118, fol. 216, n. 60.
202. Archivo de Simancas, Inq., Leg. 1665, fol. 16; Lib. 939, fol. 107; Lib. 942, fol. 31.
203. Archivo hist. nacional, Inq. de Valencia, Leg. 2, n. 16, fol. 254.--Archivo de Simancas, Inq., Lib. 83, fol. 25.

The Roman Inquisition tardily followed the example of the Spanish in a decree of 1677.--Berardi de Sollicitatione et Absolutione Complicis, p. 6 (Faventiæ, 1897).

204. "La experiencia acredita que muchos contestes, singularmente mugeres y en causas de solicitacion, nada declaran, ya por miedo, ya por vergüenza, ya por una falsa caridad, de que tiene el Santo Oficio freqüentes y lastimosas experiencias."--Instrucion que han de guardar los Comisarios, n. 21.
205. Archivo hist. nacional, Inq. de Toledo, Leg. 227, n. 7.
206. Ibidem, Inq. de Valencia, Leg. 2, n. 15.
207. Archivo de Simancas, Inq., Lib. 939, fol. 371.
208. Bibl. nacional, MSS., B, 159, fol. 161-2. For various speculations on the subject see Rod. a Cunha pro PP. Pauli V Statuto, Q. xix (Benavente, 1611).--Ant. de Sousa Opusc. circa Constit. Pauli V, Tract. ii, cap. 7-10.
209. Card. Cozza, Dubia selecta circa Solicitationem, Dub. XLII (Lovanii, 1750).
210. Archivo hist. nacional, Inq. de Valencia, Leg. 365, n. 46.
211. Bibl. nacional, MSS., V, 377, cap. XX.
212. MSS. of Royal Library of Copenhagen, 218^{b}, p. 264.
213. Archivo de Simancas, Inq., Leg. 1465, fol. 16.--MSS. of Bibl. nacional de Lima, Protocolo

223, Exp^{te} 5270.

214. Rod. a Cunha, Q. XIV, XV.--Ant. de Sousa, Tit. I, cap. 19.--Matteucci Cautela Confessarii, Lib. I, cap. 5, n. 3 (Venetiis, 1710).--Cozza, Dub. XVII.--Bibl. nacional, MSS., V, 377, cap. XX.

215. Ant. de Sousa, Tract. I, cap. XV.

216. There were many probabilist authorities who held that the fact that such acts as kissing, pressing the hands, handling the breasts, etc., were committed in the confessional did not change them from venial to mortal sins. See Del Bene de Officio S. Inquis. P. II, Dub. 237, Sect. 3, n. 3 (Lugduni, 1666). Cf. Cozza, Dub. III, n. 18.

In 1743 a lively controversy arose between the rigorists and the Jesuits over the Tatti mammillari caused by a proposition of Father Benzi S. J. that stroking the cheeks of nuns and handling their breasts were venial, when unaccompanied with depraved intentions.--Concina, Explicazione di quattro Paradossi, cap. 1 § 1 (Lucca, 1746).

217. Cozza, Dub. III, IV, V.--Fran. Bordoni Sacrum Tribunal Judicum, cap. XXIII, n. 53-61 (Romæ, 1648); Ejusd. Manuale Consultorum, Sect, XXV, n. 91 (Romæ, 1693).

218. Archivo hist. nacional, Inq. de Valencia, Leg. 365, n. 46, fol. 26.

219. Rod. a Cunha, Q. XVII.--Ant. de Sousa, Tract. I, cap. xiv.--Jo. Sánchez, Disputationes Selectæ, Disp. XI, n. 43, 44 (Ludguni, 1636).

220. Rod. a Cunha, Q. XIV.--Ant. de Sousa, Tract. I, cap. xi.--Cozza, Dub. XXXVII.--Trimarchi, p. 160.--Bibl. nacional, MSS., B, fol. 160.

221. Trimarchi, p. 145.--Cozza, Dub. XXXVIII.

222. Páramo, p. 886.

223. A Cunha, Q. IX, XI.--De Sousa, Tract. I, cap. vi, vii, xvii.--Alberghini Manuale Qualificatorum, cap. XXXI, § 1, n. 10, 11, 17.--Trimarchi, pp. 193, 199, 2O1, 212.--Cozza, Dub. IX, X, XI.--Bodoni Manuale, Sect. XXV, n. 169--Bibl. nacional, MSS., V, 377, cap. XX, §§ 5, 10.

224. Archivo hist. nacional, Inq. de Valencia, Leg. 376.--Archivo de Simancas, Inq., Registro de Solicitantes, A, 7, fol. 2 (Lib. 1002, fol. 2).

225. The more important of these decisions were--

3 There is no parvitas materiæ in solicitation.

8 When the solicitation is mutual, the confessor is to be denounced.

9 A confessor yielding to solicitation through fear is to be denounced.

10 Solicitation in other sacraments does not fall within the papal bulls.

11 Solicitation to other than carnal sins during confession does not require denunciation.

12 When a confessor praises the beauty of a penitent, if the praise is serious and without evil intention, he is not liable to denunciation; if otherwise, he is.

13 If a confessor sitting in a confessional solicits a woman standing before him without pretext of confession he is probably not liable to denunciation.

14 A confessor who makes during confession a present to the penitent, without evil intention is not liable to denunciation; otherwise he is.--Berardi de Sollicitatione, p. 5.

226. Bullar. Roman. T. VI, Append. p. 1.

227. Bullar. Benedicti PP. XIV, T. I, p. 23-4.

228. Bullar. Roman. ubi sup.

229. Bullar. Benedicti PP. XIV, loc. cit.

230. Archivo hist. nacional, Inq. de Toledo, Leg. 1; Inq. de Valencia, Leg. 365, n. 46.--Archivo de Simancas, Inq., Lib. 890.

231. Joh. Sánchez Disputt. Select., Disp. xi, n. 3, 4.--Juan Sánchez was one of the laxer moral theologians of the seventeenth century, some of whose propositions incurred papal censure, but this escaped. Hurter characterizes him as "in morum doctrina versatissimus."--Nomenclator Theol. Cathol. I, 414.

232. Ant. de Sousa, Tract. II, cap. XX.--Berardi de Sollicitatione, p. 129.--Il Consulente Ecclesiastico, Vol. IV, p. 19 (1899).--S. Alph. de Ligorio Theol. Moral. Lib. VII, n. 519. Podestà, however, tells us that in his time, in the diocese of Naples, it was reserved to the bishop.--Examen ecclesiasticum, T. II, n. 601 (Venetiis, 1788).

233. Proceso contra el Dr. Pedro Mendizabal (MS. penes me).

234. Archivo hist. nacional, Inq. de Toledo, Leg. 228, n. 18.

235. Ibidem, Inq. de Valencia, Leg. 365, n. 46, fol. 32.

236. Berardi, op. cit., pp. 36-7.

237. Archivo de Simancas, Inq. de Logroño, Procesos de fe, Leg. 1.

238. Bibl. nacional, MSS., V, 377, cap. XXI, § 6.

239. Ibidem, cap. XX, § 3.--De Sousa, Aphorism. Lib. I, cap. xxxiv, n. 40.--Alberghini, Man. Qualificator. cap. xxxi, § 1, n. 19.

240. Archivo de Simancas, Inq., Lib. 1006, fol. 25.

241. Archivo hist. nacional, Inq. de Toledo, Leg. 227, n. 4.

242. Ibidem, Leg. 1.
243. Ibidem, Inq. de Valencia, Leg. 4, n. 2, fol. 79.
244. Archivo hist. nacional, Inq. de Toledo, Leg. 1; Inq. de Valencia, Leg. 66.
245. Archivo de Simancas, Inq., Lib. 942, fol. 23; Leg. 1465, fol. 16.
246. Ibidem, Lib. 939, fol. 107; Lib. 942, fol. 38; Leg. 1465, fol. 16.
247. Archivo hist. nacional, Inq. de Valencia, Leg. 2, n. 16, fol. 264.--Archivo de Simancas, Inq., Lib. 942, fol. 52.
248. Archivo de Simancas, Inq., Leg. 1465, fol. 16.
249. Ibidem, Lib. 890.
250. Ibidem, Lib. 939, fol. 107; Lib. 941, fol. 2; Leg. 1465, fol. 16.--Archivo hist. nacional, Inq. de Valencia, Leg. 2, n. 16, fol. 254.
251. Archivo de Simancas, Inq., Lib. 939, fol. 107; Lib. 942, fol. 45; Leg. 1465, fol. 16.
252. Páramo, p. 875.
253. Archivo de Simancas, Inq., Leg. 1465, fol. 16.
254. Ibidem, Lib. 939, fol. 342.--De Sousa, Opusc. circa Constit. Pauli V, Tract. II, cap. 13, 21; Ejusd. Aphor. Inquis. Lib. 1, cap. xxxiv, n. 64, 65.--Alberghini, Man. Qualif. cap. xxxi, § 2, n. 3, 4.--Bibl. nacional MSS., V, 377, cap. xx, 9.--Archivo hist. nacional, Inq. de Valencia, Leg. 61; Inq. de Toledo, Leg. 498.--MSS. of Royal Library of Copenhagen, 218^{b}, p. 423.
255. Archivo de Simancas, Inq., Lib. 876, fol. 208.
256. Bodoni Man. Consultorum, pp. 224, 232, 235.--Cf. Trimarchum pp. 288-92.
257. MSS. of Royal Library of Copenhagen, 218^{b}, pp. 386-7.
258. Cozza, op. cit., Dub. XIV. This is still the rule. See Concil. Plenar. Americæ Latinæ, ann. 1899, Append, CXXXII, T. II, p. 761 (Romæ, 1900).
259. Archivo hist. nacional, Inq. de Valencia, Leg. 299.
260. Ibidem, Leg. 228, n. 24.
261. Archivo de Simancas, Inq., Leg. 1473 (Cartilla de Comisarios, §§ ix, x).--Ibidem, Lib. 890, fol. 156.
262. Ibidem, Lib. 83, fol. 25.
263. MSS. of Bibl. nacional, de Lima, Protocolo 233, Exp^{te} 5270.
264. Archivo de Simancas, Inq., Leg. 1465, fol. 16.
265. Páramo, p. 879.
266. A Cunha, op. cit., Q. XXIII.--De Sousa, op. cit., Tract. II, cap. 12.
267. Archivo de Simancas, Inq., Leg. 552, fol. 1.
268. Bibl. nacional, MSS., V, 377, cap. xx.--In modern practice, under the regulations issued by the Roman Inquisitors, in 1867, a first and a second denunciation only cause the accused to be watched and a third one is necessary to justify action.--Berardi, p 126.
269. Archivo hist. nacional, Inq. de Valencia, Leg. 365.
270. Archivo de Simancas, Inq., Lib. 1002, fol. 2-4.--Archivo hist. nacional, Inq. de Valencia, Leg. 66; Inq. de Toledo, Leg. 233, n. 108, fol. 90, 97, 140, 181.
271. MSS. of Royal Library of Copenhagen 218^{b}, p. 264.--Archivo hist. nacional, Inq. de Valencia, Leg. 9, n. 2, fol. 38.
272. Archivo de Simancas, Inq., Lib. 1002.
273. Ibidem, Leg. 1465, fol. 16.
274. Archivo de Simancas, Inq., Leg. 1465, fol. 16.--MSS. of Royal Library of Copenhagen, 218^{b}, p. 265.
275. Archivo de Alcalá, Hacienda, Leg. 544^{3} (Lib. 4).
276. A Cunha, Q. XXIV.--De Sousa, Tract. II, cap. 16, 18, 21.
277. Archivo de Simancas, Inq., Leg. 552, fol. 6, 22, 23, 29.

There was more wholesome severity in Rome. In 1626 the Congregation of the Inquisition reserved to itself the designation of the penalty (Collect. Decret. Sac. Congr. S. Officii, p. 397--MS. penes me). Some ten years later Trimarchus (op. cit., pp. 302, 304) after enumerating the punishments decreed by Gregory, adds that in practice, if the culprit has only once solicited an ordinary woman, deprivation of confessing suffices; if two, repeatedly, add suspension of priestly functions and, for a regular, especially if there has been scandal, perpetual reclusion in a convent or, for a secular, perpetual service in a hospital. If the penitent solicited is a nun or the wife of a magnate, or there are many women and much popular scandal, degradation or the galleys.

Although Gregory included relaxation, Benedict XIV (De Synodo Dioecesana, Lib. IX, cap. vi, n. 7) says that in no case, however aggravated, can it be found that relaxation had been inflicted, and this is repeated by Fray Manuel de Nájera in his Enchiridion canonico-morale de Confess. p. 161 (Mexico, 1764).

278. Bibl. national, MSS., V, 377, cap. xx.
279. Archivo hist. nacional, Inq. de Valencia, Leg. 290, fol. 80.

280. Ibidem, Inq. de Toledo, Leg. 229, n. 32.
281. Ibidem, Leg. 1.
282. Proceso contra Fray Estevan Ramoneda (MSS. of Am. Phil. Society).
283. Quia ex sola publica effusione seminis aut sanguinis humani ecclesia polluitur.--Clericati de Virtute Pænitentice Decisiones, p. 214 (Vinetiis, 1706).
284. MSS. of Trinity College, Dublin, Class II, Vol. IV, pp. 63, 294.--Berardi, op. cit., p. 129.--Cf. Benedicti PP. XIV de Synodo Dioecesana, Lib. VI, cap. xi, n. &.
285. MSS. of Library of Univ. of Halle, Yc, 20, T. I.
286. Ibidem, T. XI.
287. Bibl. nacional, MSS., V, 377, cap. XX, § 8.
288. Archivo de Simancas, Inq., Lib. 876, fol. 32.
289. Archivo hist. nacional, Inq. de Toledo, Leg. 231, n. 70.
290. MSS. of David Fergusson Esq.
291. Archivo hist. nacional, Inq. de Valencia, Leg. 365, n. 45, fol. 4-12.
292. MSS. of Royal Library of Copenhagen, 218^{b}, p. 387.
293. Archivo hist. nacional, Inq. de Valencia, Leg. 4, n. 2, fol. 79.
294. Archivo de Simancas, Inq., Lib. 1006.
295. Archivo hist. nacional, Inq. de Toledo, Leg. 227, n. 10; Leg. 228, n. 28.
296. Archivo de Simancas, Inq., Lib. 890.
297. Archivo de Simancas, Inq., Visitas de Barcelona, Leg. 15, fol. 5.
298. Llorente, Hist. crít., cap. XXVIII, art. 1, n. 17.
299. MSS. of Library of Univ. of Halle, Yc, 20, T. I.
300. The Dominican Maestro Alvarado, in his heated defence of the Inquisition, in 1811, calls attention to the fact that, in its later period, its penitents were largely ecclesiastics, because firstly their theology exposed them to uttering compromising propositions; secondly, "porque solos los clérigos y frailes son los que confiesan y todos saben muy bien lo peligroso de este materia y los muchos que en él han naufragado."--Cartas del Filosofo Rancio, I, 316 (Madrid, 1824).
301. Archivo hist. nacional, Inq. de Toledo, Leg. 1.
302. These statistics are compiled from various registers, covering respectively portions of the period. There are some minor breaks, which would increase the aggregate somewhat, but not materially. See Archivo hist. nacional, Inq. de Toledo, Leg. 233, n. 108; Inq. de Valencia, Leg. 66.--Archivo de Simancas, Libros 1002, 1003, 1004.

There is perhaps some interest in recording the respective responsibilities of the various classes and orders of the clergy for these delinquents, as follows:

Secular priests, canons etc 981 Franciscans, Conventual and Barefooted 552 Observantines 506 Capuchins 183 Recollects 56 Carmelites 355 Dominicans 288 Augustinians 156 Trinitarians 144 Mercenarians 131 Jesuits 92 Minims 69 Benedictines 35 Geronimites 30 San Pedro de Alcántara 29 Clérigos Menores 20 Congr. of San Filippo Neri 20 Bernardines (Cistercians) 20 Escuelas Pias 16 Basilians 16 S. Francisco de Asis 5 N. Señora de la Vitoria 5 Order of Santiago 4 Order of Calatrava 3 Theatins 3 Servites 3 Misioneros 2 Agonizantes 2 Hermits of St. Paul 2 San Juan 2 Premonstratensians 2 Ex-Jesuits 2 Carthusians 1 St. Ursula 1 San Diego 1 Not specified 38

The comparatively small number of Jesuits, who devoted themselves so greatly to the confessional, is partly explicable by the expulsion of the Society in 1767.
303. Puigblanch, La Inquisicion sin Mascara, pp. 422-5 (Cádiz, 1811).
304. Instruct. S. Inquis. Roman. 20 Feb. 1867 (Collect. Concil. Lacens. III, 353).--Berardi, op. cit.
305. A priest, who could speak from experience, concisely described, in 1820, the conditions produced by the system "En donde la doctrina infernal de la delacion tenia en una habitual consternacion á las familias y á los individuos que se correspondian con la mutua desconfianza que inspiraba el continuo recelo de encontrar en amigo, en el padre, en el hijo, en la esposa, un verdugo que armado con el puñal del fanatismo religioso contribuyese á los asesinatos naturales que solo Dios conosce y a los civiles que no son tan desconocidos."--P Antonio Bernabeu, España venturosa, p. xvi (Madrid, 1820).
306. Theologians had a storehouse of epithets with which to characterize the various classes of propositions. A few of the more usual, with their significance, are given by Alberghini (Man. Qualificator. cap. xii, n. 1-18) as follows:--

Heretical--one which is contrary to Catholic truth.

Erroneous--that which does not directly contradict the faith, but some conclusion evidently deducible from the faith.

Savoring of heresy--not contradicting the faith by evident consequence, but by very probable and morally certain consequence.

Ill-sounding--that which has a double sense, one Catholic and the other heretic, but usually accepted in the latter.

Rash--that which is not governed by reason and lacks all authority.

Scandalous or offensive to pious ears--that which gives occasion to another to err, such as "heretics are to be tolerated and not to be slain."

Schismatic or seditious--tending to disrupt the unity of the Church.

Impious--contrary to Catholic piety.

Insulting--defamatory of some Christian profession or illustrious person.

Blasphemous--insulting to God.

Simancas (Enchirid., Tit. xxiv) gives a similar list. Dandino (De Suspectis de Hæresi, pp. 477-512) a more elaborate exposition. There was no limit, however, to the vituperative vocabulary of the Church. A choice collection of additional ones will be found in the bull Auctorem fidei of Pius VI (1794), condemning the Jansenist Council of Pistoja.

307. MS. Memoria de diversos Autos, Auto 27, n. 10; Auto 37, n. 5 (See Appendix to Vol. I).

308. Archivo hist. nacional, Inq. de Toledo, Leg. 112, n. 73.

309. D. Manuel Serrano y Sanz (Revista de Archivos, Abril, 1902, pp. 260-80). This Alvaro de Montalvan was father-in-law of Francisco de Rojas, author of La Celestina, who was also a Converso.

310. Archivo de Simancas, Inq., Vistas de Barcelona, Leg. 15, fol. 9, 20.

The utterance of Clemenza Paresa seems to have been a popular saying. In 1572 Rodríguez Rúiz was penanced for it in the Canaries.--Ibidem, Canarias, Exp^{tes} de Visitas, Leg. 250, Lib. 3, fol. 8.

311. Archivo de Simancas, Inq., Canarias, Exp^{tes} de Visitas, Lib. 3, fol. 16-17.

312. Archivo hist. nacional, Inq. de Valencia, Leg. 30.

313. Rojas de Hæret. P. I, n. 2, 67, 96; P. II, n. 310-13.

314. Archivo hist. nacional, Inq. de Valencia, Leg. 299, fol. 80.

315. MSS. of the Library of Univ. of Halle, Yc, 20, T. I.

316. Elucidationes S. Officii, § 36 (Archivo de Alcalá, Hacienda, Leg. 544^{2}, Lib. 4).

317. C. Trident Sess. XXIV, De Statu Matrimonii, can. 10.--"Si quis dixerit statum conjugalem anteponendum esse statui virginitatis vel coelibatus et non esse melius ac beatius manere in virginitate aut coelibatu quam jungi matrimonio: anathema sit."

318. MSS. of Library of Univ. of Halle, Yc, 20, T. I.

319. Archivo hist. nacional, Inq. de Valencia, Leg. 299, fol. 80.

320. Archivo de Simancas, Inq., Lib. 926, fol. 25.

321. Bibl. nacional, MSS., V, 377, cap. 2.

322. S. Antonini Confessionale.

323. Archivo de Simancas, Hacienda, Leg. 25, fol. 3.

324. Ibidem, Inq., Sala 40, Lib. 4, fol. 264.

325. Schäfer, Beiträge, II, 324.

326. Archivo de Simancas, Inq., Leg. 787.

327. Ibidem, Lib. 82, fol. 228; Lib. 939, fol. 108; Lib. 942, fol. 38.--MSS. of Royal Library of Copenhagen, 218^{b}, p. 168.

328. Bibl. nacional, MSS., S, 121, fol. 54.--Archivo de Simancas, Inq., Leg. 1157, fol. 155.

329. MSS. of Library of Univ. of Halle, Yc, 20, T. I.

330. Bibl. nacional, MSS., PV, 3, n. 20.--Archivo hist. nacional, Inq. de Valencia, Leg. 99; Leg. 2, n. 10.

331. Archivo de Simancas, Inq., Lib. 939, fol. 342; Leg. 552, fol. 1.--MSS. of Royal Library of Copenhagen, 218^{b}, p. 260.

332. Archivo de Simancas, Inq., Lib. 926, fol. 25; Lib. 1002.--Archivo hist. nacional, Inq. de Toledo, Leg. 1.--MS. penes me.

333. Hurter, Nomenclator Theologiæ Catholicæ, I, 158.--Nic. Antonii Bibl nova, a.v. Ludovicus de Leon.--Greg. Mayans y Siscar, Vida del M. Luis de Leon, n. 37.--Ticknor, History of Spanish Literature, II, 87, 89 (Ed 1864).

There is considerable literature on the subject of Fray Luis's troubles with the Inquisition. The records of his first trial, omitting superfluities, occupy 925 pages in Vols. X and XI of the Coleccion de Documentos inéditos. His second trial has more recently seen the light, with an introduction by Padre Francisco Blanco García, Madrid, 1896. Fray Luis de Leon. Eine Biographie aus der Geschichte der spanischen Inquisition u. Kirche (Halle, 1866) by Dr. C. A. Wilkens is an eloquent and sympathetic account of his career, while Dr. Fr. Heinrich Reusch's Luis de Leon u. der spanische Inquisition (Bonn, 1873) is a scholarly investigation of the case, in so far as documents accessible at the time would permit. The Lic. Arango y Escandon has contributed the Proceso del P. M. Luis de Leon (Mexico, 1856, revised and enlarged in 1866), in which he justifies both the Inquisition and the sufferer. The latest contribution to the subject, based on additional documents, is by the Dominican Fray Luis G. Alonso Getino, in the Revista de Archivos (1903-4) in justification of the Inquisition. Padre Blanco has also written an Estúdio biográfico-critico de Fr. Luis de Leon, which I have not had an opportunity of consulting. The old rivalry between Dominicans and Augustinians seems to be still alive.

334. Azpilcueta Comment. Cap. Si quis autem, n. 44-47.--Coleccion de Documentos, X, 193; XI, 276.
335. Coleccion, X, 261; XI, 256, 259.
336. C. Trident. Sess. IV, De Edit. et Usu SS. Libb.
337. Coleccion, X, 115, 129.
338. Ibidem, X, 102, sqq.
339. Coleccion, X, 96-110.
340. Ibidem, X, 179.
341. Ibidem, X, 206-8.
342. Coleccion, X, 249; XI, 255-84.
343. There is no record of this in the process, but Fray Luis refers to it repeatedly both to the tribunal and to the Suprema, and there is no disclaimer.--Coleccion, XI, 48, 190, 196.
344. Coleccion, X, 562-7; XI, 7-18, 21-128.
345. Ibidem, XI, 164-86.
346. Coleccion, XI, 187-253.
347. Ibidem, XI, 351-3.
348. Coleccion, XI, 353-8.--Fray Luis attributed this unexpected mercy to the influence of Inquisitor-general Quiroga, to whom, in 1580, he dedicated his Exposition of the XXVI Psalm, with warm expressions of gratitude.--García, Segundo Proceso, p. 17.
349. Coleccion, XI, 147.
350. Coleccion, XI, 50, 52.
351. Ibidem, XI, 188, 193-4.
352. Ibidem, XI, 196-8.
353. Reusch, 113-14.--Arango y Escandon, p. 91.--Padre Alonso Getino (Revista de Archivos, Agosto-Sept., 1903) promises to give us an account of the trial of Martínez who was obliged to abjure de levi (Menéndez y Pelayo, II, 693).

Leon de Castro varied his persecution of Luis de Leon, Grajal and Martínez, by attacking the great Biblia Regia, which Arias Montano, the most learned Spaniard of the age, edited at the instance and with the support of Philip II. After its appearance with the approbation of the Holy See, de Castro, in 1575, in his zeal for the Vulgate, filled Spain, Flanders and Italy with denunciations of it and its editor. Montano, who was in Flanders, hastened to Spain by way of Italy to defend himself, but, finding much agitation on the subject in Rome, tarried there and wrote to Quiroga to protect him--an appeal which he repeated in 1579. He was not prosecuted, but the Inquisition fell foul of his biblical commentaries and placed on the Index a long list of expurgations, besides condemning some of his propositions--fortunately for him long after his death.--Coleccion de Documentos, XLI, 316, 321, 328, 387.--Index of Zapata, 1632, pp. 86-89.
354. García, Segundo Proceso, pp. 20-23, 29-30.
355. Ibidem, pp. 20-1, 26-7, 44.
356. García, pp. 28-35.
357. Ibidem, pp. 52-4.
358. Ibidem, p. 53.
359. The existing records of the trials of Sánchez are printed in Vol. II of the "Coleccion de Documentos inéditos."

The only one of his works which I have had an opportunity of examining is his "Minerva" (Salmanticæ, 1587), which sufficiently illustrates his capacity of enlivening the details of etymology and syntax with his caustic assertion of superior knowledge.
360. Coleccion, II, 1-37.
361. Ibidem, II, 40-45.
362. Coleccion, II, 40-58.
363. Coleccion, II, 57-88.
364. Ibidem, II, 89-109.
365. Coleccion, II, 109-26.
366. Ibidem, II, 127-8.
367. Ibidem, II 130-5.
368. Coleccion, II, 136-65.
369. Proceso contra Fray Joseph de Sigüenza (MSS. of Library of Univ. of Halle, Yc, 20, T. IV).
370. Archivo de Simancas, Inq., Leg. 552, fol. 1.
371. MSS. of Library of Univ. of Halle, Yc, 20, T. I.
372. Modo de Proceder, fol. 67 (Bibl. nacional, MSS., D, 122).
373. Archivo hist. nacional, Inq., Leg. 1.
374. Archivo hist. nacional, Inq. de Valencia, Leg. 45, fol. 13-33.
375. MSS. of Am. Philosophical Society.

376. Archivo hist. nacional, Inq. de Valencia, Leg. 100.
377. Archivo hist. nacional, Inq. de Valencia, Leg. 100.
378. Archivo de Simancas, Inq., Lib. 890; Lib. 435^{2}.
379. Ibidem, Lib. 890.
380. Mariana, Hist. de España, Lib. VI, n. 75.--José Amador de los Rios (Revista de España, XVII, 388).
381. Flores de las Leyes (Memorial hist. español, II, 243).
382. Partidas, P. VII, Tit. ix, ley 17; Tit. xxiii, leyes 1, 2, 3.
383. Amador de los Rios, op. cit., XVII, 382, 384-5.
384. Ibidem, XVIII, 14.
385. Flores, España Sagrada, XLIX, 188, 504.
386. Astesani de Ast Summa de Casibus Conscientiæ, P. I, Lib. i, Tit. 14.
387. Raynald. Annal, ann. 1317, n. 52-4; ann. 1318, n. 57; ann. 1320, n. 51; ann. 1327, n. 43.--Bullar. Roman. I, 204.--Ripoll, Bullar. Ord. Prædic. II, 192.
388. Ordenanzas Reales, VIII, iv, 2.
389. Ibidem, VIII, i, 9.
390. Novis. Recop. Lib. XII, Tit. iv, ley 2.
391. Tratados de Legislacion Muhamedana, pp. 143, 251 (Mem. hist. español, Tom. V).--Bleda, Corónica, p. 1025.
392. Villanueva, Viage Literario, XX, 190.--Eymerici Director, p. 202 (Ed. Venet. 1607).
393. Pulgar, Cronica, P. II, cap. iv.
394. Nueva Recop., Lib. VIII, Tit. iii, ley 7.
395. Archivo de Simancas, Inq., Lib. 3, fol. 156, 158, 170, 186; Lib. 927, fol. 446.

The parties in this case were doubtless García de Gorualan and Martin de Sória relaxed in person, and Miguel Sánchez de Romeral in effigy, as hérejes sortilegos, June 16, 1511, at Saragossa.--Libro Verde (Revista de España, CVI, 576, 581, 582). Prior to this several women had been burnt as witches, as we shall see hereafter.

396. Pragmáticas y altres Drets de Cathalunya, Lib. I, Tit. viii, cap. i, § 34; cap. 2.
397. Archivo de Simancas, Inq., Lib. 918, fol. 382.
398. Libro Verde de Aragon (Revista de España, CVI, pp. 575, 582).
399. Llorente, Hist. crít. cap. XV, Art. 1, n. 21.
400. Reprovacion de las Supersticiones, P. I, cap. i, n. 14.

This book is the Spanish classic on the subject. Maestro Pedro Ciruelo served as inquisitor in Saragossa for thirty years and was professor at Alcalá. His work appeared in Salamanca, in 1539, where it was reprinted in 1540 and 1556 and again in Barcelona in 1628, with notes by the learned Doctor Pedro Antonio Jofreu, at the instance of Miguel Santos, Bishop of Solsona.

401. Raynald. Annal., ann. 1258, n. 23.--Potthast, Regesta, n. 17,745, 18,396.--Lib. V in Sexto, Tit. ii, c. 8 § 4.
402. D'Argentré, Collect. judic. de novis Erroribus, I, II, 154.
403. Bernardi Basin Tract. de Artibus magicis, Concl. I-X.
404. Repertor. Inquisit. s. v. Sapere hæresim post v. Hæresiarcha--Pegnæ Comment. LXVII in Eymerici Director. P. II.
405. Ripoll, Bullar. Ord. Prædic., III, 301.--Cf. Alph. de Castro de justa Hæreticor. Punitione, Lib. I, cap. 13.
406. Simancæ de Cath. Institt., Tit. XXX, n. 20, 21; Tit. LXIII, n. 12.--Cf. Alphons. de Castro, loc. cit., cap. 14, 15.
407. Bibl. pública de Toledo, Sala 5, Estante 11, Tab. 3.--Archivo de Simancas, Inq., Visitas de Barcelona, Leg. 15, fol. 20.
408. Archivo de Simancas, Inq., Lib. 726.
409. Bibl. nacional, MSS., PV, 3, n. 20.
410. MSS. of Library of Univ of Halle, Yc, 20, T. I.--Catálogo de las causas seguidas ante el tribunal de Toledo, pp. 84, 326 (Madrid, 1903).

Mendo tells us (Epitome Opinionum Moralium, Append. de Matrimonio, n. 4) of similar cases in which the unfortunates were burnt.

411. Torreblanca, Epitome Delictorum sive de Magia, Lib. II, cap. ix.

The first edition of this work appeared in Seville, in 1618. My copy is of Lyons, 1678.

412. Th. Sanchez in Præcepta Decalogi Lib. II, cap. xl, n. 13.
413. Pegnæ Append. in Eymerici Director., p. 142.
414. Bulario de la Orden de Santiago, Lib. IV, fol. 118, 124, 137; Lib. V, passim.--Archivo de Simancas, Gracia y Justicia, Leg. 629.

The clause reads--"necnon de hæresi seu apostasia de fide suspectos, sortilegia manifestam hæresim sapientia, divinationes et incantationes aliaque diabolica maleficia et prestigia committentes, aut magicas et necromanticas artes exercentes, illorumque credentes, sequaces, defensores, fautores et receptatores.... per te vel alium seu alios prout juris fuerit inquirendi, procedendi et exequi seu inquiri, procedi et exequi faciendi."

415. Torreblanca, Lib. III, cap. ix, Append.; Defensa, cap. ii, p. 536.--Archivo hist. nacional, Inq. de Valencia, Leg. 299, fol. 80.

The bull, however, was not received in Valencia until 1616.--Ibidem, Leg. 6, n. 2, fol. 56.

416. Torreblanca, cap. IX, n. 25-26.
417. Nueva Recop., Lib. VIII, Tit. iii, ley 8.--Novís. Recop., Lib. XII, Tit. V, ley 2.
418. MSS. of Library of Univ. of Halle, Yc, 20, T. I.
419. Archivo de Simancas, Inq., Leg. 552, fol. 37.
420. Ibidem, Lib. 52, fol. 48.
421. Archivo hist. nacional, Inq. de Valencia, Leg. 1, n. 3, fol. 14-15.
422. Reprovacion de las Supersticiones, P. II, Cap. iii.
423. De Cath. Institt. Tit. XXI, n. 9; Tit. LXIII, n. 7.
424. Reusch, Die Indices, pp. 217, 225, 227, 236, 239.--The two prohibited books are Arcandam de nativitatibus seu fatalis dies and Johannes Schonerus de nativitatibus.
425. Córtes de Cordova del año de setenta, Peticion 71 (Alcalá, 1575).
426. Archivo de Simancas, Inq., Leg. 1157, fol. 17-20.
427. Index of Quiroga, Rule IX (Madrid, 1583, fol. 4).
428. Zanctornato, Relatione della Corte di Spagna, pp. 6, 7 (Cosmopoli, 1678).
429. Bibl. nacional, MSS., V, 377, cap. xiv, § 1.
430. Ibidem, D, 118, p. 148.
431. Archivo hist. nacional, Inq. de Toledo, Leg. 1.
432. Ibidem, Inq. de Valencia, Leg. 100.--Cf. Bedæ Opera, Ed. Migne, I, 963-66.
433. Praxis procedendi, cap. xviii, n. 3 (Archivo hist. nacional, Inq. de Valencia).--Bibl. nacional, MSS., S, 294, fol. 116.
434. Proceso contra Isabel de Montoya (MS. penes me).
435. Praxis procedendi, cap. VIII, n. 5 (Archivo hist. nacional, Inq. de Valencia).
436. MSS. of Royal Library of Copenhagen, 218^{b}, p. 382.
437. Matute y Luquin, pp. 84-105.
438. Royal Library of Berlin, Qt. 9548.
439. Reprovacion de las Supersticiones, P. I, cap. ii; P. II, cap. i; P. III, cap. v.
440. Epitome Delictorum, Lib. III, cap. i, n. 1-6.
441. Miguel Calvo (Archivo de Alcalá, Hacienda, Leg. 544^{2}, Lib. 4).--Elucidationes Sancti Officii, §§ 40, 43 (Ibidem).
442. Archivo hist. nacional., Inq. de Valencia, Leg. 2, n. 7, fol. 4, 7;n. 10, fol. 10-13.
443. Archivo de Simancas, Inq., Leg. 552, fol. 11, 13.
444. Ibidem, fol. 26, 28, 29.
445. Archivo hist. nacional, Inq. de Toledo, Leg. 2.
446. MSS. of Bibl. nacional de Lima.
447. MSS. of David Fergusson Esq.
448. Regimento do Santo Officio da Inquisição pelo Cardeal da Cunha, pp. 118-20, 123-7.
449. Llorente, Anales, II, 270.
450. Archivo hist. nacional, Inq. de Valencia, Leg. 100.
451. Proceso contra Rosa Conejos (MS. penes me).
452. Archivo de Simancas, Inq., Lib. 890.
453. Archivo hist. nacional, Inq., de Valencia, Leg. 100.
454. Archivo de Simancas, Inq., Lib. 890; Lib. 559.
455. MSS. of Library of Univ. of Halle, Yc, 20, T. I.--Archivo hist. nacional, Inq. de Toledo, Leg. 1.
456. Royal Library of Berlin, Qt. 9548.--Matute y Luquin, pp. 278-92.
457. Archivo hist. nacional, Inq. de Valencia, Leg. 100.
458. Amador de los Rios (Revista de España, XVIII, 338-40). See also Menéndez y Pelayo, Heterodoxos Españoles, I, 237.
459. P. Ricardo Cappa, La Inquisicion española, p. 242 (Madrid, 1888).

Father Cappa only enunciates the belief still taught by the Church. See S. Alph. Liguori, Theol. Moralis, Lib. III, Dub. V, and Marc, Institutiones Morales Alphonsianæ, I, 396-7 (Romæ, 1893).

460. The earliest appearance of the Sabbat in inquisitorial records would seem to be in some trials, between 1330 and 1340 in Carcassonne and Toulouse, where it connects itself curiously with remnants of the Dualism of the Cathari.--Hansen, Zauberwahn, Inquisition und Hexenprozess im Mittelalter, p. 315 (München, 1900).

461. Raynald. Annal., ann. 1437, n. 27; ann. 1457, n. 90; ann. 1459, n. 30.--Ripoll, Bullar. Ord.

Prædic. III, 193.--Bullar. Roman. I, 429.--Septimi Decretal, Lib. V, Tit. xii, cap. 1, 3, 6.--Bart. Spinæi de Strigibus, p. 14(Romæ, 1576).

462. Frag. Capitular. cap. 13 (Baluze, II, 365).--Reginon. de Eccles. Discip. II, 364.--Burchard. Decret. XI, i; XIX, 5.--Ivon. Decret., XI, 30.--Gratian. Decret. II, XXVI, V, 12.

463. S. Antonini Confessionale.--Angeli de Clavasio Summa Angelica, s. v. Interrogationes.--Bart. de Chaimis Interrogatorium, fol. 22 (Venetiis, 1480).

464. Hansen, Quellen und Untersuchungen, zur Geschichte des Hexenwahns und der Hexenverfolgung im Mittelalter, pp. 105-9 (Bonn, 1901).

465. Fortalicium Fidei, Lib. V, Consid. X.--Hansen, op. cit., pp. 113-17.

466. Martini de Arles, Tractatus de Superstitionibus, pp. 362-5, 413-15 (Francofurti ad Moenam, 1581).

Hansen (op. cit., p. 308) says that Martin of Aries is known only through this tract, of which the first edition is of 1517. Martin cites no authority later than John Nider, who died in 1438, and makes no allusion to the Inquisition, which he could scarce have failed to do had it been in existence when he wrote. His work may probably be assigned to the third quarter of the fifteenth century.

467. Bernardi Basin, Tract. de Magicis Artibus, Prop. IX.

468. Repert, Inquisitor, s. v. Xorguinæ.

469. Alonso de Spina, however (loc. cit.), knows of no gatherings at the Sabbat nearer than Dauphiny and Gascony, and these he learned from paintings of them in the Inquisition at Toulouse, which had burnt many of those concerned.

470. Libro Verde de Aragon (Revista de España, CVI, 573-6, 581-3).

471. Llorente, Añales, I, 340; Hist. crít., cap. XXXVII, art. ii, n. 41.

472. Archivo de Simancas, Inq., Lib. 72, P. I, fol. 120; P. II, fol. 50.

473. Arn. Albertini de agnoscendis Assertionibus, Q. XXIV, n. 13 (Romæ, 1572, fol. 114).

474. Archivo de Simancas, Inq., Lib. 73, fol. 215.

475. MSS. of Bodleian Library, Arch Seld. 130.

476. For the inhuman methods employed to secure confession and conviction, on the flimsiest evidence, see the very instructive essay "The Fate of Dietrich Flade" by Professor George Burr (New York, 1891), reprinted from the Transactions of the American Historical Association.

477. Mallei Malificar, P. I, Q. xiv; P. II, Q. i, C. 3, 16.--Prieriat. de Strigimagarum Lib. III, cap. 3.

The rule that the heretic or apostate who confessed and recanted was to be admitted to reconciliation was at the bottom of the anxiety of the secular magistrates to maintain their jurisdiction over witchcraft, and the relations between them and the Inquisition were the subject of much debate. Arn. Albertino argues that the Inquisition can make no distinction between witches who have and who have not committed murder; they must all be reconciled, but can again be accused of homicide before a competent judge; yet the inquisitor, to escape irregularity, must not transmit to the secular court the confessions and evidence, nor must he, in the sentences, mention these crimes, as that would be setting the judge on the track.--De agnosc. Assertionibus, Q. XXIV, n. 28, 66, 67, 68, 70, 72, 75.

478. MSS. of Bodleian Library, Arch Seld. 130.--Archivo de Simancas, Inq., Lib. 78, fol. 216.

479. Bibl. national, MSS., II, 88.--MSS. of Bodleian Library, Arch Seld. 130.

This document may safely be assumed as the source from which Prudencio de Sandoval, himself Bishop of Pampeluna and historiographer of Charles V, drew his account of the persecution of 1527 (Hist. del Emp. Carlos V, Lib. XVI, § 15) copied by Llorente (Hist. crít., cap. XV, art. 1, n. 6-9).

480. Archivo de Simancas, Inq., Lib. 76, fol. 51, 53.

There seems to have been a somewhat earlier persecution of the witches of Biscay by Fray Juan de Zumarraga, a native of Durango. At the suggestion of Charles V, who greatly admired him, he was sent there for that purpose as commissioner of the Inquisition, being specially qualified by his knowledge of the language. After discharging this duty with much ability, Charles, in 1528, sent him to Mexico as its first bishop. He took with him Fray Andrés de Olmos, who had been his assistant in Biscay. In 1548, at the age of 80 he died in the odor of sanctity and his death was miraculously known the same day over all Mexico.--Mendieta, Hist. ecles. Indiana, pp. 629, 636, 644 (Mexico, 1870)

481. Archivo de Simancas, Inq., Lib. 939, fol. 108.

482. Archivo de Simancas, Inq., Lib. 76, fol. 369.

483. Ibidem, fol. 388.

484. Arn. Albertini de agnosc. Assertionibus, Q. XXIV.--Alph. de Castro de justa hæreticor. Punitione, Lib. I, cap. xvi.

485. Archivo de Simancas, Inq., Lib. 78, fol. 144.

486. Archivo de Simancas, Inq., Sala 40, Lib. 4, fol. 191-5.

487. Ibidem, Lib. 78, fol. 215-17, 226, 258.

488. Reprovacion de las Supersticiones, P. I, cap. ii, n. 6; P. II, cap. i, n. 5-7.

489. De Cath. Institt., Tit. XXXVII, n. 6-12.

On the other hand Azpilcueta adheres to the theory of illusion and asserts it to be a mortal sin to believe that witches are transported to the Sabbat.--Manuale Confessariorum, cap. XI, n. 38.

Cardinal Toletus asserts the bodily transport of witches and all the horrors of the Sabbat, but adds that sometimes it is imaginary. Demons have power to introduce witches into houses through closed doors, where they slay infants.--Summæ Casuum Conscientiæ, Lib. IV, cap. XV.

490. MSS. of Library of Univ. of Halle, Yc, 20, T. I.--This case is not unexampled. In 1686, Sor Teresa Gabriel de Vargas, a Bernardine Recollect, charged herself with the same crime before the Madrid tribunal, but, as she added the denial of the power of God, she was reconciled for the heresy.--Archivo de Simancas, Inq., Lib. 1024, fol. 31.

Even more significant is the case of Sor Rosa de San Joseph Barrios, a Clare of the convent of San Diego, Garachico, Canaries, a woman of 25 who, in July 1773, in sacramental confession to Fray Nicolás Peraza, related how, through desire to gratify her lust, she had given herself to Satan, in a writing which disappeared from her hand, and at his command had renounced God and the Virgin and had treated the consecrated host and a crucifix with the foulest indignities. In reward for this during four years he had served her as an incubus, coming at her call about twice a month. Fray Peraza applied to the tribunal for a commission to absolve her which was granted and, on August 15th, he reported having done so, with fuller details as to her apostasy. The tribunal then decided that he had exceeded his powers; it evidently did not regard the case as hallucination for it required her to be formally reconciled and prescribed a course of life-long spiritual penance, which she gratefully accepted. An incident not readily explicable is that the bishop deprived Fray Peraza of the faculty of hearing confessions.--Birch, Catalogue of MSS. of the Inquisition in the Canary Islands, I, p. 21; II, pp. 922-30.

491. Archivo de Simancas, Inq., Lib. 927, fol. 462.

492. Archivo de Simancas, Inq., Lib. 79, fol. 226; Inq. de Logroño, Procesos de fe, Leg. 1, n. 8; Sala 40, Lib. 4, fol. 221.

493. Archivo de Simancas, Patronato Real, Leg. único, fol. 86, 87; Inq., Lib. 83, fol. 7.

494. Ibidem, Lib. 83, fol. 1.

495. MSS. of Library of University of Halle, Yc, 20, T. I.--Bibl. nacional, MSS., D, 111, fol. 127.--See Appendix.

496. Archivo de Simancas, Inq., Visitas de Barcelona, Leg. 15, fol. 5.

497. Archivo de Simancas, Inq. de Logroño, Leg. 1, Procesos de fe, n. 8.

498. Ibidem, Leg. 1, Procesos de fe, n. 8; Lib. 19, fol. 85.

499. Archivo de Simancas, Inq., Lib. 19, fol. 85.

500. Archivo de Simancas, Inq., Lib. 564, fol. 341, 343.

501. A narrative, not an official report, of this auto was printed in Logroño in 1611, a copy of which is in the Bibl. nacional, D, 118, p. 271. It was reprinted in Cádiz in 1812 and again in Madrid, in 1820, with notes by Moratin el hijo under the pseudonym of the Bachiller Gines de Posadilla (Menéndez y Pelayo, III, 281). There is another abstract of the auto, compiled from various relations by Pedro of Valencia, in the MSS. of the Bodleian Library, Arch Seld. A, Subt. 10.

Pierre de Lancre of Bordeaux, in his contemporary book on witchcraft, assumes that the outbreak in Navarre was caused by the flight of witches from the Pays de Labour, which he and his colleague had purified with merciless severity. He comments on the difference shown, in the auto of Logroño, between inquisitorial practice in Spain, where the offence was treated as spiritual and those who confessed and professed repentance were admitted to reconciliation, and that of France where it was a crime and those who confessed were burnt by the secular authorities.--Pierre de Lancre, Tableau de l'Inconstance des mauvais Angels et Demons, pp. 391, 561-2 (Paris, 1613).

502. Archivo de Simancas, Inq. de Logroño, Leg. 1, Procesos de fe, n. 8.

503. This discourse was not printed but was circulated in MS. Nicholas Antonio had two copies (Bib. nova, II, 244). There is one in the Simancas archives, Lib. 939, fol. 608, and another in the Bodleian Library. Arch Seld. A, Subt. 10.

504. The most prolific source of evidence against individuals was that obtained by requiring those who confessed to enumerate the persons whom they had seen in the aquelarres. This explains the enormous numbers of the accused during epidemics of the witchcraft craze. The value of such evidence was a disputed question, as it was argued that the demon frequently caused deception by making spectres appear in the guise of absent persons.

505. Archivo de Simancas, Inq. de Logroño, Leg. 1, Procesos de fe, n. 8.

In the Royal Library of Copenhagen (MS. 218^{b}, p. 379) there is a printed four-page set of instructions to commissioners on receiving confession and testimony as to witchcraft. It is in conformity with the above, but goes into much detail as to the interrogatories to be put, after carefully writing down the confession or deposition--a kind of cross-examination evidently suggestive of complete incredulity. It is without date, but the typography seems to be that of the seventeenth century.

506. Archivo de Simancas, Inq., Lib. 30, fol. 1.

507. Archivo de Simancas, Inq., Leg. 552, fol 1.

508. Archivo de Simancas, Inq., Leg. 552, fol. 26, 28.

509. Epitome Delictorum, Lib. II, cap. xxviii, xxxix, xl; Lib. III, cap. xiii.
510. Ibidem, Defensa, p. 517; cap. ii, n. 4, 7.
511. Reprovacion de las Supersticiones, pp. 251-63 (Ed. 1628).
512. Manuale Qualificatorum, cap. xviii, Sect 3, § 9.
513. Bibl. nacional, MSS., V, 377, cap. xiii, §§ 1, 2.
514. MSS. of Library of Univ. of Halle, Yc, 17.
515. Elucidationes S. Officii, § 42 (Archivo de Alcalá, Hacienda, Leg. 544^{2}, Lib. 4).
516. Archivo de Simancas, Inq., Leg. 552.
517. Archivo hist. nacional, Inq. de Toledo, Leg. 1.--Royal Library of Berlin, Qt. 9548.
518. Archivo hist. nacional, Inq. de Valencia, Leg. 390.
519. Ibidem, Leg. 365, n. 45, fol. 34.
520. Ibidem, Leg. 100.

It is asserted by some writers that a woman was burnt as a witch at Seville in 1780, but this is an erroneous reference to María de Dolores, relaxed there in 1780 for Molinism (supra, p. 89).

521. Cartas del Filósofo rancio, II, 493.
522. The sentence is printed by Frère Michaelis, at the end of his Pneumatologie (Paris, 1587).
523. Ragguaglio su la Sentenza di Morte in Salesburgo, p. 173(Venezia, 1751).
524. Collect. Decret. S. Congr. S^{ti} Inquisit., p. 333 (MS. penes me).--Decret. S. Congr. S. Inquisit. pp. 385-88 (Bibl. del R. Archivio di Stato in Roma, Fondo Camerale, Congr. del S. Officio, Vol. 3).

The inquisitor of Milan took no part in the trials of those accused of causing and spreading the terrible pestilence of 1630, by the use of unguents and powders furnished by the demon. His only act was to return a negative answer to the question whether it was licit to employ diabolic arts to save the city. The reckless prosecutions and savage punishments were wholly the work of the civil magistracy.--Processo originale degli Untori (Milano, 1839).

The pestilence did not extend to Spain, but the panic did, leading to the most extravagant precautions against all foreigners.--MSS. of Bodleian Library, Arch Seld. A, Subt. 11.

525. Decret. S. Congr. S. Inquis., ubi sup.
526. Decret. S. Congr. S. Inquis., ubi sup.
527. Gregor. PP. XV, Const. Omnipotentis Dei, 20 Mart. 1623 (Bullar. Roman., III, 498).

Urban VIII was equally savage in 1631, in ordering relaxation for any one who should consult diviners or astrologers about the state of the Christian Republic, or the life of the pope or of any of his kindred to the third degree (Bullar. IV, 184).

It was probably under this that the Inquisition, in 1634, relaxed Giacinto Centini and two of his accomplices and condemned four others to the galleys. He was nephew of the Cardinal of Ascoli, and procured from a diviner a forecast that Urban would die in a few years and would be succeeded by his uncle. To hasten accomplishment, figurines of wax were made representing Urban and were melted. Centini, as a noble, was beheaded and his two most guilty accomplices were hanged, before being burnt.--Royal Library of Munich, Cod. Ital. 29, fol. 104-18.

528. Instructio pro formandis processibus in causis Strygum, cum Carenæ Annotationibus (Carenæ Tract. de Off. SS. Inquisit., Lugduni, 1669, pp. 487 sqq). Carena's comments show how differently these cases were treated in Italy from the practice beyond the Alps.

See also Masini's rule forbidding action on the denunciation of those seen in the Sabbat.--Sacro Arsenale, Decima Parte, n. 141.

529. Ristretto circa li Delitti più frequenti nel S. Offizio, pp. 57-9 (MS. penes me).
530. Casus Conscientiæ Benedicti XIV, Dec. 1743, Cas. iii (Ferrariæ, 1764, p. 155).--De Servorum Dei Beatificatione, Lib. IV, P. i, cap. 3, n. 3.
531. S. Alphonsi Liguori Theol. Moralis, Lib. III, n. 26.
532. Nic. Remigii Demonolatreiæ Libri Tres. Colon. Agrip. 1596.
533. G. Plitt Henke in Realencyclopädie, VI, 97.
534. Pierre de Lancre, Tableau de l'inconstance des mauvais Anges, pp. 114, 119 (Paris, 1613).

De Lancre was a learned conseiller of the Parlement of Bordeaux and his colleague on the commission was the President d' Espaignet. It is instructive to observe that while he was drawing up his terrific relation of the manner in which they had intensified the witchcraft craze, until the churches at night would be filled with children brought there by their mothers to prevent their being carried off to the aquellares (p. 193), Inquisitor Salazar, on the other side of the Pyrenees, was extinguishing it by simple rational treatment.

535. Rogers, Scotland, Social and Domestic, p. 302. (London, 1869).
536. Commentaries, IV, 60 (Oxford, 1775).
537. Lettres à un Gentilhomme Russe, Let. I.--"L'Inquisition est un instrument purement royal; il est tout entier en la main du roi, et jamais il ne peut nuire que par la faute des ministres du prince."
538. "Sie ist kein kirchliches, sondern ein Staats institut, theilweise mit kirchlichen Formen."

(Gams, Die Kirchengeschichte von Spanien, Buch XIII, Kap. 1, § 3.) "Das neue Herrscherpaar ... gestaltete die Inquisition zu einem wichtigen Staatsinstitut." (Hergenrother, Handbuch der Kirchengeschichte, II, 765. Freiburg, 1885).

539. Hefele, Der Cardinal Ximenes, XVIII, p. 265 (Tübingen, 1851).

The most recent apologist, who assures us that the Church never used other than moral force, displays his accuracy by telling us that, in 1521, Leo X excommunicated Torquemada on account of his cruelty, against the protests of Charles V, and also that in England Henry VIII executed 70,000 victims and Queen Elizabeth 43,000.--G. Romain, L'Inquisition, son rôle religieux, politique et social, pp. 10, 11, 2^{e} Edition, Paris, 1900.

540. Ranke, Die Osmanen und die Spanische Monarchie, pp. 195-8 (Leipzig, 1877).-- Maurenbrecher, Geschichte der Katholischen Reformation, I, 45 (Nördlingen, 1880).

541. Rodrigo, Historia verdadera, I, 264; II, 87; III, 363.--Ortí y Lara, La Inquisicion, p. 2 (Madrid, 1877).--Cappa, S. J., La Inquisicion española, p. 28 (Madrid, 1888).--Pastor, Geschichte der Päpste, II, 584.

542. Llorente, Añales, II, 209, 229.--Dormer, Añales de Aragon, Lib. I, cap. 27.

543. Archivo de Simancas, Inq., Lib. 43, fol. 297.--Críticos Documentos que sirven como de segunda Parte al Proceso de Fr. Froilan Diaz, pp. 7-8 (Madrid, 1788).

544. Archivo de Simancas, Inq., Lib. 939, fol. 270.

At the same time there is no doubt that contemporary statesmen, disposed to regard with cynical incredulity the fervor of Philip's fanaticism, were apt to look upon the Inquisition as an artful instrumentality to keep the people in subjection. See the remarks of Giovanni Soranzo in Vol. I, p. 442.

545. Archivo de Simancas, Inq., Lib. 1.
546. Archivo de Simancas, Inq., Lib. 1; Lib. 2, fol. 4.
547. Llorente, Hist. crít., cap. XXVII, art. iii.
548. Danvila y Collado, La Germanía de Valencia, pp. 178, 492.
549. Llorente, Hist. crít., cap. XXVII, art. iv, n. 5-10.
550. Relazioni Venete, Serie I, T. V, p. 279.--Miscelanea de Zapata (Mem. hist. español, XI, 244).
551. Archivo de Simancas, Inq., Lib. 19, fol. 48.
552. Few episodes in Spanish history have been more exhaustively investigated than the career of Antonio Pérez and its consequences. Ample materials for its elucidation exist in the Spanish archives, in the Llorente collections preserved in the Bibliothèque nationale of France, at The Hague and in the British Museum, and these have been industriously utilized by modern writers. The contemporary sources are--

Las Obras y Relaciones de Antonio Pérez, Paris, 1654.
Proceso criminel que se fulminó contra Antonio Pérez, Madrid, 1788.
Argensola, Informacion de los sucesos del Reino de Aragon en los años de 1590 y 1591. Madrid, 1808.
Coleccion de Documentos inéditos, Vols. XII, XV, LVI.
Giambattista Confalonieri, in Spicilegio Vaticano, Vol. I, P. II, pp. 226 sqq.
Tommaso Contarini, in Relazioni Venete, Serie I, T. V, p. 401.
Cabrera, Historia de Felipe II, T. II, pp. 448, 540; T. III, pp. 529 sqq (Ed. 1876-77).
Lanuza, Historias eclesiasticas y seculares de Aragon, T. II, Lib. II, III. (Zaragoza, 1622).
The principal modern authorities are--
Llorente, Historia crítica, cap. XXXV, XXXVI.
Mignet, Antonio Pérez et Philippe II, Paris, 1854.
Pidal, Historia de las Alteraciones de Aragon en el Reinado de Felipe II, 3 vols, Madrid, 1862-3.
Muro, Vida de la Princesa de Eboli, Madrid, 1877.
Philippson (Ein Ministerium unter Philipp II, Berlin, 1895) and Major Hume (Españoles é Ingleses, Madrid, 1903) give interesting details as to the earlier events.

553. Relazioni Venete, Serie I, T. V, p. 485.

The assertion of the co-operation of the Inquisition and the Royal Council, which were habitually antagonistic, shows how little the envoy knew of the inner working of Spanish administration.

554. MSS. of Library of Univ. of Halle, Yc, 20, T. I.
555. Vida y Escritos del P. Juan de Mariana, pp. lxix-lxxviii (Historia de España, Valencia, 1783, T. I).--Alegambe, Scriptt. Soc. Jesu, p. 258.--De Backer, V, 518.

The "Tratado y Discurso sobre la Moneda de Vellon" of course was suppressed and became scarce. My copy is in MS., transcribed in 1799.

Mariana did not conceal from himself the danger to be incurred. In his address to the Reader he says--"Bien veo que algunos me tendrian por atrevido, otros por inconsiderado, pues no advierto el riesgo que corro."

556. Archivo de Simancas, Inq. de Barcelona, Córtes, Leg. 17, fol. 9.--Libro XIII de Cartas, fol. 195 (MSS. of Am. Philos. Society).

557. Llorente, Hist. crítica, cap. XXXVIII, n. 17, 19.
558. Archivo hist. nacional, Inq. de Valencia, Leg. 10, n. 2, fol. 153.
559. Bibl. nacional, MSS., H, 177, fol. 251.
560. Archivo de Simancas, Inq., Lib. 56, fol. 605.
561. Archivo hist. nacional, Inq. de Valencia, Leg. 383.
562. Bibl. nacional, MSS., Mm, 130.
563. Archivo hist. nacional, Inq. de Valencia, Leg. 100.
564. Cartas del Filósofo rancio, II, 496.
565. Archivo de Simancas, Inq., Lib. 559.
566. MS. penes me.
567. Archivo de Simancas, Inq., Lib. 559.
568. Relacion histórica de la Judería de Sevilla, p. 49 (Sevilla, 1849).
569. Córtes de Leon y de Castilla, I, 450.--Nueva Recop., Lib. VI, Tit. xviii, ley 12.
570. Dormer, Añales de Aragon, Lib. II, cap. xli.
571. Archivo de Simancas, Inq., Lib. 79, fol. 75.
572. Fueros y Observancias del Reyno de Aragon, fol. 215. Cf. fol. 194 (Zaragoza, 1624).
573. Lib. V in Sexto, Tit. vi, cap. 6.--Digard, Registres de Boniface VIII, n. 2354.--Bullar. Roman. I, 507, 718; II, 496.
574. Archivo hist. nacional, Inq. de Valencia, Leg. 2, n. 16, fol. 272.--Archivo de Simancas, Inq., Lib. 82, fol. 130; Lib. 939, fol. 115.
575. Archivo de Simancas, Inq., Lib. 83, fol. 26.
576. Argensola, op. cit., p. 199.
577. Archivo de Simancas, Inq., Visitas de Barcelona, Leg. 15, fol. 8.
578. Bibl. nacional, MSS., V, 377, cap. xxv, xxvi.
579. Bibl. nationale de France, fonds espagnol, T. 85, fol. 7.
580. Libro XIII de Cartas (MSS. of Am. Philos. Society).
581. MSS. of the Royal Library of Copenhagen, 218^{b}, p. 259.--Novís. Recop., Lib. IX, Tit. xii, ley 11.
582. Urbani PP. VIII Bull. In eminenti, 6 Mart. 1641.--Innocent PP X. Bull. Cum occasione, 31 Maii, 1653 (Bullar. V, 369, 486).

A precursor of Jansen was Michel de Bay or Baius, a theologian of Louvain, whose seventy-nine propositions were condemned by Pius V and Gregory XIII and were publicly abjured by him before the University, May 24, 1580. His name does not occur in the Spanish Indexes before that of 1632, (p. 761) where he is spoken of as a man of high reputation who abandoned his errors.

583. Letter of Benedict XIV to Inquisitor-general Prado y Cuesta (Semanário erúdito, XXX, 53).
584. Indice de 1707, I, 19, 28, 231-2, 478.
585. Nic. Anton. Biblioth. Vet. Lib. VI, cap. xi, n. 268.
586. Memorial espagnol presenté á sa Majesté Catholique contre les pretendus Jansenistes du Pays-Bas, p. 45 (s. 1. 1699).

This is a memorial drawn up by Juan de Palazol, S. J., in the name and by order of Tirso González, the Jesuit General. To it I am indebted for the details that follow.

In January 1691 a congregation of the Flemish bishops addressed to the Roman Inquisition an urgent appeal for help in their struggle with the Jansenists, whose missionary and controversial efforts were incessant and successful. It illustrates the elusory character of the theological subtilties involved that the bishops sent, as a specially successful exposure of Jansenist devices, a little book under the name of Cornelis van Craneberg, but Rome thought differently of it and condemned it by decree of March 19, 1692. Its real author was the Jesuit Jacques de la Fontaine, who was one of the most zealous champions against Jansenism.--Collectio Synodorum Archiep. Mechliniensis, I, 575.--Reusch, Der Index, II, 645.--De Backer, IV, 230.

587. Le Tellier, Recueil des Bulles et Constitutions etc. p. 125 (Mons, 1697).
588. These details are not without interest as indicating the causes which led to the establishment of the still existing schismatic see of Utrecht.
589. Suplemento á el Indice, 1739, p. 36.--Manuel F. Miguélez, Jansenismo y Regalismo en España, pp. 98 sqq. (Valladolid, 1895). Fray Miguélez is an Augustinian, seeking to vindicate St. Augustin and his Order from Jesuit attacks. His work is based on inedited documentary material.
590. Miguélez, op. cit., pp. 90-5.--Semanário erúdito, XXX, 53.
591. Miguélez, op. cit.--In connection with Padre Rábago it may be mentioned that, in 1747, when already royal confessor, he was denounced to the Santiago tribunal for solicitation, but escaped trial under the rule requiring two denunciations. Archivo hist. nacional, Inq. de Toledo, Leg. 233, n. 108, fol. 60.

The Indice Ultimo of 1790 (p. 192) records the removal of Noris's books and prohibits all writings on both sides of the affair.

592. Relazioni Venete, Serie I, T. V, p. 484.
593. Jo. Nic. von Hontheim, De Statu Ecclesiæ et legitima Potestate Romani Pontificis. Bullioni, 1763.
594. Miguélez, op. cit., pp. 274, 364, 366, 380.
595. Rafael de Vélez, Apología del Altar y del Trono, I, 442 (Madrid, 1825).-Clément, Journal de Correspondances et de Voyages pour la Paix de l'Eglise, II, 31 (Paris, 1802).

Clément, then canon and treasurer of Auxerre, and subsequently Bishop of Versailles, was a self-appointed negotiator in 1768 to prevent the schism, which he thought was impending, and to unite all the courts in opposition to Ultramontanism. His candid self-complacency and belief in his own importance give a certain life to his otherwise formless account of his mission, while his dread lest the Inquisition should obtain knowledge of what he was doing shows how thoroughly it was on the Ultramontane side.

596. Cartas del Filósofo rancio, II, 32.
597. Muriel, Historia de Carlos IV (Mem. hist. español, XXXIV, 119).
598. Menéndez y Pelayo, III, 245.
599. Clément, II, 102.
600. Llorente, Hist. crít., cap. xxix, art. iii, n. 1, 2; cap. XLIII, art. iii, n. 1.
601. Clément, op. cit., II, 44, 83-5, 296-7.
602. Ferrer del Rio, Historia de Carlos III, Lib. II, cap. ii, iv.

The trial of Dr. Benito Navarro, a Jesuit Tertiary, was printed at the time and indicates the participation of the Jesuits in the troubles, with the object of forcing the restoration to power of the Marquis of la Ensenada. Incidentally the evidence shows the enormous influence wielded by the Jesuits through having their creatures in governmental positions, where they could mislead and betray their superiors. To statesmen like Aranda, Campomanes, Roda and Floridablanca, the continued existence of the Jesuits in Spain was a manifest impossibility.

The documents connected with the expulsion are printed by Miraflores in his "Documentos á los qué se hace referencia en los apuntes historico-críticos sobre la Revolucion de España," II, 38-71 (Londres, 1834).

603. Novís. Recop., Lib. viii, Tit. i-ix.--Carta de Josef Clíment, Obispo de Barcelona, 26 de Junio, 1767.
604. MSS of Am. Philos. Society.
605. Art de Vérifier les Dates depuis l'année 1770, III, 358. A subsequent decree of March 11, 1798, permitted the ex-Jesuits to live with their kindred or in convents, provided that this was not in any royal residence (Original penes me).
606. Muriel, Hist. de Carlos IV, loc. cit.--Cartas del Filósofo rancio, II, 34.--Vélez, Apología, I, 44-6.

Yet the Acta et Decreta Synodi Dioecesance Pistoriensis anni 1786, against which the bull Auctorem fidei was directed, were not prohibited until March 18, 1801.--Suplemento al Indice Expurgatorio, p. 1 (Madrid, 1805).

On May 18, 1801, the Commissioners of the Canary tribunal at Orotava report to it that the edict has been duly read and affixed to the doors of the parish churches.--Birch, Catalogue of the MSS. of the Inq. in the Canary Islands, II, 1008.

607. Archivo hist. nacional, Inq. de Valencia, Leg. 17, n. 3, fol. 16.
608. Llorente, Hist. crít., cap. XXV, n. 33, 34; cap. XXIX, art. iii, n. 5; cap. XLIII, art. iii, n. 5.
609. Se vió á todos los jansenistas, impios y hombres desmoralizados ponerse del lado de los invasores.--Vic. de la Fuente, Hist. eclesiastica, III, 463.--Cf. Cartas del Filósofo rancio, passim.
610. Vélez. Apología del Altar y del Trono, I, 391-2.
611. G. de Castro, Il Monde Segreto, IV, 59 (Milano, 1864).--Précis historique de l'Ordre de la Franc-Maçonnerie, par J. C. B.... (Paris, 1829).--Luigi Parascandalo, La Frammassoneria figlia e erede del Manicheismo, 4 vols, 8vo (Napoli, 1865).--Ch. Van Dusen, S. J., Rome et la Franc-Maçonnerie (1896).--L'Abbé V. Davin, Les Jansénistes politiques et la Franc-Maçonnerie, p. 5 (Paris, s. d.).
612. Mariano Tirado y Rojas, La Masonería en España, I, 241-3, 252, 255-6 (Madrid, 1893).
613. Thory. Acta Latomorum, I, 35 (Paris, 1815).
614. Bullar. Roman., XV, 184.
615. Acta Latomorum, I, 43-44.
616. Compendio della vita di Giuseppe Balsamo, denominato il Conte Cagliostro, che si è estratto dal Processo contra di lui formato in Roma l'anno 1790 (Roma, 1791).

The importance attached to the case is indicated by the formal removal of the seal of secrecy and the semi-official publication of the volume. The edict imposing the death-penalty is quoted on p. 80.

617. Bullar. Bened. PP. XIV, III, 167 (Romæ, 1761).
618. Bulario de la Orden de Santiago, Lib. V, fol. 280.
619. Acta Latomorum, I, 47.

620. Fray Joseph Torrubia, Centinela contra Francs Massones, Segunda Edicion, Madrid, 1754. From the dates of the approbations it would appear that the first edition was issued in 1751 or 1752.

621. Feyjoo, Cartas, T. IV, Cart. xvi. This letter must have been written between 1751 and 1754, as it alludes to the Centinelo, while the second edition of the latter alludes to the letter. Feyjoo refers to another recent book on the subject by Fray Juan de la Madre de Dios, which I have not seen.

622. Archivo de Simancas, Inq., Lib. 879, fol. 301 B; Lib. 1024, fol 10.--Llorente, Hist. crít., cap. XLI, art. ii, n. 10-16.

623. Archivo hist. nacional, Inq. de Toledo, Leg. 108, n. 1.

The Portuguese Inquisition was as prompt as the Spanish. See "The Sufferings of John Coustos for Free-masonry," London, 1740, and it continued after the reforms of Pombal, as appears from "A Narrative of the Persecution of Hippolyto Joseph da Costa Pereira Furtado de Mendoza ... for the pretended crime of Free-masonry," 2 vols., London, 1811.

624. Tirado y Rojas, I, 269-73, 354.
625. Ibidem, I, 274-8, 289-99, 355.
626. Archivo de Simancas, Inq., Leg. 1473; Lib. 559.
627. Acta Latomorum, I, 265.
628. Archivo de Simancas, Inq., Lib. 890.
629. Ibidem, Lib. 435^{2}; Lib. 890.
630. Archivo de Simancas, Inq., Lib. 890.
631. Ibidem.
632. Archive hist. nacional, Inq. de Valencia, Leg. 100.

In this list is not included the curious case of the Bishop of Havana, Juan José Díaz de la Espada y Landa, accused of Free-Masonry in Cuba by the zealous inquisitor Elosua in 1815. The matter was transferred to Spain and was suspended November 11, 1819 (J. T. Medina, La Inquisicion de Cartagena de las Indias, p. 416). It does not seem to have interfered with the position of the good bishop, who retained his see until his death, Sept. 12, 1832 (Gams, Series Episcopp., p. 152).

633. Tirado y Rojas, II, 46, 72-3, 81-88.--Miraflores, Apuntes historico-críticos, p. 28.--Modesto Lafuente, Hist. de España, XXIX, 213-15, 333-4.

The "Memoirs of Don Juan van Halen" (London, 1830) which had an extensive circulation in many languages, are of no historical value. He was a real personage however, whose dextrous treachery in deserting the French, in 1814, is described by Toreno (Historia del Llevamiento etc., III, 323). In 1822 he was on the staff of Gen. Mina in Catalonia (Memorias del Gen. Espoz y Mina, III, 7) and, in 1838, was in high command in Valencia (Manifestacion del Gen. Córdova, p. 13).

In 1818 his name occurs as on trial in Toledo (not in Madrid, as he represents) and the charge was impeding the Inquisition, not Masonry and conspiracy--Catálogo de las causas etc., p. 131 (Madrid, 1903).

634. Martinez de la Rosa. Examen crítico de las Revoluciones de España, I, 417-18 (Paris, 1837).
635. Archivo hist. nacional, Inq. de Toledo, Leg. 1.
636. Vélez, Apología del Altar y del Trono, I, 41.
637. Clément, Journal, II, 89.
638. Archivo municipal de Sevilla, Seccion especial, Siglo XVIII, Letra A, Tomo 4, n. 55.
639. In this celebrated case I have relied chiefly on Ferrer del Rio, Hist. del Reinado de Carlos III, Lib. IV, cap. i, and on Menéndez y Pelayo, Heterodoxos, III, 205 sqq. See also Llorente, Hist. crít., cap. XXVI, art. iii, n. 13, 35, and Puigblanch, La Inquisicion sin Máscara, p. 295.

Frequent reference was made to Olavide in the debates of the Córtes of Cádiz on the suppression of the Inquisition. Señor Mexia stated that he had visited him at Baeza; that the Triunfo was merely a translation of the Abbé Lamourettes Délices de la Religion (Paris, 1788) somewhat enlarged, with the addition of a politico-economical portion, derived from the Ami des Hommes of the Marquis of Mirabeau,--Discusion del Proyecto sobre la Inquisicion, pp. 254-5. (Cádiz, 1813).

In 1831 De Custine says that there was little remaining of the prosperous colony founded by Olavide (L'Espagne sous Ferdinand VII, II, 98-107), but La Carolina, the principal town, had, in 1877, 6474 inhabitants. The district has historical interest as the scene of the victory of Las Navas de Tolosa, in 1212, and of the surrender of Bailen in 1808.

640. Llorente, Hist. crít., cap. XXVI, art. iii, n. 42.
641. Ibidem, n. 10.
642. Ibidem, cap. XXV, art. i, n. 112.--Menéndez y Pelayo, III, 255.
643. Llorente, cap. XXV, art. i, n. 89.--Art. de vérifier les Dates depuis l'année 1770, III, 355.--Modesto Lafuente, Hist. Gen. XXII, 127.--Cf. Rodrigo, Hist. verdadera, III, 365.--Discusion del Proyecto, p. 464 (Cadiz, 1813).
644. Vélez, Apología, I, 40.--Cf. Menéndez y Pelayo, III, 227.
645. Cartas escritas por el Conde de Cabarrús, pp. 81, 83, 87-9 (Vitoria, 1808).
646. Cartas del Filósofo rancio, I, 299.

647. Partidas, P. VII, Tit. xvii, ley 16.--Córtes de Leon y de Castilla, II, 378.
In the middle of the sixteenth century, branding with the letter " q" was still in force in Castile.--Rojas de Haeret., P. 1, n. 544.
648. Colmeiro, Córtes de Leon y de Castilla, II, 160, 219.--Nueva Recop., Lib. V, Tit. i, leyes 6, 7.--Novís. Recop., Lib. XII, Tit. xxviii, leyes 8, 9.
649. Memoria de diversos Autos (See Appendix to Vol. I).
650. Archivo de Simancas, Inq., Lib. 2, fol. 21.
651. Carbonell de Gestis Hæret. (Doc. de la C. de Aragon, XXVIII, 154).
652. Pragmaticas y altres Drets de Cathalunya, Lib. I, Tit. viii, cap. 1, § 4.
653. Archivo de Simancas, Inq., Lib. 933; Lib. 918, fol. 381.
654. Pragmaticas etc. de Cathalunya, Lib. I, Tit. viii, cap. 2.
655. Archivo de Simancas, Patronato Real, Inq., leg. único, fol. 38.
656. Archivo de Simancas, Inq., Lib. 3, fol. 241.
657. Concil. Hispalens., ann. 1512, cap. xxxvii (Aguirre, V, 374).
658. In the 1534 edition of his Repetitionem novam (Col. 363) Albertino says that he has treated the question extensively in his "Speculum Inquisitorum"--subsequently embodied in his "Tractatus de agnoscendis Assertionibus" as Q. XXIII (Romæ, 1572).
659. Bibl. pública de Toledo, Sala v, Est. 11, Tab. 3.
660. Simancæ de Cath. Instt., Tit. XL, n. 3; Enchirid., Tit. XII, n. 4-6.
661. Bibl. nacional, MSS., V, 377, cap. XVII.--Elucidationes S. Officii, § 33 (Archivo de Alcalá, Hacienda, Leg. 544^{2}, Lib. 4).
662. Archivo hist. nacional, Inq. de Valencia, Leg. 361, fol. 7.--MSS. of Royal Library of Copenhagen, 218^{b}, p. 418.
663. Peña, Comment. LXXXI in Eymerici Direct., P. II.--Bibl. nacional, ubi sup.--Archivo de Simancas, Inq., Lib. 921, fol. 231.
664. Archivo de Alcalá, Hacienda, Leg. 544^{2}; Lib. 10.
665. Bibl. nacional, MSS., Mm, X, 157, p. 190.
666. Archivo hist. nacional, Inq. de Valencia, Leg. 9, n. 3, fol. 313.--Archivo de Simancas, Inq., Leg. 552, fol. 42.
It was the same in Portugal, where the bishops had to yield. The question was carried to Rome and, in 1612, the Archbishop of Lisbon was commanded to hand bigamists over to the Inquisition.--Collect. Decret. S. Congr. S. Inquis., p. 361 (MS. penes me).
667. Decreta S. Congr. S. Officii, pp. 461, 466 (Bibl. del R. Archivio di Stato in Roma, Fondo Camerale, Congr. del. S. Officio, Vol. 3).
668. Archivo de Simancas, Inq., Lib. 54, fol. 117.--Ristretto cerca li Delitti più frequenti, pp. 113-141 (MS. penes me).
669. Miguel Calvo (Archivo de Alcalá, Hacienda, Leg. 544,^{2} Lib. 4).--Archivo hist. national, Inq. de Valencia, Leg. 299, fol. 80; Inq. de Toledo, Leg. 1.
670. Archivo de Simancas, Inq., Leg. 787.
671. Elucidationes S. Officii, § 33 (Archive de Alcalá, Hacienda, Leg. 544^{2}, Lib. 4)--Bibl. national, MSS., V, 377, cap. xvii, § 1.
672. MSS. of Library of Univ. of Halle, Yc, 20, T. 1.
673. Proceso contra Jos. Ant Ferro (MSS. of Am. Phil. Society).
674. Bibliothèque nationale, fonds espagnol, No. 354, fol. 242.
675. Memorias de los Vireyes del Perú, III, 38.--Archive de Simancas, Inq., Lib. 28, fol. 115.
676. MS. penes me.
677. Novís. Recop., Lib. XII, Tit. xxviii, ley 10.
678. Bibl. nacional, MSS., Mm, 93.
679. Archivo hist. nacional, Inq. de Valencia, Leg. 15, n. 11 fol. 7; n. 10, fol. 92.
680. Archivo hist. nacional, Inq. de Valencia, Leg. 15, n. 11, fol. 1-6; Inq. de Toledo, Leg. 1.
681. Ibidem, Inq. de Valencia, Leg. 15, n. 11, fol. 5.--Archivo de Alcalá, Estado, Leg. 2843.
682. Alcubilla, Códigos antiguos, II, 1908.
683. Archivo hist. nacional, Inq. de Valencia, Leg. 16, n. 5, fol. 50; Inq. de Toledo, Leg. 1, fol. 286.
684. Archivo de Simancas, Inq., Lib. 890.
685. MSS. of Library of Univ. of Halle, Yc, 20, T. I.--Archivo hist, nacional, Inq. de Toledo, Leg. 1; Inq. de Valencia, Leg. 100.--Royal Library of Berlin, Qt. 9548.
686. Nueva Recop., Lib. VIII, Tit. iv.
687. Eymerici Director, P. II, Q. XLI.--Repertor. Inquisit. s.v. Blasphemus.
688. Arguello, fol. 14.
689. Llorente, Añales, I, 278.
690. C. Hispalens. ann. 1512, cap. xxxviii (Aguirre, V, 374).

691. Pragmáticas y altres Dreta de Cathalunya, Lib. I, Tit. viii, cap. 1, 2.--Archivo de Simancas, Inq., Lib. 933.
692. Archivo de Simancas, Inq., Lib. 918, fol. 382.
693. Ibidem, Patronato Real, Inq., Leg. único, fol. 37.
694. Andres de Burgos, Reportorio de todas las Prematicas, fol. xxxix (Medina del Campo, 1551).
695. Córtes de los Reinos de Leon y de Castilla, IV, 589.
696. Nueva Recop., Lib. VIII, Tit. iv.
697. Bibl. pública de Toledo, Sala V, Est. xi, Tab. 3.
698. Archivo de Simancas, Inq., Lib. 939, fol. 106; Lib. 81, fol. 27.--Archivo hist. nacional, Inq. de Valencia, Leg. 31.
699. Archivo hist. nacional, Inq. de Valencia, Leg. 299, fol. 80.--Alberghini, Man. Qualificat., cap. xvi.

700. This was not the case in Italy where, in 1555, the Inquisition assumed jurisdiction over blasphemy. There were occasional conflicts with the secular authorities, especially in the Venetian territories, as when, in 1595, the podestà of Brescia refused to allow a blasphemer to be imprisoned by the inquisitor. The Roman Congregation protested, but the podestà prevailed and punished the offender, probably with greater severity than the Inquisition would have done. There was the same difficulty of distinction between heretical and non-heretical blasphemy. In 1606 the Congregation decided that puttana de Dio was not heretical although outside of Rome it was held to be so.--Decret. S. Cong. S. Officii, p. 29 (MSS. of Bibl. del Reale Archivio di Stato in Roma, Fondo Camerale, Congr. del. S. Officii, Vol. 3).

701. Cartas de Jesuitas (Mem. hist. español, XV, 191).--Nueva Recop., Lib. I, Tit. i, ley 10.--Autos Acordados, Lib. VIII, Tit. ii, Auto 1.
702. Archivo de Simancas, Inq., Leg. 552, fol. 13.
703. Archivo de Alcalá, Hacienda, Leg. 544^{2}, Lib. 4.
704. Ibidem.--Archivo hist. nacional, Inq. de Valencia, Leg. 299, fol. 80.--Bibl. nacional, MSS., V, 377, cap. 1.
705. Elucidationes S. Officii, § 37 (Archivo de Alcalá, ubi sup).
706. Archivo de Simancas, Inq., Leg. 552, fol. 3, 13.
707. Archivo hist. nacional, Inq. de Toledo, Leg. 1.
708. Reportorium Inquisit. S.V. Degradatio, § an clericus.
709. Simancæ de Cath. Instt., Tit. XL, n. 8-13; Ejusd. Enchirid., Tit. XII, n. 1-3.--Arnaldi Albertin. Repetitionem novam, Q. xiii, n. 47 (Ed. 1534, col. 331).

It is perhaps worth noting that the Repertorium of 1494 has no allusion to the subject under the titles Castitas, Clericus, and Matrimonium. At that time it was evidently considered to be outside of the sphere of the Inquisition.

710. Arnaldi Albertini de agnoscendis Assertionibus, Q. XXIII, n. 41. In Germany, many Catholic priests took wives. By the Interim of Charles V, in 1548, they were allowed to remain undisturbed until the Council of Trent should decide the question.--Interim, cap. XXVI, § 17.
711. C. Trident. Sess. XXIV, De Sacr. Matrimonii, can. ix. Yet the council recognized the papal power of dispensation.
712. Catálogo de las causas seguidas ante el tribunal de Toledo, pp. 306, 307.
713. MSS. of Library of Univ. of Halle, Yc, 20, T. I.
714. MSS. of Royal Library of Copenhagen, 218^{b}, p. 420.
715. Archivo hist. nacional, Inq. de Valencia, Leg. 299, fol. 80.--Elucidationes S. Officii, § 34 (Archivo de Alcalá, Hacienda, Leg. 544,^{2} Lib. 4).
716. MSS. of Library of Univ. of Halle, Yc, 20, T. I.
717. Archivo de Simancas, Inq., Leg. 552, fol. 11.
718. Archivo hist. nacional, Inq. de Toledo, Leg. 1.
719. Olmo, Relacion del Auto, p. 204.
720. Archivo hist. nacional, Inq. de Toledo, Leg. 1.
721. Ibidem, Inq. de Valencia, Leg. 100.
722. "Consentaneum visum est de sanctissimis ecclesiæ sacramentis agere, per quæ omnis vera justitia vel incipit, vel coepta augetur, vel amissa reparatur."--C. Trident. Sess. VII, De Sacramentis, Procem.
723. P. Denifle, Die älteste Tax-rolle der Apost. Pönitentiarie (Archiv f. Litt. u. K.-Geschichte, IV, 224-5).
724. Locati Opus judiciale Inquisitor., pp. 475, 476 (Romæ, 1570).--Farinacii de Hæresi, Q. CXCIII, § 1, n. 39.
725. Bullar. Roman. III, 142; IV, 144.
726. Collect. Decr. S. Congr. S. Officii, p. 50 (MS. penes me).
727. Ristretto circa li Delitti più frequenti nel S. Offizio, p. 104-5 (MS. penes me).

728. Royal Library of Munich, Cod. Ital. 185.--Bibl. del R. Archivio di Stato in Roma, Miscellanea MS., p. 729.
729. Archivo de Simancas, Inq., Lib. 939, fol. 107.--Ant. de Sousa. Opusc. circa Constit. Pauli V, p. 57.--Rod. a Cunha pro PP. Pauli V Statuto, p. 65.
730. Bullar. Roman. II, 415.
731. Archivo de Simancas, Inq., Lib. 939, fol. 108; Lib. 942, fol. 39.
732. Bibl. nacional, MSS., D, 118, fol. 114.
733. MSS. of Library of Univ. of Halle, Yc, 20, T. I.
734. Archivo de Simancas, Inq., Leg. 552, fol. 1, 11.
735. Obregon, Mexico Viejo, II, 353, 383.--Museo Mexicano, T. I, pp. 338-40 (Mexico, 1843).
736. Bibl. nacional, MSS., V, 377, cap. xix.--Miguel Calvo (Archivo de Alcalá Hacienda, Leg. 544,^{2} Lib. 4).--Elucidationes S. Officii, § 38 (Ibidem).--MSS. of Royal Library of Copenhagen, 218^{b}, p. 385.
737. Archivo de Simancas, Inq., Leg. 1183, fol. 13.
738. Archivo hist. nacional, Inq. de Toledo, Leg. 1.
739. Archivo de Simancas, Inq., Lib. 890.
740. Archivo hist. nacional, Inq. de Valencia, Leg. 100.
741. MS. Memoria de diversos Autos (see Appendix to Vol. I).
742. Bibl. nacional, MSS., V, 377, cap. xvi.
743. Elucidationes S. Officii, § 47 (Archivo de Alcalá, Hacienda, Leg. 544^{2}, Lib. 4).--MSS. of Royal Library of Copenhagen, 218^{b}, p. 332.
744. Archivo de Simancas, Hacienda, Leg. 25, fol. 3.
745. MSS. of Library of Univ. of Halle, Yc, 20, T. I.--See above, Vol. III, p. 189. Simancas (De Cath. Instt., Tit. XLVI, n. 92, 93) says that the Inquisition cannot relax for personation, however grave the case may be, which explains the necessity of the special papal brief.
746. Miscelanea de Zapata (Mem. hist, español, XI, 60). There is here evidently confusion between Almagro and Almaden.
747. Danvila y Collado, Expulsion de los Moriscos, p. 208.--Bibl. nacional, MSS., PV, 3, n. 20.
748. MSS. of Library of Univ. of Halle, Yc, 20, T. I.
749. Archivo de Simancas, Inq., Visitas de Barcelona, Leg. 15, fol. 20.
750. Llorente, Hist. crit., cap. XXIV, art. 1, n. 11.--MSS. of Library of Univ. of Halle, Yc, 20, T. I.--Archivo hist. nacional, Inq. de Toledo, Leg. 1.
751. Archivo hist. nacional, loc cit.
752. Archivo de Simancas, Inq., Leg. 552, fol. 13.
753. MSS. of Library of Univ. of Halle, Yc, 20, T. XVII.
754. Archivo de Simancas, Inq., Lib. 34, fol. 394.
755. Procesos contra Francisca Mexia y Francisca de la Serna (MSS. of David Fergusson Esq.). Fuller details of this instructive case will be found in my "Chapters from the Religious History of Spain," pp. 428-35.
756. Archivo hist. nacional, Inq. de Valencia, Leg. 100.
757. MSS. of Am. Philos. Society.
758. Decret. S. Congr. S. Officii, p. 388 (Bibl. del R. Archivio di Stato in Roma, Fondo Camerale, Congr. del S. Officio, Vol. 3).
759. Prattica per le cause del Sant' Officio, cap. 25 (MS. penes me).
760. Pellicer, Avisos históricos (Semanário erúdito, XXXIII, 116, 124, 149).
761. Bibl. national, MSS., V, 377, cap. vii, § 1.
762. MSS. of Library of Univ. of Halle, Yc, 20, T. I.
763. Archivo hist, nacional, Inq. de Toledo, Leg. 1.
764. Bibl. nacional, MSS., Bb, 122.
765. Archivo hist. nacional, Inq. de Valencia, Leg. 100.
766. Ibidem.
767. Ibidem, Leg. 1, n. 4, fol. 179.--MSS. of Royal Library of Copenhagen, 218^{b}, p. 167.
768. Cap. 1, Extra, Lib. III, Tit. xlv.
769. Archivo de Simancas, Inq., Lib. 19, fol. 70-76, 108-116.--Archivo hist. nacional, Inq. de Valencia, Leg. 6, n. 2, fol. 158 sqq.
770. Urbani PP. VIII Const. Coelestis (Bullar. Roman. IV, 85, Append, p. 33).
771. Index of 1640, Regula xvi.--Indice Ultimo, p. xxvi.
772. Discurso sobre si se le puede hacer fiesta al Premier Padre del Genero Humano Adan y darle culto y veneracion publica como á Santo, sin licencia del Romano Pontifice. Por D. Francisco Miranda y Paz. Madrid, 1636. The book was thought worthy of a refutation, which appeared in 1639 (Nic. Anton. Bibl. nova s. v. Franciscus de Miranda).
773. Padre Fidel Fita, in Boletin, 1887.--Martínez Moreno Historía del Martirio del Santo Niño de

la Guardia (Madrid, 1866).

774. The best account of these and kindred forgeries is by José Godoy Alcántara, in his Historia critica de los falsos Cronicones (Madrid, 1868). The modern President of the Canons of Sacromonte has given the other side in his El Sacro Monte de Granada (Madrid, 1883).

The influence of the Inquisition at first was adverse to the plomos. See Archivo de Simancas, Inq., Lib. 20, fol. 127, 188, 236, 319. A whole volume of the archives (Lib. 44^{1}) is occupied with papers connected with the affair from 1604 to 1636.

775. Barrantes, Aparato para la Historía de Extremadura, II, 392.

776. Archivo de Simancas, Inq., Lib. 435^{2}.

777. I have considered in some detail the development of this belief, in the "History of the Inquisition of the Middle Ages," III, 596 sqq.

778. Collect. Decretor. S. Congr. S. Officii, s. v. Conceptio (MS. penes me).--Collect. Decret. S. Congr. S. Inquisit. (Bibl. del R. Archivio di Stato in Roma, Fondo camerale, Congr. del S. Officio, Vol. 3).

779. Cartas de Jesuitas (Mem. hist. español, XIII, 450).

780. Le Tellier, Recueil des Bulles concernans les erreurs etc., p. 296 (Mons Rouen. 1697).

781. Bibl. nacional, MSS., Cc, 99, fol. 230.--Archivo hist. nacional, Inq. de Valencia, Leg. 11, n. 1, fol. 111-16.

782. Archivo hist. nacional, Inq. de Valencia, Leg. 10, n. 2, fol. 58, 90; Leg. 11, n. 2, fol. 217.

783. Ibidem, Leg. 1, n. 4, fol. 114; Leg. 11, n. 3, fol. 62.

784. Ibidem, Leg. 100.

785. C. Lateran., ann. 1179, cap. xi (Cap. 4, Extra, Lib. V, Tit. xxxi).--Très ancien Contume de Bretagne, Art. 112, 142.--Statuta criminalia Mediolani, cap. 51 (Bergomi, 1594).--Horne, Myrror of Justice, cap. iv, § 14.

786. Fuero Real de España, Lib. IV, Tit. ix, leg. 2.--Nueva Recop., Lib. VIII, Tit. xxxi, ley 1.--Ripoll, Bullar. Ord. Prædic., III, 301.--Innocent. PP. IV, Gloss in Cap. Quod nuper his, Extra, Lib. III, Tit. xxxiv.

787. Llorente, Anales, I, 327.

788. Archivo de Simancas, Inq., Lib. 933.--"En lo que toca al crimen nefando, si otras cosas no hay con ello que abiertamente sepan heregia, contra las tales personas ya sabeis que por esto no debeis vosotros proceder, ni es de vuestra jurisdiccion."

789. Escolano, Hist. de Valencia, II, 1449-70.--Boix, Hist. de la Ciudad y Reino de Valencia, I, 347.

790. Bledæ Defensio Fidei, pp. 423-4. Cf. Páramo, p. 184.

791. Bulario de la Orden de Santiago, Lib. IV, fol. 6.--Archivo de Simancas, Inq., Lib. 927, fol. 408.--Archivo hist. nacional, Inq. de Valencia, Leg. 2, n. 16, fol. 259.

792. Archivo de Simancas, Inq., Lib. 78, fol. 145.

793. Archivo de Simancas, Inq., Lib. 927, fol. 429.--Llorente, Añales, II, 373.

794. Archivo de Simancas, Inq., Lib. 939, fol. 107; Lib. 82, fol. 163.--MSS. of Bibl. nacional de Lima, Protocolo 223, Expediente, 5270.

795. Bibl. nacional, MSS., Q, 4.

796. Archivo hist. nacional, Inq. de Valencia, Leg. 2, n. 16, fol. 259.

797. Argument of Dr. Martin Real (MSS. of Bodleian Library, Arch. Seld. 130).

798. Collect. Decr. S. Congr. S. Officii, p. 396 (MS. penes me).--Decr. S. Congr. S. Inquisit., pp. 503, 539 (Bib. del R. Archivio di Stato in Roma, Fondo camerale, Congr. del S. Officio, Vol. 3).

799. Corpo Diplomatico Portugues, VI, 379; VII, 211, 235, 439; VIII, 227, 296; IX, 477; XI, 600, 656.

800. Regimiento do Santo Officio da Inquisição, Liv. III, Tit. XXV, §§ 1, 12.--Royal Library of Berlin, Qt. 9548.

801. Fueros y Actos de Corte, p. 10 (Zaragoza, 1647).

802. Archivo hist. nacional, Inq. de Valencia, Leg. 2, n. 16, fol. 270.

803. Archivo de Simancas, Inq., Lib. 927, fol. 414.

804. Archivo hist. nacional, Inq. de Valencia, Leg. 299, fol. 80; Leg. 61.--Elucidationes S. Officii, § 55 (Archivo de Alcalá, Hacienda, Leg. 544^{2}, Lib. 4).--Bibl. nacional, MSS., V, 377, cap. xxiv, § 1.

805. Archivo hist. nacional, Inq. de Valencia, Leg. 299, fol. 80.--Bibl. nacional, MSS., V, 377, cap. xxiv, § 6.

806. Archivo hist. nacional, Inq. de Valencia, Leg. 2, n. 16, fol. 259.--Parets, Sucesos de Cataluña (Mem. hist. español, XXIV, 297).

807. Archivo hist. nacional, Inq. de Valencia, Leg. 6, n. 2, fol. 52; Leg. 8, n. 2, fol. 497.

808. Bibl. nacional, MSS., V, 377, cap. xxiv, § 2.

The Inquisition was more humane than the Castilian courts. Jan. 27, 1637, two culprits were burnt in Madrid. Oct. 14, 1639, two more were burnt and a third was brought out to share the same fate, when the episcopal vicar claimed him, as he had been decoyed from the asylum of a church. Nine more were in prison at the time. Oct. 10, 1640, a man and a boy were burnt.--Cartas de Jesuitas (Mem. hist, español, XIV, 26; XV, 343).--Pellicer, Avisos históricos (Semanário erúdito, XXXI, 87, 228).

In Mexico there was a special quemadero for such cases, distinct from that of the Inquisition.--Obregon, Mexico viejo, II, 391.

809. Archivo hist. nacional, Inq. de Valencia, Leg. 61.
810. Archivo hist. nacional, Inq. de Valencia, Leg. 61.
811. Archivo de Simancas, Inq., Sala 39, Leg. 4, fol. 71.
812. Bulario de la Orden de Santiago, Lib. IV, fol. 6.--Archivo hist. nacional, Inq. de Valencia, Leg. 61; Cartas del Consejo, Leg. 5, n. 1, fol. 5.--Llorente, Hist. crít., cap. XXIV, art. 4, n. 2.--Giambattista Confalonieri (Spicilegio Vaticano, I, 461).
813. Archivo de Simancas, Inq., Lib. 82, fol. 91.
814. Bibl. nacional, MSS., PV, 3, n. 20.
815. Archivo de Simancas, Inq., Visitas de Barcelona, Leg. 15, fol. 5.
816. Archivo hist. nacional, Inq. de Valencia, Leg. 99.
817. Ibidem, Leg. 100.
818. Raynald. Annal., ann. 1258, n. 23.--Potthast, Regesta, n. 17745, 18396.--Cap. 1, Clement., Lib. V, Tit. v.
819. Repertor. Inquisit. s. v. Hæreticus, § Pertinax.

Although simony was the universally corroding vice of the Church, and although it was reckoned as a heresy, it was too profitable to the hierarchy ever to be subjected to the Inquisition. In a project of instructions for the Spanish delegates to the Lateran Council in 1512, simoniacal heresy is denounced as the universal destruction of the Church, owing to the openness with which it is practised in Rome and throughout Christendom, and they are told to labor to have it prosecuted as heresy by the Inquisition--(Döllinger, Beiträge zur politischen kirchlichen und Cultur-Geschichte, III, 204).

820. Fueros de Aragon, fol. 110. For earlier legislation of similar import see fol. 49 (Zaragoza, 1624).
821. Bulario de la Orden de Santiago, Lib. I, fol. 109. The general council here alluded to was that of Lyons, in 1273. See cap. 1, 2, in Sexto, Lib. V, Tit. v. This refers back to Concil. Lateranens. III, ann. 1179, cap. XXV.
822. Pragmaticas y altres Drets de Cathalunya, Lib. I, Tit. viii, cap. 1, § 20.--Archivo de Simancas, Inq. de Barcelona, Córtes, Leg. 17, fol. 32.--Páramo, p. 185.
823. Archivo de Simancas, Inq., Lib. 933.
824. Pragmaticas etc. de Cathalunya, Lib. I, Tit. viii, cap. 2, §§ 20, 35.
825. Argensola, Añales de Aragon, Lib. I, cap. liv.
826. Llorente, Añales, II, 298.
827. Fueros de Aragon, fol. 110.
828. Dormer, Añales de Aragon, Lib. II, cap. xli, p. 384.
829. Archivo de Simancas, Patronato Real, Inq., Leg. único, fol. 37, 38.
830. Simancas de Cath. Instt., Tit. LXVI, n. 3.
831. Archivo de Simancas, Inq., Lib. 939, fol. 106.
832. Ibidem, Visitas de Barcelona, Leg. 15, fol. 20.
833. Archivo hist. nacional, Inq. de Valencia, Leg. 100.--MSS. of Am. Phil. Society.
834. Collect. Decret. S. Congr. S. Officii, p. 125 (MS. penes me).--Decreta S. Congr. S. Inquisit., pp. 36, 515 (Bibl. del R Archivio di Stato in Romæ, Fondo camerale, Congr. del S. Officio, Vol. 3).
835. Archivo de Simancas Inq., Lib. 21, fol. 198.
836. Birch, Catalogue of MSS. of Inq. of Canaries, II, 541, 542, 559, 560.
837. MSS. of David Fergusson Esq.--Archivo de Simancas, Inq., Lib. 1002.
838. Catálogo de las causas seguidas ante el Tribunal de Toledo, p. 325.
839. Archivo hist. nacional, Inq. de Valencia, Leg. 100.
840. Archivo de Simancas, Inq., Lib. 1.
841. Ibidem, Lib. 9, fol. 6.
842. Ibidem, Sala 40, Lib. 4, fol. 164, 266.
843. Ibidem, Lib. 939, fol. 106.
844. Ant. Rodríguez Villa, La Corte y Monarquía de España, p. 95.
845. Cartas de Jesuitas (Mem. hist. español, XIII, 9, 11, 13-17, 19, 24, 27, 67-71, 73, 78-9, 119, 181, 185, 230; XIV, 395; XVII, 218; XVIII, 52, 59, 81, 105-17).--Juan de Palafox, Epist. III ad Innoc. X, n. 126 (Obras, XI, 107).--Theatro Jesuitico, p. 375.--Morale pratique des Jesuites (Cologne, 1684).
846. Cartas de Jesuitas (loc. cit., XIX, 187).
847. Archivo de Simancas, Inq., Lib. 38, fol. 12, 216, 260, 319, 320, 321, 326.
848. Archivo de Simancas, Inq., Lib. 559.
849. Archivo hist. nacional, Inq. de Toledo, Leg. 1.

850. Archivo hist. nacional, Inq. de Valencia, Leg. 100.
851. Archivo de Simancas, Inq., Lib. 939, fol. 64.
852. Royal Library of Berlin, Qt. 9548.
853. Semanário erúdito, XI, 274.
854. Archivo hist. nacional, Inq. de Toledo, Leg. 1.
855. Ibidem.
856. Archivo de Simancas, Inq., Sala 39, Leg. 4, fol. 80.
857. Archivo hist. nacional, Inq. de Toledo, Leg. 111, n. 49.
858. Bibl. nacional, MSS., Mm, 130.
859. Joaquin Lorenzo Villanueva, in "Discusion del Proyecto sobre el Tribunal de la Inquisicion," p. 432 (Cádiz, 1813).
860. V. de la Fuente, Hist. ecles., III, 381.
861. Clément, Journal, II, 124.
862. Archivo hist. nacional, Inq. de Valencia, Leg. 100.
863. Archivo hist. nacional, Inq. de Valencia, Leg. 365, n. 46, fol. 56.
864. Ibidem, Leg. 4, n. 3, fol 58.
865. MSS. of Am. Philos. Society.
866. Llorente, Hist. crít., cap. XXIX, art. iii, n. 2; cap. XLVI.--Muriel, Hist. de Carlos IV (Mem. hist, español, XXXIII, 154).
Llorente tells us that he pursued the task confided to him by Abad and in 1797 produced his "Discursos sobre el órden de procesar del Santo Oficio" which, in 1801, expand him to a smart persecution.--Memoria histórica, p. 11 (Madrid, 1812).
867. Muriel (loc. cit., XXXI, 190).--Lafuente, Hist. gen. de España., XXII, 124.--V. de la Fuente, Hist. ecles., III, 400.
868. Discusion del Proyecto, p. 473 (Cádiz, 1813).
869. Somoza de Montsoriu, Las Amarguras de Jovellanos, pp. 47-8 (Gijon, 1889).
870. Somoza, op. cit., pp. 301-5.--Muriel, op. cit., XXXII, 117. For the orthodoxy of Jovellanos, see Menéndez y Pelayo, III, 287-90.
871. Somoza, op. cit., pp. 57-60.--Discurso histórico-legal sobre el Origen, Progresos y Utilidad del Santo oficio, p. 101 (Valladolid, 1803).
872. Somoza, op. cit., pp. 77-84, 86-90, 141-2, 312-20.--Cean Bermúdez, Memorias para la Vida de D. Gaspar Melchor de Jove Llanos, p. 81 (Madrid, 1814).
873. Llorante, Hist. crít., cap, XLII, art. ii, n. 1-18.--Muriel, op. cit., xxxiv, 110-19.--Menéndez y Pelayo, III, 172-3.
874. Respuesta pacífica de un Español á la Carta sediciosa del Frances Grégoire, que se dice Obispo de Blois, pp. 3, 31, 63, 74, 75, 76, 87 (Madrid, 1798).
875. Discurso historico-legal sobre el Origen etc. del S. Oficio, pp. 126, 185, 187 (Valladolid, 1803).
876. Cartas de un Presbitero español, pp. 3, 7, 98, 121, 123, 129, 152-4 (Madrid, 1798).
877. José Clemente Carnicero, La Inquisicion justamente restablecida, I, 8 (Madrid, 1816).-- Toreno, Revolucion etc. de España, I, 160.--Llorente, Hist. crít., cap. XLIV, art. i, n. 19.--Rodrigo, Hist. verdadera, III, 486.--Menéndez y Pelayo, III, 417.
878. See Appendix.--On January 9, 1813, this letter was produced in the Córtes, by Sr. Arguelles, during the discussion on the suppression of the Inquisition.--Discusion del Proyecto, p. 143.
879. Menéndez y Pelayo, III, 386-7. For a vivid sketch of the adventurous life of Marchena see Antoine de Latour, "Espagne, Traditions, Moeurs et Littérature, p. 51 (Paris, 1869).
880. Carnicero, op. cit., I, 9.--Código de José Nap. Bonaparte, Tit. XIII, § 5 (Madrid, 1845).
881. Discusion del Proyecto, p. 148.
882. Toreno, Historia de la Revolucion, III, 106 (Paris, 1838).
883. Archivo hist. nacional, Inq. de Valencia, Leg. 100.
884. Puigblanch, La Inquisicion sin Mascara, p. 429.
885. Toreno, op. cit., II, 197-202.
886. Marliani, Histoire de l'Espagne moderne, I, 171.
887. Even Evaristo San Miguel, one of the exaltados of 1822 who, as secretary of State, was largely responsible for the follies which invited the French intervention of 1823, admits the errors of the Córtes of Cádiz. The Constitution of 1812, he says, was an exotic that took no root in the soil; the mass of the people, plunged in ignorance and misery, knew of it only by hearing from their spiritual guides that it was a tissue of impieties.--De la Guerra Civil de España, p. 88 (Madrid, 1836).
888. Toreno, II, 208, 211, 223, 249.--Coleccion de los Decretos y Ordenes que han expedido las Córtes Generales, I, 1-3 (Madrid, 1820).
889. Vélez, Apología del Altar y del Trono, I, 107-10, 113-19, 211-12 (Madrid, 1825).--Coleccion de Decretos, I, 16.

890. These letters have been repeatedly reprinted. My edition is of Madrid, 1824-5 in five volumes. Under the Restoration, Alvarado was appointed a member of the Suprema, but he can scarce have acted as he died, August 31, 1814.

891. La Inquisicion sin Máscara, pp. 5-12, 28, 299, 480-3 (Cádiz, 1811).--An English translation by William Walton appeared in London, in 1816, with a valuable Introduction.

892. Cartas del Filósofo Rancio, I, 86, 87, 96, 98, 262, 265, 268, 297; II, 21, 457, 461.

893. Marliani, op. cit., I, 175.

894. Tit. I, cap. i, art. 2, 3; Tit. II, cap. ii, art. 12 (Coleccion de Decretos, II, 98, 100).

895. Vélez, Apología, II, 116-27.--Marliani, I, 179.--Carnicero, Hist. de la Revolucion, III, 160, 184.--Coleccion de Decretos, II, 166; III, 60.

896. Vélez, Apología, I, 126-34, 212-13.--Rodrigo, III, 370.--Toreno, III, 106-7.

897. Apología de la Inquisicion, pp. 16-18 (Cadiz, 1811).--Riesco, in a speech before the Córtes, said that the functions of the Suprema were suspended on the pretext that its members had not been "purified" (Discusion del Proyecto, p. 148). All officials who had in any way been concerned with the French were required to be purified--that is, to give proofs of patriotism. This so-called purification came repeatedly in play in the kaleidoscopic changes of Spanish politics.

898. Vélez, Apología, I, 214, 384-5, 399-418.

899. Vélez, Apología, I, 134-52, 217, 219.--Toreno, III, 105-10.

900. Discusion del Proyecto, pp. 40-1, 398.

901. Discusion, pp. 38-40.--The law of the Partidas thus revived was P. VII, Tit. xxvi, ley 2, which says that heretics can be accused by any one before a bishop or his vicar, who shall examine them on the articles of faith and sacraments. If error is found he must labor to convert them by reason and persuasion when, if willing to be converted, they are to be reconciled and pardoned. If persistent they are to be handed over to the secular judge for punishment by fire or otherwise. The revival of the law was only as regards the functions of the bishops.

902. Ibidem, pp. 42-7.

903. Cartas del Filósofo Rancio, II, 453.--Menéndez y Pelayo, III, 473.--Discusion, pp 215, 229, 397.

904. Discusion del Proyecto, pp. 59, 325, 495, 564, 630-9, 683, 687.--Coleccion de Decretos, III, 215, 220.--Archivo hist. nacional, Inq. de Valencia, Leg. 100.--Archivo de Simancas, Inq., Lib. 890.

The decree concerning property continued the salaries of all officials. A subsequent decree of September 13th, regulating the national debt, applied the property of the extinguida inquisicion to that incurred in the war with France.--Coleccion, IV, 257.

905. Carnicero, La Inquisicion justamente restablecida, II, 115.

906. Vélez, Apología, I, 252-4.

907. Coleccion de Decretos, III, 26, 30, 66, 137, 211.

908. Discusion del Proyecto, pp. 683, 689-94.

909. Toreno, III, 204.

910. Memoria interesante para la Historia de las Persecuciones de la Iglesia Católica y de sus Ministros en España, Append., pp. 1-16 (Madrid, 1814).

911. Ibidem, pp. 17-20.

912. Manifesto istorico del Cardinale Pietro Gravina, pp. 63-68 (Roma, 1824).--E. Nuñez de Taboada, Le dernier soupir de l'Inquisition, pp. 43-9 (Paris, 1814).

913. Memoria interesante, Append., pp. 23-6.

914. Toreno, III, 193-203.

915. Memoria interesante, pp. ix, x, 58; Append., pp. 27-30.--Vélez, Apología, I, 262-87.

916. Taboada, op. cit., pp. 50-71.--Gravina, Manifesto istorico, pp. 68-106.

917. Vélez, Apología, I, 303.--Gravina, Manifesto istorico, pp. 106-116, 1-41.

918. Vélez, Apología, I, 260.

919. It would seem as though some of the tribunales continued to act. There is a case of a Dominican sub-deacon, Fray Tomas García, who denounced himself for saying mass to that of Valencia, which forwarded the sumaria to Cuenca, August 15, 1813.--Archivo hist. nacional, Inq. de Valencia, Leg. 100.

920. Toreno, III, 284-305.

921. Carnicero, Historia de la Revolucion, III, 169-76.

922. Miraflores, Apuntes para escribir la Historia de España, pp. 11-13 (Londres, 1834).

923. Miraflores, Documentos á los que se hace referencia en los Apuntes, I, 9-23.

924. Marliani, I, 195-200.--Toreno, III, 317, 395.--Coleccion de Decretos, I, 43; V, 87.

925. Conservatives concur with Liberals in denouncing the memory of Fernando. See Menéndez y Pelayo, III, 495 and V. de la Fuente, III, 472.

926. Toreno, III, 355-9.--Miraflores, Documentos, I, 30.--Constitucion, art. 3, 144-9, 173, 181, 187 (Coleccion de los Decretos, V, 148, 153, 182, 185).

927. Representacion y Manifiesto que algunos Diputados á las Córtes ordinarias firmaron en los mayores Apuros de su Opresion en Madrid, pp. 12, 17, 59, 60 (Madrid, 1814).

928. Toreno, III, 359, 361-4.--Koska Vayo, Historia de la Vida y Reinado de Fernando VII, II, 26, 32-5, 377 (Madrid, 1842).--Marliani, I, 206.

929. Coleccion de las Reales Cédulas etc. de Fernando VII, p. 1 (Valencia, 1814).--Toreno, III, 400.--It would be difficult to find a more slovenly piece of writing than this celebrated and fateful manifesto. Its authorship was attributed to Juan Pérez Villamil, the head of the Regency dismissed by the Córtes in March, 1813.--Toreno, III, 364.

930. Marliani, I, 208-17.--Koska Vayo, II, 48-52.--Toreno, III, 405.

931. Menéndez y Pelayo, III, 545.

932. Hervaz, Ruiz de Padron y su tiempo, pp. 101-5 (Madrid, 1898).--Archivo de Simancas, Inq., Libro 890.--His speech was issued in Coruña in 1813, under the title of "Dictamen del Dr. Antonio José Ruiz de Padron sobre la Inquisicion." Other clerical deputies who suffered reclusion in convents were Oliveros, in la Cabrera; Gallego, in the Cartuja de Jerez; Ramos, in that of Valencia; Arispe, in that of Seville; Lopez Cepero, in the Capuchins of Novelda; Antonio Larrazabal, wherever the Archbishop of Guatemala might designate, and Bernabeu, in one not ascertained. Besides these La Canal and Jaime Villanueva were recluded for editing a periodical.--V. de la Fuente, III, 471.

933. Amador de los Rios, III, 555.--When the royal decree of July 21 was received, August 16th, the cathedral was illuminated and the bells were rung, followed, August 23d and 24th, by great solemnities.--Relacion histórica de la Judería de Sevilla, pp. 46-8.

934. Rodrigo, III, 480.--Archivo de Sevilla, Seccion VI, 1ª Escribanía del Cabildo, Tomo 49, n. 14.

935. Coleccion de Cédulas de Fernando VII, p. 85.

936. Rodrigo, III, 485.--Carnicero, La Inquisicion justamente restablecida, II, 51.

937. Archivo de Simancas, Inq., Lib. 559; 890.

938. Archivo de Simancas, Inq., Lib. 559.

939. Ibidem, Lib. 890.

940. Coleccion de los Decretos, III, 220.

941. Archivo de Simancas, Inq., Lib. 559.--See Appendix.

942. Ibidem, Lib. 559.

943. Ibidem.

944. Archivo hist. nacional, Inq. de Valencia, Leg. 17, n. 4, fol. 9, 21, 36, 57, 85, 88, 93.

945. Archivo de Simancas, Inq., Lib. 559.

946. Archivo de Simancas, Inq., Lib. 559; Lib. 435^{2}.

947. Relacion de la Judería de Sevilla, pp. 49-51.

948. Archivo hist. nacional, Inq. de Valencia, Leg. 100.

949. Archivo de Simancas, Inq., Lib. 890.

950. Archivo de Simancas, Inq., Lib. 890.

951. Ibidem, Sala 39, Leg. 1473, fol. 29.

952. Ibidem, Lib. 890.

953. Ibidem.

954. Archivo de Simancas, Inq., Lib. 559.--Rodrigo, III, 489.

955. Archivo de Simancas, loc. cit.

956. Archivo de Simancas, Registro de Genealogías, n. 916, fol 4, 12.--Inq., Lib. 435^{2}; Lib. 559; Leg. 1473.

957. Archivo de Simancas, Inq., Leg. 1473.

958. Ibidem.

959. Archivo de Simancas, Inq., Lib. 890.

960. L'Espagne et ses Revolutions, p 148--quoted by Marliani, I, 235. See also Miraflores (Apuntes, pp. 23, 26) who, as an aristocrat, had no affiliation with the Liberals.

961. Many documents were gathered in the streets and sent to the United States, which have mostly perished through neglect, but some which were secured by Mr. Andrew Thorndike, then a resident of Barcelona, were presented, in 1840, to the American Philosophical Society, through whose courtesy I have been enabled to use them.

Some cases, from a similar source were translated and printed in Boston, in 1828, under the title of "Records of the Spanish Inquisition, translated from the original Manuscripts."

In Majorca the populace was more aggressive and destroyed the palace of the Inquisition.

962. Koska Vayo, II, 133-54, 170.--Miraflores, Apuntes, pp. 26-37; Documentos, I, 73-81.--Memorias de Francisco Espoz y Mina, II, 255-72.--Martínez de la Rosa, Examen crítico de las Revoluciones de España, I, 14-22.

963. Urquinaona, La España bajo el Poder arbitrario de la Congregacion Apostólica, p. 14 (Madrid, 1835).--Miraflores, Apuntes, pp. 40-5; Documentos, I, 87-91.--Cappa, La Inquisicion

española, p. 239.--Rodrigo, III, 495.
964. See Appendix.
965. Archivo de Sevilla, Seccion VII, 1820-3, Tomo XVII, n. 2.--Rodrigo, III, 495.--Coleccion de los Decretos, VI, 33.
966. Archivo de Simancas, Inq., Lib. 435^{3}.
967. España venturosa por la vida de la Constitucion y la muerte de la Inquisicion. Madrid, 1820.

Of course pamphleteers did not allow the opportunity to escape, but I have met with only two of their productions--"Memorial de la Santa Inquisicion á los Señores Ministros de Francia" and "Oracion funebre en las Exequias que se hicieron á la difunta Inquisicion en el Templo de Fanatismo de la Villa de Ignorancia, por un Ministro de la misma." Their only interest lies in their expression of the feelings of the period.

968. Coleccion de Decretos, VI, 64, 141, 155, 258; VII, 57, 60, 245, 251; IX, 384; X, 16, 17, 31.
969. H. Brück, Die geheimen Gessellschaften in Spanien, pp. 233-9, 250-60.--V. de la Fuente, III, 477-9.
970. Coleccion de los Decretos, VI, 43.
971. Modesto Lafuente, XXVII, 83.
972. Coleccion de los Decretos, VII, 36.
973. Koska Vayo, III, 42. In the reaction of 1823, Villanueva escaped to England where, as Menéndez y Pelayo tells us (Heterodoxos, III, 527), under the pressure of misery, he nearly or quite embraced Protestantism. Puigblanch, who was also a refugee, amused himself with writing violent diatribes against his fellows in misfortune and especially against Villanueva, who retorted in kind. He died in Dublin, reconciled to the Church, March 25, 1836, at the age of 80.
974. Canto, El Coloso constitucional derrocado (Orihuela, 1823).
975. Koska Vayo, III, 181.
976. Coleccion de los Decretos, VI, 145; VII, 4, 92, 105.
977. Miraflores, Apuntes, p. 65.
978. Koska Vayo, II, 317; III, 121.
979. Miraflores, Documentos, II, 76, 79.--Koska Vayo, III, 8.
980. Miraflores, Documentos, I, 214-25; II, 15.
981. Mina, Memorias, III, 16, 111-13, 159, 169.
982. Miraflores, Documentos, II, 32-99.
983. Ibidem, II, 114-72.--Koska Vayo, II, 317; III, 8.--Mina, Memorias, III, 88-9.--Châteaubriand, El Congreso de Verona, Traducela Cayetano Cortés, II, 379-80, 384.
984. Miraflores, Documentos, II, 172-4, 177-80.
985. Ibidem, pp. 174-6.
986. Miraflores, Apuntes, p. 163.
987. Ibidem, pp. 172-5.
988. Coleccion de los Decretos, X, 162.
989. Miraflores, Apuntes, pp. 185, 215; Documentos, II, 284-94--Koska Vayo, III, 72, 101-12.
990. Miraflores, Documentos, II, 240, 244; Apuntes, pp. 189, 191, 194.--Koska Vayo, III, 74.
991. Miraflores, Documentos, II, 242.
992. Miraflores, Documentos, II, 247-70.
993. Koska Vayo, III, 97-8.--Miraflores, Apuntes, pp. 219-21.
994. Miraflores, Apuntes, pp. 221-4; Documentos, II, 294-6.--Koska Vayo, III, 442.
995. Koska Vayo, III, 128.
996. Ibidem, III, 126-154.--Miraflores, Apuntes, pp. 234-44; Documentos II, 316-38.
997. Koska Vayo, III, 159-64.
998. Koska Vayo, III, 175, 184.
999. El Congreso de Verona, II, 234, 265, 268, 302, 307, 311, 317, 319, 322, 324, 339, 342.--Martínez de la Rosa, I, 372, 392, 394, 408.--Koska Vayo, III, 319.
1000. Koska Vayo, III, 185.--Miraflores, Apuntes, p. 224; Documentos, II, 296.--Urquinaona, p. 195.
1001. Javier de Burgos, Añales del Reinado de Dª Isabel II, I, 46 (Madrid, 1850).

A characteristic freak of Fernando was the establishment in Seville of a school of bull-fighting, with Don Pedro Ramiro at its head, on a salary of 12,000 reales. When Burgos became minister of Fomento, under Isabel II, he had the satisfaction of suppressing this.

1002. Rodrigo, III, 497.--Miraflores, Documentos, II, 299.--Barrantes, Aparato para la Historia de Extremadura, III, 43.
1003. El Congreso de Verona, II, 283, 302.
1004. Koska Vayo, III, 206.
1005. Rodrigo, III, 498.
1006. Martínez de la Rosa, I, 422.--Koska Vayo, III, 241.

1007. Koska Vayo, III, 222.

1008. Modesto Lafuente, XXVIII, 453-63; XXIX, 393-5.--Urquinaona, pp. 141-2.

1009. Modesto Lafuente, XXVIII, 465-71; XXIX, 7-13.--Koska Vayo, III, 305, 311.

1010. Urquinaona, p. 143.--Modesto Lafuente, XXVIII, 475.

1011. Archivo hist. nacional, Inq. de Valencia, Leg. 100.--Archivo de Simancas, Inq., Lib. 890.

1012. Archivo hist. nacional, Leg. 463, Hacienda XVI.

1013. Archivo hist. nacional, Leg. 6462.

1014. Koska Vayo, III, 207.

1015. Modesto Lafuente, XXIV, 346.--Menéndez y Pelayo, III, 524.--Vicente de la Fuente, III, 482.

1016. Modesto Lafuente, loc. cit.--V. de la Fuente, loc. cit.

1017. Pii PP. VIII Const. Cogitationes nostras, 5 Oct. 1829 (Bullar. Roman. Contin., IX, 76).

1018. Partidas, P. II, Tit. xv, ley 2.

1019. Autos Acordados, Lib. V, Tit. vii, Auto 5.

1020. Andrés Muriel, Hist. de Carlos IV (Mem. hist. español, XXIX, 14-29).

1021. Juan Pérez de Guzman (Revista de Archivos, April, 1904, p. 267).--Modesto Lafuente, XXIX, 51.

1022. Koska Vayo, III, 342, 352, 358-68.--Modesto Lafuente, XXIX. 191.

1023. Koska Vayo, III, 369-75, 387.--Modesto Lafuente, XXIX, 152.

1024. Koska Vayo, III, 380.

That the Carlists should regard the opportune resurrection of this long-buried pragmática as a fraud was not unnatural, but the records produced in its favor bear every evidence of genuineness. From them it appears that on May 31, 1789, Carlos IV summoned the Córtes to assemble on September 23d to take the oath of allegiance to his son Fernando and to transact other business. The oath was duly taken on that day; on the 30th a petition in the customary form was addressed to the king for the abrogation of the pragmática of Philip V and the restoration of the ancient law of succession. The session continued with various acts of legislation; on October 7th Carlos obtained an approval of the measure from fourteen archbishops and bishops who had joined in the oath of allegiance; on October 30th he confirmed the pragmática, but ordered absolute secrecy to be maintained with respect to it and to this all concerned took a solemn oath. Still it did not remain wholly unknown and, in December 1809, Doña Carlota, Princess of Brazil, applied to the supreme Junta Central, then ruling the kingdom, to have her possible rights to the succession under it acknowledged. The Junta was sitting in Seville; the archives were in Madrid, then in possession of the French, and inquiries were made of such survivors of the Córtes of 1789 as could be reached, who confirmed the fact of the adoption of the pragmática and of the secrecy enjoined, whereupon the Consejo de España é Indias reported in favor of the Portuguese princess's application. That these records, with their wealth of names and dates and elaborate details could be manufactured is simply incredible.--Testimonio de las Actas de Córtes de 1789 sobre la Sucesion en la Corona de España, y de los Dictámenes dados sobre esta materia; publicado por real decreto de S. M. la Reina N^{ra} S^{ra}. Año de 1833, Madrid, en la Imprenta Real.

1025. Koska Vayo, III, 393-425.

1026. Ibidem, p. 437.

1027. Quoted by Hervaz, Ruiz de Padron, p. 160.

1028. Archivo de Alcalá, Ministerio de Estado, Leg. 897, n. 30; Leg. 906, n. 87, 88.--(See Appendix.)

It will be remembered that the Duke of Medinaceli was alguazil mayor of the Madrid tribunal, and as such was drawing a yearly stipend of a thousand reales.

1029. See Appendix. The allusion to the concurrence of the Holy See is a pure assumption, seeing that, for political reasons, Isabel and the Regency were not recognised by the papacy for many years.

1030. Castillo y Ayensa, Negociaciones con Roma, I, Append, p. 156 (Madrid, 1859).

1031. Antequera, Historia de la Legislacion española, p. 419 (Madrid, 1884).

1032. Soler, Un Milagro y una Mentira, p. 5 (Valencia, 1858).

1033. Menéndez y Pelayo, III, 682-3, 686.--Hermann Dalton, Die evangelische Bewegung in Spanien, pp. 40-5 (Wiesbaden, 1872).

1034. A. Luque y Vicens, La Inquisicion, su Pro y su Contra, Segunda Edicion, Madrid, 1859.

1035. Parades, Curso de Derecho político, p. 720 (Madrid, 1883).

1036. Novísimo Código penal, arts. 236-41 (Valencia, 1872, pp. 126-7).

1037. Paredes, op cit., p. 666.

1038. See the very interesting collection of papers published by the Ateneo Cientifico y Literario of Madrid under the title Oligarquia y Caciquismo como la forma actual de Gobierno en España; urgencia y modo de cambiarla (Madrid, 1903).

This Caciquism is described as "a despotism a hundred times worse than that of the absolute kings" (p. 33).

1039. Reconstitucion y Europeizacion de España, pp. 113, 123, 289 (Madrid, 1900).--Ricardo Macías Picavea, El Problema nacional, p. 304 (Madrid, 1899).

Another eloquent exposition of the deplorable condition of public affairs in Spain is Doctor Madrazo's El Pueblo español ha muerto? (Santander, 1903).

1040. Relazioni Venete, Serie I, T. V, p. 463.

1041. Clemencin, Elogio de la Reina Isabel, p. 302 (Madrid, 1821).

1042. Cabrera, Relaciones, passim; Append. pp. 582-3.--Relazioni di Ambasciadori Lucchesi, pp. 29, 31 (Lucca, 1903).

1043. Cespedes y Meneses, Don Felipe Quarto, Lib. II, cap. i, x.

1044. A. Rodriguez Villa, La Corte y Monarquía de España, p. 110 (Madrid, 1886).

1045. Zanctornato, Relazione della Corte de España, pp. 76-82 (Cosmopoli, 1672).

1046. Relasioni Venete, Serie I, T. V, p. 396.

1047. The Córtes of 1570 complained of the sale of hidalguias, which were bought by the richer taxpayers, whose burden was thus thrown on the poor and miserable. To this Philip II replied that his necessities compelled him to it, but that more consideration would be shown in future.--Córtes de Cordova del año de setenta, fol. 5 (Alcalá, 1575).

By the censuses of 1768 and 1787 the exempt classes were--

1768. 1787. Hidalgos 722,794 480,589 Clergy 183,965 151,973 -------- -------- 906,759 632,562

Floridablanca felicitated himself on the reduction thus shown in the exemptions, resulting from greater strictness in admitting claims, while the population had increased from 9,309,804 to 10,409,879.--Censo español en el año de 1787.

1048. Dávila, Vida de Felipe III, p. 216.

1049. Libro de las Cincas Excelencias del Español que despueblan á España, fol. 163, 170 (Pamplona, 1629).

1050. Representacion al Rey D. Felipe V dirigida al mas seguro aumento del Real Erario. Hecha por D. Miguel de Zavala y Auñon, pp. 7-35, 74-97 (Madrid, 1732).

It should be observed that in none of the descriptions of the burdens imposed on the peasantry is any allusion made to what perhaps was the most grievous of all, both in amount and method of collection--the tithe by which the enormous church establishment was supported. This was wholly beyond control by the secular power and was therefore left out of consideration.

In 1820, Dr. Sebastian de Miñano, in his Cartas del Pobrecito Holgazan, gives a graphic picture of the ecclesiastical burdens of the peasant--the first fruits, the tithes and the obligatory "almsgiving" to all the neighboring convents.--Ochoa, Epistolario español, II, 616.

1051. Jovellanos, Informe en el Expediente de Ley Agraria (Obras, VII, 165-8).

The trouble still exists. In 1898 the Chamber of Agriculture of Upper Aragon states that notwithstanding large subventions to railroads and highways the greater part of the population is as isolated as ever, and it urges the expenditure of 400 or 500 millions of pesetas to convert 250,000 kilométres of mule-track into cheap wagon roads.--Reconstitucion de España, pp. 24, 89.

1052. Córtes de Leon y de Castilla, II, 344.--Jovellanos, Informe, pp. 48-80.

The exorbitant privileges of the Mesta were largely curtailed by the Córtes of Cádiz, but were promptly restored by Fernando VII, in a decree of October 2, 1514 (Coleccion de Cédulas etc., p. 170).

1053. Zavala y Auñon, pp. 104-30.--Jovellanos, p. 44.

1054. Relazioni Lucchese, p. 29.--For the multifarious laws respecting the coinage see Autos Acordados, Lib. V, Tit. xxi.

1055. Discorsos apolóxicos (Coll. de Doc. inéd., LXXI, 220).

1056. I owe this passage to Professor James Harvey Robinson's "Readings in European History," II, 25.

1057. Colmeiro, Córtes de los antiguos Reinos, II, 223.

1058. Relazioni Venete, Serie I, T. III, p. 256, 287; V, 18; VI, 360.

1059. Relazioni Lucchese, pp. 58, 70.

1060. Discurso político (Semanario erúdito, II, 143).

A modern writer attributes to the infusion of Saracen blood this characteristic--"este carácter indolente y apático, que nos impede llegar á tiempo en nuestras empresas, ó que no nos consiente llevarlas á termino bien cumplido."--Madrazo, El pueblo español ha muerto? p. 29 (Santander, 1903).

1061. Francisco Santos, El No Importe de España, pp. 149, 203 (Madrid, 1668).

1062. Dávila, Vida de Felipe III, p. 216.

1063. Pedro Fernández Navarrete, Discursos políticos, fol. 66 (Barcelona, 1621).

See also his later Conservacion de Monarquias, Discurso XLVI (Madrid, 1626) where he states that there were thirty-two universities and more than four thousand grammar-schools where Latin was taught.

1064. Semanário erúdito, XXVI, 108.--Jovellanos, Informe, p. 154.

1065. Relazioni Lucchese, p. 89.

1066. Semanário erúdito, VII, 167, 169.
1067. Juan de Valera, Disertaciones y Judicios literários, p. 201 (Madrid, 1878).--Reconstitucion de España, p. 29.
1068. See the very instructive sketch by D. Antonio Rodríguez Villa, "Patiño y Campillo," Madrid, 1882.
1069. Vida política y ministerial del Conde de Floridablanca. This, I believe, has never been printed. My copy is in MS.
1070. Córtes de los antiguos Reinos, I, 605; II, 55, 66, 134, 140, 143.
1071. Córtes de los antiguos Reinos, 1, 2, 24, 42, 43, 51, 244, 246, 289, 291, 360-1, 470.--Fuero viejo, Lib. v, Tit. ii, ley 1; Lib. I, Tit. i, ley 3.
1072. Córtes etc. III, 339-40.
1073. Ibidem, 516-18.--Autos acordados, Lib. V, Tit. x, Auto 1.
1074. Colmeiro, Córtes, II, 88, 98, 121, 147, 163, 168, 180, 192, 199, 207.--Córtes de Madrid del año de Setenta y tres, Peticion 57 (Alcalá. 1575).
1075. Bleda, Coronica de los Moros, pp. 864, 1025.
1076. Salazar, Crónica del Gran Cardenal de España, Lib. I, cap. 68 (Madrid, 1625).
1077. Dávila, Vida de Felipe III, p. 216.
1078. Cespedes y Meneses, Don Felipe Quarto, Lib, II, cap. 10.
1079. Cartas de Jesuitas (Mem. hist. español, XIII, 86).
1080. Autos Acordados, Lib. IV, Tit. i, Auto 4.
1081. Llorente, Coleccion diplomática, p. 44.
1082. Autos Acordados, Lib. V, Tit. x, Auto 3.
1083. C. Trident. Sess. XXI, De Reform. cap. 2; Sess. XXIII, De Reform. cap. 4, 5, 7, 10, 11, 12, 13, 14; Sess. XXV, De Reg. et Mon. cap. 3.
1084. Innocent. PP. XIII, Constit. Apostolici ministerii, 13 Maii, 1723. Confirmed by Benedict XIII, September 23, 1724 (Bullar. Roman. XIII, 60).
1085. Semanário erúdito, X, 149-58.
1086. Ibidem, VII, 172, 182-4; VIII, 231-33.
1087. Novís. Recop., Lib. 1, Tit. v, leyes 14, 15, 17, 18. Under Carlos III the numbers of the clergy were:

1768. 1787. Parish priests 15,639 16,689 Beneficed clergy, vicars etc. 51,408 42,707 Regular clergy, males 55,453 47,515 Do. Do. females 27,665 24,559 Servants, sacristans, acolytes, etc. 25,248 16,376 Treasurers of religious houses 8,552 4,127 -------- -------- 183,965 151,973

The falling off in 1787 is probably due to greater rigor in scrutinizing claims to exemption.
1088. Relazioni Venete, Serie I, T. V, p. 19.
1089. Ricordi sulla Spagna nell'anno 1853 (Ibidem, III, 469).
1090. Conservacion de Monarquías, Discurso XLV.
1091. Bibl. nacional, MSS., D, 118, fol. 146, n 49.
1092. Relazioni Venete, Serie I, T. V, p. 450.
1093. Ibidem, T. VI, p. 378.--Zanetornato, p. 88.

The subsidio was a grant from Paul IV to arm sixty galleys, a purpose which was speedily forgotten. The excusado was a grant from Paul V empowering the king to claim in each parish the tithe of the largest tithe-payer, but it led to difficulties in collecting and was commuted.
1094. Archivo de Simancas, Inquisicion de Granada, Expedientes varios, Leg. 2.
1095. Jovellanos, Informe, p. 88.
1096. Marina, Teoria de las Córtes, P. I, cap. xiii, n. 24 (Madrid, 1820).

The burden of the tithe was the same in France under the ancien régime. As a recent writer remarks "Les dimes étaient une des plus lourdes, peutêtre même celle qui pesait sur les campagnes de la façon la plus générale et la plus fâcheuse ... on ne devrait pas oublier que le droit en lui-même était, le plus souvent, bien moins odieux, moins funeste, que les abus auxquels il donnait lieu ou servait de prétexte."--Edme Champion, La Séparation de l'Eglise et de l'Etat en 1794 (Paris, 1903).

The tithes and first fruits were by no means the only ecclesiastical exaction which impoverished the husbandman. An anonymous Presbítero secular who, in 1828, vigorously defended the temporalities of the Church, candidly admits the oppressiveness of some of its revenues. Among those enumerated was one known as Luctuosa--the right to the best head of cattle on the death of the peasant. The lay lords had mostly commuted this for a small money payment, but the clergy farmed it out and the farmers exacted it with the utmost rigor, not only on the death of the head of a family but on that of every member, so that the survivors, in the hour of bereavement, were often stripped of the means of cultivating their holdings. In 1787 the people of the see of Lugo, after a long struggle, obtained from Carlos III a decree restricting it to the death of the head of the family and commuting it to a money payment of sixty reales when four head of cattle were owned and lesser sums for a smaller number.--Historia y Origen de las Rentas de la Iglesia de España, pp. 90-7 (Madrid, 1828).

This exaction was by no means confined to Spain. See Burn's Law Dictionary s. v. Heriot and Du Cange s. vv. Hereotum, Luctuosa.

1097. Breve Memoria (Döllinger, Beiträge zur polit. kirchl. u. Cultur-Geschichte, III, 203).
1098. C. Hispalens. ann. 1512, cap. 13, 17, 23, 26, 27 (Aguirre, T. V).--Barrantes, Aparato para la Hist. de Extremadura, I, 469.
1099. De justa Hæreticorum punitione, Lib. III, cap. 5.
1100. Comentarios, fol. 167, 260.
1101. Archivo de Simancas, Patronato Real, Inq., Leg. único, fol. 76.
1102. Synod. Oriolan., ann. 1600, cap. xxviii (Aguirre, VI, 457).
1103. Alphonsus a Castro adversus Hæreses, Lib. I, cap. xii.
1104. Relazioni Venete, Serie I, T. V, p. 79.
1105. Col. de Doc. inéd., V, 83, 85.
1106. Bleda, Corónica de los Moros, p. 910.--See Bonifacii PP. VIII. Bull. Unam Sanctam (Extrav. Commun., Lib. I, Tit. VIII, cap. 1). Also the De Regimine Principum, Lib. III, cap. x, xiii, xix, which passes under the name of Aquinas.
1107. Picatoste, La Grandeza y Decadencia de España, III, 192 (Madrid, 1887).
1108. Relazioni Venete, Serie I, T. II, p. 208.
1109. Dávila, Hist. de Felipe III, Lib. II, cap. lvii.
1110. Bulario de la Orden de Santiago, Lib. V, fol. 93, 95, 97.
1111. Relazioni Venete, Serie I, T. I, pp. 341-2; II, 61, 213; III, 222-3.
1112. Sandoval, Vida del Emp. Carlos V, II, 740, 777, 792 (Barcelona, 1625).
1113. Gachard, Correspondance de Philippe II, Tom. II, 27, 44, 58; III, 588.
1114. Pallavicini, Hist. Conc. Trident., Lib. XIV, cap. xi, n. 2.

See also the letter of St. Pius V, April 26, 1569, to the Duke of Anjou (Henry III) congratulating him on his victory over the Huguenots at Jarnac, and urging him to show himself inexorable to those who should plead for mercy towards heretics and rebels.--Pii Quinti Epistolar. Lib. V, p. 168 (Antverpiæ, 1640).

1115. Testamento y Codicilo del Rey Don Felipe II, p. 14 (Madrid, 1882).
1116. Relazioni Lucchese, p. 16.
1117. In his instructions to Colonel Lockhart, his envoy to France after the negotiation of the treaty of 1656, Cromwell tells him to explain to Cardinal Mazarin "what my principles are which led me to a closure with France rather than with Spaine ... viz. that the one gives libertie of conscience to the professors of the Protestant religion and the other persecuteing it with losse of life and estate."--Prof. C. H. Firth, in English Historical Review, October, 1906, p. 744.
1118. Coleccion de Tratados de Paz; Phelipe IV, P. VII, p. 685.
1119. MSS. of Bodleian Library, Arch Seld., 130.
1120. A. de Castro adv. Hæreses, Lib. I, cap. xiii.
1121. Comentarios, fol. 209.

Spain was not exceptional in this. In 1700, a pastoral of Archbishop Precipiano of Mechlin describes with equal energy this profanation of saints' days.--Collectio Synodorum Archiep. Mechliniensis, II, 434 (Mechliniæ, 1829).

1122. Relazioni Venete, Serie I, T. V, p. 18.--In 1565, Giovanni Soranzo makes the same statement and both remark on the facility with which Spanish troops passed over to the infidel--Ibid, p. 82.
1123. Aspilcueta de Oratione, cap. v, n. 25-35.

It was not until 1772 that Carlos III prohibited, in the churches of Madrid, the dances and gigantones and tarascas, or great pasteboard figures of giants and serpents, in the processions, as causing disorder and interfering with devotion; and in 1780 this was extended over the whole kingdom.--Novís. Recop., Lib. I, Tit. i, ley 12.

1124. Santos, El no Importe, pp. 107-31.--For a similar description by Juan de Zabaleta see his "El dia de fiesta," Obras, p. 166 (Madrid, 1728). The El no Importe was reprinted in 1787.

These profanities were not confined to Spain and were condemned by the Council of Tours in 1583 and by Archbishop Precipiano of Mechlin, in 1700.--Concil. Turonens., ann. 1583, Tit. xv (Harduin X, 1424).--(Collect. Synod. Mechlin., II, 436).

1125. Bibliothèque nationale de France, fonds Dupuy, no. 589, fol. 30.
1126. Relacion del Auto de fe de 1733. Discurso isagogico, § 2 (Lima, 1733).
1127. P. Ricardo Cappa, S. J., La Inquisicion española, Madrid, 1888.
1128. Don A. Rodríguez Villa has printed the essential portions of this memorial in the Boletin for July--September 1906, pp. 87-103. It is anonymous and without date, though he tells us that a note on the MS., in a contemporary hand, attributes it to P. Hernando de Salazar or to D. Diego Serrano de Silva, of the Suprema. It is unquestionably by a member of the Suprema, for no one else would have such knowledge of the internal affairs of the Inquisition or discourse of them so freely, even to the

sovereign. Allusion to the successes of the Dutch in Brazil assign it to the time, between 1620 and 1630, when there was so much discussion as to the Portuguese New Christians (see Vol. III, p. 275), to which this paper was doubtless a contribution.

1129. Oligarquía y Caciquismo, pp. 22, 679 (Madrid, 1903).

1130. Doctor Madrazo, while deploring the antinational policy of the ecclesiastical establishment, bears emphatic testimony to the individual virtues of the clergy, regular and secular and their efforts to realize, each in his own sphere, the ideal of Christianity. He attributes their influence on Spanish policy to the power possessed by the papacy of precipitating through them at any moment a Carlist revolt.--El Pueblo español ha muerto? pp. 140-6 (Santander, 1903).

In a very thoughtful paper, Professor Rafael Altamira and his colleagues of the University of Oviedo allude to the theocratic reaction which opposes all progress in the direction of toleration and culture and which threatens a civil war that would be the end of Spain.--Oligarquía y Caciquismo, p. 192.

1131. Relazioni Venete, Serie I, T. VI, p. 371; T. V, p. 288.--Spicilegio Vaticano, I, 461.--Relazioni Lucchese, p. 21.

1132. Ortí y Lara, La Inquisicion, p. xiv.--Macias Picavea, El Problema, p. 229.

1133. This is largely the case in the detail often given of the practices of sorcery. For these there might be some excuse offered, but there is none when wholly superfluous descriptions are included of vice too nauseous to bear transcription.

1134. Corella, Praxis Confeseionis, P. II, Perorat. n. 3.--Picatoste, III, 113-23, 158, 162.--Villa, La Corte y Monarquía, p. xvi.

1135. Chapters from the Religious History of Spain, p. 102.

1136. Döllinger u. Reusch, Moral-Streitigkeiten, I, 319.

1137. For this social anarchy see Picatoste, III, 86-9.

1138. Roda, Dictamen á una Consulta (MS. penes me).

1139. Archivo de Simancas, Inq., Lib. 69, fol. 2, 8.

1140. Corpo Diplomatico Portugues, III, 247.

1141. Relazioni Venete, Serie I, T. II, p. 40; T. III, p. 252; T. V, pp. 22, 83, 144, 288, 392, 485; T. VI, pp. 367, 412.

1142. Erasmi Epistolæ, Auctarium, p. 114 (Londoni, 1642).

1143. Mariana, Hist. de España, Lib. XXIV, cap. xvii.

1144. Archivo de Simancas, Inq. de Barcelona, Córtes, Leg. 17, fol. 74.

1145. Historia verdadera, III, 509.

1146. Die Kirchengeschichte von Spanien, Bd. III, Abt II, p. 74.--Cf. Hefele, Der Cardinal Ximenes, pp. 327 sqq.

Father Gams exposes his ignorance when he tells us that he excludes the burnings for other crimes than heresy, as if there were such, except the rare cases of unnatural crime in Aragon. He even implies that the Inquisition burnt for usury and smuggling.

1147. Hist. crít., T. IX, pp. 209, 211, 213, 214 (Madrid, 1822).

The total of Llorente's extravagant guesses, from the foundation of the Inquisition to 1808, is:
Burnt in person 31,912 Burnt in effigy 17,659 Heavily penanced 291,450 ------- 341,021
Hist. crít, IX, 233.

This is slightly modified by Gallois in his abridgement of Llorente's work (Histoire abregée de la Inquisition d'Espagne, 6e Ed., p. 351-2, Paris, 1828). He gives the figures:
Burnt alive 34,658 Burnt in effigy 18,049 Condemned to galleys or prison 288,214 ------- 340,921
It will be observed that Gallois unscrupulously classifies all personal relaxations as burnings alive and all penances as galleys or prison.

1148. Hist. de los Judíos de España, III, 492-3.

1149. Procedimientos de la Inquisicion, I, 116-17 (Madrid, 1886).

1150. Pulgar, Cronica, P. II, cap. lxxvii.

1151. L. Marinæi Siculi de Reb. Hispan., Lib. XIX.--Illescas, Hist. Pontifical, P. II, Lib. VI, c. xix.--Mariana, Hist. de España, Lib. XXIV, cap. xvii.--Páramo, p. 139.--Garibay, Comp. Hist., Lib. XVIII, cap. xvii.

1152. Hist. de los Reyes Católicos, cap. xliv.

1153. Zuñiga, Annales de Sevilla, año 1524, n. 3--Varflora, Compendio de Sevilla, P. II, cap. 1.

1154. Bernáldez, ubi sup.

1155. Lalaing, Voyage de Philippe le Beau (Gachard, Voyages des Souverains, I, 203).

1156. Zurita, Añales, Lib. XX, cap. xlix. The fact that so careful an historian as Zurita, who sought everywhere for documentary evidence, had no official statistics to cite shows that none such existed in the Suprema relating to the early years of the Inquisition.

1157. Relazioni Venete, Serie I, T. II, p. 40.

1158. Archivo hist. nacional, Inq. de Toledo, Leg. 262.--It is possible that these figures may be only of residents of Ciudad Real. Páramo (p. 170) states the numbers for the tribunal, during its two years of existence, at 52 relaxations in person, 220 in effigy and 183 reconciliations. The record just cited gives for Ciudad Real, from 1484 to 1531, 113 relaxed in person, 129 in effigy, 16 reconciled, 11 penanced, 19 absolved, 3 discharged on bail and 8 of which the sentence is not stated--all, apparently, residents of the town.

1159. Relacion de la Inquisicion Toledana (Boletin, XI, 292 sqq).

The Córdova tribunal also burned 90 residents of Chillon, who had been duped by the prophetess of Herrera (Ibidem, p. 308).

1160. Hist. crit., IX, 210.

1161. See Appendix of Vol. I. It must be borne in mind that, in the early years, small autos were held elsewhere than in the centres. Thus, in the Libro Verde there are allusions to them in Barbastro, Huesca, Monzon, Lérida and Tamarit (Revista de España, CVI, 250-1, 263-4, 266). The aggregate for these, however, would make little difference in the totals.

1162. Libro Verde (Revista de España, CVI, 570-83). The relaxations by years were:

1483--1 1495--9 1512--4 1542--1 1485--4 1496--1 1520--1 1543--1 1486--26 1497--18 1521--2 1546--2 1487--25 1498--2 1522--1 1549--1 1488--13 1499--13 1524--1 1561--4 1489--2 1500--5 1526--1 1563--1 1490--1 1502--2 1528--2 1565--1 1491--10 1505--1 1534--1 1566--1 1492--15 1506--5 1535--1 1567--2 1493--11 1510--1 1537--1 1574--2 1494--1 1511--5 1539--1

The number in 1486-7-8 is attributable to the assassination of San Pedro Arbués.

1163. Carbonell de Gestis Hæret. (Col. de Doc. de la C. de Aragon, XXVII, XXVIII).

1164. Archivo hist. nacional, Inq. de Valencia, Leg. 98, 300.

1165. Cronicon de Valladolid (Col. de Doc. inéd., XIII, 176-9, 187).

1166. Archivo de Simancas, Inq., Lib. 595.

1167. MSS. of Library of Univ. of Halle, Yc, 20, T. I.

1168. Archivo hist. nacional, Inq. de Toledo, Leg. 1.

1169. Archivo de Simancas, Inq., Lib. 1020.

1170. Royal Library of Berlin, Qt. 9548.

To illustrate the discrepancy between the facts as stated above and the reckless computations of Llorente, which have been so largely accepted, it may not be amiss to compare the facts with the corresponding figures resulting from his system of calculation, for the tribunals and periods named:

Records. Llorente. Toledo, 1483-1501. Relaxed in person 297 666 Relaxed in effigy 600 433 Imprisoned, about 200} Reconciled under edicts 5200} 6,200 Do. 1575-1610. Relaxed in person 11 252 Relaxed in effigy 15 120 Penanced 904 1,396 Do. 1648-1794. Relaxed in person 8 297 Relaxed in effigy 63 129 Penanced 1094 1,188 up to 1746. Saragossa, 1485-1502. Relaxed in person 124 584 Relaxed in effigy 32 392 Penanced 458 7,004 Barcelona, 1488-98. Relaxed in person 23 432 Relaxed in effigy 430 316 Imprisoned 116} Reconciled under edicts 304} 5,122 Valencia, 1485-1592. Relaxed in person 643 1,538 Relaxed in effigy 479 869 Tried 3104 16,677 penanced. Valladolid, 1485-92. Relaxed in person 50 424 Relaxed in effigy 6 312 Penanced ? 3,884 Majorca, 1488-1691. Relaxed in person 139 1,778 Relaxed in effigy 482 978 Penanced 975 17,861 All tribunals, 1721-27. Relaxed in person 77 238 Relaxed in effigy 74 119 Penanced 811 1,428

It will thus be seen how entirely fallacious was the guess-work on which Llorente based his system.

An even more conclusive comparison is furnished by the little tribunal of the Canaries. After 1524, Llorente includes it among the tribunals by which he multiplies the number of yearly victims assigned to each. He thus makes it responsible, from first to last, for 1118 relaxations in person and 574 in effigy. Millares (Historia de la Inquisicion en las Islas Canaries, III, 164-8) has printed the official list of the quemados during the whole career of the tribunal, and they amount in all to eleven burnt in person and a hundred and seven in effigy. The number of the latter is accounted for by the fact that, to render its autos interesting, it was often in the habit of prosecuting in absentia Moorish and negro slaves who escaped to Africa after baptism and who thus were constructively relapsed.

Dr. Schäfer (Beiträge, I, 157), after an exhaustive examination of the accessible records, has collected references to 2100 persons tried for Protestantism during the second half of the sixteenth century. Protestants were punished with special severity, but in these cases the total of relaxations in person was about 220 and in effigy about 120, and all these, as we have seen, were largely foreigners.

1171. Bernáldez, Hist. de los Reyes Católicos, cap. xliv.

1172. Archivo de Simancas, Inq., Lib. 979, fol. 40.

1173. Garau, La Fee triunfante, pp. 86, 91.

It should not be forgotten that it was only in 1790 that in England the burning of women for high and petty treason was commuted to drawing and hanging by 30 Geo. III, cap. 48 (Statutes at Large, XVI, 57).

1174. Juan de Valera, Del Influjo de la Inquisicion (Disertaciones, p. 108).--Menéndez y Pelayo, II, 707.--Ortí y Lara, La Inquisicion, p. 270.--P. Ricardo Cappa, La Inquisicion española, p. 146.

1175. Estudio del Maestre Nebrija, pp. 53-7, 97 (Madrid, 1879).

1176. Historía de España, Prólogo.

1177. Las Cinco Excelencias del Español, fol. 49, 52 (Pamplona, 1629).

1178. See tracts by Laurean Pérez of Salamanca and Gerónimo López of Saragossa in Bodleian Library, A, Subt. 16.

1179. Revista crítica de Historia y Literatura, T. VI, p. 6.

1180. Ochoa, Epistolario español, II, 182.

1181. Elógio de la Reina Católica Doña Isabel, p. 51 (Madrid, 1821).

1182. Del Influjo de la Inquisicion (Disertaciones, pp. 108, 121).

1183. Strype's Memorials, II, 214-15.--Burnet's Reformation, Vol. II, Collections, n. 33.--XXIX Car. II, c. 9 (Statutes at Large, II, 390).

1184. Archivo de Simancas, Inq., Lib. 942, fol. 53.--MSS. of Royal Library of Copenhagen, 218^{b}, p. 200.--See Appendix.

www.ingramcontent.com/pod-product-compliance
Lightning Source LLC
Chambersburg PA
CBHW020749160426
43192CB00006B/284